CURRENCY DERIVATIVES

CURRENCY DERIVATIVES

Pricing Theory, Exotic Options, and Hedging Applications

Edited by
DAVID F. DeROSA

John Wiley & Sons, Inc.

New York • Chichester • Weinhiem • Brisbane • Singapore • Toronto

For Francesca DeRosa

This book is printed on acid-free paper. ∞

Copyright © 1998 by David F. DeRosa. All rights reserved.
Published by John Wiley & Sons, Inc.
Published simultaneously in Canada.

This publication is designed to provide accurate and authoritative information in regard to the subject
matter covered. It is sold with the understanding that the publisher is not engaged in rendering
professional services. If professional advice or other expert assistance is required, the services of a
competent professional person should be sought.

Library of Congress Cataloging-in-Publication Data:

Currency derivatives: pricing theory, exotic options, and hedging
    applications / edited by David F. DeRosa.
        p.   cm.—(Wiley series in financial engineering)
    Collection of scientific articles.
    Includes bibliographical references and index.
    ISBN 0-471-25267-0 (alk. paper)
    1. Foreign exchange market.   2. Foreign exchange futures.
3. Exotic options (Finance)   4. Hedging (Finance)   I. DeRosa, David
F. II. Series.
    HG3853.C867 1998
    332.4'5—dc21 98-5653

Printed in the United States of America.

10 9 8 7 6 5 4 3 2 1

Contents

Preface

This book is a collection of scientific articles that have had an important impact on the development of the derivatives market for foreign exchange. The best example of how important academic innovation has been to the practice of trading and dealing in currency derivatives is the Black-Scholes model, which was adapted for currency options by Garman and Kohlhagen in 1983. Even the most unacademic denizen of the foreign exchange trading room knows about some of the famous "greeks" (delta, gamma, theta, rho, kappa, plus the whole raft of second-order risk measures). In the interbank market, currency options are identified by their delta and quoted in terms of implied volatility—both concepts that came from the Black-Scholes paradigm. Moreover, the management of option risk is a field that is infused with Black-Scholes terminology and concepts. The articles in this book have made a great contribution to the currency derivatives market. Some are more directly practical than others. Most are precisely focused on currency derivatives, but others are concerned with broad and general derivatives issues that have great relevance to currency derivatives.

My interest in assembling this book began with courses that I have taught at the Graduate School of Business of the University of Chicago and at the Yale School of Management under the generic title "Foreign Exchange and Its Related Derivative Instruments." Most of these papers have appeared as required reading in my courses.

David F. DeRosa
DeRosa Research and Trading, Inc.
August 1998

Acknowledgments

I would like to thank Pamela van Giessen, my editor at John Wiley & Sons, for encouraging me to put this book together. Nassim Taleb has my gratitude for advice that he gave me in choosing which articles to include. Most of all, I would like to extend my sincere admiration and thanks to the dozens of scholars who wrote these great papers that I am proud to republish in this book.

About the Contributors

GIOVANNI BARONE-ADESI is the P. Pocklington Professor at the Faculty of Business of the University of Alberta, Canada. His research is on financial derivatives and risk management. He received his Ph.D. from the University of Chicago.

DAVID S. BATES is an Associate Professor of Finance at the University of Iowa and a Research Associate of the National Bureau of Economic Research. From 1988 to 1996 he taught at the Wharton School of the University of Pennsylvania. His research primarily involves developing, estimating, and testing options pricing models, with applications to currency and stock index options. He received an S.B. in mathematics from MIT, an M.P.A. from Princeton University, and an M.A. and doctorate in economics from Princeton.

FISCHER BLACK (1938–1995) was a Partner and Director of Quantitative Strategies of Goldman, Sachs & Co. Asset Management. Previously he was a Professor of Finance at the Alfred P. Sloan School of Management of MIT and Professor of Finance at the Graduate School of Business of the University of Chicago. Dr. Black was the President of the American Finance Association in 1985. He is the author of *Exploring General Equilibrium* and *Business Cycles and Equilibrium*. Dr. Black received his A.B. in Physics from Harvard College and his Ph.D. in Applied Mathematics from Harvard University.

MARC CHESNEY is Professor of Finance and Associate Dean responsible for the Ph.D. program at Group HEC, France. Previously he was a Visiting Professor at the World Bank and held academic posts at the University of Edmonton and at the University of Geneva. His fields of interest are options pricing theory and real options. Dr. Chesney received his Ph.D. from the University of Geneva.

BRADFORD CORNELL is Professor of Finance at the Anderson Graduate School of Management at UCLA. He is also President of FinEcon, a firm that specializes in applying financial theory to business practice and litigation. His research interests are in capital budgeting and corporate valuation. He received his Ph.D. from Stanford University.

JOHN C. COX is a Nomura Professor of Finance at the Alfred P. Sloan School of Management of MIT. His expertise covers corporate finance, finance theory, and portfolio management. He is the author of *Options Markets* (with Rubinstein). He has a B.A. from Louisiana State University and a Ph.D. from the University of Pennsylvania.

EMANUEL DERMAN is a Managing Director and head of the Quantitative Strategies Group at Goldman, Sachs & Co. Prior to joining Goldman, Sachs & Co., Dr.

Derman worked for Bell Laboratories and held a number of academic positions where he did research in particle physics. His primary research interests are in valuation, modeling, and risk management systems for equity derivative products. He is co-author of the Black-Derman-Toy interest-rate model and the Derman-Kani implied tree model. Dr. Derman has a Ph.D. in theoretical physics from Columbia University.

DAVID F. DEROSA (editor of this volume) is President of DeRosa Research and Trading, Inc. He is also Adjunct Professor of Finance at Yale School of Management, where he teaches courses in International Finance and Foreign Exchange and Related Derivative Instruments. DeRosa is the author of *Managing Foreign Exchange Risk* and *Options on Foreign Exchange*. He received his A.B. degree in economics from the University of Chicago and his Ph.D. from the Graduate School of Business of the University of Chicago.

AJAY DRAVID is Co-Manager of the Salomon Brothers Asset Management equity portfolio arbitrage group. Previously he was an Assistant Professor of Finance at the Wharton School. His research interests include derivatives, asset pricing, and corporate finance. Dr. Dravid received his M.A. in Physics from SUNY, Stony Brook; an MBA in Finance from the University of Rochester; and a Ph.D. in Finance from Stanford University.

MARK B. GARMAN is Emeritus Professor of Finance at the Haas School of Business Administration of the University of California. He is the President of Financial Engineering Associates. His research interests include arbitrage, options, volatility measurement, risk management, duration-related risk measures, value at risk, and computational methods in financial engineering. Dr. Garman did his undergraduate work in physics at Stanford University. He has a Ph.D. from Carnegie-Mellon University in Systems Sciences.

HÉLYETTE GEMAN is Professor of Finance at the University of Paris IX Dauphine and at ESSEC Graduate Business School. Dr. Geman is a member of honor of the French Society of Actuaries. Her research interest is in the area of exotic options. Dr. Geman is a graduate of the Ecole Normale Superieure; she holds an M.A. in theoretical physics and a Ph.D. in mathematics from the University of Paris VI Pierre et Marie Curie and a Ph.D. in Finance from the University of Paris I Pantheon Sorbonne.

T.S. HO is Honorary Senior Research Fellow at Lancaster University School of Management, England, and Visiting Professor of Finance at the Universidade Católica Portuguesa, Porto, Portugal. Dr. Ho holds a Ph.D. in Finance, and his research interests are focused on derivatives, financial innovations, and corporate finance.

CHO H. HUI is a Senior Manager of the Hong Kong Monetary Authority in the Banking Policy Division. He heads a team to review derivative models and risk management systems in financial institutions. Prior to joining HKMA, he was a derivative and risk analyst at Citibank N.A. and NatWest Markets in Hong Kong. He holds a B.S. in physics from the University of Wisconsin at Madison and a Ph.D. in applied physics from Cornell University.

JONATHAN E. INGERSOLL JR. is the Adrian C. Israel Professor of International Trade and Finance at the Yale School of Management. Previously he was on the faculty of the Graduate School of Business at the University of Chicago. His research interests include options pricing, the pricing of derivative assets, and multiperiod financial models. Dr. Ingersoll is the author of *Theory of Financial Decision Making*. He received an S.B., S.M., and Ph.D. from MIT.

PHILIPPE JORION is a Professor of Finance at the Graduate School of Management at the University of California, Irvine. He holds an MBA and a Ph.D. from the University of Chicago and a degree in engineering from the University of Brussels. Professor Jorion has written more than fifty publications directed to academics and practitioners on the topics of risk management and international finance. He is the author of a number of books, including *Big Bets Gone Bad: Derivatives and Bankruptcy in Orange County* and *Value at Risk: The New Benchmark for Conrolling Derivatives Risk.*

PIOTR KARASINSKI is head of the Citibank interest rate options trading desk in London. He has worked on valuation models for interest rates, equity and hybrid products, and random volatility models for equities. He is the co-author of the Black-Karasinski interest rate model. Dr. Karasinski received his Ph.D. in Physics from Yale University.

STEVEN W. KOHLHAGEN manages the derivatives area for First Union Bank. Previously he was a Professor of International Finance and Economics at the University of California at Berkeley and was involved in the derivatives businesses at Bankers Trust and Lehman Brothers. Dr. Kohlhagen has a B.A. in Economics from the College of William and Mary and a Ph.D. in economics from Stanford University.

EDMOND LEVY is Assistant Director in the Specialized Derivatives Group at HSBC MIDLAND, where he is responsible for the development and risk management of foreign exchange exotic options and currency-related structured products. Prior to this, he was at BZW-Barclays Bank and Nomura Bank International plc. Dr. Levy previously lectured in Finance at Liverpool University and Econometrics at Southampton University, where he received his Ph.D.

CHRISTOPHER D. PIROS is a Senior Vice President and global fixed-income portfolio manager at Massachusetts Financial Services. Prior to joining MFS, he was a Vice President of DBL's Quantitative Asset Management Group and an Assistant Professor of Finance and Economics at Duke University's Fuqua School of Business. Dr. Piros received his Ph.D. in Economics from Harvard University.

MARK REINGANUM is the Mary Jo Vaughn Rauscher Chair in Financial Investments and Director of the Finance Institute at Southern Methodist University. His research interests include investments in general and stock market anomalies in particular. He has taught at the University of Chicago, the University of Iowa, and the University of Southern California. Dr. Reinganum has an A.B. from Oberlin College and an MBA and Ph.D. from the Graduate School of Business of the University of Chicago.

MATTHEW RICHARDSON is an Associate Professor of Finance at the Stern School of Business, New York University, and a member of the National Bureau of Economic Research. Professor Richardson teaches courses in advanced fixed-income and financial econometrics at the graduate, Ph.D., and executive levels. Professor Richardson received his Ph.D. in Finance from the Graduate School of Business at Stanford University.

PETER RITCHKEN is a Professor in the Weatherhead School of Management at Case Western Reserve University in Cleveland. He has written several books on derivatives, is the editor of *Advances in Futures and Options Research,* and has published extensively in the derivatives area. His current research interests are in pricing interest rate claims, implementing stochastic volatility options models, solving real options problems, and banking regulation issues. Dr. Ritchken received his Ph.D. in operations research from Case Western Reserve University.

STEPHEN A. ROSS is a Sterling Professor of Economics and Finance at the Yale School of Management. He is also a principal of Roll & Ross, an asset management firm. His research areas include general finance, economic theory, and real estate. He holds a B.S. from California Institute of Technology and a Ph.D. from Harvard University.

LOUIS SCOTT is Vice President in the Financial Research Group of the Fixed Income Division at Morgan Stanley Dean Witter & Co. Prior to joining Morgan Stanley in 1996, he was a Professor of Finance at the University of Georgia and at the University of Illinois at Urbana-Champaign. His research interests are in interest rate derivatives and stochastic volatility models. Dr. Scott received his Ph.D. in economics from the University of Virginia.

RICHARD C. STAPLETON is a Professor of Finance at Strathclyde University, Scotland. He teaches courses in capital markets and corporate finance and specializes his research in interest rate derivative markets and risk management of interest rate and currency-related derivatives. Dr. Stapleton's recent work includes papers on binomial methods of valuing derivatives, the pricing of American options, and the demand for futures and options.

MARTI G. SUBRAHMANYAM is the Charles E. Merrill Professor of Finance and Economics at the Stern School of New York University. His research interests are in derivatives, asset pricing theory, term structure theory, and international finance. Dr. Subrahmanyam received a B. of Tech. from the Indian Institute of Technology (Madras) and a Ph.D. in Finance and Economics from MIT.

TON-SHENG SUN is in charge of Asian research at Long-Term Capital Management. Previously he did research in fixed-income derivatives at Lehman Brothers and at Goldman, Sachs & Co. Dr. Sun received his Ph.D. in Finance from Stanford University.

STEPHEN J. TAYLOR is a Professor of Finance at Lancaster University, England. Since 1995 he has been head of the department of Accounting and Finance. His numerous publications over twenty years of research include *Modeling Financial Time Series* (Wiley), in which he presented the first description of stochastic volatility models and a pioneering analysis of GARCH models. He continues to actively research a wide range of volatility issues. Professor Taylor obtained his M.A. and Ph.D. degrees from Lancaster University, following his B.A. degree in Mathematics from Cambridge University.

JEFFREY S. WECKER is Chief Investment Officer of Caspian Quantitative Asset Management Advisers, L.L.C., which is the investment advisor for the CAM Catamaran Fund, Inc. Previously he was an Executive Director at Goldman, Sachs & Co., where he did research for the Asian derivatives group and was a member of the Quantitative Strategies Group. His research interests are in proprietary trading strategies, index arbitrage, and derivatives risk management.

ROBERT E. WHALEY is the T. Austin Finch Foundation Professor of Business Administration and Director of the Futures and Options Research Center at the Fuqua School of Business, Duke University. He has published more than fifty articles on derivatives contract valuation and market operation and holds a number of editorial positions, including Co-Editor of the *Review of Futures Markets* and Associate Editor of the *Journal of Financial Economics, Journal of Finance, Journal of Futures Markets, Journal of Derivatives,* and *Advances in Futures and Options Research.*

XINZHONG XU is employed by the Bank of England on secondment from his position as a Senior Lecturer in Accounting and Finance at the University of Manchester, England, where he teaches investment analysis and capital market theory. His research interests are in volatility modeling and forecasting, the efficiency of financial futures and options markets, and empirical tests of asset pricing models. He obtained his B.Sc. from Peking University, his MBA from Aston University, and his Ph.D. from Lancaster University.

MARC YOR is Professor of Mathematics at the University of Paris VI Pierre et Marie Curie. Professor Yor is a correspondent of the French Academy of Science. In 1993, Yor shared (with Hélyette Geman) First Prize of the Merrill Lynch award for best research in mathematical Finance. Dr. Yor holds a Ph.D. in probability theory from the University of Paris VI Pierre et Marie Curie.

Introduction: Foreign Exchange and Its Related Derivatives Instruments

DAVID F. DEROSA

THE FOREIGN EXCHANGE MARKET

The foreign exchange market comprises a network of hundreds of commercial and investment banks that deal as principals in wholesale amounts of currency. What are traded in the foreign exchange market are actual sums of foreign currency bank deposits. The basis of all foreign exchange trading is the spot transaction. This transaction, called a *deal* in the foreign exchange community, constitutes a promise to exchange sums of currencies in two bank business days. Exceptions to the rule are the Canadian dollar, which trades for one-day value against the U.S. dollar, and the Mexican peso, which trades for same-day, one-day, and two-day value against the dollar. Valid spot value dates are never U.S. banking holidays nor are they bank holidays in either currency's home country.

Spot dealers make two-way, buy or sell quotations upon request. For example, a dealer might quote 120.00–05 on dollar/yen, meaning that he would be willing to buy U.S. dollars (and sell yen) at 120.00 or sell U.S. dollars (and buy yen) at 120.05.

The largest portion of all foreign exchange trading involves the U.S. dollar. With a few well-known exceptions, foreign currencies are quoted against the dollar in terms of the number of units of foreign currency equal to one U.S. dollar (examples being U.S. dollar/German mark and U.S. dollar/Japanese yen). This is called the *European convention.* However, sterling, the Australian dollar, the New Zealand dollar, and the European currency unit are quoted the opposite way, in dollars per unit of foreign currency. This is called the *American convention.* To make matters all the more confusing to newcomers, listed currency derivatives traders at the Chicago Mercantile Exchange quote all currencies according to the American convention. Also, it is prevalent in the academic currency option literature to assume the American convention.

A lot of what is known about the size of the market comes from triennial surveys undertaken by the Bank for International Settlements. According to the April 1995 survey, some $1,230 billion of trading in foreign exchange was transacted per day in the form of spot and forward deals. The survey also revealed that the most heavily traded currency was the U.S. dollar, which was on one side of more than 83 percent of all currency deals. By currency pairs, dollar/mark accounted for over 25 percent of total trading, dollar/yen 20 percent, and sterling/dollar 10 percent. Direct transactions among the European Monetary System currencies accounted for 7 percent of the total trading. The largest trading volumes, in descending order, occurred in London, New York, and Tokyo.

Interbank dealers also transact forward foreign exchange deals. A forward foreign exchange transaction is identical in form to a spot transaction except that it settles on a spot value date that is days, weeks, months, or even years in the future. Forward dealers make bid and ask quotations for forward points. Forward points, when added or subtracted from a spot rate, produce the forward exchange rate. The forward exchange rate is called the *outright* in dealing rooms.

The difference between the forward outright and the spot exchange rate can be readily understood by a well-known no-arbitrage condition called covered interest parity. Simply explained, the forward outright must encapsulate the interest rate spread between the two currencies so as to preclude the existence of a riskless profit from investing in foreign currency money market instruments on a hedged basis. It is analogous to the principle that commodities futures prices must reflect the spot price adjusted by the commodity's cost of carry.

A SHORT HISTORY OF THE CURRENCY DERIVATIVES MARKET

Foreign exchange has shown itself to be a fertile ground for derivatives. This is because the currency market is huge in terms of trading volume and small by way of transactions costs. Foreign exchange is unique among all markets in that it is fully operational for dealing in spot, forward, and derivative instruments nearly 24 hours per day, except for weekends and prominent holidays. The currency option market can correctly claim to be the only true global option market.

The derivatives market for foreign exchange started in the listed futures and options markets of Chicago, London, and Philadelphia in the 1970s and 1980s. Trading in currency derivatives was limited to listed futures contracts and put and call options on the major exchange rates. Floor traders and a number of specialized futures and options shops ran the market.

In the 1990's the currency derivatives market "graduated upstairs" to the dealing rooms of the money-center banks that already dominated the spot foreign exchange market. This migration was motivated by a number of factors that favored the large banks. Banks had a natural advantage because they had access to the large amounts of capital that became more important as the derivatives business expanded. Banks, as mature financial institutions, knew the importance of hiring and training professionals to staff their dealing rooms. They also made heavy investments to develop risk management technology. In time, size became a factor as well. A big dealer has an advantage over the small occasional market maker because proportionately less hedging will keep him flat on the market. Hedging transactions cost money to execute. A large option book can be compared to a well-diversified portfolio. It might happen to be both long and short on the same, or nearly the same, option. The book is also likely to own both puts and calls on the same currency. Less hedging is required because elements of a large option book effectively cancel out some part of the total market exposure. The banks also enjoyed a positive externality which was created when their option market making teams were located close to their active spot dealing desks in the same room.

Contemporaneous to the migration of option trading to the inter-bank dealers came a great expansion in the use of currency derivatives by end-use counterparties. Today, a wide variety of economic entities buy and sell currency derivatives. The array includes but is not restricted to investment portfolio managers, mutual funds, private individuals, hedge funds, corporate treasurers, export and import companies, and central banks.

Once installed in the domain of the interbank foreign exchange market, derivatives trading began to key off of the full gamut of currencies. Dealers began making two-way prices on options on currencies not traded in the listed futures markets. Dealers also began to make prices on options that expire on practically any valid spot value date and at any strike.

The next phase in the development of the currency derivatives market belongs to the exotic currency option. An exotic option is any option with a nonstandard feature. The most popular exotic is the barrier option (one dealer estimates that 90% of the exotic currency option business is for barrier options). A barrier option has a defined spot exchange rate barrier level. If the barrier is ever crossed by a movement in the spot exchange rate, the option will either cease to exist or come into existence. A popular example is the knock-out option. The knock-out is otherwise the same as a standard (or *vanilla*) option except that it will cease to exist if the spot exchange rate ever breaches the assigned barrier level. There are single barrier and multiple barrier options.

A recent exotic innovation is the binary barrier option. It is a favorite of volatility traders. This option will pay at expiration a fixed sum of cash, provided that the spot exchange rate never crosses one or more defined barrier levels.

Average rate currency options have proved to be popular with foreign exchange hedgers. Average rate options define their payoff functions in terms of the average spot exchange rate over a period of time.

A quantos option is an exotic option that has a variable face amount that is geared to the market value of a foreign asset or level of a foreign stock index. Quantos options are popular with portfolio managers. The quantos innovations is that the investor can buy currency insurance in precisely the right-sized amount in advance of knowing the future value of the foreign asset. A related type of exotic currency option is the foreign stock index warrant with currency features.

All of these exotics—options, barriers and binaries, average options, quantos, and index warrants,—are discussed in depth in the articles in this volume. No pretense is made that these works exhaust the whole universe of exotic currency derivatives. At the very least such a claim would be implausible because new exotic derivatives spew forth from option dealing rooms almost everyday. Nonetheless, the papers contained here do form the core of our current understanding of currency derivatives instruments. An outline of the main sections of the book accompanied by some brief comments highlighting each of the chapters follows.

OUTLINE OF THE BOOK

Forwards and Futures on Foreign Exchange

A forward contract is a deal between counterparties to exchange sums of foreign currency on a future value date. A forward contract transacted at the current market level forward outright rate has no immediate value. Thereafter, it will take on positive or negative value with the passage of time and as exchange rates and interest rates fluctuate. To value the contract, one needs to know only the new current forward outright rate for the contract value date and the domestic interest rate. The rest is present value arithmetic, as shown in the chapter by DeRosa ("Forward and Futures Contracts on Foreign Exchange").

A futures contract is a listed derivative that pays or collects daily variation margin. By comparison, a forward contract may not generate any intermediate cash flow. The question then arises as to whether there can be any substantial difference in the forward outright and the futures price. In the most simple case, the interest rate can be assumed to be nonstochastic. Cox, Ingersoll, and Ross (CIR) ("The Relation between Forward Prices and Futures Prices") demonstrate that this implies that the forward and futures prices must be equal. The proof comes from constructing a rollover futures hedge, which is described in the DeRosa article. However, in the stochastic interest rate case, CIR show that forward and futures prices need not be equal. In practice, arbitrageurs look to quickly take advantage of any discrepancy between forward prices and futures prices but do not get satisfaction on a regular basis, according to Cornell and Reinaganum ("Forward and Futures Prices: Evidence from the Foreign Exchange Markets") who find only insignificant differences between forward and futures prices. The Cornell and Reinganum chapter also demonstrates that the key condition—covariance between futures prices and interest rates—in the CIR framework that allows forward prices to deviate from futures prices in the stochastic interest rate case is absent in the foreign exchange market.

Currency Option Pricing Models

The Garman and Kohlhagen chapter ("Foreign Currency Option Values") is the single most influential scientific analysis of currency derivatives. The importance of this work has already been acknowledged in the preface. The Garman and Kohlhagen model for European exercise puts and calls on foreign currency is a direct application of the Black and Scholes (1973). Their innovation is in the explicit recognition of the role of both foreign and domestic interest rates in determining the option's value. As in the Black-Scholes model, the value of call and put options is derived from the solution of a partial differential equation subject to terminal boundary constraints at expiration. The approach taken by these authors also has roots in earlier works by Samuelson and Merton (1969) and Black (this volume). The Samuelson and Merton work on stock warrants introduces the theoretical construct of a share of stock that pays a dividend that varies proportionately with the stock price. In effect, one could say that Garman and Kohlhagen use the interest rate on the foreign currency in a way that is analogous to the way Samuelson and Merton use their proportional dividend. Garman and Kohlhagen work primarily with options on spot foreign exchange, but they also derive another formulation based on forward foreign exchange. This second approach is reminiscent of Black's 1976 work, "The Pricing of Commodity Contracts" (contained in this volume), because their forward exchange rate can be seen as substituting for Black's futures price. However one chooses to understand Garman and Kohlhagen's work, there should be no confusion about the enormity of the importance of that paper for the currency option market.

Black and Scholes and Garman and Kohlhagen assume that instantaneous percentage changes in the spot exchange rate follow a simple diffusion process, or alternatively that the spot exchange rate itself is a log-normal variate. Ingersoll ("Valuing Foreign Exchange Rate Derivatives with a Bounded Exchange Process") considers the pricing of various currency derivatives in an environment in which the movement in a spot exchange rate is restricted by effective boundaries. The foremost example in recent memory of such an exchange rate regime is the European Exchange Rate Mechanism experiment.

Ingersoll's topic is interesting because the existence of exchange rate boundaries works subtle changes on the value of currency options. On one hand, upside and downside boundaries limit the extent to which an option could eventually rise or fall into or out of the money. On the other hand, he has to consider that boundaries dampen the instantaneous volatility of the spot process, and in the case of American options, impact the early exercise decision.

American exercise options constitute a small yet not insignificant portion of the currency option market, with the listed options of the Philadelphia Stock Exchange and the Chicago Mercantile Exchange being noteworthy examples. Experience shows that American exercise currency options are in fact commonly subject to early exercise. On theoretical grounds, American exercise currency options can be valued with the binomial option pricing model of Cox,

Ross, and Rubinstein (1979) but practitioners have always searched for faster computational alternatives. Barone-Adesi and Whaley ("Efficient Analytic Approximation of American Option Values") invent a clever algorithm that solves the quadratic approximation model of MacMillan (1986) for the value of American options. Ho, Stapleton, and Subrahmanyam ("A Simple Technique for the Valuation and Hedging of American Options") joined the competition for the title of fastest American option approximation recipe, with a technique that is based on the value of a hypothetical European option that is twice exercisable. Both of these chapters have been of substantial assistance to traders of American currency options.

Currency Futures Options

Currency futures options trade on the Chicago Mercantile Exchange and account for at least half of all trading in listed currency derivatives. Upon exercise a currency futures option delivers a position in a currency futures contract. Black's chapter ("The Pricing of Commodity Contracts") is a classic in the field of derivatives. It contains a unified framework for understanding forward contracts, futures contracts, and commodity options (now called futures options). This work influenced Cox, Ingersoll, and Ross in the development of their work on forwards and futures. Its importance for Garman and Kohlhagen has already been noted. The only shortcoming that this chapter has from a practitioner's point of reference is that the futures option model is for European exercise options, whereas the currency futures options that trade on the Chicago Mercantile Exchange feature American exercise. This is where Whaley's chapter ("On Valuing American Futures Options") picks up the thread. This chapter addresses a number of fundamental issues for American exercise futures options, including put-call parity (which takes the form of an inequality because of the possibility of early exercise) and the optimality of early exercise. Not surprisingly, Whaley uses the quadratic approximation model (which is the subject of his chapter with Barone-Adesi) to value American futures options.

Implied Volatility in Currency Derivatives

Implied volatility functions as a price in the currency derivatives market. Options and other derivative instruments are quoted and traded in bid and ask levels of implied volatility. Professional option traders spend a good deal of time trying to understand patterns of movement in implied volatility. Xu and Taylor ("The Term Structure of Volatility Implied by Foreign Exchange Options") study the term structure of implied volatility of options on four of the currencies that traded on the Philadelphia Stock Exchange during the period from January 1985 to November 1989. Sample implied volatility showed great variance across the term structure over time, and the slope of the term structure freely changed back and forth from positive to negative. Another significant finding was that the term structures of the four currencies taken at a common point of time bear resemblance to each other. In a second study, Taylor and Xu ("The Magnitude of Implied Volatility Smiles: Theory and Empirical Evidence for Exchange Rates") investigate the strike structure of Philadelphia currency option implied volatility. A well-known feature of all option markets is the famous "smile." That phenomenon refers to the relative higher implied volatility for out-of-the-money options compared to the at-the-money options. Smiles do exist in foreign exchange option markets, as Taylor and Xu find, but they are generally less pronounced than the ones observed in equity and equity index derivative instruments. One popular theoretical explanation for the observed smile phenomenon is that the option market may be pricing actual spot exchange rate volatility as a stochastic variable rather than as a fixed constant. Taylor and Xu find corroborating evidence for this conjecture but caution that the observed Philadelphia smiles are larger in magnitude than this theory predicts.

Jump Process and Stochastic Volatility Models for Currency Derivatives

Two classes of models challenge the supremacy of the Garman-Kohlhagen model for currency options. One is the jump process option model, first developed by Merton (1976), which alters the stochastic process generating exchange rates to create a mixed jump-diffusion process. The jump element is represented by a Poisson variable that adds discontinuous shocks to the ordinary diffusion process. Jorion ("On Jump Processes in the Foreign Exchange and Stock Markets") finds evidence that foreign exchange markets exhibit significant jump behavior in the period between January 1974 and December 1985. He believes that this finding has relevance for understanding the pricing of out-of-the-money currency options. Bates ("Dollar Jump Fears, 1984–1992: Distributional Abnormalities Implicit in Currency Futures Options) is quite simply a tour de force in derivatives modeling and statistical methodology. In one of the many clever parts of the chapter Bates develops a jump-diffusion option model that he then fits to observed currency futures options data. This allows him to observe implied levels of not only volatility, but skewness and kurtosis as well. His findings are not at odds with the concept that the market price of currency futures options has at times incorporated allowances for jump process movements in exchange rates.

   The second class of challenger option models comprises the random variance models. Random variance option models have the advantage that the volatility parameter is allowed freedom to wander. However, they are mathematically complex and require computationally expensive procedures such as simulation analysis to be put into useful practice. Added to that, Chesney and Scott ("Pricing European Currency Options: A Comparison of the Modified Black-Scholes Model and a Random Variance Model") find only slight advantage to using the random variance model for currency options instead of the Garman-Kohlhagen model with timely refreshment of market levels of implied volatility.

Barrier, Binary, and Average Currency Options

As was noted in an earlier section, barrier options have attracted a significant audience in the foreign exchange community. Single-barrier puts and calls are now so prevalent that some believe they should no longer be described as exotic options. Closed-form solutions for single-barrier options are well known, starting with Merton (1973). In practice, single-barrier options are dealt either with the barrier located out of the money (a knock-out option) or with the barrier placed in the money (a kick-out option). As a matter of fact, placement of the barrier turns out to be a substantial determinant of the subsequent behavior of the option (see DeRosa 1996 and 1992).

Some practitioners choose to value single-barrier currency options with the binomial option model, despite the existence of closed-form solutions. Sometimes this is necessary because barrier options have been known to carry the American exercise privilege. However, binomial values for barrier options can be seriously biased. Moreover, expanding the number of nodes in the binomial tree, a standard remedy to raise precision, does not always work. Boyle and Lau (1994) trace the origin of the problem to the positioning of the barrier inside the adjacent layers of nodes in the lattice. Ritchken ("On Pricing Barrier Options") provides an efficient and mechanically simple fix: move to a trinomial lattice. Ritchken's trick is to construct the trinomial lattice so that the barrier level is exactly hit after an integer number of successive moves.

Double-barrier options have achieved a foothold in the marketplace, although they are admittedly less popular than single-barrier options. A double-barrier option is knocked out when the underlying price transits either one of the two barrier levels. Valuation and hedging considerations for these options are much more complex than for single-barrier options. Geman and Yor ("Pricing and Hedging Double-Barrier Options: A Probabilistic Approach") can value these options and are able to produce hedge ratios, but they have to resort to advanced applied mathematics (Laplace transforms and Bessel processes).

Volatility traders find the double-barrier binary option to be useful for expressing short volatility views. This option promises to pay a fixed sum of money at expiration, provided that neither of two defined barriers is breached during the option's life. It is considered to be a short volatility bet because, when there is little or no movement in the spot rate, there is a good probability that the option will be in the money, so to speak, at expiration. Hui ("One-Touch Double Barrier Binary Option Values") works within the Black-Scholes framework to arrive at the value of this exotic option for both European and American exercise.

All of the major dealers quote average rate foreign exchange options. Hedgers favor their use because they usually sell for a lower price than a vanilla option. This may be the case because the value at expiration of the average option is a function of an average of spot rates over time, whereas the vanilla depends only on the spot rate at expiration. In point of fact, the valuation of these exotic options is said to be one of the most complex topics in option theory. Average options are considerably less complicated if the averaging process is based on the geometric mean of the spot levels. Unfortunately, the average option that is in demand is one that is based on the arithmetic average. Not to despair, Levy ("Pricing European Average Rate Currency Options") has a closed-form pricing model for the arithmetic average option.

Quantos Options and Equity Warrants with Special Currency Features

Quantos options are currency options that have expandable and contractible face amounts. These options are found primarily in the international portfolios of institutional investors. The size of the face amount is geared to the value of the international investment in local currency terms. Derman, Karasinski, and Wecker ("Understanding Guaranteed Exchange-Rate Contracts in Foreign Stock Investments") derive valuation formulas for guaranteed exchange rate (i.e., quantos) forward contracts and quantos options. Piros ("The Perfect Hedge: To Quanto Or Not to Quanto") expands on the valuation and hedging of the quantos option. He then provides a thorough consideration of the benefits and costs to using quantos products for hedging. Finally, quantos options sometimes exist in less explicit forms, and some equity derivative products have quantos features. This is the subject of Dravid, Richardson, and Sun ("Pricing Foreign Index Contingent Claims: An Application to Nikkei Index Warrants").

REFERENCES

Boyle, P., and S. H. Lau. "Bumping Up Against the Barrier with the Binomial Method." *Journal of Derivatives,* 1, 4 (1994): 6-14.

Black, Fischer, and Myron Scholes. "The Pricing of Options and Corporate Liabilities." *Journal of Political Economy* 81 (May–June 1973): 637-54.

Cox, John C., Stephen A. Ross, and Marc Rubinstein. "Option Pricing: A Simplified Approach." *Journal of Financial Economics* 3 (September 1979): 229-63.

DeRosa, David F. *Managing Foreign Exchange Risk: Advanced Strategies for Global Investors, Corporations, and Financial Institutions.* Chicago: Irwin Professional Publishing, 1996.

DeRosa, David F. *Options on Foreign Exchange.* Chicago: Probus Publishing, 1992.

MacMillan, Lionel W. "Analytic Approximation for the American Put Option." *Advances in Futures and Options Research* 1 (1986): 119-40.

Merton, Robert C. "Option Pricing When Underlying Stock Returns Are Discontinuous." *Journal of Financial Economics* 3 (January/March 1976): 125-44.

Merton, Robert C. "Theory of Rational Option Pricing." *Bell Journal of Economics and Management Science* 4 (Spring 1973): 141-83.

Samuelson, Paul A., and Robert Merton. "A Complete Model of Warrant Pricing that Maximizes Utility." *Industrial Management Review* 10 (Winter 1969): 17-46.

PART ONE

Forwards and Futures Contracts on Foreign Exchange

The Relation between Forward Prices and Futures Prices

JOHN C. COX
JONATHAN E. INGERSOLL, JR.
STEPHEN A. ROSS

This paper consolidates the results of some recent work on the relation between forward prices and futures prices. It develops a number of propositions characterizing the two prices. These propositions contain several testable implications about the difference between forward and futures prices. Many of the propositions show that equilibrium forward and futures prices are equal to the values of particular assets, even though they are not in themselves asset prices. The paper then illustrates these results in the context of two valuation models and discusses the effects of taxes and other institutional factors.

INTRODUCTION

Forward markets and futures markets have long played an important role in economic affairs. In spite of the attention that they have collectively received, virtually no consideration has been given to the differences between the two types of markets. Indeed, most of the academic literature has treated them as if they were synonymous. Similarly, most practitioners have viewed the differ-

This paper is a substantial expansion of part of the 1977 version of Cox, Ingersoll and Ross (1978). We are grateful to our many colleagues who provided helpful comments and suggestions on that paper. Special thanks go to Fischer Black, Douglas Breeden, Robert Merton, Merton Miller, George Oldfield, and the referee, John Long. This research was supported by the Center for the Study of Futures Markets at Columbia University and by the National Science Foundation under Grants Nos. SOC 77-18087 and SOC 77-22301.

Reprinted with permission from the *Journal of Financial Economics;* Vol. 9; Cox, Ingersoll, and Ross; 1981; Elsevier Science SA, P.O. Box 564, 1001 Lausanne, Switzerland.

ences as irrelevant administrative details and acted as if the two served exactly the same economic functions. Given the similarity of the two markets, such conclusions are quite understandable, but they are nevertheless incorrect. Forward markets and futures markets differ in fundamental ways.

An individual who takes a long position in a forward contract agrees to buy a designated good or asset on a specified future date, the maturity date, for the forward price prevailing at the time the contract is initiated. On the maturity date, then, the forward price must equal the spot price of the underlying good or asset. No money changes hands initially or during the lifetime of the contract, only on the maturity date. The equilibrium forward price must thus continually change over time in a way such that newly created forward contracts will always have a zero value when they are initiated.

A futures contract is similar in many ways, but there is an important difference. An individual who takes a long position in a futures contract nominally agrees to buy a designated good or asset on the maturity date, for the futures price prevailing at the time the contract is initiated. Hence, the futures price must also equal the spot price on the maturity date. Again, no money changes hands initially. Subsequently, however, as the futures price changes, the party in whose favor the price change occurred must immediately be paid the full amount of the change by the losing party. As a result, the payment required on the maturity date to buy the underlying good or asset is simply its spot price at that time. The difference between that amount and the initial futures price has been paid (or received) in installments throughout the life of the contract. Like the forward price, the equilibrium futures price must also continually change over time. It must do so in such a way that the remaining stream of future payments described above always has a value of zero.

The difference in the payment schedules is clearly explained in a seminal article by Black (1976). While Black's discussion is completely correct, it is unfortunately presented in the context of a constant interest rate. As it turns out, this obscures a basic economic difference between the two types of markets. With a constant interest rate, the two are essentially equivalent and forward prices are equal to futures prices, but in general this is not true.

Several studies in addition to ours have independently noted the critical role of stochastic interest rates. To our knowledge, the first to do so was Margrabe (1976). Working in a continuous-time framework. Margarbe shows that if forward and futures prices are equal there will be an arbitrage opportunity unless a certain special condition is satisfied; constant interest rates are sufficient but not necessary for this condition to be met. Merton (1979) uses a discrete-time arbitrage argument to derive a way to sign the difference between forward and futures prices. Although Merton considers only forward and futures contracts on Treasury bills, his approach is such that this involves no loss of generality. Jarrow and Oldfield (1981) provide a perspicuous discussion of the contractual differences and use an arbitrage argument to show the importance of stochastic interest rates. They also show the connection between forward contracts and options. Richard and Sundaresan (1981) derive a continuous-time equilibrium model and use it to analyze forward and futures contracts. Sundaresan (1980) employs the Richard and Sundaresan model to develop and test a number of explicit formulas for forward and futures prices. French (1981) examines a discrete-time utility-based model of forward and futures pricing and undertakes several empirical tests of his results.

One purpose of our paper is to consolidate some of the results of these studies. In so doing, we hope to help clarify the relation between forward prices and futures prices. Section 2 develops a number of propositions characterizing the two prices. These propositions contain several testable implications about the difference between forward and futures prices. Many of the propositions show that equilibrium forward and futures prices are equal to the values of particular assets. This allows one to apply any framework for valuing assets to the determination of forward and futures prices, even though they are not in themselves asset prices. Section 3 illustrates some of these results in a simple two-period framework with a complete set of state prices. Section 4 then uses the propositions developed in section 2 to examine forward and futures prices in the context of a continuous-time valuation model. This model gives a basis for obtaining explicit formulas for equilibrium forward and futures prices and hence provides further opportunities for empirical testing. In section 5, we conclude the paper with some comments and conjectures about the effects of taxes and other institutional factors.

SOME FUNDAMENTAL PROPOSITIONS ABOUT FORWARD PRICES AND FUTURES PRICES

For the most part, our results in this section are based on arbitrage arguments and are thus quite general. They are consequences of what is sometimes called the law of one price: investment strategies which have the same payoffs must have the same current value. To concentrate on the basic issues, we assume perfect frictionless markets. Hence, we shall ignore both taxes and transactions costs until section 5.

We shall use the following notation:

s = maturity date of the forward and futures contracts,
$V(s)$ = price at time s of the good or asset on which the contracts are written,
$P(t)$ = price at time t of a default-free discount bond paying one dollar at time s.
$G(t)$ = forward price at time t,
$H(t)$ = futures price at time t,
R_t = one plus the spot interest rate prevailing from time t to time $t + 1$.

Our first two propositions express forward prices and futures prices in terms of assets making particular payments on the maturity date:

PROPOSITION 1. *The forward price $G(t)$ is the value at time t of a contract which will pay at time s the amount*

$V(s)/P(t)$.   (1)

Proof. Consider the following strategy: take a long position in $1/P(t)$ forward contracts and place the amount $G(t)$ in bonds maturing at time s. The current investment required is $G(t)$. There are no interim payoffs, and the payoff at time s is

$$\frac{1}{P(t)}\,[G(s) - G(t)] + \frac{G(t)}{P(t)} = \frac{V(s)}{P(t)}. \quad \blacksquare$$ (2)

PROPOSITION 2. *The futures price $H(t)$ is the value at time t of a contract which will pay at time s the amount*

$$V(s) \prod_{k=t}^{s-1} R_k.$$ (3)

Proof. Consider the following strategy: at time t, take the amount $H(t)$ and continually reinvest it and the accumulated interest in one-period bonds until time s. At each time $j, j = t, t + 1, \ldots, s - 1$, take a long position in $\Pi_{k=t}^{j} R_k$ futures contracts. Liquidate each contract after one period and continually re-invest the (possibly negative) proceeds and accumulated interest in one period bonds until time s. The current investment required for this strategy is $H(t)$. The payoff at time s is

$$H(t) \prod_{k=t}^{s-1} R_k + \sum_{j=t}^{s-1} \left(\prod_{k=t}^{j} R_k\right)[H(j + 1) - H(j)]\left(\prod_{k=j+1}^{s-1} R_k\right)$$

$$= H(s) \prod_{k=t}^{s-1} R_k = V(s) \prod_{k=t}^{s-1} R_k. \quad \blacksquare$$ (4)

Propositions 1 and 2 show that the distinction between forward prices and futures prices is very much like the distinction between "going long" and "roll-ing over shorts" in the bond market. Each price is equal to the value of a claim which will pay a particular number of units of the underlying good or asset on the maturity date. For the forward price, this number is the total return which will be earned on an investment in a discount bond maturing at time s. For the futures price, it is the total return which will be earned from a policy of contin-ual reinvestment in one-period bonds. This characterization draws attention to an important difference between futures prices and forward prices: futures prices will depend on the correlation of spot prices and interest rates, while forward prices will not.

Jarrow and Oldfield (1981) show that forward and futures contracts can be used to create a portfolio which will give a sure return on the maturity date if interest rates are constant, but not if they are random. Propositions 1 and 2, taken together, give essentially the same conclusion. Proposition 2 is identical to a result derived by Richard and Sundaresan (1981) using their equilibrium model and by French (1981) using a discrete-time arbitrage approach. Our next three propositions follow immediately from Propositions 1 and 2.

PROPOSITION 3. [Black (1976)]. *If interest rates are non-stochastic, then G(t) = H(t).*

Proof. If interest rates are non-stochastic, then

$$\frac{1}{P(t)} = \prod_{k=t}^{s-1} R_k. \ \blacksquare \tag{5}$$

If there is only one period remaining before the maturity date, $1/P(t)$ will always equal R_t. Consequently, there will be no difference between forward and futures contracts in any one-period model or in any two-period model where all goods are consumed in the final period.

PROPOSITION 4. *If V(s) is non-stochastic, then G(t) = H(t) = V(s).*

Proof. If $V(s)$ is non-stochastic, then a current investment of the amount $V(s)$ in bonds maturing at time s produces a payoff at that time of $V(s)/P(t)$, so $G(t) = V(s)$. Similarly, a current investment of $V(s)$ in a strategy of rolling over one-period bonds gives a payoff at time s of $V(s)\prod_{k=1}^{s-1}R_k$, so $H(t) = V(s)$. $\blacksquare$

PROPOSITION 5. *Let $h_i(t)$ be the futures price and $g_i(t)$ be the forward price at time t of a good i whose spot price at time s is $v_i(s)$). If*

$$V(s) = \sum_i a_i v_i(s) \quad \text{for some constants } a_i.$$

then

$$H(t) = \sum_i a_i h_i(t) \quad \text{and} \quad G(t) = \sum_i a_i g_i(t).$$

Proof. This follows immediately from the linearity in $V(s)$ of the right-hand side of (1) and (3). $\blacksquare$

This result states that the futures price of a portfolio is equal to a corresponding portfolio of futures prices and the same is true for forward prices. If the payoffs were not linear, then this conclusion would not hold; for example, it is well known that an option on a portfolio is not the same as a portfolio of options. While Proposition 5 is quite obvious, it is nevertheless very useful. One example is provided by the forward and futures prices of non-callable government bonds. These bonds can be thought of as portfolios of discount bonds. Consequently, any method for finding the futures price of a discount bond will also give the futures prices for all coupon bonds.

Our next proposition expresses the difference between forward prices and futures prices in terms of the relation between futures prices and bond prices.

It is very similar to a result of Merton (1979). Loosely stated, it says that if futures prices and bond prices are positively correlated, then the futures price is less than the forward price; if they are negatively correlated, then the futures price is greater than the forward price. In this and the following propositions, we shall occasionally refer to a continuous-time, continuous-state economy. By this, we mean an economy in which trading takes place continuously and in which all variables relevant to the equilibrium follow diffusion processes.

PROPOSITION 6. $G(t) - H(t)$ *is the value at time t of a payment of*

$$-\sum_{j=t}^{s-1} [H(j + 1) - H(j)]\left[\frac{P(j)}{P(j + 1)} - 1\right]\bigg/P(t), \tag{6}$$

to be received at time s. For a continuous-time, continuous-state economy, this sum becomes

$$\int_t^s H(u)[\text{cov } H(u), P(u)]du/P(t), \tag{7}$$

where [cov H(u), P(u)] stands for the local covariance of the percentage changes in H with the percentage changes in P. Hence, [cov H(u), P(u)] > 0 for all u implies $G(t) > H(t)$ and [cov H(u), P(u)] < 0 for all u implies $G(t) < H(t)$.

Proof.   Consider the following strategy, which requires no investment. Take a short position in a forward contract at time t. In each period j, $j = t, \ldots, s - 1$, take a long position in $P(j)$ futures contracts, liquidate them after one period, and place the (possibly negative) proceeds in bonds with maturity date s. At time s, the payoff to this strategy is

$$G(t) - G(s) + \sum_{j=t}^{s-1} P(j)[H(j + 1) - H(j)]\left(\frac{1}{P(j + 1)}\right)$$

$$= G(t) - G(s) + \sum_{j=t}^{s-1} [H(j + 1) - H(j)]$$

$$+ \sum_{j=t}^{s-1} [H(j + 1) - H(j)]\left[\frac{P(j)}{P(j + 1)} - 1\right]$$

$$= H(s) - G(s) + G(t) - H(t)$$

$$+ \sum_{j=t}^{s-1} [H(j + 1) - H(j)]\left[\frac{P(j)}{P(j + 1)} - 1\right]. \tag{8}$$

Since this strategy requires no investment, the current values of this payoff must be zero. Now note that $G(s) = H(s)$ and that the current value of a certain payment of $G(t) - H(t)$ at time s is $P(t)[G(t) - H(t)]$. Consequently, $G(t) - H(t)$ is the current value of a payment at time s of

$$-\sum_{j=1}^{s-1} [H(j + 1) - H(j)]\left[\frac{P(j)}{P(j + 1)} - 1\right]\bigg/P(t).$$

Hence, in a continuous-time, continuous-state economy, if the local covariance of the percentage changes in H and P will always have one sign from t to s, then $G(t) - H(t)$ has the same sign.   ■

Like Proposition 2, the following proposition equates the futures price, which is not itself the value of an asset, with another quantity which is the value of an asset. This allows us to apply any equilibrium framework for valuing assets to the determination of equilibrium futures prices. Proposition 8 establishes an analogous result for forward prices.

PROPOSITION 7.   *$H(t)$ is the value at time t of a contract which gives a payment of $V(s)$ at time s and a flow from time t to time s of the prevailing spot rate times the prevailing futures price. That is, $H(t)$ is the value at time t of a contract which pays $V(s)$ at time s and $(R_u - 1)H(u)$ at each time $u + 1$ for $u = t, t + 1, \ldots, s - 1$.*

Proof.   Consider strategy A: continually reinvest the payouts received from this security and the accumulated interest in one-period bonds. At time s, the proceeds will be

$$\sum_{j=t}^{s-1} (R_j - 1)H(j) \prod_{k=j+1}^{s-1} R_k + V(s). \tag{9}$$

But since $V(s) = H(s)$, this can be rewritten as

$$H(t) \prod_{k=t}^{s-1} R_k + \sum_{j=t}^{s-1} [H(j + 1) - H(j)] \prod_{k=j+1}^{s-1} R_k. \tag{10}$$

Now consider strategy B: invest $H(t)$ in a one-period bond at time t and then continually reinvest the proceeds in one-period bonds. Take a long position in one futures contract and continually reinvest the (possibly negative) proceeds received at the end of each period in one-period bonds. At time s, the proceeds of strategy B will be

$$H(t) \prod_{k=t}^{s-1} R_k + \sum_{j=t}^{s-1} [H(j + 1) - H(j)] \prod_{k=j+1}^{s-1} R_k. \tag{11}$$

This is the same as the proceeds of strategy A. Since the current value of B is $H(t)$, the current value of A must also be $H(t)$.   ■

PROPOSITION 8.   *$G(t)$ is the value at time t of a contract which pays $V(s)$ at time s and the flow*

$$(R_u - 1)G(u) + [G(u + 1) - G(u)]\left[\frac{P(u + 1)}{P(u)} - 1\right], \tag{12}$$

at each time $u + 1$ for $u = t, \ldots, s - 1$.

Proof.   Let strategy A be the following: continually reinvest the payouts received from this security and the accumulated interest in one-period bonds. At time s the proceeds will be

$$
\sum_{j=t}^{s-1} (R_j - 1) G(j) \prod_{k=j+1}^{s-1} R_k
$$
$$
+ \sum_{j=t}^{s-1} [G(j+1) - G(j)] \left[\frac{P(j+1)}{P(j)} - 1 \right] \prod_{k=j+1}^{s-1} R_k + V(s). \tag{13}
$$

Since $G(s) = V(s)$, this can be rewritten as

$$
G(t) \prod_{k=t}^{s-1} R_k + \sum_{j=t}^{s-1} [G(j+1) - G(j)] \prod_{k=j+1}^{s-1} R_k
$$
$$
+ \sum_{j=t}^{s-1} [G(j+1) - G(j)] \left[\frac{P(j+1)}{P(j)} - 1 \right] \prod_{k=j+1}^{s-1} R_k
$$
$$
= G(t) \prod_{k=t}^{s-1} R_k + \sum_{j=t}^{s-1} [G(j+1) - G(j)] \left[\frac{P(j+1)}{P(j)} \right] \prod_{k=j+1}^{s-1} R_k. \tag{14}
$$

Now consider strategy B: invest $G(t)$ in a one-period bond at time t and then continually reinvest the proceeds in one-period bonds. At each time $j, j = t, \ldots, s - 1$, take a long position in $1/P(j)$ forward contracts. Close out each contract after one period, thereby locking in the amount $G(j+1) - G(j)$ to be received at time s. Obtain the present value of this amount, $P(j + 1)[G(j + 1) - G(j)]$, and invest it in one-period bonds. Continually reinvest the proceeds in one-period bonds thereafter. At time s, the proceeds of strategy B will be

$$
G(t) \prod_{k=t}^{s-1} R_k + \sum_{j=t}^{s-1} [G(j+1) - G(j)] \left[\frac{P(j+1)}{P(j)} \right] \prod_{k=j+1}^{s-1} R_k. \tag{15}
$$

This is identical to the proceeds of strategy A. Since the current value of B is $G(t)$, the current value of A must also be $G(t)$.   ∎

Propositions 7 and 8 are useful not only in their own right, but also for obtaining Proposition 9. This proposition shows for forward prices a result analogous to Proposition 6 for futures prices. It expresses the difference between forward prices and futures prices in terms of the relation between forward prices and bond prices.

PROPOSITION 9.   *$G(t) - H(t)$ is the value at time t of a payment of*

$$
\left(\prod_{k=t}^{s-1} R_k \right) \left[\sum_{j=t}^{s-1} [G(j+1) - G(j)] \left[\frac{P(j+1)}{P(j)} - 1 \right] \right], \tag{16}
$$

to be received at time s. For a continuous-time, continuous-state economy, the above expression becomes

$$
\left[\exp\left(\int_t^s \log R(u) \, du \right) \right] \int_t^s G(u)[\text{cov } G(u), P(u)] \, du. \tag{17}
$$

Hence, [cov G(u), P(u)] > 0 for all u implies G(t) > H(t) and [cov G(u), P(u)] < 0 for all u implies G(t) < H(t).

Proof. Propositions 7 and 8 imply that $H(t) - G(t)$ is the current value of a contract which pays

$$(R_u - 1)[H(u) - G(u)] - [G(u + 1) - G(u)]\left[\frac{P(u + 1)}{P(u)} - 1\right], \tag{18}$$

at each time $u + 1$ for $u = t, \ldots, s - 1$. Consider the following strategy.

Over each period j, take a long position in $\Pi_{k=t}^{j} R_k$ of these contracts. Do this with no net investment in the following way. If the current value of the contract is positive, borrow the amount and use the first component of the payout, which will be positive, to repay the borrowing; if the current value is negative, lend the amount and use the proceeds of the lending to make restitution for the first component of the payout, which will be negative. After doing this, the remaining proceeds at time $j + 1$ from the position taken at time j will be

$$\left[[H(j + 1) - G(j + 1)] - [H(j) - G(j)]\right.$$
$$\left. - [G(j + 1) - G(j)]\left[\frac{P(j + 1)}{P(j)} - 1\right]\right]\prod_{k=t}^{j} R_k. \tag{19}$$

Invest this amount in one period bonds at time $j + 1$ and then continually reinvest it and the accumulated interest in one-period bonds. At time s the total proceeds from all positions taken from t to s will be

$$\left[\sum_{j=t}^{s-1}[H(j + 1) - G(j + 1)] - [H(j) - G(j)]\right.$$
$$\left. - \sum_{j=1}^{s-1}[G(j + 1) - G(j)]\left[\frac{P(j + 1)}{P(j)} - 1\right]\right]\prod_{k=t}^{s-1} R_k. \tag{20}$$

Note that since $G(s) = H(s)$, then

$$\sum_{j=t}^{s-1}[[H(j + 1) - G(j + 1)] - [H(j) - G(j)]] = G(t) - H(t). \tag{21}$$

Since the entire position requires no net investment, its current value must be zero. The current value of the amount $[G(t) - H(t)]\Pi_{k=t}^{s-1}R_k$ received at time s is $G(t) - H(t)$. Consequently, $G(t) - H(t)$ is the current value of a payment at time s of

$$\left(\prod_{k=t}^{s-1} R_k\right)\left[\sum_{j=t}^{s-1}[G(j + 1) - G(j)]\left[\frac{P(j + 1)}{P(j)} - 1\right]\right]. \tag{22}$$

Hence, for a continuous-time, continuous-state economy, if [cov $G(u)$, $P(u)$] always has one sign, then $G(t) - H(t)$ has the same sign. ∎

Note that Propositions 6 and 9 show the relation between forward and futures prices when both forward and futures markets exist simultaneously. If we find, for example, that $G(t) > H(t)$, this does not imply that replacing a forward market with a futures market will result in a lower price. Such a change could conceivably affect the equilibrium valuation of all assets and lead instead to a higher price. At the present time, simultaneous forward and futures markets are available for certain U.S. Treasury and Government National Mortgage Association securities, some foreign currencies, and a number of commodities. However, the forward contracts are typically traded with standardized times to maturity rather than standardized maturity dates. In these cases, corresponding forward and futures contracts exist simultaneously only on the days for which a standardized time to maturity in the forward market coincides with a standardized maturity date in the futures market.

Up to this point, nothing that we have said has depended on the existence of a spot market or on the characteristics of the underlying good or asset. Indeed, this good or asset need not even exist at the current time. This could be the case, for example, with a perishable commodity before the next crop is harvested. However, if there is a spot market, or an options market, then we can express our results in terms of spot prices and option prices.

If $V(s)$ is the price at time s of a currently traded good or asset, then

$$G(t) = O(t)/P(t), \tag{23}$$

where $O(t)$ is the current value of a European call option with maturity date s and exercise price zero. [The strategy of buying $1/P(t)$ options gives a payoff at time s of $V(s)/P(t)$.] In that case

$$[G(j+1) - G(j)]\left[\frac{P(j+1)}{P(j)} - 1\right] = \frac{O(j)}{P(j)}\left[\frac{O(j+1)}{O(j)} - 1\right]\left[\frac{P(j+1)}{P(j)} - 1\right] \\ - \frac{O(j+1)}{P(j+1)}\left[\frac{P(j+1)}{P(j)} - 1\right]^2, \tag{24}$$

and for continuous-time, continuous-state economies this becomes

$$G[\text{cov } G, P] = (O/P)[\text{cov } O, P - \text{var } P]. \tag{25}$$

If the asset makes no payouts between t and s, then $O(t) = V(t)$. This immediately leads to a result which was obtained in a different way by Margrabe (1976):

(i) $\text{cov } V, P > \text{var } P$ implies $G(t) > H(t)$,

(ii) $\text{cov } V, P < \text{var } P$ implies $G(t) < H(t)$. $\tag{26}$

For Treasury bills, V is itself a discount bond maturing at some time after s. We would thus expect V and P to be highly correlated and var $V >$ var P. Hence, we would expect cov $V, P >$ var P and $G(t) > H(t)$. For an asset which is a hedge against bond price fluctuations (i.e., is negatively correlated with bond prices), we would have cov $V, P <$ var P and $G(t) < H(t)$.

With the existence of a spot market, we can also obtain another result somewhat similar to Proposition 6, but involving payouts depending on the spot price rather than the futures price. This gives an additional way to determine the futures price. It also allows us to express the relation between futures prices and spot prices in terms of the relation between the interest rate and the spot rental rate on the good or asset. By the spot rental rate at time u, we mean the fraction of the beginning-of-period spot price which would have to be paid at the end of the period to obtain the full use of the good or asset during the period, including the right to receive any payouts such as dividends.

PROPOSITION 10. *Let Y_u be the spot rental rate at time u. Then $H(t) - V(t)$ is equal to the value of a contract which gives a payment of*

$$[(R_u - 1 - Y_u)V(u)] \prod_{k=t}^{u-1} R_k, \tag{27}$$

at each time $u + 1$ for $u = t, t + 1, \ldots, s - 1$. Consequently, if the spot interest rate is always greater (less) than the spot rental rate, then the futures price is greater (less) than the spot price.

Proof. Let $Z(t)$ be the value at time t of the contract described. Consider the following strategy. At time t, take a long position in one contract and buy one unit of the good or asset in the spot market for $V(t)$. Finance the spot purchase by rolling over one-period loans. The total investment required is thus $Z(t)$. At each time j, for $j = t + 1, \ldots, s - 1$, use the payment received from the contract and the proceeds from spot rental over the previous period to increase the number of units of the spot good or asset held from $\prod_{k=t}^{j-1} R_k$ to $\prod_{k=t}^{j} R_k$. The total value of the position at time s is

$$V(s) \prod_{k=t}^{s-1} R_k - V(t) \prod_{k=t}^{s-1} R_k. \tag{28}$$

Using Proposition 2, the current value of this amount is $H(t) - V(t)$. Consequently, $Z(t) = H(t) - V(t)$. If all of the payments given by the contract are positive (negative), then its current value must be positive (negative), so $H(t) > V(t)$ $H(t) < V(t)$). ∎

Our final proposition relates our results to the continuous-time capital asset pricing model (CAPM). It is stated in terms of the CAPM in consumption form as derived by Breeden (1979), but the same conclusions hold for the original multi-factor model of Merton (1973).

PROPOSITION 11. *Futures prices will satisfy the capital asset pricing model for arbitrary $V(s)$, but forward prices will do so only if interest rates are non-stochastic.*

Proof. Consider the dollar return from holding over one period a long position in $1/P(t)$ forward contracts and the amount $G(t)$ in one-period bonds. The dollar return is

$$\frac{1}{P(t)} \left[P(t + 1)[G(t + 1) - G(t)]\right] + R_t G(t). \tag{29}$$

Denote the expected value of the dollar return as μG. The CAPM in consumption form says that

$$\mu G - R_t G = \beta_{C,K}\left(\frac{\mu_M M - R_t M}{\beta_{C,M}}\right), \tag{30}$$

where

$$\beta_{C,K} = \text{cov}\left[\frac{P(t + 1)}{P(t)} [G(t + 1) - G(t)], C(t + 1) - C(t)\right]\Big/\sigma_C^2,$$

$C(t)$ is aggregate consumption at time t, $M(t)$ is the value of the market portfolio at time t, and K is the portfolio described above. Consequently, we can write

$$\begin{aligned} E&\left(\frac{P(t + 1)}{P(t)} [G(t + 1) - G(t)]\right) \\ &= \text{cov}\left(\frac{P(t + 1)}{P(t)} [G(t + 1) - G(t)], C(t + 1) - C(t)\right) \\ &\quad \times \left(\frac{\mu_M M - R_t M}{\sigma_C^2 \beta_{C,M}}\right), \end{aligned} \tag{31}$$

where E indicates expectation. Also, we have

$$\begin{aligned} \frac{P(t + 1)}{P(t)} &[G(t + 1) - G(t)] \\ &= [G(t + 1) - G(t)] + \left(\frac{P(t + 1)}{P(t)} - 1\right)[G(t + 1) - G(t)]. \end{aligned} \tag{32}$$

Thus, in the limit for continuous-time, continuous-state economies,

$$\begin{aligned} \text{cov}&\left(\frac{P(t + 1)}{P(t)} [G(t + 1) - G(t)], C(t + 1) - C(t)\right) \\ &= \text{cov}[G(t + 1) - G(t), C(t + 1) - C(t)], \end{aligned} \tag{33}$$

so forward prices can satisfy the CAPM only if

$$E\left(\left(\frac{P(t + 1)}{P(t)} - 1\right)[G(t + 1) - G(t)]\right)\Big/[(t + 1) - t] \to 0 \tag{34}$$

in the limit, which will be true for arbitrary V only if interest rates are nonstochastic.

Consequently, any attempt to apply the CAPM to a series of forward prices will be misdirected. However, a slight modification of this line of reasoning shows that changes in future prices, when combined with a portfolio as described above, will satisfy the CAPM in consumption form, as is discussed in Breeden (1980). ∎

This concludes our series of propositions relating forward prices and futures prices. Although we hope that our list contains the most important propositions, it is not meant to be exhaustive; we have not found a general way to characterize all possible relations between the two prices.

In the remainder of this section, we discuss how some of the features of forward and futures contracts could be combined. Forward contracts provide an easy way for an individual to lock in at time t the amount he will have to pay at time s for one unit of the underlying good or asset. By taking a long position in a forward contract, the individual can arrange today to buy the good on the maturity date for a price of $G(t)$. An important implication of our results is that futures contracts cannot in general provide exactly the same service. An exact hedging strategy using only (a finite number of) futures contracts may not be possible, and even if possible, it would typically require more information than is needed when employing forward contracts.

It may appear that this is a necessary consequence of the resettlement feature of futures contracts. This would be unfortunate, since resettlement may provide certain advantages. With forward contracts significant implicit or explicit collateral may be necessary; with futures contracts the requirements would be much smaller. Futures markets thus to a large extent separate the actual transactions in the good from the issues of collateralization and financing, while forward markets do not. However, it is easy to specify a contract which will meet the dual requirements of providing a simple exact hedging procedure and requiring only minimal collateral. This is in fact exactly what would be accomplished with a forward contract which had to be settled and rewritten continually.

To make this more precise, we introduce a quasi-futures contract, which is exactly the same as a regular futures contract, except that at the end of each period the person in whose favor the price change occurred is paid not the full amount of the change, but instead the present value that this full amount would have if it were paid on the maturity date. If we denote the quasi-futures price at time t as $Q(t)$, then an individual having a long position in such a contract receives at each time $j + 1$, for $j = t, \ldots, s - 1$, the amount $P(j + 1)[Q(j + 1) - Q(j)]$. If the individual invests the (possibly negative) proceeds received at each time $j + 1$ in bonds maturing at time s, then the value of his position at time s will be

$$\sum_{j=t}^{s-1} P(j + 1)[Q(j + 1) - Q(j)]\left(\frac{1}{P(j + 1)}\right) = V(s) - Q(t). \tag{35}$$

This strategy allows the individual to arrange today to buy the good on the maturity date for a designated price $Q(t)$. Since the strategy requires no net investment, it is equivalent to a forward contract, and hence $Q(t) = G(t)$.

A TWO-PERIOD EXAMPLE

In this section, we give a simple example in which forward and futures prices can be found directly and use it to illustrate some of our propositions. In the next section, we shall reverse this procedure and use the propositions to de-termine forward and futures prices in a more complex setting.

For our first example, we consider a two-period model with a complete system of state prices. We shall supplement our earlier notation in the following way:

p_i = price at time t of a claim which will pay one dollar at time $t + 1$ if the economy is in state i at time $t + 1$,

p_{ij} = price at time $t + 1$ of a claim which will pay one dollar at time $t + 2$ if the economy is in state i at time $t + 1$ and state j at time $t + 2$,

V_{ij} = price of the underlying good or asset at time $t + 2$ if the economy is in state i at time $t + 1$ and state j at time $t + 2$,

H_i = futures price at time $t + 1$ if the economy is in state i at time $t + 1$.

As before, $G(t)$ and $H(t)$ stand for the current forward price and futures price, respectively.

At time $t + 2$, the value of a forward contract written at time t will be

$$V_{ij} - G(t),\tag{36}$$

and the current value of this amount is

$$\sum_{i,j} p_i p_{ij} [V_{ij} - G(t)].\tag{37}$$

Since no money changes hands initially, both parties will be willing to enter into the contract only if its current value is zero. Consequently,

$$G(t) = \sum_{i,j} p_i p_{ij} V_{ij} \Big/ \sum_{i,j} p_i p_{ij}.\tag{38}$$

The current value of a bond paying one dollar at time $t + 2$ is $\sum_{i,j} p_i p_{ij}$, so this verifies that $G(t)$ can be found as shown in Proposition 1.

Now we turn to determining the current futures price. Note that at time $t + 1$ the futures contract is the same as a forward contract, so

$$H_i = \sum_i p_{ij} V_{ij} \Big/ \sum_j p_{ij}.\tag{39}$$

At time t, the holder of a futures contract knows that he will receive at time $t + 1$ the amount

$$H_i - H(t),\tag{40}$$

the current value of which is

$$\sum_i p_i [H_i - H(t)].\tag{41}$$

Again, since no money changes hands when the contract is initiated, this current value must be zero, so

$$H(t) = \sum_i p_i H_i \bigg/ \sum_i p_i = \sum_i p_i \bigg[\sum_j p_{ij} V_{ij} \bigg/ \sum_j p_{ij}\bigg] \bigg/ \sum_i p_i$$

$$= \sum_{i,j} p_i p_{ij} \bigg(1 \bigg/ \sum_i p_i\bigg)\bigg(1 \bigg/ \sum_j p_{ij}\bigg) V_{ij}. \tag{42}$$

Since $R_t = 1/\Sigma_i p_i$ and $R_{t+1} = 1/\Sigma_i p_{ij}$, this result illustrates Proposition 2. The current futures price is the same as the value of a claim which will pay at time $t + 2$ the amount V_{ij} times the total return from rolling over one-period bonds.

If interest rates are non-stochastic, then $\Sigma_j p_{ij}$ is the same for all i, and $\Sigma_{i,j} p_i p_{ij} = (\Sigma_i p_i)(\Sigma_j p_{ij})$. Hence, it is apparent by inspection that $G(t) = H(t)$. Similarly, if V_{ij} is a constant, then it is obvious that $G(t) = H(t)$.

FUTURES PRICES AND FORWARD PRICES IN CONTINUOUS-TIME, CONTINUOUS-STATE ECONOMIES

Propositions 2, 7 and 10 show how to construct assets whose current value must be equal to the current futures price. Propositions 1 and 8 do the same for forward prices. These results enable us to apply any intertemporal valuation model to the determination of forward and futures prices.

For our second example, we shall use a valuation framework which has become standard in finance. It has been shown by various arguments that in a continuous-time, continuous-state economy the value of any contingent claim F will satisfy the fundamental partial differential equation

$$\frac{1}{2} \sum_{i,j} (\text{cov } X_i, X_j) F_{X_i X_i} + \sum_i (\mu_i - \phi_i) F_{X_i} + F_t$$
$$- r(X, t)F + \delta(X, t) = 0, \tag{43}$$

where subscripts on F indicate partial derivatives and X is a vector containing all variables necessary to describe the current state of the economy. The remaining symbols are as follows: μ_i is the local mean of changes in X_i, cov X_i, X_j is the local covariance of the changes in X_i with the changes in X_j, $r(X, t)$ is the spot interest rate, $\delta(X, t)$ is the continuous payment flow (if any) received by the claim, and ϕ_i is the factor risk premium associated with X_i.

A number of studies have derived equations similar to (43) based on arbitrage arguments. For example, see Brennan and Schwartz (1979), Garman (1977), and Richard (1978). In these models, the factor risk premiums and the processes driving the state variables are determined exogenously or remain unspecified.

A somewhat different approach leading to the same type of equation is taken in Cox, Ingersoll and Ross (1978). In that paper, an intertemporal equilibrium model is developed in which all economic variables, including the interest rate and the factor risk premiums, are endogenously determined and explicitly identified in terms of individual preferences and production possibilities. Richard and Sundaresan (1981) extend this model to include multiple goods and use it to examine forward and futures contracts. In that setting, Sundaresan (1980) develops several explicit formulas for forward and futures prices. Most of our results in this section are special cases of their results.

Proposition 7 states that the futures price is equal to the value of an asset which receives a continual payout flow of $(R_u - 1)H(u)$ and the amount $V(s)$ at time s. In the present application, this would correspond to $\delta(X, t) = r(X, t)H(X, t)$ and $H(X, s) = V(X, s)$. The futures price must thus satisfy the partial differential equation

$$\frac{1}{2} \sum_{i,j} (\text{cov } X_i, X_j) H_{X_i X_j} + \sum_i (\mu_i - \phi_i) H_{X_i} + H_t = 0, \tag{44}$$

with terminal condition $H(X, s) = V(X, s)$.

Two results from Cox, Ingersoll and Ross (1978) will be useful in characterizing futures prices. Lemma 4 of that paper shows that with $\delta = 0$ the solution of (43) for a claim paying $\theta(X(s))$ at time s can be written as

$$\hat{E}\left[\theta(X(s))\left[\exp\left(-\int_t^s r(X(u))du\right)\right]\right], \tag{45}$$

where $\hat{E}$ indicates expectation taken with respect to a risk-adjusted process for the state variables. The risk adjustment is accomplished by reducing the local mean of each underlying variable by the corresponding factor risk premium. Proposition 2 states that the futures price is the same as the current value of an asset which will receive a single payment of $\theta(X(s)) = V(X(s))[\exp(\int_t^s r(X(u))du)]$ at time s. Consequently, we can write the futures price as the risk-adjusted expected spot price at time s,

$$H(X, t) = \hat{E}[V(X(s))]. \tag{46}$$

An immediate application of theorem 4 of Cox, Ingersoll and Ross (1978) shows that the futures price can be written in yet another way as

$$H(X, t) = E\left[V(X(s))\left[\exp\left(\int_t^s r(X(u))du\right)\right]\left(\frac{J_W(s)}{J_W(t)}\right)\right], \tag{47}$$

where E indicates expectation with respect to the actual process (with no risk-adjustment) for the state variables and $J_W(\cdot)$ is the marginal utility of wealth of the representative individual. Given proposition 2, this is an intuitively sensible result. Since H is the value of a security which will pay $V(X(s))\exp[\int_t^s r(X(u))du]$ at time s, (47) simply says that the value of this security is the expectation of its marginal-utility-weighted payoffs.

Forward prices can be obtained in a very straightforward way. From Proposition 1, $G(X, t)$ will equal $(1/P(t))$ times the solution to (43) with $\delta = 0$ and $F(X, s) = V(X, s)$. Similarly, we can write

$$G(X, t) = \hat{E}\left[V(X(s))\left[\exp\left(-\int_t^s r(X(u))du\right)\right]\right]\Big/P(t) = E\left[V(X(s))\left(\frac{J_W(s)}{J_W(t)}\right)\right]\Big/P(t). \tag{48}$$

As we have noted, an important historical role of forward and futures markets has been to provide a mechanism by which individuals can lock in today the price which they will have to pay for a good or asset on a future date. The simple strategy of taking a long position in one forward contract will accomplish exactly that, but the corresponding strategy of taking a long position in one futures contract will not. However, this does not rule out the possibility of achieving the same outcome by using futures contracts in a more complicated strategy. In the present context, with say n state variables, the results of Black (1976) indicate that we should be able to find a controlled hedging portfolio, along the lines of Merton (1977), containing n futures contracts and borrowing or lending at the spot interest rate r which will require no subsequent investment and will duplicate the payoff to a forward contract on the maturity date.

To pursue this without unnecessary complications, we shall consider the case of $n = 1$; generalization to an arbitrary number of state variables is straightforward. Let π be the value of the hedging portfolio, and let α be the number of futures contracts held in this portfolio. Further, let $D(t)$ be the value at time t of a forward contract written at time q; if q is the current time t, then $D(t) = 0$. Consider the following strategy. At time t, make an investment of $D(t)$ in the hedging portfolio. Place this amount in spot lending (rolling over shorts). At each time τ, take a long position in $D_X(\tau)/H_X(\tau)$ futures contracts, using (41) and (42) to find D and H in terms of X and t. Invest all money received from the futures position in spot lending and finance all money due by spot borrowing. If it is always possible to trade at equilibrium futures prices and interest rates, then this hedging portfolio will have the same value as the forward contract on the maturity date. To see this, consider the following argument. Let $w(t)$ be the Wiener process driving the state variable, and let LH denote the differential generator of H, $LH \equiv 1/2\sigma^2(X)H_{XX} + \mu_X H_X + H_t$, where $\sigma^2(X)$ is the local variance of the changes in X. From Ito's formula, the value of the hedging portfolio will follow the stochastic differential equation

$$d\pi(t) = r(X, t)\pi(t)dt + \alpha(X, t)dH(t). \tag{49}$$

Hence, the value of the portfolio at time s is

$$\pi(s) = \left[\exp\left(\int_t^s r(u)du\right)\right]\left[\pi(t) + \int_t^s \left[\exp\left(-\int_t^z r(u)du\right)\right]\alpha(z)LH(z)dz\right.$$
$$\left. + \int_t^s \left[\exp\left(-\int_t^z r(u)du\right)\right]\alpha(z)H_X(z)\sigma(z)dw(z)\right]. \tag{50}$$

Now note that (43) implies that $LD = \phi_X D_X + rD$ and (44) implies that $LH = \phi_X H_X$, so $LH = (LD - rD)/(D_X/H_X)$. Substituting this expression for LH into (50) and letting $\alpha = D_X/H_X$ gives

$$\pi(s) = \exp\left(\int_t^s r(u)du\right)\left[\pi(t) \int_t^s \left[\exp\left(-\int_t^z r(u)du\right)\right](LD(z) - r(z)D(z))dz\right.$$
$$\left. + \int_t^s \left[\exp\left(-\int_t^z r(u)du\right)\right]D_X(z)\sigma(z)dw(z)\right]$$
$$= D(s) + \left[\exp\left(\int_t^s r(u)du\right)\right][\pi(t) - D(t)]. \tag{51}$$

Since $\pi(t) = D(t)$, then $\pi(s) = D(s)$, so the hedging portfolio will have the same value as a forward contract on the maturity date. The particular nature of the payoff received by a forward contract played no role in the argument, so there is no problem in specifying a more general payoff. Similarly, with multiple state variables, both traded assets and futures contracts can be included in the hedging portfolio. However, readers should be aware that our discussion has not gone into certain technical difficulties connected with continuous trading [see Harrison and Kreps (1979)].

An important advantage of the framework used in this example is that it can easily be specialized to produce testable explicit formulas. An illustration of this is its application to the term structure of interest rates. For instance, under the additional assumptions of logarithmic utility and a technology which leads to a spot interest rate following the stochastic differential equation

$$dr = \kappa(\mu - r)dt + \sigma\sqrt{r}\,dw, \tag{52}$$

it is shown in Cox, Ingersoll and Ross (1978) that the prices of discount bonds will satisfy the partial differential equation

$$\frac{1}{2}\sigma^2 rP_{rr} + [\kappa\mu - (\kappa + \lambda)r]P_r + P_t - rP = 0, \tag{53}$$

where κ, μ and σ are the parameters of the interest rate process and λr is the local covariance of changes in the interest rate with percentage changes in aggregate wealth (the market portfolio).

Now consider the forward and futures prices for contracts with maturity date s on a discount bond paying one dollar at time T, with $T > s$. Straightforward application of the methods discussed earlier shows that

$$G(t) = \left(\frac{A(T - t)}{A(s - t)}\right) \exp[-r(B(T - t) - B(s - t))], \tag{54}$$

and

$$H(t) = A(T - s)\left[\frac{\eta}{B(T - s) + \eta}\right]^{2\kappa\mu/\sigma^2} \exp\left[-r\left(\frac{\eta B(T - s)e^{-(\kappa + \lambda)(s - t)}}{B(T - s) + \eta}\right)\right], \tag{55}$$

where

$$A(T - t) = \left[\frac{2\gamma e^{[(\kappa + \lambda + \gamma)(T - t)]/2}}{(\gamma + \kappa + \lambda)(e^{\gamma(T - t)} - 1) + 2\gamma}\right]^{2\kappa\mu/\sigma^2},$$

$$B(T - t) = \frac{2(e^{\gamma(T - t)} - 1)}{(\gamma + \kappa + \lambda)(e^{\gamma(T - t)} - 1) + 2\gamma},$$

$$\gamma = [(\kappa + \lambda)^2 + 2\sigma^2]^{1/2}, \quad \eta = \frac{2(\kappa + \lambda)}{\sigma^2(1 - e^{-(\kappa + \lambda)(s - t)})}.$$

Note that since $A(0) = 1$ and $B(0) = 0$, $G(s) = H(s)$, as of course it must. For all $t < s$, $G(t) > H(t)$, confirming the observation made about Treasury bill futures in the discussion following Proposition 9. It is apparent by inspection that forward and futures prices are decreasing convex functions of the interest rate, as is also true of bill prices in this model. However, unlike the bill prices, the forward prices and futures prices can be increasing functions of the time to maturity for sufficiently high interest rates.

This approach can be generalized in a number of ways. For example, the simple mean-reverting drift for the interest rate in (52) can be replaced with exponentially weighted extrapolative and regressive components, as in the De Leeuw–Malkiel term structure hypotheses [see Cox, Ingersoll and Ross (1981)]. Although the resulting forward and futures prices are more complicated than (54) and (55), they still retain the simple exponential form. Furthermore, Proposition 5 shows that our results for discount bonds can be immediately applied to coupon bonds.

Formulas such as (54) and (55) make predictions about simultaneous prices in different markets, and hence offer interesting opportunities for empirical testing. However, the empirical magnitude of the effect introduced by the continual resettlement feature of futures contracts remains an open question. Capozza and Cornell (1979) analyzed futures prices and implicit forward prices in the Treasury bill market and found that, except for very short maturities, forward prices exceeded futures prices and that the difference increased with time to maturity. Rendleman and Carabini (1979) independently reached a similar but less definitive conclusion. These findings are generally consistent with the qualitative predictions of (26). However, Rendleman and Carabini have examined (54) and (55) for a range of parameter values and have concluded that the implied differences do not fully explain the observed differences between forward prices and futures prices in the Treasury bill market. This may indicate that one of the generalizations mentioned above will be more appropriate. Another possible explanation for the observed discrepancies lies in various tax effects which we have thus far ignored but shall consider in the next section.

THE EFFECTS OF TAXES AND OTHER INSTITUTIONAL FACTORS

We shall postpone a complete discussion of taxes until another occasion, but some informal comments and conjectures may still be worthwhile. The simplest way to introduce taxes into the setting of section 4 is as follows. Taxes are collected continuously at constant rates which are the same for all individuals. Capital gains are taxed as they accrue, rather than when realized, with full loss offsets. The dollar receipts from futures price changes are taxed as capital gains.

In such a world, investors will be concerned with their after-tax returns and will value contingent claims accordingly. For any given claim F, let the tax rate for capital gains be c and the tax rate for payouts and interest income be d. It can then be shown that the fundamental valuation equation becomes

$$\frac{1}{2} \sum_{i,j} (\text{cov } X_i, X_j) F_{X_i X_j} + \sum_i (\mu_i - \phi_i) F_{X_i}$$
$$+ F_t - \left(\frac{1-d}{1-c}\right) r(X, t) F + \left(\frac{1-d}{1-c}\right) \delta(X, t) = 0. \tag{56}$$

Since the last two terms will not apply for a futures price, taxes of this type will have no direct effect upon its value. Of course, there will be indirect effects, since taxes will in general affect the factor risk premiums and the current values and stochastic processes of all endogenously determined state variables. However, if we are considering the comparative effect of a change only in the tax rate applicable to futures markets, then these general equilibrium effects would presumably be negligible or non-existent, and the futures prices would remain unchanged. Notice, too, that for Treasury bills $\delta = 0$ and $c = d$, since their price changes are taxed at the rate for ordinary income. Hence, their valuation equation would remain the same as well.

The actual tax law is of course more complex than this, particularly with regard to Treasury bill futures. It currently appears that a gain on a long position in a Treasury bill futures contract will be taxed as a long-term or short-term capital gain, depending on whether the holding period is longer or shorter than six months. On the other hand, if the position shows a loss, by taking delivery and selling the Treasury bills, the basis can be taken to be the original futures price and the loss will be considered as an ordinary loss. If the taxes are collected on the maturity date and all individuals are taxed at the same rate, then a modification of the above analysis can be used to find the futures price. With this type of tax, the terminal condition will depend on the initial value, so a recursive procedure is necessary. The problem is first solved with an arbitrary parameter replacing the initial value in the terminal condition. This parameter is then varied until the initial value and the parameter value are equal. As one would expect, other things equal, this tax option results in a higher futures price.

We have not gone through this analysis explicitly only because we are not convinced of its relevance. Additional considerations may bring us full circle. Although we cannot provide a formal model which includes both differential taxes and transactions costs, it seems likely to us that the agents with transactions costs low enough to be able to conduct arbitrage operations are likely to be professionals who are taxed at the same rate for all trading income and who consequently derive no benefit from the special tax option. The actions of arbitrageurs would thus tend to keep futures prices near the levels we have predicted; simultaneously, individuals who cannot conduct arbitrage operations could nevertheless obtain tax advantages at these prices. Cornell (1980) has persuasively advanced this point of view and has provided some interesting empirical support. If the actions of arbitrageurs did not effectively determine the Treasury bill futures price, then one would expect a discontinuous change in the price (though not in the after-tax returns to the marginal investor) when a contract changes from long-term to short-term tax treatment, but Cornell found no evidence of this.

Some additional institutional factors may have an effect on the futures price in particular markets. In the basic futures contract we described, the seller of the contract can on the maturity date close out his position either by taking an offsetting long position or by delivering the specified amount of the underlying good or asset. In many markets, the seller has somewhat more flexibility than this. He may have one or more of three additional alternatives which we will refer to as a quality option, a quantity option, and a timing option.

The quality option allows the seller some discretion in the good which can be delivered. For example, several different types of a particular grain may all be acceptable. If the spot price of one of the types would always be less than the others, then this is the one the seller would choose, and the contract would in effect become an ordinary futures on that type. The situation is only slightly more complicated when the price ordering is not always the same. In that case, all of our results would hold, or would require only minor modification, when $V(s)$ is replaced by the minimum of the spot prices of the acceptable goods on the maturity date.

The quantity option allows the seller some choice in the amount of the good which is to be delivered. In this case, the futures price is quoted on a per unit basis, so the choice concerns only the scale of the contract. In perfect, competitive markets, as we have assumed, the quantity option will be a matter of indifference and will have no effect on the futures price.

The timing option gives the seller some flexibility in the delivery date of the good. In this case, delivery can be made at any time during a designated period beginning on the maturity date. Typically, the designated period is one month or less. Since delivery can be postponed, the futures price will not necessarily be equal to the spot price on the maturity date. Clearly, the futures price cannot be greater than the spot price during the designated period. If it were, then it would be possible to make an arbitrage profit by simultaneously selling a futures contract, purchasing the good in the spot market, and making delivery. Consequently, we must append to any valuation framework the arbitrage condition $H(\tau) \leqq V(\tau)$ for all τ such that $s \leqq \tau \leqq s'$ and $H(s') = V(s')$, where s' is the end of the designated period. Readers familiar with option pricing theory will note the similarity to the arbitrage condition for an American option. We can now use Proposition 10 to give a sufficient condition for the effective delivery date to be s or s'. According to this proposition, if the spot rental rate is always greater than the spot interest rate, then the futures price with maturity date s' is always less than the spot price. Consequently, the arbitrage condition will always be satisfied and the futures price can be determined as if the maturity date were s'. On the other hand, if the rental rate is always less than the interest rate, then the arbitrage condition cannot be satisfied for any maturity date later than s and all deliveries would be made at that time. In this case, the futures price can thus be determined as if the maturity date were s.

REFERENCES

Black, Fischer, 1976, The pricing of commodity contracts, Journal of Financial Economics 3, 167–179.

Brennan, Michael J. and Eduardo S. Schwartz, 1979, A continuous time approach to the pricing of bonds, Journal of Banking and Finance 3, 133-155.

Breeden, Douglas T., 1979, An intertemporal asset pricing model with stochastic consumption and investment opportunities, Journal of Financial Economics 7, 265-296.

Breeden, Douglas T., 1980, Consumption risk in futures markets, Journal of Finance 35, 503-520.

Capozza, Dennis R. and Bradford Cornell, 1979, Treasury bill pricing in the spot and futures markets, Review of Economics and Statistics 61, 513-520.

Cornell, Bradford, 1980, Taxes and the pricing of Treasury bill futures contracts, Unpublished working paper (Graduate School of Management, University of California, Los Angeles, CA).

Cox, John C., Jonathan E. Ingersoll, Jr. and Stephen A. Ross, 1978, A theory of the term structure of interest rates. Research paper no. 468 (Graduate School of Business, Stanford University, Stanford, CA).

Cox, John C., Jonathan E. Ingersoll, Jr. and Stephen A. Ross, 1981, A reexamination of traditional hypotheses about the term structure of interest rates, Journal of Finance 36, 769-800.

French, Kenneth R., 1981, The pricing of futures contracts, Unpublished working paper (Graduate School of Management, University of Rochester, Rochester, NY).

Garman, Mark B., 1977, A general theory of asset valuation under diffusion processes, Working paper no. 50, Research Program in Finance (Institute of Business and Economic Research, University of California, Berkeley, CA).

Harrison, J. Michael and David M. Kreps, 1979, Martingales and arbitrage in multiperiod securities markets, Journal of Economic Theory 20, 381-408.

Jarrow, Robert A. and George S. Oldfield, 1981, Forward contracts and futures contracts, Journal of Financial Economics, this issue.

Margrabe, William, 1976, A theory of forward and futures prices, Unpublished working paper (The Wharton School, University of Pennsylvania, Philadelphia, PA).

Merton, Robert C., 1973, An intertemporal capital asset pricing model, Econometrica 41, 867-887.

Merton, Robert C., 1977, On the pricing of contingent claims and the Modigliani-Miller theorem, Journal of Financial Economics 5, 241-249.

Merton, Robert C., 1979, Unpublished class notes (Sloan School of Management, Massachusetts Institute of Technology, Cambridge, MA).

Rendleman, Richard J., Jr. and Christopher E. Carabini, 1979, The efficiency of the Treasury bill futures market, Journal of Finance 34, 895-914.

Richard, Scott F., 1978, An arbitrage model of the term structure of interest rates, Journal of Financial Economics 6, 33-57.

Richard, Scott F. and M. Sundaresan, 1981, A continuous time equilibrium model of forward prices and future prices in a multigood economy, Journal of Financial Economics, this issue.

Sundaresan, M., 1980, A study of commodity futures prices, Unpublished doctoral dissertation (Graduate School of Industrial Administration, Carnegie-Mellon University, Pittsburgh, PA).

2

Forward and Futures Contracts on Foreign Exchange

DAVID F. DEROSA

F oreign exchange is the largest of all the financial markets. The majority of transactions occur in the interbank market in the form of spot and forward deals. But there is also a non-trivial amount of trading done in listed futures contracts on a few of the major currencies. For certain there are some obvious institutional differences between a forward and a futures contract, mostly having to do with the timing of payment and collection of profits and losses. Nonetheless, it is difficult to establish any meaningful economic difference between forward exchange rates and the implied forward rate obtained from currency futures prices.

SPOT AND FORWARD EXCHANGE RATES

Spot and forward exchange are traded in an over-the-counter market where money center banks act as the dealers. Usually, a bank is on the "other side" of every trade.

The spot exchange rate is a quote for the exchange of two currencies in two business days (except in the cases of the Canadian dollar and Mexican peso versus the U.S. dollar, where delivery is in one business day).[1] The spot rate is normally given as a bid-ask quotation.

For example, a quote on dollar-yen of 99.00/10 means that a dealer is willing to buy dollars for yen at 99.00 yen per dollar or sell dollars for yen at the rate of 99.10 yen per dollar. Unfortunately, two conventions for the quotation of spot and forward rates have evolved. In the American convention, currency is quoted

Reprinted with permission from Institutional Investor, *Derivatives Quarterly*, Fall 1994, 488 Madison Avenue, New York, NY 10022.

in terms of U.S. dollars per unit of foreign exchange (i.e., one British pound equals $1.50). The British pound, Australian dollar, New Zealand dollar, and ECU are quoted American. All the other currencies are quoted European, which means as the number of units of foreign currency equal to one dollar (i.e., 99.00 yen per one U.S. dollar or 1.55 German marks per one U.S. dollar). To make matters even more confusing, most exchange-traded currency futures and options quote currencies American, even some that are quoted European in spot and forward markets.

The forward exchange rate is a quote for settlement (or "value") at a more distant date in the future than spot settlement. A forward rate can be negotiated for any settlement date, but indications are usually given for one month, three months, six months, or one year in the future.

The forward exchange rate, also called the outright, is sometimes quoted in two parts, one being the spot bid or ask, and the other called the forward points. Forward points are either added or subtracted from the spot rate to arrive at the forward exchange rate. For example, if the forward points on dollar-yen for settlement in one year are quoted $-2.97/-2.95$, the outright would be 96.03/96.15, using 99.00/10 as the spot rate. Note that the negative sign indicates that the forward points should be subtracted from the spot bid or ask.

THE INTEREST PARITY THEOREM AND THE FORWARD EXCHANGE RATE

The Interest Parity Theorem (IPT) is the linkage between forward exchange rates and interest rates.

The basic concept is that the market sets the forward rate in relation to spot in order to absorb the interest rate differential between two currencies (known as the interest rate spread). This is a "no free lunch" idea: You cannot hop between currencies, picking up yield advantage, and lock up a guaranteed profit by using the forward market. The forward rate acts as the "spoiler."

For example, suppose that a U.S. dollar-based investor is attracted by a substantial yield spread offered by the British pound over the U.S. dollar. If the investor converts dollars to pounds for the purpose of investing in high-yielding sterling paper, there is no guarantee of any yield pick-up because the future level of the spot exchange rate is unknown. That is the rate at which the investor would later have to exchange pounds back into dollars. The future spot might be higher than the initial spot, in which case the investor would make an even greater profit; or lower than the initial spot, in which case some or all of the yield differential would be lost. In fact, if the spot exchange rate falls by a great enough amount, the investment could suffer a negative return in dollars, meaning that the exchange rate loss is greater than the interest earned on the pounds.

The exchange rate risk could be hedged by selling the future value of the pounds versus the dollar in the forward market. But at what forward rate? If there were a 500-basis point spread between sterling and dollar one-year interest rates and if the spot exchange rate were $1.80 per pound, then the only one-year forward rate that would make economic sense would be $1.72. At any other rate, riskless arbitrage would be possible. To see this, take the example of $100. This converts to 55.56 British pounds at the spot rate. This sum invested at, say, 13% would become 62.78 pounds in one year.

Comparing this to the alternative of keeping the funds in dollars, say, at 8%, and compounding to $108 after one year, we see that the forward rate must be

$$\frac{108.00 \text{ USD}}{62.78 \text{ GBP}} = 1.72 \text{ USD/GBP}$$

At this rate, the investor would be indifferent between the U.S. dollar note yielding 8% and the pound note yielding 13%, working with simple interest.

What has just been described is the Interest Parity Theorem, which can be written mathematically as

American Quotation Convention

$$F = Se^{(R_d - R_f)\tau}$$

European Quotation Convention

$$F' = S'e^{(R_f - R_d)\tau}$$

where F is the forward rate quoted American convention with delivery in τ years; S is the spot rate quoted American; R_d is the domestic interest rate; and R_f is the foreign currency interest rate. F' and S' are the forward and spot rates for currencies quoted European convention. Note that these expressions use continuously compounded interest rates for algebraic simplicity. The difference between the forward rate and the spot rate is called the forward points.

THE VALUATION OF FORWARD CONTRACTS

A currency forward contract is an agreement between two counterparties to exchange currencies at a fixed rate, called the delivery price, on a settlement day sometime in the future. In most instances, a forward contract is negotiated at a delivery price equal to the prevailing forward exchange rate; the initial value of such a forward contract is zero. Thereafter, the value of the contract assumes positive or negative values as a function of exchange rates, the domestic and foreign interest rates, and the remaining time to settlement. On the settlement day, T, the value of a forward contract to buy one unit of foreign exchange, denoted as V_T, is equal to the spot rate at settlement, S_T, minus the delivery price established when the parties enter into the contract, F_0. This paradigm assumes American quotation.

To exit a forward contract, a second closing transaction must be executed any time before the settlement day, and it forms the basis of how to value a forward contract. The closing transaction must also settle on the same settlement date. If the first contract bought foreign exchange, the closing contract must sell the same quantity of currency. If the first sold foreign exchange, the second must buy the same quantity of currency. Either way, on the settlement day, there will be some positive or negative residual of the other currency that must be settled. The net present value of this residual amount of currency is the value of the forward contract at any time before expiration.

Suppose that on day t, when time $\tau = (T - t)$ remains before settlement, we wish to value a forward contract to buy one unit of foreign exchange. Our forward contract is to pay F_0 in dollars and receive one unit of the foreign currency. What is the value of this exchange? Today, the value of F_0 dollars at time T is

$$F_0 e^{-R_d \tau}$$

The value of one unit of foreign currency at time T is

$$e^{-R_f \tau}$$

but in dollars it is

$$S_t e^{-R_f \tau}$$

Because we pay the dollars and receive the foreign currency, the value today of the forward contract is

$$V_t = S_t e^{-R_f \tau} - F_0 e^{-R_d \tau}$$

CURRENCY FUTURES CONTRACTS

Currency futures contracts are listed on the Chicago Mercantile Exchange's International Monetary Market (CME (IMM)), the Singapore Monetary Exchange (SIMEX), the Philadelphia Board of Trade, and the MidAmerica Commodities Exchange.[2] By trading volume, the most important currency futures exchange is the CME (IMM). It lists futures on the Australian dollar, British pound, Canadian dollar, French franc, German mark, Japanese yen, and the Swiss franc. The SIMEX currency futures are identical in all respects to the CME (IMM) futures, except that SIMEX does not trade in the Australian dollar, French franc, Swiss franc, or Canadian dollar.

Listed futures contracts have fixed specifications with respect to expiration date, size, and minimum price fluctuation (Figure 2-1). For example, the CME (IMM)'s yen futures contract terminates trading on the second business day before the third Wednesday of the delivery month, has a notional value of 12,500,000 yen, and a minimum price fluctuation of $12.50 per contract.

The convention in futures markets is to quote all currencies in the American style. Currency futures are traded in pits in an "open outcry" environment similar to futures contracts on agricultural and other financial commodities.

Each futures exchange has a clearinghouse. The CME (IMM) and SIMEX own their respective clearinghouses. One role of a clearinghouse is to interpose itself

FIGURE 2-1   Listed Currency Futures Contracts Chicago Mercantile Exchange
("IMM") and Singapore International Monetary Exchange
("SIMEX")

Currency	Size in Foreign Currency Units	Minimum Fluctuation**	Value of One Point	Minimum Price Change	Position Accountability	Opening Limits in Points
Australian Dollar	100,000	0.0001	$10.00	$10.00	6,000	200
British Pound*·***	62,500	0.0002	$6.25	$12.50	10,000	400
Canadian Dollar	100,000	0.0001	$10.00	$10.00	6,000	200
German Mark*·***	125,000	0.0001	$12.50	$12.50	10,000	200
Japanese Yen*·***	12,500,000	0.000001	$12.50	$12.50	10,000	200
Swiss Franc***	125,000	0.0001	$12.50	$12.50	10,000	200
Deutschemark/ Japanese Yen	125,000DM	0.01 Yen	0.01 Yen	1,250 Yen	6,000	1.50
French Franc	500,000FF	0.00002	$5.00	$10.00	2,000	500

Notes:
*Denotes listing on SIMEX.
**U.S. $ per unit of foreign currency, except for cross-rates.
***Subject of position accountability levels.
Additional Specifications:

Months	January, March, April, June, July, September, October, December, plus spot month
Trading Hours	IMM: 7:20am–2:00pm CST
	SIMEX: 8:15am–5:15pm Singapore time
	SIMEX: 6:15pm–3:15am Chicago time
Last Trade Day	Second business day before third Wednesday
First Delivery Day	Third Wednesday
Opening Limits	Apply to first fifteen minutes of IMM trading only. After expiration of the opening price limits, there is a schedule of sequential expanded daily price limits.

between each buyer and seller of every currency futures contract in order to act as a guarantor of contract performance. In addition, traders can operate on a net basis regardless of the fact that their long and short positions might have been initiated against different counterparties. A long position involves the purchase of the futures contract, while a short position entails the sale of a contract.

The clearinghouse for each futures exchange sets initial and maintenance margin requirements. The term "margin" is misleading; "good faith deposit" is more accurate. Initial margin is the deposit that an investor must provide upon opening a long or short position. Maintenance margin is the minimum allowable equity per contract in an investor's account.

The CME (IMM) minimum initial and maintenance margin rules differentiate "speculators" from "hedgers"; CME members are automatically considered hedgers (Figure 2-2). The CME (IMM) also has a separate set of margin rules for intracurrency spread trades such as long one March, short one June Swiss franc futures; as well as intercurrency spread trades, such as a position that is long Australian dollar futures and simultaneously short Canadian dollar futures.

Initial margin can be met with cash or U.S. Treasury securities, but in the case of the latter, a "haircut" will be applied, meaning that the security will count as something less than 100 cents on the dollar.

More important than initial margin is daily variation margin, by which gains and losses on futures are settled every day. Variation margin is based on the daily settlement price. In theory, the settlement price will be the last bona fide price at the close of a trading session. In practice, however, determination of a fair settlement price can be difficult.

For one thing, because of the nature of the open outcry system, many trades might occur simultaneously at the close. In this case, the settlement price can be the average of the highest and lowest trades done at the close. Also, when no trade is done at the close, special procedures may be in force that take into account the historical relationship between contract months.

Long positions in futures contracts receive positive variation margin and pay negative variation margin. Short futures positions do just the opposite: they pay positive variation margin and receive negative variation margin.

When a position is opened, that day's variation margin is calculated based on the spread between the traded price and the day's settlement price. Thereafter, the daily variation margin is based on the spread between the settlement price that day and the settlement price of the previous day. On a day when a position is closed, the amount required to settle is based on the spread between the traded price and the previous day's settlement price.

CURRENCY FUTURES CONTRACTS COMPARED TO FORWARD CONTRACTS

Several differences between futures and forwards emerge from this discussion. But the distinguishing difference seems to turn on the practice of settling vari-

FIGURE 2-2 Margin Requirements on Listed Currency Futures Contracts Chicago Mercantile Exchange ("IMM")

		Speculators		Hedgers and CME Members	
Currency	Size	Initial ($)	Maintenance ($)	Initial ($)	Maintenance ($)
Australian Dollar	100,000	1,080	800	800	800
British Pound	62,500	1,215	900	900	900
Canadian Dollar	100,000	743	550	550	550
German Mark	125,000	1,350	1,000	1,000	1,000
Japanese Yen	12,500,000	2,565	1,900	1,900	1,900
Swiss Franc	125,000	1,755	1,300	1,300	1,300
French Franc	500,000	1,350	1,000	1,000	1,000

Source: Minimum performance bond/margin requirements and contract specifications, Chicago Mercantile Exchange, revised January 30, 1992.

ation margin. Futures gains and losses are settled daily, while there are no intermediate cash flows associated with forward contracts. How do futures contracts differ from forward contracts? More to the point, is there any reason to believe that the implicit forward rate embodied in the futures price should be systematically different from the actual forward exchange rate?

Suppose that on expiration day T, the futures price converges on the spot rate, which we can write as:

$$f_T = S_T$$

Before expiration, the difference between the futures price and the spot exchange rate is:

$$f_t - S_t$$

defined as the futures basis.

The mark-to-market process resets the value of the futures contract to zero each day. Also, each day's cash flow from the mark-to-market must be invested in the case of a profit, or financed in the case of a loss.

The nature of the interest rate at which this can be done is the focus in the theoretical literature on the distinction between futures and forward contracts. In a simple case, one could assume that the interest rate is known with perfect certainty (i.e., it is non-stochastic). Cox, Ingersoll, and Ross (CIR) [1981], building on earlier work by Black [1976], demonstrate that the futures price must equal the forward exchange rate if this assumption holds. Another way to express their conclusion is to say that if the interest rate were known with perfect certainty, the futures price, like the forward exchange rate, must obey the Interest Parity Theorem. This means that the futures' basis would have to be equal to the forward points for settlement on the futures' expiration day.

CIR's proof of this theorem demonstrates that a rolling series of futures contracts can perfectly duplicate a forward contract, at least in the non-stochastic interest rate case. In their rollover futures hedge, the number of futures contracts $e^{-Rd\tau}$ is adjusted each day as a function of the known interest rate and the remaining time to expiration.

In other words, at time $t = 0$, the hedge would consist of e^{-RdT} contracts. The next day, an incremental amount of contracts would be added, making the total $e^{-Rd(T-1)}$. Finally, there would be one whole contract at expiration when $t = T$.

Our explanation of the CIR proof para-phrases Whaley [1986] and Stoll and Whaley [1986]. Consider two portfolios, A and B. Portfolio A consists of a long forward contract negotiated at time $\tau = 0$ at the prevailing forward outright F_0 (quoted American-style), to receive one unit of foreign exchange on day T plus a long position in riskless zero-coupon bonds that mature on day T. The bonds have maturity value equal to F_0 worth of domestic currency; their initial present value is equal to F_0 multiplied by the present value factor using the continuously compounded domestic interest rate, $e^{-Rd\tau}$. On day T, when the bonds mature and the forward contract settles, Portfolio A will be worth the spot exchange rate S_T. This is because the forward contract will be worth the spot exchange rate minus the forward delivery price, F_0, and the bond will mature and pay an amount equal to F_0.

Portfolio B consists of a rollover futures position that expires on day T plus a long position in riskless zero-coupon bonds that mature on day T. The initial futures price is denoted as f_0. Enough bonds are purchased to make their maturity value equal to f_0; their present value is equal to f_0 multiplied by $e^{-Rd\tau}$.

The daily mark-to-market in the rollover program is invested or financed at the domestic interest rate R_d. The value of Portfolio B on expiration day T will be equal to S_T. This is because the profit or loss on the futures contracts will be marked to market each day in an amount equal to

$$e^{-Rd(T-t)}[f_t - f_{t-1}]$$

where f_t is the futures price at the end of trading on day t and f_{t-1} is the futures price from the previous day. The future value of this amount on day T will be equal to

$$e^{-Rd(T-t)}[f_t - f^{t-1}]e^{Rd(T-t)} = [f_t - f_{t-1}]$$

and the sum of all the future values of the daily mark-to-market will be equal to

$$[f_1 - f_0]$$

plus $[f_2 - f_1]$

plus   . . .

plus $[S_T - f_{T-1}]$

which will equal $S_T - f_0$.

Note that the futures price at expiration, f_T, is assumed to converge on the spot rate, S_T. When combined with the matured zero-coupon bonds, with maturity value f_0, the value of Portfolio B, like that of Portfolio A, will be equal to S_T. Using the no-arbitrage rule, CIR conclude that the futures price, f_0, must equal the forward exchange rate, F_0.

CONCLUSION

As noted earlier, the foreign exchange market is the largest of all the financial markets. Transactions in the foreign exchange market are executed in the interbank and futures markets. The majority of trading is conducted in the interbank market by means of spot and forward exchange deals. These types of transactions are traded in the over-the-counter market. Currency futures are traded on established exchanges such as the Chicago Mercantile Exchange and the Singapore International Monetary Exchange. The spot exchange rate is a quote for the exchange of two currencies, with a delivery in two days for the majority of currencies.

Forward exchange quotes are for contracts that settle at more distant dates in the future. These contracts call for the exchange of currencies at a fixed rate, on the settlement date that is typically one, three, six, or twelve months in the future. Forward exchange rates and interest rates are linked by means of the Interest Parity Theorem (IPT). IPT holds that the market sets the forward rate by taking into consideration the spot rate and the interest rate spread between two currencies.

Futures contracts traded on exchanges have fixed specifications with respect to expiration date, size, and minimum price fluctuation. Each futures contract has a guarantee of contract performance backed by the exchange's clearinghouse. Futures contracts are marked to market each day and traders are required to deposit margin to ensure performance. Although there are several differences between futures contracts and forward contracts, the most notable is the practice of settling variation margin in the futures market.

More important, however, is the question of whether the implicit forward rate in the futures price is any different from the actual forward exchange rate. If it is assumed that the interest rate is known with perfect certainty, several proofs have shown that the futures price must equal the forward exchange rate.

REFERENCES

Black, Fischer. "The Pricing of Commodity Contracts." *Journal of Financial Economics,* 3 (January-March 1976), pp. 167–179.

Cox, J. C., Jonathan E. Ingersoll, and Stephen A. Ross. "The Relationship between Forward and Futures Prices." *Journal of Financial Economics,* 9 (December 1981), pp. 321–346.

DeRosa, David F. *Managing Foreign Exchange Risk: Advanced Strategies for Global Investors, Corporations, and Financial Institutions.* Chicago, IL: Irwin Professional Publishing, 1996.

———. *Options on Foreign Exchange.* Chicago, IL: Probus Publishing, 1992.

Stoll, Hans R., and Robert E. Whaley. "New Options Instruments: Arbitrageable Linkages and Valuation." *Advances in Futures and Options Research,* 1 (1986), pp. 25–62.

Whaley, Robert E. "Valuation of American Futures Options: Theory and Empirical Tests." *Journal of Finance,* 61 (March 1986), pp. 127–149.

ENDNOTES

1. The assumed value date for the Canadian dollar and Mexican peso is the next bank business day. However, spot trades for the same value date are done early in the trading day. Moreover, two-day

settlement can be accommodated by combining one-day spot with one day's worth of forward points.

2. Currency futures are also listed on Sao Paulo's Bolsa de Mercadonas and Futuros, the Sydney Futures Exchange, Barcelona's Mercado de Futuros Financieros, Amsterdam's Financial Futures Market, the New Zealand Futures Exchange, and the Tokyo International Financial Futures Exchange.

3

Forward and Futures Prices: Evidence from the Foreign Exchange Markets

BRADFORD CORNELL
MARC R. REINGANUM

E mpirical studies of the Treasury bill market have revealed differences between the futures price (or rate) and the implicit forward price derived from the term structure of interest rates.[1] These differences have generally been attributed to market "imperfections" such as taxes and transaction costs. (See, for example, Arak [1], Capozza and Cornell [2], and Rendelman and Carabini [6]). Recently, however, Cox, Ingersoll, and Ross [3], henceforth CIR, derived a model in which forward and futures prices need not be equal, even in perfect markets without taxes, as long as interest rates are stochastic.

The significance of the CIR effect may be hard to investigate using only data from the bill market, because of the potentially complicating effects of taxes and transaction costs unique to this market. By using data from the foreign exchange market, we are able to eliminate the tax effect and reduce the impact of transaction costs. The question we address is whether the discrepancies observed in the Treasury Bill market are also observed in the foreign exchange market. If they are, then we have evidence that the differences are due to a combination of the CIR effect and the transaction costs common to both markets. If they are not, then either the magnitude of the CIR effect is much less in the foreign exchange market, or the Treasury Bill results are due to the unique tax treatment and transaction costs of that market.

This paper is organized as follows. In Section I the trading mechanics of the forward and futures markets in foreign exchange are discussed. Section II re-

The authors would like to thank Michael Brennan, John Cox, and Jon Ingersoll as well as participants at finance workshops at UC Berkeley and UCLA for helpful comments. Research assistance was provided by Tom Hay.

Reprinted with permission from the *Journal of Finance;* Vol. XXXVI, No. 36; Cornell and Reinganum; 1981; American Finance Association.

views the explanations for the discrepancies between the forward and futures prices for Treasury Bills. The institutional differences between the foreign exchange and bill markets are also summarized to show which of these explanations cannot apply to the foreign exchange market. In Section III, the data are described and the empirical results are presented. The conclusions are summarized in the final section.

FORWARD AND FUTURES TRADING IN FOREIGN EXCHANGE

The forward market in foreign exchange is handled almost exclusively by banks at the retail level. An agent who wants to take a forward position contacts a bank to request a quote. If the agent accepts a bank's quote, a forward contract is established. The contract specifies the amount of foreign exchange to be delivered, the date of delivery, and the price. If the agent decides to close out his position prior to the delivery date, a covering transaction with the bank must be arranged.

For example, suppose the agent decides to purchase one million Swiss Francs, six months forward. He contacts Citibank which gives him a quote of .6201/.6205. He accepts the quote and contracts to buy one million Swiss Francs in six months at $.6205. Three months later the agent decides to cover his position. He contacts Citibank, which gives him a quote of .6250/.6255 for *three* forward francs. If he accepts the price of .6250, Citibank nets out his position on their books and pays him (.6250 − .6205) 1,000,000 = $4,500.

If the agent is a good customer of Citibank, no margin need be posted to make the forward contract. In addition, no money changes hands until either the position is covered or delivery occurs. Most contracts in the forward market are settled by delivery.

Unlike the forward market, the futures market deals in standardized contracts. Both contract size and the delivery date are specified in advance by the exchange. Trading in these standardized contracts is conducted by open auction on the floor of the exchange. Rather than matching individual buyers and sellers, however, the clearing house of the exchange takes the opposite side of each position. The clearing house, therefore, is the seller for every buyer and the buyer for every seller. An agent who places an order to buy Swiss Francs in the futures market has a contract to buy from the clearing house. If he later decides to cover the position, he places an order to sell Swiss Francs for the same delivery date. When that order is executed, the clearing house nets out his position on its books. Over 95% of the positions in the foreign exchange futures market are covered prior to delivery.

For the clearing house to perform its function, all profits and losses must be settled on a daily basis. This procedure, called "marking to the market," requires that funds change hands each day, even if the positions are not covered. In addition to marking to the market, traders are also required to post a performance bond, called margin, when a position is opened. The margin requirement, however, may be satisfied by pledging Treasury Bills so the opportunity cost is zero. For this reason, we shall ignore the margin requirement for the remainder of the paper.[2]

A simple example illustrates how the market works. The standardized Swiss Franc contract calls for delivery of 125,000 francs. Contracts trade for delivery in March, June, September, and December up to two years in the future. If today's date were 3 June and our agent wanted to buy one million Swiss Francs six months hence, the best he could do would be to trade the December contract that calls for delivery on the third Wednesday in December (16 December in 1981). To contract to buy one million Swiss Francs, he would place an order to go long eight December futures contracts. For illustration, suppose his order was filled at $.6200. If the futures price fell to .6190 the next day, the agent would have incurred a loss of $1,000 (.001 × 125.000 × 8 = $1,000). This would have to be paid to the clearing house before the following day's opening. Since all profits and losses are settled daily, nothing special happens when a contract is covered. The profit or loss for the final day is cleared, and the position is netted out on the books of the clearing house.

EXPLANATIONS FOR A DISCREPANCY BETWEEN FORWARD AND FUTURES PRICES

The Settling up Problem and the Cox-Ingersoll-Ross Model

From the preceding section, it is clear that an agent who took a long position in the futures market and a short position of the same size in the forward market would not necessarily have a riskless position, because the futures position must be settled daily. If the daily interest rate at which inflows can be invested (or the outflows can be financed) is stochastic, the forward-futures hedge is risky.

Cox, Ingersoll, and Ross [3] derive an expression for the difference between the forward and futures price caused by the settling up procedure. Their model is based on the insight that a forward contract can be duplicated by a combination of a futures contracts and daily borrowing or lending. Because two assets with identical cash flows must have the same price in equilibrium, relative valuation equations for forward and futures contracts can be derived.

To express the CIR solution, we use their notation:

t = current time
s = maturity date for forward and futures contracts
$H(t)$ = futures price at time t
$G(t)$ = forward price at time t
$P(t)$ = price at time t of a discount bond paying one dollar at time s.

$$\text{cov}(H(u), P(u)) = \lim_{\Delta u \to 0} \text{cov}\left[\frac{H(u + \Delta u)}{H(u)}, \frac{P(u + \Delta u)}{P(u)}\right] \Big/ \Delta u$$

In terms of the preceding notation, CIR show that the difference between the forward and futures price, $H(t) - G(t)$, is equal to the current *value* of the payment flow given by:

$$\sum_{j=t}^{s-1} [H(j + 1) - H(j)]\left[\frac{P(j)}{P(j + 1) - 1}\right] \tag{1a}$$

For a continuous-time, continuous-state economy, this reduces to

$$-\int_s^t H(u)[\text{cov}[H(u), P(u)]]du \tag{1b}$$

It is important to note that Expressions (1a) and (1b) are stochastic and that the difference between the forward and futures price is not equal to the payment flow, but equal to its present value. To obtain an explicit solution, therefore, a complete valuation model is required.

Differential Tax Treatment

The Treasury Bill futures market provides the individual investor with a unique tax option. Suppose the investor takes long position in a contract with over six months to maturity. If he has a gain at maturity, he closes out his futures position and reports the profit as long-term *capital* gain. If he has a loss, he takes delivery of the bills and sells them in the cash market, thereby generating an *ordinary* loss. The same potential does not exist on a short position, because all profits on short positions are taxed as short-term capital gains irrespective of the holding period.[3] Commercial dealers in bills, on the other hand, are taxed at ordinary income rates on all gains and losses.

The tax option creates an added demand for long positions in futures contracts with a maturity of over six months. This increased demand may tend to drive the futures price above the implied forward price. Any differential between the forward and futures price, however, presents commercial dealers with an arbitrage opportunity. The equilibrium differential between the forward and futures price, therefore, is indeterminate. Demand side analysis implies the differential must equal the value of the tax option, while supply side analysis implies the differential should be zero. In the "real world," any differences between these two extremes could be observed although a priori one might expect the difference to be closer to the side of the market with the smaller transaction costs.

Even in markets such as foreign exchange, where taking delivery will not produce ordinary loss, individuals will still have a preference for the long side of the market, because positions held for more than six months are taxed as long-term capital gains. The investor takes a long position in a contract with over six months to maturity and closes it out just prior to the six-month deadline if he has a loss (reporting a short-term loss) or holds it just past the six-month deadline if he has a gain (reporting a long-term gain). Whether or not this preference for the long side leads to a bias in the futures price for foreign exchange again depends on the behavior of commercial dealers.

Unfortunately, our data do not allow us to test for the existence of the tax effect in the foreign exchange futures markets. The only forward and futures contracts which have an identical maturity of six months or more are the one-year contracts. Trading in the International Monetary Market futures contracts with a maturity of one year is very sporadic. It is common for contracts of that maturity to go several days, or even weeks, without trading. Thus, we confine ourselves to contracts of one, two, three, and six months maturity. For such contracts, all profits and losses from futures trading are short term. Under these circumstances, individual traders are taxed symmetrically on short and long positions, so that there is no reason for the futures and forward price to diverge because of tax effects.[4]

Special Costs of Short-Selling Bills

There is no explicit forward market in Treasury Bills. To establish a forward position, the investor must short a cash bill. Because the short seller cannot match the guarantee provided by the U.S. government, he must pay a premium. Evidence cited by Capozza and Cornell [2] indicates that this premium is approximately 50 basis points per year.

The arbitrage does not face this problem in the foreign exchange market. The existence of an explicit forward market obviates the need for cash transactions completely. Eliminating the cost of shorting cash bills significantly narrows the boundaries on the forward-futures price differential set by the no arbitrage condition.

Transaction Costs and Differential Default Risk

Transaction costs produce a band around the equilibrium forward-futures differential within which arbitrage is not profitable. Even within the band, however, there are forces which should drive the differential toward its equilibrium level. Assume, for example, that the equilibrium differential is zero, but that the futures price is currently above the forward price. Agents who had already decided to take a short position would be attracted to the futures market, while those desiring a long position would gravitate toward the forward market. Such behavior on the part of investors would push the differential toward equilibrium.

Comparative default risk is difficult to assess. The clearing house stands behind all futures contracts, while forward contracts are guaranteed by the contracting parties. The contracting parties, however, are generally major banks, corporations, and governmental bodies. In both cases, therefore, the probability of default is small.

Predictions of the Theories

The main distinctions between the bill market and the foreign exchange market are the tax treatment and the existence of forward trading. If either the tax effect or the cost of shorting cash bills is responsible for the discrepancy between forward and futures prices, then the discrepancy should not be observed in our foreign exchange sample. On the other hand, if the discrepancy is due to the CIR effect, then it should be observable in the foreign exchange market, unless the value of the payment flow given by (1a) or (1b) is much less for foreign exchange than for Treasury Bills. Finally, we have argued that neither transaction costs nor differential default risk should produce a substantial difference between forward and futures prices in the foreign exchange market.

DATA AND EMPIRICAL TESTS

All our data were provided by the International Monetary Market of the Chicago Mercantile Exchange, henceforth referred to as the IMM. Until 1978 the IMM was the only futures market for foreign exchange in the United States. Recently other exchanges, such as the Commodity Exchange of New York, have begun trading foreign exchange futures, but the volume on these competing exchanges is insignificant over our sample period.

Our sample begins with the June 1974 futures contract. Foreign exchange futures trading on the IMM began on 16 May 1972, but trading was very thin until mid-1974. For this reason we chose the later starting date. The sample runs through the June 1979 futures contract.

The currencies studied are the British Pound, Canadian Dollar, German Mark, Japanese Yen, and Swiss Franc. These were the only currencies actively traded on the IMM over the entire sample period. There was also an active forward market in each of these five currencies. The futures prices we use are the daily closing prices. Closing times on the IMM range from 1:15 P.M., Chicago time, for the Swiss Franc to 1:25 P.M. for the Japanese Yen. The forward prices the IMM provided us were given to the exchange by Continental Illinois Bank. The forward quotes are for 1:00 P.M., Chicago time. Since the forward and futures prices are not recorded at the same instant, some random variation between the two prices will be observed. This random error, though, will not bias the results. (Only a trend in prices would produce bias, but any trends which might exist are far too small to be significant over an interval of half an hour or less.)

Another potential problem is the daily price limit imposed by the exchange. Suppose, for example, that the Swiss Franc closed the previous day at $.6200. Currently, daily price changes in the futures market are limited to $.0100. If the price in the forward market, which has no limit, rises to $.6350 the next day, the futures price would rise to $.6300 and trading would stop. Traders would not be willing to sell until the price hit $.6350, but the limit rule prevents the price from rising to that level. The result is a spurious divergence of the forward and futures price. Fortunately, limit moves have been very rare in the foreign exchange futures market, and our sample contains only two such occurrences, both for the Swiss Franc. When computing our statistics, these two observations are eliminated.

Finally, we have the problem that bid and ask quotes are not both available throughout the entire sample period in the forward market. The problem is not that data for specific days are missing, but rather that the IMM did not report the ask quotes for months at a time. While we do have a complete series of bid prices, about one-third of the ask prices are missing. If only bid prices are used, however, the difference between the futures price and the forward price will be overstated by approximately one-half the bid-ask spread. To adjust for this bias, we first computed all statistics, including standard errors, using the bid prices. Next, we computed the mean bid-ask spread from observations when both prices were available. Lastly, we adjusted the mean difference between the futures and forward price by one-half of the mean bid-ask spread. The standard errors were not adjusted.

The results are reported in Table 3-1. The most striking fact is the small mean discrepancy between the futures and forward price. Only two of the mean differences are significantly different from zero: the three-month maturity for the British Pound and the one-month maturity for the Canadian Dollar. (Note that if we had attempted to adjust the standard errors to take account of variance in the bid-ask spread, the standard errors would be higher and the t-statistics would be smaller.) Both the Canadian and British results, however, are affected by the existence of several large negative observations in 1974 and 1975, when futures trading was very thin. Deleting just two observations, for example, switches the sign of the mean difference in both cases.

The results are economically, as well as statistically, insignificant. With the same two exceptions, the adjusted mean difference between the futures price and the forward price is less than the bid-ask spread in the forward market. Even in these two cases, the mean difference is less than twice the bid-ask spread, which is still too small for arbitragers to exploit on average.

Arbitrage profits can be made when the mean difference is zero, if there are instances when the differences between the forward and futures prices exceed the cost of transacting. (Obviously such discrepancies would have to be both positive and negative for the mean to be zero.) This possibility is investigated in Figures 3-1 and 3-2. The three-month maturity for the German Mark and Swiss Franc is used in the figures because futures trading is more active for these contracts, particularly in the earlier years. The figures show the difference between the futures price and the adjusted forward price oscillating in a narrow range around zero. The *maximum* discrepancy of 17 points is only about three times the bid-ask spread in the forward market and only 0.40 percent of the average forward price. Since potential arbitragers must undertake two trades in both the futures and forward market, even the maximum discrepancy is not of economic significance.

These results are in sharp contrast to those in the Treasury Bill market, where average differences between forward and futures prices were five percent of the futures price or as high as ten times the bid-ask spread in the cash market

TABLE 3-1   Future vs. Forward Prices Statistics for Price Differentials

Currency	Maturity	Mean (Fut-For)[c] (1)	t-statistic (2)	Mean (Ask-Bid) (3)	N (4)
British Pound[a]	1	− 3.26	0.39	15.65	21
	2	− 13.91	− 1.48	15.24	21
	3	− 32.16**	− 4.05	19.83	21
	6	− 17.89	− 1.54	20.16	21
Canadian Dollar[a]	1	− 4.73*	− 2.59	4.18	21
	2	1.16	0.74	4.06	21
	3	0.51	0.57	4.72	21
	6	− 1.37	− 0.37	5.01	21
German Mark[a]	1	0.26	0.27	4.82	21
	2	1.31	1.15	5.00	21
	3	2.01	1.55	4.56	21
	6	0.34	0.19	5.42	21
Japanese Yen[b]	1	3.06	1.54	5.29	20
	2	− 1.91	− 1.24	6.79	17
	3	− 1.71	− 0.70	7.22	20
	6	− 4.17	− 0.95	10.79	17
Swiss Franc[a]	1	3.99	1.15	6.53	20
	2	− 0.47	− 0.23	6.35	21
	3	0.71	0.26	5.83	21
	6	2.16	1.04	7.89	20

[a]Each unit is $.0001
[b]Each unit is $.000001
[c]Forward price is equal to the observed bid price plus one-half the mean bid-ask spread.
*Significant at 5% level
**Significant at 1% level

were observed for three-month contracts.[5] No discrepancies of that magnitude are found in the foreign exchange market.

It is possible that the conflicting results for the two markets are consistent with the CIR effect, because the value of the cash flow represented by (1a) or (1b) may be quite different for different futures contracts. To investigate this possibility, we computed the covariance between percentage changes in the futures price and percentage changes in the discount bond price for Treasury Bill futures and for several foreign exchange futures contracts. We used a limited number of contracts, because all the data had to be collected and entered by hand.

The maturity dates for the chosen futures contracts were September 1977, June 1978, and March 1979. These contracts were selected because the maturity of the Treasury Bill and foreign exchange contracts differed only by one day.[6] (For other contracts the difference was eight, or even fifteen, days.) For the

FIGURE 3-1   German Mark Spread: Three-Month Maturity

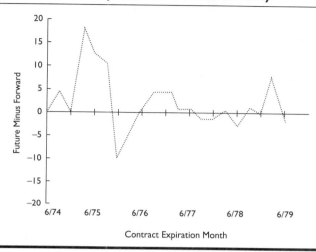

FIGURE 3-2   Swiss Franc Spread: Three-Month Maturity

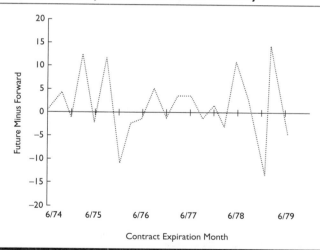

discount bond price, we used the bid price of the cash Treasury Bill which matured on the same day as the Treasury Bill futures contract. Both cash and futures prices for bills were stated in terms of a maturity value of 100, so a typical price would be 96.751. (In the case of the futures market, the prices were computed from the IMM index, but the index itself was not employed).

Foreign exchange futures prices were stated in terms of the dollar price of foreign exchange as quoted on the IMM.

A sample of forty trading days was used to estimate the covariance. In each case the sample begins 60 days, or about three months, before the maturity of the futures contract. The estimation results are reported in Table 3-2. In addition to the covariances, the t-statistics from regressions of the percentage change in the discount bond price on the percentage change in the futures price are also reported.

The covariances are all very small, on the order of 1.0×10^{-7} or less. It may seem surprising that the covariance for the foreign exchange futures exceeds that for Treasury Bill futures, since cash bill prices and bill futures prices are more highly correlated than cash bill prices and foreign exchange futures prices. It turns out, however, that foreign exchange futures prices are much more variable than bill prices, and this effect swamps the impact of the correlation when computing the covariance.

The economic significance of our covariance estimates can be approximated by returning to (1b) and making the simplifying assumption that the covariance is equal to our estimated value during the life of the futures contract. For Treasury Bills, furthermore, we know that $H(u)$ will always be less than 100. Since the present value of a risky payment stream typically will be less than the size of the stream, it follows that

$$|H(t) - G(t)| = \left| \text{Val}\left[\int_s^t H(u)[\text{cov}(H(u), P(u))]du \right] \right|$$

$$|H(t) - G(t)| = \left| \text{Val}\left[C \int_s^t H(u)du \right] \right|$$

$$|H(t) - G(t)| \leq \left| C \int_s^t 100du \right|$$

$$|H(t) - G(t)| \leq |C100(t - s)|$$

Substituting the maximum value of the estimated covariance for Treasury Bills,

TABLE 3-2   Covariance Estimates

Maturity Date	Treasury Bills	German Mark	Swiss Franc
March 1979	-3.98×10^{-9}	3.36×10^{-8}	-1.08×10^{-8}
	(-0.68)[a]	(-0.15)	(-0.04)
June 1978	1.25×10^{-8}	-2.63×10^{-7}	-3.38×10^{-7}
	(3.12)	(-1.73)	(-1.73)
September 1977	3.58×10^{-9}	1.62×10^{-7}	1.47×10^{-7}
	(1.28)	(1.61)	(1.48)

[a] t-statistic from regression of percentage change in price of discount bond on percentage change in futures price.

$C = 1.25 \times 10^{-8}$, and setting $t - s$ equal to sixty trading days, or ninety calendar days before maturity, yields

$$|H(t) - G(t)| \leq 1.25 \times 10^{-8} \times 100 \times 60$$

$$|H(t) - G(t)| \leq 7.5 \times 1^{-5}.$$

This means, for example, that if the forward price were 96.000, the futures price would be 96.00075; a very small difference in light of the fact that Treasury Bill prices are only stated to three decimal points. In terms of yield, the difference is less than *one-tenth* of a basis point.

Such a precise bound cannot be placed on the differential in the case of foreign exchange futures because there is not a known limit on $H(u)$. Suppose, nonetheless, that we pick a high upper bound for $H(u)$, such as $1.00 for the mark and the franc. Even with this inflated figure and the maximum covariance, the absolute value of the differential is only

$$|H(t) - G(t)| = 3.38 \times 10^{-7} \times 1. \times 60 \; 2.0 \times 10^{-5}$$

which is less than 1 percent of the bid-ask spread.

Rendleman and Carabini [6] and French [4] also estimated the equilibrium forward-futures differential. Rendleman and Carabini assumed that a simple valuation model held, so that a closed form solution to (1b) could be derived. Using that solution, they concluded that the differential should be approximately 3–4 basis points for contracts with 270 days to maturity, and less for contracts with shorter maturities. Though higher than our estimate, this is still an insignificant difference compared to the bid-ask spread in the cash market which is at least 10 basis points for 270 day contracts, and the observed differential which has exceeded 100 basis points. French, on the other hand, assumed that the nominal interest rate and the marginal utility of the commodity on which the futures contract is written are uncorrelated. This is not an appropriate assumption for financial futures, so his results are not directly comparable with ours. Nonetheless, French also found discrepancies of the same order of magnitude.

In light of these results, it is not surprising that forward and futures prices were found to be nearly identical in the foreign exchange market. With such small covariances, the CIR model predicts that the two prices should be indistinguishable. For this reason, another explanation must be sought for the differential observed in the Treasury Bill market.

SUMMARY AND CONCLUSIONS

The large discrepancies between forward and futures prices found in the Treasury Bill market were not found in the foreign exchange market. The foreign exchange data reveal that mean differences between forward and futures prices are insignificantly different from zero, both in a statistical and economic sense. The mean discrepancy is less than the mean bid-ask spread in the forward market in 18 of the 20 cases, and barely exceeds it in the other two. Even when individual observations were analyzed, the maximum difference rarely exceeded two bid-ask spreads.

Such results are consistent with the Cox-Ingersoll-Ross model because the relevant covariance is so small that forward and futures prices should be indistinguishable in equilibrium. Unfortunately, this covariance term is even smaller in the case of Treasury Bill futures. Explanations for the Treasury Bill results, therefore, must rely on conditions unique to the market. Two obvious candidates are the tax treatment of bills and the cost of establishing forward positions, which requires shorting cash bills.

REFERENCES

M. Arak. "Taxes, Treasury Bills, and Treasury Bill Futures." Unpublished manuscript. Federal Reserve Bank of New York, 1980.

D. Capozza and B. Cornell. "Treasury Bill Pricing in the Spot and Futures Market." *Review of Economics and Statistics* 61 (November 1979), 513-20.

J. C. Cox, J. E. Ingersoll, and S. A. Ross. "The Relationship Between Forward and Futures Prices." Unpublished manuscript, University of Chicago, 1980.

K. R. French. "The Pricing of Futures Contracts." Unpublished manuscript, University of Rochester, 1981.

R. W. Lang and R. H. Rasche. "A Comparison of Yields on Futures Contracts and Implied Forward Rates." *Federal Reserve Bank of St. Louis Monthly Review* 60 (December 1978), 21-30.

R. J. Rendleman and C. F. Carabini. "The Efficiency of the Treasury Bill Futures Market." *Journal of Finance* 34 (September 1979) 895-914.

A. J. Vignola and C. J. Dale. "Is the Futures Market for Treasury Bills Efficient?" *Journal of Portfolio Management* 5 (Winter 1979), 78-81.

ENDNOTES

1. The papers include Capozza and Cornell [2], Lang and Rosche [5], Rendleman and Carbini [6], and Vignola and Dale [7].

2. Traders who qualify as hedgers may have the margin requirement waived.

3. It should be noted that the IRS did not formally decide to tax Treasury Bill futures in this fashion until 1978. Prior to that time confusion existed as to whether Treasury Bill futures would be considered capital assets, like other futures contract, or whether they would be taxed like cash Treasury Bills.

4. Actually, the tax treatment on long and short positions under six months may not be symmetric. If delivery on a long position is accepted, then taxes could be postponed and converted to long term if the underlying asset is held long enough.

5. See Cornell and Capozza [21].

6. For many commodities delivery can occur any time during the month of maturity. This makes the definition of maturity ambiguous. Fortunately, this problem does not occur in the case of Treasury Bills or foreign exchange, because delivery for both occurs on the day after trading ends.

PART TWO

Currency Option Pricing Models

4

Foreign Currency Option Values

MARK B. GARMAN
STEVEN W. KOHLHAGEN

oreign exchange options (hereafter 'FX options') are an important new
market innovation. They provide a significant expansion in the available
risk-control and speculative instruments for a vital source of risk, namely
foreign currency values. The purpose of this paper is to develop the relevant
pricing formulas for FX options.

The deliverable instrument of an FX option is a fixed amount of underlying
foreign currency. In the standard Black-Scholes (1973) option-pricing model,
the underlying deliverable instrument is a non-dividend-paying stock. The difference between the two underlying instruments is readily seen when we compare their equilibrium forward prices. When interest rates are constant (as in
the Black-Scholes assumptions), the forward price of the stock must, by arbitrage, command a forward premium equal to the interest rate. But in the foreign
currency markets, forward prices can involve either forward premiums or dis-
counts. This is because the forward value of a currency is related to the ratio of
the prices of riskless bonds traded in each country. The familiar arbitrage relationship ('interest rate parity') correspondingly asserts that the forward exchange premium must equal the interest rate *differential,* which may be either
positive or negative. Thus both foreign and domestic interest rates play a role
in the valuation of these forward contracts, and it is therefore logical to expect
that such a role extends to options as well. That this is indeed the case we shall
see below.

The authors gratefully acknowledge comments contributed during the course of this research by
Fischer Black, Robert Geske, Richard Roll, and Terry Turner, without implicating them in any errors
contained herein.

Reprinted with permission from *Journal of International Money and Finance;* Vol. 2; Garman
and Kohlhagen; *Foreign Currency Option Values;* 1983; Elsevier Science Ltd., Oxford, England.

DEVELOPMENT

We use notation as follows:

S = the spot price of the deliverable currency (domestic units per foreign unit)
F = the forward price of the currency delivered at option maturity
K = exercise price of option (domestic units per foreign unit)
T = time remaining until maturity of option
$C(S, T)$ = the price of an FX call option (domestic units per foreign unit)
$P(S, T)$ = the price of an FX put option (domestic units per foreign unit)
r_D = the domestic (riskless) interest rate
r_F = the foreign (riskless) interest rate
σ = volatility of the spot currency price
μ = drift of the spot currency price
$N(\cdot)$ = cumulative normal distribution function
α = the expected rate of return on a security
δ = the standard deviation of the security rate of return

Our assumptions are the usual ones for an option-pricing model, that:

1. Geometric Brownian motion governs the currency spot price: i.e., the differential representation of spot price movements is $dS = \mu S dt + \sigma S dz$, where z is the standard Wiener process.
2. Option prices are a function of only one stochastic variable, namely S.
3. Markets are frictionless.
4. Interest rates, both in the domestic and foreign markets, are constant.[1]

As is also usual, our analysis shall pertain to European FX options: options which can be exercised only on their maturity date. The American options, which may be exercised at any time prior to maturity, are discussed later.

The key to understanding FX option pricing is to properly appreciate the role of foreign and domestic interest rates. We do this by comparing the advantages of holding an FX option with those of holding its underlying currency. As is well known, the risk-adjusted expected excess returns of securities governed by our assumptions must be identical in an arbitrage-free continuous-time economy.[2] That is, we must have

$$\frac{\alpha_i - r_D}{\delta_i} = \lambda, \text{ for all } i \tag{1}$$

where λ does not depend on the security considered.[3] Applying this fact to the ownership of foreign currency, we have[4]

$$\frac{(\mu + r_F) - r_D}{\sigma} = \lambda \tag{2}$$

That is, the expected return from holding the foreign currency is μ, the 'drift' of the exchange rate (domestic units per foreign unit), plus the riskless capital growth arising from holding the foreign currency in the form of an asset (e.g., foreign treasury notes and CD's) paying interest at the rate of r_F. The denominator of the left-hand-side of equation (2) is σ, since this is the standard deviation of the rate of return on holding the currency. (Note that μ, σ, r_F, and r_D are all dimensionless quantities, so there is no issue of conversion between foreign and domestic terms.)

Next, letting $C(S, T)$ be the price of a European call option with time T left to maturity, (1) implies

$$\frac{\alpha_C - r_D}{\delta_C} = \lambda \tag{3}$$

where α_C and δ_C are the call option's expected rate of return and standard deviation of same, respectively. By Ito's lemma, we have

$$\alpha_C C = \frac{1}{2} \sigma^2 S^2 \frac{\partial^2 C}{\partial S^2} + \mu S \frac{\partial C}{\partial S} - \frac{\partial C}{\partial T} \tag{4}$$

and

$$\delta_C C = \sigma S \frac{\partial C}{\partial S} \tag{5}$$

Substituting (4) and (5) into (3) yields

$$\frac{\frac{1}{2} \sigma^2 S^2 \frac{\partial^2 C}{\partial S^2} + \mu S \frac{\partial C}{\partial S} - \frac{\partial C}{\partial T} - r_D C}{\sigma S \frac{\partial C}{\partial S}} = \lambda \tag{3'}$$

Thus equating (2) and (3) we have

$$\frac{\sigma^2}{2} S^2 \frac{\partial^2 C}{\partial S^2} - r_D C + (r_D S - r_F S) \frac{\partial C}{\partial S} = \frac{\partial C}{\partial T} \tag{6}$$

The latter equation is reminiscent of models proposed by Samuelson (1965) and Samuelson and Merton (1969), in which the dividend rate of a stock is presumed to be proportional to the level of the stock price. Indeed, there is a similar interpretation for foreign currency options. Consider r_F as the 'dividend rate' of the foreign currency. However, this rate is in foreign terms, so to convert to domestic terms, one would naturally multiply it by the spot exchange rate S. The Samuelson-Merton model has not received a great deal of attention in the literature, probably because of its rather strained assumption of a proportional dividend policy. That is, under their model, a firm must constantly monitor its stock price and adjust a continuously paid dividend as a fixed fraction of that price. This is rather impractical as a realistic dividend policy. But in the foreign exchange context, the 'adjustment of dividends' takes place in an automatic fashion, since the conversion from foreign to domestic currency terms at the market exchange rate is natural for dimensional consistency within (6).

SOLUTIONS

The solution to (6) for a European FX call option must obey the further boundary condition that $C(S, 0) = \max[0, S - K]$, yielding[5] the valuation formula

$$C(S, T) = e^{-r_F T}SN(x + \sigma\sqrt{T}) - e^{-r_D T}KN(x) \tag{7}$$

where

$$x \equiv \frac{\ln(S/K) + \{r_D - r_F - (\sigma^2/2)\}T}{\sigma\sqrt{T}}$$

Note that both the foreign interest rate r_F, and the interest differential, $r_D - r_F$, play distinct roles in the solution.

Of course, equation (6) governs all securities satisfying our original assumptions. Thus the European FX put option also satisfies that differential equation, but with the boundary condition $P(S, 0) = \max[0, K - S]$. Hence the solution to the European FX put option is given as

$$P(S, T) = e^{-r_F T}S[N(x + \sigma\sqrt{T}) - 1] - e^{-r_D T}K[N(x) - 1] \tag{8}$$

where x is as defined for the call option.[6]

COMPARATIVE STATICS

The partial derivatives of formula (7) are also of interest, and these are computed below. Foremost in significance is the 'hedge ratio':

$$\frac{\partial C}{\partial S} = e^{-r_F T}N(x + \sigma\sqrt{T}) > 0 \tag{9}$$

Other partial derivatives are:

$$\frac{\partial C}{\partial K} = -e^{-r_D T}N(x) < 0 \tag{10}$$

$$\frac{\partial C}{\partial \sigma} = e^{-r_D T}K\sqrt{T}N'(x) > 0 \tag{11}$$

$$\frac{\partial C}{\partial r_D} = Te^{-r_D T}KN(x) > 0 \tag{12}$$

$$\frac{\partial C}{\partial r_F} = -Te^{-r_F T}SN(x + \sigma\sqrt{T}) < 0 \tag{13}$$

and

$$\frac{\partial C}{\partial T} \equiv -r_F e^{-r_F T}SN(x + \sigma\sqrt{T}) + r_D e^{-r_D T}KN(x) + \frac{e^{-r_D T}\sigma}{2\sqrt{T}}KN'(x) \tag{14}$$

Interpreting, when other variables (significantly the spot rate) are held constant, FX European call values rise when the domestic interest rate increases, and fall when the foreign rate increases. Increases in volatility uniformly give rise to increases in FX option prices, while increases in the strike price cause FX call option prices to decline. However, the sign of the time derivative is ambiguous. In-the-money calls tend to have negative signs for this derivative when the time to maturity is short. The situation is exacerbated when the calls become deep-in-the-money or when foreign interest rates rise well above domestic rates. Of course, a negative time derivative could not pertain to an American FX option, and so we see that the European formulas for calls (and puts) are clearly inadequate descriptions of their American counterparts in these cases. (See also the discussion by Merton (1973) for the proportional-dividend case.)

The derivatives of the European FX put options are obtained analogously from (8), with the obvious changes in sign for the derivatives involved.

RELATIONSHIP TO CONTEMPORANEOUS FORWARD PRICE

Asserting the familiar relationship known as 'interest rate parity' (Keynes, 1923), the forward price of currency deliverable contemporaneously[7] with the maturation of the option is[8]

$$F = e^{(r_D - r_F)T} S \tag{15}$$

Substituting this relation into the solution (7) gives the alternate solution[9]

$$C(F, T) = \{FN(x + \sigma\sqrt{T}) - KN(x)\}e^{-r_D T} \tag{16}$$

where

$$x \equiv \frac{\ln(F/K) - (\sigma^2/2)T}{\sigma\sqrt{T}}$$

Note that with this substitution the call value depends only upon F and r_D; it does not depend independently upon S and r_F. That is, given the current domestic rate of interest, all option-relevant information concerning the foreign interest rate and the spot currency price is reflected in the forward price.

The European put value formula is analogous:

$$P(F, T) = \{F[N(x + \sigma\sqrt{T}) - 1] - K[N(x) - 1]\}e^{-r_D T} \tag{17}$$

We now augment some conclusions regarding comparative statics, this time using the forward-based formula (16). The derivative of the call value with respect to forward price is given as

$$\frac{\partial C}{\partial F} = e^{-r_D T} N(x + \sigma\sqrt{T}) > 0 \tag{18}$$

However, some caution should be observed in applying this latter derivative as a 'hedge ratio'. This is because the forward price is not equivalent to the value of a forward contract, the latter being the important determinant of current wealth at risk. Rather, the forward price is a parameter, not unlike a strike price, which is continuously adjusted so as to make the value of the forward contract identically zero. Consequently, the forward price must be discounted by the factor $e^{(r_F - r_D)T}$ to properly reflect current values, and hence the correct 'hedge ratio' between wealth at risk in forward and option contract positions is as given previously in (9).

With regard to other partial derivatives, we have

$$\frac{\partial C}{\partial K} = -e^{-r_D T} N(x) < 0 \tag{19}$$

and

$$\frac{\partial C}{\partial \sigma} = e^{-r_D T} K \sqrt{T} N'(x) > 0 \tag{20}$$

exactly as before. However, the sign of the domestic interest rate partial derivative is just the opposite of the previous section:

$$\frac{\partial C}{\partial r_D} = -e^{-r_D T} T \{ F N(x + \sigma \sqrt{T}) - K N(x) \} = -TC < 0 \tag{21}$$

That is, if the contemporaneous forward rate is held constant, an increase in domestic interest rates results in a decrease in FX call values. Finally, we have

$$\frac{\partial C}{\partial T} = -r_D C + e^{-r_D T} \frac{\sigma}{2\sqrt{T}} K N'(x) \tag{22}$$

Again the last derivative is ambiguous in sign, reflecting the European, as opposed to American, nature of the options treated.

COMMENTS ON AMERICAN FX OPTIONS

As noted previously, the European formulas will not serve to adequately price American FX options. (See also Samuelson (1965), Samuelson and Merton (1969), and Merton (1973).) Early exercise is decidedly a factor in pricing the American options,[10] and affects primarily the deep-in-the-money options (particularly calls on currencies with negative forward premiums and puts on currencies with positive forward premiums). Of course, American FX options must conform to the basic differential equation (6). However, the boundary conditions differ from the European case inasmuch as the option prices must never be less than the immediate conversion value, e.g.

$$C(S, T) \geq \max[0, S - K]$$

for all T. Following the methodology of Merton (1973), it can also be shown that

$$C(S, T) \geq \max[0, Se^{-r_F T} - Ke^{-r_D T}]$$

for both the European and American cases.

Analytic solutions for the above type of boundary conditions problem seem quite difficult to derive. Therefore numerical methods, such as proposed by Brennan and Schwartz (1977), Parkinson (1977), or Cox, Ross and Rubinstein (1979) (all recently reviewed by Geske and Shastri (1982)), are indicated for the evaluation of such American options.

CONCLUSIONS

The appropriate valuation formulas for European FX options depend importantly on both foreign and domestic interest rates. The present paper has developed such formulas, and these are closely related to the proportional-dividend model when the spot prices are given, and to the commodity-pricing model when contemporaneous forward prices are given. The comparative statics are as might be expected, with two exceptions: the reaction of FX option prices to interest rate changes depends upon the nature of the concommitant changes required in either the spot or forward currency markets. Finally, American FX option values exceed the European FX option values most markedly for deep-in-the-money options, particularly for calls on currencies with negative forward premiums and puts on currencies with positive forward premiums.

REFERENCES

Brennan, M. and E. Schwartz, 'The Valuation of American Put Options', *J. Finance*, May 1977, 32: 449–462.

Black, F., 'The Pricing of Commodity Contracts', *J. Financial Econ.*, January 1976, 3: 167–179.

Black, F. and M. Scholes, 'The Pricing of Options and Corporate Liabilities', *J. Pol. Econ.*, May/June 1973, 81: 637–654.

Cox, J., S. Ross and M. Rubinstein, 'Option Pricing: A Simplified Approach', *J. Financial Econ.*, September 1979, 7: 229–263.

Geske, R. and K. Shastri, 'Valuation by Approximation: A Comparison of Alternative Option Valuation Techniques', working paper, Graduate School of Management, UCLA, 1982.

Keynes, J., *A Tract on Monetary Reform*, London: Macmillan, 1923.

Merton, R. C., 'Theory of Rational Option Pricing', *Bell J. Econ. and Management Sci.*, Spring 1973, 4: 141–183.

Parkinson, M. 'Option Pricing: The American Put', *J. Business*, January 1977; 50: 21–36.

Samuelson, P. A., 'Rational Theory of Warrant Pricing', *Ind. Management Rev.*, Spring 1965, 6: 13–31.

Samuelson, P. and R. Merton, 'A Complete Model of Warrant Pricing that Maximizes Utility', *Ind. Management Rev.*, Winter 1969, 10: 17–46.

Shapiro, A., *Multinational Financial Management*, Boston: Allyn and Bacon, 1982.

ENDNOTES

1. The analysis could be extended without much difficulty to stochastic interest rates, by assuming that the market is 'neutral' towards the sources of uncertainty driving such rates. In this case, volatility parameters must be redefined to incorporate the variances and covariances of interest rate movements as well as spot price movements. However, we forego this extension in the interest of clarity.

2. This is true, however, for only the case where there is a single source of uncertainty considered; multiple sources give rise to multiple volatility factors and risk premia, which are better expressed in alternative forms. Also, it is important to emphasize that the invariance of the risk-adjusted excess return is a pure arbitrage result, and does not depend upon any specific asset pricing model in a continuous-time (diffusion) setting.

3. In general, λ may depend on time and the state variables involved; however, in this particular case it is a constant.

4. The more usual presentation of our formula (2) would be $\mu = (r_D - r_F) + \lambda\sigma$, emphasizing that the expected return can be decomposed into an interest-rate-related drift and a risk premium. The form given emphasizes the invariance of risk premia across securities, in order to compare these.

5. The solution proceeds analogously to Merton's (1973) description of the proportional-dividend model, replacing his dividend rate d by the foreign interest rate, as noted previously.

6. Alternatively, we could use put-call parity to determine the put option formula without resolving (6).

7. At the current writing, FX options are traded on the Philadelphia Stock Exchange and were designed to mature concurrently with the IMM currency futures contracts, in March, June, September, and December.

8. For an introduction to exchange rate relationships, see for example the recent text by Shapiro (1982). This particular relationship is a pure-arbitrage result which employs riskless bonds of maturity identical to the forward contract, which of course can be created when instantaneous interest rates are constant.

9. This solution, although derived in a somewhat different fashion, is equivalent to Black's (1976) commodity option-pricing formula, showing that FX options may be treated on the same basis as commodity options generally, provided that the contemporaneous forward instruments exist.

10. At typical currency parameter values, it is not unusual to see a 10–20% difference between American and European values for certain in-the-money options.

5

Valuing Foreign Exchange Rate Derivatives with a Bounded Exchange Process

Jonathan E. Ingersoll, Jr.

INTRODUCTION

In recent years, the number and variety of foreign exchange based financial products have expanded enormously. OTC and private party derivatives have also increased in scope and importance. At the same time, the once free-floating exchange rates, which might well be characterized by the standard lognormal distribution of option pricing theory, have been more tightly fixed relative to one another, particularly in the European Economic Community.

Of course, this change has really been a more formal adoption of policies which have long been in place. The 1946 Bretton Woods Agreement established fixed exchange rates between most currencies. Under this understanding, the various countries agreed to keep their currencies within a narrow band of a parity value.

In 1973 floating exchange rates were adopted. However, the central banks of many countries still attempted to hold their exchange rate within a particular range relative to gold or some other currency, usually the dollar. In the first half of the 1980s exchange rates relative to the dollar were typically allowed to

The author would like to thank Ken French and Geert Rouwenhorst for their comments and suggestions.

Reprinted with permission from *Review of Derivatives Research;* Vol. I, Issue 2; Jonathan E. Ingersoll, Jr.; 1996; Kluwer Academic Publishers.

fluctuate more while the yen and the mark took on more important roles. The mid to late 1980s were characterized by cooperative stabilization attempts such as the Plaza Agreement in September 1985 which succeeded in lowering the value of the dollar against the currencies of its major trading partners.

The European Economic Community adopted a much more tightly controlled system known as the Exchange Rate Mechanism (ERM) in March 1979. Under the ERM each member country was, and is, required to maintain its exchange rate with the European Currency Unity (ECU) within certain bands. After several realignments of the currencies in the early 1980s, the ERM stabilized with bands of $\pm$ 2-1/4% of parity with the ECU for each currency.[1]

In September 1993, Italy and the U.K. could not maintain their currencies within the bands and were required to leave the ERM. In August 1993 the bands for six of the remaining members (Belgium, Denmark, France, Ireland, Portugal, and Spain) were relaxed to $\pm$ 15%. These wider bands are still in effect with only Germany and the Netherlands maintaining the more narrow bands of 2-1/4%.

This paper examines the effects of targeted exchange rates with strict bounds on the value of foreign exchange options and other derivative contracts. A bounded stochastic process limits the range of the exchange rate at the option's maturity and hence the uncertainty of its payoff. This tends to decrease the value of a simple put or call. On the other hand, the bounds also keep the exchange rate in a small range around the strike price. As this is the region in which an option's time or insurance value is highest,[2] there is also a tendency for option values to be enhanced. Both of these effects are important for realistic choices of parameter values. Overall the presence of bounds can have a material effect on option values.

The models developed here may also be applicable for pricing derivatives on agricultural products or other assets in whose markets the government may support prices.

Section 2 of this paper reviews some of the basic relations. Section 3 discusses bounded processes while section 4 discusses the particular process employed here. Sections 5 and 6 derive various models to solve derivative pricing problems.

BASIC RELATIONS

The notation we employ uses starred letters to denote foreign (franc) values. The dollar value at time t of a default-free zero-coupon loan paying one dollar at time T is $B(t; T)$. The time t value in francs of a default-free zero-coupon loan paying one franc at time T is $B^*(t; T)$. The domestic and foreign continuously compounded rates of interest are r and r^*. (These rates are not necessarily assumed to be constant.) The dollar-franc spot exchange rate (i.e., the value in dollars of one franc) is x_t. The franc-dollar exchange rate is $x_t^* = 1/x_t$.

The most common foreign exchange derivatives are forward contracts and their exchange traded counterparts, futures contracts. To prevent arbitrage the forward price for the delivery of francs must be $x_t B^*(t; T)/B(t; T)$ dollars. The forward price for the delivery of dollars is the reciprocal, $x_t^* B(t; T)/B^*(t; T)$ francs.

The futures foreign exchange rates for francs or dollars at time T are z_{tT} and z_{tT}^*. As shown by Cox, Ingersoll, and Ross (1981) the futures price may differ from the forward price due to the daily marking to market.[3]

There are numerous other foreign exchange derivative contracts trading, and new contract types are being designed continually. Even the simple options listed on the various exchanges throughout the world come in more than two dozen varieties. In this paper we concentrate on puts and calls. The same techniques can be applied to the more complex contracts.

There are sixteen simple options of interest. Each option can be a put or call, American or European in style, written on francs or dollars, and denominated in francs or dollars.[4] The values of these sixteen types are closely related by three simple rules, however, so there is only one basic pricing problem for European options and two basic problems for American options. Most listed foreign exchange options are European style, except on the Philadelphia Exchange where both types are traded.

The first relation is simply a change of numeraire. If c is the dollar value of a contract, then c/x (or cx^*) is the franc value of this same contract. This rule applies to both American and European options and, in fact, any security.

The second rule is international put-call equivalence which relates domestic puts to foreign calls and vice versa (see Giddy 1983). A foreign call on dollars is identical to a domestic put on francs. In particular a call on one dollar with a strike price of K^* francs is the same as K^* puts on one franc each with a strike of $1/K^*$ dollars. The price of the foreign option on dollars would usually be quoted in francs so combining rules

$$c^*(x^*; K^*) = K^* p(x; 1/K^*)/x = K^* x^* p(1/x^*; 1)$$

$$p^*(x^*; K^*) = K^* c(x; 1/K^*)/x = K^* x^* c(1/x^*; 1).$$

$$(1)$$

Again this rule applies to both American and European options. Although the Black-Scholes function is homogeneous of degree one in its arguments, option values need not be in general. In particular the formula developed in this paper is not homogeneous of any degree. It is therefore improper to "simplify" the right-most terms of (1) to $p(K^*; x^*)$ and $c(K^*; x^*)$.

The foreign exchange version of put-call parity is put-call forward-exchange parity (see Giddy 1983). A European put and a call on one franc each with a strike price of k dollars and maturing at time T are related by

$$p(x, t; k, T) = c(x, t; k, T) - xB^*(t; T) + kB(t; T). \qquad (2)$$

Here the foreign bond price, $B^*(\cdot)$, serves as a "dividend" adjustment for the foregone interest. Put-call parity only holds for European options.

To further complicate option taxonomy, there are also *future-style options* or, more precisely, options with futures-style margining.[5] A futures-style option is not really an option at all. It is a futures contract on an option-like payoff. As with any futures contract, no money (other than a bilateral performance guarantee margin) is paid up front. Each day the contract is marked to market, and the long (short) parties' margin accounts are credited (debited) with any increase in the futures option price.[6] The difference between a futures-style option and a regular futures contract is the final settlement price at maturity. With a regular futures contract, the final settlement price must peg to x_T. The final settlement price for a futures-style option pegs to $\text{Max}[x_T - k, 0]$ for a call or $\text{Max}[k - x_T, 0]$ for a put.

Cox, Ingersoll, and Ross (1981) have shown that any futures price is equal to the risk-neutral expected value of the spot price at maturity. So for example, $z_{tT} = \hat{E}_t[x_T]$. For a futures-style call, the "spot price" at maturity is $\text{Max}[x_T - k, 0]$ so the futures-style call price at time t is $\hat{E}_t[\text{Max}(x_T - k, 0)]$ and similarly for futures-style puts.

Cox, Ingersoll, and Ross (1981) also proved that futures prices could be treated like asset prices for the purposes of valuation including the use of the risk-neutral method. Therefore, the change of numeraire and international put-call equivalence rules are valid for futures-style options. Futures-style put-call parity is different though. The relation is

$$p_{\text{futures-style}}(x_t, t; k, T) = c_{\text{futures-style}}(x_t, t; k, T) - z_{tT} + k. \tag{3}$$

Futures-style put-call parity has no discounting since futures prices, including futures-style option prices, are all expectations of prices in the future and not discounted expectations.[7]

Exchange-listed foreign exchange options are commonly written with a futures price as the basis. Since the futures price for immediate delivery must equal the spot price, futures and spot based European options are identical if the futures has the same maturity as the option. Therefore, with no loss of generality, we can assume the basis for the option expiring at time T' is a futures which expires at T (with $T' \leq T$). For options on the spot price we just set $T = T'$. The same basic rules given above apply to options with futures price bases.[8]

American options on the spot and the futures exchange rates, however, are not identical due to differing payoffs at early exercise. A call with a spot price basis has a payoff of $x_t - k$ upon exercise while a call with a futures price basis is worth $z_{tT} - k$.

BOUNDED EXCHANGE RATES

We model the exchange rate dynamics under the assumption that one or both governments will intercede to stabilize the foreign exchange market. Specifically we conjecture the governments act, together or alone, to keep the exchange rate in the range $a(t)$ to $b(t)$ at time t.

Although only the bounds prevailing at the maturity of a European option directly affect its payoff, we need to recognize the effect of the bounds at earlier times on the dynamic behavior of the exchange rate and consequently on the probability distribution of the option's payoff. Furthermore, the behavior of the spot exchange rate and the two countries' interest rates must be linked in order to prevent arbitrage opportunities.[9] In particular, necessary conditions for the absence of arbitrage are

$$a(T) \le a(t) \frac{B^*(t; T)}{B(t; T)}$$

$$b(T) \le b(t) \frac{B^*(t; T)}{B(t; T)} \tag{4}$$

for all $T > t$.

For example, suppose the latter condition fails to hold. Then when the exchange rate is at its upper bound, the domestic bond market dominates the foreign bond market. An investment of $b(t)$ dollars (or one franc) in foreign bonds will be repatriated at time T for $x(T)/B^*(t; T)$ dollars. As $x(T)$ is bounded by $b(T)$, the repatriated dollars can be no more than $b(T)/B^*(t; T)$. Now if the no-arbitrage condition above fails to hold, this in turn is less than $b(t)/B(t; T)$. But this last amount, which is more than can be earned in the foreign bond market, is the guaranteed result in the domestic bond market.

It is clear from (4) that the exchange rate and the two countries' interest rates must be linked to prevent arbitrage. For example if the exchange rate bounds are constant over time, then both countries' interest rates cannot be (unless they are equal) since one of the two inequalities in (4) could not hold for large T. On the other hand if the interest rates are stochastic, pricing problems are complex. Fortunately the problems can be simplified by using the futures price as the basis for the option since, as shown in Proposition 1, the barrier behavior of the futures price is straight forward.

PROPOSITION 1. *If the spot exchange rate at time T will be bounded between $a(T)$ and $b(T)$, then the futures price at time t for delivery at time T must also bounded between $a(T)$ and $b(T)$ for all $t \le T$.*

Proof. For any probability distribution the expectation with respect to any information set must lie within the range of the support of the random variable, so $a(T) \le \hat{E}_t[x_T] \le b(T)$, and the proposition follows immediately since $z_{tT} = \hat{E}_t[x_T]$. ∎

If this proposition is violated, than an arbitrage opportunity will exist in the futures market. For example, if the futures price exceeds the upper bound, $b(T)$, then shorting a futures contract must realize a profit although its timing is uncertain. By suitably hedging the futures contract to eliminate the timing uncertainty an arbitrage can be created.

Given Proposition 1, knowledge of the futures exchange rate process is sufficient to price futures-style options, and knowledge of the futures exchange rate and domestic interest rate processes is sufficient for pricing ordinary options. If we wished to price these options as a function of the current exchange rate, we would need the dynamics of the spot exchange rate and both countries' interest rates. In addition we would need to verify that these dynamics did not violate the no-arbitrage condition of Proposition 1.

We assume the futures price for delivery of francs at time T follows the diffusion process

$$dz_{tT} = \mu(\cdot)dt + \Gamma(z; t; T)d\omega \tag{5}$$

in the bounded region $a(T) \leq z_{tT} \leq b(T)$. As in the Black-Scholes model, the expected change, μ, can have almost arbitrary functional form and may depend on either interest rate or other, possibly stochastic, variables. Only the diffusion function, Γ, will affect the pricing of derivatives. We assume that $\Gamma(\cdot)$ depends on only z, t and T.

The expected change need not be specified to price derivatives. All that is required is the expected change under the equivalent risk-neutral (or martingale) process, $\hat{\mu}(\cdot)$. Since the futures price is the risk-neutral expectation of the spot price at maturity, applying the law of iterated expectations we have

$$\hat{E}_t[z_{t+dt,T}] = \hat{E}_t\hat{E}_{t+dt}[x_T] = \hat{E}_t[x_T] = z_{tT}. \tag{6}$$

Therefore, the risk-neutral expected change in the futures price is $\hat{\mu} = 0$, or, equivalently, the risk-neutral expected payoff from entering a futures contract is zero.

To fully define the stochastic process, the behavior of the exchange rate at the barriers must be specified. The barriers may be accessible or inaccessible. Accessible barriers may be reflecting or absorbing.[10] The accessibility of a barrier depends on μ and Γ. In particular for a lower barrier to be inaccessible either $\Gamma \to 0$ or $\mu \to \infty$ must hold as $z \to a$. For an upper barrier to be inaccessible either $\Gamma \to 0$ or $\mu \to \infty$ must hold as $z \to b$.[11]

Modeling the barriers for the futures price as accessible absorbing barriers seems inappropriate as it cuts off all further uncertainty once the barrier is reached. Under this assumption, the exchange rate would eventually become fixed at one barrier or the other. Making the barriers accessible and reflecting would appear to be a better choice but actually admits arbitrage. At an upper (lower) reflecting barrier, the futures price can only drop (rise); therefore, a short (long) position in the futures contract, which requires no investment and must make money over the next instant, is an arbitrage.

Adopting inaccessible barriers seems to be the best choice. Inaccessible barriers could result from the government(s) taking more and more drastic stabilization measures as the barrier was approached so that it could never be reached.

A SPECIFIC MODEL OF BOUNDED EXCHANGE RATES

The lognormal model of Black and Scholes, $\Gamma(z, t; T) = \sigma z$, is the standard for option pricing and has been employed by many in the foreign exchange market. A natural extension of the lognormal case for a bounded exchange rate stochastic process is a diffusion coefficient of $\Gamma(z, t; T) = (z - a)(1 - z/b)\sigma(t; T)$. For this choice, the martingale or risk-neutral stochastic process equivalent to (5) is[12]

$$dz = (z - a)(1 - z/b)\sigma(t; T)d\hat\omega. \tag{7}$$

This model is a natural extension of the lognormal model for two reasons. First, it obviously includes the lognormal as the special case $a = 0$ and $b = \infty$. Second, as in the lognormal model, the evolution of the reciprocal of the basis (and hence the franc-dollar exchange rate) has the same functional form for its variance as does the basis with lower and upper barriers of $1/b$ and $1/a$. By Itô's lemma

$$d\left(\frac{1}{z}\right) = \mu_{1/z}(\cdot)dt + \sigma(t; T)\left(\frac{1}{z} - \frac{1}{b}\right)\left(1 - \frac{a}{z}\right)d\omega. \tag{8}$$

The variance of this proces depends on the futures price. It vanishes at both barriers making them inaccessible as shown in Proposition 2 below. It is highest at the midpoint of the range $(a + b)/2$. The logarithmic variance also depends on the futures price vanishing at the barriers and achieving its maximum at the geometric midpoint $\sqrt{ab}$. We permit the volatilities of distinct futures prices (indexed by T) to differ; in addition, the volatility of any particular futures price may change over time as its maturity date approaches or conditions vary.

PROPOSITION 2. *Assuming $\sigma(t; T)$ is uniformly bounded, the barriers a and b for the risk-neutral stochastic process in (7) are inaccessible. A sufficient condition for the barriers to be inaccessible for the original stochastic process (5) is that the drift have a weak tendency away from each barrier. I.e., ($\exists a' > a$) such that $\mu(z) \geq 0$ ($\forall z < a'$), and ($\exists b' < b$) such that $\mu(z) \leq 0$ ($\forall z > b'$).*

Proof. Define $\xi \equiv 1/2\ln[(z - a)/(b - z)]$. The domain of ξ is the real line with $-\infty$ and ∞ corresponding to $z = a$ and $z = b$, respectively. By Itô's lemma the stochastic process for ξ is

$$d\xi = \frac{e^{2\xi} - 1}{e^{2\xi} + 1} v^2 dt + \frac{(e^\xi + e^{-\xi})^2}{2(b - a)} \mu(\cdot)dt + vd\omega$$

$$= \tanh(\xi)v^2 dt + \frac{2}{(b - a)} \cosh^2(\xi)\mu(\cdot)dt + vd\omega$$

where $v \equiv \frac{b - a}{2} \sigma.$ (9)

The first term is uniformly bounded in absolute value by $v^2 dt$. The second term is nonnegative for all $\xi < 1/2\ln[(a' - a)/(b - a')]$. Therefore at smaller values, the evolution of ξ stochastically dominates that of the random walk process $dw = -v^2 dt + v dw$. Since $-\infty$ is inaccessible for w, it is also inaccessible for ξ, and, therefore, a is inaccessible for z. Similar reasoning shows that b is also inaccessible. The risk-neutral stochastic process for ξ is

$$d\xi = \frac{e^{2\xi} - 1}{e^{2\xi} + 1} v^2 dt + v d\hat\omega = v^2 \tanh(\xi)dt + v d\hat\omega, \tag{10}$$

and the same proof is valid with $\mu = 0$. ∎

    As shown in (10), the risk-neutral expected change in ξ positive and increasing for $\xi > 0$ and negative and decreasing for $\xi < 0$. Therefore, in the long run, ξ tends to $\pm\infty$. In fact when ξ is positive (negative) there is a non-zero risk-neutral probability that it will never subsequently become negative (positive).[13] Correspondingly, the risk-neutral probability density for z tends to accumulate near one of its barriers, and when z is below (above) the midpoint, $(a + b)/2$, there is a non-zero risk-neutral probability that it will never subsequently rise above (fall below) the midpoint.

    The risk-neutral probability density function for the maturity-T futures price at time s conditional on the futures price at time t can be determined by stochastically integrating (10) or from the second derivative of the price of an option as shown in the Appendix. It is

$$\text{Prob}\{z_{sT} \in (z, z + dz) | z_{tT} = z_0\}$$
$$= \frac{1}{v} e^{-v^2/8} \sqrt{\frac{(z_0 - a)(1 - z_0/b)}{(z - a)^3(1 - z/b)^3}} \, \phi\!\left(\frac{1}{v} \ln\!\left[\frac{z_0 - a}{z - a} \frac{1 - z/b}{1 - z_0/b}\right]\right)$$

where $v^2(t, s; T) = (1 - a/b)^2 3 \displaystyle\int_t^s \sigma^2(\tau; T)d\tau \tag{11}$

and $\phi(u) \equiv e^{-u^2/2}/\sqrt{2\pi}$ is the standard normal density function.

    Figure 5-1 illustrates this distribution for a typical case. Plotted is the probability density for the exchange rate in six, twelve and eighteen months. The barriers are $\pm 10\%$ from the midpoint of the range. The propositional standard deviation is constant over time and 6% per year (measured at the midpoint). The initial futures price is 2% below the midpoint. The most obvious characteristic of the distribution is its bimodal shape after eighteen months. As noted previously, the probability that the exchange rate will be found close to one of the two barriers tends to accumulate. Over the shorter interval (or, equivalently, if the process has a smaller variance), the distribution may be unimodal; however, it is always "flatter" through the mid-range than the lognormal distribution.

    Of course, the density function for the true process can have a shape which is quite different from that for the risk-neutral process. The true process is not restricted to have an expected change of zero, and could, for example, have a central tendency toward some interior point of the permissible range resulting in a unimodal density regardless of the time period involved.

FIGURE 5-1 **Probability density function for the stochastic process dz =
3D(z − a)(1 − z/b)dω̂. The standard deviation is 6% measured at
the midpoint of the range. The barriers are ±10% of the
midpoint and the initial value is 2% below the midpoint.**

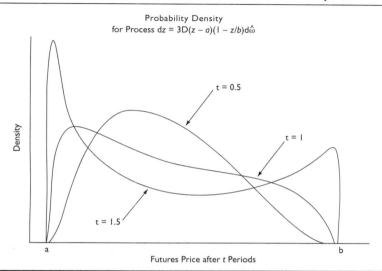

Probability Density
for Process dz = 3D(z − a)(1 − z/b)dω̂

t = 0.5

t = 1

t = 1.5

Density

a   b

Futures Price after t Periods

PRICING EUROPEAN DERIVATIVES FOR THE BOUNDED PROCESS

Provided the domestic interest rate, r, is constant, the fundamental partial differential equation for pricing ordinary options and other derivatives for the postulated exchange rate dynamics in (7) is

$$0 = \frac{1}{2} \sigma^2(t; T)(z - a)^2(1 - z/b)^2 f_{zz} - rf + f_t. \tag{12}$$

The appropriate condition at maturity, T', depends on the contract being valued. For most contracts, we need not impose other boundary conditions since the two barriers are inaccessible as previously demonstrated. However, some contracts, such as American options, may have an "early-exercise" boundary within the barriers. For these contracts, additional conditions will be required.

We could value contracts by taking the expectation of their payoffs with respect to the risk-neutral probability distribution in (11). A simpler approach is to define a new function $g(\zeta, t) \equiv (1 - a/b)f(z, t)/[(1 - k/b)(1 - z/b)]$ in terms of the new variable $\zeta \equiv (z - a)/(1 - z/b)$. As shown in the Appendix, the partial differential equation for g and its maturity condition when the option is a call are

$$0 = \frac{1}{2} \sigma^2(t; T)(1 - a/b)^2 \zeta^2 g_{\zeta\zeta} - rg + g_t$$

(13)

subject to $\quad g(\zeta, T') = \text{Max} \left[0, \zeta - \dfrac{k - a}{1 - k/b} \right]$.

This is the Black-Scholes equation and maturity condition for a call with strike price of $(k - a)/(1 - k/b)$ on an asset with price ζ paying dividends continuously at the rate r. Using the Black-Scholes call function and reexpressing the value in the original variables gives a price of

$$
\begin{aligned}
c(z, t; k, T') &= \frac{1}{1 - a/b} e^{-r(T' - t)} \mathcal{C}\Big((z - a)(1 - k/b), T' - t; \\
&\qquad (k - a)(1 - z/b), \frac{v^2}{T' - t}, 0\Big) \\
&= \frac{1}{1 - a/b} e^{-r(T' - t)} [(z - a)(1 - k/b)\Phi(b^+) \\
&\qquad - (k - a)(1 - z/b)\Phi(b^-)]
\end{aligned}
$$

where $\quad b^{\pm} \equiv \dfrac{1}{v(t, T'; T)} \left[\ln\!\left(\dfrac{z - a}{k - a} \dfrac{1 - k/b}{1 - z/b} \right) \pm \dfrac{1}{2} v^2(t, T'; T) \right]$ (14)

where v is defined in (11), $\Phi(\cdot)$ is the standard cumulative normal distribution function, and $\mathcal{C}(S, \tau; K, \sigma^2, r)$ is the Black-Scholes call option function for a call maturing in τ years with a strike price K on a stock with price S and logarithmic variance of σ^2 when the interest rate is r.

A futures price is an expectation of a future value and not an expectation discounted to the present like an asset price.[14] Therefore, the same partial differential equation, without the discounting term, $-rf$, holds for futures-style derivatives which are futures prices as explained previously. This equation is now valid even when the domestic interest rate is stochastic, as is evident from its absence in the equation. With the same substitution we can derive the futures-style call price as

$$
\begin{aligned}
c_{\text{futures-style}}(z, t; k, T') &= \frac{1}{1 - a/b} \mathcal{C}\Big((z - a)(1 - k/b), T' - t; \\
&\qquad (k - a)(1 - z/b), \frac{v^2}{T' - t}, 0\Big).
\end{aligned}
$$

(15)

The put and futures-style put prices can be determined by using the appropriate put-call parity relation.

Table 5-1 gives the values of three-month and one-year futures-style call options for different bounds for the exchange rate dynamics. In each case the parameter σ has been selected so the instantaneous standard deviation of percentage changes in the exchange rate at its current level is 10% per year. That is $\sigma(z - a)(1 - z/b) = 0.1 \cdot z$. The values of regular call options are smaller by the factor $e^{-r(T' - t)}$. The call option price is also plotted in Figure 5-2. Note that the call reaches its minimum and maximum values of 0 and $(b - k)$ when the futures exchange rate hits the barriers a and b, respectively.

TABLE 5-1 Value of foreign exchange futures-style call as a percent of the strike price as given by equation (15). Interest rate is $r = 5\%$. Volatility parameter, σ, gives an annualized percentage standard deviation of 10% at the current futures price, $\sigma = z/[(z - \alpha)(1 - z/b)] \cdot 10\%$. Barriers are proportionally symmetric about the strike price; e.g., if $a = 0.8k$, then $b = k/0.8 = 1.25k$.

z/k	Range of Exchange Rate (a, b) as a Fraction of the Strike Price k				
	0, ∞	0,5, 2.0	0.8, 1.25	0.9, 1.11	0.95, 1.052
	Three months to maturity				
0.90	0.030	0.033	0.078	†	†
0.92	0.095	0.099	0.145	0.544	†
0.94	0.252	0.256	0.293	0.485	†
0.96	0.572	0.574	0.591	0.658	0.502
0.98	1.134	1.133	1.128	1.107	0.980
1.00	1.994	1.993	1.978	1.922	1.719
1.02	3.170	3.170	3.164	3.142	3.009
1.04	4.630	4.632	4.648	4.709	4.586
1.06	6.310	6.314	6.351	6.527	†
1.08	8.139	8.144	8.192	8.545	†
1.10	10.057	10.061	10.112	10.508	†
	One year to maturity				
0.90	0.712	0.738	0.994	†	†
0.92	1.085	1.101	1.245	1.021	†
0.94	1.585	1.591	1.633	1.538	†
0.96	2.229	2.225	2.184	1.950	0.513
0.98	3.028	3.017	2.922	2.570	1.490
1.00	3.988	3.975	3.859	3.463	2.433
1.02	5.106	5.095	4.997	4.637	3.538
1.04	6.376	6.371	6.323	6.069	4.615
1.06	7.785	7.789	7.817	7.696	†
1.08	9.317	9.331	9.452	9.329	†
1.10	10.954	10.977	11.202	10.526	†

†The futures price z is confined to the open interval a to b.

At-the-money call options are lower in value when the exchange rate is bounded (after equating the variances). When the exchange rate is near either barrier, narrowing the range first increases the option price as the variance parameter σ must be increased to keep the instantaneous properties the same. Further increases lower the option's value as its potential profitability is cut off. The latter effect is less important in the three-month option as over a short period a distant barrier has little effect on the option payoff. Note in particular, when $z = 110$, moving the barrier from 125 to 111 (and increasing σ) decreases the price of the long term option but not the short term option.

FIGURE 5-2   Value of a futures-style call option as a function of the futures price z for the risk-neutral stochastic process $dz = 3D(z - a)$ $(1 - z/b)d\hat{\omega}$.

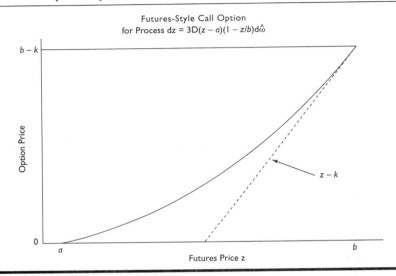

Futures-Style Call Option
for Process $dz = 3D(z - a)(1 - z/b)d\hat{\omega}$

FIGURE 5-3   Value of standard and futures-style call options as functions of maturity for the risk-neutral stochastic process $dz = 3D(z - a)$ $(1 - z/b)d\hat{\omega}$.

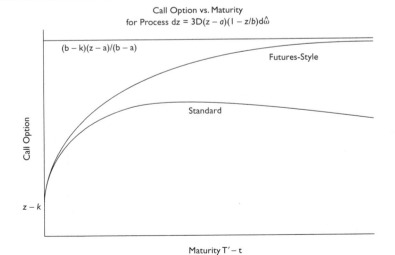

Call Option vs. Maturity
for Process $dz = 3D(z - a)(1 - z/b)d\hat{\omega}$

As shown in Table 5-1, the futures-style call prices are increasing in maturity. The implied comparative static, $\partial c_{fs}/\partial T' > 0$, can be verified directly. This can most easily be explained by examining futures-style put-call parity (3). Since futures-style put prices must be positive, $c_{fs} > z_{tT} - k$. Therefore, parity guarantees that there is no early exercise premium for an American futures-style call and that European and American futures-style calls have the same price. An American option price must be increasing in maturity since moving the expiration date back only increases the holder's rights so the same must be true for the European futures-style option. The comparative static $\partial p_{fs}/\partial T' > 0$ also holds as can be confirmed by put-call parity. Similar reasoning applies. The futures-style call option prices increase to limits of [15]

$$c_{\text{futures-style}}(z, t; k, \infty) = \frac{z - a}{b - a}(b - k)$$

$$p_{\text{futures-style}}(z, t; k, \infty) = \frac{b - z}{b - a}(k - a). \tag{16}$$

For ordinary options a change in maturity has an indeterminate effect. Clearly short-maturity options which are out-of-the-money will be increasing functions of maturity. On the other hand, the value of a futures-style option has an upper bound as shown in (16), and since the price of an ordinary option is equal to the discounted value of the price of a futures-style option, for sufficiently great maturities, the value of an ordinary option must be decreasing in maturity, approaching zero in the limit (figure 5-3).

The hedge ratios for these options are

$$\Delta_c = e^{r(T'-t)}\left[\frac{b - k}{b - a}\Phi(b^+) + \frac{k - a}{b - a}\Phi(b^-)\right]$$

$$\Delta_p = e^{-r(T'-t)} - \Delta_c. \tag{17}$$

As usual the call delta is positive, and the put delta is negative. In addition, these deltas are always less than one in absolute value, so the options always have less absolute price risk than does the futures price itself. In fact the deltas for the standard puts and calls are smaller in absolute value than $e^{-r(T'-t)}$. The deltas for the futures-style options are larger in absolute value by a factor of $e^{r(T'-t)}$, though they are still less than one.

The option's elasticities, or omegas, are plotted in Figure 5-4. Because they are proportional to the ratios of the option's deltas to their prices, the discount factors cancel making both standard and futures-style omegas the same. Neither the call nor the put omega is monotonic; instead each option has its lowest risk relative to that of the futures price at some interior point of the possible exchange rates. However, it can be shown that the standard deviation of the rate of return on a call (put) is monotonically decreasing (increasing) in the futures price since the return risk on the futures price itself is smaller near both barriers.

Most of the other usual option comparative statics hold for this model:

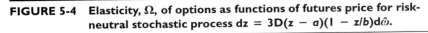

FIGURE 5-4   **Elasticity, Ω, of options as functions of futures price for risk-neutral stochastic process dz = 3D(z − a)(1 − z/b)dω̂.**

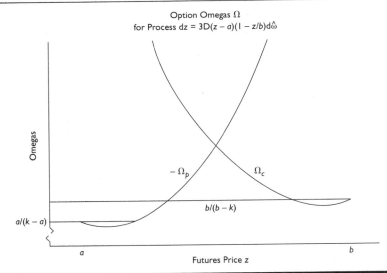

$$\frac{\partial c}{\partial k} < 0 \quad \frac{\partial p}{\partial k} > 0$$

$$\frac{\partial c}{\partial \sigma} > 0 \quad \frac{\partial p}{\partial \sigma} > 0 \tag{18}$$

$$\frac{\partial c}{\partial r} < 0 \quad \frac{\partial p}{\partial r} < 0.$$

An increase in the strike price decreases (increases) the value of a call (put). An increase in volatility increases both option prices.[16] The one difference is that an increase in the domestic interest rate decreases both option prices. Recall that an increase in the interest rate holding the futures price fixed is a decrease in the spot exchange rate. The comparative statics for the futures-style and ordinary options are the same except in one case. As is obvious from the partial differential pricing equation, futures-style option prices are independent of the domestic interest rate (for a given futures price).

The foreign interest rate does not affect the option prices (other than through the futures price) so the foreign yield curve need not be flat or even nonstochastic for this model. The effect of foreign interest rates on European option prices comes entirely through changes in the futures foreign exchange price.

The call's value is an increasing function of the level of the upper barrier. This is an expected result as increasing the upper barrier (i) makes it more likely the option will mature in-the-money and (ii) increases the potential profitability of the call in those cases. Less obviously, increasing b also increases the instantaneous variance of the exchange rate at all levels of z. Since increasing the lower bound, a, also makes the option's maturing in-the-money more likely, it is perhaps surprising that the call's value is a decreasing function of the lower barrier. The reason behind this counterintuitive result can be seen in the exchange rate dynamics. Increasing the lower bound decreases the variance of the exchange rate at any level and this more than offsets the increased probability of ending in the money. A similar result holds for puts. The values of both options increase with an increase in the range (a, b).

PRICING AMERICAN DERIVATIVES FOR THE BOUNDED PROCESS

Many listed foreign exchange options have American-style exercise. Even though there are no dividends paid on foreign exchange futures (or on currencies), the right to exercise these options before maturity generally has positive value. Merton's (1973) proposition that call options written on shares of stock with no dividend payments should never be exercised prior to maturity does not apply in this case. The futures price basis does not have an risk-neutral expected rate of return equal to the interest rate and, in this sense, it behaves as if it paid a dividend. Furthermore, we saw previously that their prices may be decreasing in maturity which indicates that an early exercise is optimal in some cases.[17]

To value an American option we must append the no-arbitrage-by-exercise conditions, $c(z, t; k) \geq z - k$ or $p(z, t; k) \geq k - z$, to the partial differential equations. As is the case for ordinary options, no closed-form solution exists for finite-maturity American options when early exercise is optimal; however, several approximations have been developed for ordinary puts and calls which can be adapted to the bounded dynamics of this paper. For example, any of the numerical methods for dealing directly with the partial differential pricing equation can be employed. The simplest approach is probably to apply the standard binomial model to the pricing equation (13) in the transformed variable ζ.[18]

Other quicker methods can also be used. Here we adapt the approximation developed by Barone-Adesi and Whaley (1987). This method is based on the perpetual option problem which we tackle first.

For a perpetual American option on a futures price with the bounded dynamics studied in this paper, the pricing equation is the ordinary differential equation

$$\frac{1}{2}(z - a)^2(1 - z/b)^2\sigma^2 f'' - rf = 0. \tag{19}$$

This equation is identical to the standard pricing partial differential equation (12) without the time derivative term. The boundary and optimal exercise conditions are $c(z_c) = z_c - k$ and $c'(z_c) = 1$ for calls and $p(z_p) = k - z_p$ and $p'(z_p) = -1$ for puts. The call and put options are exercised when the futures price reaches the exercise points, z_c and z_p respectively. The high-contact or smooth-pasting conditions, $c'(z_c) = 1$ and $p'(z_p) = -1$, ensure that the exercise points are optimal in each case.

The general solution to a homogeneous, linear, second-order differential equation is a linear combination of two solutions. In this case

$$f(z) = C_1(z - a)^\alpha (b - z)^{1-\alpha} + C_2(z - a)^{1-\alpha}(b - z)^\alpha$$

$$\text{where} \quad \alpha \equiv \frac{1}{2}\left(1 + \sqrt{1 + \frac{8r}{\sigma^2(1 - a/b)^2}}\right). \tag{20}$$

Since $\alpha > 1$, the second solution becomes unbounded as z approaches a. But the call price should be small when $z \approx a$; therefore, only the first solution is valid, and $C_2 = 0$. Similarly the first solution becomes unbounded as z approaches b so for a put option, $C_1 = 0$. The remaining constant and the optimal exercise point can be determined from the boundary and optimal exercise conditions. For perpetual call and put options we have

$$c(z, t; k, \infty) = (z_c - k)\left(\frac{z - a}{z_c - a}\right)^\alpha \left(\frac{b - z}{b - z_c}\right)^{1-\alpha}$$

$$\text{where} \quad z_c \equiv \frac{ab - [\alpha b + (1 - \alpha)a]k}{\alpha a + (1 - \alpha)b - k} \tag{21a}$$

$$p(z, t; k, \infty) = (k - z_p)\left(\frac{z - a}{z_p - a}\right)^{1-\alpha}\left(\frac{b - z}{b - z_p}\right)^\alpha$$

$$\text{where} \quad z_p \equiv \frac{ab - [\alpha a + (1 - \alpha)b]k}{\alpha b + (1 - \alpha)a - k}. \tag{21b}$$

The prices z_c and z_p are the optimal exercise prices for the call and put respectively.

For the lognormal process, the optimal exercise points are proportional to the strike price, so any perpetual option must be in-the-money by a certain percentage amount before it is exercised. For the bounded process in this paper, calls and puts cannot be in-the-money by more than $b - k$ or $k - a$, respectively. Nevertheless, for all parameter values, it is true that $a < z_p < k < z_c < b$, so all options are exercised within the bounded region. When the futures price is close to either of the boundaries, its return variance is small. This keeps the value of an option alive small so the opportunity cost of exercise is low offsetting the small gain realized.

As shown in the appendix, under the Barone-Adesi and Whaley method, the early exercise premium for an American option is approximated as $f_{Am}(z, t) - f_{Eu}(z, t) \approx [1 - e^{-r(T'-t)}]\pi(z)$ where π satisfied an ordinary differential equation like (19) for perpetual options. The American options are worth

$$c_{Am}(z, t) \approx c_{Eu}(z, t) + [\tilde{z}_c - k - c_{Eu}(\tilde{z}_c, t)]\frac{(\tilde{z} - a)^{\tilde{\alpha}}(b - z)^{1-\tilde{\alpha}}}{(\tilde{z}_c - a)^{\tilde{\alpha}}(b - \tilde{z}_c)^{1-\tilde{\alpha}}}$$

$$p_{Am}(z, t) \approx p_{Eu}(z, t) + [k - \tilde{z}_p - p_{Eu}(\tilde{z}_p, t)]\frac{(\tilde{z} - a)^{1-\tilde{\alpha}}(b - z)^{\tilde{\alpha}}}{(\tilde{z}_p - a)^{1-\tilde{\alpha}}(b - \tilde{z}_p)^{\tilde{\alpha}}}$$

$$\text{where} \quad \tilde{\alpha} \equiv \frac{1}{2}\left(1 + \sqrt{1 + \frac{8r}{\sigma^2(1 - a/b)^2}[1 - e^{-r(T'-t)}]^{-1}}\right) \tag{22}$$

and c_{Eu} and p_{Eu} are the values of the corresponding European options with the same strike price. The estimated current optimal exercise points, $\tilde{z}_c$ and $\tilde{z}_p$, must be determined numerically by solving the high-contact equations

$$\tilde{z}_c - k - c_{Eu}(\tilde{z}_c, t) = [1 - \partial c_{Eu}(\tilde{z}_c, t)/\partial z] \frac{(\tilde{z}_c - a)(b - \tilde{z}_c)}{(1 - \tilde{\alpha})a + \tilde{\alpha}b - \tilde{z}_c}$$

(23)

$$k - \tilde{z}_p - p_{Eu}(\tilde{z}_p, t) = [1] - \partial p_{Eu}(\tilde{z}_p, t)/\partial z] \frac{(\tilde{z}_p - a)(b - \tilde{z}_p)}{a\tilde{\alpha} + (1 - \tilde{\alpha})b - \tilde{z}_p}.$$

Table 5-2 gives the values of representative European and American calls on a bounded foreign exchange process. The parameter values are $r = 5\%$ and $\tau = 1$ year. The volatility parameter is selected so that the local standard deviation is 10%.

Figure 5-5 plots the differences, $C_{fs} - C_{Eu}$ and $C_{Am} - C_{Eu}$. For low futures prices, both differences are small since there is little likelihood that any of the options will expire in the money. As the futures price increases, the value of the early exercise premium on the American options also increases. A futures-style option is worth more than a standard option; furthermore, there is no early exercise premium for an American futures-style option so $C_{fs} - C_{Eu}$ must be larger than $C_{Am} - C_{Eu}$ as shown.

CONCLUSION

This paper has presented a model for valuing foreign exchange derivatives when the exchange rate process is bounded. Both European and approximate American formulae have been given.

A bound on the stochastic process of the basis asset can have a large effect on the price of the derivative. Bounds, of course, limit the profit that can be realized, but they also limit how far an option can fall out-of-the-money. In addition the presence of bounds can significantly alter the optimal exercise policy for an American option.

This model can also be applied to other situations in which the basis may have an upper or lower bound. This, for example, may be a good model of cash flows or earnings in some cases. Modelling agricultural commodities with price supports is another obvious example.

In addition, the stochastic process may provide a useful approximation in other problems. For example, if we model the interest adjusted stock price $Z \equiv Se^{-rt}$ as following a risk-neutral process with an upper bound $dZ = \sigma Z(1 - Z/b)d\hat{\omega}$, then its logarithmic volatility (and that of the stock) will be smaller at higher prices. This may be an effective alternative to the constant elasticity of variance model.

TABLE 5-2 Value of European and American foreign exchange call option as a percent of the strike price as given by equations (14) and (22).

| | One year to maturity Range of Exchange Rate (a, b) as a Fraction of the Strike Price k | | | | | |
| | 0, ∞ | | 0.8, 1.25 | | 0.9, 1.11 | |
z/k	Eu	Am	Eu	Am	Eu	Am
0.92	1.032	1.049	1.184	1.203	0.971	0.998
0.94	1.508	1.531	1.553	1.578	1.463	1.492
0.96	2.120	2.151	2.078	2.110	1.855	1.889
0.98	2.880	2.923	2.779	2.822	2.445	2.489
1.00	3.793	3.850	3.671	3.729	3.294	3.355
1.02	4.857	4.934	4.753	4.833	4.411	4.499
1.04	6.065	6.167	6.015	6.124	5.773	5.902
1.06	7.405	7.541	7.436	7.581	7.321	7.512
1.08	8.862	9.041	8.991	9.182	8.874	9.168

Maturity is $T' - t = 1$. Interest rate is $r = 5\%$. Volatility parameter, σ, gives an annualized percentage standard deviation of 10% at the current futures price, $\sigma = z/[z - a)(1 - z/b] \cdot 10\%$. Barriers are proportionally symmetric about the strike price; e.g., if $a = 0.8k$, then $b = k/0.8 = 1.25k$.

FIGURE 5-5 Excess value of futures-style and American call options as functions of futures price for risk-neutral stochastic process $dz = 3D(z - a)(1 - z/b)d\hat{\omega}$.

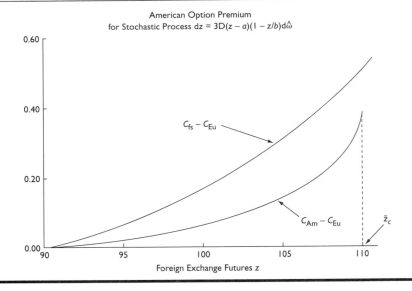

American Option Premium
for Stochastic Process $dz = 3D(z - a)(1 - z/b)d\hat{\omega}$

$C_{fs} - C_{Eu}$

$C_{Am} - C_{Eu}$

$\bar{z}_c$

Foreign Exchange Futures z

APPENDIX

Derivation of the Reduced Pricing Equation and the Option Price

This appendix presents the details of the paper's derivations. The reduced option pricing equation (13) is derived first. From this, the option's price (14) is determined. The risk-neutral probability density for the bounded exchange rate process (11) is derived from the second derivative of the option price with respect to the strike price. Finally, the American approximation formulae (22) are determined.

Let $\zeta \equiv (z - a)/(1 - z/b)$. Then

$$\frac{\partial \zeta}{\partial z} = \frac{1}{1 - z/b} + \frac{1}{b} \frac{z - a}{(1 - z/b)^2} = \frac{1 - a/b}{(1 - z/b)^2}. \tag{A1}$$

Now let $f(z, t) \equiv (1 - k/b)(1 - z/b)g(\zeta, t)/(1 - a/b)$. The partial derivatives of f are

$$\frac{\partial f}{\partial t} = \frac{(1 - k/b)(1 - z/b)}{1 - a/b} \frac{\partial g}{\partial t}$$

$$\frac{\partial f}{\partial z} = \frac{1 - k/b}{1 - a/b} \left[-\frac{1}{b} g + (1 - z/b) \frac{\partial g}{\partial \zeta} \frac{\partial \zeta}{\partial z} \right] = -\frac{1 - k/b}{b - a} g + \frac{1 - k/b}{1 - z/b} \frac{\partial g}{\partial \zeta}$$

$$\frac{\partial^2 f}{\partial z^2} = \left[-\frac{1 - k/b}{b - a} \frac{\partial g}{\partial \zeta} + \frac{1 - k/b}{1 - z/b} \frac{\partial^2 g}{\partial \zeta^2} \right] \frac{1 - a/b}{(1 - z/b)^2} + \frac{1 - k/b}{(1 - z/b)^2} \frac{1}{b} \frac{\partial g}{\partial \zeta}$$
$$= \frac{(1 - k/b)(1 - a/b)}{(1 - z/b)^3} \frac{\partial^2 g}{\partial \zeta^2}. \tag{A2}$$

Substituting these partial derivatives into (12) and collecting terms gives

$$0 = \frac{(1 - k/b)(1 - z/b)}{1 - a/b} \left[\frac{1}{2} \sigma^2(t; T)(1 - a/b)^2 \frac{(z - a)^2}{(1 - z/b)^2} g_{\zeta\zeta} - rg + g_t \right] \tag{A3}$$

which is the partial differential equation in (13) in the text. If f is a call option, the condition for g at maturity is

$$g(\zeta, T') = \frac{1 - a/b}{(1 - k/b)(1 - z/b)} f(z, T') = \text{Max}\left[\frac{1 - a/b}{(1 - k/b)(1 - z/b)} (z - k), 0 \right]$$
$$= \text{Max}\left[\frac{(z - a)(1 - k/b) - (1 - z/b)(k - a)}{(1 - k/b)(1 - z/b)}, 0 \right]$$
$$= \text{Max}\left[\zeta - \frac{k - a}{1 - k/b}, 0 \right] \tag{A4}$$

which is the boundary condition in (13) in the text.

This will be recognized as Merton's (1973) time-varying volatility version of the standard Black-Scholes partial differential equation for a call option with a strike price of $(k - a)/(1 - k/b)$ on a basis asset ζ with a continuous dividend at the constant yield of r. Therefore,

$$g(\zeta, t) = \mathscr{C}\left(\zeta e^{-r(T'-t)}, T' - t; \frac{k - a}{1 - k/b}, \frac{v^2(t, T'; T)}{T' - t}, r\right)$$

where $\quad v^2(t, T'; T) \equiv (1 - a/b)^2 \int_t^{T'} \sigma^2(s; T)ds$ (A5)

and $\mathscr{C}(S, \tau; K, \sigma^2, r)$ is the Black-Scholes option function for a call maturing in τ years with a strike price K on a stock with price S and logarithmic variance of σ^2 when the interest rate is r.

Expressing the original function $f(z, t) \equiv (1 - k/b)(1 - z/b)g(\zeta, t)/(1 - a/b)$ by substituting for $\zeta \equiv (z - a)/(1 - z/b)$ gives

$$f(z, t; k, T') = \frac{(1 - k/b)(1 - z/b)}{1 - a/b}$$

$$\times \mathscr{C}\left(\frac{z - a}{1 - z/b} e^{-r(T'-t)}, T' - t; \frac{k - a}{1 - k/b}, \frac{v^2}{T' - t}, r\right)$$

$$= \frac{1}{1 - a/b} e^{-r(T'-t)}\mathscr{C}\left((z - a)(1 - k/b), T' - t;\right.$$

$$\left.\times (k - a)(1 - z/b), \frac{v^2}{T' - t}, 0\right)$$

$$= \frac{1}{1 - a/b} e^{-r(T'-t)}[(z - a)(1 - k/b)\Phi(b^+)$$

$$- (k - a)(1 - z/b)\Phi(b^-)]$$ (A6)

where

$$b^{\pm} \equiv \frac{1}{v(t, T'; T)}\left[\ln\left(\frac{z - a}{k - a}\frac{1 - k/b}{1 - z/b}\right) \pm \frac{1}{2} v^2(t, T'; T)\right]$$

$\Phi(\cdot)$ is the standard cumulative normal distribution function, and v is defined as above.[19]

Derivation of the Probability Distribution for the Process dz = (z − a)(1 − z/b)dω

The probability density function for the futures price can be derived from the call option price as $e^{r(T'-t)}\partial^2 c/\partial k^2$ (see e.g., Ingersoll 1987). Recall that the derivatives of the Black-Scholes option price with respect to the stock price and the strike price are $\partial\mathscr{C}/\partial S = \Phi(b^+)$ and $\partial\mathscr{C}/\partial K = e^{-rt}\Phi(b^-)$. Therefore, the probability density that the futures price at time T' is equal to k can be obtained as

$$e^{r(T'-t)}\frac{\partial c}{\partial k} = \frac{1}{1 - a/b}\left[\Phi(b^+)\frac{z - a}{-b} - \Phi(b^-)(1 - z/b)\right]$$

$$e^{r(T'-t)}\frac{\partial^2 c}{\partial k^2} = -\frac{1}{b - a}[(z - a)\phi(b^+) + (b - z)\phi(b^-)]\frac{\partial b^{\pm}}{\partial k}$$

$$= \frac{1}{v}\frac{1}{(b - k)(k - a)}[(z - a)\phi(b^+) + (b - z)\phi(b^-)]$$ (A7)

where $\phi(\cdot)$ is the standard normal density function. This can be simplified to[20]

$$\text{Prob}\{z_{T'T} \in (z, z + dz) | z_{tT} = z_0\} = \frac{(b - a)(b - z_0)}{v(b - z)^2(z - a)}$$

$$\times \phi\left(\frac{1}{v(t, T'; T)} \left[\ln\left(\frac{z_0 - a}{z - a} \frac{1 - z/b}{1 - z_0/b}\right) - \frac{1}{2} v^2(t, T'; T) \right]\right). \tag{A8}$$

After expanding the argument of $\phi(\cdot)$, the density can also be expressed as

$$\text{Prob}\{z_{T'T} \in (z, z + dz) | z_{tT} = z_0\}$$

$$= \frac{1}{v} e^{-v^2/8} \sqrt{\frac{(z_0 - a)(1 - z_0/b)}{(z - a)^3(1 - z/b)^3}} \phi\left(\frac{1}{v} \ln\left[\frac{z_0 - a}{z - a} \frac{1 - z/b}{1 - z_0/b}\right]\right) \tag{A9}$$

which illustrates the symmetry in $z - a$ and $1 - z/b$.

Derivation of the Approximate American Solution

For the Barone-Adesi and Whaley approximation the early exercise premium for an American option is expressed as $f(z, t) \equiv f_{\text{Am}}(z, t) - f_{\text{Eu}}(z, t) = \psi(t)\pi(z; \psi)$ where $\psi(t) \equiv 1 - e^{-r(T'-t)}$. Since both the American and European option prices satisfy the same linear partial differential equation, the premium, which is just a portfolio of these two, does as well. The partial derivatives of f expressed in terms of π and ψ are $f_z = \psi\pi_z, f_{zz} = \psi\pi_{zz}$, and $f_t = \psi_t\pi + \psi\pi_\psi \psi_t$. Since $\psi_t = -re^{-r(T'-t)} = r(\psi - 1)$, the partial differential equation for π is

$$\psi\left[\frac{1}{2} (z - a)^2(1 - z/b)^2\sigma^2\pi_{zz} - \frac{r}{\psi} \pi + r(\psi - 1)\pi_\psi\right] = 0. \tag{A10}$$

This equation is an exact description of the early exercise premium. The approximation consists of assuming the final term can be ignored. This is reasonable since for short maturities $\psi \approx 1$ and for long maturities $\pi_\psi \approx 0$. This is also the reason for valuing the premium $f_{\text{Am}}(z, t) - f_{\text{Eu}}(z, t)$ rather than the American option price directly since its time sensitivity is smaller. The approximation, $\tilde{\pi}(z; \psi) \approx \pi(z, \psi)$ then only depends on the current value of ψ, and hence time, parametrically. It satisfies the ordinary differential equation used to value perpetual options (19) with an adjusted interest rate of r/ψ

$$\frac{1}{2} (z - a)^2(1 - z/b)^2\sigma^2\tilde{\pi}'' - \frac{r}{\psi} \tilde{\pi} \approx 0. \tag{A11}$$

As before the solution is the linear combination

$$\pi(z, \psi) \approx \tilde{\pi}(z; \psi) = C_1(z - a)^{\tilde{\alpha}}(b - z)^{1-\tilde{\alpha}} + C_2(z - a)^{1-\tilde{\alpha}}(b - z)^{\tilde{\alpha}}$$

$$\text{where} \quad \tilde{\alpha} \equiv \frac{1}{2}\left(1 + \sqrt{1 + \frac{8r/\psi(t)}{\sigma^2(1 - a/b)^2}}\right). \tag{A12}$$

Like α, the approximation exponent, $\tilde{\alpha}$, is greater than one so $C_1 = 0$ for puts and $C_2 = 0$ for calls. The remaining constant is determined from the boundary condition. The call is worth $c_{\text{Eu}}(z, t) + \psi(t)C_1(z - a)^{\tilde{\alpha}}(b - z)^{1-\tilde{\alpha}}$. At the approximately optimal exercise point, $\tilde{z}_c$, it is exercised for $\tilde{z}_c - k$ so

$$C_1 = \frac{\tilde{z}_c - k - c_{\mathrm{Eu}}(\tilde{z}_c, t)}{\psi(t)(\tilde{z}_c - a)^{\tilde{\alpha}}(b - \tilde{z}_c)^{\tilde{\alpha}}}. \tag{A13}$$

The constant C_2 for the put is determined similarly. The American options are therefore worth approximately

$$c_{\mathrm{Am}}(z, t) \approx c_{\mathrm{Eu}}(z, t) + \frac{\tilde{z}_c - k - c_{\mathrm{Eu}}(\tilde{z}_c, t)}{(\tilde{z}_c - a)^{\tilde{\alpha}}(b - \tilde{z}_c)^{1 - \tilde{\alpha}}} (z - a)^{\tilde{\alpha}}(b - z)^{1 - \tilde{\alpha}}$$

$$ \tag{A14}$$

$$p_{\mathrm{Am}}(z, t \approx p_{\mathrm{Eu}}(z, t) + \frac{k - \tilde{z}_p - p_{\mathrm{Eu}}(\tilde{z}_p, t)}{(\tilde{z}_p - z)^{1 - \tilde{\alpha}}(b - \tilde{z}_p)^{\tilde{\alpha}}} (z - a)^{1 - \tilde{\alpha}}(b - z)^{\tilde{\alpha}}.$$

The estimated (current) optimal exercise points, $\tilde{z}_c$ and $\tilde{z}_p$, must be determined numerically. This can be done by maximizing C_{Am} with respect to $\tilde{z}_c$ or, equivalently, solving the high-contact equations

$$\tilde{z}_c - k - c_{\mathrm{Eu}}(\tilde{z}_c, t) = [1 - \partial c_{\mathrm{Eu}}(\tilde{z}_c, t)/\partial z] \frac{(\tilde{z}_c - a)(b - \tilde{z}_c)}{(1 - \tilde{\alpha})a + \tilde{\alpha}b - \tilde{z}_c}$$

$$ \tag{A15}$$

$$k - \tilde{z}_p - p_{\mathrm{Eu}}(\tilde{z}_p, t) = [1 - \partial p_{\mathrm{Eu}}(\tilde{z}_p, t)/\partial z] \frac{(\tilde{z}_p - a)(b - \tilde{z}_p)}{a\tilde{\alpha} + (1 - \tilde{\alpha})b - \tilde{z}_p}.$$

REFERENCES

Barone-Adesi, G., and R. E. Whaley. (1987). "Efficient Analytic Approximation of American Option Values," *The Journal of Finance* 42, 301–320.

Black, F., and M. Scholes. (1973). "The Pricing of Options and Corporate Liabilities," *Journal of Political Economy* 81, 637–654.

Cox, J. C., and S. A. Ross. (1976). "The Valuation of Options for Alternative Stochastic Processes," *Journal of Financial Economics* 3, 145–166.

Cox, J. C., J. E. Ingersoll, Jr., and S. A. Ross. (1981). "The Relation Between Forward Prices and Futures Prices," *Journal of Financial Economics* 9, 321–346.

Garman, M. B., and S. W. Kohlhagen. (1983). "Foreign Currency Option Values," *Journal of International Money and Finance* 2, 231–238.

Giddy, I. (1983). "Foreign Exchange Options," *Journal of Futures Markets* 3, 143–166.

Grabbe, J. O. (1983). "The Pricing of Call and Put Options on Foreign Exchange," *Journal of International Money and Finance* 2, 239–253.

Ingersoll, J. E., Jr. (1987). *Theory of Financial Decision Making*. Totowa, N.J.: Rowman & Littlefield.

Ingersoll, J. E., Jr. (1991). "An Approximation for Valuing American Puts and Other Financial Derivatives Using 'Barrier' Options," unpublished working paper.

Karlin, S., and H. M. Taylor. (1981). *A Second Course in Stochastic Processes*. New York: Academic Press.

Lieu, D. (1990). "Option Pricing with Futures Style Margining," *Journal of Futures Markets* 10, 327–338.

Merton, R. C. (1973). "Theory of Rational Option Pricing," *Bell Journal of Economics and Management Science* 4, 141–183.

Merton, R. C. (1977). "On the Pricing of Contingent Claims and the Modigliani-Miller Theorem," *Journal of Financial Economics* 5, 125–144.

Shastri, K., and K. Tandon. (1986). "On the Use of European Models to Price American Options on Foreign Currency," *Journal of Futures Markets* 6, 93–108.

ENDNOTES

1. Later members, Portugal, Spain, and the United Kingdom, were only required to keep their currencies within approximately 6% of par. Although the permitted ranges are precise, the 2-1/4% and 6% requirements are approximate because changes in the values of the various currencies also change the value of the ECU.

2. An option's time value is the excess over the amount by which it is in-the-money. For a call the time value is the price less the greater of zero or the exchange rate minus the strike price. For a put the time value is the price less the greater of zero or the strike price minus the exchange rate.

3. The futures foreign exchange rate depends on the stochastic processes driving the spot exchange rate and the interest rates. If the domestic interest rate is constant or uncorrelated with changes in the foreign interest rate and spot exchange rate, then futures exchange rates are the same as forward exchange rates for all maturities, $z_{tT} = x_t B^*(t; T)/B(t; T)$. See Cox, Ingersoll, and Ross (1981) for details.

4. Recently several exchanges have introduced cross-rate futures which are denominated in a third currency. For example, Deutschmark-Franc and Deutschmark-Yen futures are traded in dollars on the FINEX. These cross-rate futures prices can be converted into any of the currencies simply by using the relevant exchange rate.

5. See Lieu (1990) for a more detailed development of futures-style options. Futures-style options on foreign exchange, interest rates, and stock indices are traded on the London International Financial Futures Exchange. The Chicago Board of Trade and the Chicago Mercantile Exchange are awaiting CFTC approval to trade futures-style options.

6. Also as for any futures contract, the futures-style option price is not the value of the contract but that *settlement price* for which the contract currently has a value of zero.

7. Futures-style put-call parity can be derived as

$$p_{fs}(x_t, t; k, T) = \hat{E}[\text{Max}(k - x_T, 0)] = \hat{E}[\text{Max}(x_T - k, 0) - x_T + k]$$
$$= c_{fs}(x_t, t; k, T) - \hat{E}[x_T] + k = c_{fs}(x_t, t; k, T) - z_{tT} + k.$$

8. Put-call parity as given in (2) remains valid. It can also be expressed in terms of the futures price as

$$p(z_{tT}, t; k, T') = c(z_{tT}, t; k, T') - B(t; T')(z_{tT} - k)$$

provided the domestic interest rate is nonstochastic.

9. See Ingersoll (1987, chap. 17) for a discussion of the arbitrage opportunities that can arise with bounded processes.

10. Behavior at an inaccessible barrier need not be described as it cannot be reached. There are a number of other accessible barrier types, such as elastic or sticky. Most of these alternatives cannot be explained in an elementary fashion, and, in any case, seem inappropriate as models of exchange rates. See Karlin and Taylor (1981) for a discussion of the barrier classification.

11. Neither condition alone is sufficient. For example for the square root process, $dz = c\,dt + v\sqrt{z}\,d\omega$ $\mathcal{C}(z) \to 0$ as z approaches 0, but zero is accessible only if $v^2 > 2c$.

12. Since $\hat{E}_t[dz] = 0$, z is a local martingale under the risk-neutral process. Since z is bounded whether or not the barriers are accessible, it is a martingale as well. The risk-neutral process is an

equivalent martingale to the original processes only if both have the same type of barriers. A sufficient condition for both processes to have inaccessible barriers is given in proposition 2.

13. For the random walk diffusion $dw = -\mu dt + \sigma d\omega$ with $\mu > 0$, the probability that w will never rise to w' starting from w_0 is $\exp[-2(w' - w_0)\mu/\sigma^2]$. Therefore, the risk-neutral probability that ξ will never rise from ξ_0 to ξ' (with $\xi_0 < \xi' < 0$) is greater than $\exp[-2(\xi' - \xi_0)|\tanh(\xi')|/v^2]$. Obviously the risk-neutral probability that ξ will rise to positive values or z will rise above the midpoint $(a + b)/2$ is even less.

14. See Cox, Ingersoll, and Ross (1981) for a complete discussion.

15. For distant times, the risk-neutral probability distribution becomes more and more concentrated near the two barriers a and b. Therefore, in the limit as the maturity grows, the futures-style option prices can be determined exactly with the binomial model. The returns per dollar realized in the "up" and "down" states are b/z and a/z so the risk-neutral probability of the "up" step which gives a zero expected change is $(1 - a/z)/(b/z - a/z) = (z - a)/(b - a)$.

16. The comparative static with respect to volatility, $\partial c/\partial\sigma$, measures the change with respect to a uniform increase in the function $\sigma(t; T)$.

17. The prices of the futures-style options are increasing in maturity. For these options the American right of early exercise is zero. It pays to exercise a futures-style call early only if $c_{fs}(z_{tT}, t) \leq z_{tT} - k$. However, the futures price and the futures-style options price are each the risk-neutral expectation of the payoff. Provided the event $z_{T'T} < k$ is possible, $\hat{E}[\text{Max}(z_{T'T} - k, 0)] > \hat{E}[z_{T'T}] - k$, and the inequality above cannot hold.

18. As proved by Merton (1973), optimal early exercise is characterized by the high-contact conditions, $\partial f/\partial z = \pm 1$, for calls and puts, respectively. Using the expressions for $\partial f/\partial z$ in equation (A2) in the Appendix, we can show that $\partial f/\partial z = \pm 1$ and $f(z, t) = \pm(z - k)$ together imply that $\partial g/\partial \zeta = \pm 1$ so the problem in the transformed variable ζ has the same optimal exercise point.

19. The second equality follows from the homogeneity of the Black-Scholes function, $\lambda\mathscr{C}(S, \tau; X) = \mathscr{C}(\lambda S, \tau; \lambda X)$.

20. This last relation uses the property

$$Z\phi(b^+) = \phi(b^-) \quad \text{where} \quad b^\pm = \frac{\ln Z \pm \frac{1}{2}v^2}{v}.$$

6

Efficient Analytic Approximation of American Option Values

GIOVANNI BARONE-ADESI
ROBERT E. WHALEY

O ptions written on a wide variety of commodities and commodity futures contracts[1] now trade in the U.S. and Canada. Nearly all these options are American style[2] and thus have early exercise premiums implicitly embedded in their prices. Unlike the European-style option-pricing problems, however, analytic solutions for the American option-pricing problems have not been found, and the pricing of American options has usually resorted to finite-difference, binomial, or, more recently, compound-option approximation methods. While these approximation methods yield accurate American option values, they are cumbersome and expensive to use.

The purpose of this paper is to provide an accurate, inexpensive method for pricing American call and put options written on commodities and commodity futures contracts. The development of the "quadratic" approximation method is contained in the first section. Commodity option and commodity futures option contracts are defined, the underpinnings of commodity option valuation are discussed, and the solutions to the European call and put option-pricing problems are presented. Unlike the non-dividend-paying stock option case, it is shown that the American call option written on a commodity, as well as the American put option, may optimally be exercised prior to expiration. The approximation methods for the American call and put option values are then

This research was supported by the Futures and Options Research Center at The Fuqua School of Business, Duke University. Comments and suggestions by Fred D. Arditti, David Emanuel, Hans R. Stoll, Stuart M. Turnbull, Vera Zeidan, Luigi Zezza, and an associate editor of this *Journal of Finance* are gratefully acknowledged.

Reprinted with permission from the *Journal of Finance;* Vol. XLII, No. 2; Barone-Adesi and Whaley; 1987; American Finance Association.

derived in the manner in which MacMillan [13] approximated the solution to the American put option on a non-dividend-paying stock pricing problem. In the following section, the programming of the approximations is considered, and the results of comparisons of the finite-difference, compound-option, and quadratic approximation methods are presented and discussed. Comparisons are also made to heuristic option-pricing methods. The final section contains a summary.

VALUATION EQUATIONS FOR COMMODITY OPTIONS

In this section, the theory of pricing commodity and commodity futures option contracts is reviewed, and the approximations for the American call and put options are presented. At the outset it is useful to clearly define the terms "commodity option" and "commodity futures option." In the context in which the terms will be used here, a commodity option represents the right to buy or sell a specific commodity at a specified price within a specified period of time. The exact nature of the underlying commodity varies and may be anything from a precious metal such as gold or silver to a financial instrument such as a Treasury bond or a foreign currency. Usually the commodity option is labeled by the nature of the underlying commodity. For example, if the commodity option is written on a common stock, it is referred to as a "stock option," and, if the commodity option is written on a foreign currency, it is referred to as a "foreign currency option." If the underlying commodity is a futures contract, the options are referred to as "commodity futures options" or simply "futures options."

To begin, the focus will be on a general commodity option-pricing model. The assumptions used in the analysis are consistent with those introduced by Black and Scholes [3] and Merton [15]. First, the short-term interest rate, r, and the cost of carrying the commodity, b, are assumed to be constant, proportional rates. For a non-dividend-paying stock, the cost of carry is equal to the riskless rate of interest (i.e., $b = r$), but, for most other commodities, this is not the case. In Merton's [15] constant, proportional dividend-yield option-pricing models, for example, the cost of carrying the stock is the riskless rate, r, less the dividend yield, d (i.e., $b = r - d$). In Garman and Kohlhagen's [9] foreign currency option-pricing models, the cost of carrying the foreign currency is the domestic riskless rate, r, less the foreign riskless rate, r^* (i.e., $b = r - r^*$). However, that is not to say that the cost of carry is always below the riskless rate of interest. For the traditional agricultural commodities such as grain and livestock, the cost of carry exceeds the riskless rate by costs of storage, insurance, deterioration, etc.

In the absence of costless arbitrage opportunities, the assumption of a constant, proportional cost of carry suggests that the relationship between the futures and underlying commodity prices is

$$F = Se^{bT}, \tag{1}$$

where F and S are the current futures and spot prices, respectively, and T is the time to expiration of the futures contract. This relationship will prove useful later in this section.

A second common assumption in the option-pricing literature is that the underlying commodity price-change movements follow the stochastic differential equation,

$$dS/S = \alpha dt + \sigma dz, \tag{2}$$

where α is the expected instantaneous relative price change of the commodity, σ is the instantaneous standard deviation, and z is a Wiener process. It is worthwhile to note that, if the cost-of-carry relationship (1) holds and if equation (2) describes the movements of the commodity price through time, then the movements of the futures price are described by the equation,

$$dF/F = (\alpha - b)dt + \sigma dz. \tag{3}$$

That is, the expected instantaneous relative price change of the futures contract is $\alpha - b$ and the standard deviation of relative commodity price relatives is equal to the standard deviation of futures price relatives.[3]

Finally, assuming that a riskless hedge between the option and the underlying commodity may be formed, the partial differential equation governing the movements of the commodity option price (V) through time is

$$\frac{1}{2} \sigma^2 S^2 V_{SS} + bSV_S - rV + V_t = 0. \tag{4}$$

This equation, which first appeared in Merton [15], is the heart of the commodity option-pricing discussion contained herein. Note that, when the cost-of-carry rate b is equal to the riskless rate of interest, the differential equation (4) reduces to that of Black and Scholes [3], and, when the cost of carrying the underlying commodity is 0, the Black [2] commodity futures option differential equation is obtained. Both the non-dividend-paying stock and the futures option-pricing problems are special cases of this more general commodity option-pricing problem.

European Commodity Options

The differential equation (4) applies to calls and puts and to European options and American options. To derive the European call formula, the terminal boundary condition, $\max(0, S_T - X)$, is applied. Merton shows indirectly that, when this terminal boundary condition is applied to equation (4), the value of a European call option on a commodity is

$$c(S, T) = Se^{(b-r)T}N(d_1) - Xe^{-rT}N(d_2), \tag{5}$$

where $d_1 = [\ln(S/X) + (b + 0.5\sigma^2)T]/\sigma\sqrt{T}$, $d_2 = d_1 - \sigma\sqrt{T}$, and $N(\cdot)$ is the cumulative univariate normal distribution.[4] When the lower boundary condition for the European put, $\max(0, X - S_T)$, is applied to the partial differential equation (4), the pricing equation is

$$p(S, T) = Xe^{-rT}N(-d_2) - Se^{(b-r)T}N(-d_1),$$ (6)

where all notation is as defined above.

American Commodity Options

The European call formula (5) provides a convenient way of demonstrating that, under certain conditions, the American call option may be exercised early. Suppose $b < r$, as is the case with most of the non-common-stock commodity options traded. As the commodity price, S, becomes extremely large relative to the exercise price of the option, the values of $N(d_1)$ and $N(d_2)$ approach one and the European call value approaches $Se^{(b-r)T} - Xe^{-rT}$. However, the American option may be exercised immediately for $S - X$, which may be higher than the European option value when $b < r$. Thus, the American call option may command a higher price than the European call option because of the early exercise privilege. If $b \geq r$, as in the case of an option on a non-dividend-paying stock (i.e., $b = r$), the lower price bound of the European option will have a greater value than the exercisable proceeds of the American option for all levels of commodity price, so there is no possibility of early exercise and the European call option model (5) will accurately price American call options. For the American puts, there is always some possibility of early exercise, so the European formula (6) never applies. A more detailed explanation of the conditions for early exercise of the call and put options written on commodities is provided in Stoll and Whaley [19].

The valuation of American commodity options therefore involves addressing the early exercise feature of the options. When the American option boundary conditions are applied to (4), analytic solutions are not known and approximations must be used. The most common approach uses finite-difference methods. The first applications along these lines were by Schwartz [18], who valued warrants written on dividend-paying stocks, and by Brennan and Schwartz [5], who priced American put options on non-dividend-paying stocks.[5] Recently, Ramaswamy and Sundaresan [16] and Brenner, Courtadon, and Subrahmanyam [6] used finite-difference methods to price American options written on futures contracts.

The most serious limitation of using finite-difference methods to price American options is that they are computationally expensive. To ensure a high degree of accuracy, it is necessary to partition the commodity price and time dimensions into a very fine grid and enumerate every possible path the commodity option price could travel during its remaining time to expiration. This task is cumbersome and can only be efficiently accomplished with the use of a mainframe computer.

An alternative approximation method was recently introduced by Geske and Johnson [10]. Their compound-option approximation method is computationally less expensive than numerical methods and offers the advantages of being intuitively appealing and easily amenable to comparative-statics analysis.

However, while being about twenty times more computationally efficient than numerical methods, the compound-option approach is still not inexpensive since it requires the evaluation of cumulative bivariate, trivariate, and sometimes higher order multivariate normal density functions. Needless to say, such integral evaluations require the assistance of fairly sophisticated programs and are not practical on anything below the level of a fast microcomputer.

Johnson [12] and others provide heuristic techniques for valuing American put options on non-dividend-paying stocks. Although these techniques are very fast computationally, they are specific to the stock option-pricing problem and are not directly comparable to the general commodity option-pricing approximations discussed herein. In addition, the accuracy of heuristic techniques is frequently sensitive to the parameter range used in the option-pricing problem, a point that we will return to in the simulation results of the next section.

The American commodity option-pricing approximation method derived here is accurate, is amenable to comparative-statics analysis, and can be programmed on a hand-held calculator. The method is based on MacMillan's [13] quadratic approximation of the American put option on a non-dividend-paying stock valuation problem. To explain the derivation of our approximation, the problem of pricing an American call option on a commodity is addressed.

Quadratic Approximation of the American Call Value

The key insight into the quadratic approximation approach is that, if the partial differential equation (4) applies to American options as well as European options, it also applies to the early exercise premium of the American option. For an American call option written on a commodity, the early exercise premium $\varepsilon_C(S, T)$ is defined as

$$\varepsilon_C(S, T) = C(S, T) - c(S, T),\tag{7}$$

where $C(S, T)$ is the American commodity option value and $c(S, T)$ is the European commodity option value as described by equation (5). The partial differential equation for the early exercise premium is therefore

$$\frac{1}{2}\sigma^2 S^2 \varepsilon_{SS} - r\varepsilon + bS\varepsilon_S + \varepsilon_t = 0.\tag{8}$$

For ease of exposition, two simplifications are made. First, in place of time t evolving from the present toward the option's expiration t^*, time T evolving from the option's expiration to the present, that is, $T = t^* - t$, is used. Thus, $\varepsilon_T = -\varepsilon_t$. Second, equation (8) is multiplied by $2/\sigma^2$, and, third, the notational substitutions $M = 2r/\sigma^2$ and $N = 2b/\sigma^2$ are made. Equation (8) now reads as

$$S^2 \varepsilon_{SS} - M\varepsilon + NS\varepsilon_S - (M/r)\varepsilon_T = 0.\tag{9}$$

The early exercise premium is then defined as $\varepsilon_C(S, K) = K(T)f(S, K)$. It therefore follows that $\varepsilon_{SS} = Kf_{SS}$ and $\varepsilon_T = K_T f + KK_T f_K$. Substituting the partial derivative expressions into (9), factoring K, and gathering terms on Mf yield

$$S^2 f_{SS} + NS f_S - Mf \left[1 + (K_T/rK)(1 + K f_K/f)\right] = 0. \tag{10}$$

Choosing $K(T) = 1 - e^{-rT}$, substituting into (10), and simplifying give

$$S^2 f_{SS} + NS f_S - (M/K)f - (1 - K)M f_K = 0. \tag{11}$$

Up to this point, the analysis has been exact, and no approximation has been made. The approximation will be made in equation (11); the last term on the left-hand side will be assumed to be equal to 0. For commodity options with very short (long) times to expiration, this assumption is reasonable since, as T approaches 0 (∞), f_K approaches 0 (K approaches 1), and the term, $(1 - K)M f_K$, disappears. As an approximation, therefore, the last term is dropped, and the approximation of the early exercise premium differential equation is

$$S^2 f_{SS} + NS f_S - (M/K)f = 0. \tag{12}$$

Equation (12) is a second-order ordinary differential equation with two linearly independent solutions of the form aS^q. They can be found by substituting $f = aS^q$ into (12):

$$aS^q[q^2 + (N - 1)q - M/K] = 0. \tag{13}$$

The roots of (13) are $q_1 = [-(N - 1) - \sqrt{(N - 1)^2 + 4M/K}]/2$ and $q_2 = [-(N - 1) + \sqrt{(N - 1)^2 + 4M/K}]/2$. Note that, because $M/K > 0$, $q_1 < 0$ and $q_2 > 0$.

The general solution to (12) is

$$f(S) = a_1 S^{q_1} + a_2 S^{q_2}. \tag{14}$$

With q_1 and q_2 known, a_1 and a_2 are left to be determined. With $q_1 < 0$ and $a_1 \neq 0$, the function f approaches ∞ as the commodity price S approaches 0. This is unacceptable since the early exercise premium of the American call becomes worthless when the commodity price drops to zero. The first constraint to be imposed is, therefore, $a_1 = 0$, and the approximate value of the American call option written on a commodity will be written as

$$C(S, T) = c(S, T) + Ka_2 S^{q_2}. \tag{15}$$

To find an appropriate constraint on a_2, consider equation (15). As $S = 0$, $C(S, T) = 0$ since both $c(S, T)$ and $Ka_2 S^{q_2}$ are equal to 0. As S rises, the value of $C(S, T)$ rises for two reasons: $c(S, T)$ rises and $Ka_2 S^{q_2}$ rises, assuming $a_2 > 0$. In order to represent the value of the American call, however, the function on the right-hand side of (15) should touch, but not intersect, the boundary imposed by the early exercise proceeds of the American call, $S - X$. Below the critical commodity price S^* implied by the point of tangency, the American call value is represented by equation (15). Above S^*, the American call value is equal to its exercisable proceeds, $S - X$, and the fact that $a_2 S^{q_2}$ rises at a faster and faster rate above S^* is not of concern.

To find the critical commodity price S^*, the exercisable value of the American call is set equal to the value of $C(S^*, T)$ as represented by (15), that is,

$$S^* - X = c(S^*, T) + Ka_2S^{*q_2}, \tag{16}$$

and the slope of the exercisable value of the call, one, is set equal to the slope of $C(S^*, T)$, that is,

$$1 = e^{(b-r)T}N[d_1(S^*)] + Kq_2a_2S^{*q_2-1}, \tag{17}$$

where $e^{(b-r)T}N[d_1(S^*)]$ is the partial derivative of $c(S^*, T)$ with respect to S^* and where $d_1(S^*) = [\ln(S^*/X) + (b + 0.5\sigma^2)T]/\sigma\sqrt{T}$. Thus, there are two equations, (16) and (17), and two unknowns, a_2 and S^*. Isolating a_2 in (17) yields

$$a_2 = \{1 - e^{(b-r)T}N[d_1(S^*)]\}/Kq_2S^{*q_2-1}. \tag{18}$$

Substituting (18) into (16) and simplifying results in a critical commodity price, S^*, that satisfies

$$S^* - X = c(S^*, T) + \{1 - e^{(b-r)T}N[d_1(S^*)]\}S^*/q_2. \tag{19}$$

Although S^* is the only unknown value in equation (19), it must be determined iteratively. An efficient algorithm for finding S^* is presented in the next section. With S^* known, equation (16) provides the value of a_2. Substituting (18) into (15) and simplifying yields

$$C(S, T) = c(S, T) + A_2(S/S^*)^{q_2}, \quad \text{when } S < S^*, \text{ and}$$
$$\tag{20}$$
$$C(S, T) = S - X, \quad\quad \text{when } S \geq S^*,$$

where $A_2 = (S^*/q_2)\{1 - e^{(b-r)T}N[d_1(S^*)]\}$. Note that $A_2 > 0$ since S^*, q_2, and $1 - e^{(b-r)T}N[d_1(S^*)]$ are positive when $b < r$. Equation (20) is therefore an efficient analytic approximation of the value of an American call option written on a commodity when the cost of carry is less than the riskless rate of interest. When $b \geq r$, the American call will never be exercised early, and valuation equation (5) applies.[6]

In equation (20), it is worthwhile to note that the early exercise premium of the American call option on a commodity approaches 0 as the time to expiration of the option approaches 0. As T gets small, $N[d_1(S^*)]$ approaches 1,[7] $\{1 - e^{(b-r)T}N[d_1(S^*)]\}$ approaches 0, A_2 approaches 0, and, thus, $A_2(S/S^*)^{q_2}$ approaches 0.

Quadratic Approximation of the American Put Value

Before proceeding with a discussion of how to use this quadratic approximation, it is useful to note how the approximation would change for the American put option on a commodity. Since the partial differential equation (8) applies to the early exercise premium of the American put

$$\varepsilon_p(S, T) = P(S, T) - p(S, T), \tag{21}$$

equations (9) through (14) of the analysis remain the same. In (14), it is now the term $a_1S^{q_1}$ that is of interest since the early exercise premium of the American put must approach 0 as S approaches positive infinity. The term, $a_2S^{q_2}$, violates this boundary condition, so a_2 is set equal to zero and the approximate value of the American put option becomes

$$P(S, T) = p(S, T) + Ka_1S^{q_1}. \tag{22}$$

Again, the values of the coefficient a_1 and the critical commodity price S^{**} must be determined, and the necessary steps pattern those used in determining a_2 and S^*. The value of a_1 is

$$a_1 = -\{1 - e^{(b-r)T}N[-d_1(S^{**})]\}/Kq_1S^{**q_1-1}, \tag{23}$$

where $-e^{(b-r)T}N[-d_1(S^{**})]$ is the partial derivative of $p(S^{**}, T)$ with respect to S^{**} and where $a_1 > 0$ since $q_1 < 0$ and since all other terms are positive. The critical commodity price S^{**} is determined by solving

$$X - S^{**} = p(S^{**}, T) - \{1 - e^{(b-r)T}N[-d_1(S^{**})]\}S^{**}/q_1. \tag{24}$$

With S^{**} known, the approximate value of an American put option written on a commodity (22) becomes

$$P(S, T) = p(S, T) + A_1(S/S^{**})^{q_1}, \quad \text{when } S > S^{**}, \text{ and} \tag{25}$$

$$P(S, T) = X - S, \quad \text{when } S \leq S^{**},$$

where $A_1 = -(S^{**}/q_1)\{1 - e^{(b-r)T}N[-d_1(S^{**})]\}$. Note that $A_1 > 0$ since $q_1 < 0$, $S^{**} > 0$, and $N[-d_1(S^{**})] < e^{-bT}$.

American Commodity Futures Options

Up to this point, the focus of the discussion has been on the valuation of commodity options where the cost of carrying the underlying commodity is a constant, proportional rate b. If b is set equal to certain specific values, however, specific commodity option-valuation equations are obtained. For example, the cost of carrying any futures position is equal to 0. Thus, to obtain the commodity futures option-valuation results, simply set b equal to zero in the approximation just described. The approximate value of an American call option on a futures contract is given by equation (20), where the futures price, F, is substituted for the commodity price, S, and where the cost of carry, b, is set equal to zero. The approximate value of an American put option on a futures contract is given by equation (25), where similar substitutions are made. Both of these American futures option-price approximations are used in Whaley [21].

American Stock Options

Another special case of the commodity option-valuation framework is the non-dividend-paying stock option. The cost of carrying the underlying stock is assumed to be equal to the riskless rate of interest; in other words, b is set equal to r in the above approximation. It is worthwhile to point out that, since $b = r$ for this option-pricing problem, the American call will be valued using the European formula (5). The resulting approximation for the American put is that of MacMillan [13].

Summary

The quadratic approximation techniques for pricing the American call and put options on a commodity have now been derived. Before presenting some simulation results intended to show the accuracy of the techniques, it is worthwhile to reiterate that they are useful in a wide range of option-pricing problems. The futures option and the stock option cases are only two examples. American options on foreign currencies, on stock indexes with continuous dividend yields, on precious metals such as gold and silver, and on long-term debt instruments with continuous coupon yields can be accurately priced within this framework.

IMPLEMENTATION AND SIMULATION OF APPROXIMATION METHOD

In the approximation procedure outlined in the last section, only one step, the determination of the critical commodity price S^*, is not straightforward. In this section, an efficient algorithm for determining S^* is presented, and then simulated results from the quadratic approximation method are compared with results for the finite-difference and compound-option approximation methods.

An Algorithm for Determining S*

To find the critical commodity price S^*, it is necessary to solve equation (19). Since this cannot be done directly, an iterative procedure must be developed.[8] To begin, evaluate both sides of equation (19) at some seed value, S_1, that is,

$$\text{LHS}(S_i) = S_i - X, \text{ and} \tag{26a}$$

$$\text{RHS}(S_i) = c(S_i, T) + \{1 - e^{(b-r)T}N[d_1(S_i)]\}S_i/q_2, \tag{26b}$$

where $d_1(S_i) = [\ln(S_i/X) + (b + 0.5\sigma^2)T]/\sigma\sqrt{T}$ and $i = 1$. Naturally, it is unlikely that $\text{LHS}(S_i) = \text{RHS}(S_i)$ on the initial guess of S_1, and a second guess must be made. To develop the next guess S_{i+1}, first find the slope b_i of the RHS at S_i, that is,

$$b_i = e^{(b-r)T}N[d_1(S_i)](1 - 1/q_2) + [1 - e^{(b-r)T}n[d_1(S_i)]/\sigma\sqrt{T}]/q_2, \tag{27}$$

where $n(\cdot)$ is the univariate normal density function. Next, find where the line tangent to the curve RHS at S_i intersects the exercisable proceeds of the American call, $S - X$, that is,

$$\text{RHS}(S_i) + b_i(S - S_i) = S - X,$$

and then isolate S to find S_{i+1},

$$S_{i+1} = [X + \text{RHS}(S_i) - b_i S_i]/(1 - b_i). \tag{28}$$

Equation (28) will provide the second and subsequent guesses of S, with new values of (26a), (26b), (27), and (28) computed with each new iteration. The iterative procedure should continue until the relative absolute error falls within an acceptable tolerance level; for example,

$$|\text{LHS}(S_i) - \text{RHS}(S_i)|/X < 0.00001. \tag{29}$$

Seed Value

The iterative technique outlined here converges reasonably quickly by setting the seed value S_1 equal to the option's exercise price X and by imposing the tolerance criterion (29). The speed with which the algorithm finds the critical commodity price, however, can be improved by using a starting point closer to the solution.

To arrive at an approximate value of the critical commodity price, consider the information contained in equation (19). If the time to expiration of the call option is equal to 0, the critical commodity price above which the option will be exercised is the exercise price of the option, X. At the other extreme, if the time remaining to expiration is infinite, the critical commodity price may be solved exactly by substituting $T = +\infty$ in (19), that is,

$$S^*(\infty) = X/[1 - 1/q_2(\infty)], \tag{30}$$

where $q_2(\infty) = [-(N - 1) + \sqrt{(N - 1)^2 + 4M}]/2$. Equation (19) also shows that the critical commodity price is an increasing function of time to expiration of the option.

With this and other information from the call option-pricing problem in hand, it is possible to derive an approximate analytic solution to finding the critical commodity price. Such a derivation is provided in the Appendix. The final form of the approximation is

$$S^* = X + [S^*(\infty) - X][1 - e^{b_2}], \tag{31}$$

where $b_2 = -(bT + 2\sigma\sqrt{T})\{X/[S^*(\infty) - X]\}$. Note that (31) satisfies the critical commodity-price restrictions when $T = 0$ and $T = +\infty$.

For the put option-pricing problem, the critical commodity price must satisfy equation (24). At $T = 0$, the critical price is again the exercise price of the option, and, at $T = +\infty$,

$$S^{**}(\infty) = X/[1 - 1/q_1(\infty)], \tag{32}$$

where $q_1(\infty) = [-(N - 1) - \sqrt{(N - 1)^2 + 4M}]/2$. It is worthwhile to point out that, when the cost of carry b is equal to the riskless rate of interest r, this result is exactly the same as Merton's [15]. In equation (24), the critical commodity price is a decreasing function of time to expiration, and an approximate analytic expression for the critical commodity price is

$$S^{**} = S^{**}(\infty) + [X - S^{**}(\infty)]e^{b_1}, \tag{33}$$

where $b_1 = (bT - 2\sigma\sqrt{T})\{X/[X - S^{**}(\infty)]\}$.[9]

Equations (31) and (33) provide the seed values for the iterative procedures that determine the critical commodity price in the American call and the American put option algorithms. Both are straightforward computations, and their use usually ensures convergence in three iterations or less.

Simulation Results

Tables 6-1 through 6-4 contain a sensitivity analysis of the theoretical European and American commodity option values for a variety of cost-of-carry parameters. In Tables 6-1 and 6-2, for example, the cost-of-carry parameter (b) is set equal to -0.04 and 0.04, respectively. Thus, the values in these tables may be thought of as being American foreign currency option prices, where the foreign riskless rate of interest is greater than and less than the domestic interest rate, respectively. In Table 6-3, the cost-of-carry parameter is set equal to 0, so the resulting option values are for American commodity futures options. Finally, in Table 6-4, the cost of carry is set equal to the riskless rate of interest. Since this is the non-dividend-paying stock option case, only American put option values are reported.[10]

In the first three tables, three methods for pricing the American commodity options are used: (a) the implicit finite-difference approximation method with commodity price steps of 0.10 and time steps of 0.20 days or 0.0005479 years, (b) the compound-option approximation method using a three-point extrapolation, and (c) the quadratic approximation method. The European model values are included to provide an indication of the magnitude of the early exercise premium on American options. In the fourth table, the values of Johnson's [12] heuristic technique are also provided.

Commodity Option Results

Judging by the results reported in Tables 6-1 and 6-2, the quadratic approximation is very accurate. The option prices for this method are within pennies of the implicit finite-difference method.[11] The most extreme errors occur for the in-the-money options where the volatility parameter is set equal to 0.40 and where the cost of carry is -0.04 for the calls and 0.04 for the puts (see Tables 6-1 and 6-2), but even there the degree of mispricing, when compared with the finite-difference method, is less than three tenths of one percent. Considering that the quadratic approximation costs roughly 2000 times less, this result is impressive.

The compound-option valuation method appears to do about as well as the quadratic approximation at pricing American options. For options at or out of the money, both techniques provide accurate option values. In-the-money options have minor mispricing errors, but on a proportionate basis the errors are trivial. The overwhelming advantage of using the quadratic approximation, how-

TABLE 6-1　Theoretical American Commodity Option Values Using Finite-Difference, Compound-Option, and Quadratic Approximation Methods (Cost of Carry (b) = −0.04 and Exercise Price (X) = 100)

Option Parameters[a]	Commodity Price S	Call Options				Put Options			
		European c(S, T)[b]	American C(S, T)			European p(S, T)[b]	American P(S, T)		
			Finite-Difference Method[c]	Compound-Option Method[d]	Quadratic Approximation Method[e]		Finite-Difference Method[c]	Compound-Option Method[d]	Quadratic Approximation Method[e]
r = 0.08, σ = 0.20, T = 0.25	80	0.03	0.03	0.03	0.03	20.41	20.41	20.41	20.42
	90	0.57	0.58	0.58	0.59	11.25	11.25	11.25	11.25
	100	3.42	3.52	3.52	3.52	4.40	4.40	4.40	4.40
	110	9.85	10.35	10.38	10.31	1.12	1.12	1.12	1.12
	120	18.62	20.00	19.97	20.00	0.18	0.19	0.18	0.18
r = 0.12, σ = 0.20, T = 0.25	80	0.03	0.03	0.03	0.03	20.21	20.23	20.23	20.25
	90	0.56	0.58	0.57	0.59	11.14	11.14	11.14	11.15
	100	3.39	3.50	3.49	3.51	4.35	4.35	4.35	4.35
	110	9.75	10.32	10.36	10.29	1.11	1.11	1.11	1.11
	120	18.43	20.00	19.97	20.00	0.18	0.18	0.18	0.18
r = 0.08, σ = 0.40, T = 0.25	80	1.05	1.06	1.05	1.07	21.43	21.44	2.144	21.46
	90	3.23	3.27	3.27	3.28	13.91	13.91	13.92	13.93
	100	7.29	7.40	7.41	7.41	8.27	8.26	8.27	8.27
	110	13.25	13.52	13.51	13.50	4.52	4.52	4.52	4.52
	120	20.73	21.29	21.30	21.23	2.29	2.29	2.29	2.30
r = 0.08, σ = 0.20, T = 0.50	80	0.21	0.21	0.21	0.23	20.95	20.96	20.96	20.98
	90	1.31	1.36	1.36	1.39	12.63	12.63	12.63	12.64
	100	4.46	4.71	4.69	4.72	6.37	6.37	6.37	6.37
	110	10.16	11.00	11.03	10.96	2.65	2.65	2.65	2.65
	120	17.85	20.00	19.98	20.00	0.92	0.92	0.92	0.92

[a]The notation in this column is as follows: r = riskless rate of interest; σ = standard deviation of the commodity price-change relative; and T = time to expiration.

[b]Values are computed using equations (5) and (6).

[c]Values are computed using the implicit finite-difference method with commodity price steps of 0.10 and time steps of 0.20 days or 0.0005479 years.

[d]Values are computed using the three-point extrapolation of the compound-option valuation approach.

[e]Values are computed using the quadratic approximation equations (20) and (25).

TABLE 6-2 Theoretical American Commodity Option Values Using Finite-Difference, Compound-Option, and Quadratic Approximation Methods (Cost of Carry (b) = 0.04 and Exercise Price (X) = 100)

		Call Options				Put Options			
			American C(S, T)				American P(S, T)		
Option Parameters[a]	Commodity Price S	European c(S, T)[b]	Finite-Difference Method[c]	Compound-Option Method[d]	Quadratic Approximation Method[e]	European p(S, T)[b]	Finite-Difference Method[c]	Compound-Option Method[d]	Quadratic Approximation Method[e]
r = 0.08, σ = 0.20, T = 0.25	80	0.05	0.05	0.05	0.05	18.87	20.00	19.99	20.00
	90	0.85	0.85	0.85	0.85	9.76	10.22	10.25	10.18
	100	4.44	4.44	4.44	4.44	3.46	3.55	3.54	3.54
	110	11.66	11.66	11.66	11.66	0.78	0.79	0.79	0.80
	120	20.90	20.90	20.90	20.90	0.11	0.11	0.11	0.12
r = 0.12, σ = 0.20, T = 0.25	80	0.05	0.05	0.05	0.05	18.68	20.00	19.99	20.00
	90	0.84	0.84	0.84	0.84	9.67	10.20	10.23	10.16
	100	4.40	4.40	4.40	4.40	3.42	3.52	3.52	3.53
	110	11.55	11.55	11.55	11.55	0.77	0.78	0.78	0.79
	120	20.69	20.69	20.69	20.69	0.11	0.11	0.11	0.12
r = 0.08, σ = 0.40, T = 0.25	80	1.29	1.29	1.29	1.29	20.11	20.59	20.60	20.53
	90	3.82	3.82	3.82	3.82	12.74	12.95	12.94	12.93
	100	8.35	8.35	8.35	8.35	7.36	7.46	7.46	7.46
	110	14.80	14.79	14.80	14.80	3.91	3.95	3.95	3.96
	120	22.71	22.71	22.71	22.72	1.93	1.94	1.94	1.95
r = 0.08, σ = 0.20, T = 0.50	80	0.41	0.41	0.41	0.41	18.08	20.00	19.96	20.00
	90	2.18	2.18	2.18	2.18	10.04	10.75	10.79	10.71
	90	2.18	2.18	2.18	2.18	10.04	10.75	10.79	10.71
	100	6.50	6.50	6.50	6.50	4.55	4.77	4.75	4.77
	110	13.42	13.42	13.42	13.42	1.68	1.74	1.74	1.76
	120	22.06	22.06	22.06	22.06	0.51	0.53	0.53	0.55

[a] The notation in this column is as follows: r = riskless rate of interest; σ = standard deviation of the commodity price-change relative; and T = time to expiration.

[b] Values are computed using equations (5) and (6).

[c] Values are computed using the implicit finite-difference method with commodity price steps of 0.10 and time steps of 0.20 days or 0.0005479 years.

[d] Values are computed using the three-point extrapolation of the compound-option valuation approach.

[e] Values are computed using the quadratic approximation equations (20) and (25).

TABLE 6-3 Theoretical American Futures Option Values Using Finite-Difference, Compound-Option, and Quadratic Approximation Methods (Cost of Carry (b) = 0.00 and Exercise Price (X) = 100)

| | | Call Options | | | | Put Options | | | |
| | | | American C(F, T) | | | | American P(F, T) | | |
Option Parameters[a]	Futures Price F	European c(F, T)[b]	Finite-Difference Method[c]	Compound-Option Method[d]	Quadratic Approximation Method[e]	European p(F, T)[b]	Finite-Difference Method[c]	Compound-Option Method[d]	Quadratic Approximation Method[e]
r = 0.08, σ = 0.20, T = 0.25	80	0.04	0.04	0.04	0.04	19.64	20.00	20.00	20.00
	90	0.70	0.70	0.70	0.70	10.50	10.59	10.58	10.58
	100	3.91	3.92	3.93	3.93	3.91	3.92	3.93	3.93
	110	10.74	10.82	10.81	10.81	0.94	0.94	0.94	0.94
	120	19.75	20.03	20.04	20.02	0.14	0.14	0.14	0.15
r = 0.12, σ = 0.20, T = 0.25	80	0.04	0.04	0.04	0.04	19.45	20.00	19.99	20.00
	90	0.69	0.69	0.69	0.70	10.40	10.53	10.53	10.53
	100	3.87	3.89	3.90	3.90	3.87	3.89	3.90	3.90
	110	10.63	10.76	10.76	10.75	0.94	0.93	0.93	0.93
	120	19.55	20.01	20.02	20.00	0.14	0.14	0.14	0.15
r = 0.08, σ = 0.40, T = 0.25	80	1.16	1.16	1.16	1.17	20.77	20.94	20.94	20.93
	90	3.52	3.53	3.53	3.53	13.32	13.39	13.39	13.39
	100	7.81	7.83	7.84	7.84	7.81	7.83	7.84	7.84
	110	14.01	14.08	14.08	14.08	4.21	4.22	4.22	4.23
	120	21.71	21.87	21.86	21.86	2.10	2.11	2.11	2.12
r = 0.08, σ = 0.20, T = 0.50	80	0.30	0.30	0.30	0.30	19.51	20.06	20.09	20.04
	90	1.70	1.71	1.71	1.72	11.31	11.48	11.47	11.48
	100	5.42	5.46	5.47	5.48	5.42	5.46	5.57	5.48
	110	11.73	11.90	11.89	11.90	2.12	2.14	2.14	2.15
	120	19.91	20.36	20.37	20.34	0.69	0.69	0.69	0.70

[a]The notation in this column is as follows: r = riskless rate of interest; σ = standard deviation of the commodity futures price-change relative; and T = time to expiration.

[b]Values are computed using equations (5) and (6).

[c]Values are computed using the implicit finite-difference method with commodity futures price steps of 0.20 days or 0.0005479 years.

[d]Values are computed using the three-point extrapolation of the compound-option valuation approach.

[e]Values are computed using the quadratic approximation equations (20) and (25).

TABLE 6-4   Theoretical American Put Option on Stock Values Using Finite-Difference, Compound-Option, Quadratic, and Johnson Approximation Methods (Exercise Price (X) = 100)

Option Parameters[a]	Stock Price S	European c(S, T)[b]	Put Options			
			American P(S, T)			
			Finite-Difference Method[c]	Compound-Option Method[d]	Quadratic Approximation Method[e]	Johnson Method[f]
b = r = 0.08, σ = 0.20, T = 0.25	80	18.09	20.00	20.00	20.00	20.00
	90	9.05	10.04	10.07	10.01	10.56
	100	3.04	3.22	3.21	3.22	3.21
	110	0.64	0.66	0.66	0.68	0.65
	120	0.09	0.09	0.09	0.10	0.09
b = r = 0.12, σ = 0.20, T = 0.25	80	17.13	20.00	20.01	20.00	20.00
	90	8.26	10.00	0.96	10.00	10.00
	100	2.63	2.92	2.91	2.93	2.90
	110	0.52	0.55	0.55	0.58	0.53
	120	0.07	0.07	0.07	0.08	0.07
b = r = 0.08, σ = 0.40, T = 0.25	80	19.45	20.32	20.37	20.25	20.08
	90	12.17	12.56	12.55	12.51	12.52
	100	6.94	7.11	7.10	7.10	7.12
	110	3.63	3.70	3.70	3.71	3.72
	120	1.76	1.79	1.79	1.81	1.80
b = r = 0.08, σ = 0.20, T = 0.50	80	16.65	20.00	19.94	20.00	20.00
	90	8.83	10.29	10.37	10.23	10.73
	100	3.79	4.19	4.17	4.19	4.17
	110	1.31	1.41	1.41	1.45	1.38
	120	0.38	0.40	0.40	0.42	0.39

[a]The notation in this column is as follows: b = cost of carrying underlying stock; r = riskless rate of interest; σ = standard deviation of the stock price-change relative; and T = time to expiration.

[b]Values are computed using equations (5) and (6).

[c]Values are computed using the implicit finite-difference method with stock price steps of 0.10 and time steps of 0.20 days or 0.0005479 years.

[d]Values are computed using the three-point extrapolation of the compound-option valuation approach.

[e]Values are computed using the quadratic approximation equations (20) and (25).

[f]Values are computed using the Johnson [12] method.

ever, lies in the fact that its computational cost is approximately 100 times less than the compound-option approximation.

Commodity Futures Option Values

In Table 6-3 the simulation results for futures options are reported. With the cost-of-carry parameter set equal to 0, the quadratic approximation shows even more precision across the parameter ranges considered. The largest errors are on the order of one tenth of one percent.

Stock Option Values

Table 6-4 contains the simulation results for the special case where the cost of carry is equal to the riskless rate of interest, that is, for American options written on non-dividend-paying stocks. Since the call will not rationally be exercised early, only put option values appear in the table. The quadratic approximation method used here is that of MacMillan [13].

With respect to the quadratic approximation and the compound-option approach, the results are qualitatively similar to the previous tables. Slightly larger mispricing errors occur for in-the-money options, but, even in the case where the volatility parameter is set equal to 0.40, the degree of mispricing is less than four tenths of one percent.

Unlike the previous tables, Table 6-4 contains an additional column of values under the heading "Johnson Method." Johnson [12] provides a heuristic technique for valuing American put options on non-dividend-paying stocks.[12] His technique is slightly faster than the quadratic approximation; however, its validity appears to break down for put options that are slightly in the money. Consider the put option values for the first set of parameters. When the stock price is 80, all techniques yield an option value equal to 20.00. This is because the current stock price is below the critical stock price, so that the value of the American put is simply equal to its exercisable proceeds. However, if the stock price is 90, as seen in the second row of the table, the current stock price is in excess of the critical stock price and the approximation methods are invoked. While the quadratic approximation produces an absolute mispricing error of 0.03 (or 0.3 percent) relative to the finite-difference value, the Johnson technique produces a 0.52 (or 5.18 percent) error.

For the second and third set of option-pricing parameters, the Johnson technique produces reasonable values, but, for the fourth set of parameters, the first in-the-money put option again has a large mispricing error. This is indicative of the problems one faces when using heuristic procedures. While the option prices may be well behaved in general, they may lead to serious mispricing errors for arbitrary combinations of parameters.

Long-Term Option Values

The parameters of the options in Tables 6-1 through 6-4 were chosen so as to represent typical exchange-traded options with times to expiration of less than six months. The most actively traded options, in fact, have maturities of less than three months. In the interest of completeness, however, it is worthwhile to point out that over-the-counter markets for long-term options are slowly developing, particularly in the area of U.S. Treasury obligations, and the impact of the time-to-expiration parameter on the accuracy of the approximation methods is of particular importance. For this reason, simulations are performed using times to expiration of up to three years. Table 6-5 contains the three-year time-to-expiration results.

The results in Table 6-5 show that all the approximation method results are weakened considerably. In some cases, the three-point extrapolation compound-option method does better than the quadratic approximation, and in other cases vice versa. The Johnson technique produces the largest mispricing errors for the American put option on a non-dividend-paying stock.

Based on the results of Table 6-5 and the other simulation results (not reported here) using time-to-expiration parameters of between 0.5 and 3 years, it is reasonable to use either the three-point compound-option extrapolation method or the quadratic approximation method for pricing commodity options with less than one year to expiration, with the obvious preference being for the quadratic approximation method because of its computational expediency. For times to expiration beyond one year, finite-difference or binomial option-pricing methods should be used to ensure pricing accuracy.

SUMMARY

More than thirty commodity option and commodity futures option contracts now trade in a variety of markets in the U.S. and Canada. These options are, in general, American style and, as such, are exercisable at any time up to and including the expiration day of the option. Previous attempts at pricing these options have been accurate but computationally expensive. This paper provides simple, inexpensive approximations for valuing exchange-traded American call and put options written on commodities as well as commodity futures contracts.

APPENDIX

Derivation of Analytic Approximation of Critical Commodity Price S*:

Equation (19) shows that the critical commodity price is an increasing function of time to expiration of the option bounded by the exercise price when $T = 0$ and by

$$S^*(\infty) = X/[1 - 1/q_2(\infty)], \tag{A1}$$

where $q_2(\infty) = [-(N - 1) + \sqrt{(N - 1)^2 + 4M}]/2$ when $T = +\infty$. To derive an approximate analytic equation for the critical commodity price as a function of time, consider the call option holder's dilemma when the time to expiration

TABLE 6-5   Theoretical American Commodity Option Values Using Finite-Difference, Compound-Option, Quadratic, and Johnson Approximation Methods (Exercise Price (X) = 100)

Option Parameters[a]	Commodity Price S	Call Options				Put Options				
		European c(S, T)[b]	American C(S, T)			European p(S, T)[b]	American P(S, T)			
			Finite-Difference Method[c]	Compound-Option Method[d]	Quadratic Approximation Method[e]		Finite-Difference Method[c]	Compound-Option Method[d]	Quadratic Approximation Method[e]	Johnson Method[f]
b = −0.04, r = 0.08, σ = 0.20, T = 3.00	80	1.93	2.34	2.31	2.52	24.78	25.66	25.59	26.25	
	90	3.75	4.76	4.71	4.97	19.62	20.08	20.05	20.64	
	100	6.36	8.49	8.54	8.67	15.25	15.50	15.51	15.99	
	110	9.75	13.79	14.08	13.88	11.67	11.80	11.83	12.22	
	120	13.87	20.89	21.29	20.88	8.81	8.88	8.91	9.23	
b = 0.00, r = 0.08, σ = 0.20, T = 3.00	80	3.79	3.98	3.99	4.20	19.52	22.20	22.35	22.40	
	90	6.81	7.25	7.23	7.54	14.68	16.21	16.18	16.50	
	100	10.82	11.70	11.65	12.03	10.82	11.70	11.65	12.03	
	110	15.71	17.31	17.28	17.64	7.85	8.37	8.34	8.69	
	120	21.35	24.02	24.11	24.30	5.62	5.93	5.93	6.22	
b = 0.04, r = 0.08, σ = 0.20, T = 3.00	80	6.88	6.88	6.88	6.97	14.59	20.35	20.60	20.33	
	90	11.49	11.48	11.49	11.62	10.33	13.50	13.69	13.56	
	100	17.20	17.19	17.22	17.40	7.17	8.94	8.95	9.11	
	110	23.80	23.80	23.85	24.09	4.90	5.91	5.85	6.12	
	120	31.08	31.08	31.18	31.49	3.32	3.90	3.85	4.12	
b = 0.08, r = 0.08, σ = 0.20, T = 3.00	80					10.25	20.00	19.44	20.00	20.00
	90					6.78	11.69	11.96	11.63	12.89
	100					4.41	6.93	7.06	6.96	6.69
	110					2.83	4.15	4.13	4.26	3.71
	120					1.80	2.51	2.45	2.64	2.16

[a]The notation in this column is as follows: b = cost of carrying underlying stock; r = riskless rate of interest; σ = standard deviation of the commodity price-change relative; and T = time to expiration.

[b]Values are computed using equations (5) and (6).

[c]Values are computed using the implicit finite-difference method with commodity price steps 0.10 and time steps of 0.20 days or 0.0005479 years.

[d]Values are computed using the three-point extrapolation of the compound-option valuation approach.

[e]Values are computed using the quadratic approximation equations (20) and (25).

[f]Values are computed using the Johnson [12] method.

of the option is some arbitrarily small time increment, Δ. If the call is exercised at time Δ, the exercisable proceeds are $S(\Delta) - X$, which will earn interest to become $[S(\Delta) - X](1 + r\Delta)$ at $T = 0$. On the other hand, if the option holder chooses to leave the call position open, the worth of the call is equal to the expected terminal value of the option, $E[S(0) - X|S(0) > X]$. Thus, the critical commodity price above which the call option holder will choose to exercise early is determined by

$$[S^*(\Delta) - X](1 + r\Delta) = E[S^*(0) - X|S^*(0) > X]. \tag{A2}$$

To evaluate the right-hand side of (A2), represent the commodity price at the expiration of the option using the Cox-Ross-Rubinstein [7] risk-neutral binomial approach, that is,

$$S^*(0) = S^*(\Delta)(1 + b\Delta \pm \sigma\sqrt{\Delta}). \tag{A3}$$

Equation (A3) says that, in a risk-neutral world, the expected rate of return on commodity S is equal to its cost of carry, $b\Delta$, plus or minus the stochastic component, $\sigma\sqrt{\Delta}$, with equal probabilities. Thus, the expected value of holding the call to expiration is

$$E[S^*(0) - X|S^*(0) > X] = 0.5[S^*(1 + b\Delta + \sigma\sqrt{\Delta}) - X], \tag{A4}$$

and, if (A4) is substituted into (A2), the critical commodity price is determined by

$$(S^*(\Delta) - X)(1 + r\Delta) = 0.5[S^*(1 + b\Delta + \sigma\sqrt{\Delta}) - X]. \tag{A5}$$

Rearranging equation (A5) to isolate $S^*(\Delta)$ provides

$$S^*(\Delta) = [X(1 + 2\Delta r)]/[1 + (2r - b)\Delta - \sigma\sqrt{\Delta}], \tag{A6}$$

which, in turn, provides the approximations

$$\begin{aligned} S^*(\Delta) &\approx X(1 + 2\Delta r)[1 - (2r - b)\Delta + \sigma\sqrt{\Delta}] \\ &\approx X(1 + b\Delta + \sigma\sqrt{\Delta}). \end{aligned} \tag{A7}$$

Equation (A7) ignores terms of order higher than Δ. Moreover, Δ is assumed to be small enough to make opportunities of exercising the call at intermediate times before expiration negligible. Therefore, equation (A7) holds exactly only in the case where Δ approaches 0.

To approximate S^* for arbitrary times to expiration, expand $S^*(0)$ around $S^*(\Delta)$, that is,

$$S^*(0) = S^*(\Delta) + (\delta S^*/\delta T)_{T=\Delta}\Delta. \tag{A8}$$

(The reason for choosing $T = \Delta$ in lieu of $T = 0$ as the origin of the expression (A8) is that at $T = 0$ the slope is discontinuous.) Substituting (A7) for $S^*(\Delta)$ and recalling that $S^*(0) = X$, it follows that the critical commodity price satisfies the differential equation

$$\delta S^*/\delta T = S^*(0)(b + \sigma/\sqrt{\Delta}) \tag{A9}$$

in a neighborhood of $T = 0$, with boundary condition $S^*(0) = X$. The general solution of (A9) is of the exponential form, with exponent $(bT + 2\sigma\sqrt{T})$.

Now, drawing the results together, the critical commodity price function is bounded at $T = 0$ and at $T = +\infty$ and has a slope described by the differential equation (A9). An appropriate final form for the critical commodity price of an American call option is therefore

$$S^* = X + [S^*(\infty) - X][1 - e^{b_2}], \tag{A10}$$

where $b_2 = -(bT + 2\sigma\sqrt{T})\{X/[S^*(\infty) - X]\}$. A parallel analysis can be made in deriving an approximate analytical critical commodity price equation for the American put option.

REFERENCES

M. R. Asay. "A Note on the Design of Commodity Contracts." *Journal of Futures Markets* 2 (Spring 1982), 1-7.

F. Black. "The Pricing of Commodity Contracts." *Journal of Financial Economics* 3 (January-March 1976), 167-79.

———— and M. S. Scholes. "The Pricing of Options and Corporate Liabilities." *Journal of Political Economy* 81 (May-June 1973), 637-54.

E. C. Blomeyer. "An Analytic Approximation for the American Put Price for Options on Stocks with Dividends." *Journal of Financial and Quantitative Analysis* 21 (June 1986), 229-33.

M. J. Brennan and E. S. Schwartz. "The Valuation of American Put Options." *Journal of Finance* 32 (May 1977), 449-62.

M. Brenner, G. R. Courtadon, and M. Subrahmanyam. "Option on the Spot and Options on Futures." *Journal of Finance* 40 (December 1985), 1303-17.

J. C. Cox, S. A. Ross, and M. Rubinstein. "Option Pricing: A Simplified Approach." *Journal of Financial Economics* 3 (September 1979), 229-63.

J. C. Cox and M. Rubinstein. *Options Markets.* Englewood Cliffs, NJ: Prentice-Hall, 1985.

M. Garman and S. Kohlhagen. "Foreign Currency Option Values." *Journal of International Money and Finance* 2 (December 1983), 231-37.

R. Geske and H. E. Johnson. "The American Put Valued Analytically." *Journal of Finance* 39 (December 1984), 1511-24.

R. Geske and K. Shastri. "Valuation by Approximation: A Comparison of Alternative Valuation Techniques." *Journal of Financial and Quantitative Analysis* 20 (March 1985), 45-71.

H. E. Johnson. "An Analytic Approximation for the American Put Price." *Journal of Financial and Quantitative Analysis* 18 (March 1983), 141-48.

L. W. MacMillan. "Analytic Approximation for the American Put Option." *Advances in Futures and Options Research* 1 (1986), 119-39.

P. Mehl. *Trading in Privileges on the Chicago Board of Trade.* U.S. Department of Agriculture, Circular No. 323, December 1934.

R. C. Merton. "The Theory of Rational Option Pricing." *Bell Journal of Economics and Management Science* 4 (Spring 1973), 141-83.

K. Ramaswamy and S. M. Sundaresan. "The Valuation of Options on Futures Contracts." *Journal of Finance* 40 (December 1985), 1319-40.

R. Roll. "An Analytical Valuation Formula for Unprotected American Call Options on Stocks with Known Dividends." *Journal of Financial Economics* 5 (November 1977), 251–58.

E. S. Schwartz. "The Valuation of Warrants: Implementing a New Approach." *Journal of Financial Economics* 4 (January 1977), 79–93.

H. R. Stoll and R. E. Whaley. "The New Option Instruments: Arbitrageable Linkages and Valuation." *Advances in Futures and Options Research* 1 (1986), 25–62.

R. E. Whaley. "On the Valuation of American Call Options on Stocks with Known Dividends." *Journal of Financial Economics* 9 (June 1981), 207–11.

———. "Valuation of American Futures Options: Theory and Empirical Tests." *Journal of Finance* 41 (March 1986), 127–50.

ENDNOTES

1. Options on physical commodities (i.e., commodity options) were traded in the U.S. as early as the late 1800's. (See Mehl [14].) These options convey the right to buy or sell a certain physical commodity at a specified price within a specified period of time. The Commodity Exchange Act of 1936, however, banned trading in such options. Recently the CFTC introduced a pilot program allowing the various exchanges to reintroduce commodity options. Active trading now occurs not only in options on physical commodities such as gold and foreign currencies but also in options on commodity futures contracts (i.e., commodity futures options) such as wheat and livestock.

2. The Chicago Board Options Exchange now lists European-style options on selected foreign currencies and the S&P 500 Composite Stock Index.

3. This result is noted in Black [2].

4. It is interesting to note that substitution of the cost-of-carry relationship (1) into the European commodity formula (5) yields the Black [2] commodity futures option-pricing equation. This was first pointed out by Black and then later by Asay [1].

5. Geske and Shastri [11] provide a comprehensive analysis of the merits of the explicit, implicit, and binomial finite-difference approximation methods. Cox, Ross, and Rubinstein [7] and Cox and Rubinstein [8] provide detailed discussions of the binomial option-pricing framework.

6. In coding the American call option-pricing algorithm, first check whether the cost of carry b is less than the riskless rate of interest r. If not, then price the call using the European pricing formula.

7. The term $N[d_1(S^*)]$ approaches 1 rather than 0 as T approaches 0 because the critical commodity price S^* is always greater than or equal to the exercise price X.

8. Iterative solution to (19) for each of the options on a single underlying commodity is unnecessary. The critical commodity price in (19) is proportional in X; thus, if the critical commodity price S_1^* is computed for an option with exercise price X_1, the critical commodity price for a second option with a different exercise price X_2 is simply $S_2^* = (S_1^*/X_1)X_2$.

9. For very large values of b and T, the influence of b must be bounded in the put exponent to ensure critical prices monotonically decreasing in T. A reasonable upper bound on b is $0.6\sigma/\sqrt{T}$, so the critical commodity price declines at least with a velocity $e^{-1.4\sigma\sqrt{T}}$.

10. Recall that, when the cost of carry is greater than or equal to the riskless rate of interest, the American call option will not be exercised early.

11. Here, the finite-difference method is assumed to provide the "true" value of the American commodity option.

12. When the underlying stock pays known discrete dividends, both the American call and put options written on the stock may be optimally exercised early. Roll [17] and Whaley [20] provide the analytic solution to the American call option-pricing problem where the stock pays known discrete dividends. Analytic solutions to the American put option-pricing problem have not been found; however, Geske and Johnson [10] and Blomeyer [4] provide heuristic techniques for approximating the put option values.

7

A Simple Technique for the Valuation and Hedging of American Options

T. S. Ho
RICHARD C. STAPLETON
MARTI G. SUBRAHMANYAM

I n a well-known article, Geske and Johnson [1984] suggest a way of estimating the value of an American option by pricing a series of compound-
or multiple-exercisable options and then using Richardson extrapolation to
obtain a value for the continuously exercisable option. They show that the
estimated value using the Richardson approximation is very close to the values
obtained using standard numerical techniques.

In this article, we propose and test an alternative, much simpler, technique
for valuing American-style options. The technique requires the estimation of just
two option prices: a European option and a twice-exercisable (i.e., a compound)
option. These option prices can be computed essentially instantaneously, and
hence the American option values can be rapidly computed for a large book of
options with little computational effort.

The technique we suggest is based on an observed approximately exponential relationship between the value of an American-style option and the number of exercise points allowed up to the maturity date. If only one exercise point
is allowed, the option is European and has a value of $x_1\%$ of the asset price,

This article is part of research previously presented at the European Finance Association Conference,
Rotterdam, The Netherlands, and at the Financial Options Research Centre, Warwick University,
U.K. The authors acknowledge the able research assistance of Jingzhi Huang and the comments of
John Chang. They are grateful to an anonymous referee for helpful comments and suggestions that
improved the article.

Reprinted with permission from Institutional Investor, *Journal of Derivatives*, Fall 1994, 488
Madison Avenue, New York, NY 10022.

where x_1 depends upon the strike price of the option, the volatility of the underlying asset, the time to maturity, and the interest rate.

If two exercise points are allowed, the option is a compound option that effectively turns into a European option once the first exercise date is passed. Say this option has a value of x_2% of the underlying asset price. Then, our technique predicts the continuously exercisable option price given only x_1 and x_2.

PREVIOUS WORK ON ESTIMATION OF AMERICAN OPTION PRICES USING SIMPLE TECHNIQUES

Many option products, ranging from equity options such as warrants to fixed-income products such as mortgage-backed securities and corporate securities, have early exercise features that influence their valuation and hedging. Since closed-form solutions to the valuation and hedging problems of such American-style options are impossible to achieve, researchers have focused on numerical methods.

Examples are the binomial approach of Cox, Ross, and Rubinstein [1979] or the finite-difference methods of Brennan and Schwartz [1977], Parkinson [1977], and Courtadon [1982]. Unfortunately, these methods are computationally intensive and become difficult to implement if frequent revaluation of a book of American-style options is necessary.

Faced with this computational problem, Geske and Johnson [1984] (GJ) propose a method based on a few multiple-exercisable options, i.e., options that can be exercised only on a given number of dates. Although the method can be used to value any American-style option, GJ use the case of American-style put options as an example.

The essence of the GJ argument can be explained quite simply. Let P_1 be the price of a European option with maturity T. Let P_2 and P_3 be the prices of multiple-exercisable options, exercisable on two or three dates, respectively. The twice-exercisable option can be exercised at times T/2 and T. The three-times-exercisable option can be exercised at times T/3, 2T/3, and T.

GJ show that a particular form of the Richardson extrapolation can be employed to predict the price of the (continuously exercisable) American option, P. Their estimation formula using P_1, P_2, and P_3 is[1]

$$P_{GJ} = P_3 + \frac{7}{2}(P_3 - P_2) - \frac{1}{2}(P_2 - P_1) \tag{1}$$

The GJ method also yields hedge ratios, because in differential form

$$\frac{\partial P_{GJ}}{\partial S} = \frac{\partial P_3}{\partial S} + \frac{7}{2}\left(\frac{\partial P_3}{\partial S} - \frac{\partial P_2}{\partial S}\right) - \frac{1}{2}\left(\frac{\partial P_2}{\partial S} - \frac{\partial P_1}{\partial S}\right) \tag{2}$$

where S is the price of the underlying asset.

There have been a number of extensions and modifications of the GJ technique. Omberg [1987] points out that there may be some convergence problems with the GJ procedure. These problems arise due to the fact that the exercise points used in the P_3 calculation do not include all those used in the P_2 calculation. As a result, it is possible that the condition $P_1 < P_2 < P_3$ does not hold, and this can lead to nonconvergence of the GJ procedure. This problem may be overcome, at some computational cost, by using a series of prices P_1, P_2, P_4, . . . , which must necessarily converge.

Another interesting modification of the GJ procedure is suggested by Bunch and Johnson [1992]. They propose using only the P_1 and P_2 calculations, although these prices then become the values of the European and twice-exercisable option that have the highest values for alternative exercise dates in the period until expiration. Bunch and Johnson show that their "maximum price" method works well for options that are not deep-in-the-money and is more computationally efficient than the GJ method, since the GJ method requires the evaluation of higher-order (at least trivariate) multivariate normal distributions.

Breen [1991] simplifies the calculations by showing that the GJ methodology can be applied to a binomial option pricing model. His "accelerated binomial" option pricing model combines the computational efficiency of the GJ methodology with the simplicity of the binomial model.

The technique that we suggest is closely related to, but also differs significantly from, these contributions. First, as in Bunch and Johnson [1992], we use only P_1 and P_2 values. For American options with a constant exercise price, we do not need the "maximum price" procedure. Also, our exponential formula differs from the Richardson approximation used by those authors.

Second, our technique does not require Breen's [1991] binomial model, since we require only P_1 and P_2 estimates, which can be obtained *analytically* using at most the bivariate cumulative normal density function.

Finally, since we employ only P_1 and P_2, our technique does not suffer from the non-convergence problems discussed in Omberg [1987]. Our incremental contribution to this literature is to show that a small change in the approximating method, using an exponential relationship in place of the linear approximation used by GJ, can produce accurate American option prices with dramatically reduced computational time, in fact almost instantaneously.

In a related article, Johnson [1983] uses an alternative approach involving only European options.[2] Johnson shows that the American put value can be approximated by a portfolio of a European put with a strike price equal to that of the American option, and a European put with a compounded strike price. His formula relies on empirically estimated relationships to determine the portfolio weights, which in turn change with the option strike price.

Our method does not rely on such empirical estimation, since it is a fixed function of P_1 and P_2. Also, our formula applies to options regardless of the depth-in-the-money of the option.

Estimates of American option prices can be obtained with similar computational time using the quadratic approximation method suggested by Barone-Adesi and Whaley [1987] (BW).[3] This approach is specific to the stochastic process assumed for the underlying asset price and applies in the case of assets paying a continuous dividend. For options with a significant time premium, our method appears to improve on the accuracy of the BW method.

ESTIMATION OF AMERICAN OPTION PRICES WITH MULTIPLE-EXERCISABLE OPTIONS

An American contingent claim is one that can be exercised at any one time up to the final maturity, T. One way to consider such a claim is that it is the limiting case of a series of claims that are exercisable at one of two, three, . . . , n dates, where n is very large.

Mathematically, if P_n is the price of a claim that is exercisable at one of n dates, then we have a series of prices:

$P_1, P_2, P_3, \ldots, P_n$

and the value of the American-style claim is

$$P = \lim_{n \to \infty} P_n \qquad (3)$$

where the prices $P_1, P_2, \ldots, P_n$, and P are all prices at time 0, the valuation date.

We assume here that the exercise dates are equally distanced from each other. Also, P refers to the price of *any* American-style contingent claim (for example, the simple put or call option). As n increases, the price of the claim approaches its asymptotic value P. In practical terms, P_1 provides the "base level" of the option price, and P_2 (in comparison to P_1) gives a good first approximation of the American premium. The additional prices, $P_3, \ldots, P_n$ fill in the remainder of the value.

The essence of our simple approach is that P_1 and P_2 alone provide a large percentage of the information required for estimating P. Let us define $\hat{P}$ as our estimate of P, where $\hat{P}$ is a function of $P_1, P_2, \ldots, P_n$. Then, our method uses a function

$\hat{P} = f(P_1, P_2)$

The key point to note here is that we wish to restrict the "predictor option prices" to *just* P_1 and P_2. Our motivation is to save computational time without sacrificing too much accuracy.

The European price, P_1, can be calculated instantaneously from the Black and Scholes formula. The twice-exercisable option price can be obtained almost instantaneously using a bivariate normal probability distribution. Proceeding to P_3 and P_4 would rapidly increase the computational time, as pointed out by

Bunch and Johnson [1992]. Hence, it is most desirable to be able to predict P with only P_1 and P_2.[4]

In Figure 7-1, we plot multiple-exercisable option prices, P_1 and P_2, for various American put options for which both European and American prices are reported in Geske and Johnson [1984, Table I, p. 1519]. The striking feature of Figure 7-1 is the asymptotic behavior of the series of prices $P_1, P_2, \ldots, P_\infty$. The suggestion is that there is an exponential relationship between the price P_n and the number of exercise points, n.

Of course, this relationship differs from option to option depending on the volatility of the underlying stock, the time-to-maturity, and the depth-in-the-money. In each case, however, it appears that the relationship can be modeled as an exponential function.

Suppose then, that for any option and for all n, the n-times-exercisable option is related to the American price, P, by the exponential relationship

$$P = P_n \exp\left(\frac{\alpha}{n}\right) \tag{4}$$

where α is a constant. Substituting for n = 1 and simplifying, Equation (4) can be written as

FIGURE 7-1   European Values and Asymptotic Values of American Puts

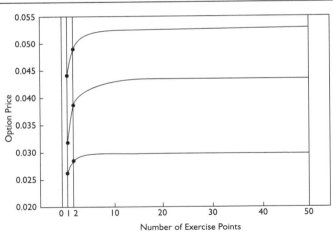

Notes: Plots of once-, twice-, and n-exercisable option prices, P_1, P_2, and P_n, where n = 50, for three American puts, P(S, T; K, r, σ). The P_1 values are the Black-Scholes European put prices, and the $P_{n=50}$ values are the Parkinson put prices determined by numerical methods, as reported in Geske and Johnson's Table I [1984, p. 1519]. The P_2 values are the twice-exercisable prices computed using the formula shown in the appendix. All three options have stock price, S = $1, time-to-maturity, T = 1, and exercise price, K = $1. The top curve (■) plots the option with a risk-free rate, r = 0.08, and an asset volatility, σ = 0.2; the middle curve ($\diamond$) with r = 0.12 and σ = 0.2; and the bottom curve (+) with r = 0.03, and σ = 0.1.

$$P_n = P_1 \exp(\alpha) \exp\left(-\frac{\alpha}{n}\right) \tag{5}$$

It can be seen that P_n is a positive, increasing function of n and reaches an asymptotic value

$$P = \lim_{n \to \infty} P_n = P_1 \exp(\alpha) \tag{6}$$

Hence, the exponential function in Equation (4) has the same overall shape as that observed for the option prices in Figure 7-1. In order to determine the constant, α, assume that Equation (4) holds for all n, and examine specifically the twice-exercisable option, P_2. Substituting n = 2 in Equation (4), we have

$$P_2 = P_1 \exp\left(\frac{\alpha}{2}\right) \tag{7}$$

Now, we can eliminate the unknown parameter α by substituting Equation (7) into Equation (6). A little manipulation yields

$$P = P_1 \exp\{2(\ln P_2 - \ln P_1)\}$$

and

$$P = \frac{P_2^2}{P_1} \tag{8}$$

The formula in Equation (8) relating P, American price, to the European price P_1 and the twice-exercisable option price P_2, relies on the assumption that Equation (4) holds exactly for all n. Of course, Equation (4) is really only an approximation, and P in Equation (8) is only an estimate of the true American price. It follows that we should write

$$\hat{P} = \frac{P_2^2}{P_1} \tag{9}$$

where $\hat{P}$ is the estimated American option price.[5]

Finally, note that Equation (9) can be written in logarithmic form

$$\log \hat{P} = \log P_2 + (\log P_2 - \log P_1) \tag{10}$$

Intuitively, Equation (10) suggests that, in logarithmic terms, the value of an American option can be estimated using the value of a twice-exercisable option as the basis and adding the difference between the value of the twice-exercisable option and the European option to it.

HEDGE RATIOS FOR AMERICAN OPTIONS

Option traders require hedge ratios and other risk parameters to aid the management of their positions. Typically, they need to know the sensitivity of the option prices to changes in the underlying asset spot price (delta), the volatility of the asset (vega), and the time-to-maturity (theta), as well as the sensitivity of the option's delta to changes in the spot price (gamma).

In general, these partial derivatives are difficult to compute for American-style options, since the computations would involve perturbations of the rather complex computations. Using the estimating Equation (9), approximate hedge ratios can be obtained. For example, the estimated delta is obtained by differentiating Equation (9) to obtain

$$\hat{\Delta} = \frac{\partial \hat{P}}{\partial S} = \hat{P}\left(\frac{2\Delta_2}{P_2} - \frac{\Delta_1}{P_1}\right) \tag{11}$$

where S is the stock price, and $\Delta_2 = \partial P_2/\partial S$ and $\Delta_1 = \partial P_1/\partial S$ are the hedge ratios of the twice-exercisable and the European options, respectively.

The other hedge ratios can be computed in an analogous manner. The option's gamma, given by

$$\hat{\Gamma} = \frac{\partial^2 \hat{P}}{\partial S^2} = \hat{P}\left(\frac{2\Delta_1^2}{P_1^2} - \frac{4\Delta_1\Delta_2}{P_1 P_2} + \frac{2\Delta_2^2}{P_2^2} - \frac{\Gamma_1}{P_1} + \frac{2\Gamma_2}{P_2}\right) \tag{12}$$

can be computed by further differentiating Equation (11) with respect to S.

Similarly, the option's vega,[6] theta, and rho are given by

$$\hat{V} = \frac{\partial \hat{P}}{\partial \sigma} = \hat{P}\left(\frac{2V_2}{P_2} - \frac{V_1}{P_1}\right) \tag{13}$$

$$\Phi = \frac{\partial \hat{P}}{\partial T} = \hat{P}\left(\frac{2\Phi_2}{P_2} - \frac{\Phi_1}{P_1}\right) \tag{14}$$

$$\hat{R} = \frac{\partial \hat{P}}{\partial r} = \hat{P}\left(\frac{2R_2}{P_2} - \frac{R_1}{P_1}\right) \tag{15}$$

where the partial derivatives in the case of the once- and twice-exercisable option are subscripted by 1 and 2, respectively.

The computational advantage of this approach to American option pricing and hedging is now apparent. The hedge ratios, which are often required for several hundred option positions, can be computed given the corresponding hedge ratios for P_1 and P_2. Those for P_1 are simply obtained from the Black and Schole model. The hedge ratios and other risk parameters for P_2 can be computed analytically using the formula of Geske and Johnson [1984, p. 1514]. (See Appendix.)

SIMULATION OF THE VALUE, HEDGE RATIO, AND RISK PARAMETERS OF AN OPTION BOOK

We now test our "simple" American option pricing formula by computing the value, the hedge ratio, and risk parameters of a set of options. In order to illustrate the comparative performance of our approximation, we use a standard portfolio of options analyzed previously by Cox and Rubinstein [1985] and Geske and Johnson [1984].

The options considered are all American put options on a stock whose current price is $40. These options range from being out-of-the-money (strike price of $35) through at-the-money (strike price of $40) to in-the-money (strike price of $45).

The volatility parameter of the underlying asset varies from 20% to 40%, covering the typical range for equity options. The continuously compounded risk-free rate is constant across maturities at 0.0488 (the continuously compounded rate that yields 5% on an effective basis). The options considered have expiration dates varying from 30 days to 250 days from today.

In Table 7-1, we illustrate the accuracy of prices computed using the approximation in Equation (9). The first seven columns are as reported in Geske and Johnson's Table I [1984, p. 1519]. In column (9), we show the American option values computed by our approximation.

The differences between our approximation and the values computed by Cox and Rubinstein [1985] using numerical methods are shown in column (10). Apart from the in-the-money options, our values are within one or two cents of the Cox and Rubinstein values in virtually every case and hence well within the typical bid-ask spread.

Furthermore, the errors in the approximation have to be viewed in a portfolio context. In most practical cases, one is valuing and hedging a whole book of options and not each option individually. The issue, therefore, is whether there is a significant and consistent bias in the value and hedge ratio of the whole portfolio of options.

The answer to this question is negative. For example, the value of all the options in the table, viewed as a portfolio, is $78.84, or within 0.09% of the Cox and Rubinstein number of $78.91.

Although the options are, in general, valued extremely accurately by our simple method, there are some individual biases apparent from the computations. In-the-money options are overvalued, and the out-of-the-money options are undervalued by the approximation. In the worst case, where volatility is only 20%, the long-maturity in-the-money option is overvalued by seven cents.

The in-the-money bias is counteracted by a high-volatility bias, however. Note that when volatility is 40%, even the in-the-money puts are accurately valued. In any event, from a practical standpoint, the error would still be within the typical bid-ask spread even for in-the-money options.[7]

Table 7-2 shows the deltas and gammas for the options considered in Table 7-1. The American option hedge ratios (delta) computed using Equation (11) shown in column (8) are computed from the deltas for P_1 and P_2 shown in the Appendix. Column (9) shows that the differences between our hedge ratios and those obtained by Geske and Johnson are small in most cases. As we can see, in no case is the hedge ratio off by more than ± 0.02. The difference is even less significant for the total portfolio of options.

TABLE 7-1   Comparison of American and European Option Values

Option Parameters				GJ Estimation Method	CR Binomial Method	BS European Put Price	Exponential Approximation Method		Pricing Difference
r (1)	K (2)	σ (3)	T (4)	P_{GJ} (5)	P_{CR} (6)	P_1 (7)	P_2 (8)	$\hat{P}$ (9)	$\hat{P} - P_{CR}$ (10)
0.0488	35	0.2	0.0833	0.0062	0.01	0.0061	0.0061	0.0062	0.00
0.0488	35	0.2	0.3333	0.1999	0.20	0.1959	0.1963	0.1968	0.00
0.0488	35	0.2	0.5833	0.4321	0.43	0.4168	0.4199	0.4231	−0.01
0.0488	40	0.2	0.0833	0.8528	0.85	0.8396	0.8437	0.8483	0.00
0.0488	40	0.2	0.3333	1.5807	1.58	1.5214	1.5473	1.5739	−0.01
0.0488	40	0.2	0.5833	1.9905	1.99	1.8806	1.9335	1.9881	0.00
0.0488	45	0.2	0.0833	4.9985	5.00	4.8384	4.9181	5.0000	0.00
0.0488	45	0.2	0.3333	5.0951	5.09	4.7791	4.9546	5.1359	0.05
0.0488	45	0.2	0.5833	5.2719	5.27	4.8389	5.0828	5.3384	0.07
0.0488	35	0.3	0.0833	0.0774	0.08	0.0770	0.0770	0.0771	0.00
0.0488	35	0.3	0.3333	0.6969	0.70	0.6863	0.6879	0.6898	−0.01
0.0488	35	0.3	0.5833	1.2194	1.22	1.1885	1.1959	1.2036	−0.02
0.0488	40	0.3	0.0833	1.3100	1.31	1.2982	1.3014	1.3053	0.00
0.0488	40	0.3	0.3333	2.4817	2.48	2.4268	2.4487	2.4713	−0.01
0.0488	40	0.3	0.5833	3.1733	3.17	3.0627	3.1098	3.1579	−0.01
0.0488	45	0.3	0.0833	5.0599	5.06	4.9781	5.0275	5.0767	0.02
0.0488	45	0.3	0.3333	5.7012	5.71	5.5276	5.6305	5.7352	0.03
0.0488	45	0.3	0.5833	6.2365	6.24	5.9713	6.1262	6.2852	0.05
0.0488	35	0.4	0.0833	0.2466	0.25	0.2455	0.2455	0.2458	0.00
0.0488	35	0.4	0.3333	1.3450	1.35	1.3293	1.3321	1.3352	−0.01
0.0488	35	0.4	0.5833	2.1568	2.16	2.1123	2.1231	2.1342	−0.03
0.0488	40	0.4	0.0833	1.7679	1.77	1.7568	1.7595	1.7630	−0.01
0.0488	40	0.4	0.3333	3.3632	3.38	3.3329	3.3525	3.3727	−0.01
0.0488	40	0.4	0.5833	4.3556	4.35	4.2466	4.2901	4.3345	−0.02
0.0488	45	0.4	0.0833	5.2855	5.29	5.2347	5.2649	5.2954	0.01
0.0488	45	0.4	0.3333	6.5093	6.51	6.3756	6.4467	6.5188	0.01
0.0488	45	0.4	0.5833	7.3831	7.39	7.1644	7.2804	7.3985	0.01

The first seven columns are similar to those reported in Table I of Geske and Johnson [1984, p. 1519]. Columns (1) to (4) represent the parameter inputs for r, the continuously compounded risk-free rate; K, the strike price; σ, the volatility; and T, the time to expiration. The stock price in all cases is $40. The remaining columns refer to put option prices in dollars. Column (5) shows the Geske-Johnson put option values, P_{GJ}. Column (6) indicates the American put option values computed by the Cox and Rubinstein [1985] numerical method, which we use as a benchmark. Columns (7) and (8) show the once-exercisable (Black-Scholes), P_1, and the twice-exercisable put option values, P_2 [Equation (A-1) in the Appendix], respectively. Column (9) shows the American put option values, $\hat{P}$, using our approximation, where $\hat{P} = P_2^2/P_1$. Column (10) shows the differences between the American put option value using our approximation in column (9), P, and the Cox and Rubinstein values, P_{CR}, in column (6).

TABLE 7-2 Hedge Ratios and Convexity Parameters for European and American Options

				Hedge Ratios (Deltas)					Convexity (Gammas)		
Option Parameters				GJ	BS	Exponential Method		Difference	BS	Exponential Method	
r	K	σ	T	Δ_{GJ}	Δ_1	Δ_2	$\hat{\Delta}$	$\hat{\Delta} - \Delta_{GJ}$	Γ_1	Γ_2	$\hat{\Gamma}$
(1)	(2)	(3)	(4)	(5)	(6)	(7)	(8)	(9)	(10)	(11)	(12)
0.0488	35	0.2	0.0833	−0.008	−0.008	−0.008	−0.008	0.000	0.009	0.009	0.009
0.0488	35	0.2	0.3333	−0.090	−0.088	−0.088	−0.089	−0.001	0.035	0.035	0.035
0.0488	35	0.2	0.5833	−0.134	−0.128	−0.130	−0.132	0.002	0.034	0.035	0.036
0.0488	40	0.2	0.0833	−0.470	−0.461	−0.465	−0.470	0.000	0.172	0.177	0.181
0.0488	40	0.2	0.3333	−0.443	−0.421	−0.435	−0.449	−0.006	0.085	0.091	0.097
0.0488	40	0.2	0.5833	−0.427	−0.396	−0.417	−0.439	−0.012	0.063	0.069	0.076
0.0488	45	0.2	0.0833	−1.000	−0.974	−0.985	−0.997	0.003	0.026	0.020	0.013
0.0488	45	0.2	0.3333	−0.888	−0.794	−0.835	−0.878	0.010	0.062	0.063	0.064
0.0488	45	0.2	0.5833	−0.805	−0.695	−0.746	−0.801	0.004	0.057	0.062	0.066
0.0488	35	0.3	0.0833	−0.052	−0.051	−0.051	−0.051	0.001	0.030	0.030	0.030
0.0488	35	0.3	0.3333	−0.174	−0.171	−0.172	−0.172	0.002	0.037	0.037	0.038
0.0488	35	0.3	0.5833	−0.213	−0.206	−0.208	−0.211	0.002	0.031	0.032	0.033
0.0488	40	0.3	0.0833	−0.470	−0.464	−0.467	−0.469	0.001	0.115	0.117	0.118
0.0488	40	0.3	0.3333	−0.442	−0.428	−0.436	−0.445	−0.003	0.057	0.059	0.062
0.0488	40	0.3	0.5833	−0.425	−0.406	−0.418	−0.431	−0.006	0.042	0.045	0.048
0.0488	45	0.3	0.0833	−0.926	−0.898	−0.912	−0.926	0.000	0.051	0.051	0.051
0.0488	45	0.3	0.3333	−0.726	−0.691	−0.715	−0.739	−0.013	0.051	0.054	0.057
0.0488	45	0.3	0.5833	−0.651	−0.608	−0.637	−0.667	−0.016	0.042	0.045	0.049
0.0488	35	0.4	0.0833	−0.106	−0.106	−0.106	−0.106	0.000	0.040	0.040	0.040
0.0488	35	0.4	0.3333	−0.226	−0.222	−0.224	−0.225	0.001	0.032	0.033	0.033
0.0488	35	0.4	0.5833	−0.254	−0.247	−0.250	−0.253	0.001	0.026	0.027	0.027
0.0488	40	0.4	0.0833	−0.467	−0.463	−0.465	−0.466	0.001	0.086	0.087	0.088
0.0488	40	0.4	0.3333	−0.437	−0.426	−0.432	−0.438	−0.001	0.042	0.044	0.045
0.0488	40	0.4	0.5833	−0.418	−0.403	−0.412	−0.421	−0.003	0.032	0.033	0.035
0.0488	45	0.4	0.0833	−0.835	−0.823	−0.833	−0.842	−0.007	0.056	0.058	0.059
0.0488	45	0.4	0.3333	−0.646	−0.627	−0.642	−0.656	−0.010	0.041	0.043	0.045
0.0488	45	0.4	0.5833	−0.580	−0.556	−0.574	−0.593	−0.013	0.032	0.035	0.037

The first six columns are as reported in Table I of Geske and Johnson [1984, p. 1519]. Columns (1) to (4) represent the parameter inputs for r, the continuously compounded risk-free rate; K, the strike price; σ, the volatility; and T, the time to expiration. The stock price in all cases is \$40. Column (5) shows the Geske-Johnson put option hedge ratios, Δ_{GJ}. Columns (6) and (7) represent the hedge ratios for the once-exercisable (Black-Scholes), Δ_1, and twice-exercisable options, Δ_2, respectively. Columns (8) gives our estimated value of the hedge ratio for the American put options using an approximation: $\Delta = \partial \hat{P}/\partial S = \hat{P}\,(2\delta_2/P_2 - \Delta_1/P_1)$. Column (9) represents the differences between the hedge ratios using our approximation in column (8), Δ, and the corresponding ones using the Geske-Johnson approximation, Δ_{GJ}, in column (5). Columns (10) and (11) show the convexity (gamma) parameters for the once-exercisable (Black-Scholes) and twice-exercisable options. Column (12) represents the convexity parameter for the American put option using our approximation [Equation (12)].

The ease of computation using our method is readily apparent in these calculations. The usual methods of computing the values are laborious, since they generally involve perturbing the current parameter inputs. Our method, being a direct one, economizes substantially on the computational effort.

ESTIMATION OF PRICES OF LONG-MATURITY CALL AND PUT OPTIONS ON DIVIDEND-PAYING STOCKS

Perhaps the closest competitor to our exponential estimate, $\hat{P}$, is the quadratic approximation method discussed in detail by Barone-Adesi and Whaley [1987] (BW). In Table 7-3, we compare put option prices estimated using the two methods for a range of parameter values assuming that no dividends are paid. For these short-maturity options, either method can be used to obtain accurate estimates although some inaccuracy occurs, using either method, in the case of deep-in-the-money options.

A simple adjustment in the calculation of P_1 and P_2 allows us to extend the exponential method to the case of puts and calls where the stock pays a continuous dividend. This extension then covers the case of foreign exchange, futures, and index options.[8]

In Table 7-4, we compare $\hat{P}$ estimates for a range of dividend yields, y, and for various other parameter values. The accuracy of $\hat{P}$ is again approximately the same as for the BW method, although the $\hat{P}$ estimate is relatively accurate for out-of-the-money options.

A more rigorous test of the predictive ability of $\hat{P}$ versus the BW method is provided by the case of long-maturity options. In Table 7-5 we compare both put and call prices with those obtained by Barone-Adesi and Whaley for three-year maturity options on dividend-paying stocks.

The BW method significantly misprices both puts on high-yielding stocks, and calls on low-yielding stocks. This mispricing is avoided by the $\hat{P}$ method.

Also, the $\hat{P}$ method performs significantly better than the BW method when the yield equals the risk-free interest rate. This suggests that the $\hat{P}$ method may represent a significant improvement in the case of futures options and foreign-exchange options where the cost of carry is low. The BW method tends to outperform our method in the case of long-dated puts on zero dividend-paying stocks.

In Table 7-6, we examine the accuracy of $\hat{P}$ for put and call options with maturities up to five years for dividend and non-dividend-paying stocks. The aim is to show the possible limitations of the $\hat{P}$ estimate: when it should be used and when it should not.

The top half of Table 7-6 considers options on dividend-paying stocks, with the dividend yield equal to the risk-free interest rate. Here, both call and put options are accurately priced for one-year maturities. For a three-year maturity, in-the-money options are slightly overpriced. For five-year maturity options, the biases get larger, and the method should not be used for in-the-money options.

TABLE 7-3 Comparison of American Put Option Values on Stocks Using Finite-Difference, Barone-Adesi and Whaley Quadratic, and Ho, Stapleton, and Subrahmanyam Exponential Methods: Zero Dividend Case

						American Put Option Values		
						Finite-Difference Method	Quadratic Approximation Method	Exponential Approximation Method
Dividend Yield	Other Option Parameters				Stock Price			
y	r	σ	T	K	S	P_{FD}	P_{BW}	$\hat{P}$
(1)	(2)	(3)	(4)	(5)	(6)	(7)	(8)	(9)
0.00	0.08	0.20	0.25	100	80	20.00	20.00	20.00
0.00	0.08	0.20	0.25	100	90	10.04	10.01	10.12
0.00	0.08	0.20	0.25	100	100	3.22	3.22	3.22
0.00	0.08	0.20	0.25	100	110	0.66	0.68	0.65
0.00	0.08	0.20	0.25	100	120	0.09	0.10	0.09
0.00	0.12	0.20	0.25	100	80	20.00	20.00	20.02
0.00	0.12	0.20	0.25	100	90	10.00	10.00	10.00
0.00	0.12	0.20	0.25	100	100	2.92	2.93	2.95
0.00	0.12	0.20	0.25	100	110	0.55	0.58	0.54
0.00	0.12	0.20	0.25	100	120	0.07	0.08	0.07
0.00	0.08	0.40	0.25	100	80	20.32	20.25	20.48
0.00	0.08	0.40	0.25	100	90	12.56	12.51	12.62
0.00	0.08	0.40	0.25	100	100	7.11	7.10	7.08
0.00	0.08	0.40	0.25	100	110	3.70	3.71	3.66
0.00	0.08	0.40	0.25	100	120	1.79	1.81	1.77
0.00	0.08	0.20	0.50	100	80	20.00	20.00	20.00
0.00	0.08	0.20	0.50	100	90	10.29	10.23	10.46
0.00	0.08	0.20	0.50	100	100	4.19	4.19	4.22
0.00	0.08	0.20	0.50	100	110	1.41	1.45	1.38
0.00	0.08	0.20	0.50	100	120	0.40	0.42	0.38

The first eight columns are based on the option parameters and results of American put option prices reported in Barone-Adesi and Whaley's Table IV [1987, p. 315]. Columns (1) to (6) represent the parameter inputs (annualized) for y, the dividend yield; r, the continuously compounded risk-free rate; σ, the volatility; T, the time to expiration; K, the strike price; and S, the stock price. The remaining columns refer to put option prices in dollars. Column (7) shows the implicit finite-difference American put option values, P_{FD}, computed with stock price steps of 0.10, and time steps of 0.20 days, which we use as a benchmark. Column (8) lists the American put option values computed by the quadratic approximation method of Barone-Adesi and Whaley [1987, Equation (25), p. 308]. Column (9) tabulates the American put option values, $\hat{P}$, using our approximation, where $\hat{P} = P_2^2/P_1$.

In the bottom half of Table 7-6 we consider options on stocks paying a zero dividend. Here, $\hat{P}$ is again accurate for one-year options, but is less reliable for the three-year and five-year maturities.

Generally, Table 7-6 reveals a systematic overpricing of in-the-money options, which increases with maturity.

TABLE 7-4   **Comparison of American Put Option Values on Stocks Using Finite-Difference, Barone-Adesi and Whaley Quadratic, and Ho, Stapleton, and Subrahmanyam Exponential Methods: Continuous Dividend Case**

						American Put Option Values		
Dividend Yield	Other Option Parameters				Stock Price	Finite-Difference Method	Quadratic Approximation Method	Exponential Approximation Method
y	r	σ	T	K	S	P_{FD}	P_{BW}	$\hat{P}$
(1)	(2)	(3)	(4)	(5)	(6)	(7)	(8)	(9)
0.04	0.08	0.20	0.25	100	80	20.00	20.00	20.00
0.04	0.08	0.20	0.25	100	90	10.22	10.18	10.31
0.04	0.08	0.20	0.25	100	100	3.55	3.54	3.53
0.04	0.08	0.20	0.25	100	110	0.79	0.80	0.78
0.04	0.08	0.20	0.25	100	120	0.11	0.12	0.11
0.08	0.12	0.20	0.25	100	80	20.00	20.00	20.00
0.08	0.12	0.20	0.25	100	90	10.20	10.16	10.29
0.08	0.12	0.20	0.25	100	100	3.52	3.53	3.51
0.08	0.12	0.20	0.25	100	110	0.78	0.79	0.77
0.08	0.12	0.20	0.25	100	120	0.11	0.12	0.11
0.04	0.08	0.40	0.25	100	80	20.59	20.53	20.69
0.04	0.08	0.40	0.25	100	90	12.95	12.93	12.97
0.04	0.08	0.40	0.25	100	100	7.46	7.46	7.43
0.04	0.08	0.40	0.25	100	110	3.95	3.96	3.92
0.04	0.08	0.40	0.25	100	120	1.94	1.95	1.93
0.04	0.08	0.20	0.50	100	80	20.00	20.00	20.00
0.04	0.08	0.20	0.50	100	90	10.75	10.71	10.89
0.04	0.08	0.20	0.50	100	100	4.77	4.77	4.76
0.04	0.08	0.20	0.50	100	110	1.74	1.76	1.71
0.04	0.08	0.20	0.50	100	120	0.53	0.55	0.52

The first eight columns are based on the option parameters and results of American put option prices reported in Table II of Barone-Adesi and Whaley [1987, p. 313]. Columns (1) to (6) represent the parameter inputs (annualized) for y, the dividend yield; r, the continuously compounded risk-free rate; σ, the volatility; T, the time to expiration; K, the strike price; and S, the stock price. The remaining columns refer to put option prices in dollars. Column (7) shows the implicit finite-difference American put option values, P_{FD}, computed with stock price steps of 0.10, and time steps of 0.20 days, which we use as a benchmark. Column (8) lists the American put option values computed by the quadratic approximation method of Barone-Adesi and Whaley [1987, Equation (25), p. 308]. Column (9) tabulates the American put option values, $\hat{P}$, using our approximation, where $\hat{P} = P_2^2/P_1$. Note that the results of $\hat{P}$ for American call option prices computed using our approximation are identical to those reported in Barone-Adesi and Whaley's Table II for the finite-difference and the quadratic approximation methods, where their cost of carry, b, = 0.04. In our notation, b = r − y. The results for American call option prices are, therefore, not reported here, since in this case there is no early exercise, and American call prices are equal to the corresponding European option prices.

TABLE 7-5 Comparison of Long-Maturity American Call and Put Option Values Using Finite-Difference, Barone-Adesi and Whaley Quadratic, and Ho, Stapleton, and Subrahmanyam Exponential Methods: Continuous Dividend Case

Option Parameters						American Call Options			American Put Options		
y	r	σ	T	K	S	C_{FD}	C_{BW}	$\hat{C}$	P_{FD}	P_{BW}	$\hat{P}$
(1)	(2)	(3)	(4)	(5)	(6)	(7)	(8)	(9)	(10)	(11)	(12)
0.12	0.08	0.20	3.00	100	80	2.34	2.52	2.31	25.66	26.25	25.96
0.12	0.08	0.20	3.00	100	90	4.76	4.97	4.87	20.08	20.64	20.18
0.12	0.08	0.20	3.00	100	100	8.49	8.67	8.91	15.50	15.99	15.50
0.12	0.08	0.20	3.00	100	110	13.79	13.88	14.55	11.80	12.22	11.78
0.12	0.08	0.20	3.00	100	120	20.89	20.88	21.66	8.88	9.23	8.86
0.08	0.08	0.20	3.00	100	80	3.98	4.20	3.93	22.20	22.40	22.88
0.08	0.08	0.20	3.00	100	90	7.25	7.54	7.24	16.21	16.50	16.59
0.08	0.08	0.20	3.00	100	100	11.70	12.03	11.83	11.70	12.03	11.83
0.08	0.08	0.20	3.00	100	110	17.31	17.64	17.71	8.37	8.69	8.36
0.08	0.08	0.20	3.00	100	120	24.02	24.30	24.73	5.93	6.22	5.87
0.04	0.08	0.20	3.00	100	80	6.88	6.97	6.88	20.35	20.33	20.80
0.04	0.08	0.20	3.00	100	90	11.48	11.62	11.49	13.50	13.56	14.06
0.04	0.08	0.20	3.00	100	100	17.19	17.40	17.20	8.94	9.11	9.24
0.04	0.08	0.20	3.00	100	110	23.80	24.09	23.83	5.91	6.12	5.99
0.04	0.08	0.20	3.00	100	120	31.08	31.49	31.15	3.90	4.12	3.86
0.00	0.08	0.20	3.00	100	80				20.00	20.00	20.00
0.00	0.08	0.20	3.00	100	90				11.69	11.63	12.09
0.00	0.08	0.20	3.00	100	100				6.93	6.96	7.29
0.00	0.08	0.20	3.00	100	110				4.15	4.26	4.30
0.00	0.08	0.20	3.00	100	120				2.51	2.64	2.52

Columns (1) to (8), (10), and (11) are based on the option parameters and results of American call and put option prices reported in Barone-Adesi and Whaley, Table V [1987, p. 313]. Columns (1) to (6) represent the parameter inputs (annualized) for y, the dividend yield; r, the continuously compounded risk-free rate; σ, the volatility; T, the time to expiration; K, the strike price; and S, the stock price. The remaining columns refer to call and put option prices in dollars. Columns (7) and (10) show the implicit finite-difference American call, C_{FD}, and put, P_{FD}, option values, computed with stock price steps of 0.10, and time steps of 0.20 days, which we use as a benchmark. Columns (8) and (11) list the American call, C_{BW}, and put, P_{BW}, option values computed by the quadratic approximation method of Barone-Adesi and Whaley [1987, Equations (20) and (25), pp. 307 and 308, respectively]. Columns (9) and (12) tabulate the American call, $\hat{C}$, and put option values, $\hat{P}$, using our approximation Equation (9).

CONCLUSIONS

Options practitioners deal with an array of American-style options ranging from warrants on stocks to mortgage-backed securities. The computation of option values, hedge ratios, and risk parameters in these cases is often quite laborious. This means that it is virtually impossible to revalue and rehedge a book of op-

TABLE 7-6   **Pricing Biases of the Ho, Stapleton, and Subrahmanyam Exponential Method Relative to the Cox and Rubinstein Binomial Method for Long-Maturity American Call and Put Options**

					American Call Options		American Put Option	
Dividend Yield	Other Option Parameters			Exercise Price	CR Binomial Method	HSS Exponential Method	CR Binomial Method	HSS Exponential Method
y	r	σ	T	K	C_{CR}	$\hat{C}$	P_{CR}	$\hat{P}$
(1)	(2)	(3)	(4)	(5)	(6)	(7)	(8)	(9)
0.08	0.08	0.20	1.00	35.00	5.84	5.89	1.05	1.04
0.08	0.08	0.20	1.00	40.00	3.00	2.99	3.00	2.99
0.08	0.08	0.20	1.00	45.00	1.36	1.35	6.15	6.18
0.08	0.08	0.20	3.00	35.00	7.02	7.20	2.53	2.52
0.08	0.08	0.20	3.00	40.00	4.68	4.73	4.68	4.73
0.08	0.08	0.20	3.00	45.00	3.07	3.06	7.55	7.74
0.08	0.08	0.20	5.00	35.00	7.64	8.01	3.35	3.39
0.08	0.08	0.20	5.00	40.00	5.52	5.70	5.52	5.70
0.08	0.08	0.20	5.00	45.00	4.01	4.06	8.29	8.68
0.08	0.08	0.30	1.00	35.00	7.03	7.06	2.25	2.24
0.08	0.08	0.30	1.00	40.00	4.49	4.48	4.49	4.48
0.08	0.08	0.30	1.00	45.00	2.77	2.75	7.54	7.57
0.08	0.08	0.30	3.00	35.00	9.04	9.24	4.57	4.56
0.08	0.08	0.30	3.00	40.00	6.97	7.06	6.97	7.06
0.08	0.08	0.30	3.00	45.00	5.42	5.42	9.89	10.09
0.08	0.08	0.30	5.00	35.00	10.05	10.50	5.77	5.88
0.08	0.08	0.30	5.00	40.00	8.20	8.49	8.20	8.49
0.08	0.08	0.30	5.00	45.00	6.76	6.92	11.04	11.53
0.00	0.08	0.20	1.00	35.00			0.59	0.58
0.00	0.08	0.20	1.00	40.00			2.11	2.15
0.00	0.08	0.20	1.00	45.00			5.22	5.33
0.00	0.08	0.20	3.00	35.00			1.17	1.20
0.00	0.08	0.20	3.00	40.00			2.77	2.92
0.00	0.08	0.20	3.00	45.00			5.58	5.74
0.00	0.08	0.20	5.00	35.00	No early		1.40	1.49
0.00	0.08	0.20	5.00	40.00	exercise in		3.00	3.21
0.00	0.08	0.20	5.00	45.00	these zero		5.71	5.86
0.00	0.08	0.30	1.00	35.00	dividend cases:		1.63	1.61
0.00	0.08	0.30	1.00	40.00	American		3.56	3.59
0.00	0.08	0.30	1.00	45.00	option value		6.46	6.59
0.00	0.08	0.30	3.00	35.00	= Black-Scholes		2.95	3.00
0.00	0.08	0.30	3.00	40.00	European		4.97	5.16
0.00	0.08	0.30	3.00	45.00	option		7.67	7.99
0.00	0.08	0.30	5.00	35.00	value, P_1		3.53	3.70

TABLE 7-6 **Pricing Biases of the Ho, Stapleton, and Subrahmanyam Exponential Method Relative to the Cox and Rubinstein Binomial Method for Long-Maturity American Call and Put Options (Continued)**

					American Call Options		American Put Option	
Dividend Yield	Other Option Parameters			Exercise Price	CR Binomial Method	HSS Exponential Method	CR Binomial Method	HSS Exponential Method
y	r	σ	T	K	C_{CR}	$\hat{C}$	P_{CR}	$\hat{P}$
(1)	(2)	(3)	(4)	(5)	(6)	(7)	(8)	(9)
0.00	0.08	0.30	5.00	40.00			5.56	5.90
0.00	0.08	0.30	5.00	45.00			8.19	8.65

Columns (1) to (5) represent the parameter inputs (annualized) for y, the dividend yield; r, the continuously compounded risk-free rate; σ, the volatility; T, the time to expiration; and K, the strike price. The stock price, S, in all cases is $40. The remaining columns refer to call and put option prices in dollars. Columns (6) and (8) show the Cox and Rubinstein [1985] binomial method American call, C_{CR}, and put option, P_{CR}, values computed 150 time steps. Columns (7) and (9) show the American call, $\hat{C}$, and put option, $\hat{P}$, using our approximation Equation (9).

tions on a real-time basis. Furthermore, given the complexity of the calculations, it is often difficult to gain an intuitive understanding of the magnitudes of the values resulting from the calculations.

Our method is at once both computationally efficient and intuitively appealing. Its computational efficiency results from the need to compute just two different numbers for each parameter (value, hedge ratios, etc.) and extrapolate from these. The intuitive appeal comes from the exponential nature of the approximation used—the analyst can readily see by how much the American-style feature affects the value and hedging compared to similar twice-exercisable and European options.

The exponential estimate $\hat{P}$ is generally accurate for options of up to three years' maturity. It also applies, as does the Barone-Adesi and Whaley [1987] quadratic approximation, to assets paying continuous dividends. It cannot, however, in its simple form, cope with discrete dividends paid at arbitrary times up to the option maturity. For these options the technique would need to be extended along the lines of Bunch and Johnson's [1992] "maximum price" method.

In contrast to the Barone-Adesi and Whaley [1987] quadratic approximation, however, our general $\hat{P}$ prediction method makes no specific assumptions regarding the process followed by the underlying asset. Neither does it necessarily assume non-stochastic interest rates or volatility.

Our exponential method, like the Geske and Johnson [1984] and the Bunch and Johnson [1992] methods, is simply a method for predicting the American option price, given P_1 and P_2. Hence, it is potentially applicable to price American options under stochastic interest rates and/or stochastic volatility.[9]

Also, the general approach could be applied to other path-dependent and exotic options. Such extensions are hard to envisage in the case of the Barone-Adesi and Whaley approximation.

While similar in spirit to the method suggested previously by Bunch and Johnson [1992], our technique is quite different for the case of longer-dated American options. The underpricing effect of using the Bunch and Johnson [1992] two-point estimation, $2P_2 - P_1$, grows larger as the maturity of the option increases. This can be corrected either by a Geske and Johnson [1984] estimation with three or more points, or by using the Bunch and Johnson [1992] maximum method, but far more easily by using our "exponential" method.

APPENDIX

Comparative Statics of a Twice-Exercisable American Option

Consider an American option on a dividend-paying stock. Assume that the option is twice-exercisable at times t_1 and t_2 from today. Geske and Johnson [1984] show that the price of the option is given by

$$P_2 = \delta(Kw_2 - Sw_1) \tag{A-1}$$

where

$$w_1 = e^{-yt_1}N_1(-\delta d'_1) + e^{-yt_2}N_2(\delta d'_1, -\delta d''_1; -\rho) \tag{A-2}$$

$$w_2 = e^{-rt_1}N_1(-\delta d'_2) + e^{-rt_2}N_2(\delta d'_2, -\delta d''_2; -\rho) \tag{A-3}$$

with $\delta = 1$ for a put option and $\delta = -1$ for a call option, and where N_1 and N_2 are the standard cumulative univariate and bivariate normal distributions, respectively,[10] with parameters

$$d'_1 = \frac{\ln(S/S_1^*) + \left(r - y + \frac{1}{2}\sigma^2\right)t_1}{\sigma\sqrt{t_1}} \tag{A-4}$$

$$d''_1 = \frac{\ln(S/K) + \left(r - y + \frac{1}{2}\sigma^2\right)t_2}{\sigma\sqrt{t_2}} \tag{A-5}$$

$$d'_2 = d'_1 - \sigma\sqrt{t_1} \tag{A-6}$$

$$d''_2 = d''_1 - \sigma\sqrt{t_2} \tag{A-7}$$

$$\rho = \sqrt{t_1/t_2} \tag{A-8}$$

The critical stock price, S_1^*, is obtained by solving the relationship:[11]

$$\delta(K - S''_1) = P_1(S''_1, t_2 - t_1; K, r, y, \sigma) \tag{A-9}$$

where

$$P_1(S_1^*, t_2 - t_1; K, r, y, \sigma) = \delta[Ke^{-r(t_2-t_1)}N_1(-\delta d_2) - S_1^*e^{-y(t_2-t_1)}N_1(-\delta d_1)] \quad \text{(A-10)}$$

and

$$d_1 = \frac{\ln(S_1^*/K) + \left(r - y + \frac{1}{2}\sigma^2\right)(t_2 - t_1)}{\sigma\sqrt{(t_2 - t_1)}} \quad \text{(A-11)}$$

$$d_2 = d_1 - \sigma\sqrt{(t_2 - t_1)} \quad \text{(A-12)}$$

The hedge ratio of the twice-exercisable option, Δ_2, can be obtained as follows. From Geske and Johnson [1984], we have

$$\frac{\partial P_2(S, t_1, t_2; K, r, y, \sigma)}{\partial S} = -\delta w_1 \quad \text{(A-13)}$$

It follows from (A-2) that the hedge ratio for a twice-exercisable option is

$$\Delta_2 = \frac{\partial P_2}{\partial S} = -\delta[e^{-yt_1}N_1(-\delta d_1') + e^{-yt_2}N_2(\delta d_1', -\delta d_1''; -\rho)] \quad \text{(A-14)}$$

The convexity (gamma) of the twice-exercisable option is given by

$$\Gamma_2 = \frac{\partial \delta_2}{\partial S} = \frac{n_1(d_1')}{S\sigma\sqrt{t_1}}\left[e^{-yt_1} - e^{-yt_2}N_1\left(\frac{\delta d_1'' - \rho\delta d_1'}{\sqrt{1 - \rho^2}}\right)\right]$$
$$+ \frac{n_1(d_1'')}{S\sigma\sqrt{t_2}}e^{-yt_2}N_1\left(\frac{\delta d_1' - \rho\delta d_1''}{\sqrt{1 - \rho^2}}\right) \quad \text{(A-15)}$$

where $n_1(\cdot)$ is the univariate normal density function.

The other risk management parameters can be obtained in a similar fashion, although the derivations are somewhat involved.

REFERENCES

Abramowitz, M., and I. Stegun, eds. *Handbook of Mathematical Functions with Formulas, Graphs, and Mathematical Tables.* New York: Dover Publications, Inc., 1972, 9th Edition.

Amin, K. I., and J. N. Bodurtha, Jr. "Discrete-Time Valuation of American Options with Stochastic Interest Rates." *Review of Financial Studies,* forthcoming, 1994.

Barone-Adesi, G., and R. E. Whaley. "Efficient Analytic Approximation of American Option Values." *Journal of Finance,* 42 (June 1987), pp. 301–302.

Blomeyer, E. C. "An Analytic Approximation for the American Put Price for Options on Stocks with Dividends." *Journal of Financial and Quantitative Analysis,* 21 (June 1986), pp. 229–233.

Breen, R. "The Accelerated Binomial Option Pricing Model." *Journal of Financial and Quantitative Analysis,* 26 (June 1991), pp. 153–164.

Brennan, M. J., and E. S. Schwartz. "The Valuation of American Put Options." *Journal of Finance,* 32 (May 1977), pp. 449–462.

Bunch, D. S., and H. E. Johnson. "A Simple and Numerically Efficient Valuation Method for American Puts Using a Modified Geske-Johnson Approach." *Journal of Finance,* 47 (June 1992), pp. 809–816.

Courtadon, G. R. "A More Accurate Finite Difference Approximation for the Valuation of Options." *Journal of Financial and Quantitative Analysis,* 17 (December 1982), pp. 697–703.

Cox, J. C., S. A. Ross, and M. Rubinstein. "Option Pricing: A Simplified Approach." *Journal of Financial Economics,* 7 (September 1979), pp. 229–263.

Cox, J. C., and M. Rubinstein, *Options Markets.* Englewood Cliffs, NJ: Prentice-Hall, 1985.

Donnelly, T. G., "Algorithm 462: Bivariate Normal Distribution [S15]." *Communications of the Association for Computing Machinery,* 16 (1973), p. 638.

Drezner, Z. "Computation of the Bivariate Normal Integral." *Mathematics of Computations,* 32 (January 1978), pp. 277–279.

Geske, R. "The Valuation of Corporate Liabilities as Compound Options." *Journal of Financial and Quantitative Analysis,* 12 (November 1977), pp. 541–552.

Geske, R., and H. E. Johnson, "The American Put Valued Analytically." *Journal of Finance,* 39 (December 1984), pp. 1511–1542.

Hornbeck, R. *Numerical Methods.* Englewood Cliffs, NJ: Quantum Publishers, Inc./Prentice-Hall, Inc., 1975.

Johnson, H. E. "An Analytical Approximation of the American Put Price." *Journal of Financial and Quantitative Analysis,* 18 (June 1983), pp. 141–148.

Omberg, E. "A Note on the Convergence of the Binomial Pricing and Compound Option Models." *Journal of Finance,* 42 (June 1987), pp. 463–469.

Owen, D. B. "Tables for Computing Bivariate Normal Probabilities." *Annals of Mathematical Statistics,* 27 (1956), pp. 389–419.

Parkinson, M. "Option Pricing: The American Put." *Journal of Business,* 50 (January 1977), pp. 21–36.

ENDNOTES

1. See Geske and Johnson [1984, p. 1523, Equation A2]:

2. Blomeyer [1986] extends Johnson's method to dividend-paying stocks.

3. The computational time for the BW method is approximately $1/100$ of that required for the three-point GJ method (see Barone-Adesi and Whaley [1987, p. 312]). Hence it is similar in scale to that of the GJ two-point estimation method, reported by Bunch and Johnson [1992, p. 815], which is $1/60$ of that required for the GJ three-point method. Since our proposed method uses a similar amount of time to that of the GJ two-point method, we conclude that the computation times of our method and the BW method must be similar. In fact, both are virtually instantaneous on a PC-486 DX2 66MHz machine.

4. According to Bunch and Johnson [1992], methods requiring P_1, P_2, and P_3 are sixty times more expensive than those requiring only P_1 and P_2.

5. Note that in the case of deep-in-the-money options, Equation (9) can occasionally give $\hat{P}$ values outside the no-arbitrage boundaries. To recognize the possibility of immediate exercise, the estimate is changed in the applications to $\hat{P} = \max[P_2^2/P_1, \delta(K - S)]$, where K is the strike price, and S the stock price, with $\delta = 1$ for a put option, and $\delta = -1$ for a call option.

6. Vega is also referred to as kappa.

7. Note that the prices produced by our approximation, in the case of these examples, are similar to those obtained by Bunch and Johnson [1992] using a two-point GJ approximation. For longer-

dated options, however, Equation (9) produces quite different predicted values. If, for example, P_1 = 1, P_2 = 1.5, Equation (9) gives $\hat{P}$ = 2.25, while the two-point GJ method gives $\hat{P}$ = 2.00.

8. A FOREX option can be valued as an option on an asset that pays a continuous dividend equal to the foreign interest rate. A futures option is akin to an option on an asset that pays a dividend equal to its risk-free rate of interest; that is, where the cost of carry is zero.

9. In these cases the possible savings in computational time are very large indeed. For an idea of the computational time in the case of stochastic interest rates, see, for example, Amin and Bodurtha [1994].

10. The univariate normal distribution function used in the simulations is based on the polynomial approximation in Abramowitz and Stegun [1972, Equation 26.2.17, p. 932]. Given the underlying assumption that stock prices follow a geometric Brownian motion, the correlation coefficient, ρ, for the twice-exercisable option is always $\sqrt{t_1/t_2}$ (see Geske [1977, p. 584]). The algorithm used in the simulations for computing the cumulative bivariate normal probabilities is based on the FOR-TRAN implementation of Owen [1956] by Donnelly [1973], with the "central error function" re-placed with that suggested in Abramowitz and Stegun [1972]. Alternative algorithms are the IMSL's MDBNOR subroutine, which uses the Owen [1956] polynomial approximation, and Drezner [1978].

11. The critical stock price is computed by a Newton-Raphson numerical method (see Hornbeck [1975], p. 67]) with the epsilon error for finding the root set at 0.0001, and a starting (seeding) stock price of $S - \sigma\sqrt{t_1/t_2}$. Convergence is quite quick, usually between two to six iterations.

PART THREE

Currency Futures Options Pricing Models

8

The Pricing of Commodity Contracts

FISCHER BLACK

INTRODUCTION

The market for contracts related to commodities is not widely understood. Futures contracts and forward contracts are often thought to be identical, and many people don't know about the existence of commodity options. One of the aims of this paper is to clarify the meaning of each of these contracts.[1]

The spot price of a commodity is the price at which it can be bought or sold for immediate delivery. We will write p for the spot price, or $p(t)$ for the spot price at time t.

The spot price of an agricultural commodity tends to have a seasonal pattern: it is high just before a harvest, and low just after a harvest. The spot price of a commodity such as gold, however, fluctuates more randomly.

Predictable patterns in the movement of the spot price do not generally imply profit opportunities. The spot price can rise steadily at any rate lower than the storage cost for the commodity (including interest) without giving rise to a profit opportunity for those with empty storage facilities. The spot price can fall during a harvest period without giving rise to a profit opportunity for growers, so long as it is costly to accelerate the harvest.

The futures price of a commodity is the price at which one can agree to buy or sell it at a given time in the future without putting up any money now.

The author is grateful for comments on earlier drafts by Michael Jensen, Myron Scholes, Edward Thorp, and Joseph Williams. This work was supported in part by the Center for Research in Security Prices (sponsored by Merrill Lynch, Pierce, Fenner & Smith Inc.) at the Graduate School of Business, University of Chicago.

Reprinted with permission from the *Journal of Financial Economics;* Vol. 3; Fischer Black; 1976; Elsevier Science SA, P.O. Box 564, 1001 Lausanne, Switzerland.

We will write x for the futures price, or $x(t, t^*)$ for the futures price at time t for a transaction that will occur at time t^*.

For example, suppose that it is possible today to enter into a contract to buy gold six months from now at $160 an ounce, without either party to the contract being compensated by the other. Both parties may put up collateral to guarantee their ability to fulfill the contract, but if the futures price remains at $160 an ounce for the next six months, the collateral will not be touched. If the contract is left unchanged for six months, then the gold and the money will change hands at that time. In this situation, we say that the six month futures price of gold is $160 an ounce.

The futures price is very much like the odds on a sports bet. If the odds on a particular baseball game between Boston and Chicago are 2:1 in favor of Boston, and if we ignore the bookie's profit, then a person who bets on Chicago wins $2 or loses $1. No money changes hands until after the game. The odds adjust to balance the demand for bets on Chicago and the demand for bets on Boston. At 2:1, balance occurs if twice as many bets are placed on Boston as on Chicago.

Similarly, the futures price adjusts to balance demand to buy the commodity in the future with demand to sell the commodity in the future. Whenever a contract is opened, there is someone on each side. The person who agrees to buy is long the commodity, and the person who agrees to sell is short. This means that when we add up all positions in contracts of this kind, and count short positions as negative, we always come out with zero. The total long interest in commodity contracts of any type must equal the total short interest.

When the two times that specify a futures price are equal, the futures price must equal the spot price,

$$x(t, t) \equiv p(t). \tag{1}$$

Expression (1) holds for all times t. For example, it says that the May futures price will be equal to the May spot price in May, and the September futures price will be equal to the September spot price in September.

Now let us define the three kinds of commodity contracts: forward contracts, futures contracts, and option contracts. Roughly speaking, a forward contract is a contract to buy or sell at a price that stays fixed for the life of the contract; a futures contract is settled every day and rewritten at the new futures price; and an option contract can be exercised by the holder when it matures, if it has not been closed out earlier.

We will write v for the value of a forward contract, u for the value of a futures contract, and w for the value of an option contract. Each of these values will depend on the current futures price $x(t, t^*)$ with the same transaction time t^* as the contract, and on the current time t, as well as on other variables. So we will write $v(x, t)$, $u(x, t)$ and $w(x, t)$. The value of the short side of any contract will be just the negative of the value of the long side. So we will treat v, u, and w as the values of a forward contract to buy, a long futures contract, and an option to buy.

The value of a forward contract depends also on the price c at which the commodity will be bought, and the time t^* at which the transaction will take place. We will sometimes write $v(x, t, c, t^*)$ for the value of a long forward contract. From the discussion above, we know that the futures price is that price at which a forward contract has a current value of zero. We can write this condition as

$$v(x, t, x, t^*) \equiv 0. \tag{2}$$

In effect, eq. (2) says that the value of a forward contract when it is initiated is always zero. When it is initiated, the contract price c is always equal to the current futures price $x(t, t^*)$.

Increasing the futures price increases the value of a long forward contract, and decreasing the futures price decreases the value of the contract. Thus we have

$$v(x, t, c, t^*) > 0, \quad x > c,$$
$$\tag{3}$$
$$v(x, t, c, t^*) < 0, \quad x < c.$$

The value of a forward contract may be either positive or negative.

When the time comes for the transaction to take place, the value of the forward contract will be equal to the spot price minus the contract price. But by eq. (1), the futures price $x(t, t^*)$ will be equal to the spot price at that time. Thus the value of the forward contract will be the futures price minus the spot price,

$$v(x, t^*, c, t^*) = x - c. \tag{4}$$

Later we will use equation (4) as the main boundary condition for a differential equation describing the value of a forward contract.

The difference between a futures contract and a forward contract is that the futures contract is rewritten every day with a new contract price equal to the corresponding futures price. A futures contract is like a series of forward contracts. Each day, yesterday's contract is settled, and today's contract is written with a contract price equal to the futures price with the same maturity as the futures contract.

Eq. (2) shows that the value of a forward contract with a contract price equal to the futures price is zero. Thus the value of a futures contract is reset to zero every day. If the investor has made money, he will be given his gains immediately. If he has lost money, he will have to pay his losses immediately. Thus we have

$$u(x, t) \equiv 0. \tag{5}$$

Technically, eq. (5) applies only to the end of the day, after the futures contract has been rewritten. During the day, the futures contract may have a positive or negative value, and its value will be equal to the value of the corresponding forward contract.

Note that the futures price and the value of a futures contract are not at all the same thing. The futures price refers to a transaction at times t^* and is never zero. The value of a futures contract refers to time t and is always zero (at the end of the day).

In the organized U.S. futures markets, both parties to a futures contract must post collateral with a broker. This helps to ensure that the losing party each day will have funds available to pay the winning party. The amount of collateral required varies from broker to broker.

The form in which the collateral can be posted also varies from broker to broker. Most brokers allow the collateral to take the form of Treasury Bills or marginable securities if the amount exceeds a certain minimum. The brokers encourage cash collateral, however, because they earn the interest on customers' cash balances.

The value of a futures customer's account with a broker is entirely the value of his collateral (at the end of the day). The value of his futures contracts is zero. The value of the collateral posted to ensure performance of a futures contract is not the value of the contract.

As futures contracts are settled each day, the value of each customer's collateral is adjusted. When the futures price goes up, those with long positions have money added to their collateral, and those with short positions have money taken away from their collateral. If a customer at any time has more collateral than his broker requires, he may withdraw the excess. If he has less than his broker requires, he will have to put up additional collateral immediately.

Commodity options have a bad image in the U.S., because they were recently used to defraud investors of many millions of dollars. There are no organized commodity options markets in this country. In the U.K., however, commodity options have a long and relatively respectable history.

A commodity option is an option to buy a fixed quantity of a specified commodity at a fixed time in the future and at a specified price. It differs from a security option in that it can't be exercised before the fixed future date. Thus it is a 'European option' rather than an 'American option'.

A commodity option differs from a forward contract because the holder of the option can choose whether or not he wants to buy the commodity at the specified price. With a forward contract, he has no choice: he must buy it, even if the spot price at the time of the transaction is lower than the price he pays.

At maturity, the value of a commodity option is the spot price minus the contract price, if that is positive, or zero. Writing c^* for the exercise price of the option, and noting that the futures price equals the spot price at maturity, we have

$$
\begin{aligned}
w(x, t^*) &= x - c^*, \quad x \geqq c^*, \\
&= 0, \qquad\quad x < c^*.
\end{aligned} \tag{6}
$$

Expression (6) looks like the expression for the value of a security option at maturity as a function of the security price.

THE BEHAVIOR OF THE FUTURES PRICE

Changes in the futures price for a given commodity at a given maturity give rise to gains and losses for investors with long or short positions in the corresponding futures contracts. An investor with a position in the futures market is bearing risk even though the value of his position at the end of each day is zero. His position may also have a positive or negative expected dollar return, even though his investment in the position is zero.

Since his investment is zero, it is not possible to talk about the percentage or fractional return on the investor's position in the futures market. Both his risk and his expected return must be defined in dollar terms.

In deriving expressions for the behavior of the futures price, we will assume that taxes are zero. However, tax factors will generally affect the behavior of the futures price. There are two peculiarities in the tax laws that make them important.

First, the IRS assumes that a gain or loss on a futures contract is realized only when the contract is closed out. The IRS does not recognize, for tax purposes, the fact that a futures contract is effectively settled and rewritten every day. This makes possible strategies for deferring the taxation of capital gains. For example, the investor can open a number of different contracts, both long and short. The contracts that develop losses are closed out early, and are replaced with different contracts so that the long and short positions stay balanced. The contracts that develop gains are allowed to run unrealized into the next tax year. In the next year, the process can be repeated. Whether this process is likely to be profitable depends on the special factors affecting each investor, including the size of the transaction costs he pays.

Second, the IRS treats a gain or loss on a long futures position that is closed out more than six months after it is opened as a long-term capital gain or loss, while it treats a gain or loss on a short futures position as a short-term capital gain or loss no matter how long the position is left open. Thus if the investor opens both long and short contracts, and if he realizes losses on the short contracts and gains on the long contracts, he can convert short-term gains (from other transactions) into long-term gains. Again, whether this makes sense for a particular investor will depend on his transaction costs and other factors.

However, we will assume that both taxes and transaction costs are zero. We will further assume that the capital asset pricing model applies at each instant of time.[2] This means that investors will be compensated only for bearing risk that cannot be diversified away. If the risk in a futures contract is independent of the risk of changes in value of all assets taken together, then investors will not have to be paid for taking that risk. In effect, they don't have to take the risk because they can diversify it-away.

The usual capital asset pricing formula is

$$E(\tilde{R}_i) - R = \beta_i[E(\tilde{R}_m) - R]. \tag{7}$$

In this expression, $\tilde{R}_i$ is the return on asset i, expressed as a fraction of its initial value; R is the return on short-term interest-bearing securities; and $\tilde{R}_m$ is the return on the market portfolio of all assets taken together. The coefficient β_i is a measure of the extent to which the risk of asset i cannot be diversified away. It is defined by

$$\beta_i = \text{cov}(\tilde{R}_i, \tilde{R}_m)/\text{var}(\tilde{R}_m). \tag{8}$$

The market portfolio referred to above includes corporate securities, personal assets such as real estate, and assets held by non-corporate businesses. To the extent that stocks of commodities are held by corporations, they are implicitly included in the market portfolio. To the extent that they are held by individuals and non-corporate businesses, they are explicitly included in the market portfolio. This market portfolio cannot be observed, of course. It is a theoretical construct.

Commodity contracts, however, are not included in the market portfolio. Commodity contracts are pure bets, in that there is a short position for every long position. So when we are taking all assets together, futures contracts, forward contracts, and commodity options all net out to zero.

Eq. (7) cannot be applied directly to a futures contract, because the initial value of the contract is zero. So we will rewrite the equation so that it applies to dollar returns rather than percentage returns.

Let us assume that asset i has no dividends or other distributions over the period. Then its fractional return is its end-of-period price minus its start-of-period price, divided by its start-of-period price. Writing P_{i0} for the start-of-period price of asset i, writing $\tilde{P}_{i1}$ for its end-of-period price, and substituting from eq. (8), we can rewrite eq. (7) as

$$E\{(\tilde{P}_{i1} - P_{i0})/P_{i0}\} - R = [\text{cov}\{(\tilde{P}_{i1} - P_{i0})/P_{i0}, \tilde{R}_m\}/\text{var}(\tilde{R}_m)][E(\tilde{R}_m) - R]. \tag{9}$$

Multiplying through by P_{i0}, we get an expression for the expected dollar return on an asset,

$$E(\tilde{P}_{i1} - P_{i0}) - RP_{i0} = [\text{cov}(\tilde{P}_{i1} - P_{i0}, \tilde{R}_m)/\text{var}(\tilde{R}_m)][E(\tilde{R}_m) - R]. \tag{10}$$

The start-of-period value of a futures contract is zero, so we set P_{i0} equal to zero. The end-of-period value of a futures contract, before the contract is re-written and its value set to zero, is the change in the futures price over the period. In practice, commodity exchanges set daily limits which constrain the reported change in the futures price and the daily gains and losses of traders. We will assume that these limits do not exist. So we set $\tilde{P}_{i1}$ equal to $\Delta\tilde{P}$, the change in the futures price over the period,

$$E(\Delta\tilde{P}) = [\text{cov}(\Delta\tilde{P}, \tilde{R}_m)/\text{var}(\tilde{R}_m)][E(\tilde{R}_m) - R]. \tag{11}$$

In effect, we have applied expression (10) to a futures contract, and have come up with expression (11), which refers to the change in the futures price. For the rest of this section, we can forget about futures contracts and work only with the futures price.

Writing β^* for the first factor on the right-hand side of eq. (11), we have

$$E(\Delta\tilde{P}) = \beta^*[E(\tilde{R}_m) - R]. \tag{12}$$

Expression (12) says that the expected change in the futures price is proportional to the 'dollar beta' of the futures price. If the covariance of the change in the futures price with the return on the market portfolio is zero, then the expected change in the futures price will be zero,[3]

$$E(\Delta\tilde{P}) = 0, \quad \text{when} \quad \text{cov}(\Delta\tilde{P}, \tilde{R}_m) = 0. \tag{13}$$

Expressions (12) and (13) say that the expected change in the futures price can be positive, zero, or negative. It would be very surprising if the β^* of a futures price were exactly zero, but it may be approximately zero for many commodities. For these commodities, neither those with long futures positions nor those with short futures positions have significantly positive expected dollar returns.

FUTURES PRICES AND SPOT PRICES

When eq. (13) holds at all points in time, the expected change in the futures price will always be zero. This means that the expected futures price at any time t' in the future, where t' is between the current time t and the transaction time t^*, will be equal to the current futures price. The mean of the distribution of possible futures prices at time t' will be the current futures price.[4]

But the futures price at time t^* is the spot price at time t^*, from expression (1). So the mean of the distribution of possible spot prices at time t^* will be the current futures price, when eq. (13) always holds.

Even when (13) doesn't hold, we may still be able to use eq. (12) to estimate the mean of the distribution of possible spot prices at time t^*. To use (12), though, we need to know β^* at each point in time between t and t^*, and we need to know $E(\tilde{R}_m) - R$.

A farmer may not want to know the mean of the distribution of possible spot prices at time t^*. He may be interested in the discounted value of the distribution of possible spot prices. In fact, it seems plausible that he can make his investment decisions as if β^* were zero, even if it is not zero. He can assume that the β^* is zero, and that the futures price is the expected spot price.

To see why this is so, note that he can hedge his investments by taking a short position in the futures market. By taking the right position in the future market, he can make the β of his overall position zero. Assuming that the farmer is not concerned about risk that can be diversified away, he should make the same investment decisions whether or not he actually takes offsetting positions in the futures market.

In fact, futures prices provide a wealth of valuable information for those who produce, store, and use commodities. Looking at futures prices for various transaction months, participants in this market can decide on the best times to plant, harvest, buy for storage, sell from storage, or process the commodity. A change in a futures price at time t is related to changes in the anticipated distribution of spot prices at time t^*. It is not directly related to changes in the spot price at time t. In practice, however, changes in spot prices and changes in futures prices will often be highly correlated.

Both spot prices and futures prices are affected by general shifts in the cost of producing the commodity, and by general shifts in the demand for the commodity. These are probably the most important factors affecting commodity prices. But an event like the arrival of a prime producing season for the commodity will cause the spot price to fall, without having any predictable effect on the futures price.

Changes in commodity prices are also affected by such factors as the interest rate, the cost of storing the commodity, and the β of the commodity itself.[5] These factors may affect both the spot price and the futures price, but in different ways.

Commodity holdings are assets that form part of investors' portfolios, either directly or indirectly. The returns on such assets must be defined to include such things as the saving to a user of commodities from not running out in the middle of a production run, or the benefit to anyone storing the commodity of having stocks on hand when there is an unusual surge in demand. The returns on commodity holdings must be defined net of all storage costs, including deterioration, theft, and insurance premiums. When the returns on commodity holdings are defined in this way, they should obey the capital asset pricing model, as expressed by eq. (7), like any other asset. If the β of the commodity is zero, as given in eq. (7), then we would expect the β^* of a futures contract to be approximately zero too, as given in eq. (12). And vice versa.

The notion that commodity holdings are priced like other assets means that investors who own commodities are able to diversify away that part of the risk that can be diversified away. One way this can happen is through futures markets: those who own commodities can take short positions, and those who hold diversified portfolios of assets can include long positions in commodity contracts.

But there are other ways that the risk in commodity holdings can be largely diversified away. The most common way for risk to be spread is through a corporation. The risk of a corporation's business or assets is passed on to the holders of the corporation's liabilities, especially its stockholders. The stockholders have, or could have, well diversified portfolios of which this stock is only a small part.

Thus if stocks of a commodity are held by a corporation, there will normally be no need for the risk to be spread through the futures market. (There are special cases, however, such as where the corporation has lots of debt outstanding and the lenders insist that the commodity risk be hedged through the futures market.) There are corporations at every stage in a commodity's life cycle: production, distribution, and processing. Even agricultural commodities are generally produced by corporations these days, though the stock may be closely held. Any of these corporate entities can take title to the stocks of commodities, no matter where they are located, and thus spread the risk to those who are in the best position to bear it. For example, canners of tomatoes often buy a farmer's crop before the vines are planted. They may even supply the vines.

This means that a futures market does not have a unique role in the allocation of risk. Corporations in the commodity business play the same role. Which kind of market is best for this role depends on the specifics of such things as transaction costs and taxes in each individual case. It seems clear that corporations do a better job for most commodities, because organized futures markets don't even exist for most commodities. Where they do exist, most of the risk is still transferred through corporations rather than through futures markets.

Thus there is no reason to believe that the existence of a futures market has any predictable effect on the path of the spot price over time. It is primarily the storage of a commodity that reduces fluctuations in its price over time. Storage will occur whether or not there is any way of transferring risk. If there were no way to transfer risk, the price of a seasonal commodity might be somewhat higher before the prime production periods than it is now. But since there are good ways to transfer risk without using the futures market, even this benefit of futures markets is minimal.

I believe that futures markets exist because in some situations they provide an inexpensive way to transfer risk, and because many people both in the business and out like to gamble on commodity prices. Neither of these counts as a major benefit to society. The big benefit from futures markets is the side effect: the fact that participants in the futures markets can make production, storage, and processing decisions by looking at the pattern of futures prices, even if they don't take positions in that market.

This, of course, assumes that futures markets are efficient. It assumes that futures prices incorporate all available information about the future spot price of a commodity. It assumes that investors act quickly on any information they receive, so that the price reacts quickly to the arrival of the information. So quickly that individual traders find it very difficult to make money consistently by trading on information.

THE PRICING OF FORWARD CONTRACTS AND COMMODITY OPTIONS

We have already discussed the pricing of futures contracts and the behavior of futures prices. In order to derive formulas for the other kinds of commodity contracts, we must make a few more assumptions.

First, let us assume that the fractional change in the futures price over any interval is distributed log-normally, with a known variance rate s^2. The derivations would go through with little change if we assumed that the variance rate is a known function of the time between t and t^*, but we will assume that the variance rate is constant.

Second, let us assume that all of the parameters of the capital asset pricing model, including the expected return on the market, the variance of the return on the market, and the short-term interest rate, are constant through time.

Third, let us continue to assume that taxes and transaction costs are zero.

Under these assumptions, it makes sense to write the value of a commodity contract only as a function of the corresponding futures price and time. If we did not assume the parameters of the capital asset pricing model were constant, then the value of a commodity contract might also depend on those parameters. Implicitly, of course, the value of the contract still depends on the transaction price and the transaction time.

Now let us use the same procedure that led to the formula for an option on a security.[6] We can create a riskless hedge by taking a long position in the option and a short position in the futures contract with the same transaction date. Since the value of a futures contract is always zero, the equity in this position is just the value of the option.

The size of the short position in the futures contract that makes the combined position riskless is the derivative of $w(x, t)$ with respect to x, which we will write w_1. Thus the change in the value of the hedged position over the time interval Δt is

$$\Delta w - w_1 \Delta x. \tag{14}$$

Expanding Δw, and noting that the return on the hedge must be at the instantaneous riskless rate r, we have the differential equation[7]

$$w_2 = rw - \frac{1}{2} s^2 x^2 w_{11}. \tag{15}$$

Note that this is like the differential equation for an option on a security, but with one term missing. The term is missing because the value of a futures contract is zero, while the value of a security is positive.

The main boundary condition for this equation is expression (6).[8] Using standard methods to solve eqs. (15) and (6), we obtain the following formula for the value of a commodity option:

$$w(x, t) = e^{r(t-t^*)}[xN(d_1) - c^*N(d_2)],$$

$$d_1 = \left[\ln \frac{x}{c^*} + \frac{s^2}{2}(t^* - t)\right]\bigg/ s\sqrt{(t^* - t)}, \tag{16}$$

$$d_2 = \left[\ln \frac{x}{c^*} - \frac{s^2}{2}(t^* - t)\right]\bigg/ s\sqrt{(t^* - t)}.$$

This formula can be obtained from the original option formula by substituting $xe^{r(t-t^*)}$ for x everywhere in the original formula.[9] It is the same as the value of an option on a security that pays a continuous dividend at a rate equal to the stock price times the interest rate, when the option can only be exercised at maturity.[10] Again, this happens because the investment in a futures contract is zero, so an interest rate factor drops out of the formula.

Eq. (16) applies to a 'European' commodity option, that can only be exercised at maturity. If the commodity option can be exercised before maturity, the problem of finding its value becomes much more complex.[11] Among other things, its value will depend on the spot price and on futures prices with various transaction dates before the option expires.

Eq. (16) also assumes that taxes are zero. But if commodity options are taxed like security options, then there will be substantial tax benefits for high tax bracket investors who write commodity options.[12] These benefits may be passed on in part or in full to buyers of commodity options in the form of lower prices. So taxes may reduce the values of commodity options.

Compared with the formula for a commodity option, the formula for the value of a forward contract is very simple. The differential equation it must satisfy is the same. Substituting $v(x, t)$ for $w(x, t)$ in eq. (15), we have

$$v_2 = rv - \frac{1}{2} s^2 x^2 v_{11}.$$

(17)

The main boundary condition is eq. (4), which we can rewrite as

$$v(x, t^*) = x - c.$$

(18)

The solution to (17) and (18) plus the implicit boundary conditions is

$$v(x, t) = (x - c)e^{r(t - r^*)}.$$

(19)

Expression (19) says that the value of a forward contract is the difference between the futures price and the forward contract price, discounted to the present at the short-term interest rate. It is independent of any measure of risk. It does not depend on the variance rate of the fractional change in the futures price or on the covariance rate between the change in the futures price and the return on the market.

REFERENCES

Black, F., 1975, Fact and fantasy in the use of options, Financial Analysts Journal 31, July/Aug.

Black, F. and M. Scholes, 1973, The pricing of options and corporate liabilities, Journal of Political Economy 81, May/June, 637–654.

Brennan, M. J., 1958, The supply of storage, American Economic Review 48, March, 50–72.

Chicago Board of Trade, 1973, Commodity trading manual (Board of Trade of the City of Chicago, Chicago, Ill.)

Cootner, P. H., 1960a, Returns to speculators: Telser versus Keynes, Journal of Political Economy 68, Aug., 396–404.

Cootner, P. H., 1960b, Rejoinder, Journal of Political Economy 68, Aug., 415–418.

Dusak, K., 1973, Futures trading and investor returns: An investigation of commodity market risk premiums, Journal of Political Economy 81, Nov./Dec., 1387–1406.

Jensen, M. C., 1972, Capital markets: Theory and evidence, Bell Journal of Economics and Management Science 3, Autumn, 357–398.

Merton, R. C., 1973, The theory of rational option pricing, Bell Journal of Economics and Management Science 4, Spring, 141–183.

Telser, L., 1958, Futures trading and the storage of cotton and wheat, Journal of Political Economy 66, June, 233–255.

Telser, L., 1960, Returns to speculators: Telser versus Keynes, Reply, Journal of Political Economy 67, Aug., 404–415.

Thorp, E., 1973, Extensions of the Black-Scholes options model, Bulletin of the International Statistical Institute, Proceedings of the 39th Session, 522–529.

ENDNOTES

1. For an introduction to commodity markets, see Chicago Board of Trade (1973).

2. For an introduction to the capital asset pricing model, see Jensen (1972). The behavior of futures prices in a model of capital market equilibrium was first discussed by Dusak (1973).

3. In the data she analyzed on wheat, corn, and soybean futures, Dusak (1973) found co-variances that were close to zero.

4. The question of the relation between the futures price and the expected spot price is discussed under somewhat different assumptions by Cootner (1960a, 1960b) and Telser (1960).

5. Some of the factors affecting changes in the spot price are discussed by Brennan (1958) and Telser (1958).

6. The original option formula was derived by Black and Scholes (1973). Further results were obtained by Merton (1973).

7. For the details of this expansion, see Black and Scholes (1973, p. 642 or p. 646).

8. Another boundary condition and a regularity condition are needed to make the solution to (15) and (6) unique. The boundary condition is $w(0, t) = 0$. The need for these additional conditions was not noted in Black and Scholes (1973).

9. Thorp (1973) obtains the same formula for a similar problem, related to the value of a security option when an investor who sells the underlying stock short does not receive interest on the proceeds of the short sale.

10. Merton (1973) discusses the valuation of options on dividend-paying securities. The formula he obtains (f. 62) should be eq. (16), but he forgets to substitute $xe^{r(t-t')}$ for x in d_1 and d_2.

11. See Merton (1973) for a discussion of some of the complexities in finding a value for an option that can be exercised early.

12. For a discussion of tax factors in the pricing of options, see Black (1975).

9

On Valuing American Futures Options

ROBERT E. WHALEY

O ptions on futures contracts were introduced in the U.S. only four years ago.[1] Now more than 20 different futures option contracts are actively traded on every major futures exchange. The Chicago Mercantile Exchange (CME) trades options based on the S&P 500, the West German mark, the British pound, the Swiss franc, Eurodollars, live cattle, and live hogs. The Chicago Board of Trade (CBT) has U.S. Treasury bond, U.S. Treasury note, silver, corn and soybean futures options. The New York Futures Exchange (NYFE) has NYSE composite index equity futures options, and the Commodity Exchange (CMX) has gold and silver futures options. Even the smaller exchanges, such as the Kansas City Board of Trade (KC), the Minneapolis Grain Exchange (MPLS), the MidAmerica Commodity Exchange (MCE), the New York Cotton Exchange (CTN), and the Coffee, Sugar, and Cocoa Exchange (CSCE) now maintain active secondary markets in futures option contracts.

The alacrity with which these new contingent claims have captured the attention of financial analysts and portfolio managers argues for a review and extension of the fundamentals of futures option valuation. In 1976, Black provided a framework for analyzing commodity futures options.[2] His work was explicitly directed at pricing "European" futures options—that is, options that may be exercised only at expiration. The "American" options currently trading, however, may be exercised at any time up to and including the expiration day.

Although much has been written about futures options since the first contract applications were placed before the Commodity Futures Trading Commission (CFTC) in the early 1980s, most of the work has deferred to Black's European futures option pricing results.[3] Not until very recently has substantive

This research was supported by the Institute for Financial Research, University of Alberta. Comments and suggestions by Warren Bailey, Bruce Cooil, Theodore E. Day, Thomas S.Y. Ho, and H.R. Stoll on an earlier version of this paper are gratefully acknowledged.

progress been made in understanding the value of the early exercise privilege of American futures options and in providing more computationally efficient methods for pricing American options.[4]

This article clarifies the principles and intuition underlying European futures option pricing, extends these principles and intuition to American futures option pricing, and provides a simple and computationally efficient method for pricing American futures options. Most of the published work on futures option pricing actually represents work on forward option pricing. While the distinction between a forward and a futures contract is not particularly important in pricing European options, it is of critical importance in pricing their American counterparts. We thus begin with a short discussion of the difference between forward and futures contracts.

FUTURES VS. FORWARD CONTRACTS

Before considering futures option pricing relations, it is useful to distinguish between a futures contract and a forward contract. A *forward contract* is an agreement to deliver the underlying asset at a future time T at a price specified today. Payment for the asset takes place at time T, and no intermediate payments are made. A *futures contract* is similar to a forward contract, except that intermediate cash payments (receipts) are made as losses (profits) are incurred when the futures position is marked to market each day during the contract's life. These profits and losses accumulate interest during the contract's life so that, in general, the terminal value of a long futures contract position differs from that of a long forward contract position.

Although the terminal values of the two contract positions differ, the price of a forward contract, f, will equal the price of a futures contract, F, if the gains and losses on the futures position accumulate at a known riskless rate of interest.[5] To see this, consider two portfolios in a market that affords no costless arbitrage opportunities. The first portfolio consists of a long position of fe^{-rT} riskless bonds and a long forward contract.[6] The second consists of a long position of Fe^{-rT} riskless bonds and a long "rollover" futures position, where $e^{-r(T-1)}$ futures contracts are purchased the first day, $e^{-r(T-2)}$ the second day, $e^{-r(T-3)}$ the third day, and so on.[7] The number of futures contracts purchased increases by a factor of e^r each day, so that on the last day exactly one long futures contract is held.[8]

As Table 9-1 shows, the value of each portfolio position at time T equals the underlying commodity price, S_T. This being the case, the initial values of the portfolios must also be the same; otherwise arbitrageurs would step in to earn costless profits. The price of the forward contract must equal the price of the futures contract.

Futures Options Vs. Stock Options

A *futures option contract* is similar to an option on a stock, in the sense that it provides its holder with the right to buy or sell the underlying security at the

TABLE 9-1   Transactions for Futures-Forward Contract Price Equivalence

	Foward Portfolio		Futures Portfolio	
Position	Initial Value	Terminal Value	Initial Value	Terminal Value
Long Bonds	fe^{-rT}	f	Fe^{-rT}	F
Long Forward Contract	0	$S_T - f$		
Long "Rollover" Futures Position			0	$S_T - F$
Net Value	fe^{-rT}	S_T	Fe^{-rT}	S_T

exercise price of the option. Unlike a stock option, however, a futures option does not involve a cash exchange in the amount of the exercise price when the futures option is exercised.

Upon exercise, a futures option holder merely acquires a long or short futures position with a futures price equal to the exercise price of the option. When the futures contract is marked to market at the close of the day's trading, the option holder is free to withdraw in cash an amount equal to the futures price less the exercise price in the case of a call or the exercise price less the futures price in the case of a put. Exercising a futures option is thus tantamount to receiving in cash the exercisable value of the option.

PUT-CALL PARITY

In stock option markets, arbitrageurs and floor traders hold the prices of the put, the call and the underlying stock in a certain configuration by engaging in conversion and reverse conversion trading strategies.[9] The essential feature of these strategies is the recognition that the payoff contingencies posed by a long call position may be duplicated by a portfolio consisting of a long stock, a long put and some riskless borrowing. Therefore, if the price of the call exceeds the sum of the prices of the portfolio's securities, the arbitrageur can earn a costless profit by selling the call and buying the portfolio (i.e., by enacting a conversion). Conversely, if the price of the call is less than the sum of the prices of the portfolio's securities, a costless profit can be earned by buying the call and selling the portfolio (i.e., enacting a reverse conversion).[10]

In futures option markets, the same principles apply. Arbitrageurs who continually search for and take advantage of costless profit opportunities force particular configurations of futures option prices. These configurations are expressed in the form of pricing relations that have come to be known as "put-call parity theorems."

In addition to the assumption that the marketplace is free of costless arbitrage opportunities, this analysis requires that markets are frictionless (i.e., there are no transaction or similar costs) and that individuals can borrow or lend risklessly at a continuously compounded rate of interest rate, r. Neither of these assumptions is particularly restrictive; arbitrageurs pay minimal transaction costs, and the riskless rate is fairly constant over short intervals of time.

European Futures Options

The put-call parity relation for European futures options is as follows:[11]

$$C(F, T; X) - p(F, T; X) = (F - F)e^{-rT}, \tag{1}$$

where $c(f, T; X)$ and $p(f, T; X)$ are the prices of a European call and put, respectively, with exercise price X and time to expiration T.

This relation is driven by a conversion arbitrage portfolio consisting of (a) a long position in the futures contract, (b) a long position in the European put, (c) a short position in the call, and (d) a long position of $(F - X)e^{-rT}$ bonds. The long futures position is identical to that used above. On the first day, $e^{-r(T-1)}$ contracts are purchased, on the second $e^{-r(T-2)}$, $e^{-r(T-3)}$ on the third, and so on. Table 9-2 gives the initial and terminal values of this portfolio. Because the terminal value of the portfolio is certain to be zero, the initial value must also equal zero, and therefore Equation (1) must hold.

Note that this conversion arbitrage strategy calls for daily revision of the futures position. Earlier researchers using a static "buy-and-hold" futures contract position erroneously treated the futures contract as a forward contract in their proofs of European put-call parity and realized the correct pricing relation only because the options were European in nature.[12] If this approach were used in deriving American put-call parity, the resulting relation would be misspecified.

American Futures Options

The put-call parity relation for American futures options, like that for American spot options, is represented by two inequalities, as follows:[13]

TABLE 9-2 Arbitrage Transactions for Put-Call Parity of European Futures Options

Position	Initial Value	Terminal Value $F_T < X$	Terminal Value $F_T \geq X$
Long "Rollover" Futures	0	$F_T - F$	$F_T - F$
Long Put Option	$-p(F, T; X)$	$X - F_T$	0
Short Call Option	$+c(F, T; X)$	0	$-(F_T - X)$
Long $(F - X)e^{-rT}$ Bonds	$-(F - X)e^{-rT}$	$F - X$	$F - X$
Net Value	$c(F, T; X) - p(F, T; X)$ $-(F - X)e^{-rT}$	0	0

$$Fe^{-rT} - X \le C(F, T; X) - P(F, T; X) \le F - Xe^{-rT}, \tag{2}$$

where $C(F, T; X)$ and $P(F, T; X)$ are the prices of an American call and put, respectively, with exercise price X and time to expiration T.

This relation is driven by two separate sets of arbitrage transactions. The left-hand-side of Equation (2) requires a reverse conversion arbitrage portfolio consisting of (a) a long position in the call, (b) a short position in the put, (c) a short position in the futures, and (d) a short position of $Fe^{-rT} - X$ bonds. Here, the short futures position is just the opposite of the rollover strategy applied to derive European put-call parity. That is, $e^{-r(T-1)}$ futures contracts are sold the first day, $e^{-r(T-1)}$ futures contracts are sold the first day, $e^{-r(T-2)}$ the second day $e^{-r(T-3)}$ the third day, and so on. Table 9-3 presents the initial, intermediate, and terminal values of the overall portfolio.

As Table 9-3 shows, if the put option is not exercised early, the terminal value of the portfolio is certain to be positive. The only uncertainty faced by the portfolio holder rests with the short position in the put, because it may be exercised against the portfolio holder at any time during the option's life. If the put option is exercised early, however, the payment of the exercise price is more than covered by riskless borrowing, and the assumed long futures position is less than fully offset by the short futures position established at the outset. The net value of the portfolio at early exercise thus equals the sum of three components, each of which has a value at least equal to zero. With the intermediate and terminal values of this portfolio being nonnegative, the initial value must be nonpositive, so the left-hand-side inequality of Equation (2) must hold.

To understand the right-hand inequality of Equation (2), consider a conversion arbitrage portfolio consisting of (a) a long position in the put, (b) a long position in the futures, (c) a short position in the futures and (d) a long position of $F - Xe^{-rT}$ bonds. Here the long futures position differs slightly from the rollover strategy described earlier. The investor purchases e^{r} futures on the first day, e^{2r} the second day, e^{3r} the third day, and so on. Each day the number of

---

TABLE 9-3 Arbitrage Transactions for Put-Call Parity of American Futures Options, $Fe^{-rT} - X \le C(F, T; X) - P(F, T; X)$

Position	Initial Value	Intermediate Value	Terminal Value $F_T < X$	Terminal Value $F_t \ge X$
Long Call Option	$-C(F, T; X)$	C_t	0	$F_T - X$
Short Put Option	$+P(F, T; X)$	$-(X - F_t)$	$-(X - F_T)$	0
Short Futures	0	$-(F_t - F)e^{-r(T-t)}$	$-(F_T - F)$	$-(F_T - F)$
Short $Fe^{-rT} - X$ Bonds	$+Fe^{-rT} - X$	$-[Fe^{-r(T-t)} - Xe^{rt}]$	$-(F - Xe^{rT})$	$-(F - Xe^{rT})$
Net Value	$Fe^{-rT} - X$ $-[C(F, T; X)$ $-P(F, T; X)]$	$C_t + F_t[1 - e^{-r(T-t)}]$ $+X(e^{rt} - 1)$	$X(e^{rT} - 1)$	$X(e^{rT} - 1)$

futures contracts bought increases by a factor of e^r, and on the last day e^{rT} contracts are held. Table 9-4 gives the initial, intermediate, and terminal values of these portfolios. As the intermediate and terminal values of the portfolio are certain to be nonnegative, the initial value must be nonpositive and the right-hand side of Equation (2) must hold.

In summary, certain futures option pricing relations are dictated by the absence of costless arbitrage opportunities in an efficiently operating market-place. For the American-style futures options trading in the U.S. today, the put-call parity condition of Equation (2) represents one such relation. If it is violated in any of the existing futures option markets, either the reverse conversion arbitrage strategy depicted in Table 9-3 or the conversion arbitrage strategy depicted in Table 9-4 may be enacted to earn a costless arbitrage profit. The relation does *not* depend on the nature of the commodity underlying the futures contract: It applies to agricultural futures option contracts, as well as those written on financial instruments, currencies and precious metals.

VALUATION EQUATIONS

By far the more interesting pricing relations from a financial analyst's standpoint are valuation equations. They provide the guidance in the never-ending search to identify mispriced securities and to tailor the risk-return properties of contingent claims within a portfolio context.

Unlike the put-call parity relations, valuation equations require an assumption about the nature of the underlying futures price distribution. In option pricing theory, the most common assumption is that the price of the instrument underlying the option contract is lognormally distributed. This assumption is intuitively appealing, because the lowest price a security can attain is zero and the highest price is unlimited. The lognormal price distribution assumption is used to obtain the following futures option pricing results.

TABLE 9-4   **Arbitrage Transactions for Put-Call Parity of American Futures Options, $C(F, T; X) - P(F, T; X) \leq F - Xe^{-rT}$**

			Terminal Value	
Position	Initial Value	Intermediate Value	$F_T < X$	$F_T \geq X$
Long Put Option	$-P(F, T; X)$	P_t	$X - F_T$	0
Long Futures	0	$(F_t - F)e^{rt}$	$(F_T - F)e^{rT}$	$(F_T - F)e^{rT}$
Short Call Option	$+C(F, T; X)$	$-(F_t - X)$	0	$-(F_T - X)$
Long $F - Xe^{-rT}$ Bonds	$-(F - Xe^{-rT})$	$Fe^{rt} - Xe^{-r(T-t)}$	$Fe^{rT} - X$	$Fe^{rT} - X$
Net Value	$\begin{array}{c} C(F, T; X) \\ -P(F, T; X) \\ -(F - Xe^{-rT}) \end{array}$	$\begin{array}{c} P_t + F_t(e^{rT} - 1) \\ +X[1 - e^{-r(T-t)}] \end{array}$	$F_t(e^{rT} - 1)$	$F_t(e^{rT} - 1)$

European Futures Options

As noted, Black derived the valuation equation for a European call option on futures contracts. If futures prices are lognormally distributed, and if a riskless hedge may be formed between the European call and its underlying futures contract, the value of a European call may be expressed as follows:[14]

$$c(F, T; X) = e^{-rT}[FN_1(d_1) - XN_1(d_2)], \tag{3}$$

where

$$d_1 = [\ln(F/X) + 0.5\sigma^2 T]/\sigma\sqrt{T}, \text{ and}$$

$$d_2 = d_1 - \sigma\sqrt{T},$$

and where $c(F, T; X)$ is the price of a European call with exercise price X and time to expiration T. The current futures price is F, the riskless rate of interest is r, and the instantaneous standard deviation of the relative price changes in the futures contract is σ. The term $N_1(d)$ is the probability that a unit normally distributed random variable x will be less than or equal to d.

Equation (3) may seem without intuitive appeal, but it is not. It merely says that the current value of the call equals the present value of its expected value at expiration. At expiration time T, the futures option is worthless if it is out-of-the-money (i.e., if $F_T < X$) and it is worth $F_T - X$ if it is in-the-money (i.e., $F_T > X$).

The expected value of the call option at expiration is thus the expected difference between the futures price and the exercise price conditional upon the option being in-the-money times the probability that the call option will be in-the-money. This is precisely the meaning of the term $FN_1(d_1) - XN_1(d_2)$ in Equation (3). The term e^{-rT} is the appropriate discount factor by which the expected expiration value is brought back to the present.[15] The term $N_1(d_2)$ is the probability that the futures price will exceed the exercise price at the option's expiration.[16]

American Futures Options

Although the Black model is commonly used to price futures options, it may seriously understate the value of an American call option on a futures contract because it fails to account for the potential benefit of exercising the option early. Consider deep in-the-money call options. If Equation (3) is used to price the futures option, the call's value will be $e^{-rT}(F - X)$, because the values of $N(d_1)$ and $N(d_2)$ are approximately equal to one. The American call, however, can be exercised immediately for $F - X$, which is greater than the European call price by an amount equal to $(F - X)(1 - e^{-rT})$. In other words, the Black model underprices a deep in-the-money call by an amount equal to the present value of the interest that could be earned on the exercisable proceeds of the option if the option were exercised immediately.

In general, there is always some probability that a call option will go deep in-the-money, so the American call option price must include a premium that accounts for the potential benefit of early exercise. Figure 9-1 shows that the exercisable value of the American call option, $F - X$, always exceeds the lower price boundary of the corresponding European futures option, $(F - X)e^{-rT}$, so the American call may be worth more "dead" than "alive."[17] The difference between the curves $C(F, T; X)$ and $c(F, T; X)$ is the amount of the early exercise premium. The curve $C(F, T; X)$ intersects the exercisable value of the American call at a futures price level where it is optimal to exercise the option immediately.

A technical explanation of the analytical valuation equation for an American call option on a futures contract is beyond the scope of this paper.[18] An intuitively appealing approximation method based upon the valuation equation is discussed below, however.

A Compound Valuation Approach

Consider the following sequence of "pseudo-American" call option prices. The first element of the sequence, C_1, is the price of a call option that can be exercised only at expiration; the second element, C_2, is the price of a call that can be exercised exactly one-half of the way through the call's life or at expiration; the third element, C_3, is the price of a call that can be exercised exactly one-third of the way through the option's life, two-thirds of the way through the

---

FIGURE 9-1 **European and American Call Option Prices as a Function of the Underlying Futures Contract Price**

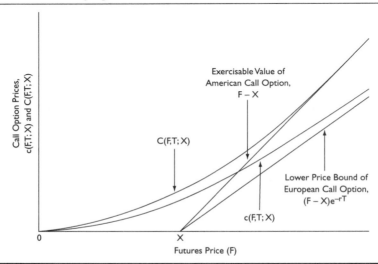

option's life or at expiration, and so on. The value of each new call option introduced into the sequence has a greater value than the previous element, because it offers additional early exercise opportunity. If the sequence is continued indefinitely, the limiting value will be the price of a pseudo-American call with an infinite number of early exercise opportunities or, equivalently, the price of an American call option written on a futures contract.

The formula for the limiting value of the sequence has an infinite number of terms, hence is not a practical means of estimating the values of American call options written on futures contracts. All is not lost, however. The American call can be accurately priced by combining the first three elements of the sequence as follows:[19]

$$C(F, T; X) = 0.5C_1 - 4C_2 + 4.5C_3. \tag{4}$$

The values of C_1, C_2, and C_3 are used to extrapolate the limiting value of the sequence.

The problem, then, becomes one of pricing the first three pseudo-American call options. The value of C_1 is easily computed using Equation (3), because this pseudo-American call option has no early exercise opportunities. As noted earlier, C_1 is simply the present value of the expected terminal value of the call conditional on the call finishing in-the-money times the probability that the call will finish in-the-money.

The value of C_2 can also be expressed as a present value formula. This time, however, the value is the sum of two components—(a) the present value of the expected early exercise value of the call half-way through the option's life conditional upon the call being exercised early times the probability that the call will be exercised early, and (b) the present value of the expected terminal value of the call conditional upon the call not being exercised early and being in-the-money at expiration times the probability that the call is not exercised early and is in-the-money at expiration.

The obvious question to ask at this point is, what determines whether the option will be exercised early at time t? The answer lies in considering the call option holder's dilemma at the early exercise opportunity at time t. Figure 9-2 illustrates this. Just prior to the early exercise instant, the exercisable proceeds of the call are $F_t - X$. If the call option holder chooses not to exercise, he is left with a European call option with a value of $c(F_t, T - t; X)$. The critical futures price F_t^* is determined by the intersection of $F_t - X$ and $c(F_t, T - t; X)$, or:

$$F_t^* - X = c(F_t^*, T - t; X). \tag{5}$$

At this point, the option holder is indifferent about early exercise of his option. If the futures price at time t, F_t, is below F_t^*, the option is worth more alive than dead and will be held to expiration. If F_t is above F_t^*, the option is worth more dead than alive and will be exercised early. Note that, given Equation (3), the value of F_t^* may be computed, although a numerical search procedure is required.[20]

FIGURE 9-2   Call Option Price as a Function of Futures Price at the Early Exercise Instant t

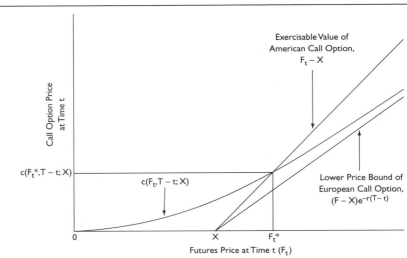

With the value of F_t^* determined, the call option pricing formula may be solved. The value of C_2 is as follows:

$$C_2 = e^{-rt}[FN_1(a_1) - XN_1(a_2)]$$
$$+ e^{-rT}[FN_2(-a_1, b_1; -\sqrt{1/2}) - XN_2(-a_2, b_2; -\sqrt{1/2})], \tag{6}$$

where

$$a_1 = [\ln(F/F_t^*) + 0.5\sigma^2 t]/\sigma\sqrt{t}$$

$$a_2 = a_1 - \sigma\sqrt{t},$$

$$b_1 = [\ln(F/X) + 0.5\sigma^2 T]/\sigma\sqrt{T},$$

$$b_2 = b_1 - \sigma\sqrt{T}, \text{ and } t = T/2.$$

$N_1(a)$ represents the probability that a unit normally distributed variable x will be less than or equal to a, and $N_2(a, b; \rho)$ is the probability that two unit normally distributed random variables x and y with correlation ρ will be less than or equal to a and b, respectively.[21] The first term in brackets in Equation (6) is the expected call option value at the early exercise instant conditional upon early exercise times the probability that the call is exercised early. The second bracketed term is the expected call option value at expiration conditional upon the call not being exercised early and being in-the-money at expiration times the probability that the call is not exercised early and is in-the-money at expiration.

$N_1(a_2)$ is the probability that the call will be exercised early, and $N_2(-a_2, b_2; -\sqrt{1/2})$ represents the probability that the call will not be exercised early and will be in-the-money at expiration. The formula for C_3 is derived in a similar fashion.

Results

Table 9-5 presents call option values for C_1, C_2, and C_3, as well as the approximation value from Equation (4), denoted as $C(F, T; X)_a$. Note that the call with one early exercise opportunity has a greater value than the call with no early exercise, and the call with two early exercise opportunities has a greater value than the call with one early exercise opportunity. Each additional early exercise opportunity adds value to the option.

Table 9-5 also includes a column labelled $C(F, T; X)_n$. These American futures option values were computed using numerical methods. These methods, while accurate in the sense that they account for the "infinite" number of early exercise opportunities offered the American option holder, are computationally expensive and are not sensible for microcomputer applications.[22] It is encouraging, however, that the extrapolated values $C(F, T; X)_a$ very closely match the numerically estimated values. Furthermore, they do so at *less than 5 percent of the computational cost* and can be easily programmed on a microcomputer!

Table 9-6 presents a sensitivity analysis of the theoretical European and American futures option values for a variety of option pricing parameters. It is important to see how well the extrapolation method works for reasonable ranges of inputs in the option pricing formula. Although the valuation equations for put option contracts are not presented here, their specifications are easily derived from the call option pricing results provided, and their values are included in Table 9-6.

Note that the extrapolation method yields option prices within a penny or so of the numerical method. Assuming the numerical method provides the

TABLE 9-5   Valuation of an American Call Option on a Futures Contract Using the Compound Option Valuation Approach ($X = 100$, $r = 0.12$, $\sigma = 0.20$, $T = 0.25$)

Futures Price (F)	American Call Option Price Sequence			Analytic Approx. $C(F, T; X)_a$	Numerical Approx. $C(F, T; X)_n$
	$C_1(F, T; X)$	$C_2(F, T; X)$	$C_3(F, T; X)$		
80	0.04	0.04	0.04	0.04	0.04
90	0.69	0.69	0.69	0.69	0.69
100	3.87	3.88	3.88	3.90	3.89
110	10.63	10.71	10.73	10.76	10.76
120	19.55	19.80	19.88	20.02	20.01

TABLE 9-6   Theoretical European and American Futures Option Values (exercise price (X) = 100)

Option Parameters	Futures Price (F)	Call Options			Put Options		
		European $c(F, T; X)$	American		European $p(F, T; X)$	American	
			$C(F, T; X)_a$	$C(F, T; X)_n$		$P(F, T; X)_a$	$P(F, T; X)_n$
$r = 0.12$	80	0.04	0.04	0.04	19.45	19.99	20.00
$\alpha = 0.20$	90	0.69	0.69	0.69	10.40	10.53	10.53
$T = 0.25$	100	3.87	3.90	3.89	3.87	3.90	3.89
	110	10.63	10.76	10.76	0.93	0.93	0.93
	120	19.55	20.02	20.01	0.14	0.14	0.14
$r = 0.16$	80	0.04	0.04	0.04	19.25	19.99	20.00
$\sigma = 0.20$	90	0.68	0.69	0.69	10.29	10.49	10.48
$T = 0.25$	100	3.83	3.87	3.86	3.83	3.87	3.86
	110	10.52	10.70	10.71	0.92	0.92	0.92
	120	19.36	20.01	20.00	0.14	0.14	0.14
$r = 0.12$	80	1.15	1.15	1.15	20.56	20.84	20.84
$\sigma = 0.40$	90	3.48	3.50	3.49	13.19	13.30	13.30
$T = 0.25$	100	7.73	7.78	7.77	7.73	7.78	7.77
	110	13.87	13.98	13.98	4.17	4.19	4.18
	120	21.49	21.74	21.74	2.08	2.09	2.08
$r = 0.12$	80	0.29	0.29	0.29	19.13	20.04	20.01
$\sigma = 0.20$	90	1.67	1.68	1.68	11.09	11.35	11.36
$T = 0.50$	100	5.31	5.38	5.38	5.31	5.38	5.38
	110	11.50	11.76	11.77	2.08	2.10	2.10
	120	19.51	20.28	20.24	0.68	0.68	0.68

"true" value of the American futures option (and considering the numerical method's computational cost), this result is impressive. Note also that the degree of mispricing is greater, the further the option is in-the-money and the longer is its time to expiration. Even under these circumstances, however, the relative error is less than two-tenths of 1 percent. A final observation is that out-of-the-money options generally have negligible early exercise premiums. This suggests that it may be appropriate to apply the computationally less expensive Black model, Equation (3), to approximate the values of out-of-the-money American futures options.

It should be emphasized that the results presented here apply to all futures option contracts, independent of the nature of the commodities underlying the futures. Futures options written on financial instrument, foreign currency, precious metal and agricultural futures contracts all follow the valuation principles discussed. Such general results are not available, however, for options written on the spot commodities themselves.

ENDNOTES

1. Although not futures options *per se,* commodity options were introduced in the U.S. as early as the mid-1800s. The Commodity Exchange Act of 1936, however, banned trading in options on all domestic, regulated commodities, and it was not until 1982 that the commodity futures options appeared on the scene. For some early perspectives on agricultural options trading, see P. Mehl, *Trading in Privileges on the Chicago Board of Trade* (Washington, D.C.: United States Department of Agriculture, Circular No. 323, December 1934).

2. See F. Black, "The Pricing of Commodity Contracts," *Journal of Financial Economics* 3 (1976), pp. 167-179.

3. See, for example, E. Moriarty, S. Phillips and P. Tosini, "A Comparison of Options and Futures in the Management of Portfolio Risk," *Financial Analysts Journal,* January/February 1981, pp 61-67; M. R. Asay, "A Note on the Design of Commodity Contracts," *Journal of Futures Markets* 2 (1982), pp. 1-7; and A. Wolf, "Fundamentals of Commodity Options on Futures," *Journal of Futures Markets* (1982), pp 391-408.

4. See R. E. Whaley, "Valuation of American Futures Options: Theory and Empirical Tests," *Journal of Finance,* March 1986.

5. J. C. Cox, J. E. Ingersoll and S. A. Ross, "The Relation Between Forward and Futures Prices," *Journal of Financial Economics* 9 (1982), pp. 321-346, demonstrate that the price of a futures contract is equal to the price of a forward contract when interest rates are nonstochastic.

6. The riskless bonds used throughout the study may be thought of as Treasury bills with time T remaining to maturity.

7. The concept of a "rollover" futures strategy was introduced by Cox, Ingersoll and Ross, "The Relation Between Forward and Futures Prices," *op. cit.*

8. To understand the nature of the rollover strategy, consider the first day's settlement activity. At the beginning of the first day, $e^{-r(T-1)}$ futures contracts are purchased at price F_0. At the end of the day, the contracts are marked to market, and the long registers a gain (loss) of $e^{-r(T-1)}(F_1 - F_0)$. On the second day, the gain is $e^{-r(T-2)}(F_2 - F_1)$, and on the third day, $e^{-r(T-3)}(F_3 - F_2)$. If each of these daily gains (losses) is then invested at the riskless rate until the end of the futures contract life, the terminal value of the rollover futures position will be as follows:

$$e^{-r(T-1)}(F_1 - F_0)e^{r(T-1)} + e^{-r(T-2)}(F_2 - F_1)e^{r(T-2)} + e^{-r(T-3)}(F_3 - F_2)e^{r(T-3)} + \dots$$
$$+ e^{-r(T-t)}(F_t - F_{t-1})e^{r(T-t)} + \dots + (F_T - F_{T-1}) = F_T - F_0 = S_T - F_0.$$

Note that it is this long rollover futures position that provides the same terminal value as a single long forward contract.

9. Conversion and reverse conversion trading strategies are explained in detail in L. G. McMillan, *Options as a Strategic Investment: A Comprehensive Analysis of Listed Stock Option Strategies* (New York: New York Institute of Finance, 1980), pp. 238-240.

10. R. C. Merton, "The Theory of Rational Option Pricing," *Bell Journal of Economics and Management Science* 4 (1973), pp. 141-183, provides a comprehensive analysis of the rational stock option pricing relations.

11. In H. R. Stoll, "The Relationship Between Put and Call Option Prices," *Journal of Finance* 24 (1969), pp. 802-824, put-call parity for European stock options was shown to be:

$$c(S, T; X) - p(S, T; X) = S - Xe^{-rT}$$

The structure of this put-call parity condition is the same as that demonstrated for European futures options [i.e., Equation (1)], if the futures, futures options and the stock options expire at the same instant and if the cost-of-carry relation $F = Se^{rT}$ holds.

12. See Moriarty, Phillips and Tosini, "A Comparison of Options and Futures," *op. cit.* and Wolf, "Fundamentals of Commodity Options on Futures," *op. cit.*

13. This relation first appeared in H. R. Stoll and R. E. Whaley, "New Option Instruments: Arbitrageable Linkages and Valuation," *Advances in Futures and Option Research* 1(A) 1986: 25–62. A partial result appears in K. Ramaswamy and S. Sundaresan, "The Valuation of Options on Futures Contracts," *Journal of Finance,* December 1985.

14. It is worthwhile to note that the Black model is not unlike the Black-Scholes model for pricing the European call option on a non-dividend-paying stock. (See F. Black and M. Scholes, "The Pricing of Options and Corporate Liabilities," *Journal of Political Economy* 81 (1973), pp. 637–659.) If the cost-of-carry relation $F = Se^{rT}$ is substituted into Equation (3), one obtains the Black-Scholes model:

$$c(S, T; X) = SN(d_1) - Xe^{-rT}N(d_2)$$

where $d_1 = [\ln(S/X) + (r + 0.5\sigma^2)T]/\sigma\sqrt{T}$. This result was first noted by F. Black, "The Pricing of Commodity Contracts," *op. cit.* and then later by M. R. Asay, "A Note on the Design of Commodity Contracts," *Journal of Futures Markets* 2 (1982), pp. 1–7.

15. This interpretation of the Black model invokes the risk-neutrality argument that appears in J. C. Cox and S. A. Ross, "The Valuation of Options for Alternative Stochastic Processes," *Journal of Financial Economics* 3 (1976), pp. 145–166. If a riskless hedge may be formed between the futures option and the underlying futures contract, the value of the option is the same for risk-neutral investors and for risk-averse investors. Thus, for mathematical tractability, assume investors are risk-neutral. The appropriate discount rate to use in the present value computation is, therefore, the riskless rate of interest.

16. The pricing equation for a European put option on a futures contract may be derived by substituting the European call option valuation Equation (3) into the put-call parity Equation (1). The value of the European put option is as follows:

$$p(F, T; X) = e^{-rT}[XN(-d_2) - FN(-d_1)],$$

where d_1 and d_2 are the same as they were defined for Equation (3). Here, the term in brackets is the expected value of the put option at expiration conditional upon the option being in-the-money at expiration times the probability that the put option will finish in-the-money; $N(-d_2)$ is the probability that the futures price will be below the exercise price at expiration. Note that when the European call and put options have the same exercise price and time to expiration, the probability that the call will finish in-the-money, $N(d_2)$, and the probability that the put will finish in-the-money, $N(-d_2)$, sum to one.

17. As Merton ("The Theory of Rational Option Pricing," *op. cit.*) demonstrates, because the exercisable value of an American call option on a non-dividend-paying stock, $S - X$, is always less than the lower price bound of the corresponding European option, $S - Xe^{-rT}$, the American call option is always worth more "alive" than "dead" and will thus not be exercised early.

18. The approach used parallels the methodology used by R. Geske and H. E. Johnson, "The American Put Valued Analytically," *Journal of Finance* 39 (1984), pp. 1511–1524, in deriving the analytical formula for an American put option on a stock. The compound option valuation approach was also used to price the American call option on a dividend-paying-stock. See R. Roll, "An Analytic Valuation Formula for Unprotected American Call Options on Stocks with Known Dividends," *Journal of Financial Economics* 5 (1977), pp. 251–258; R. Geske, "A Note on an Analytical Formula for Unprotected American Call Options on Stocks with Known Dividends," *Journal of Financial Economics* 7 (1979), pp. 375–380; and R. E. Whaley, "On the Valuation of American Call Options on Stocks with Known Dividends," *Journal of Financial Economics* 9 (1981), pp. 207–211.

19. The derivation of these weights is provided in R. Geske and H. E. Johnson, "The American Put Valued Analytically," *op. cit.*

20. As a numerical example, consider a futures option with an exercise price (X) of 100 and a time to expiration (T) of 0.25. Also, suppose that the riskless rate of interest (r) is 12 per cent and that the standard deviation of the relative price changes in the futures contract (σ) is 20 per cent. The critical futures price F_t^* above which the call option holder will exercise his option at the early exercise opportunity t is 111.84.

21. Methods for evaluating the probabilities $N_1(\cdot)$ and $N_2(\cdot)$ are available in M. Abramowitz and I. Stegum, *Handbook of Mathematical Functions* (Washington, D.C.: National Bureau of Standards).

22. A variety of numerical methods have been applied to American option pricing problems. An interested reader may refer to M. J. Brennan and E. S. Schwartz, "Finite Difference Methods and Jump Processes Arising in the Pricing of Contingent Claims: A Synthesis," *Journal of Financial and Quantitative Analysis* 13 (1978), pp. 461–474, and R. Geske and K. Shastri, "Valuation by Approximation: A Comparison of Alternative Valuation Techniques," *Journal of Financial and Quantitative Analysis* 20 (1985).

PART FOUR

Implied Volatility in Currency Derivatives

10

The Magnitude of Implied Volatility Smiles: Theory and Empirical Evidence for Exchange Rates

STEPHEN J. TAYLOR
XINZHONG XU

INTRODUCTION

At any moment of time implied volatilities vary for different times to option expiry T and different exercise prices X. A matrix of implied volatilities is frequently available, with columns ordered by T and rows ordered by X. Rational expectations of the average volatility during the next T years will vary with T whenever volatility is believed to be stochastic. Thus the rows of the implied volatility matrix provide information about the term structure of expected future volatility. Xu and Taylor (1994) have explained how this term structure can be estimated from a row of the implied volatility matrix. In this paper we present theoretical and empirical results for the columns of the matrix.

Hull and White (1987) and Stein and Stein (1991) have shown that it is rational for the implied volatility to vary with X when the asset volatility is believed to be stochastic. When special assumptions are made, their equations and calculations show that a plot of theoretical implieds against X displays a

Xinzhong Xu was employed at the Financial Options Research Centre at the University of Warwick when the results in this paper were obtained and the first draft of this paper was written. The authors thank the Philadelphia Stock Exchange for providing data.

Reprinted with permission from *The Review of Futures Markets;* Vol. 13; Stephen J. Taylor and Xinzhong Xu; 1994.

'smile': the function has a U-shape and the minimum implied occurs at a value of X very near to the forward price of the underlying asset. Shastri and Wethyavivorn (1987) show that a 'smile effect' is predicted by theory when prices follow a mixed jump-diffusion process. We present new theoretical results. Further results are given in the similar but independent study by Heynen (1993).

There have been several attempts to decide if option prices have a 'strike bias.' However, we are only aware of a few empirical studies which explore the idea that a 'smile effect' is the appropriate form of strike bias, although traders often remark that they know implieds 'smile'. Shastri and Wethyavivorn (1987) concluded that exchange rate implieds were a U-shaped function of the exchange rate divided by X, for options traded in 1983 and 1984. Sheikh (1991) has argued that a U-shaped pattern occurred for S&P-100 options during various subperiods between 1983 and 1985. Fung and Hsieh (1991) discuss informally some empirical 'smile' pictures. Heynen (1993) has shown that U-shaped functions can describe a dataset of EOE stock index implieds obtained from nine months of transaction prices. Our study fits U-shaped functions to seven years of currency implieds.

Section 2 reviews notation and definitions, followed by theoretical results in Sections 3 through 5. Stochastic volatility is shown to be a sufficient reason for smiles to exist. The theoretical effects are of economic importance especially when T is a relatively short time. Section 6 describes empirical estimates of the magnitude of the smile effect for spot currency options traded at the Philadelphia Stock Exchange from November 1984 to January 1992. A general effect is found although it is more pronounced than predicted by the theory we develop. Conclusions are stated in Section 7.

NOTATION AND DEFINITIONS

To develop the theoretical results we consider European options, traded upon an asset which pays dividends at a continuous rate. The fair price for a call option when the asset price follows geometric Brownian motion is represented by

$$c(S, T, X, r, d, V), \quad V = \sigma^2,$$

or simply $c(X, V)$, with S the spot price, T the time to expiry, X the exercise price, r the riskfree interest rate, d the dividend rate and σ the volatility (which is constant for the assumed price model). Time t is measured in years and the present time is $t = 0$.

When volatility is stochastic and therefore depends upon t let

$$V(t) = \sigma^2(t),$$

$$\bar{V} = \frac{1}{T} \int_0^T V(t)dt$$

and suppose the conditional distribution $\bar{V} \mid V(0)$ has probability density function $f(\nu)$ for which the mean and variance are respectively $\mu_{\bar{V}}$ and $\sigma_{\bar{V}}^2$.

The fair price in a world of stochastic volatility is represented by

$C(\ldots X, \ldots)$.

When firstly the price and the volatility both follow diffusion processes within the general structure discussed by Hull and White (1987), secondly volatility risk is not priced and thirdly the price and volatility differentials are uncorrelated, $C(X)$ is given by the following integral:

$$C(X) = \int_0^\infty c(X, \nu)f(\nu)d\nu. \tag{1}$$

It is emphasised that (1) and hence our subsequent analysis does not apply when the price and volatility differentials are correlated. For each X there is a Black-Scholes implied volatility corresponding to the fair price given by a stochastic volatility process. This implied quantity is defined by:

$$C(X) = c(X, \sigma_{imp}^2(X)). \tag{2}$$

THEORETICAL APPROXIMATIONS

Series expansions of $c(X, V)$ around $V = \mu_{\bar{V}}$ permit theoretical analysis of the smile effect. A quadratic approximation is required in (1) and a linear approximation in (2) to ensure that σ_{imp}^2 depends upon X. Then:

$$C(X) \approx \int_0^\infty f(\nu)\left[c(X, \mu_{\bar{V}}) + (\nu - \mu_{\bar{V}})\frac{\partial c}{\partial \nu} + \frac{1}{2}(\nu - \mu_{\bar{V}})^2 \frac{\partial^2 c}{\partial \nu^2}\right]d\nu$$

$$= c(X, \mu_{\bar{V}}) + \frac{1}{2}\sigma_{\bar{V}}^2 \frac{\partial^2 c}{\partial V^2} \tag{3}$$

and

$$C(X) \approx c(X, \mu_{\bar{V}}) + [\sigma_{imp}^2(X) - \mu_{\bar{V}}]\frac{\partial c}{\partial V}. \tag{4}$$

From (3) and (4):

$$[\sigma_{imp}^2(X) - \mu_{\bar{V}}]\frac{\partial c}{\partial V} \approx \frac{1}{2}\sigma_{\bar{V}}^2 \frac{\partial^2 c}{\partial V^2}$$

and so

$$\sigma_{imp}^2(X) \approx \mu_{\bar{V}} + \frac{1}{2}\sigma_{\bar{V}}^2 \frac{\partial^2 c/\partial V^2}{\partial c/\partial V} \tag{5}$$

with the partial derivatives evaluated at $V = \mu_{\bar{V}}$. These partials are functions of X and other variables.

The ratio of the second partial derivative to the first partial derivative of c, with respect to V, can be calculated from the following familiar equations:

$$c(X, V) = Se^{-dT}N(d_1) - Xe^{-rT}N(d_2),$$

$$d_1 = \frac{\ln(S/X) + \left(r - d + \frac{1}{2} V\right)T}{(VT)^{1/2}},$$

$$d_2 = d_1 - (VT)^{1/2},$$

$$\frac{\partial c}{\partial V} = \frac{1}{2} Se^{-dT}\phi(d_1)T^{1/2}V^{1/2},$$

$$\frac{\partial^2 c}{\partial V^2} = \frac{1}{4} Se^{-dT}\phi(d_1)T^{1/2}V^{1/2}(d_1 d_2 - 1),$$

and hence

$$\frac{\partial^2 c/\partial V^2}{\partial c/\partial V} = \frac{d_1 d_2 - 1}{2V}. \tag{6}$$

Using the forward price $F = Se^{(r-d)T}$,

$$d_1(X) = \frac{\ln(F/X) + \frac{1}{2} VT}{(VT)^{1/2}}$$

and thus

$$d_1(X)d_2(X) = \frac{[\ln(F/X)]^2 - \frac{1}{4} V^2 T^2}{VT}. \tag{7}$$

Also,

$$d_1(X)d_2(X) - d_1(F)d_2(F) = \frac{[\ln(F/X)]^2}{VT}. \tag{8}$$

Substituting (7) into (6), then replacing V by $\mu_{\bar{V}}$ and finally substituting (6) into (5) gives the following approximation:

$$\sigma^2_{imp}(X) \approx \mu_{\bar{V}} + \frac{\sigma^2_{\bar{V}}}{4\mu_{\bar{V}}} [d_1(X)d_2(X) - 1] \tag{9}$$

$$= \mu_{\bar{V}} + \frac{\sigma^2_{\bar{V}}}{4\mu_{\bar{V}}} \left[\frac{[\ln(F/X)]^2 - \mu_{\bar{V}}T - \frac{1}{4} \mu^2_{\bar{V}}T^2}{\mu_{\bar{V}}T}\right]. \tag{10}$$

From (7) and (9) the approximate implied volatility is minimised when $X = F$. Furthermore, the quadratic term $[\ln(F/X)]^2$ predicts a theoretical smile.

The height of the smile can be approximated if it is assumed that the second term on the right of (9) is small compared with the first term. This assumption gives

$$\sigma_{imp}(X) \approx \mu_{\bar{V}}^{1/2}\left[1 + (d_1(X)d_2(X) - 1)\frac{\sigma_{\bar{V}}^2}{8\mu_{\bar{V}}^2}\right].$$ (11)

From (8), an approximate *height* is given by

$$\sigma_{imp}(X) - \sigma_{imp}(F) \approx [\ln(F/X)]^2 \frac{\sigma_{\bar{V}}^2}{8T\mu_{\bar{V}}^{2.5}}.$$ (12)

From (8) and (11) it can also be shown that an approximate *relative height* is given by

$$\frac{\sigma_{imp}(X)}{\sigma_{imp}(F)} \approx 1 + [\ln(F/X)]^2 \frac{\sigma_{\bar{V}}^2}{8T\mu_{\bar{V}}^3}.$$ (13)

Several manuscripts, some unpublished, contain subsets of equations (1)–(8), whilst equations (9)–(13) are believed to be new.

A plot of theoretical implied volatilities against the exercise price will display a quadratic function (approximately) of $\ln(F/X)$ with the magnitude of the smile effect being dependent upon T, $V(0)$ and the parameters of the process defining $\{V(t), 0 < t \le T\}$.

ACCURACY OF THE APPROXIMATIONS

The approximations have been evaluated for one of the most frequently specified continuous-time stochastic processes for volatility. This process is an Ornstein-Uhlenbeck (O-U) process for the logarithm of volatility, studied by Scott (1987), Wiggins (1987) and Chesney and Scott (1989). These authors have considered discrete-time approximations to this process, as also have Taylor (1986, 1994), Harvey, Ruiz and Shephard (1994) and Jacquier, Polson and Rossi (1994).

Recall $\sigma(t) = \sqrt{V(t)}$ and denote the unconditional mean and variance of $\ln(\sigma(t))$ by α and β^2 respectively. The diffusion model for volatility is then:

$$d(\ln \sigma) = \Phi(\alpha - \ln \sigma)dt + (2\Phi)^{1/2}\beta dW.$$ (14)

with Φ a positive parameter which controls the rate of reversion towards the mean level α and with $W(t)$ a standardised Wiener process. For the 'half-life' h, equal to $(\ln 2)/\Phi$:

$$E[\ln \sigma(h)|\sigma(0)] = \frac{1}{2}[\alpha + \ln(\sigma(0))].$$

Monte Carlo methods have been used to calculate exact implied volatilities when the volatility logarithm follows the above O-U process. These methods require a discrete-time approximation to (14). The discrete-time process is also required for the calculation of $\mu_{\bar{V}}$ and $\sigma_{\bar{V}}^2$ and hence the approximate implieds given by (11) and the approximate relative smile heights given by (13).

A discrete-time approximation to (14) which matches the mean, variance and half-life is the following AR(1) process:

$$\ln(\sigma_{t+\Delta t}) - \ln(\sigma_t) = (1 - \phi)(\alpha - \ln(\sigma_t)) + \beta(1 - \phi^2)^{1/2}\epsilon_{t+\Delta t} \tag{15}$$

with

$$\phi = \exp(-(\ln 2)(\Delta t)/b)$$

and $\{\epsilon_{\Delta t}, \epsilon_{2\Delta t}, \ldots\}$ a set of i.i.d. standardised Normal variables. For model (15) and $T = N(\Delta t)$, straightforward mathematics and calculations provide the conditional mean and variance of

$$\bar{V}_{discrete} = \frac{1}{N}\sum_{j=0}^{N-1} V_{j(\Delta t)} = \frac{1}{N}\sum_{j=0}^{N-1} \sigma_{j(\Delta t)}^2$$

for any specified initial variance $V(0)$. All the calculations based upon the discrete process in this paper assume Δt is $T/100$ for an option expiring after time T.

The accuracy of the approximations derived in Section 3 has been evaluated by considering parameter values similar to the empirical estimates reported for currencies by Taylor (1994) and Harvey, Ruiz and Shephard (1994). The parameter α was chosen so that $\sigma(t)$ has median value equal to 10%. The parameter β was chosen to be 0.4 and results are given for the initial volatility $\sigma(0)$ equal to one of the lower quartile $Q_1 = \exp(\alpha - 0.674\beta) = 7.6\%$, the median $Q_2 = \exp(\alpha) = 10\%$ and the upper quartile $Q_3 = \exp(\alpha + 0.674\beta) = 13.1\%$. The half-life b was set equal to 30 days.

Table 10-1 presents results when:

$T = 0.5, 1, 2$ or 4 half-lives,
$X/F = 0.92, 0.96, 1, 1.04$ or 1.08,
$\sigma(0) = Q_1, Q_2$ or Q_3,
$r = d = 0.06$, and
$S = F = 100$.

Columns 3 to 6 list the exact implieds $\sigma_{imp}(X)$, the approximate implieds given by equation (11), the exact relative heights $\sigma_{imp}(X)/\sigma_{imp}(F)$ and the approximate relative heights given by equation (13). Sufficient Monte Carlo replications were performed to ensure that the standard errors of the exact implieds were less than 0.00001.

It can be seen from Table 10-1 that the approximations are close to the exact results when X/F equals 0.96, 1 or 1.04 but the approximations are sometimes inaccurate when X/F equals 0.92 or 1.08. Both the exact and approximate results show that smile magnitudes decrease as either T or $\sigma(0)$ increases.

FURTHER RESULTS FOR ORNSTEIN-UHLENBECK PROCESSES

Equation (13) predicts that empirical estimates of $\sigma_{imp}(X)/\sigma_{imp}(F)$ may depend upon X/F and the function

TABLE 10-1 Accuracy of smile approximations when the logarithm of volatility follows an O-U process

Panel A: Initial volatility $\sigma(0) = Q_1 = 7.6\%$

T (days)	X	exact implied %	approx. implied (11) %	exact ratio	approx. ratio (13)	$\sqrt{\mu_{\bar{v}}}$
15	92	n/a				
15	96	8.85	9.01	1.078	1.097	
15	100	8.21	8.20	1.000	1.000	8.33
15	104	8.81	8.94	1.073	1.090	
15	108	n/a				
30	92	n/a				
30	96	9.19	9.29	1.059	1.074	
30	100	8.68	8.64	1.000	1.000	8.89
30	104	9.15	9.24	1.055	1.068	
30	108	n/a				
60	92	10.53	11.04	1.124	1.181	
60	96	9.69	9.71	1.035	1.043	
60	100	9.36	9.29	1.000	1.000	9.68
60	104	9.67	9.68	1.033	1.040	
60	108	10.39	10.79	1.109	1.154	
120	92	10.76	10.88	1.060	1.076	
120	96	10.32	10.28	1.016	1.018	
120	100	10.16	10.08	1.000	1.000	10.50
120	104	10.30	10.26	1.014	1.017	
120	108	10.68	10.76	1.052	1.065	

Panel B: Initial volatility $\sigma(0) = Q_2 = 10\%$

T (days)	X	exact implied %	approx. implied (11) %	exact ratio	approx. ratio (13)	$\sqrt{\mu_{\bar{v}}}$
15	92	n/a				
15	96	10.82	10.91	1.050	1.060	
15	100	10.31	10.29	1.000	1.000	10.46
15	104	10.79	10.86	1.047	1.055	
15	108	n/a				
30	92	11.97	12.61	1.138	1.198	
30	96	10.93	10.99	1.030	1.047	
30	100	10.52	10.48	1.000	1.000	10.77
30	104	10.90	10.95	1.036	1.044	
30	108	11.79	12.29	1.121	1.169	
60	92	11.79	12.12	1.093	1.127	
60	96	11.06	11.05	1.025	1.030	
60	100	10.79	10.71	1.000	1.000	11.13
60	104	11.04	11.03	1.023	1.028	
60	108	11.66	11.92	1.081	1.108	
120	92	11.59	11.67	1.048	1.059	
120	96	11.20	11.16	1.013	1.014	
120	100	11.06	10.99	1.000	1.000	11.41
120	104	11.19	11.14	1.011	1.013	
120	108	11.52	11.57	1.041	1.051	

TABLE 10-1 **Accuracy of smile approximations when the logarithm of volatility follows an O-U process (Continued)**

Panel C: Initial volatility $\sigma(0) = Q_3 = 13.1\%$

T (days)	X	exact implied %	approx. implied (11) %	exact ratio	approx. ratio (13)	$\sqrt{\mu_{\bar{v}}}$
15	92	n/a				
15	96	13.36	13.41	1.032	1.036	
15	100	12.95	12.93	1.000	1.000	13.13
15	104	13.33	13.37	1.029	1.033	
15	108	14.25	14.63	1.101	1.129	
30	92	14.00	14.39	1.095	1.126	
30	96	13.12	13.14	1.026	1.030	
30	100	12.79	12.74	1.000	1.000	13.08
30	104	13.09	13.11	1.024	1.028	
30	108	13.85	14.15	1.083	1.107	
60	92	13.35	13.55	1.067	1.087	
60	96	12.73	12.70	1.018	1.021	
60	100	12.51	12.43	1.000	1.000	12.87
60	104	12.71	12.68	1.016	1.019	
60	108	13.23	13.39	1.058	1.074	
120	92	12.61	12.66	1.037	1.045	
120	96	12.27	12.23	1.005	1.011	
120	100	12.16	12.09	1.000	1.000	12.51
120	104	12.27	12.22	1.009	1.010	
120	108	12.55	12.57	1.032	1.039	

Parameters
$S = 100, r = 0.06, d = 0.06$
median $\sigma(t) = Q_2 = 10\%$
standard deviation of $\ln(\sigma(t)) = \beta = 0.4$
lower quartile for $\sigma(t) = Q_1 = 7.6\%$
upper quartile for $\sigma(t) = Q_3 = 13.1\%$
half-life $h = 30$ days

$$R(T) = \frac{\sigma_V^2}{8T\mu_V^3}. \tag{16}$$

It is helpful for empirical work to understand how R depends upon T and $\sigma(0)$.

Table 10-2 presents some relevant results when $\ln(\sigma(t))$ follows an O-U process. The parameters α and h are as before but now β is one of 0.2, 0.4 or 0.6. Once more $\sigma(0) = Q_1$, Q_2 or Q_3. Panel A of Table 10-2 lists values for both $\sigma_V^2/(8\mu_V^3)$ and σ_V^2, with $\bar{V}$ approximated by $\bar{V}_{discrete}$. These functions of T are unimodal. Panel B of Table 10-2 lists the values of T which maximise these functions for the nine combinations of β and $\sigma(0)$. Most of the maxima are at between two and four 'half-lives.'

The function $R(T)$ decreases as T increases for each of the nine combinations. It is difficult to say at what rate the function $R(T)$ decreases. When β is

TABLE 10-2 Selected Conditional Moments for $\bar{V}$ When the Logarithm of Volatility Follows on O–U Process

Panel A: Conditional moment functions

β	T (days)	$\sigma_{\bar{V}}^2/(8\mu_{\bar{V}}^3)$			$10^6\sigma_{\bar{V}}^2$		
		$\sigma(0) = Q_1$	Q_2	Q_3	$\sigma(0) = Q_1$	Q_2	Q_3
0.2	15	0.457	0.357	0.279	1.97	3.06	4.73
0.2	30	0.708	0.566	0.451	3.53	5.05	7.24
0.2	60	0.882	0.734	0.608	5.37	6.88	8.87
0.2	120	0.813	0.714	0.623	6.06	6.95	8.03
0.4	15	2.401	1.469	0.896	6.44	15.36	36.78
0.4	30	3.641	2.339	1.490	14.42	29.17	59.56
0.4	60	4.280	2.997	2.058	28.18	45.51	74.88
0.4	120	3.581	2.807	2.140	38.38	49.56	65.66
0.6	15	7.246	3.479	1.659	14.08	51.35	188.57
0.6	30	10.837	5.637	2.874	44.43	124.82	357.19
0.6	60	11.882	7.104	4.070	124.89	246.84	506.17
0.6	120	8.770	6.251	4.205	214.40	303.83	452.33

Panel B: Values of T which maximise the conditional moment functions

β	$\sigma_{\bar{V}}^2/(8\mu_{\bar{V}}^3)$			$\sigma_{\bar{V}}^2$		
	$\sigma(0) = Q_1$	Q_2	Q_3	$\sigma(0) = Q_1$	Q_2	Q_3
0.2	71	80	90	107	87	68
0.4	60	74	93	134	98	66
0.6	50	67	91	156	111	72

The conditional moments depend on the initial volatility $\sigma(0)$
Parameters
median $\sigma(t) = Q_2 = 10\%$
standard deviation of $\ln(\sigma(t)) = \beta$
lower quartile for $\sigma(t) = Q_1 = 10\%/\exp(0.674\beta)$
upper quartile for $\sigma(t) = Q_3 = 10\%*\exp(0.674\beta)$
half-life $h = 30$ days

0.4, $R(T)$ is, very approximately, proportional to $T^{-0.5}$ when T is around one half-life and proportional to T^{-1} when T is around 2.5 half-lives. The function is proportional to T^{-2} for large T.

Table 10-2 confirms that $R(T)$ decreases as $\sigma(0)$ increases and, for each T, $R(T)$ is approximately proportional to $1/\sigma(0)$. Also $R(T)$ increases with β.

Analytic results can be obtained when $V(t)$, rather than its logarithm, follows an O-U process. Of course it is then impossible to guarantee that $V(t)$ is positive. Suppose the unconditional mean and variance of $V(t)$ are μ_V and σ_V^2, and:

$$dV = \Phi(\mu_V - V)dt + (2\Phi)^{1/2}\sigma_V dW \tag{17}$$

with Φ positive and $W(t)$ a standardised Wiener process. The 'half-life' h again equals $(\ln 2)/\Phi$, with:

$$E[V(b)\,|\,V(0)] \;=\; \frac{1}{2}\,(\mu_V + V(0)).$$

Adapting the analysis presented in Cox and Miller (1972, Sec. 5.8) gives the following results for the first two conditional moments:

$$\mu_{\bar{V}} \;=\; E[\bar{V}\,|\,V(0)] \;=\; \mu_V + [V(0) - \mu_V]\!\left(\frac{1 - e^{-\Phi T}}{\Phi T}\right), \tag{18}$$

and

$$\sigma_{\bar{V}}^2 \;=\; \mathrm{var}(\bar{V}\,|\,V(0)) \;=\; \frac{2\sigma_V^2}{\Phi^2 T^2}\left[\Phi T - (1 - e^{-\Phi T}) - \frac{1}{2}(1 - e^{-\Phi T})^2\right]. \tag{19}$$

The conditional variance as a function of T is unimodal and converges to zero as $T \to 0$ or $T \to \infty$. The maximum of this function is at $T = 1.89/\Phi$ (approx.) which is 2.73 'half-lives' (approx.). The conditional variance depends on neither $\mu_{\bar{V}}$ nor $V(0)$. From (19),

$$\sigma_{\bar{V}}^2 \approx \frac{2}{3}\,\sigma_V^2(\Phi T) \quad \text{as } T \to 0,$$
$$= 0.28\sigma_V^2 \quad \text{when } T = (\ln 2)/\Phi,$$
$$= 0.38\sigma_V^2 \quad \text{when } T = 1.89/\Phi,$$
$$\approx 2\sigma_V^2/(\Phi T) \quad \text{as } T \to \infty.$$

The theoretical magnitude of the smile effect as a function of T depends particularly upon $\sigma_{\bar{V}}^2/T$. This quantity is essentially constant for small T, is proportional to T^{-1} near to 2.73 'half-lives' and is proportional to T^{-2} for large T.

It is concluded that when either $V(t)$ or its logarithm follows an O-U process then the theoretical relative smile height is

(i) a decreasing function of T, and
(ii) a decreasing function of $\sigma(0)$.

It is also concluded that, in theory, 'large' smiles should be found at those markets whose prices have 'high' values of $\mathrm{var}(V(t))$.

EMPIRICAL ESTIMATES OF SMILE MAGNITUDES

Currency Data

The primary source database for the options prices is the transaction report compiled daily by the Philadelphia Stock Exchange (PHLX). Only the closing call and put options prices and the simultaneous spot exchange rate quotes for the (British) Pound, (German) Mark, (Japanese) Yen and (Swiss) Franc against the US Dollar have been used. All eight datasets start on November 5, 1984; Pound calls and puts, Mark calls and Yen calls end on January 8, 1992 while the other four datasets end on November 22, 1989. These dates were determined by the availability of the PHLX data. However, the transaction report is not available for some trading days and then prices have been collected manually from the Wall Street Journal (WSJ). Approximately 10% of our implied volatilities are calculated from WSJ prices.

The domestic and foreign interest rates used are London euro-currency rates, collected from Datastream. This source provides overnight, seven days, one month, three months, six months and one year interest rates. For intermediate times, we simply use linear interpolation.

Often applied exclusion criteria have been used to remove uninformative options records from the database. Option prices less than 0.05 cents are eliminated as transaction costs including the bid-ask spread and liquidity premia are then large relative to the options prices. We also remove options with less than 10 calendar days to expiry because of well-known expiration effects.

Calculation of Implied Volatility

Implied volatilities have been calculated from American model prices. The model prices are approximated by the very accurate functions derived in Barone-Adesi and Whaley (1987). The calculations of implied volatility used an interval subdivision method, which always converged to an unique solution.

Estimation of $\sigma_{imp}(F)$

In order to empirically examine the relative smile effect, we require estimates of the implied volatility when the exercise price is exactly equal to the forward price. These estimates are required for all values of T found in the datasets. Estimates have been obtained by fitting the term structure model developed in Xu and Taylor (1994) to nearest-the-money options whose exercise prices minimise $|X - F|$. This methodology provides approximate estimates of the at-the-money implied volatilities.

The volatility term structure model involves two factors representing short-term and long-term volatility expectations. These volatility expectations are assumed to be mean reverting. The average squared volatility over a general time interval is a linear function of squared short- and long-term expected volatilities.

A Kalman filtering method has been applied to obtain both parameter estimates for the term structure model and time series of volatility expectations estimates. Estimates of at-the-money implied volatility are then calculated using equation (7) in Xu and Taylor (1994). These estimates are denoted by

$\hat{\sigma}_{imp}(F, T)$.

The Regression Model

Let M denote the 'moneyness' of an option defined by

$M = \ln(F/X)$.

Guided by the general conclusions about theoretical smiles given in Section 5, the following regression model has been estimated using ordinary least squares:

$$\frac{\sigma_{imp}(X, T)}{\hat{\sigma}_{imp}(F, T)} = a_0 + a_1 \frac{M}{\sqrt{T}} + a_2 \frac{M^2}{\sqrt{T}} + a_3 \frac{M}{T} + a_4 \frac{M^2}{T}$$

$$+ a_5 \frac{M^2}{\sqrt{T}\hat{\sigma}_{imp}(F, T)} + a_6 \frac{M^2}{T\hat{\sigma}_{imp}(F, T)} + \text{residual.} \qquad (20)$$

The smile theory developed in Section 3 assumes that asset price and volatility differentials are uncorrelated and consequently smile effects are functions of M^2; the sign of M is then irrelevant and we say the smile is symmetric. The assumption of uncorrelated differentials is known to be satisfactory for currencies; see, for example, Taylor (1994). The symmetric smile prediction can be assessed by fitting the above regression specification which permits the relationship between implied volatility ratios and M to be asymmetric. Additional variables can be included in the regression model but it has been found that explanatory variables such as M and M^2 do not change the functions fitted to implied volatility ratios. The values of the regression statistic R^2 range from 0.34 to 0.52 for the eight currency datasets when model (20) is estimated.

Results

Five figures are used to summarise the regression results for the Mark options. These clearly demonstrate the existence of smile effects in the prices of these options. These figures all show the fitted regression relationships when the at-the-money volatility is 12%. Further figures, available from the authors, make clear that similar implied volatility smiles are found for the other three currencies.

Figure 10-1 summarises the implied volatility smiles given by the regression estimates for Mark calls. Six curves representing six different maturities ranging from 10 days to 360 days are plotted. Implied volatility smiles are most pronounced for short maturity options and become smaller when the time to maturity becomes longer as predicted by theory. There is little evidence of asymmetry in these implied volatilities. Similar smiles have been obtained for Mark puts as in Figure 10-2, although the magnitude of the effects for the puts is slightly larger than those for the calls. The results presented here are broadly consistent with those of Shastri and Wethyavivorn (1987) for two earlier years although they simply examined average implied volatilities across different maturities and different levels of moneyness.

Figures 10-3 and 10-4 plot implied volatility smiles when the regression model is estimated for subsets of the Mark calls data, respectively, when the time to maturity is first restricted to be 10 to 30 days and second with the restriction from 31 to 60 days. The magnitude of the smiles on Figures 10-3 and 10-4 are extremely close to those on Figure 10-1. Furthermore, the curves for T = 30 days on Figures 10-3 and 10-4 are almost identical. These observations confirm that the results are robust against the selection of maturities T.

FIGURE 10-1   Implied Volatility Smiles (Mark Calls)

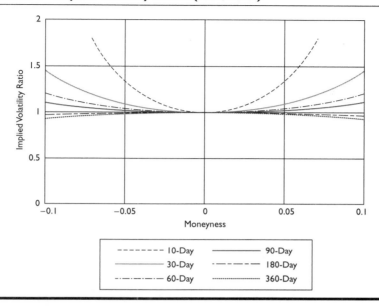

FIGURE 10-2   Implied Volatility Smiles (Mark Puts)

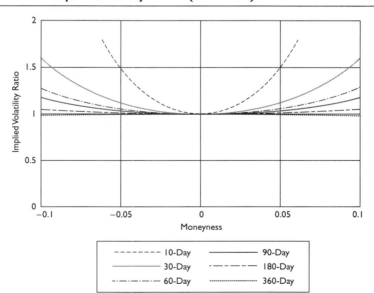

FIGURE 10-3   Implied Volatility Smiles (Mark Calls: 10–30 Days)

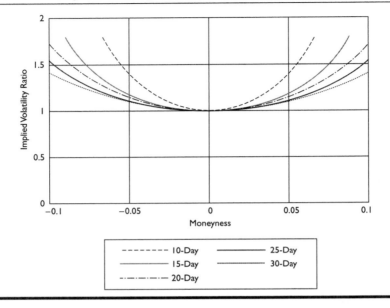

FIGURE 10-4   Implied Volatility Smiles (Mark Calls: 31–60 Days)

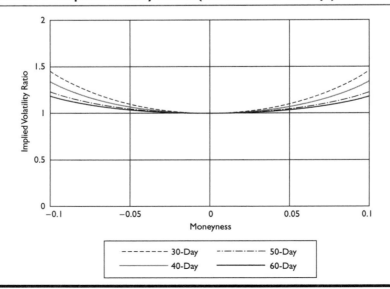

Figure 10-5 presents the results for 30-day implied volatility smiles for Mark calls on a year-to-year basis. The variation between years is small during the first six years, although it seems the magnitude of the volatility ratio has increased gradually for in-the-money options. Asymmetry in the fitted curves is more evident than for the full sample estimates. The 'skewness' changed from negative to positive sometime around 1988. The regression R^2 values for the seven years vary from 0.35 to 0.51.

Comparing Table 10-1 with Figure 10-1 we find that the empirical implied ratios are larger than the theoretical ratios. The magnitudes of the empirical smiles are very approximately twice the magnitude of the theoretical smiles. This might be explained by our assumptions about the price process (for example, no jumps) or by market imperfections (for example, transaction costs).

CONCLUSIONS

The 'smile effect' has been shown, by theoretical methods, to be a logical consequence of stochastic variation in asset volatility. Implied volatilities are approximately a quadratic function of $\ln(F/X)$, whose minimum is at $X = F$, when asset price and volatility differentials are uncorrelated and volatility risk is not priced. This conclusion is probably true for some risk functions when volatility

FIGURE 10-5   30-Day Implied Volatility Smiles (Mark Calls: 1985–1991)

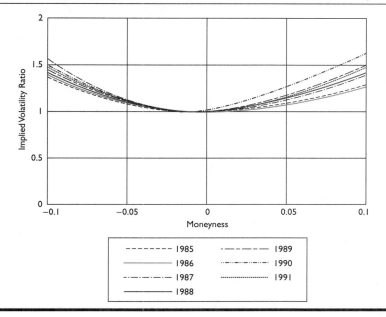

risk is priced although we have not proved this conjecture. The curvature of the quadratic function depends on the time to maturity T of the option and several volatility parameters including the present level, the long-run median level (when this exists) and the variance of future average volatility. The magnitude of the smile is a decreasing function of T. It is concluded that implied volatilities ought to be functions of both T and X, even when there are no term structure effects so that at-the-money options have the same implieds for all T.

The empirical evidence for exchange rate options supports the theoretical predictions, although the empirical smiles are larger than predicted by the theory.

REFERENCES

Barone-Adesi, G. and R. E. Whaley, 1987, Efficient analytic approximation of American option values, Journal of Finance 42, 301–320.

Chesney, M. and L. O. Scott, 1989, Pricing European currency options: a comparison of the modified Black-Scholes model and a random variance model, Journal of Financial and Quantitative Analysis 24, 267–284.

Cox, D. R. and H. D. Miller, 1972, The Theory of Stochastic Processes (Chapman and Hall, London).

Fung, W. K. H. and D. A. Hsieh, 1991, Empirical analysis of implied volatility: stocks, bonds and currencies, conference paper presented at the Financial Options Research Centre, University of Warwick.

Harvey, A. C., E. Ruiz and N. G. Shephard, 1994, Multivariate stochastic variance models, Review of Economic Studies 61, 247–264.

Heynen, R., 1994, An empirical investigation of observed smile patterns, The Review of Futures Markets 13(2), 317–354.

Hull, J. and A. White, 1987, The pricing of options on assets with stochastic volatilities, Journal of Finance 42, 281–300.

Jacquier, E., N. G. Polson and P. E. Rossi, 1994, Bayesian analysis of stochastic volatility models, Journal of Business and Economic Statistics 12(4), October 1994, pages 371–389.

Scott, L. O., 1987, Option pricing when the variance changes randomly: theory, estimation, and an application, Journal of Financial and Quantitative Analysis 22, 419–438.

Shastri, K. and K. Wethyavivorn, 1987, The valuation of currency options for alternate stochastic processes, Journal of Financial Research 10, 283–293.

Sheikh, A. M., 1991, Transactions data tests of S&P 100 call option pricing, Journal of Financial and Quantitative Analysis 26, 459–475.

Stein, E. M. and J. C. Stein, 1991, Stock price distributions with stochastic volatility: an analytic approach, The Review of Financial Studies 4, 727–752.

Taylor, S. J., 1986, Modelling Financial Time Series (John Wiley, Chichester).

Taylor, S. J., 1994, Modeling stochastic volatility: a review and comparative study, Mathematical Finance 4, 183–204.

Wiggins, J. B., 1987, Option values under stochastic volatility: theory and empirical estimates, Journal of Financial Economics 19, 351–372.

Xu, X. and S. J. Taylor, 1994, The term structure of volatility implied by foreign exchange options, Journal of Financial and Quantitative Analysis 29, forthcoming March.

11

The Term Structure of Volatility Implied by Foreign Exchange Options

Xinzhong Xu
Stephen J. Taylor

INTRODUCTION

Options provide information about the expected future volatility of the underlying asset. Implied volatilities at any moment in time vary, however, for different times to option expiry T and different exercise prices X. A matrix of implied volatilities is frequently available, say with columns ordered by T and rows ordered by X. Rational expectations of the average volatility during the next T years will vary with T whenever volatility is believed to be stochastic. Thus, the rows of the implied volatility matrix may provide information about the term structure of expected future volatility. This paper describes and illustrates meth-

Xu was at the Financial Options Research Centre, University of Warwick, when the paper was written and revised. The authors thank JFQA Managing Editor Jonathan Karpoff, an anonymous JFQA referee, Les Clewlow, Gordon Gemmill, Teng-Suan Ho, Stewart Hodges, Richard Stapleton, participants at seminars held at City University, Lancaster University, Oxford University, and Warwick University, and participants at the 1992 meetings of the European and French Finance Associations for their helpful comments and advice. The authors thank the Philadelphia Stock Exchange for providing their currency options data.

Reprinted with permission from *Journal of Financial and Quantitative Analysis;* Vol. 29, No. 1; Xinzhong Xu and Stephen J. Taylor; 1994.

ods for estimating this term structure from one row of the implied volatility matrix, corresponding to nearest-the-money options.

We model both the term structure of expected volatility and the time series characteristics of the term structure. Section II describes a simple specification for the term structure at one moment in time. The specification involves two "factors" representing short-term expected volatility and long-term expected volatility. Thus, the specification is more general than the single factor approach of Stein (1989). The term structure specification is particularly appropriate when a satisfactory model for asset prices is GARCH(1, 1). This model has often been recommended in empirical studies (see Bollerslev, Chou, and Kroner (1992)). Section III describes two estimation methods. A Kalman filter formulation has many advantages and allows estimation of time series models for the long-term expected volatility and the spread between short- and long-term expected volatility; examples are given for AR(1) models.

The empirical examples are for spot currency options on the British pound, German mark, Japanese yen, and Swiss franc quoted against the U.S. dollar. Daily implied volatilities are modeled for the five-year period from January 1985 to November 1989. Section IV describes the Philadelphia Stock Exchange options data. Section V presents the empirical estimates of the term structure. Volatility expectations are shown to revert from their short-term level towards their long-term level with a half-life of approximately four weeks. There are considerable fluctuations in the spread between short- and long-term expectations and frequent changes in the slope of the term structure. There are also significant changes in long-term volatility expectations, which can be modeled either by an AR(1) process or a random walk. Section VI presents conclusions.

The term structure of implied volatilities has also been discussed by Poterba and Summers (1986), Stein (1989), Franks and Schwartz (1991), Diz and Finucane (1993), and Heynen, Kemna, and Vorst (1994). Only two values of T are considered at any moment of time in these papers. Any number of T values can be studied using the estimation methods presented here and the number can vary from day to day. Time series studies involving one implied volatility per day are reported in several papers (for example, Merville and Pieptea (1989) and Day and Lewis (1992)), but such studies ignore term structure effects because T then varies from day to day. Our empirical analysis shows that it is possible to estimate interesting time series models for both short- and long-term expected currency volatility using the Kalman filter.

Stein (1989) directly examined the term structure of implied volatilities, using two daily time series on implied volatilities for S&P 100 index options over the period December 1983 to September 1987. The values of T were less than one month for the first series and between one and two months for the second series. Based on the assumption that the volatility is mean reverting, as supported by his data, Stein claimed that the elasticity of volatility changes is larger than suggested by rational expectations theory: long-maturity options tend to "overreact" to changes in the implied volatility of short-maturity options. This conclusion has been disputed by Diz and Finucane (1993) following their analysis of similar S&P 100 index data. Furthermore, Heynen, Kemna, and Vorst (1994) found that their conclusion about overreaction depended on the model used to represent changes in asset price volatility. They considered one year of European Options Exchange data and two values of T, one varying between zero and three months, the other between six and nine months.

Resnick, Sheikh, and Song (1993) have used stock options data to show that investors perceive monthly differences in return variability and, hence, the implied volatility term structure is not flat. The monthly differences are economically significant.

A MODEL FOR THE TERM STRUCTURE

Volatility is defined in our term structure model in the usual way and is always expressed in annual terms. Thus, the volatility for some time period is the annualized standard deviation of the change in the price logarithm during the same period of time. It is supposed that each year is divided into n smaller intervals of time. These intervals might be calendar days or they might be trading days and so they commence when a market closes on one day and end when the market next closes; alternatively the durations of the intervals might be one week.

Market agents will have expectations at time t about the volatility during future time periods. Suppose they form expectations of the quantities,

$$\text{Var}(\text{Ln } P_{t+\tau} - \text{Ln } P_{t+\tau-1}), \quad \tau = 1, 2, \ldots, \tag{1}$$

where P refers to the price of the asset upon which options are traded. These expectations can be annualized by multiplying them by n. After doing this, let $\sigma_{t,t+\tau}$ denote the volatility expectation at time t for time interval $t + \tau$, so

$$\sigma_{t,t+\tau}^2 = n \text{ Var}(\text{Ln}(P_{t+\tau}/P_{t+\tau-1})|M_t), \tag{2}$$

where M_t is the information set used by the options market.

Our term structure model is intended to be as simple as is reasonably possible. The model supposes that the expectations $\sigma_{t,t+\tau}$ are functions of at most three parameters. The first is the short-term expectation α_t for the next time interval,

$$\alpha_t = \sigma_{t,t+1}. \tag{3}$$

The second parameter is the long-term expectation μ_t, given by assuming that the expectations converge for distant intervals,

$$\mu_t = \lim_{\tau \to \infty} \sigma_{t,t+\tau}. \tag{4}$$

Expectations are assumed to revert towards the time-dependent level μ_t as τ increases. The third parameter, ϕ, controls the rate of reversion towards μ_t and ϕ is assumed to be the same for all t. It is more practical to suppose that reversion applies to variances than to standard deviations, as follows,

$$\sigma_{t,t+\tau}^2 - \mu_t^2 = \phi(\sigma_{t,t+\tau-1}^2 - \mu_t^2), \quad \tau > 1. \tag{5}$$

It then follows that the expectation for time interval $t + \tau$ depends upon $\alpha_t, \mu_t,$ ϕ, and τ, thus,

$$\sigma_{t,t+\tau}^2 = \mu_t^2 + \phi^{\tau-1}(\alpha_t^2 - \mu_t^2), \quad \tau > 0. \tag{6}$$

Market agents have mean-reverting expectations when $0 < \phi < 1$. Stein (1989) used an equation similar to the special case of (6) given by constant μ_t. Constant expectations as τ varies, consistent with the Black-Scholes paradigm, are only obtained when $\phi = 0$ or $\phi = 1$.

Our preference for a simple model only permits three shapes for a graph of $\sigma_{t,t+\tau}$ against τ. The expectations are either monotonic increasing or monotonic decreasing as τ increases, or they are the same for all τ. Graphs of the expectations cannot contain spikes, perhaps aligned with seasonal events or the anticipated release of particularly important information.

The preceding equations summarize expectations made at time t for unit time intervals commencing at later times. The expected volatility at time t for an interval of general length T, from time t to time $t + T$, is the square root of

$$v_T^2 = \frac{1}{T} \sum_{\tau=1}^{T} \sigma_{t,t+\tau}^2 = \mu_t^2 + \frac{1 - \phi^T}{T(1 - \phi)}(\alpha_t^2 - \mu_t^2), \tag{7}$$

here assuming that subsequent asset prices, $\{P_{t+\tau}, \tau > 0\}$, follow a random walk. The numbers $v_T, T = 1, 2, 3, \ldots$, define the term structure of expected average volatility at time t; note the units for T are time intervals in (7), not years. We are interested in using implied volatilities from options prices to estimate the time series $\{\alpha_t\}$ and $\{\mu_t\}$ and also the mean-reversion parameter ϕ. This can be achieved because (7) shows that v_T^2 is a linear function of α_t^2 and μ_t^2.

ESTIMATION METHODS

Two methods have been developed for estimating the term structure model. The first method seeks the best match between the model and a dataset of implied volatilities. This method makes few assumptions about the time series properties of the series $\{\alpha_t\}$ and $\{\mu_t\}$. The method is also very quick. The second method supposes that $\{\alpha_t\}$ and $\{\mu_t\}$ follow autoregressive processes (possibly with unit roots) and then uses the Kalman filter to provide estimates of both the term structure and the parameters of the models assumed for $\{\alpha_t\}$ and $\{\mu_t\}$. This method requires substantially more computer resources.

Notation

The time t is now supposed to count trading days. On day t, there will be implied volatility information for N_t expiry dates, supposed to be represented by a single number for each expiry date. It is a feature of our datasets that N_t varies from day to day. Let $y_{j,t}$ denote the implied volatility for option expiry date j on day

t and suppose the times to expiry are $T_{j,t}$, measured in calendar days, with $T_{1,t} < T_{2,t} < \ldots < T_{N_t,t}$.

A Regression Method

Forward implied variances $f_{j,t}$ can be calculated from the implied volatilities. At time t, the forward variance for the time interval from $t + T_{j-1,t}$ to $t + T_{j,t}$ is

$$f_{j,t} = \frac{T_{j,t}y_{j,t}^2 - T_{j-1,t}y_{j-1,t}^2}{T_{j,t} - T_{j-1,t}}. \tag{8}$$

This is an annualized number. When $j = 1$, $T_{0,t} = 0$ in (8).

The forward implied variance can be compared with the expected value for the appropriate part of the term structure. The forward expected variance $g_{j,t}$ is

$$g_{j,t} = \frac{1}{T_{j,t} - T_{j-1,t}} \left(\sum_{\tau=T_{j-1,t}+1}^{T_{j,t}} \sigma_{C(t),C(t)+\tau}^2 \right), \tag{9}$$

where $C(t)$ is the calendar day count corresponding to the passage of t trading days and τ is measured in calendar days. From (6) it can be seen that the forward expected variance is a linear combination of α_t^2 and μ_t^2. The combination is

$$g_{j,t} = \mu_t^2 + x_{j,t}(\alpha_t^2 - \mu_t^2), \quad \text{with} \tag{10}$$

$$x_{j,t} = \frac{\phi^{T_{j-1,t}} - \phi^{T_{j,t}}}{(1 - \phi)(T_{j,t} - T_{j-1,t})}, \tag{11}$$

assuming $\phi < 1$.

Let n now denote the number of days for which there are implied volatilities. We wish to find estimates of

$$\phi, \quad \alpha_1, \alpha_2, \ldots, \alpha_n, \quad \mu_1, \mu_2, \ldots, \mu_n,$$

giving small values for the differences,

$$e_{j,t} = f_{j,t} - g_{j,t}, \quad 1 \le j \le N_t, \quad 1 \le t \le n.$$

Our estimates are given by minimizing sums of terms $e_{j,t}^2$ for various ϕ, followed by choosing ϕ to be the value giving the smallest sum across all times t. We could estimate α_t and μ_t using the implied volatilities for period t alone, providing $N_t \ge 2$. These estimates are rather erratic because the difference $e_{j,t}$ are nontrivial. There are many possible explanations for nontrivial differences including bid/ask spreads and nonsynchronous options and asset prices (Day and Lewis (1988)), incorrectly priced options, and misspecification of the term structure model. Less erratic estimates for period t can be obtained by using the implied volatilities for a time window $t - k$ to $t + k$. This will be a reasonable method when it can be assumed that the volatility term structure is approximately constant within the time window.

The estimation method can be summarized by three steps. Step 1 involves selecting a set of plausible values for ϕ, say $\phi_1, \ldots, \phi_m$. Step 2 involves finding the best estimates $\hat{\alpha}_{i,t}, \hat{\mu}_{i,t}$, when $\phi = \phi_i, i = 1, \ldots, m$. As $g_{j,t}$ is a linear function of $x_{j,t}$, from (10), these estimates are given for period t by regressing $f_{j,s}$ on $x_{j,s}$, with $1 \leq j \leq N_s$ and $t - k \leq s \leq t + k$. From (10), the estimated intercept is $\hat{\mu}_{i,t}^2$ and the sum of the estimated slope and the estimated intercept is $\hat{\alpha}_{i,t}^2$. These estimates are obtained for $t = k + 1, \ldots, n - k$, and the sum of the squared regression errors calculated, summing over the three variables j, s, and t. Call the sum $S(\phi_i)$ when $\phi = \phi_i$. Step 3 gives $\hat{\phi}$ as the value that minimizes $S(\phi_i)$, and the time series of estimates $\{\hat{\alpha}_t\}$ and $\{\hat{\mu}_t\}$ as the regression estimates when $\phi = \hat{\phi}$. When this method was implemented for our data, it was found that $\hat{\phi}$ is essentially the same for all k between one and 10. Consequently, results are reported in Section V. A with $k = 5$.

The Kalman Filter Method

The expected squared volatility over any period of time is a linear function of the current values of $\alpha_t^2 - \mu_t^2$ and μ_t^2, from (7). This suggests a Kalman filter method is ideal for estimating the term structure, day by day, if a set of squared implied volatilities is considered to be the expected squared volatility (from the term structure model) plus a set of measurement errors that can be attributed to option mispricing, nonsynchronous observations, and other issues. The Kalman filter formulation has several attractive properties: i) it permits comparisons of models for the time series behavior of the state variables, ii) all the parameters can be obtained by maximizing a quasi-likelihood function, iii) the number of observations N_t can vary from day to day, and iv) it can be extended to give results for several assets simultaneously, thus permitting the identification of common factors in the term structures of similar assets.

There are many ways to define the state variables and to model their time series characteristics. One credible example is presented here and further examples are evaluated in Section V.B. We suppose $\{\alpha_t^2\}$ and $\{\mu_t^2\}$ are stationary processes and have the same mean value $\bar{\mu}$. The state variables are taken to be $\alpha_t^2 - \mu_t^2$ and $\mu_t^2 - \bar{\mu}$, which both have zero mean and are unlikely to be highly correlated with each other. This choice is preferred to $\alpha_t^2 - \bar{\mu}$ and $\mu_t^2 - \bar{\mu}$ because these variables will probably have substantial covariation. The simplest plausible model for each of the chosen state variables is an AR(1) process. Independence between the state variables will be assumed. This gives the following state equations,

$$S_t = \begin{pmatrix} \alpha_t^2 - \mu_t^2 \\ \mu_t^2 - \bar{\mu} \end{pmatrix}, \quad \text{a } 2 \times 1 \text{ vector,}$$

$$S_t = \begin{pmatrix} \phi_1 & 0 \\ 0 & \phi_2 \end{pmatrix} S_{t-1} + \varepsilon_t,$$

$$E[\varepsilon_t] = 0, \quad E[\varepsilon_t \varepsilon_t'] = \begin{pmatrix} \sigma_1^2 & 0 \\ 0 & \sigma_2^2 \end{pmatrix}. \tag{12}$$

The observation equation for the Kalman filter is written as

$$Y_t = Z_t S_t + \xi_t. \tag{15}$$

Here Y_t is a $N_t \times 1$ vector of squared implied volatilities minus $\bar{\mu}$, S_t is the 2×1 vector of state variables that summarize the term structure of expected volatility, Z_t is a $N_t \times 2$ matrix of state coefficients, and ξ_t is a $N_t \times 1$ vector of measurement errors. We have

$$Y_t = \begin{pmatrix} y_{1,t}^2 - \bar{\mu} \\ \cdot \\ \cdot \\ y_{N_t,t}^2 - \bar{\mu} \end{pmatrix} \quad \text{and} \quad Z_t = \begin{pmatrix} z_{1,t} & 1 \\ \cdot & \cdot \\ \cdot & \cdot \\ z_{N_t,t} & 1 \end{pmatrix}, \quad \text{with} \tag{16}$$

$$z_{j,t} = \frac{1 - \phi^{T_{j,t}}}{T_{j,t}(1 - \phi)} \tag{17}$$

from (7). The measurement errors are assumed to have zero means. Specification of their covariance matrix H_t is far from straightforward. Our preliminary results were based on the assumption that this matrix is diagonal with all N_t diagonal terms equal to the same number,

$$H_t = E[\xi_t \xi_t'] = \text{diag}(\sigma_0^2, \ldots, \sigma_0^2). \tag{18}$$

Assuming uncorrelated measurement errors, so $E[\xi_s \xi_t'] = 0$ when $s \neq t$, concludes the specification of this particular model.

Sequential application of the Kalman filter to increasing information sets $I_t = \{Y_1, Y_2, \ldots, Y_t\}$ yields the minimum mean square linear estimators (MMSLE) of the state variables, $E[S_t | I_t]$, using standard updating equations; these can be found in Harvey ((1989), Ch. 3). The MMSLE are 2×1 vectors from which can be calculated the $N_t \times 1$ prediction error vectors,

$$\nu_t = Y_t - Z_t \begin{pmatrix} \phi_1 & 0 \\ 0 & \phi_2 \end{pmatrix} E[S_{t-1} | I_{t-1}], \tag{19}$$

and the term structure estimates,

$$\begin{pmatrix} \hat{\alpha}_t^2 \\ \hat{\mu}_t^2 \end{pmatrix} = \begin{pmatrix} \bar{\mu} \\ \bar{\mu} \end{pmatrix} + \begin{pmatrix} 1 & 1 \\ 0 & 1 \end{pmatrix} E[S_t | I_t]. \tag{20}$$

Equations (12)–(18) specify a model having seven parameters, summarized by the vector

$$\theta = (\phi, \phi_1, \phi_2, \sigma_0^2, \sigma_1^2, \sigma_2^2, \bar{\mu}).$$

A quasi-maximum likelihood estimate of θ can be obtained because the likelihood function is the product of conditional densities $f(Y_t | I_{t-1})$ and these densities depend, through θ, upon the prediction errors ν_t and their covariance matrices $F_t = E[\nu_t \nu_t' | I_{t-1}]$. Following the arguments of Harvey ((1989), p. 126), the quasi-log-likelihood function is as follows, given by assuming the prediction errors are multivariate normal,

$$\mathrm{Ln}\ L(Y_1, Y_2, \ldots, Y_n) = \sum_{t=1}^{n} \mathrm{Ln}\ f(Y_t | I_{t-1})$$

$$= -\frac{1}{2} \sum_{t=1}^{n} (N_t\ \mathrm{Ln}(2\pi) + \mathrm{Ln}(\det F_t) + \nu_t' F_t^{-1} \nu_t). \qquad (21)$$

This function can be maximized using standard subroutines. We used the NAG subroutine E04JAF for our optimizations.

DATA AND COMPUTATION OF IMPLIED VOLATILITY

The Market

The Philadelphia currency options market is the world's leading exchange in European and American-style options on spot currencies, with markets in the Deutsche mark, Japanese yen, Swiss franc, British pound, French franc, Australian dollar, Canadian dollar, and European currency unit. Total volume in these contracts represented approximately $2 billion in underlying value each trading day in 1990. The expiry months always include March, June, September, and December. Two nearby months are also traded so that $N_t = 6$ when trade occurs for all the expiry months.

Data Sources

The primary source database for this study is the transaction report compiled daily by the Philadelphia Stock Exchange (PHLX). This report contains the following information for each option traded during a day: a date (the trade date before February 1987; for February 1987 onwards, the date on which the report was compiled, usually one day later), the style (call or put, European or American) and currency, expiration month, exercise price, number of trades, number of contracts traded, the opening, closing, lowest, and highest option prices, and the simultaneous spot exchange rate quotes. Only the closing option prices have been used. The database studied here contains options prices for the seven currencies mentioned above and the ECU from November 5, 1984, to November 21, 1989. However, the transaction report is not available for some trading days during the above period; for some others, the report is not complete or, in a few cases, is in some way clearly erroneous.

Prices have been collected manually from the Wall Street Journal (WSJ) whenever necessary. Approximately 10 percent of our implied volatilities are calculated from WSJ prices. The WSJ options prices and the associated spot prices are not simultaneous; we discuss the consequences of this nonsimultaneity in detail in Section V.B.

All the results presented in this paper are for the period commencing January 2, 1985. The prices for November and December 1984 are only used to commence the Kalman filter calculations.

The interest rates used are London euro-currency rates, collected from Datastream. This source provides overnight, seven days, one month, three months, six months, and one year interest rates. For intermediate times, we simply use linear interpolation. There is unlikely to be a simultaneity problem with the option data as the trading times are similar.

The London euro-currency interest rates were chosen because they consist of the maximum number of different maturities that we could use to make the interest rates used in calculating implied volatility as accurate as possible. Furthermore, they ensure the foreign and domestic interest rates are contemporaneous and are offered by the same institutions.

Data Selection and Revisions

Results have been obtained for American style options on four currencies, British pound, Deutsche mark, Japanese yen, and Swiss franc, separately for calls and puts. Results for the other three currencies have not been sought because trading was thin, in particular during the early part of the period studied.

Two essential changes have been made to the original data. First, we changed all the report compilation dates to the appropriate trading dates. Second, as the options expire on the Saturday before the third Wednesday of the expiration month but settle on the third Wednesday of that month, we have multiplied each option premium by $e^{R_d(4/365.25)}$, with R_d the relevant domestic (i.e., dollar) interest rate.

Several exclusion criteria were used to remove uninformative options records from the database. Five criteria are first listed and then explained. We use standard notation, with S the spot rate, X the exercise price, T the time to expiry measured in years, and R_f the foreign interest rate:

i) Options with time to expiration less than 10 calendar days.
ii) Options violating European boundary conditions, $c < Se^{-R_fT} - Xe^{-R_dT}$, $p < Xe^{-R_dT} - Se^{-R_fT}$.
iii) Options violating American boundary conditions, $C < S - X$, $P < X - S$.
iv) Options with premia less than or equal to 0.01 cents.
v) Options that are far in- or out-of-the-money: $X < 0.8S$ or $X > 1.2S$.

Criterion i was used to eliminate options with small times to maturity as the implied volatilities then behave erratically.

Criteria ii and iii eliminate options violating the boundary conditions for European and American options. As the American options could be exercised at any time up to expiration, both boundary conditions must be satisfied, otherwise a riskless arbitrage could arise. Where an option price violates a rational pricing bound, there are good reasons for suspecting that trades could not be made at this price.

Criterion iv is used to exclude options for which the necessarily discrete market prices are particularly likely to distort calculations of implied volatility.

Criterion v is used to eliminate those options that are either deep in-the-money or deep out-of-the-money. As their implied volatilities are extremely sensitive to a small change in the option price, they could distort calculations of implied volatility. Furthermore, these options trade without much volume and are thus unrepresentative.

Preliminary calculations showed that a very small number of extreme outliers ought to be removed because of their excessive influence on the model estimates. After all the exclusions, there are at least three maturities for between 75 percent and 90 percent of the days in each of the eight datasets studied.

Computation of Implied Volatility

Implied volatilities have been calculated from American model prices. The model prices are approximated by the very accurate functions derived in Barone-Adesi and Whaley (1987). The calculations of implied volatility used an interval subdivision method, which always converges to an unique solution.

It was decided to calculate the implied volatilities only from the closing prices of the nearest-the-money options; the nearest-the-money option on some day for a specific T is the option whose exercise price minimizes $|S - S|$. Nearest-the-money options were chosen for two reasons. First, given the widely reported "strike bias" or "smile effect" (Shastri and Wethyavivorn (1987), Sheikh (1991), Taylor and Xu (1993)), including out-of-the-money and in-the-money options would introduce further noise into the term structure estimates; in theory, the smile effect can be a consequence of stochastic volatility (Hull and White (1987), Stein and Stein ((1991), Table 1)). Second, the approximation that the implied volatility of a rationally priced option will equal the mean expected volatility over the time to expiry is generally considered more satisfactory for an at-the-money option than for all other options (Stein (1989), Day and Lewis (1992), Heynen, Kemna, and Vorst (1994)).

RESULTS

Results from the Regression Method

The regression method described in Section III.B produces an estimate of ϕ, the mean-reversion parameter for volatility expectations, by fitting term structures to implied volatilities within windows containing $2k + 1$ trading days. Table 11-1 lists the estimates of ϕ when $k = 5$. These are very similar across currencies, ranging from 0.968 to 0.980. The median of the eight ϕ estimates is 0.975 corresponding to a "half-life" of 27 calendar days by solving the equation $0.975^b = 0.5$. The call and put estimates can be seen to be very similar: the two smallest estimates are for the yen, the third and fourth in magnitude are for the pound, the fifth and sixth are for the mark, and the two largest are for the Swiss franc.

TABLE 11-1 Regression Method Estimates of the Term Structure Parameter ϕ when $k = 5$

Options	Full Sample (85.01–89.11)	Subsample 1 (85.01–87.06)	Subsample 2 (87.07–89.11)
BPC	0.973	0.967	0.980
BPP	0.973	0.965	0.983
DMC	0.976	0.967	0.986
DMP	0.977	0.972	0.983
JYC	0.968	0.939	0.979
JYP	0.972	0.964	0.976
SFC	0.978	0.979	0.978
SFP	0.980	0.978	0.981

BPC refers to British pound calls, BPP to British pound puts, etc.

Table 11-1 also provides estimates of the parameter ϕ for two subperiods, the first from January 1985 to June 1987 and the second from July 1987 to November 1989. Again the differences between the estimates from call and put options are very similar except for the yen in the first period. Most of the estimates of ϕ in the second period are higher than their counterparts in the first period although the differences are fairly small. The range is much greater for the first period, from 0.939 to 0.979, than for the second period, from 0.976 to 0.986. The median values are 0.967 and 0.981, respectively, for the first and second periods, corresponding to "half-lives" equal to 21 and 36 calendar days. These estimates of the "half-life" provide the important result that the market does not expect volatility shocks to persist for long, i.e., their effect is expected to disappear quickly.

Figure 11-1 summarizes the term structure of volatility expectations for mark calls. Very similar numbers are obtained for mark puts as expected. Figure 11-1 shows the time series estimates of the 15-day expectations (from Equation (6) with $\tau = 15$) and the long-term expectations μ_t. The 15-day expectations (Equation 6) are very similar to the 30-day expected average volatilities (Equation 7). We chose to plot estimates for 15-day expectations rather than expectations estimates for the next day to avoid extrapolation beyond the limits implied by our data; recall $T \geq 10$ calendar days in all the calculations. Further figures, available from the authors, make clear that volatility expectations for the three European currencies have been extremely similar with the yen close to the European currencies after mid-1987.

Five conclusions are suggested by Figure 11-1. First, the difference between 15-day and long-term expectations is often several percent so the implied volatilities reveal a significant term structure. Second, the estimates of the 15-day and long-term expectations frequently cross over, so the slope of the term structure often changes. Crossovers occur, very approximately, at an average rate of once every two to three months. Third, the long-term expected volatility varies

**FIGURE 11-1   Estimated Volatility Expectations
(Regression Method, DM Calls)**

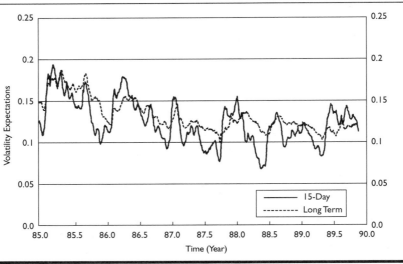

significantly. This will become clearer when the results from the Kalman filter are analyzed. Fourth, as might be expected, the estimated 15-day volatility expectation is much more variable over time than the estimated long-term expectation. Finally, the implied volatility process may not have been stationary in the sense that the average level appears to have been higher in 1985 than in the later years 1986 to 1989, although historic estimates of volatility are also high in 1985.

Results from the Kalman Filter

There are seven parameters in the time-varying term structure model described in Section III.C. The parameter ϕ continues to measure the rate of reversion in volatility expectations towards the long-term level. The spread between short- and long-term expected squared volatility is assumed to follow an AR(1) process with AR parameter ϕ_1, mean zero, and residual variance σ_1^2. The long-term expected squared volatility is assumed to independently follow an AR(1) process with AR parameter ϕ_2, mean $\bar{\mu}$, and residual variance σ_2^2.

The final parameter in III.C is the variance of the measurement errors when the model is fitted to squared implied volatilities. One parameter for the measurement error variances has been found to be insufficient to give a satisfactory model for our implied volatilities data. The magnitude of the measurement errors is larger, on average, for the WSJ observations because of nonsimultaneous spot and options prices. Furthermore, we have noted that the magnitude of the measurement errors increases, on average, as T decreases, for both data sources. Our preferred model has nine parameters with three parameters (σ_P^2, σ_T^2, and σ_W^2) used to define the dispersion matrix for the measurement errors ξ_t. The following diagonal matrix is preferred,

$$H_t = \mathrm{E}[\xi_t \xi_t'] = \mathrm{diag}\left(\sigma_S^2 + \frac{\sigma_T^2}{T_{1,t}}, \ldots, \sigma_S^2 + \frac{\sigma_T^2}{T_{N_t,t}}\right),$$

$\sigma_S^2 = \sigma_P^2$ for PHLX prices,

$\quad = \sigma_W^2$ for WSJ prices. (22)

Results are discussed in some detail for this nine-parameter model and then for simplifications (e.g., $\phi_2 = 1$) and, finally, for more general models (e.g., H_t is not diagonal).

The Preferred Model

Table 11-2 gives the parameter estimates obtained by maximizing the quasi-log-likelihood function (Equation 21) defined by the Kalman filter. Panel A presents the estimates and approximate standard errors for the complete five-year period from 1985 to 1989. The standard errors have been calculated from the information matrix using numerical second derivatives, although the reliability of the usual likelihood theory in this context is unknown to us because the matrices of state coefficients, Z_t, are time-dependent. Panel B presents the estimates for the two subperiods, from January 1985 to June 1987 and from July 1987 to November 1989.

The square root of an estimate $\bar{\mu}$ is an estimate of the median level of volatility expectations. These median estimates are smaller for the yen than for the European currencies and they decrease from the first subperiod to the second subperiod for all currencies.

The Kalman filter estimates of ϕ are very similar to the estimates for the regression method. The average of the Kalman estimate minus the regression estimate is almost zero and the differences only vary from -0.006 to 0.004. The Kalman filter estimates of ϕ range from 0.967 to 0.980 for the full samples, with median 0.974 and "half-life" equal to 27 calendar days. The Kalman filter estimates of ϕ, like those for the regression method, are generally larger for the second subperiod. The median and "half-life" for the first subperiod are 0.966 and 20 days, with a range from 0.947 to 0.981. The corresponding figures are 0.980, 35 days, 0.975 and 0.983 for the second subperiod.

Some models for asset returns imply estimates of ϕ and ϕ_1 should be similar if expectations are formed rationally. A GARCH(1, 1) model for returns is one example. The estimates of ϕ_1 are nontrivially smaller than the estimates of ϕ, but the former estimates are associated with trading days and the latter estimates with calendar days. The median estimate of ϕ_1 for the full samples is 0.966, and the associated "half-life" is 20 trading days or approximately 29 calendar days, compared with 27 calendar days for ϕ. The subperiod median estimates of ϕ_1 are very similar: 0.964 and 0.972.

TABLE 11-2   Estimated Parameters for the Preferred Term Structure Model

Options	ϕ	ϕ_1	ϕ_2	$\sqrt{\bar{\mu}}$	σ_P^2 (10^{-6})	σ_W^2 (10^{-6})	σ_T^2 (10^{-5})	$\sigma_1^2/(1-\phi_1^2)$ (10^{-5})	$\sigma_2^2/(1-\phi_2^2)$ (10^{-5})
Panel A. Estimates, 1985–1989[a]									
BPC	0.9714	0.9685	0.9972	0.1279	1.14	3.82	9.03	6.39	8.53
	(0.0019)	(0.0078)	(0.0021)	(0.0281)	(0.08)	(0.59)	(0.71)	(1.47)	(6.43)
BPP	0.9666	0.9631	0.9959	0.1334	2.08	8.99	6.99	7.79	8.06
	(0.0027)	(0.0087)	(0.0026)	(0.0212)	(0.12)	(0.95)	(0.77)	(1.71)	(5.08)
DMC	0.9756	0.9709	0.9934	0.1292	0.63	3.36	5.98	4.92	3.29
	(0.0012)	(0.0071)	(0.0033)	(0.0112)	(0.04)	(0.38)	(0.39)	(1.14)	(1.59)
DMP	0.9766	0.9689	0.9916	0.1280	0.37	14.16	7.26	4.77	2.65
	(0.0012)	(0.0074)	(0.0035)	(0.0089)	(0.04)	(1.25)	(0.41)	(1.06)	(1.10)
JYC	0.9717	0.9511	0.9838	0.1127	0.99	3.99	4.87	3.90	1.18
	(0.0018)	(0.0098)	(0.0053)	(0.0048)	(0.06)	(0.47)	(0.46)	(0.72)	(0.37)
JYP	0.9733	0.9524	0.9844	0.1099	0.33	2.57	5.09	3.56	0.95
	(0.0013)	(0.0083)	(0.0037)	(0.0045)	(0.03)	(0.32)	(0.32)	(0.56)	(0.21)
SFC	0.9772	0.9680	0.9773	0.1353	1.35	5.47	10.84	5.66	3.03
	(0.0018)	(0.0082)	(0.0064)	(0.0054)	(0.10)	(0.76)	(0.79)	(1.29)	(0.81)
SFP	0.9799	0.9640	0.9876	0.1309	0.53	9.02	13.24	4.82	2.26
	(0.0016)	(0.0086)	(0.0047)	(0.0065)	(0.08)	(1.18)	(0.84)	(1.04)	(0.81)
Panel B. Subperiod Estimates[b]									
BPC - Sub 1	0.9651	0.9700	0.9978	0.1248	1.46	1.56	9.08	16.46	
- Sub 2	0.9798	0.9737	0.9807	0.1167	0.47	7.99	6.26	4.16	0.40
BPP - Sub 1	0.9557	0.9652	0.9965	0.1414	2.55	8.85	8.35	14.61	12.94
- Sub 2	0.9811	0.9701	0.9692	0.1173	1.30	10.66	6.23	3.69	0.57
DMC - Sub 1	0.9667	0.9683	0.9921	0.1388	0.78	3.70	6.80	6.45	4.40
- Sub 2	0.9832	0.9764	0.9810	0.1193	0.36	3.24	5.62	4.11	0.31
DMP - Sub 1	0.9705	0.9636	0.9883	0.1384	0.42	7.74	8.45	6.21	3.22
- Sub 2	0.9816	0.9768	0.9803	0.1173	0.25	17.92	6.35	3.66	0.32
JYC - Sub 1	0.9474	0.9300	0.9847	0.1164	1.39	2.14	3.19	5.00	1.92
- Sub 2	0.9814	0.9616	0.9826	0.1084	0.05	3.76	9.95	4.19	0.39
JYP - Sub 1	0.9655	0.9443	0.9830	0.1130	0.35	2.75	5.31	3.34	1.54
- Sub 2	0.9752	0.9564	0.9834	0.1065	0.32	2.62	4.67	4.04	0.30
SFC - Sub 1	0.9783	0.9716	0.9648	0.1463	1.29	6.89	15.53	5.02	3.36
- Sub 2	0.9770	0.9579	0.9769	0.1230	1.07	5.52	7.18	6.34	0.52
SFP - Sub 1	0.9805	0.9596	0.9793	0.1409	0.51	6.82	17.98	4.37	2.42
- Sub 2	0.9790	0.9737	0.9849	0.1206	0.17	11.34	10.70	5.09	0.44

[a]The numbers in parentheses are the estimated standard deviations of the parameter estimates calculated from the information matrix using numerical second derivatives.
[b]The first subsample is from January 1985 to June 1987 and the second from July 1987 to November 1989.

All the estimates of ϕ_2 exceed 0.975 for the complete datasets and half of these estimates exceed 0.99. The "half-lives" for the median estimates are 66 trading days for the complete period, 51 trading days for the first subperiod, and 36 trading days for the second subperiod.

The penultimate column of Table 11-2 shows estimates of $\sigma_1^2/(1 - \phi_1^2)$, which is the variance of the spread term. The variation in the spread term is similar across the subperiods for three currencies but not for the pound, which has smaller values in the later subperiod. The final column gives estimates of $\sigma_2^2/(1 - \phi_2^2)$, which is the variance of long-term expectations. The numbers document a substantial fall over the five years in the variability through time of these expectations. An approximate 95-percent probability interval for the long-term volatility expectation can be obtained from $\sigma_2^2/(1 - \phi_2^2)$ and $\bar{\mu}$. An example is an interval from 10.4 percent to 13.3 percent for the mark, using the call estimates for the later subperiod. A corresponding interval for 15-day volatility expectations can be calculated by additionally using $\sigma_1^2/(1 - \phi_1^2)$ and ϕ. This gives 6 percent to 16 percent for the same mark source.

The small estimated values of σ_P^2 and σ_T^2 indicate that the time-varying term structure model fits the PHLX data reasonably well. A very approximate standard deviation for the difference between an observed implied volatility ($y_{j,t}$) and the correct term structure value (ν_t, Equation 7) is given by the square root of ($\sigma_P^2 + T_{j,t}^{-1}\sigma_T^2)/(4\bar{\mu})$ for PHLX observations. Typical values are 0.8 percent for a 15-day option and 0.4 percent for a 180-day option (from mark calls, full sample). The relative inaccuracy of the WSJ source is confirmed by the higher estimates for σ_W^2 than for σ_P^2. The illustrative approximate standard deviations for WSJ observations increase to 1.0 percent and 0.8 percent, respectively for 15- and 180-day options.

Figure 11-2 compares the Kalman filter estimates of volatility expectations with the regression method estimates. It can be seen that the estimates of 60-day expected average volatilities (from Equation 7) are very similar and this is

FIGURE 11-2 Estimated 60-Day Expected Average Volatilities (Regression Method and Kalman Filter, DM Calls)

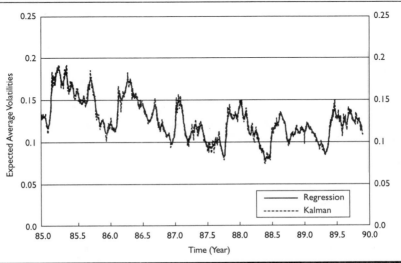

also true for 15-day and long-term expectations. Further figures, not presented here, indicate that the plotted series are less smooth for the filter method, particularly for the 15-day expectations, because the regression method uses overlapping 11-day windows. Also, the differences between the expectations obtained from call and put options are more variable for the Kalman filter.

Simpler Models

To help evaluate certain simplifications of the preferred specification of the time-varying term structure model, we present comparisons of the maximum quasi-log-likelihoods for the nine-parameter model with the corresponding figures for special cases requiring fewer parameters. The usual likelihood-ratio tests provide some insight. Cautious interpretations of log-likelihood differences are necessary, however, not least because several model parameters may have varied during the five-year period. The results for seven simplifications are summarized in Table 11-3, Panel A.

To emphasize that term structure effects exist, the model has been fitted with the restriction that the spread term is always zero ($\sigma_1 = \phi = \phi_1 = \alpha_0^2 - \mu_0^2 = 0$). The maximum log-likelihood then falls by more than 700 for each of the eight datasets. The possibility of constant long-term expectations through time ($\sigma_2 = \phi_2 = 0$) is also not credible as the maximum log-likelihood always falls by more than 500 for this model. Likewise, we can confidently disregard the idea that the two sources provide implied volatilities of equal accuracy ($\sigma_P = \sigma_W$), and we can reject the assumption that the model fits with the same accuracy for all times to expiry ($\sigma_T = 0$).

The joint hypothesis that both the spread between short- and long-term expectations and the long-term expectations follow random walks ($\phi_1 = \phi_2 = 1, \bar{\mu}$ undefined) gives likelihood-ratio test values ranging from 20.52 to 39.02, which could be compared with χ_3^2 if we trust the usual asymptotic theory. The test values strongly suggest that the joint hypothesis is doubtful. The more plausible hypothesis that the long-term expectation alone follows a random walk ($\phi_2 = 1, \bar{\mu}$ undefined) can be accepted for the pound and the mark using standard theory and a 5-percent significance level.

The hypothesis that the spread term reverts towards zero through trading time (weekdays less holidays) at the same rate as the term structure displays reversion in calendar time towards long-term expectations ($\phi_1^{4.8} = \phi^7$) is supported by all the datasets with the maximum value of the likelihood-ratio test statistic equal to 1.50.

More General Models

There are many ways to add a tenth parameter to the preferred model. The results for five generalizations are summarized in Table 11-3, Panel B, although none of them give substantial improvements for a majority of the datasets. The generalizations nearly always change the estimate of ϕ and ϕ_1 by negligible amounts. A few estimates of ϕ_2 change nontrivially, especially for the Swiss franc data.

TABLE 11-3 Comparisons of the Maximum Quasi-Log-Likelihoods for the Preferred Time-Varying Term Structure Model with the Figures for Alternative Models

	Parameters	Changes in Log-Likelihood[a]		
		Minimum	Maximum	Significant[b]
Panel A Simplifications				
Flat Term Structures	6	− 1644.81	− 720.71	8
Constant Long-Term Expectations	7	− 1413.26	− 579.41	8
Measurement Error Variance				
Same for Both Sources	8	− 466.56	− 22.13	8
Same for All T	8	− 250.64	− 52.05	8
Random Walks for:				
Spreads and Long-Term Expectations	6	− 19.51	− 10.26	8
Long-Term Expectations	7	− 6.80	− 0.90	4
Same Reversion Rate in the Spread				
and the Term Structure	8	− 0.75	− 0.01	0
Panel B Generalizations				
Average Spread Not Zero	10	0.05	1.21	0
State Variables Correlated	10	0.06	5.31	3
Correlated Measurement Errors	10	0.22	45.08	3
Mean Long-Term Expectation Varies				
with Time	10	0.38	9.01	3
σ_T^2 Depends on Data Source	10	0.01	36.33	4

The simplifications and generalizations are defined completely in Section V.B.

[a]The change in the quasi-log-likelihood function is the maximum of the function for the particular simplification or generalization minus the maximum for the preferred nine-parameter model. Each row of the table summarizes eight changes, four for pound, mark, yen, and franc call options, and four for put options.

[b]Number of significant test values out of eight at the 5-percent level. In Panel A, the test value is minus twice the change and the null hypothesis is that the preferred model is no better than the simplification. In Panel B, the test value is twice the change and the null hypothesis is that the generalization is no better than the preferred model. Test values are compared with a chi-squared distribution with degrees-of-freedom given by the number of extra parameters in the alternative hypothesis. The test values must be interpreted with caution.

A variation that deserves evaluation is to remove the assumption that $\{\alpha_t^2\}$ and $\{\mu_t^2\}$ have the same mean value, i.e., on average, the term structure is flat. Figure 11-1, at first sight, suggests that, on average, the term structure slopes upwards. Defining different means for $\{\alpha_t^2\}$ and $\{\mu_t^2\}$ gives a ten-parameter model. The difference between the square root of the estimated long-term mean and the square root of the estimated short-term mean ranges from a minimum of 0.002 for yen calls to a maximum of 0.011 for pound calls, implying a positive average slope. However, the increases in the maximum quasi-log-likelihoods are all small and insignificant.

The spread innovation is assumed to be uncorrelated with the long-term innovation in (14), which implies that there is no correlation between the spread and long-term variables. Adding a parameter for correlation between the innovation terms gives small correlation estimates; they vary from 0.03 to 0.28.

The covariance matrix H_t for the measurement errors is assumed to be diagonal in the preferred model. An extra parameter can be added by assuming that all the off-diagonal elements in the associated correlation matrix are equal. Except for the Swiss franc, the estimated common correlation term is very small (range -0.05 to 0.04) and the changes in the log-likelihood are unimportant. There is far more correlation between the measurement errors for the exceptional currency, 0.28 for the calls and 0.13 for the puts with large changes in the log-likelihood. Three parameters define the diagonal terms of H_t in (22). Increasing this to four, by allowing σ_T^2 to differ for the PHLX and WSJ sources improves some of the model fits but has no discernible effect upon the six parameters that do not appear in H_t.

Figure 11-1 and the subperiod estimates of $\bar{\mu}$ suggest that the mean of the process for long-term expectations may have declined as time progressed. Replacing $\bar{\mu}$ by $\mu_0 + \mu_1 t$ leads to negative estimates of μ_1 as expected, but the increases in the log-likelihood are not large.

CONCLUSIONS

Two methods for estimating the time-varying term structure of volatility expectations have been illustrated. These methods assume that expectations revert monotonically from a short-term value towards a long-term level as the horizon of the expectations increases. The regression method is elementary and obtains many of the conclusions provided by the technically more demanding Kalman filter method. The filter method, however, also permits estimation of time series models for volatility expectations and comparisons between models. Independent autoregressive models for long-term expectations and the spread between short- and long-term expectations are preferred for currency markets.

Our study of volatility expectations for four currencies provides five further conclusions. First, there are significant term structure effects. Fifteen-day and long-term volatility expectations often differ by several percent, which causes implied volatilities to vary significantly across maturities. Second, the term structure sometimes slopes upwards, sometimes downwards, and its direction (up or down) frequently changes. The direction changes, on average, approximately once every two or three months. Third, there are significant variations in long-term volatility expectations, although these expectations change more slowly than both short-term expectations and the spread between short- and long-term expectations. Fourth, the term structures of the pound, mark, Swiss franc, and yen at any moment in time have been very similar. Finally, there are nonstationary elements in the term structure in the sense that some of the parameters of the preferred autoregressive models changed during the five years investigated.

The volatility expectations provide insights into how the currency options market behaves. A constant volatility assumption is not made by the market. Volatility shocks are assumed to be transitory with an estimated half-life of approximately only one month. There is no evidence that the currency options market overreacts because this half-life is indistinguishable from the half-life for the mean-reverting spread between short- and long-term expectations. This is contrary to the equity results of Stein (1989), who assumed constant long-term expectations.

The volatility term structure estimates summarize the market's beliefs about volatility for all future periods. These estimates are expected to be more informative than forecasts obtained from historic prices alone. The estimates can be used to enhance hedging strategies and to value options for all maturities T including those that are not traded at exchanges.

Day and Lewis (1992) and Lamoureux and Lastrapes (1993) have estimated ARCH models for returns using implied volatility information, but disregarding term structure effects. Further research should estimate ARCH models for asset returns using the information in historic returns and short- and long-term volatility expectations. The conditional variance should then depend on short-term expectations alone if the options market is efficient. Xu and Taylor (1993) use this ARCH methodology and conclude that the PHLX currency options market is informationally efficient.

REFERENCES

Barone-Adesi, G., and R. E. Whaley. "Efficient Analytic Approximation of American Option Values." *Journal of Finance,* 42 (June 1987), 301–320.

Bollerslev, T.; R. Y. Chou; and K. F. Kroner. "ARCH Modeling in Finance: a Review of the Theory and Empirical Evidence." *Journal of Econometrics,* 52 (April 1992), 5–59.

Day, T. E., and C. M. Lewis. "The Behaviour of the Volatility Implicit in the Prices of Stock Index Options." *Journal of Financial Economics,* 22 (Oct. 1988), 103–122.

———. "Stock Market Volatility and the Information Content of Stock Index Options." *Journal of Econometrics,* 52 (April 1992), 267–287.

Diz, F., and T. J. Finucane. "Do the Options Markets Really Overreact?" *Journal of Futures Markets,* 13 (June 1993), 299–312.

Franks, J. R., and E. S. Schwartz. "The Stochastic Behaviour of Market Variance Implied in the Prices of Index Options." *The Economic Journal,* 101 (Nov. 1991), 1460–1475.

Harvey, A. C. *Forecasting, Structural Time Series Models and the Kalman Filter.* Cambridge, UK: Cambridge Univ. Press (1989).

Heynen, R.; A. G. Z. Kemna; and T. Vorst. "Analysis of the Term Structure of Implied Volatilities." *Journal of Financial and Quantitative Analysis,* 29 (March 1994), 31–56.

Hull, J., and A. White. "The Pricing of Options on Assets with Stochastic Volatilities." *Journal of Finance,* 42 (June 1987), 281–300.

Lamoureux, C. G., and W. D. Lastrapes. "Forecasting Stock Return Variance: Toward an Understanding of Stochastic Implied Volatilities." *Review of Financial Studies,* 6 (Summer 1993), 293–326.

Merville, L. J., and D. R. Pieptea. "Stock Price Volatility, Mean-Reverting Diffusion, and Noise." *Journal of Financial Economics,* 24 (Sept. 1989), 193–214.

Poterba, J. M., and L. H. Summers. "The Persistence of Volatility and Stock Market Fluctuations." *American Economic Review,* 76 (Dec. 1986), 1142–1151.

Resnick, B. G.; A. M. Sheikh; and Y. Song. "Time Varying Volatilities and Calculation of the Weighted Implied Standard Deviation." *Journal of Financial and Quantitative Analysis,* 28 (Sept. 1993), 417–430.

Shastri, K., and K. Wethyavivorn. "The Valuation of Currency Options for Alternate Stochastic Processes." *Journal of Financial Research,* 10 (No. 2, 1987), 283–293.

Sheikh, A. M. "Transaction Data Tests of S&P 100 Call Option Pricing." *Journal of Financial and Quantitative Analysis,* 26 (Dec. 1991), 459–475.

Stein, E. M., and J. C. Stein. "Stock Price Distributions with Stochastic Volatility: An Analytic Approach." *Review of Financial Studies,* 4 (Winter 1991), 727–752.

Stein, J. C. "Overreactions in the Options Market." *Journal of Finance,* 44 (Sept. 1989), 1011–1023.

Taylor, S. J., and X. Xu. "The Magnitude of Implied Volatility Smiles: Theory and Empirical Evidence for Exchange Rates." *Review of Futures Markets,* 13 (1994), 355–380.

Xu, X., and S. J. Taylor. "Conditional Volatility and the Informational Efficiency of the PHLX Currency Options Market." *Journal of Banking and Finance,* 19 (1995), 803–821.

PART FIVE

Jump Process and Stochastic Volatility Models for Currency Derivatives

12

Dollar Jump Fears, 1984–1992: Distributional Abnormalities Implicit in Currency Futures Options

DAVID S. BATES

Currency option pricing models premised upon the Black-Scholes assumption of geometric Brownian motion (GBM) exhibit severe specification error when fitted to market data. Systematic pricing errors—or, equivalently, different implicit volatilities for different strike prices and maturities—are repeatedly found. For instance, Bodurtha and Courtadon's (1987) study of the Philadelphia foreign currency options market over February 28, 1983, to March 25, 1985, found that out-of-the-money Deutsche mark call options were systematically underpriced and in-the-money call options were overpriced using the previous day's implicit volatility. Hsieh and Manas-Anton (1988) found a skewed U-shape in implicit volatilities in 1984 DM futures options traded on the Chicago Mercantile Exchange, with a tendency for higher implicit volatilities to accompany higher strike prices. More recent attention has focused on the so-called 'volatility smile,' or U-shaped pattern in implicit volatilities for different strike prices; e.g., Cao's (1992) study of foreign currency options over 1987–89.

The evidence of specification error indicates that the conditional distributions implicit in foreign currency option prices deviate substantially from the lognormal distribution assumed by Black and Scholes. The asymmetric moneyness biases observed by Bodurtha and Courtadon over 1983–85 indicate a positively skewed implicit distribution for the \$/DM spot exchange rate. The subsequent 'volatility smile' evidence of 'overpriced' out-of-the-money call and put

Reprinted with permission from *Journal of International Money and Finance;* Vol. 15, No. 1; David S. Bates; *Dollar Jump Fears, 1984-1992;* 1996; Elsevier Science Ltd., Oxford, England.

options over 1987–89 is characteristic of a leptokurtic distribution; the options would not be overpriced under fatter-tailed distributions' higher probabilities of pay-off. Numerous time series studies have, of course, indicated substantial abnormalities in daily or weekly log-differenced exchange rates. Foreign currency option prices indicate that such abnormalities may continue to be of concern at the monthly or quarterly horizon corresponding to typical option maturities.

Three approaches have been employed in attempting to achieve an implicit distribution more compatible with observed option prices. Stochastic interest rate models such as Grabbe (1983), Amin and Jarrow (1991), and Hilliard et al. (1991) relax the standard assumption of constant domestic and foreign interest rates. Unfortunately, most of these models still imply lognormal implicit distributions (or, equivalently, that all European options should have the same implicit volatility), and therefore cannot explain the systematic biases of the GBM model.[1] Chesney and Scott (1989), Jorion (1989), and Cao (1992) have explored the possibility that the option pricing biases are related to the stochastic evolution of the instantaneous conditional volatility—a randomization known to induce excess kurtosis. Finally, models with independent fat-tailed shocks to the exchange rate have been proposed: McCulloch's (1985, 1987) stable-Paretian model, Borensztein and Dooley's (1987) pure-jump model, and Jorion's (1989) jump-diffusion model.

This paper falls into the last category, and examines the ability of a jump-diffusion model to explain systematic deviations in implicit distributions from the benchmark assumption of lognormality. Since Merton's (1976) assumption of diversifiable jump risk is untenable for currency options, a jump-diffusion model is developed for pricing American options on foreign currency futures when jump exchange risk is systematic. The theoretical development parallels Bates (1991), but with closer attention to numeraire issues relevant for currency options. A closely related model is in Perraudin and Sørensen (1994).

This paper has three empirical objectives. The first is descriptive: to document the extent to which abnormalities in implicit distributions have been important over time in options on foreign currency futures. Such a history is interesting both for identifying when market participants were most concerned about exchange rate abnormalities (as reflected in the prices they were willing to pay for options), and for generating 'stylized facts' to be matched by future option pricing models. Two methods are used in chronicling these deviations. The 'skewness premium' metric of Bates (1991, 1994a), defined as the percentage deviation of call from put prices for options equally out-of-the-money, is used as an atheoretic measure of implicit skewness that can shed light on which distributional hypotheses can and cannot explain observed deviations from GBM prices. The second method uses model-specific daily estimates of the volatility, skewness, and excess kurtosis implicit in currency futures option prices. The methodology generalizes the common practice of estimating implicit volatilities assuming geometric Brownian motion, which is nested within the jump-diffusion specification.

Second, this paper examines the extent to which abnormalities implicit at times in foreign currency futures option prices can predict subsequent abnormalities in realized log-differenced foreign currency futures prices. The $/DM distributions inferred from options using the jump-diffusion model do in fact predict future abnormalities in the $/DM futures price distribution, although the predictions are not unbiased. No informational content whatsoever is found in $/yen futures option prices.

The third objective of the paper is to examine the extent to which option pricing anomalies can shed light on the puzzlingly strong rejections of uncovered interest rate parity. As discussed in the surveys of Hodrick (1987), Froot and Thaler (1990), and Lewis (1995), one of the central puzzles of international finance is the apparently predictable divergence between domestic and foreign money market returns denominated in a common currency. The simple trading strategy of switching between two currencies based on which has the higher interest rate has been found to be significantly profitable for assorted industrialized countries' currencies and various subperiods; the higher interest rates have not tended to be offset by capital losses from exchange rate movements. And although this divergence could potentially be explained by a risk premium, no explicit model has yet succeeded both in explaining the magnitude of the profit opportunities, and in satisfying Fama's (1984) argument that *if* it is a risk premium, it must be a highly time-varying one.[2]

If the profit opportunities are not attributable to risk premiums, then there must either be expectational errors, or the econometric evidence is unreliable. The expectational error hypothesis has been explored by various studies that have employed survey data as a proxy for market expectations.[3] A theoretical justification is provided by Lewis (1989), who postulates and tests a model of Bayesian learning about a regime shift during the 1980s. Studies challenging the reliability of the econometric evidence have focussed on small-sample problems originating in peso problems and bubbles (Evans, 1986), learning (Lewis, 1989), and regime shifts (Engel and Hamilton, 1990).

If there is a peso problem underlying observed rejections of uncovered interest parity, then it should be discernable in option prices. If, for instance, fears of a dollar crash deterred investors from investing in high-interest dollars in the early 1980s, then those fears should be reflected in positively skewed $/FC distributions—which can in fact be inferred from Bodurtha and Courtadon (1987). But even symmetric jump fears and the associated leptokurtosis can create small-sample problems for the asymptotic distribution theory used in market efficiency tests, as discussed in Krasker (1980). This paper therefore reruns the standard tests of uncovered interest parity, exploiting the information provided by option prices regarding skewness and excess kurtosis in the conditional distribution.

The first section of this chapter presents the jump-diffusion model for pricing American options on foreign currency futures under systematic exchange rate jump risk. The second section discusses the diagnostics of implicit distributions, while the third examines the forecasting ability of those distributions and implications for tests of uncovered interest parity. The final section concludes.

PRICING OPTIONS UNDER SYSTEMATIC EXCHANGE RATE JUMP RISK

Actual versus 'Risk-Neutral' Distributions

The fundamental distributional assumption underlying the option pricing model presented in this paper is the following:

ASSUMPTION 1: The \$/FC spot exchange rate is assumed to follow a geometric jump-diffusion with normally distributed jump-contingent changes in the log of the exchange rate:

$$\frac{dS}{S} = (\mu - \lambda \bar{k})dt + \sigma dZ + (e^{\gamma} - 1)dq, \tag{1}$$

where

μ = is the expected rate of appreciation of foreign currency:
Z = is a standard Wiener process:
λ = is the frequency of jumps:
$\bar{k}$ = $E(e^{\gamma} - 1)$ is the mean percentage jump in the exchange rate:
γ, = the random jump in the log of the exchange rate, conditional on a jump occurring, is normally distributed $N[\ln(1 + \bar{k}) - 1/2\delta^2, \delta^2]$; and
q = is a Poisson counter with frequency λ: $\text{Prob}(dq = 1) = \lambda dt$.

All parameters are assumed constant over the relevant option horizon of 1–4 months. The notation $\Delta S/S \equiv k \equiv e^{\gamma} - 1$ will occasionally be used below for the percentage change conditional on a jump.

In the presence of jump risk, options can no longer be priced via no-arbitrage conditions. Instead, the jump risk must be priced either by assuming that the jump risk is nonsystematic or by imposing restrictions on preferences and technologies sufficient to price the jump risk.[4] Since the exchange rate is a fundamental economic variable affecting international consumption and investment decisions, the latter approach will be followed. Without loss of generality, the dollar will be used as the measurement currency.

ASSUMPTION 2: *Aggregate preferences can be represented by a price-taking international consumer-investor with time-separable, state-independent von Neumann-Morgenstern preferences of the form*

$$E_t \int_t^{\infty} \frac{e^{-\rho s}}{1 - R} \left[\left(\frac{C_s}{Q_s} \right)^{1-R} - 1 \right] ds, \tag{2}$$

where C_s is dollar expenditure on consumption goods at time s and $Q = P^{\alpha}(SP^*)^{1-\alpha}$ is the price deflator given world expenditure shares α and (1

$- \alpha)$ on dollar-denominated and foreign goods, respectively. Given consumption of foreign goods, the price deflator jumps synchronously with the exchange rate:

$$dQ/Q = (\pi - \lambda \bar{k}_q)dt + \sigma_q dZ_q + (e^{\gamma_q} - 1)dq. \tag{3}$$

ASSUMPTION 3: *The dollar value of optimally invested world wealth follows a geometric jump-diffusion of the form*

$$dW/W = (\mu_w - \lambda \bar{k}_w - C/W)dt + \sigma_w dZ_w + (e^{\gamma_w} - 1)dq, \tag{4}$$

where q is the same Poisson counter with frequency λ as in (1) and (3) above, and γ, γ_w, and γ_q have a trivariate normal distribution with constant parameters:

$$\begin{pmatrix} \gamma \\ \gamma_w \\ \gamma_q \end{pmatrix} \sim N \left[\begin{pmatrix} \ln(1 + \bar{k}) - \dfrac{1}{2}\delta^2 \\ \ln(1 + \bar{k}_w) - \dfrac{1}{2}\delta_w^2 \\ \ln(1 + \bar{k}_q) - \dfrac{1}{2}\delta_q^2 \end{pmatrix}, \begin{pmatrix} \delta^2 \delta_{sw} \delta_{sq} \\ \delta_{sw} \delta_w^2 \delta_{wq} \\ \delta_{sq} \delta_{wq} \delta_q^2 \end{pmatrix} \right]. \tag{5}$$

The parameters π, μ_w and σ_w will be assumed constant below.

The second assumption is consistent with an international economy in which domestic and foreign agents both have log utility ($R = 1$) and are consequently effectively homogeneous despite deviations from purchasing power parity. More general preferences in the absence of purchasing power parity imply agents are heterogeneous, with preferences of the representative agent consequently dependent upon the international distribution of wealth. For those generalized preferences, one must implicitly assume that aggregation issues and the evolution of wealth distribution can be ignored when pricing foreign currency options.[5]

The third assumption regarding the distribution of optimally invested wealth is consistent with a jump-diffusion extension of the Cox et al. (1985) production economy (Ahn and Thompson, 1988; Bates, 1988).[6] In general some or all of the parameters of the wealth process may be stochastic. Absent any direct information regarding the intrinsically unobservable distribution of jumps in the world market index, the assumption of a time-invariant lognormal distribution is plausible and convenient.

Under these assumptions, it is shown in the appendix that options are priced *as if* investors were risk-neutral in dollar terms and the \$/FC exchange rate followed the jump-diffusion

$$dS/S = (r - r^* - \lambda' k')dt + \sigma dZ' + k' dq', \tag{6}$$

where:

$\lambda' = \lambda[1 + E(n)]$;
$n \equiv \Delta(J_w/Q)/J_w/Q$ is the jump-contingent percentage change in the marginal utility of dollar wealth:

Z' is a standard Wiener process;

q' is a Poisson counter with frequency λ';

$\bar{k}' = \bar{k} + \text{Cov}(k, n)/1 + E(n) = (1 + \bar{k})e^{-R\delta_{sw} - (1-R)\delta_{sq}} - 1$;

$\ln(1 + k')$ is normally distributed $N[\ln(1 + \bar{k}') - 1/2\delta^2, \delta^2]$;

and R is the coefficient of relative risk aversion. The expressions for λ' and $\bar{k}'$ in terms of moments and covariances of the pricing kernel n are quite general, and do not depend upon Assumptions 2 and 3. The role of those assumptions is to ensure constant λ' and $\bar{k}'$, to generate a convenient lognormal distribution for $\ln(1 + k')$, and to imply constant domestic and foreign interest rates r and r^*. Only under quite stringent conditions will the risk-neutral and actual distributions coincide exactly; e.g., when there exist risk-neutral US investors who do not consume foreign goods. On the other hand, calibrations using standard assumptions about relative risk aversion suggest it is unlikely that the risk-neutral and actual parameters would deviate substantially.[7]

The 'risk-neutral' jump-diffusion, which summarizes the relevant Arrow–Debreu state-contingent prices for evaluating contingent claims, depends upon the choice of measurement currency. In particular, (6) is appropriate for generating the *dollar* prices of contingent claims as functions of the \$/FC exchange rate. Suppose instead one wanted the foreign currency price $V^*(S^*, t)$ of a contingent claim as a function of the FC/\$ exchange rate $S^* = S^{-1}$. The appropriate pricing kernel is then the jump-contingent percentage change in the marginal utility of *foreign-currency* denominated wealth, and the relevant 'risk-neutral' jump-diffusion is of the form

$$\frac{dS^*}{S^*} = \left[r^* - r - \lambda''E''\left(\frac{\Delta S^*}{S^*}\right)\right]dt + \sigma Z'' + (e^{\gamma''} - 1)dq'', \tag{7}$$

where

$\lambda'' = \lambda[1 + E(n^*)]$;

$n^* \equiv \Delta(SJ_w/Q)/SJ_w/Q$ is the jump-contingent percentage change in the marginal utility of foreign currency-denominated wealth;

q'' is a Poisson counter with frequency λ'';

$1 + E''(\Delta S^*/S^*) = 1/(1 + \bar{k}')$; and

γ'' is normally distributed $N[-\ln(1 + \bar{k}') - 1/2\delta^2, \delta^2]$.

It is not correct to take an Itô transformation of (6) using $S^* = S^{-1}$ to get the risk-neutral measure for S^*.

The incompatibility of the dollar- and foreign currency-based 'risk-neutral' specifications of the exchange rate is another manifestation of Siegal's paradox. If, for instance, investors are genuinely risk-neutral in dollar terms with respect to jump risk, then they cannot be risk-neutral in foreign currency terms. The issue is resolved by the existence of numeraire-specific risk premiums built into the 'risk-neutral' probability measures—in particular, into the difference between λ' and λ''.

Option Pricing

Given that domestic and foreign interest rates are constant under the assumptions of the model, futures and forward prices are identical. Consequently, the risk-neutral process for the futures price $F_{t,T} = Se^{(r-r^*)(T-t)}$ is a jump-diffusion martingale similar to (6) above:

$$dF/F = -\lambda' \bar{k}' dt + \sigma dZ' + k' dq'. \tag{8}$$

European call options on foreign currency futures with strike price X are priced at the discounted expected terminal payoff under the risk-neutral distribution given by (8):

$$c(F, T; X) = e^{-r(T+\Delta t_1)} \sum_{n=0}^{\infty} Prob'(n \text{ jumps}) E'_t[\max(F_{t+T} - X, 0)|n \text{ jumps}]$$

$$= e^{-r(T+\Delta t_1)} \sum_{n=0}^{\infty} \left[e^{-\lambda' T} \frac{(\lambda' T)^n}{n!} \right] [Fe^{b(n)T} N(d_{1n}) - XN(d_{2n})] \tag{9}$$

where:

$$b(n) = -\lambda' \bar{k}' + \frac{n\ln(1 + \bar{k}')}{T},$$

$$d_{1n} = \frac{\ln(F/X) + b(n)T + \frac{1}{2}(\sigma^2 T + n\delta^2)}{\sqrt{\sigma^2 T + n\delta^2}},$$

and

$$d_{2n} = d_{1n} - \sqrt{\sigma^2 T + n\delta^2}.$$

T is the time to maturity, while Δt_1 is the delivery lag upon terminal exercise. European put option values can be obtained from call option values using put-call parity:

$$p(F, T; X) = c(F, T; X) + e^{-r(T+\Delta t_1)}(F - X). \tag{10}$$

Studies of foreign currency options traded on the Philadelphia Stock Exchange have exploited the fact that either American call prices or American put prices are well approximated by their European counterparts, depending on whether the domestic/foreign interest differential is positive or negative. No similar approximation is valid for the American foreign currency futures options traded on the Chicago Mercantile Exchange. Instead, it is necessary to take into account the extra value accruing to both calls and puts from the ability to exercise the options prior to maturity—the 'early-exercise premium.' This study uses a slightly modified version of the analytic approximations to the early-exercise premiums derived in Bates (1991):

$$P(F, T; X) = \begin{cases} p(F, T; X) + XA_1 \left(\dfrac{F/X}{y_p^*}\right)^{q_1} & \text{for } F/X \geq y_p^* \\ e^{-r\Delta t_2}(X - F) & \text{for } F/X < y_p^* \end{cases} \tag{11}$$

$$
C(F, T; X) = \begin{cases} c(F, T; X) + XA_2\left[\dfrac{F/X}{y_c^*}\right]^{q_2} & \text{for } F/X < y_c^* \\[2ex] e^{-r\Delta t_2}(F - X) & \text{for } F/X \geq y_c^* \end{cases}
\tag{12}
$$

where:

$A_1 = e^{-r\Delta t_2}(1 - y_p^*) - p(y_p^*, T; 1);$

$A_2 = e^{-r\Delta t_2}(y_c^{*1} - 1) - c(y_c^*, T; 1);$

Δt_2 is the delivery lag upon early exercise;

the variables q_1 and q_2 are the negative and positive roots to:

$$
\frac{1}{2}\sigma^2 q^2 - \left(\lambda'\bar{k}' + \frac{1}{2}\sigma^2\right)q - \frac{r}{1 - e^{-rT}}
$$
$$
+ \lambda'[(1 + \bar{k}')^q e^{1/2 q(q-1)\delta^2} - 1] = 0;
\tag{13}
$$

y_p^*, the critical futures price/strike price ratio for immediate exercise of puts, is given implicitly by

$$
e^{-r\Delta t_2}(1 - y_p^*) = p(y_p^*, T; 1) - \left(\frac{y_p^*}{q_1}\right)[e^{-r\Delta t_2} + p_F(y_p^*, T; 1)];
\tag{14}
$$

and y_c^*, the critical futures price/strike price ratio for immediate exercise of calls, is given by

$$
e^{-r\Delta t_2}(y_p^* - 1) = c(y_c^*, T; 1) + \left(\frac{y_c^*}{q_2}\right)[e^{-r\Delta t_2} - c_F(y_c^*, T; 1)].
\tag{15}
$$

American foreign currency futures options traded on the Chicago Mercantile Exchange expire two Fridays (12 days) prior to the third Wednesday of the contract month, that Wednesday being the underlying future's delivery date. Exercise of an option on any trading day yields a position at the strike price in the underlying futures the following business day, which can then be marked to market and closed out without incurring margin requirements. For these options, T is the time until the last trading day, Δt_1 is the 3 calendar day lag upon terminal exercise, and Δt_2 is the 1 business day lag upon early exercise.

The accuracy of the approximations is examined in Bates (1991). For DM and yen futures options of less than 6 months maturity, the approximation error is typically substantially less than 0.01 ¢/DM or 0.0001 ¢/¥, the size of one price tick.

ESTIMATION

Data

This study uses the options on Deutsche mark and yen futures traded on the Chicago Mercantile Exchange (CME), which began trading on January 24, 1984 and March 5, 1986, respectively.[8] While pre-dated by the foreign currency options traded since 1983 on the Philadelphia Stock Exchange (PHLX), the futures options were typically more actively traded, and have the advantage of being a much cleaner data set with readily available underlying futures prices.[9] The longer time span of the PHLX yen options is somewhat illusory given virtually no trading in those options over 1984–85. Both markets are currently dwarfed by the interbank foreign currency options market. However, the interbank market predominantly trades at-the-money options, which contain information only about implicit volatilities and not about higher moments.[10]

The foreign currency futures options market evolved substantially over 1984–92, with the number of maturities and the range of strike prices available generally increasing. For instance, whereas futures options were initially available only for March, June, September, and December expiration dates, serial options on the nearest other two months were introduced in 1987. Similarly, DM options were initially available only for integer strike prices (in ¢/DM) falling within a ±2-1/2 cent band around the integer strike closest to the previous day's settlement price, plus strike prices opened previously. Currently, the relevant band for integer strikes (¢/DM or ¢/100¥) is ±6 cents, and there have been half-cent strikes since 1990 for both DM and yen futures options. Given that past contracts can trade until expiration, the range of strike prices available for a given quarterly maturity at any time depends upon the past movements of the futures price during the history of that maturity of option.[11]

Transactions data for call and put options on Deutsche mark and yen futures and for the underlying futures contracts were obtained from the CME from inception of the options contracts through December 31, 1992. The data consist of the time and price of every transaction in which the price changed from the previous transaction. Bid and ask prices are also recorded if the bid is above or the ask is below the price of the previous transaction. There is no information given regarding the volume of the transactions at a particular price.

Four restrictions were applied to the data. First, the bid and ask data were discarded, since no transactions were conducted at those prices. Second, only contracts of a single maturity were considered for any day: namely, quarterly contracts with maturities between 1 and 4 months (28–116 days). Longer maturities were too thinly traded, and shorter maturities were too near maturity to contain much information about implicit distributions. Third, to avoid days with thin trading, at least 20 call and 20 put transactions were required for a day's data to be retained. Finally, transactions in at least 4 strike classes for calls and 4 for puts were required, to ensure a 'moneyness' range sufficient to provide a good picture of the underlying distribution.

The nearest futures transaction of comparable maturity preceding each options transaction was used as the underlying futures price, provided elapsed time was less than 5 minutes. If not, and if there existed a shorter-maturity futures transaction during the preceding 5 minutes, a comparable-maturity futures price was inferred using the average comparable-maturity/short-term futures price ratio computed from synchronous pairs of futures transactions observed over the day.[12] Otherwise the option record was discarded. Lapsed time between the futures and options transactions averaged about 30 seconds for both DM and yen options. The daily risk-free interest rate used in pricing options was interpolated from that day's 1- and 3-month Treasury bill yields. While admittedly inconsistent with the constant interest rate assumptions, Amin and Jarrow's (1991) model indicates that using the contemporaneous discount factor captures the major impact of stochastic interest rates upon foreign currency futures option prices.[13]

The above criteria eliminated 237 out of 2262 days over 1984–92 for DM futures options, mostly in the first two years. For yen options, 537 out of 1728 days over 1986–92 were eliminated, largely because of thin trading after mid-1991. The resulting data set averages 162 (146) transactions per day in DM (yen) futures options. Overall, 58% of the DM transactions and 50% of the yen transactions were calls. Most transactions involved out-of-the-money or at-the-money transactions; in-the-money options were thinly traded. The relative activity in calls versus puts varied considerably over time; see Figure 12-1.

The Skewness Premium

A nonparametric diagnostic of the skewness of the distribution implicit in option prices is provided by the *skewness premium,* defined as the percentage deviation of x percent out-of-the-money call prices from x percent out-of-the-money put prices:

$$SK(x) \equiv \frac{C(F, T; X_c)}{P(F, T; X_p)} - 1 \tag{16}$$

where:

FIGURE 12-1   Call transactions relative to total call and put transactions: DM and yen futures options, 1984–92.

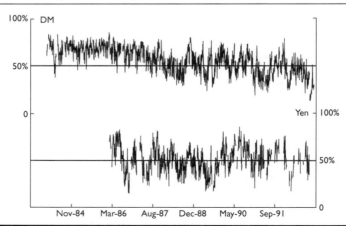

$$X_p = \frac{F}{1 + x} < F < X_c = F(1 + x), x > 0.$$

As discussed in Bates (1991, 1994a), the skewness premium for European options in general and American futures options should be roughly between 0 percent and x percent inclusive for the standard essentially symmetric distributions typically considered: arithmetic and geometric Brownian motion, 'standard' constant elasticity of variance processes, jump-diffusions with mean-zero jumps (under the risk-neutral distribution), and the Hull and White (1987) stochastic volatility process. Greater positive skewness arising from positive-mean jumps or a positive correlation between volatility and exchange rate innovations will be reflected in a skewness premium greater than x percent. Conversely, negative-mean jumps or a negative correlation between volatility and exchange rate shocks pushes the premium below x percent and possibly negative.

Since call and put transactions are not typically symmetrically out-of-the-money synchronously, measurement of the skewness premium requires interpolation from the available set of option prices over a given interval. For this study, prices of all call and put transactions within any given day were pooled. The daily representative call and put options price/futures price ratios for options 0 percent, 2 percent, 4 percent and 6 percent out-of-the-money (OTM) were interpolated using the constrained cubic spline methodology of Bates (1991) illustrated in Figure 12-2. The fits of the cubic splines were generally excellent, with median standard errors of .029 percent and .020 percent for

---

FIGURE 12-2   March 25, 1986 prices of calls and puts on DM futures: transaction prices, constrained cubic spline, and early exercise values, as a fraction of the underlying futures price.

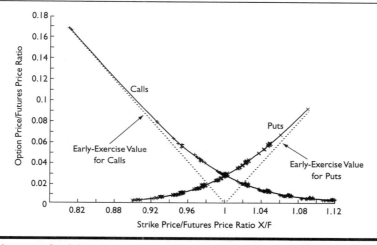

Cubic splines were fitted through the data subject to convexity, slope, and early-exercise constraints.

calls and puts, respectively—roughly 1 to 2 price ticks. There were exceptions on individual days, however, as well as variations over time in the noisiness of options markets. Most notable was the increase in option price dispersion in the $/DM options market accompanying and following the Exchange Rate Mechanism (ERM) currency crisis in September 1992; see Figure 12-3.

Skewness premiums over 1984–92 for DM and over 1986–92 for yen were generated as the percentage difference between interpolated call and put prices using options at-the-money and 2 percent, 4 percent and 6 percent out-of-the-money:

$$S\hat{K}(x) = [\hat{C}(x) - \hat{P}(x)]/\hat{P}(x)$$

with estimated standard error $\sigma_{SK} = (\hat{C}/\hat{P})[(\hat{\sigma}_c/\hat{C})^2 + (\hat{\sigma}_p/\hat{P})^2]^{1/2}$ computed assuming that the interpolation error for calls was uncorrelated with the error for puts.[14]

Despite the noisiness of estimated skewness premiums evident in Figures 12-4 and 12-5, persistent deviations away from the $[0, x]$ range of standard distributional hypotheses are periodically observed. Over most of 1984–87, for instance, the $/DM implicit distribution was persistently more positively skewed than the lognormal.[15] The 4 percent $/DM skewness premium oscillated over 1988–92 with occasional persistent sign changes, while the September 1992 devaluations of the lira and pound were followed by a temporary negative surge in the $/DM premium. The 4 percent $/yen skewness premium appears substantially correlated with the $/DM premium over most of 1986–92, suggesting that it was predominantly US-specific factors moving both premiums. Not sur-

FIGURE 12-3   Overall fit of splines, as a percentage of the underlying futures price.

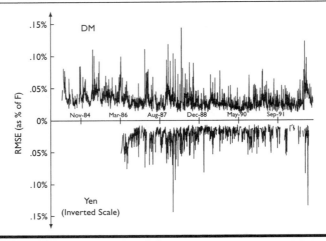

Standard errors of .02% of F correspond roughly to 1 − 1-1/2 price ticks for DM and yen futures options.

FIGURE 12-4 and FIGURE 12-5   Percentage deviation of call form put prices (skewness premium) and associated standard errors for options 4% out-of-the-money, 1984–92.

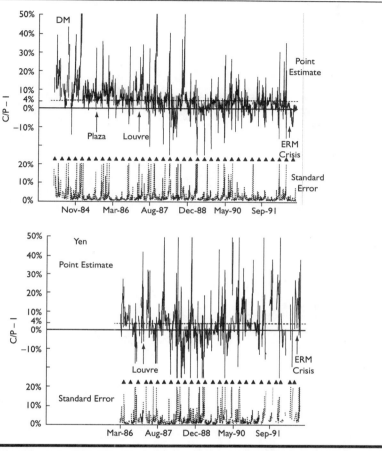

Deviations above (below) the [0%, 4%] range indicate greater positive (negative) skewness than that implied by standard distributional hypotheses. Triangles (▲) indicate shifts in the delivery date of the 1–4 month options.

prisingly, the September 1992 ERM crisis had little impact on the $/yen premium. Given the noisiness of the series, it is not clear whether the major international exchange rate agreements affecting the $/DM and $/yen exchange rates during this period (the Plaza Agreement of September 22, 1985, and the Louvre Accord of February 21, 1987) influenced the skewness premiums.

The performance of the 2 percent and 6 percent skewness premiums were qualitatively similar to that of the 4 percent, and are consequently not shown.[16] As indicated in Table 12-1, deviations from the [0, x] range of standard distributional hypotheses were observed over more than half of the period for both DM and yen futures options; more frequently above than below. The deviations were typically but not invariably too large to be attributable to interpolation error. The null hypothesis that $SK(x) \in [0, x]$ was rejected at 5 percent significance for 33–45 percent of the days (depending on currency and moneyness), and rejected at 1 percent significance for 27–39 percent of the days.

Estimation of Jump-Diffusion Parameters

A more explicit characterization of the distribution implicit in option prices can be obtained by fitting the jump-diffusion model of the first section to intradaily option prices. The option price/futures price ratios within a given day were

TABLE 12-1 Skewness premium $(C − P)/P$ for options at-the-money and 2 percent, 4 percent, and 6 percent out-of-the-money: summary statistics, and frequency of rejection over 1984–92 of the null hypothesis H_0: $0 \le (C − P)/P \le x\%$ for options $x\%$ out-of-the-money.

DM: January 24, 1984– December 31, 1992 (2025 days)	ATM options	2% OTM options	4% OTM options	6% OTM options
Number of observations of $(C − P)/P$	1959	2023	1964	1482
Mean (%)	0.1	2.2	5.2	7.7
Standard deviation (%)	1.6	3.2	11.4	21.0
Distribution of $(C − P)/P$ (%)				
less than 0%	48	20	21	29
within [0%, x%] range		34	32	26
greater than x%	52	46	47	45
Frequency of rejection of H_0: $(C − P)/P \in [0, x\%]$ (%)				
at 5% significance	40	33	38	35
at 1% significance	29	27	32	30
Yen: March 5, 1986–December 31, 1992 (1192 days)				
Number of observations of $(C − P)/P$	1089	1191	1102	617
Mean (%)	0.1	1.9	4.8	11.3
Standard deviation (%)	1.9	4.4	16.7	59.3
Distribution of $(C − P)/P$ (%)				
less than 0%	50	29	35	38
within [0%, x%] range		26	22	18
greater than x%	50	45	44	45
Frequency of rejection of H_0: $(C − P)/P \in [0, x\%]$ (%)				
at 5% significance	45	42	45	40
at 1% significance	33	34	39	34

assumed to be the corresponding model prices plus a random additive disturbance term:

$$\frac{V_j}{F_j} = \frac{V(F_j, T; X_j, \sigma, \lambda', \bar{k}', \delta)}{F_j} + \epsilon_j, \quad j = 1, \ldots, NOBS_t. \tag{17}$$

A cross-sectional data sample of calls and puts with identical maturities was used. The implicit parameters σ_t, λ'_t, $\bar{k}'_t$, and δ_t for each day were estimated via nonlinear least squares using the quadratic hillclimbing software of Goldfeld and Quandt, GQOPT method GRADX, six starting values per day. Similar regressions were run for all days in the 1984–92 data sample. The implicit parameters were not constrained to be constant over time.

The jump-diffusion option pricing model appears to suffer from a nonlinear identification problem, in that quite different parameter values can yield virtually identical option prices. For instance, there were two equilibria for 98-day DM options on March 2, 1984 with identical root mean squared error:

$(\sigma, \lambda', \bar{k}', \delta) = (8.195\%, 2.209 \text{ jumps/yr}, 2.227\%, 4.591\%)$ and

$(\sigma, \lambda', \bar{k}', \delta) = (9.508\%, 0.266 \text{ jumps/yr}, 11.689\%, 0.054\%)$.

This is not necessarily a problem, in that what matters primarily is the implicit distribution rather than the parameters generating it. The probability density and distribution functions are indistinguishable at the 98-day horizon for the two sets of parameters above, and both are substantially positively skewed and leptokurtic. However, an implication of the identification problem is that the time series of parameter estimates are volatile and uninformative. Consequently, only relatively stable transformations of the parameter estimates are reported below; in particular, the implicit moments.

The implicit expected jump component $\lambda'\bar{k}'$ shown in Figure 12-6 mirrors the 4 percent skewness premium, albeit with somewhat less noise. Substantial upside risk on DM was observed in 1984–85, while perceptions of downside risk on DM followed the September 1992 devaluations of the lira and pound. Substantial oscillation over 1986–92 in the number of implicit expected jumps per year was observed for both DM and yen futures options.

A particularly striking result is the strong direct relationship between the implicit expected jump size and the relative trading activity in calls versus puts shown in Figure 12-1. For yen futures options the implicit mean jump size was invariably positive in periods in which more calls were traded than puts, and negative when the reverse was true. A similar relationship held for DM futures options for 77 percent of the 2025 days in the 1984–92 data sample; see Table 12-2. Since in-the-money calls and puts are thinly traded, this implies that the periods of positive-mean implicit jumps coincided with relatively heavy trading in OTM calls, while negative-mean implicit jumps coincided with heavy trading in OTM puts. Similarly, relative trading activity was directly related to whether the 4 percent skewness premium was above or below its 4 percent benchmark.

The implicit variance, skewness, and excess kurtosis of $\ln(F_{t+T}/F_t)$ under the risk-neutral distribution are given by:

FIGURE 12-6   Expected jumps pear year $\lambda'\bar{k}'$ implicit in 1–4 month DM and yen futures options, 1984–92.

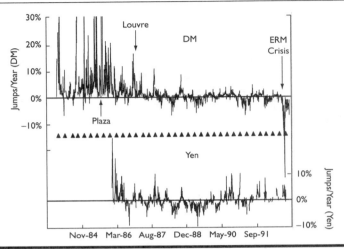

Triangles (▲) indicate shifts in the delivery date of the options.

TABLE 12-2   Distribution of expected jumps per year $\lambda'\bar{k}'$ versus call/put trading activity

Relative call transactions activity	Implicit jumps/year—$/DM Number of days (% of total)		Implicit jumps/year—$/yen Number of days (% of total)	
	$\lambda'\bar{k}' < 0$	$\lambda'\bar{k}' > 0$	$\lambda'\bar{k}' < 0$	$\lambda'\bar{k}' > 0$
Less than 50%	598 (30%)	60 (3%)	594 (50%)	0 (0%)
Greater than 50%	416 (21%)	951 (47%)	0 (0%)	598 (50%)

Table shows distribution of days sorted by two criteria: 1) whether the expected number of jumps per year inferred from futures options is positive or negative; 2) whether calls were less or more actively traded than puts.

$$v^2T = \{\sigma^2 + \lambda'[(\bar{\gamma}')^2 + \delta^2]\}T, \tag{18}$$

$$SKEW = \frac{\lambda'\bar{\gamma}'[(\bar{\gamma}')^2 + 3\delta^2]}{v^3\sqrt{T}}, \tag{19}$$

$$XKURT = \frac{\lambda'[(\bar{\gamma}')^4 + 6(\bar{\gamma}')^2\delta^2 + 3\delta^4]}{v^4T}, \tag{20}$$

where $\bar{\gamma}' \equiv \ln(1 + \bar{k}') - 1/2\delta^2$, and are shown in Figures 12-7, 12-8, and 12-9. The implicit volatilities from the jump-diffusion model were typically close to but slightly (0–1%) higher than the no-jump implicit volatilities estimated using

FIGURE 12-7   Annualized volatility $\{\sigma^2 + \lambda'[(\bar{\gamma}')^2 + \delta^2]\}^{1/2}$ implicit in 1–4 month DM and yen futures options, 1984–92.

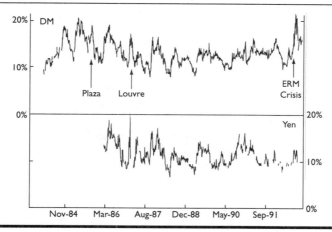

FIGURE 12-8   1–4 month skewness of $\ln(F_{t+T}/F_t)$ implicit in DM and yen futures options, 1984–92.

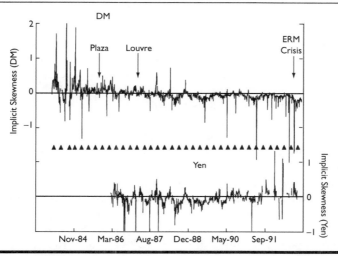

Triangles (▲) indicate shifts in the delivery date of the options, with an associated jump in option maturity from one month to four months.

FIGURE 12-9   **1–4 month excess kurtosis of $\ln(F_{t+T}/F_t)$ implicit in DM and yen futures options, 1984–92.**

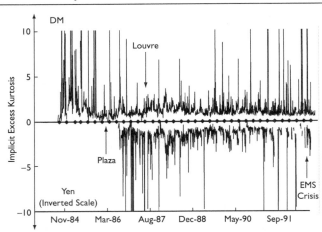

Diamonds (♦) indicate shifts in the delivery date of the options, with an associated jump in option maturity from one month to four months.

the Barone-Adesi and Whaley American option pricing formula. However, extreme jump parameters were occasionally estimated (e.g., a large jump on average every 200 years) for which implicit volatilities deviated more substantially. The fluctuations in implicit monthly skewness largely mirrored the expected jumps per year and were also directly related to relative trading activity in calls. Implicit excess kurtosis was substantially noisier, given the quartic sensitivity to implicit mean jump size and jump dispersion. However, some persistent components in excess kurtosis are apparent, including generally higher levels in 1984–88 than in 1989–92 for both DM and yen futures options.

The jump-diffusion model predicts that implicit excess kurtosis should quadruple as the option maturity declines from 4 months to 1 month, and should drop by 75 percent on days in which the quarterly revision in delivery date causes a reverse jump increase in option maturity. Figure 12-9 shows that this implication is rejected. While implicit excess kurtosis does tend to increase as option maturity shrinks, and does tend to drop at jump increases in option maturity, the magnitude of the maturity effects is not as large as predicted.[17] On the other hand, the maturity profile of excess kurtosis is equally inconsistent with standard stochastic volatility models, which predict that implicit excess kurtosis should be directly rather than inversely related to option maturity.

The jump-diffusion model typically fits option prices as well as the constrained cubic spline fits shown in Figure 12-3. The abnormalities captured by the jump-diffusion model vary in importance over time. The model fit DM futures options substantially better than the no-jumps geometric Brownian motion

(GBM) model in 1984 through early 1985 (see Figure 12-10), with reductions in standard errors of 1–2 price ticks. GBM also did poorly for both DM and yen futures options during the 1-1/2 years following the Louvre Accord. Thereafter, relaxing the no-jumps constraint improved standard errors by less than 1/2 price tick for DM and futures options—except after the lira and pound devaluations in September 1992, when substantial negative implicit skewness appeared in DM options. The daily reductions in standard errors are typically highly significant statistically under an F-test. However, it is not clear whether standard statistical inference is compatible with implicit parameter estimation under nonlinear ordinary least squares, given that GBM option pricing residuals are highly correlated in the presence of specification error.

THE INFORMATIONAL CONTENT OF IMPLICIT DISTRIBUTIONS

Given that the distributions implicit in option prices occasionally deviate substantially and persistently from the benchmark lognormal distribution, two questions arise. First, do the implicit abnormalities predict subsequently abnormal behavior in foreign currency futures prices? And second, can the 'peso problem' implications of implicit skewness and excess kurtosis explain the puzzlingly strong rejections of uncovered interest parity? The equivalent hypothesis for futures prices is that they follow a martingale, which was rejected by Hodrick

---

FIGURE 12-10   **Reduction in standard errors from relaxing the Black-Scholes no-jump ($\lambda = 0$) constraint.**

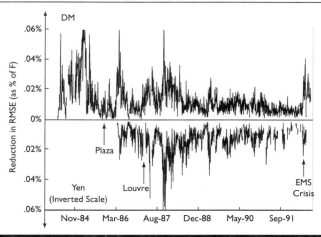

The reductions are the difference in root mean squared error between the jump-diffusion and geometric Brownian motion models re-estimated daily on 1–4 month DM and yen futures options, 1984–92. Reductions of 0.2% of F represent an improvement in standard errors of roughly 1 − 1-1/2 price ticks.

and Srivastava (1987). If peso problem abnormalities are present and inferable from option prices, then conditioning on that information should reveal that standard tests of the futures martingale hypothesis lack power.

Option prices of course contain no information about the conditional mean of the distribution, but do potentially contain substantial information about higher moments. To examine the above questions, it is assumed that the conditional distribution of the log-differenced futures price is a jump-diffusion with parameters related to those estimated from option prices:

$$\ln F_{t+\Delta t} - \ln F_t = \left[c_0 + c_1(r_t - r_t^*) + \frac{1}{2} V_t - \Lambda_t \bar{k}_t' \right] \Delta t + \sqrt{V_t} \Delta W + \sum_{n=1}^{N_t} \gamma_{nt} \tag{21}$$

where:

$E_t(F_{t+\Delta t}/F_t) = e^{[c_0 + c_1(r_t - r_t^*)]\Delta t}$ is the conditional mean;

ΔW is distributed $N(0, \Delta t)$;

γ_{nt} for $n = 1, \ldots, N_t$ are independent random variables distributed $N(\ln(1 + \bar{k}_t') - 1/2\delta_t^2, \delta_t^2) \equiv N(\gamma_t', \delta_t^2)$;

the number of jumps N_t has a Poisson distribution: $\text{Prob}(N_t = n) = w_n(\Lambda_t \Delta t) = \exp(-\Lambda_t \Delta t)(\Lambda_t \Delta t)^n/n!$;

$V_t = cv_0 + cv_1\sigma_t^2$ is the conditional variance per year, with non-negative cv_0 and cv_1;

$\Lambda_t = cl_0 + cl_1\lambda_t'$ is the conditional jump frequency per year, with non-negative cl_0 and cl_1;

$\langle \sigma_t, \lambda_t', \bar{k}_t', \delta_t \rangle$ are the jump-diffusion parameters estimated from date-t options.

The parameter vector $\theta = \langle c_0, c_1, cv_0, cv_1, cl_0, cl_1 \rangle$ is estimated via maximum likelihood subject to non-negativity constraints on the last four parameters, using the likelihood function

$$L(\theta) = \prod_{t=0}^{T} \sum_{n=0}^{\infty} \frac{w_n(\Lambda_t \Delta t)}{\sqrt{2\pi(V_t + n\delta_t^2)}}$$

$$\times \exp\left\{ -\frac{\left\{ \ln(F_{t+\Delta t}/F_t) - \left[c_0 + c_1(r_t - r_t^*) - \frac{1}{2} V_t - \Lambda_t \bar{k}_t' \right] \Delta t - n\bar{\gamma}_t \right\}^2}{2(V_t + n\delta_t^2)} \right\}. \tag{22}$$

Noon quotes for short-term futures were selected for Wednesdays on which there existed corresponding implicit parameters. The typical time interval was therefore one week, although there were numerous occasions (especially for the yen) in which thin trading in options markets implied a longer interval. The futures contract maturity was the shortest maturity such that futures contracts of the same maturity existed at the next available Wednesday.[18] One-month Eurocurrency interest rates were used for the interest differential.

Linear transformations of the implicit parameters were used rather than the parameters themselves for three reasons. First, other studies have found implicit volatilities to be biased predictors of future volatility. Estimating a linear transformation potentially exploits the information implicit in options more optimally, and permits tests of unbiasedness of that information. Second, the estimation involves a maturity mismatch between the option horizon (1–4 months) and the futures holding period (typically 1 week). Since jump-diffusions imply strong inverse relationships between the length of the holding period and the extent of skewness and excess kurtosis that do not appear justified, the extrapolation from 1–4 month to 1-week holding periods may be improved by a linear transformation. Finally, as discussed in the first section, the actual jump parameters can in principle deviate from the parameters implicit in option prices because of a jump risk premium.

Tests of the futures martingale hypothesis conditional on options information are reported in Table 12-3 for DM and yen futures. Tests were initially run under the no-jumps (Black-Scholes) assumption, under various parameter restrictions. The restriction $cv_1 = 0$ ignores the information implicit in options, and is essentially equivalent to a standard regression test of the martingale hypothesis.[19] The restriction $[cv_0, cv_1] = [0, 1]$ assumes implicit volatilities are unbiased estimates of future volatility, while the unrestricted estimates of $[cv_0, cv_1]$ allow for bias.

As shown in Table 12-3, implicit volatilities do contain statistically significant information regarding \$/DM futures price, while the hypothesis that the volatility forecasts are unbiased cannot be rejected. Furthermore, adjusting for conditional heteroskedasticity based on implicit volatilities substantially increases the power of the test relative to the homoskedasticity restriction $cv_1 = 0$, with P-values dropping from .33 to .10 − .15. The ability to reject unbiasedness is still weak, but that is not uncommon for univariate tests. As found elsewhere, point estimates suggest it is the spot exchange rate rather than the futures rate that follows a martingale.[20]

The jump-diffusion distributions implicit in 1–4 month options describe the *ex post* distribution of (predominantly weekly) log-differenced \$/DM futures prices very poorly; worse even than the conditionally homoskedastic specification. However, the implicit distributions do contain substantial information, in that the optimal linear transformations significantly increase the likelihood relative to optimally transformed no-jump implicit variances. Furthermore, the inferred conditional abnormalities are important. The hypothesis that the jump-diffusion parameters out-perform Black-Scholes implicit variances only because the extra parameters (cl_0, cl_1) allow a better modelling of conditional variance is rejected, with a P-value of .035.[21]

There is no evidence, however, that these abnormalities create 'peso problem' effects for tests of uncovered interest parity. Standard errors on parameter estimates are comparable for the optimally transformed lognormal and jump-diffusion implicit distributions, while likelihood ratio tests of unbiasedness yield comparable P-values.

The comparable results for \$/yen futures prices are uninformative. The most striking result from Table 12-3 is that the distributions implicit in \$/yen futures options—both implicit volatilities and higher moments—contain no information whatsoever for the subsequent evolution of the \$/yen futures price.

TABLE 12-3 Tests of the futures martingale hypothesis conditional on distributions implicit in foreign currency futures options. Wednesday noon futures prices. DM: 1984–92; Yen: 1986–92. All parameters are in annualized units. Standard errors are in parentheses. P-values are from likelihood ratio tests.

DM	cond. mean c_0	c_1	cond. variance cv_0	cv_1	jump frequency cl_0	cl_1	ln L	H_0: $c_0 = c_1 = 0$ (P-value)
Using 'Black-Scholes' implicit volatilities								
1.	6.67%	−.91	.0165	0			1080.06	.330
	(4.53)	(1.36)	(.0011)					
2.	7.40%	−2.41	0	1			1089.06	.103
	(4.37)	(1.33)						
3.	7.28%	−2.10	.0030	.808			1089.68	.154
	(4.41)	(1.36)	(.0028)	(.192)				
Using implicit jump-diffusion parameters								
4.	5.81%	−4.28	0	1	0	1	950.53	.000
	(1.22)	(.45)						
5.	8.07%	−2.12	.0112	.393	.0085	.258	1092.59	.108
	(4.35)	(1.33)	(.0015)	(.183)	(.2334)	(.139)		

yen	cond. mean c_0	c_1	cond. variance cv_0	cv_1	jump frequency cl_0	cl_1	ln L	H_0: $c_0 = c_1 = 0$ (P-value)
Using 'Black-Scholes' implicit volatilities								
1.	8.01%	−2.33	.0139	0			640.47	.336
	(5.51)	(2.28)	(.0013)					
2.	9.09%	−4.46	0	1			631.02	.005
	(4.74)	(1.93)						
3.	8.17%	−2.57	.0119	.154			640.63	.313
	(5.48)	(2.29)	(.0034)	(.263)				
Using implicit jump-diffusion parameters								
4.	−5.03%	−1.84	0	1	0	1	571.22	.001
	(1.63)	(.41)						
5.	8.00%	−2.33	.0139	.000[a]	.0084	.000[a]	640.47	.340
	(5.52)	(2.29)	(.0013)		(.3375)			

[a]Non-negativity constraint binding.

SUMMARY AND CONCLUSIONS

This paper has shown that the \$/DM and \$/yen distributions implicit in futures options have varied substantially over 1984–92 and 1986–92, respectively. Evidence came first from the nonparametric 'skewness premium' measure of skewness, based upon relative prices of out-of-the-money calls and puts. Further evidence came from fitting a jump-diffusion option pricing model to the options data, enabling scrutiny of implicit volatility, skewness, and excess kurtosis. $/DM implicit skewness was substantially positive during the strong-dollar period of 1984 and early 1985 and oscillated substantially thereafter, typically in tandem with $/yen implicit skewness. A strong direct relationship was found between implicit skewness and relative trading activity in calls *versus* puts.

There are, of course, alternate explanations than jump fears for the non-normal distributions implicit in currency futures option prices: stochastic interest rates, stochastic volatility, and market frictions. It seems unlikely, however, that stochastic interest rates can explain the implicit abnormalities. Interest rate/exchange rate correlations affect European option prices in standard stochastic interest rate models primarily through an impact on implicit volatilities; higher implicit moments are unaffected.[22] A stochastic interest rates explanation therefore either requires interest rate processes substantially different from those typically considered, or requires a substantial impact from stochastic interest rates on the early-exercise premium of the (predominantly at- and out-of-the-money) American futures options examined in this study.

Stochastic volatility models can generate option pricing biases in the direction of those observed in this study. Such models imply leptokurtic distributions, and positive or negative skewness depending on the correlation between exchange rate and volatility shocks. Whether such models can generate sufficiently large biases under plausible volatility parameters seems unlikely, however.[23]

An alternate possibility is that the strongly skewed implicit distributions in 1984 and early 1985 represent some form of option mispricing or market frictions in a new, illiquid market. Such explanations become especially plausible in light of the strong relationship between relative activity in calls *versus* puts and implicit skewness. If options transactions are largely buyer-initiated, it might seem reasonable to assume that option writers faced with heavier demand for OTM calls than for OTM puts would charge more for the calls, generating positive implicit skewness. But it is not clear whether option writers' optimal response to asymmetric demand *is* asymmetric pricing, if the true distribution of the underlying asset is symmetric.[24] Furthermore, every transaction must have a buyer and a seller, and it is unclear why the option purchasers are willing to pay the higher price if their perceived distribution is essentially symmetric and lognormal. The underlying question also remains as to why the relative trading volume in calls and puts should fluctuate over time, given the intrinsic symmetry of foreign exchange markets.

Consequently, it seems likely that the distributions implicit in option prices are in fact a barometer of market sentiment. In particular, it appears that fears of a dollar crash against the Deutsche mark did accompany the final stage of appreciation of the dollar in late 1984 and early 1985. The asymmetric crash fears rapidly diminished after early 1985. Perceptions of symmetric jump risk appear to have persisted through end-1988, with the following 1989–92 period more normally distributed. Furthermore, the perceived abnormalities implicit in $/DM futures options over 1984–92 appear to have been validated by subsequent \$/DM futures price behavior, although the same cannot be said for \$/yen futures options. It does not appear, however, that the 'peso problem' implications of the substantial skewness and excess kurtosis evident at times in currency futures options can explain observed rejections of uncovered interest parity.

APPENDIX: OPTION PRICING UNDER SYSTEMATIC EXCHANGE RATE JUMP RISK

International Capital Asset Pricing Model

Define r and r^* as the instantaneous dollar and DM interest rates, respectively. Let

$$J(W/Q, t) \equiv \max_{\{C_t\}} E_t \int_t^\infty e^{-\rho s} U(C_s/Q_s) ds \tag{A1}$$

be the indirect utility of real wealth of the representative international investor given the optimal consumption strategy. By a standard perturbation argument, the incremental real gain from borrowing at the nominally riskless dollar interest rate and investing uncovered in a foreign money market investment must be zero in equilibrium:

$$E_t\left[J_w\left(\frac{W_{t+dt}}{Q_{t+dt}}, t \right) Q_{t+dt}^{-1} \left(\frac{S_{t+dt}}{S_t} e^{r^* dt} - e^{r dt} \right) \right] = 0. \tag{A2}$$

Dividing by the current marginal utility of dollar wealth J_w/Q and rearranging yields the standard result

$$E_t\left(\frac{dS}{S} \right) + (r^* - r) dt = -E_t\left[\frac{d(J_w/Q)}{J_w/Q} \frac{dS}{S} \right] + o(dt), \tag{A3}$$

where $o(dt)$ involves terms of less than order dt. The foreign currency has a positive risk premium if foreign currency appreciation tends to coincide with low marginal utility of dollar wealth. The Itô expansion of $d(J_w/Q)/(J_w/Q)$ given synchronous jumps in real wealth and Q is given by

$$\frac{d[J_w(W/Q, t)/Q]}{J_w/Q} = \left[\frac{W J_{ww}}{Q J_w}\left(\frac{dW}{W} - \frac{dQ}{Q} \right) - \frac{dQ}{Q} \right]_{\text{no jumps}} + \frac{\Delta(J_w/Q)}{J_w/Q} dq + O(dt), \tag{A4}$$

where $O(dt)$ involves terms of order dt or less, and

$$\frac{\Delta(J_w/Q)}{J_w/Q} = \frac{J_w[We^{\gamma_w}/(Qe^{\gamma_q}), t]}{J_w(W/Q, t)} e^{-\gamma_q} - 1 \equiv m e^{-\gamma_q} - 1 \tag{A5}$$

is the jump-contingent percentage change in the marginal utility of dollar wealth. Plugging (A4) into (A3) and ignoring terms of order $o(dt)$ yield the following equilibrium condition for jump-diffusion processes.

PROPOSITION 1. *When the exchange rate follows a jump-diffusion process with systematic jump risk, the instantaneous foreign currency risk premium is*

$$\frac{E_t(dS/S)}{dt} - (r - r^*) = R\left(\frac{W}{Q}, t\right)\sigma_{sw} + \left[1 - R\left(\frac{W}{Q}, t\right)\right]\sigma_{sq} - \lambda E_t\left[(me^{-\gamma_q} - 1)\frac{\Delta S}{S}\right], \quad \text{(A6)}$$

where:

$R(W/Q, t) = -(W/Q)J_{ww}/J_w$ is the instantaneous coefficient of relative risk aversion;

$\sigma_{sw} = \text{Cov}(dS/S, dW/W)/dt$ is the instantaneous covariance per unit time between percentage changes in the exchange rate and dollar wealth conditional on no jumps;

$\sigma_{sq} = \text{Cov}(dS/S, dQ/Q)/dt$ is the instantaneous covariance per unit time between percentage changes in the exchange rate and the price deflator conditional on no jumps; and

$me^{-\gamma_q} - 1$, the jump-contingent percentage change in the marginal utility of dollar wealth, is defined in (A5) above.

The first two terms are discussed in Adler and Dumas (1983). $R\sigma_{sw}$ represents the compensation for systematic risk conditional upon no jumps, while $(1 - R)\sigma_{sq}$ is an adjustment term given returns are written in nominal rather than real terms. The third term represents the compensation for systematic nominal jump risk, given that real wealth, the price deflator, and the exchange rate all jump synchronously. Only under quite stringent conditions will the last term vanish; e.g. when there exist risk-neutral US investors who do not consume foreign goods.

The above proposition is written using the dollar as measurement currency. By Itô calculus, a symmetric expression holds when the foreign currency is used:

$$\frac{E_t(dS^*/S^*)}{dt} - (r^* - r) = R\sigma_{s^*w^*} + (1 - R)\sigma_{s^*q^*} - \lambda E_t\left[(me^{-\gamma_{q^*}} - 1)\frac{\Delta S^*}{S^*}\right], \quad \text{(A7)}$$

where $S^* = S^{-1}$, $W^* = W/S$, $Q^* = Q/S$, $\gamma_{q^*} = \gamma_q - \gamma$, and $\Delta S^*/S^* = e^{-\gamma} - 1$. As functions of $W/Q = W^*/Q^*$, R and m are invariant to the choice of measurement currency. It is straightforward to show that assumptions 1–3 imply (under additional transversality conditions) the following:

1. $J_w(W/Q, t) = Ae^{-\rho t}(W/Q)^{-R}$;
2. the coefficient of relative risk aversion $R(W/Q, t)$ is constant;
3. the distribution of $me^{-\gamma_q} = e^{-R\gamma_w - (1-R)\gamma_q}$ is state-independent and lognormal;
4. the domestic and foreign interest rates r and r^* are constant.

Absent the last two conditions, it would be necessary when pricing options either to specify how r, r^* and $me^{-\gamma_q}$ will evolve in the future, or to assume that option prices are insensitive to the future evolution of those variables.

Valuation of Contingent Claims

Proposition 1 holds for any investment, with dS/S and r^* re-interpreted as the instantaneous capital gain and dividend yield on the asset, respectively. Consequently, it also holds for contingent claims. Writing the dollar price of the option as $V(S, t)$, the equilibrium expected return β on the claim is given by

$$(\beta - r)V = SV_s R\sigma_{sw} + (1 - R)SV_s\sigma_{sq} - \lambda E_t[(me^{-\gamma_q} - 1)\Delta V], \tag{A8}$$

where $\Delta V = V(Se^{\gamma}, t) - V$ is the random jump in the price of the option conditional on a jump occurring. By Itô's Lemma, the expected return on the claim also satisfies

$$\beta V = V_t + (\mu - \lambda\bar{k})SV_s + \frac{1}{2}\sigma^2 V_{ss} + \lambda E_t(\Delta V). \tag{A9}$$

Combining (A6), (A8), and (A9) yields the fundamental integro-differential equation for pricing contingent claims on foreign currency in the presence of jumps.

PROPOSITION 2. *The dollar price $V(S, t)$ of a contingent claim on foreign currency satisfies the equation*

$$V_t + \left[r - r^* - \lambda E\left(me^{-\gamma_q}\frac{\Delta S}{S}\right)\right]SV_s + \frac{1}{2}S^2 V_{ss} + \lambda E(me^{-\gamma_q}\Delta V) = rV \tag{A10}$$

subject to claim-specific boundary conditions.

It is convenient to transform the probability measure and rewrite (A10) in a form representing option pricing in an equivalent risk-neutral world. Exploiting the bivariate lognormality of $1 + \Delta S/S$ and $me^{-\gamma_q}$ yields the following proposition.

PROPOSITION 3. *The dollar price $V(S, t)$ of contingent claim on foreign currency satisfies the equation*

$$V_t + (r - r^* - \lambda'\bar{k}')SV_s + \frac{1}{2}S^2 V_{ss} + \lambda'E[V(Se^{\gamma'}, t) - V] = rV \tag{A11}$$

subject to claim-specific boundary conditions. Equivalently, contingent claims are priced as if investors were risk-neutral in dollar terms and the $/FC exchange rate followed the jump-diffusion

$$dS/S = (r - r^* - \lambda'\bar{k}')dt + \sigma dZ' + (e^{\gamma'} - 1)dq', \tag{A12}$$

where:

$\lambda' \equiv \lambda E(me^{-\gamma_q}) = \lambda E[e^{-R\gamma_w - (1-R)\gamma_q}]$
Z' is a standard Wiener process;
q' is a Poisson counter with frequency λ';
$\bar{k}' = (1 + \bar{k})e^{-R\delta_{sw} - (1-R)\delta_{sq}} - 1$;
γ' is normally distributed $N[\ln(1 + \bar{k}') - 1/2\delta^2, \delta^2]$.

Proof: See Bates (1991), Appendix I.

Suppose instead one wanted the foreign currency price $V^*(S^*, t)$ of a contingent claim as a function of the FC/\$ exchange rate $S^* = S^{-1}$. The relevant integro-differential equation is then[25]

$$V_t^* + \left[r^* - r - \lambda E\left(me^{-\dot{\gamma}_q}\frac{\Delta S^*}{S^*} \right) \right] S^* V_{s^*}^* + \frac{1}{2}(S^*)^2 V_{s^* s^*}^* + \lambda E(me^{-\lambda_{q^*}}\Delta V^*)$$
$$= r^* V^*.$$

(A13)

The associated 'risk-neutral' jump-diffusion is of the form

$$\frac{dS^*}{S^*} = \left[r^* - r - \lambda'' E''\left(\frac{\Delta S^*}{S^*} \right) \right] dt + \sigma dZ'' + (e^{\gamma''} - 1)dq''$$

(A14)

where:

$\lambda'' = \lambda E(me^{-\dot{\gamma}_q}) = \lambda E(me^{-\gamma_q + \gamma_s})$;

q'' is a Poisson counter with frequency λ'';

$1 + E''(\Delta S^*/S^*) = 1/(1 + \bar{k}')$; and

γ'' is normally distributed $N\{ -\ln(1 + \bar{k}') - 1/2\delta^2, \delta^2 \}$.

REFERENCES

Adler, Michael and Bernard Dumas, 'International portfolio choice and corporation finance: A synthesis,' *Journal of Finance,* June 1983, **38:** 925–984.

Ahn, Chang Mo and Howard E. Thompson, 'Jump-diffusion processes and the term structure of interest rates,' *Journal of Finance,* March 1988, **43:** 155–174.

Akgiray, Vedat and G. Geoffrey Booth, 'Mixed diffusion-jump process modeling of exchange rate movements,' *Review of Economics and Statistics,* November 1988, **70:** 631–637.

Amin, Kaushik I. and Robert A. Jarrow, 'Pricing foreign currency options under stochastic interest rates,' *Journal of International Money and Finance,* September 1991, **10:** 310–329.

Bates, David S., 'Pricing options on jump-diffusion processes,' Rodney L. White Center working paper 37–88, October 1988.

Bates, David S., 'The crash of '87; Was it expected? The evidence from options markets,' *Journal of Finance,* July 1991, **46;** 1009–1044.

Bates, David S., 'The skewness premium: Option pricing under asymmetric processes,' Wharton School working paper, May 1994 (1994a).

Bates, David S., 'Jumps and stochastic volatility: Exchange rate processes implicit in PHLX Deutsche mark options,' Wharton School working paper, August 1994 (1994b).

Bodurtha, James N., Jr. and Georges R. Courtadon, 'Tests of an American option pricing model on the foreign currency options market,' *Journal of Financial and Quantitative Analysis,* June 1987, **22:** 153–167.

Borensztein, Eduardo R. and Michael P. Dooley, 'Options on foreign exchange and exchange rate expectations,' *IMF Staff Papers,* December 1987, **34:** 642–680.

Cao, Charles, 'Pricing foreign currency options with stochastic volatility,' University of Chicago working paper, November 1992.

Chesney, Marc and Louis O. Scott, 'Pricing European currency options: A comparison of the modified Black-Stoles model and a random variance model.' *Journal of Financial and Quantitative Analysis,* Sept. 1989, **24:** 267-284.

Cox, John C., Jonathan E. Ingersoll, Jr., and Stephen A. Ross, 'An intertemporal general equilibrium model of asset prices,' *Econometrica,* March 1985, **53:** 363-384.

Dominguez, Kathryn M., 'Are foreign exchange forecasts rational? New evidence from survey data,' *Economics Letters,* 1986, **21:** 227-281.

Dumas, Bernard, 'Two-person dynamic equilibrium in the capital market,' *Review of Financial Studies,* 1989, **2:** 157-188.

Engel, Charles M. and James D. Hamilton, 'Long swings in the dollar: Are they in the data and do markets know it?' *American Economic Review,* September 1990, **80:** 689-713.

Evans, George W., 'A test for speculative bubbles in the sterling-dollar exchange rate: 1981-84,' *American Economic Review,* September 1986, **76:** 621-636.

Evans, John S., *International Finance: A Markets Approach,* Fort Worth, TX: The Dryden Press, 1992.

Fama, Eugene F., 'Forward and spot exchange rates,' *Journal of Monetary Economics,* November 1984, **14:** 319-338.

Frankel, Jeffrey A. and Kenneth A. Froot, 'Forward discount bias: Is it an exchange risk premium?' *Quarterly Journal of Economics,* February 1989, **104:** 139-161.

Froot, Kenneth A. and Richard H. Thaler, 'Anomalies: Foreign exchange,' *Journal of Economic Perspectives,* Summer 1990, **4:** 179-192.

Grabbe, J. Orlin, 'The pricing of call and put options on foreign exchange,' *Journal of International Money and Finance,* December 1983, **2:** 239-253.

Hilliard, Jimmy E., Jeff Madura and Alan L. Tucker, 'Currency option pricing with stochastic domestic and foreign interest rates,' *Journal of Financial and Quantitative Analysis,* June 1991, **26:** 139-151.

Hodrick, Robert J., *The Empirical Evidence on the Efficiency of Forward and Futures Foreign Exchange Markets,* New York: Harwood Academic Publishers, 1987.

Hodrick, Robert J. and Sanjay Srivastava, 'Foreign currency futures,' *Journal of International Economics,* February 1987, **22:** 1-24.

Hsieh, David A. and Luis Manas-Anton, 'Empirical regularities in the Deutsche mark futures options,' *Advances in Futures and Options Research,* 1988, **3:** 183-208.

Hull, John and Alan White, 'The pricing of options on assets with stochastic volatility,' *Journal of Finance,* June 1987, **42:** 281-300.

Jorion, Philippe, 'On jump processes in the foreign exchange and stock markets,' *Review of Financial Studies,* 1989, **1:** 427-445.

Krasker, Williams S., 'The peso problem in testing for efficiency of forward exchange markets,' *Journal of Monetary Economics,* April 1980, **6:** 269-276.

Leland, Hayne E., 'Option pricing and replication with transactions costs,' *Journal of Finance,* December 1985, **40:** 1283-1301.

Lewis, Karen K., 'Changing beliefs and systematic rational forecast errors with evidence from foreign exchange,' *American Economic Review,* September 1989, **79:** 621-636.

Lewis, Karen K., 'International financial markets,' in Gene Grossman and Kenneth Rogoff, eds., *Handbook of International Economics,* Amsterdam: North Holland, 1995.

Malz, Allan M., 'Option prices and the distribution of exchange rates: The case of mark/Paris,' Columbia University working paper, March 1994.

McCulloch, J. Huston, 'The valuation of European options with log-stable uncertainty,' Ohio State University working paper, July 1985.

McCulloch, J. Huston, 'Foreign exchange option pricing with log-stable uncertainty,' in Sarkis J. Khoury and Gosh Alo, eds., *Recent Developments in International Banking and Finance,* Lexington, MA: Lexington Books, 1987.

Merton, Robert C., 'Option pricing when underlying stock returns are discontinuous,' *Journal of Financial Economics,* January/March 1976, **3**: 125–144.

Naik, Vasantitilak and Moon Hoe Lee, 'General equilibrium pricing of options on the market portfolio with discontinuous returns,' *Review of Financial Studies,* 1990, **3**: 493–522.

Perraudin, William R. M. and Bent E. Sørensen, 'Continuous time international arbitrage pricing: Theory and estimation,' Brown University working paper, January 1994.

Ramaswamy, Krishna and Suresh M. Sundaresan, 'The valuation of options on futures contracts,' *Journal of Finance,* December 1985, **40**: 1319–1340.

Scott, Louis O., 'Pricing stock options in a jump-diffusion model with stochastic volatility and interest rates: Applications of Fourier inversion methods,' University of Georgia working paper, May 1993.

ENDNOTES

1. The square root interest rate processes used in Scott (1993) are an exception, and can in principle generate implicit distributions that are not lognormal. Scott finds only small biases in short-term option prices from the stochastic interest rate component of his model.

2. See Lewis (1995) for a recent survey of risk premium explanations of uncovered interest parity rejections.

3. Examples of this approach include Dominguez (1986) and Frankel and Froot (1989).

4. The major example of the former approach is Merton (1976). Examples of the latter approach include Ahn and Thompson (1988), Naik and Lee (1990), and Bates (1988, 1991). Perraudin and Sørensen (1994) pursue the alternate approach of directly restricting the pricing kernel, and derive an option pricing model substantially identical to the one presented below.

5. For an illustration of the impact of investor heterogeneity upon market equilibrium, see Dumas (1989). In principle, investor heterogeneity could matter more when jumps can occur than the small impact seen in Dumas' no-jump model. First, some default-free interpersonal contracts may not be feasible in the presence of jumps. Second, jump-contingent redistributions of wealth and the resulting general equilibrium changes in the investment opportunity set could be larger, implying a more substantial hedge factor *ex ante* with respect to such redistributions.

6. Naik and Lee (1990) derive a similar specification in a jump-diffusion extension of a Lucas exchange economy.

7. Suppose for instance that foreign assets constitute two-thirds of world wealth, *local-currency* returns are unaffected by exchange rate jumps, and exchange rate jumps have a mean and standard deviation of 9 percent—a combination implying substantial systematic exchange rate risk. If investors have log utility, then $\lambda' = .92\lambda$ and the 'risk-neutral' mean jump size is 8.5 percent—essentially the same as the actual parameters.

8. Evans (1992) points out that although it is customary to identify the options with the International Money Market (IMM) where the underlying futures are traded, the options are actually traded at the CME's Index and Option Market (IOM) division.

9. See Bates (1994b) for an examination of PHLX Deutsche mark options over 1984–91.

10. An exception is the interbank *risk reversal* contract examined in Malz (1994).

11. Different rules apply to serial options, which trade for a shorter period of time. The strike price range upon introduction of a new serial option includes any strike prices actively traded at adjacent quarterly maturities.

12. This ratio is quite stable intradaily for currency futures, and reflects the domestic/foreign interest differential.

13. Amin and Jarrow price European futures options. Ramaswamy and Sundaresan (1985) use an alternate square root interest rate process and conclude that expected drift in interest rates affects the early exercise premium of American futures options, but that the stochastic component does not.

14. Details of the estimation of constrained cubic splines and computation of standard errors are available from the author.

15. These deviations are consistent with the tendency reported by Bodurtha and Courtadon (1987) of option pricing formulas premised upon geometric Brownian motion to underprice OTM Deutsche mark call options traded on the Philadelphia Stock Exchange during February 28, 1983 to March 25, 1985, and to overprice in-the-money DM call options.

16. The 2 percent and 6 percent skewness premiums typically move in proportion to the 4 percent premium, with a scale factor of about 1/2 and 1-1/2, respectively. For example, the 0 percent, 2 percent, 4 percent, and 6 percent skewness premiums on November 26, 1984 DM futures options were about 0 percent, 10 percent, 20 percent, and 30 percent, respectively. This proportionality has also been found in S&P 500 futures options (Bates, 1991).

17. Implicit excess kurtosis fell for 27 out of 36 days on which the maturity of DM futures options increased, and 22 out of 26 days for yen futures options. The median percentage change was -25 percent for DM, -44 percent for yen.

18. For example, June 1984 options on March 5, 1984 were used to predict the March 1984 futures prices transition from March 5 to March 12. On March 12, June 1984 options were used to predict the June 1984 futures price transition from March 12 to March 19.

19. The estimates would be exactly equivalent to ordinary least squares if all data were at regular time intervals.

20. The underlying spot exchange rate follows a martingale if $(c_0, c_1) = (0, -1)$.

21. Modelling the conditional variance as $cv_{;0} + cv_1\sigma_t^2 + [cl_0 + cl_1\lambda_t'][(\bar{\gamma}_t')^2 + \delta_t^2]$, setting the actual jump frequency to zero, and optimizing over the parameter vector yields a log likelihood of 1089.25, which is essentially the same as using the optimally transformed 'Black-Scholes' implicit volatilities.

22. See, e.g. Grabbe (1983), Hillard et al. (1991), and Amin and Jarrow (1991).

23. Chesney and Scott (1989) found little difference between Black-Scholes and stochastic volatility option prices for parameters estimated from exchange rate time series.

24. Binomial option pricing models with transactions costs such as Leland (1985) imply a higher implicit volatility for all options, but no asymmetries in the implicit distribution.

25. The incredulous can confirm that (A13) is consistent with (A10) by plugging $V(S, t) = SV^*(S^{-1}, t)$ into (A10).

13

On Jump Processes in the Foreign Exchange and Stock Markets

PHILIPPE JORION

T he objective of this article is to analyze and compare the empirical distribution of returns in the stock market and in the foreign exchange market. There are a number of reasons why a better understanding of the stochastic processes driving prices in these markets would be useful. Many financial models rely heavily on the assumption of a particular stochastic process, while relatively little attention is paid to the empirical fit of the postulated distribution. As a result, models like option pricing models are applied indiscriminately to various markets such as the stock market and the foreign exchange market when the underlying processes may be fundamentally different. The foreign exchange market, for instance, is characterized by active exchange rate management policies that do not have counterparts in the stock market. A systematic comparison of these two markets, à la Frenkel and Mussa (1980), could reveal interesting insights into the behavior of stock prices and exchange rates.

This article compares the empirical fit of two classes of distributions as alternatives to the usual continuous diffusion process. First, it is important to examine if discontinuities are present in the data, given that many continuous-time models are based on the assumption that asset prices have continuous sample paths. Evidence of discontinuities would indicate that one of the basic building blocks of many financial models is inconsistent with the data. Recently,

This research was supported by the Faculty Research Fund of the Graduate School of Business, Columbia University. Part of this research was developed while the author was visiting Northwestern University. The author thanks Michael Brennan, Jerome Detêmple, Jon Ingersoll, and David Hsieh, the referee, for helpful comments. Address reprint requests to Dr. Jorion, Graduate School of Business, Columbia University, New York, NY 10027.

Reprinted by permission of Oxford University Press; *Review of Financial Studies;* No. 1, pp. 427–445; Philippe Jorion; 1988.

Jarrow and Rosenfeld (1984) and Ball and Torous (1985) have found evidence that *daily* stock returns are characterized by lognormally distributed jumps, which indicates that the assumption of stationary lognormal processes may be suspect for common stocks. These discontinuities are not apparent in monthly and weekly data. Whether these results carry to the foreign exchange market is an open question.

The findings of discontinuities, however, may not be quite unexpected given the observed leptokurtosis in the distribution of exchange rates. In fact, any process that can generate "fat" tails could potentially lead to the rejection of the stationary diffusion process against the postulated alternative. The rejection of the diffusion process may be due to the assumption of stationary parameters instead of the existence of discontinuities. Because diffusion processes with time-varying parameters are consistent with continuous-time models, the question is whether any observed jump process disappears when specific allowance is made for time-varying parameters. As a first approach, this article considers a tractable specification of time-varying second moments: the autoregressive conditional heteroskedastic (ARCH) model, first proposed by Engle (1982). This article employs maximum-likelihood estimation, which allows formal tests of the fit of various models through nested hypotheses.

Finally, the article attempts to address the question of economic versus statistical significance by illustrating the implications of the results for the pricing of options. Ball and Torous (1985) report that the existence of jumps in common stock returns leads to relatively small deviations between the Black-Scholes and Merton option valuation models and thus may not be operationally significant for the stock option market. On the other hand, Bodurtha and Courtadon (1987) recently documented systematic biases in the American option pricing model applied to currency options. If jump components are relatively more important for exchange rates, these results could be explained by discontinuities in exchange rates.

This article is organized as follows. Section 1 presents a review of the issues and literature on the distribution of exchange rate movements. The methodology and models used are presented in Section 2. Section 3 analyzes the results of the maximum-likelihood estimation applied to the monthly and weekly U.S. dollar/German mark ($/DM) exchange rate, as well as to the U.S. value-weighted stock market index. The importance of these results for the pricing of foreign currency options is demonstrated in Section 4. Section 5 contains a few concluding comments.

ISSUES AND LITERATURE REVIEW

The empirical literature on distributions in the foreign exchange market has grown largely as an extension of the abundant literature on distributions in the stock market, without much consideration to potential differences in the structure of the two markets. No study has looked at the existence of jump processes in the sample path of exchange rates. Yet this is an important topic, given its implications for the use of continuous-time models in international finance as well as for models of exchange rate determination.

There is no reason why the information arrival process should be the same in the foreign exchange market and in the stock market. During fixed-exchange-rate regimes, discontinuities obviously occur when parity values are realigned. But even with flexible exchange rates, realignments in cross-exchange rates, for example, within the European Monetary System, could be reflected in the exchange rate vis à vis the dollar. In addition, jumps in exchange rates may be generated by discontinuities in the arrival of "news," which Mussa (1979) and Frenkel (1981) argued should be the predominant cause of exchange rate movements, or by changes in monetary policies directed at affecting the external value of a currency, which Flood and Hodrick (1986) labeled "process switching."

There is some empirical evidence on the distributional characteristics of exchange rate movements, but less than for the stock market. It is a documented fact[1] that the distribution of changes in exchange rates exhibits fatter tails than would be expected from a normal distribution. Given this result, the empirical distribution could be potentially explained by one of the three possible classes of models: (1) a stationary process, such as a Paretian stable or a Student's t distribution, with fatter tails than the normal model, (2) a mixture of stationary distributions, such as two normal distributions with different means or variances, or a mixture of a normal and jump process, or (3) a distribution such as the normal distribution with time-varying parameters. Any of these choices could improve the fit over the normal distribution. A number of these models have been applied to the foreign exchange market, usually independently, and it is not clear which of these hopefully parsimonious representations is most appropriate. McFarland, Pettit, and Sung (1982), for example, document a day-of-the-week effect, which implies different distributional parameters, but argue that *weekly* changes in exchange rates are appropriately characterized by stable Paretian distributions. Friedman and Vandersteel (1982) and Boothe and Glassman (1987), on the other hand, suggest that exchange rate changes can be described by normal distributions with time-dependent parameters. This is confirmed by Hsieh (1988), who shows that the distributions of daily exchange rates are characterized by time-varying parameters. The problem with these studies is that the proposed models have not been formally pitted against each other. Thus, it would be of considerable interest to compare two classes of models and formally test whether one is more appropriate than the other.

The first model considered in this study will be the jump-diffusion process, which could explain the skewness in exchange rate distributions reported by Calderon-Rossell and Ben-Horim (1982) and So (1987). A possible alternative that is consistent with continuous-time financial models is that of a diffusion process with time-varying parameters. The model chosen here is the ARCH process, introduced by Engle (1982), in which the conditional variance is a deterministic function of past data. This model was first applied to the foreign exchange market by Domowitz and Hakkio (1985). The simplest specification is a first-order model in which the conditional variance is a linear function of the past squared innovation. This could be easily extended to more general specifications. Both models will be tested and compared to each other. The question is whether discontinuities can be identified even after allowing for diffusion processes with time-varying parameters. Comparative results will be reported for both the foreign exchange market and the stock market, which may yield some insights into differences in the structures of the two markets.

METHODOLOGY

This section briefly presents the stochastic processes under investigation as well as the maximum-likelihood estimation procedure. Detailed derivations are contained in the Appendix. Define x_t as the logarithm of price relatives $\ln(P_t/P_{t-1})$, where P is either the dollar price of the foreign currency or the dollar price of the normalized stock market index. The assumption that prices follow the diffusion process $dP_t/P_t = \alpha\, dt + \sigma\, dz_t$ implies that $x_t \sim N(\mu, \sigma^2)$ or is normally distributed with mean $\mu \equiv \alpha - \sigma^2/2$ and variance σ^2, both defined per unit time. In discrete time,

$$\ln(P_t/P_{t-1}) = \mu + \sigma z \tag{1}$$

where z is a standard normal deviate.

Discontinuities can be modeled by the mixed jump-diffusion process $dP_t/P_t = \alpha\, dt + \sigma\, dz_t + dq_t$, in which the Poisson process dq_t is characterized by a mean number of jumps occurring per unit time λ as well as a jump size Y, which is assumed independently lognormally distributed $\ln Y \sim N(\theta, \delta^2)$. Thus x_t can be written as

$$\ln(P_t/P_{t-1}) = \mu + \sigma z + \sum_{t=1}^{n_t} \ln Y_i \tag{2}$$

where n_t is the actual number of jumps during the interval.

But the observed leptokurtosis could also be explained by a diffusion model with time-varying second moments. The alternative explored here is that of a first-order ARCH process,[2] in which the conditional variance is defined as a nonstochastic function of the last squared innovation. Conditional on information at $t - 1$, the distribution of x_t is given by

$$\ln(P_t/P_{t-1})|t - 1 = \mu + \sqrt{h_t}\, z$$
$$h_t \equiv E_{t-1}(\sigma_t^2) = \alpha_0 + \alpha_1(x_{t-1} - \mu)^2 \tag{3}$$

in which α_1 is the autoregressive parameter inducing heteroskedasticity.

The question as to whether time-varying second moments can fully account for the observed fat tails can be answered by considering a specification combining both ARCH and jump processes:

$$\ln(P_t/P_{t-1})|t - 1 = \mu + \sqrt{h_t}z + \sum_{i=1}^{n_t} \ln Y_i \tag{4}$$

This model can be used as an alternative against which the hypothesis of a pure ARCH process [Equation (3)] can be tested.

The parameters of interest are estimated by numerical maximization of the likelihood function of the parameter vector ϕ given the observations x, $L(\phi; x)$. The likelihood functions and the first-order conditions are derived in the Appendix. Maximum-likelihood estimation presents a number of advantages in this context.[3] The estimates are consistent and invariant, with normal asymptotic distributions with known parameters. In addition, maximum-likelihood estimation permits formal tests of the relative fit of various distributions. *Nested* hypotheses can be tested using the *generalized* likelihood ratio $\Lambda = \sup_{\phi \in \Phi_0} L(\phi; x)/\sup_{\phi \in \Phi} L(\phi; x)$ of the maximized-likelihood functions under the null and under the enlarged parameter space Φ, which also includes the alternative hypothesis Φ_1. Under the null Φ_0, the statistic $-2 \ln \Lambda$ has a chi-square distribution with degrees of freedom equal to the difference in the number of parameters between the two models. Thus, the improvement in the maximized likelihood indicates to what extent an enlarged specification helps in fitting the data.

It should be emphasized that the alternative hypothesis must include the null hypothesis as a special case to employ this test. Results based on a *simple* likelihood ratio—defined as the ratio of the maximized likelihood for one model to the maximized likelihood for another model—are only suggestive, because they only indicate which model is more "likely" and are not formal tests of hypotheses. One model, for instance, may require estimating many more parameters than the other and thus may yield a higher value of the maximized likelihood, when it is not clear whether the improvement is due to a better functional fit or a greater number of parameters.[4] If one wants to decide between non-nested models, such as the ARCH, and the mixed jump-diffusion process, the criterion for model selection should explicitly penalize for the number of parameters. Schwarz (1978) suggested choosing the model *a posteriori* most probable. A simple approximation to this bayesian approach is to choose the model with the lowest value of the "Schwarz Criterion"

$$SC = -2 \ln L(\hat{\phi}; x) + (\ln T)K$$

where K is the number of parameters. Here the trade-off between precision and parsimony is clear.

EMPIRICAL RESULTS

The following data sources were used in the empirical analysis. Daily observations for exchange rates were obtained from Data Resources International for the period June 1973 to December 1985. Daily stock market returns were taken from the Center for Research in Security Prices (CRSP) database, which provides a value-weighted market index of all quoted NYSE and AMEX stocks. End-of-month and end-of-week data were sampled from the daily files. Because 1973 was a year of transition from fixed to flexible exchange rates, all samples start in January 1974.[5] Given the complex distributional changes observed for different days of the week,[6] daily data will not be investigated here. The analysis focuses on monthly and weekly data; which are the data usually chosen for tests of asset pricing models and of models of exchange rate determination. For conciseness, only detailed results for the $/DM rate are presented in this article; the analysis was also performed for the British pound and the Japanese yen with similar results.

Table 13-1 shows summary statistics for monthly and weekly logarithmic changes in the $/DM exchange rate and in the value-weighted stock market. The departures from the normal density are apparent from the high excess

TABLE 13-1   Summary statistics for the $/DM rate and value-weighted CRSP index for the period January 1974–December 1985

	$/DM rate		Value-weighted CRSP index	
	Monthly	*Weekly*	*Monthly*	*Weekly*
Mean	0.000695	0.000134	0.009942	0.002277
Standard deviation	0.033505	0.014338	0.046482	0.021956
Skewness	0.0323	0.2510	0.0593	0.0702
	(0.16)	(2.56)	(0.29)	(0.72)
Excess kurtosis	1.5588*	3.291*	0.894	2.922*
	(3.82)	(16.81)	(2.19)	(14.92)
Autocorrelations ρ-lags:				
1	−0.045	0.069	0.030	−0.005
2	0.129	0.020	−0.046	−0.018
3	0.083	0.023	0.037	0.144*
4	0.006	0.044	0.052	−0.017
5	0.009	−0.058	0.140	−0.082
6	−0.053	−0.015	−0.142	0.078
7	0.042	−0.006	−0.082	−0.036
8	0.078	0.035	−0.053	−0.056
9	−0.066	0.036	−0.071	0.079
10	0.064	0.046	0.003	−0.059
11	0.065	0.035	−0.062	−0.103*
12	−0.119	0.019	0.097	0.107*
Standard error (ρ)	0.083	0.040	0.083	0.040
Box-Pierce (P-value)	7.575	10.707	9.864	43.238*
	[0.817]	[0.554]	[0.628]	[0.00002]
Number of observations (T)	144	626	144	626

Asymptotic t-statistics in parentheses and marginal significance level in brackets. Under the normality assumption, the skewness and excess kurtosis coefficients should be zero.
*Significant at the 1 percent level.

kurtosis coefficients, especially for weekly data. Normal densities imply zero coefficients of skewness and excess kurtosis. The high asymptotic t-statistics clearly reveal "fat-tailed" distributions. The pattern of autocorrelation, on the other hand, indicates little serial correlation.[7]

To provide a check on the methodology, a jump-diffusion process was estimated for the $/DM exchange rate over the fixed-rate period January 1959 to May 1971.[8] Over this 12-year period, there were two revaluations of the mark, which should be prime candidates for jumps. Indeed, as shown in Table 13-2, the χ_3^2 statistic of 266.7 amounts to a very strong rejection of the pure diffusion process. After the jump component is factored in,[9] the volatility of the remaining diffusion process drops dramatically, and the drift term becomes much smaller, which is consistent with small movements within the support points around the parity exchange rate. As expected, fixed-exchange-rate regimes are characterized by discontinuities that can be modeled by jump processes. The question now is whether such discontinuities also exist in flexible-exchange-rate regimes.

Tables 13-3 and 13-4 show the estimated coefficients for models (1) to (4) as well as tests of various hypotheses on the distribution of the logarithmic change in the $/DM exchange rate and in the stock market index. A comparison between the stock market and the exchange rate provides interesting results. First, it should be noted that floating exchange rates are typically less volatile than the stock market. Annualizing weekly variances by $\sqrt{52}$, for instance, the volatility of the mark is about 10.2 percent per annum, compared with 15.8 percent for the value-weighted stock market.

Turning now to the empirical fit of the various stochastic processes, a simple diffusion model seems to provide an adequate description of monthly stock returns: none of the χ^2 tests are significant, and the SC criterion is minimized for the simple diffusion model. This is consistent with the findings of Fama

---

TABLE 13-2 Jump-diffusion process for the $/DM rate for the fixed-rate period January 1959–April 1971

	Process parameters					
Lognormal		Jump				Test of
μ $(\times 10^2)$	σ $(\times 10^4)$	λ	θ $(\times 10^4)$	δ^2 $(\times 10^4)$	Log-likelihood	diffusion χ_3^2
0.095	0.446*				531.35	
(1.74)	(8.60)					
−0.018	0.040*	0.0625*	0.0180	0.00033	664.71	266.7*
(−1.0)	(7.53)	(2.58)	(2.44)	(1.99)		

Diffusion process: $\ln(P_t/P_{t-1}) \sim N(\mu, \sigma^2)$. Jump process: intensity λ, jump size $\ln Y \sim N(\theta, \delta^2)$. Asymptotic t-statistics in parentheses. The German mark was revalued by 5 percent on March 2, 1961, and 9.29 percent on October 26, 1969. The χ^2 statistic tests the hypothesis of a pure diffusion process against a jump-diffusion model with constant parameters. Monthly observations ($T = 148$).
*Significant at the 1 percent level.

TABLE 13-3 Stochastic processes for the $/DM rate, January 1974–December 1985

	Process parameters							Test of diffusion model against				
	Lognormal		Jump			ARCH	Log				Goodness	Schwarz
μ ($\times 10^2$)	σ^2 ($\times 10^4$)	λ	θ ($\times 10^4$)	δ^2 ($\times 10^4$)	α_1	likelihood	Mixed, χ^2_4	Jump, χ^2_3	ARCH, χ^2_1	of fit, χ^2_{19}	criterion, SC
Monthly												
0.070 (0.251)	11.15* (8.48)					285.21				24.75 [0.17]	−560.5
−0.015 (−0.06)	5.08* (5.04)	0.40 (0.55)	0.21 (0.25)	15.56 (1.53)		290.15		9.88 [0.020]		18.76 [0.47]	−555.5
0.052 (0.19)	9.56* (7.77)				0.126 (1.51)	287.79			5.16 [0.023]	23.32 [0.23]	−560.7†
0.039 (0.15)	5.14* (4.81)	0.32 (0.39)	0.03 (0.02)	14.24 (1.21)	0.118 (1.40)	290.89	11.37 [0.023]	6.18 [0.103]			
Weekly												
0.0134 (0.23)	2.052* (17.69)					1769.52				68.28* [0.0]	−3526.2
0.0531 (1.28)	0.173* (4.49)	1.32 (1.66)	−0.022 (−0.52)	1.38* (6.25)		1813.42		87.80* [0.0]		14.08 [0.78]	−3594.6†
0.0143 (0.26)	1.456* (14.73)				0.324* (4.37)	1792.08			45.12* [0.0]	60.49* [0.0]	−3564.8
0.0567 (1.48)	0.088* (2.90)	1.16 (1.24)	−0.014 (−0.24)	1.23* (5.05)	0.271* (3.96)	1829.96	120.9* [0.0]	75.76 [0.0]			

Diffusion process: $x_t \sim N(\mu, \sigma^2)$. Jump process: intensity λ, jump size $\ln Y \sim N(\theta, \delta^2)$. ARCH process: $x_t \sim N(\mu, h_t)$, with $h_t = \sigma^2 + \alpha_1(x_{t-1} - \mu)^2$. Asymptotic t-statistics in parentheses; marginal significance levels in brackets; † denotes best model according to SC criterion, which allows us to compare nonnested models by explicitly penalizing for a larger number of parameters. The 1 percent critical levels for the χ^2_4, χ^2_3, and χ^2_1 are 13.3, 11.3, and 6.6, respectively. These statistics, respectively, test the hypothesis of a pure diffusion process with constant parameters against a mixed jump-ARCH, a jump-diffusion, and an ARCH model. The degrees of freedom correspond to the additional number of parameters in the alternative hypothesis. The χ^2_3 statistics of 6.18 and 75.76 test the ARCH model against a mixed jump-ARCH model. Number of observations is 144 for monthly data and 626 for weekly data.
*Significant at the 1 percent level.

TABLE 13-4 Stochastic processes for the CRSP value-weighted index January 1974–December 1985

| Process parameters | | | | | | Log likelihood | Test of diffusion model significance | | | Goodness of fit, χ^2_{19} | Schwarz criterion, SC |
| Lognormal | | Jump | | | ARCH | | | | | | |
$\mu\,(\times 10^2)$	$\sigma^2\,(\times 10^4)$	λ	$\theta\,(\times 10^4)$	$\delta^2\,(\times 10^4)$	α_1		Mixed, χ^2_4	Jump, χ^2_3	ARCH, χ^2_1		
Monthly											
0.994*	21.46*					238.06				20.25	−466.2†
(2.58)	(8.48)									[0.38]	
0.858	10.77*	0.51	0.27	21.3		240.26		4.39		18.46	−455.7
(2.37)	(4.84)	(0.36)	(0.26)	(1.31)				[0.22]		[0.49]	
1.134*	19.04*				0.107	239.36			2.60	14.51	−463.8
(2.96)	(7.83)				(1.27)				[0.107]	[0.75]	
0.993*	9.27*	0.65	0.06	15.7	0.089	240.62	5.11	2.52			
(2.68)	(4.02)	(0.16)	(0.06)	(1.00)	(0.72)		[0.276]	[0.472]			
Weekly											
0.228*	4.813*					1502.75				46.16*	−2992.6
(2.60)	(17.69)									[0.0]	
0.280*	2.882*	0.17	−0.33	11.2		1529.06		52.60*		32.44	−3025.9†
(3.61)	(12.87)	(1.30)	(−0.71)	(2.40)				[0.0]		[0.03]	
0.255*	3.846*				0.199*	1517.12			28.74*	45.29*	−3014.9
(3.11)	(15.50)				(3.50)				[0.0]	[0.0]	
0.299*	2.459*	0.12	−0.45	12.3	0.162*	1539.79	74.07*	45.34*			
(3.94)	(11.78)	(1.54)	(−0.78)	(2.26)	(3.37)		[0.0]	[0.0]			

See notes for Table 13-3.

(1976) and more recently of Jarrow and Rosenfeld (1984). For the monthly $/DM rate, on the other hand, the hypothesis of a pure diffusion process is rejected against both the jump-diffusion and ARCH models: the marginal significance level of the respective χ_3^2 and χ_1^2 is about 2 percent for both alternatives. Similar conclusions hold for the χ_4^2 test of diffusion against combined ARCH and jump. These results must be qualified, however, given that the distributional assumptions are only valid asymptotically and that χ^2 tests tend to reject too often in small samples. The SC criterion suggests that the ARCH model is a posteriori most probable, by a small margin, over the diffusion model. Overall, these results do not present overwhelming evidence against the diffusion model for monthly exchange rate movements.

The analysis of weekly data is shown in the lower parts of Tables 13-3 and 13-4. The χ_3^2 tests indicate that the jump-diffusion model is a significant improvement over the simple diffusion model in both the foreign exchange and stock markets. The results for the stock market are in contrast with those of Jarrow and Rosenfeld (1984), who reported no significant jump process for weekly stock market returns from 1962 to 1978. Further, Table 13-5 shows a summary of the χ_3^2 tests of no jump component for four weekly subperiods and three currencies. The subperiod analysis indicates that the jump process identified for the stock market is not spread evenly over the four subperiods. The jump process for the exchange rate, however, is significant for each of the four subperiods considered. Thus, the distribution of weekly exchange rate changes seems to be consistently characterized by discontinuities.

TABLE 13-5   Comparative tests of stochastic processes for weekly subperiods January 4, 1974–December 31, 1985

Period (weekly)	T	$/DM Jump, χ_3^2	$/DM ARCH, χ_1^2	$/yen Jump, χ_3^2	$/yen ARCH, χ_1^2	$/£ Jump, χ_3^2	$/£ ARCH, χ_1^2	Value weighted CRSP index Jump, χ_3^2	Value weighted CRSP index ARCH, χ_1^2
Jan. 1974– Dec. 1976	157	13.20* [0.0042]	5.90*† [0.015]	108.9*† [0.0]	22.01* [0.0]	25.76*† [0.0]	14.95* [0.0001]	16.06* [0.0011]	11.19*† [0.0008]
Jan. 1977– Dec. 1979	156	35.87* [0.0]	40.30*† [0.0]	26.56*† [0.0]	0.04 [0.844]	55.90*† [0.0]	14.11* [0.0002]	17.72*† [0.0005]	2.32 [0.127]
Jan. 1980– Dec. 1982	157	15.57*† [0.0014]	1.11 [0.292]	6.63 [0.085]	0.35 [0.551]	15.57*† [0.0014]	0.00 [0.997]	3.52 [0.318]	0.94 [0.333]
Jan. 1983– Dec. 1985	154	14.54* [0.0022]	5.25† [0.022]	46.11*† [0.0]	5.12 [0.023]	23.91* [0.0]	8.76*† [0.003]	6.20 [0.102]	0.01 [0.909]
Jan. 1974– Dec. 1985	626	87.80*† [0.0]	45.12* [0.0]	119.8*† [0.0]	12.53* [0.0]	97.74*† [0.0]	32.92* [0.0]	52.60*† [0.0]	28.74* [0.0]

Numbers in brackets are marginal significance levels. The χ_3^2 statistics test the null of a diffusion process against the jump-diffusion process. The alternative hypothesis for the χ_1^2 statistics in the ARCH process.
†indicates most likely model among diffusion, mixed jump-diffusion, or ARCH models, according to SC criterion. No † indicates that diffusion model is best.
*Significant at the 1 percent level.

For weekly data, however, the normal distribution is also rejected against the alternative of a first-order ARCH process: the χ_1^2 statistic is highly significant for the \$/DM exchange rate and for the stock market. The economic significance of the ARCH process parameters can be illustrated as follows. If there were no movement in the \$/DM rate in the previous week, the conditional variance would be 0.0001456 per week, which translates into a weekly standard deviation of 8.7 percent. In contrast, if the previous weekly exchange rate movement were 3 percent—which is not an exceptional movement given the reported volatilities—the conditional variance would increase to 0.0001456 + $0.324(0.03)^2$, for an annual volatility of 15.1 percent, which is nearly twice the previous number! Clearly, the estimates of the ARCH process provided in Table 13-3 suggest economically important movements in exchange rate volatility. The figures for the stock market, on the other hand, yield a relatively less important ARCH effect: the same 3 percent movement in the stock market would increase the volatility from 14.1 to 17.1 percent per annum. It is also interesting to note that rejections of the null hypothesis of a constant variance are systematically weaker for the stock market than for the \$/DM rate.

Because both jump and ARCH components have been identified in weekly exchange rate movements—which was to be expected given the existence of fat tails—the question arises as to which of the two processes provides a superior description of the data. The values of the SC criterion in the right-hand columns of Tables 13-3 and 13-4 indicate that, even explicitly penalizing for its large number of parameters, the jump-diffusion process is a posteriori more probable than either the diffusion or the ARCH model for weekly data.

Further, given the evidence of heteroskedasticity in weekly data, one should test whether discontinuities still appear in the conditional distribution of returns. The fourth model in Tables 13-3 and 13-4 is a combined jump-ARCH process, which can be used to test this hypothesis. The χ_3^2 statistic tests the added significance of the jump process over and above the simple ARCH process. The values of the statistics are 75.76 and 45.34 for the \$/DM rate and the stock market index, respectively, which are highly significant. This suggests that discontinuities are present in the distribution of weekly exchange rates even after explicitly accounting for heteroskedasticity. These results could explain why Hsieh (1988) reports substantial leptokurtosis in the residuals of a more complex ARCH model, in which both the mean and variance of daily spot rate changes are allowed to vary over time. Similarly, Engle and Bollerslev (1986) also find that the residuals from a generalized ARCH (GARCH) model display fatter tails than those expected from a normal distribution.[10]

The last task of this section is to ascertain whether the assumptions underlying the maximum-likelihood estimation are appropriate for this data set. This is important because the estimation technique relies heavily on a correct specification of the likelihood function. Tables 13-3 and 13-4 show goodness-of-fit test statistics for the first three models, obtained as follows. First, the observations $\{x_t\}$ were sorted in order of increasing magnitude and classified into N = 20 equally sized groups. Knowledge of the density function for each distribution allows us to compute a theoretical number of observations in each group. The goodness of fit between the actual and theoretical distributions is tested by summing the squares of the differences between the observed and theoretical number of outcomes in each group. Asymptotically, this test statistic has a χ^2_{N-1} distribution.[11] The predicted number of observations was computed from numerical integration of the relevant density functions over each interval.[12] Tables 13-3 and 13-4 show that the models fit well the data for monthly observations but that the diffusion and ARCH models are not quite appropriate for weekly data. The jump–diffusion process, on the other hand, does not seem incorrectly specified, which supports the general conclusions of this section.

IMPLICATIONS FOR OPTION PRICING

The finding of marked jump processes in exchange rates has important implications for the pricing of currency options. Recently, Bodurtha and Courtadon (1987) tested the ability of the American option valuation model to explain the pricing of currency options quoted on the Philadelphia Stock Exchange. Focusing on the relative pricing error, the model seems to underprice short-term out-of-the-money options by as much as 29 percent. At-the-money and in-the-money options are generally slightly over-priced, with the bias most pronounced for short-maturity options.[13] These results are in contrast with what has been found generally for stock options.[14]

As suggested by Bodurtha and Courtadon (1987), the directions of these biases are generally consistent with a mixed jump-diffusion process. Consider the price of an out-of-the-money call option close to maturity. If the exchange rate follows a diffusion process, the chance of exercising the option at maturity may be quite small; with a jump process, however, one jump may be sufficient to move the option in the money, which implies that a diffusion model will underprice the option.[15] Thus the issue is whether the empirically observed large biases can be fully accounted for by a jump process, which is the subject of this section.

Consider the sensitivity of the European[16] call option valuation model to the introduction of a mixed jump-diffusion process for exchange rates. The Black-Scholes formula assumes a lognormal diffusion process; modified for foreign currency options,[17] it can be written as

$$F_e(S,\ \tau;\ r,\ r^*,\ \sigma^2,\ K) \equiv e^{-r^*\tau}C(S,\ \tau;\ r\ -\ r^*,\ \sigma^2,\ K) \tag{5}$$

where C is the usual Black-Scholes pricing formula for call options, S is the spot rate expressed in dollars per unit of the foreign currency, τ is the time to expiration on a per annum basis, r and r^* are the domestic and foreign rates of interest, σ^2 is the annual variance, and K is the strike price. The foreign rate of interest can be interpreted as the continuous dividend yield on the underlying asset. With an added jump component, Merton's (1976) valuation model[18] can be extended to the case of currency options as

$$F(S, \tau; r, r^*, \sigma_0^2, \lambda, \theta, \delta^2, K) \equiv e^{-r^*\tau} \sum_{j=0}^{\infty} \frac{e^{-\lambda T e^{\theta+\delta^2/2}}(\lambda T e^{\theta+\delta^2/2})^j}{j!}$$

$$\cdot \; C\left(S, \tau; r - r^* + j\frac{\theta + \delta^2/2}{\tau} - \lambda(e^{\theta+\delta^2/2} - 1), \sigma_0^2 + j\frac{\delta^2}{\tau}, K\right) \qquad (6)$$

where σ_0^2 is now the variance of the pure diffusion process and λ, θ, and δ^2 are the parameters of the jump process, defined previously. An investor ignoring the jump component would estimate the total variance of an assumed diffusion process as $\sigma^2 = \sigma_0^2 + \lambda\delta^2$, on which the diffusion option price F_e will be based. For example, from the weekly data in Tables 13-3 and 13-4, the annual volatility of the \$/DM rate would be 10.2 percent, against a volatility of 15.8 percent for the value-weighted stock market.

The extent of the mispricing can be measured by the relative difference[19] $\epsilon = (F - F_e)/F$, using the parameters previously estimated from weekly data over the period 1974 to 1987. F_e is computed from Equation (5) with $\sigma^2 = \sigma_0^2 + \lambda\delta^2$, and F is computed from Equation (6) using the same values of σ_0^2, λ, and δ^2. The analysis is performed for \$/DM currency call options and hypothetical call options on the value-weighted stock market.

Tables 13-6 and 13-7 show relative and absolute mispricing errors for typical option parameters. The options have been classified by time to maturity and by the ratio S/K, taken to represent in-, at-, and out-of-the-money classes. All prices are scaled by the strike price. For stock options, the out-of-the-money option is defined here by a spot price level of 0.95. For currency options, a different

---

TABLE 13-6 Hypothetical options: relative pricing differences in percent [$\epsilon = (F - F_e)/F$; parameters: $K = 1$, $r = 5\%$, $r^* = 5\%$]

	Months to maturity							
	0.50	0.75	1	1.5	3	4.5	6	9
$/DM options								
Out-of-the-money	17.15	4.63	0.72	−1.23	−0.99	−0.68	−0.50	−0.32
($S = 0.9678$)	(0.86)	(0.49)	(0.15)	(−1.14)	(−1.43)	(−1.53)	(−1.60)	(−1.67)
At-the-money	−4.62	−2.78	−1.98	−0.93	−0.61	−0.40	−0.29	−0.19
($S = 1.00$)	(−1.52)	(−1.58)	(−1.66)	(−1.78)	(−1.76)	(−1.70)	(−1.62)	(−1.43)
In-the-money	0.31	0.23	0.15	−0.05	−0.09	−0.10	−0.09	−0.07
($S = 1.0322$)	(2.12)	(1.34)	(0.69)	(−0.24)	(−0.54)	(−0.66)	(−0.68)	(−0.67)
Stock index options								
Out-of-the-money	12.81	−0.87	−4.46	−4.50	−2.95	−1.61	−0.98	−0.49
($S = 0.95$)	(0.72)	(−0.06)	(−0.41)	(−0.80)	(−0.90)	(−1.01)	(−1.18)	(−1.18)
At-the-money	−7.37	−6.12	−5.26	−3.09	−1.86	−0.91	−0.50	−0.21
($S = 1.00$)	(−1.41)	(−1.20)	(−1.10)	(−0.98)	(−0.91)	(−0.83)	(−0.73)	(−0.44)
In-the-money	−0.79	−1.19	−1.40	−1.28	−0.84	−0.37	−0.16	−0.02
($S = 1.05$)	(−0.37)	(−0.49)	(−0.56)	(−0.68)	(−0.65)	(−0.49)	(−0.30)	(−0.06)

Asymptotics t-statistics in parentheses. Stochastic process parameters taken from Tables 13-3 and 13-4, weekly data. Error measured as "true" jump-diffusion price minus Black-Scholes price divided by true price: $(F - F_e)/F$, where $F = F(S, \tau; r, r^*, \sigma_0^2, \lambda, \theta, \delta^2, K)$, $F_e = F_e(S, \tau; r, r^*, \sigma^2, K)$, and $\sigma^2 = \sigma_0^2 + \lambda\delta^2$.

TABLE 13-7   Hypothetical options: absolute pricing difference in cents $[\epsilon = F - F_e$; parameters: $K = 1, r = 5\%, r^* = 5\%]$

	Months to maturity							
	0.50	0.75	1	1.5	3	4.5	6	9
$/DM options								
Out-of-the-money	1.05	0.57	0.14	−0.61	−0.76	−0.78	−0.74	−0.64
(S = 0.9678)	(1.80)	(0.67)	(0.16)	(−1.04)	(−1.80)	(−2.36)	(−2.72)	(−3.23)
At-the-money	−3.66	−2.75	−2.27	−1.52	−1.21	−0.97	−0.82	−0.65
(S = 1.00)	(−2.32)	(−2.40)	(−2.57)	(−2.78)	(−2.69)	(−2.48)	(−2.25)	(−1.83)
In-the-money	1.03	0.84	0.53	−0.18	−0.37	−0.43	−0.43	−0.39
(S = 1.0322)	(2.11)	(1.80)	(0.71)	(−0.24)	(−0.54)	(−0.67)	(−0.69)	(−0.64)
Stock index options								
Out-of-the-money	1.10	−0.15	−1.24	−3.26	−3.39	−2.77	−2.17	−1.49
(S = 0.95)	(0.70)	(−0.06)	(−0.42)	(−0.84)	(−0.97)	(−1.13)	(−1.37)	(−1.32)
At-the-money	−8.81	−9.07	−9.06	−7.64	−5.68	−3.44	−2.16	−1.10
(S = 1.00)	(−1.47)	(−1.25)	(−1.15)	(−1.03)	(−0.97)	(−0.88)	(−0.78)	(−0.45)
In-the-money	−4.00	−6.10	−7.33	−7.37	−5.20	−2.55	−1.15	−0.20
(S = 1.05)	(−0.38)	(−0.49)	(−0.57)	(−0.69)	(−0.66)	(−0.50)	(−0.31)	(−0.06)

See notes to Table 13-6.

definition of the out-of-the-money options was used to account for the lower volatility of exchange rates. Specifically, the amount by which the stock option was out of the money (0.05) was multiplied by the ratio of the volatilities to yield $0.05 \times 10.2/15.8 = 0.0322$. Thus, the out-of-the-money currency option was taken as the one for which the exchange rate was 0.9678. With this adjustment, the probability of ending in the money is the same for the currency and stock options, based on a simple diffusion process. In the same fashion, in-the-money options are defined by a spot price of 1.05 and 1.0322 for stock options and currency options, respectively. The other parameters were fixed at $r = 5$ percent and $r^* = 5$ percent for the dollar and foreign interest rates.

Some noticeable differences appear in the mispricing of currency and stock options. Using the estimated parameters, the Black-Scholes model underprices short-term out-of-the-money currency options by about 17 percent, which can partly explain the 29 percent underpricing reported by Bodurtha and Courtadon (1987). This result can be traced to the ratio $\lambda\delta^2/(\lambda\delta^2 + \sigma_0^2)$, which represents the fraction of the variance caused by the jump component; this ratio is 96 percent for the $/DM rate, much higher than the 36 percent figure for the stock market.[20] As a result, the diffusion process underestimates the likelihood of a jump that would bring one of those out-of-the-money short-lived DM call options into the money. The mispricing is weaker for stock market options, which is in line with the interpretation of Ball and Torous (1985), who report few operational discrepancies between the two option valuation models. Finally, the extent of the mispricing decreases as the time to maturity increases, as observed empirically.

One shortcoming of this analysis is that it does not take into account the estimation error in the process parameters. Given the invariance property of maximum-likelihood estimators, these reported pricing errors are also maximum-likelihood estimates. But it would also be interesting to construct asymptotic standard errors for the reported point estimates. These could be used to test whether the reported pricing errors are significantly different from zero given the sampling variation in the data and the dependence of the pricing errors on the estimated parameters. As Table 13-6 shows, the results from the asymptotic *t*-statistics are generally inconclusive for the *relative* pricing errors. However, the *absolute* pricing discrepancy for the shortest-term out-of-the-money currency option has a *t*-value of 1.8. Thus, there is some evidence that the reported underpricing of short-term out-of-the-money currency options is not due to sampling variation.

At-the-money call options appear overpriced in both markets, and significantly so for currency options. Pricing errors for options in the money seem relatively small. Finally, the extent of the mispricing decreases with the time to maturity. Most of these results are consistent with empirical observations in the currency options market.

In summary, the estimates of mixed jump-diffusion processes reveal that ignoring the jump component in exchange rates can lead to serious mispricing errors for currency options. This can account in large part for the large pricing errors reported in previous empirical tests of option pricing models in the foreign currency options market. On the other hand, smaller discrepancies were found in stock market options, which can be explained by the fact that discontinuities are harder to identify in the stock market index.

CONCLUSIONS

This article has investigated the existence of discontinuities in the sample path of exchange rates and of a value-weighted U.S. stock market index. It was found that exchange rates display significant jump components, which are more manifest than in the stock market. These discontinuities seem to arise even after explicit allowance is made for possible heteroskedasticity in the usual diffusion process and appear very strongly in weekly data but less so in monthly data. The statistical analysis was performed side by side for the foreign exchange market and the stock market, and it suggests important differences in the structure of these markets.

The economic importance of this result was illustrated for the currency options market, for which it was shown that ignoring the jump component can induce serious mispricing of currency options. Previous models of currency options have always relied on the assumption of continuous sample paths for exchange rates. Using the estimated parameters, numerical examples showed that about two-thirds of the 29 percent biases reported for short-term out-of-the-money options can be explained by a mixed jump–diffusion process. Consequently, successful models of short-term movements in exchange rates should be consistent with these empirical findings.

APPENDIX: MAXIMUM-LIKELIHOOD ESTIMATION

This Appendix briefly summarizes the maximum-likelihood estimation method used in the article. If prices follow a diffusion process with constant drift parameter $E[\Delta P/P] = \alpha$ and constant variance $V[\Delta P/P] = \sigma^2$, the logarithm of price relatives $x_t \equiv \ln(P_t/P_{t-1})$ is normally distributed with mean $\mu \equiv \alpha - \sigma^2/2$ and variance σ^2. With T independent observations, the logarithm of the likelihood function $L(\phi; x)$, viewed as a function of the parameter vector $\phi = (\mu, \sigma^2)$, can be written as

$$l_N = -\frac{T}{2}\ln(2\pi) + \sum_{t=1}^{T} \ln\left[\frac{1}{\sqrt{\sigma^2}} \exp\left(\frac{-(x_t - \mu)^2}{2\sigma^2}\right)\right] \tag{A1}$$

Consider now a Poisson process where λ is the mean number of jumps occurring per unit time and where the jump size Y has a posited distribution $\ln Y \sim N(\theta, \delta^2)$. The log-likelihood function for the mixed jump–diffusion process is

$$l_J = -T\lambda - \frac{T}{2}\ln(2\pi) + \sum_{t=1}^{T} \ln\left[\sum_{j=0}^{\infty} \frac{\lambda^j}{j!} \frac{1}{\sqrt{\sigma^2 + \delta^2 j}} \exp\left(\frac{-(x_t - \mu - \theta j)^2}{2(\sigma^2 + \delta^2 j)}\right)\right] \tag{A2}$$

In order to numerically optimize the above function, the infinite sum has to be truncated after some value of N. Ball and Torous (1985) derived a formula for an upper bound on the truncation error, which could be used to select a desirable N. In practice, truncation at $N = 10$ provides satisfactory accuracy for all parameter values encountered in this article.

Leptokurtic distributions can also arise because of time-varying parameters instead of discontinuities. One such model is an ARCH process introduced by Engle (1982). This is a tractable specification where the conditional variance h_t is explicitly modeled as a nonstochastic function of past squared innovations. Because economic theory has little to say about the appropriate number of lags to include, the simplest specification chosen here is the first-order ARCH model, where the conditional volatility can be written as

$$h_t = \alpha_0 + \alpha_1 \epsilon_t^2 = \alpha_0 + \alpha_1(x_{t-1} - \mu)^2 \tag{A3}$$

with ϵ_t defined as $x_t - \mu$. In the absence of heteroskedasticity, the parameter α_1 should be zero, in which case α_0 represents the variance of a stationary diffusion process. This could be expanded to include a weighted average of a number of past observations, or in general any predetermined information. The log-likelihood function for this ARCH model is

$$l_A = -\frac{T}{2}\ln(2\pi) + \sum_{t=1}^{T} \ln\left[\frac{1}{\sqrt{h_t}} \exp\left(\frac{-(x_t - \mu)^2}{2h_t}\right)\right] \tag{A4}$$

If the conditional distribution of ϵ has a Poisson distribution, the log-likelihood function can be written as

$$l_{AJ} = -T\lambda - \frac{T}{2}\ln(2\pi) + \sum_{t=1}^{T}\ln\left[\sum_{j=0}^{\infty}\frac{\lambda^{j}}{j!}\frac{1}{\sqrt{b_t + \delta^2 j}}\exp\left(\frac{-(x_t - \mu - \theta j)^2}{2(b_t + \delta^2 j)}\right)\right] \quad (A5)$$

This likelihood function includes the jump process, the ARCH process, and the normal process as special cases. Therefore it can be used to construct a generalized likelihood ratio $\Lambda = \sup_{\phi \in \Phi_0} L(\phi; x)/\sup_{\phi \in \Phi} L(\phi; x)$, where the likelihood functions have been maximized (1) over the parameter space $\phi \in \Phi_0$ under the null hypothesis and (2) over the parameter space $\phi \in \Phi = \Phi_0 \cup \Phi_1$, which includes the alternative Φ_1. Under the null hypothesis, the statistic -2 in Λ has a chi-square distribution with degrees of freedom equal to the number of parameters between the two models. This asymptotic result holds because the two hypotheses Φ_0 and Φ are nested in the parameter space.

REFERENCES

Ball, C., and W. Torous, 1985, "On Jumps in Common Stock Prices and Their Impact on Call Option Pricing," *Journal of Finance,* 40, 155-173.

Bodurtha, J., and G. Courtadon, 1987, "Tests of the American Option Pricing Model in the Foreign Currency Options Market," *Journal of Financial and Quantitative Analysis,* 22, 153-167.

Boothe, P., and D. Glassman, 1987, "The Statistical Distribution of Exchange Rates: Empirical Evidence and Economic Implications," *Journal of International Economics,* 22, 297-319.

Borensztein, E., and M. Dooley, 1987, "Options on Foreign Exchange and Exchange Rate Expections," *IMF Staff Papers,* 34, 643-680.

Calderon-Rossell, J., and M. Ben-Horim, 1982, "The Behavior of Foreign Exchange Rates," *Journal of International Business Studies,* 13, 99-111.

Domowitz, I., and C. Hakkio, 1985, "Conditional Variance and the Risk Premium in the Foreign Exchange Market," *Journal of International Economics,* 19, 47-66.

Engle, R., 1982, "Autoregressive Conditional Heteroscedasticity with Estimates of the Variance of United Kingdom Inflation," *Econometrica,* 50, 987-1007.

Engle, R., and T. Bollerslev, 1986, "Modelling the Persistende of Conditional Variances," *Econometric Reviews,* 5, 1-47.

Fama, E., 1976, *Foundations of Finance,* Basic Books, New York.

Farber, A., R. Roll, and B. Solnik, 1977, "An Empirical Study of Risk under Fixed and Flexible Exchange," *Carnegie-Rochester Conference Series on Public Policy,* 5, 235-265.

Flood, R., and R. Hodrick, 1986, "Asset Price Volatility, Bubbles, and Process Switching," *Journal of Finance,* 41, 831-842.

Frenkel, J., 1981, "Flexible Exchange Rates, Prices and the Role of 'News': Lessons from the 1970's," *Journal of Political Economy,* 89, 665-705.

Frenkel, J., and M. Mussa, 1980, "The Efficiency of Foreign Exchange Markets and Measures of Turbulence," *American Economic Review,* 70, 374-381.

Friedman, D., and S. Vandersteel, 1982, "Short-Run Fluctuations in Foreign Exchange Rates: Evidence from the Data 1973–79," *Journal of International Economics,* 13, 171–186.

Garman, M., and S. Kohlhagen, 1983, "Foreign Currency Option Values," *Journal of International Money and Finance,* 2, 231–238.

Hsieh, D., 1988, "The Statistical Properties of Daily Foreign Exchange Rates: 1974–1983," *Journal of International Economics,* 24, 129–145.

Hsieh, D., and L. Manas-Anton, 1988, "Empirical Regularities in the Deutsche Mark Futures Options," *Advances in Futures and Options Research,* 3, 183–208.

Jarrow, R. and E. Rosenfeld, 1984, "Jump Risks and the Intertemporal Capital Asset Pricing Model," *Journal of Business,* 57, 337–351.

Jarrow, R., and A. Rudd, 1983, *Option Pricing,* Irwin, Homewood, Ill.

Jorion, P., and N. Stoughton, 1989, "An Empirical Investigation of the Early Exercise Premium of Foreign Currency Options," forthcoming in *Journal of Futures Market.*

Kendall, M., and A. Stuart, 1967, *The Advanced Theory of Statistics,* vol. 2, *Inference and Relationship,* Haffner, New York.

Kon, S., 1984, "Models of Stock Returns—A Comparison," *Journal of Finance,* 39, 147–165.

McBeth, J., and L. Merville, 1980, "Tests of the Black-Scholes and Cox Option Valuation Models," *Journal of Finance,* 35, 285–301.

McFarland, J., R. Pettit, and S. Sung, 1982, "The Distribution of Foreign Exchange Price Changes: Trading Day Effects and Risk Measurement," *Journal of Finance,* 37, 693–715.

Merton, R., 1976, "Option Pricing When Underlying Stock Returns Are Discontinuous," *Journal of Financial Economics,* 3, 125–144.

Mussa, M., 1979, "Empirical Regularities in the Behavior of Exchange Rates and Theories of the Foreign Exchange Market," *Carnegie-Rochester Conference on Public Policy,* 11, 9–57.

Rogalski, R., and J. Vinso, 1978, "Empirical Properties of Foreign Exchange Rates," *Journal of International Business Studies,* 9, 69–79.

Schwarz, G., 1978, "Estimating the Dimensions of a Model," *Annals of Statistics,* 6, 461–464.

Shastri, K., and K. Tandon, 1986, "On the Use of European Models to Price American Options on Foreign Currency," *Journal of Futures Markets,* 6, 93–108.

So, J., 1987, "The Distribution of Foreign Exchange Price Changes: Trading Day Effects and Risk Measurement—A Comment," *Journal of Finance,* 42, 181–188.

Wasserfallen, W., and H. Zimmermann, 1985, "The Behavior of Intra-Daily Exchange Rates," *Journal of Banking and Finance,* 9, 55–72.

Westerfield, J., 1977, "An Examination of Foreign Exchange Risk under Fixed and Floating Rate Regimes," *Journal of International Economics,* 7, 181–200.

ENDNOTES

1. See, for instance, Farber, Roll, and Solnik (1977), Westerfield (1977), McFarland, Pettit, and Sung (1982), and Wasserfallen and Zimmermann (1985) for monthly, weekly, daily, and intradaily exchange rates, respectively.

2. This is the simplest model that captures the time variation in second moments. It could be extended to include autocorrelation and/or time variation in first and second moments, as in Hsieh (1988).

3. Unfortunately, the method cannot be applied to the estimation of stable distributions, whose densities, with few exceptions, are not known in closed form.

4. This procedure has been used by Rogalski and Vinso (1978), who argue that the Student's t-distribution is more appropriate than the stable distribution for weekly changes in flexible exchange rates. See also Kon (1984) for tests involving stock market prices.

5. This allows monthly and weekly returns to start at the same date and also allows the use of some presample data for the ARCH process.

6. See, for example, McFarland, Pettit, and Sung (1982) and Hsieh (1988).

7. Some autocorrelation coefficients for weekly stock market returns seem abnormally high. For this series, the Box-Pierce statistic also rejects the hypothesis that the correlation coefficients are jointly zero. This effect, however, can be attributed to a few observations in 1975 and is restricted to a short sample period. Hsieh (1988) also argued that rejections in such tests can be caused by incorrect estimates of standard errors due to heteroskedasticity.

8. The monthly data were taken from various issues of Pick's currency yearbook.

9. The estimated jump intensity $\lambda = 0.0625$ is greater than what would be expected from two realignments in 148 months ($\lambda = 2/148 = 0.013$). This parameter is negatively correlated with θ, the drift of the log of the jump size, whose estimated value of 1.8 percent is less than the average size of a devaluation. As λ is overestimated and θ is underestimated, these parameters imply more frequent and smaller jumps than actually occurred. Although the jump process parameters are jointly significant, the imprecision in their estimated values can be attributed to the small number of jumps observed in the sample.

10. The results in this article were also reproduced with a GARCH(1, 1) process, which actually provides a better fit than the simplest ARCH(1) model because it allows more persistence in the variances. The GARCH(1, 1) model was also rejected in favor of a more general alternative including jumps.

11. The statistic $\sum_{j=1}^{N}(M_j - MP_j)^2/MP_j$, where M_j and MP_j are the observed and predicted number of outcomes, respectively, has an asymptotic distribution which is actually bounded between a χ_{N-1}^2 and a χ_{N-1-k}^2, where k is the number of parameters estimated by maximum likelihood. See, for instance, Kendall and Stuart (1967). A conservative test was used here, given that the distribution is only valid asymptotically.

12. For the ARCH process, innovations divided by the conditional volatility should follow a standard normal distribution.

13. Similar results are reported by Borensztein and Dooley (1987) and Hsieh and Manas-Anton (1989), the latter for options on mark *futures*.

14. McBeth and Merville (1980), for instance, find that out-of-the-money options are overpriced by the Black-Scholes model, while in-the-money options seem mostly underpriced.

15. Similarly, deep in-the-money options could also appear too expensive relative to a diffusion model: the "insurance" feature of the option, virtually worthless with a diffusion process, should be greater when jumps are present.

16. As Shastri and Tandon (1986) showed, the difference in the valuation of American and European options is small for most call options, especially in cases where the foreign interest rate is lower than the U.S. interest rate, which is typical of the German mark. For instance, Jorion and Stoughton (1989) analyzed the value of the early exercise premium from market data and found that it averages 2 percent for $/DM call options.

17. See, for instance, Garman and Kohlhagen (1983).

18. See also Jarrow and Rudd (1983). The Merton model relies on the assumption that the jump component is diversifiable and therefore not priced. This allows the risk of the jump component to be eliminated through a risk-neutral argument.

19. This definition is consistent with that of Bodurtha and Courtadon (1987) and thus can be used for comparing numerical results.

20. Holding this ratio constant, the mispricing would be even more important for a process characterized by large jumps that occur infrequently; that is, for a smaller λ and larger δ^2.

14

Pricing European Currency Options: A Comparison of the Modified Black-Scholes Model and a Random Variance Model

MARC CHESNEY
LOUIS SCOTT

INTRODUCTION

In recent years, markets for foreign currency options have developed in the U.S., Europe, and around the world. These new markets can be used to hedge foreign currency risks in a manner that is not easily available in forward markets or futures markets. For example, with currency options, one can purchase insurance against an adverse change in the exchange rate. In addition, traders and investors can achieve risk-return tradeoffs with currency options that are not generally available in other markets. We use two alternative option pricing mod-

The authors have benefited by comments from *JFQA* Managing Editor Paul Malatesta, Alan White, a *JFQA* referee, and participants at the 1988 Finance Conference at HEC-ISA. The first author would like to acknowledge financial support from the University of Geneva and the Geneva Stock Exchange. The research for this paper was completed while both authors were at the University of Illinois at Urbana-Champaign.

Reprinted with permission from *Journal of Financial and Quantitative Analysis;* Vol. 24, No. 3; Marc Chesney and Louis Scott; 1989.

els to study prices from Geneva, Switzerland, for calls and puts on the dollar/Swiss franc exchange rate.

Most option pricing models are designed to price European options that can be exercised only at maturity. The foreign currency options traded in the U.S. are primarily American options that can be exercised prior to maturity. It is well known that the early exercise feature on American foreign currency options has value. In this paper, we analyze prices on European options so that we have a unique opportunity to assess the performance of our option pricing models. We use the modified Black-Scholes model for foreign currency options and a random variance model to focus on two issues. First, can these models explain the actual option prices observed? Second, can the model be used to generate a profitable trading strategy?

ALTERNATIVE MODELS FOR PRICING EUROPEAN CURRENCY OPTIONS

We first consider the modified Black-Scholes model that has been developed by Garman and Kohlhagen (1983), Grabbe (1983), and Biger and Hull (1983). In this model, the spot exchange rate follows a diffusion process

$$dS = \mu S dt + \sigma S dz,$$

where S is the domestic price of foreign currency (ratio of foreign currency to domestic currency). Both the foreign and domestic interest rates, r_f and r_d, and the instantaneous standard deviation, σ, are assumed to be constant. The modified Black-Scholes formula for the European call is

$$C(S, t) = S_t e^{-r_f(T-t)} N(d_1) - X e^{-r_d(T-t)} N(d_2), \tag{1}$$

where

$$d_1 = \ln(S_t/X) + (r_d - r_f + 1/2\sigma^2)(T - t)/\sigma\sqrt{T - t},$$
$$d_2 = d_1 - \sigma\sqrt{T - t},$$

and $N(x)$ is the distribution function for a standard normal random variable. T represents maturity and X is the strike price. The foreign interest rate enters the model because we earn the foreign interest rate whenever we take a long position in the foreign currency. Without the foreign interest rate, the model is identical to the usual Black-Scholes model. Prices for European puts can be easily obtained via the put-call parity theorem: $P(S, t) = C(S, t) + e^{-r_d(T-t)}X - e^{-r_f(T-t)}S_t$.

With the Black-Scholes model, we are assuming that changes in foreign exchange rates are lognormally distributed, but recent empirical tests by Bollerslev (1987) and Wasserman and Zimmerman (1986) indicate rejection of this lognormal model. One explanation for the rejection of the lognormal model is the possibility that the variance of $\ln(S_t/S_{t-1})$ changes randomly. To incorporate randomly changing variance rates, we apply the results of recent papers by Hull and White (1987), Scott (1987), and Wiggins (1987). In the alternative random variance model, we have a second stochastic equation for volatility

$$dS = \mu S dt + \sigma S dz_1,$$

$$d\sigma = \sigma \left[\frac{1}{2} \gamma^2 + \beta(\bar{a} - \ln\sigma) \right] dt + \gamma\sigma dz_2, \tag{2}$$

with $E(dz_1 dz_2) = \delta dt$. The $d\sigma$ equation is set up so that $\ln\sigma$ is a mean-reverting process: $d\ln\sigma = \beta(\bar{a} - \ln\sigma)dt + \gamma dz_2$.[1] To keep the model simple, we assume that the foreign and domestic interest rates are nonstochastic as in the Black-Scholes model.

To price a European call option in this model, we use the results of Theorem 3 and Lemma 4 in Cox, Ingersoll, and Ross (1985a). The fundamental partial differential equation for a contingent claim in Theorem 3 includes aggregate wealth and state variables for the economy. Cox, Ingersoll, and Ross (1985b), in their companion paper, show that we can drop the wealth variable if the utility function is a constant relative risk aversion utility function and the payoffs of the contingent claim do not depend directly on wealth. The resulting partial differential equation for a European call option, $C(Y, t)$, in the notation of Cox, Ingersoll, and Ross is

$$\frac{1}{2} \sum_{i=1}^{k} \sum_{j=1}^{k} C_{y_i y_j}(\text{Cov } Y_i, Y_j) + \sum_{i=1}^{k} C_{y_i}(\mu_i - \phi_i) + C_t - r_d C = 0,$$

where Y is the vector of state variables, μ_i is the instantaneous mean for Y_i, and ϕ_i is the risk premium associated with state variable Y_i. The subscripts indicate partial derivatives. In our model, the two state variables are the exchange rate and volatility. Let Y_1 be the exchange rate and $\mu_1 = \mu S$. Let Y_2 be the volatility and $\mu_2 = \sigma[1/2\gamma^2 + \beta(\bar{a} - \ln\sigma)]$. Since the foreign currency is a traded asset and investors can earn the foreign interest rate on funds invested in the foreign currency, $\mu S = (r_d - r_f)S + \phi_s S$, where $\phi_s S$ is the risk premium for the exchange rate. The fundamental partial differential equation for our option pricing function $C(S, \sigma, t)$ becomes

$$\frac{1}{2} C_{11}\sigma^2 S^2 + C_{12}\delta\gamma\sigma^2 S + \frac{1}{2} C_{22}\gamma^2\sigma^2 + C_1 S(r_d - r_f)$$

$$+ C_2 \left[\sigma\left(\frac{1}{2} \gamma^2 + \beta(\bar{a} - \ln\sigma) \right) - \phi_\sigma \right] + C_3 - r_d C = 0, \tag{3}$$

where the subscripts on C represent partial derivatives with respect to the first, second, and third variables in the option pricing function $C(S, \sigma, t)$. Hull and White (1987) and Scott (1987) have shown that riskless arbitrage is not enough to produce a unique option pricing function with random volatility. Here, we use the equilibrium asset pricing model of Cox, Ingersoll, and Ross to derive an option pricing function.

The solution to the partial differential equation in (3) can be found by applying Lemma 4 of Cox, Ingersoll, and Ross

$$C(S, \sigma, t) = \hat{E}_t\left\{e^{-r_d(T-t)} \max[0, S_T - X]\right\},\tag{4}$$

where $\hat{E}$ is the risk-adjusted expectations operator. The expectation is taken conditional on what is known at time t, namely S_t and σ_t, and the risk adjustment is incorporated by taking the expectation with respect to the following set of equations

$$dS = (r_d - r_f)Sdt + \sigma Sdz_1,$$
$$d\sigma = \left(\sigma\left[\frac{1}{2}\,gamma^2 + \beta(\bar{a} - \ln\sigma)\right] - \phi_\sigma\right)dt + \gamma\sigma dz_2.\tag{5}$$

At this point, we assume that the correlation between volatility changes and exchange rate changes is zero.[2] With $\delta = 0$, we can solve part of the expectation in (4) analytically by using results in Scott ((1987), p. 425) and Hull and White ((1987a), pp. 284–286).

$$C(S, \sigma, t) = \int_0^\infty [e^{-r_f(T-t)}S_t N(d_1) - e^{-r_d(T-t)}XN(d_2)]d\hat{F}(V),\tag{6}$$

where

$$d_1 = \ln(S_t/X) + (r_d - r_f)(T - t) + 1/2V/\sqrt{V},$$
$$d_2 = d_1 - \sqrt{V},$$

$V = \int_t^T \sigma_{(s)}^2 ds$, and $\hat{F}$ is the distribution function of V using the risk-adjusted $d\sigma$ process in (5). One method for computing option prices in Equation (6) is the Monte Carlo method. We simulate the random variable V by simulating σ over discrete intervals from t to T and plugging each value of V into the function enclosed in brackets in (6), which is the Black-Scholes formula with V in place of $\sigma^2(T - t)$. The sample mean converges in probability to the option pricing function in (6) as the number of simulations increases to infinity. When we use the antithetical variate method described in Boyle (1977), we find that 1,000 simulations of V are sufficient to obtain accurate prices.[3] To price European puts, we simply price the European call and apply the put-call parity theorem.

ESTIMATING THE PARAMETERS OF THE VOLATILITY PROCESS

For our empirical analysis, we use the modified Black-Scholes formula in (1) and the random variance model in (6). For the Black-Scholes model, all of the parameters except the variance rate are observable. A variety of methods is available for estimating the variance rate and most researchers use the implied standard deviation (ISD) from observed option prices as the current estimate of volatility, σ. Alternatively, one can use historical estimates of σ from changes in the foreign exchange rate. We use both methods for estimating σ in the Black-Scholes model. For the random variance model, we need the current volatility (σ_t), the parameters of the volatility process, and the risk premium associated with σ_t. The fixed parameters of the volatility process can be estimated from data on the foreign exchange rate and we describe our estimation technique in this section. Given the parameters and the risk premium for volatility, we can estimate σ_t as the ISD from actual option prices using the random variance model. Estimating the risk premium for volatility is particularly difficult. One method that we try is to use an initial set of option prices and find that value for the risk premium that yields the best fit.

The estimates for the parameters of the volatility process are computed by methods described in Scott (1988). First, we note that the mean-reverting process for $\ln\sigma$ implies the following model for $\ln\sigma_t$ at discrete points

$$\ln\sigma_t = \bar{a}(1 - e^{-\beta}) + e^{-\beta}\ln\sigma_{t-1} + \varepsilon_t,$$

where $E(\varepsilon_t^2) = \sigma_t^2 = \gamma^2(1 - e^{-2\beta}/2\beta$.

For the estimation, we rewrite the model as follows

$$\ln\sigma_t = a + \rho\ln\sigma_{t-1} + \varepsilon_t,$$

and we estimate a, ρ, and σ_ε^2. These parameters are simple functions of $\bar{a}$, β, and γ, and one can recover estimates of $\bar{a}$, β, and γ from the estimates $\hat{a}$, $\hat{\rho}$, and $\hat{\sigma}_\varepsilon^2$. Over a small time interval, we use the following approximation with the autoregressive process for $\ln\sigma_t$,

$$\Delta\ln S_t = m + \sigma_{t-1}u_t,$$

where m is the mean and u_t is a standard normal random variable. To estimate the parameters, we work with $x_t \equiv \Delta\ln S_t - m$ and compute estimates for a variety of moments. First, we observe that

$$E(x_t^2) = \exp\left\{2\left(\frac{a}{1-\rho}\right) + 2\left(\frac{\sigma_\varepsilon^2}{1-\rho^2}\right)\right\},$$

$$E(x_t^4) = 3\exp\left\{4\left(\frac{a}{1-\rho}\right) + 8\left(\frac{\sigma_\varepsilon^2}{1-\rho^2}\right)\right\}.$$

To estimate ρ, we observe that $\ln|x_t| = \ln\sigma_{t-1} + \ln|u_t|$ has an autoregressive-moving average representation that is an ARMA (1,1) as follows

$$(1 - \rho L)\ln|x_t| = b^* + (1 - \theta L)e_t,$$

where θ, b^*, and the variance of e_t are functions of the model parameters. We estimate the ARMA (1, 1) model for $\ln|x_t|$ to obtain an estimate of ρ, and then use the sample estimates of $E(x_t^2)$ and $E(x_t^4)$ to infer estimates of a and σ_ε^2. We then let $y_t \equiv \ln|x_t| - \rho\ln|x_{t-1}|$, and estimate the following covariance to obtain an estimate of δ, the correlation coefficient between u_t and ε_t,

$$\text{Cov}(y_t, x_{t-1}) = E[(\varepsilon_{t-1} + \ln|u_t| - \rho\ln|u_{t-1}|)\sigma_{t-2}u_{t-1}]$$

$$= \delta\sigma_\varepsilon \exp\left\{\left(\frac{a}{1-\rho}\right) + \frac{1}{2}\left(\frac{\sigma_\varepsilon^2}{1-\rho^2}\right)\right\}.$$

Since we are using the method of moments to estimate these parameters, we can use the techniques described in Hansen (1982) to compute an asymptotic variance matrix from which we can calculate standard errors. Our method-of-moments estimators may be biased in small samples, but they are consistent estimators: that is, any biases approach zero as the sample size gets large. To calculate the series x_t, we must use the sample mean of $\ln S_t$, which is a consistent estimator of the mean, m.

To estimate the parameters of the volatility process, we use roughly four years of data on daily exchange rates, and our data source is the *Bank and Quotation Record*. Since we are using the estimates to price options for the year 1984, we use data from November 1979 to December 1983 in our estimation.[4] The estimation results are contained in Table 14-1. The sample kurtosis for $\Delta \ln S_t$ is 4.97, and this estimate is more than three standard errors above three, which is the theoretical value for a normally distributed random variable. The δ estimate is very close to zero, and the t statistic for a test of the null hypothesis that $\delta = 0$ is -0.009. Because the δ estimate is insignificant, we use the random variance model in Equation (6). The estimates for a, ρ, and σ_ε in Table 14-1 are used to simulate values of V for our calculations in the random variance model.

The implied estimates for the original parameters are $\bar{a} = -4.9676$, $\beta = 0.021255$, and $\gamma = 0.073198$. Using the parameter estimates, we get a mean-reverting level of 0.006960 for σ_t; on an annual basis this mean-reverting level is 0.11048, which can be interpreted as a long-run average annual standard deviation. Using either the ρ estimate or the β estimate, one can compute a mean half-life for the model. The mean half-life has the following interpretation. Suppose $\ln \sigma_t$ experiences a deviation or shock from its mean-reverting level, $\bar{a}$. If there are no more random shocks, then the amount of time needed to eliminate half of the deviation is measured by the mean half-life. Our parameter

TABLE 14-1   Parameter Estimates for the Volatility Process Sample Period: November 1979 to December 1983

Parameter	Estimate	Standard Error
a	-0.1044736	0.077678
σ_ε^2	0.00524573	0.004026
ρ	0.9789692	0.015658
δ	-0.00653396	0.763883
Sample Kurtosis $= 4.97$		
Mean Level for σ, Daily $= 0.006960$		
Annual $= 0.110480$		

$$T = 1023$$

$$\ln \sigma_t = a + \rho \ln \sigma_{t-1} + \varepsilon_t$$

Notes: σ_ε^2 is the variance of ε_t, and δ is the correlation coefficient between stock price changes and volatility changes. The sample size T is 1,023 trading days, σ_t is the instantaneous standard deviation, and the mean level for σ represents a long-run average.

estimates imply that the mean half-life for $\ln\sigma$ is 32.6 trading days, or roughly 6-1/2 weeks. The parameter estimates also imply that the long-run two standard error range for σ is from 0.00342 to 0.01416.

EMPIRICAL RESULTS WITH PRICES ON EUROPEAN OPTIONS

In this section, we use the modified Black-Scholes model and the random variance model to price calls and puts on the dollar/Swiss franc exchange rate, and we compare the prices to bid-ask quotes for European calls and puts traded in Switzerland. Our data set consists of prices on foreign currency options traded by Credit Suisse First Boston (CSFB) Futures Trading in Geneva. We use the same data source that was used by Chesney and Loubergé (1987). CSFB writes and buys calls and puts denominated in Swiss francs on the spot rate of the U.S. dollar. The options can be exercised only at maturity (the third Wednesday of March, June, September, or December), which means that they are of the European type. The option prices are quoted in Swiss centimes and the value of each contract is $50,000. The striking prices are quoted in Swiss francs, and the interval between two striking prices is 5 Swiss centimes.

Data for the year 1984 were collected from *Finanz und Wirtschaft*, a financial newspaper published twice a week in Zurich. We use three sets of data. The first set includes prices of call options and put options on U.S. dollars quoted in Geneva at 2:00 p.m. on Tuesdays and Fridays. CSFB Futures Trading communicates these prices to *Finanz und Wirtschaft*. Typically, 18 different call and put prices are quoted. We have bid and ask prices corresponding to 3 striking prices (in-, at-, and out-of-the money) for the next 3 standardized maturities. The second data set is the spot price of the currency (U.S. dollar) quoted on the same days at the same time (2:00 p.m.) on the foreign exchange market. These prices are also communicated to *Finanz und Wirtschaft* by CSFB Futures Trading. The third data set includes the Eurodollar and Euro-Swiss franc rates observed on the same days at 11:00 a.m. These interest rates are official middle rates for maturities of 1, 2, 3, 6, and 12 months communicated to *Finanz und Wirtschaft* by CSFB. The relevant interest rates for our currency options are computed by interpolating between the two closest interest rates.[5]

The option prices for the random variance model are calculated by the Monte Carlo method, and we use the parameter estimates from Section III for the volatility process. We find that the antithetical variate method described in Boyle (1977) substantially reduces the number of simulations required to produce accurate prices. All of our calculations with the random variance model are done on a Cray X-MP supercomputer, and we find that 1,000 simulations are sufficient.[6] The accuracy of our simulated prices can be assessed by calculating the large sample standard errors for the sample means. To illustrate the level of accuracy that we achieve, we have computed call prices and standard errors for a variety of representative options. The calculations are shown in Table 14-2 and we find that for the longest maturities, the largest standard errors are less

TABLE 14-2 Call Option Prices and Standard Errors in the Random Variance Option Pricing Model Monte Carlo Simulation, 1,000 Simulations Strike Price = 200 centimes r_d = 0.09 per annum r_f = 0.11 per annum

Spot Rate (Centimes)	Time-to-Maturity	Option Price (Centimes)	Standard Error
180	30	0.0665	0.0016
	60	0.3386	0.0051
	90	0.6607	0.0079
	120	0.9829	0.0096
	150	1.2934	0.0104
	180	1.5880	0.0110
	210	1.8711	0.0115
	240	2.1389	0.0116
	270	2.3904	0.0118
200	30	3.6383	0.0041
	60	4.8876	0.0075
	90	5.7347	0.0101
	120	6.3964	0.0117
	150	6.9416	0.0127
	180	7.4025	0.0134
	210	7.8113	0.0142
	240	8.1726	0.0146
	270	8.4923	0.0149
220	30	19.6281	0.0024
	60	19.5978	0.0066
	90	19.6507	0.0098
	120	19.7222	0.0115
	150	19.7949	0.0125
	180	19.8608	0.0131
	210	19.9256	0.0138
	240	19.9827	0.0141
	270	20.0290	0.0144

Note: 100 centimes = 1 Swiss franc.

than 0.015 centimes so that the 95-percent confidence intervals are smaller than ±0.03 centimes. The 95-percent confidence intervals are much smaller for many of the options.

To estimate the implied standard deviations (ISD's) for both the Black-Scholes model and the random variance model, we use at-the-money call options, and minimize the sum of squared errors between the model prices and actual prices. Since our price quotes are bid-ask quotes, we use the midpoint of the bid-ask spread. For at-the-money options, we use those calls that have strike prices within 5 centimes of the spot rate. Using prices on a given day, we minimize

$$\min_{\sigma_t} F = \sum_{i=1}^{P} (C_i(S_t, \sigma_t, t) - W_{it})^2,$$

where W_{it} is the midpoint of the bid-ask spread. To reduce the number of iterations required to find the ISD, we use both first and second partial derivatives of F with respect to σ.

In addition, we would like to allow for a risk premium in the volatility process. One method of estimation is to infer a value from option prices. If we assume that the volatility risk premium has the form $\phi_\sigma = \lambda\sigma$, where λ is a constant, then the risk-adjusted process for $\ln\sigma$ becomes $d\ln\sigma = [\beta(\bar{a} - \ln\sigma) - \lambda]dt + \gamma dz_2$. In this case, λ becomes an adjustment on the mean-reverting level for $\ln\sigma$ and, in our discrete model, we have

$$\ln\sigma_t = (a - \lambda^*) + \rho\ln\sigma_{t-1} + \varepsilon_t.$$

We use prices on at-the-money calls from December 1983 to find the value for λ^* that yields the best fit. For this initial set of option prices, we set σ_t and λ^* to minimize the sum of squared errors between the model prices and the midpoints of the bid-ask spread. We find that σ is relatively low during December 1983 and the early months of 1984; all of the daily ISD's are below the mean-reverting level of σ, which is 0.00696 per trading day. With these option prices, we estimate a positive value for λ^*, which implies a significant downward adjustment in the mean-reverting level for σ from 0.00696 to 0.00387. This adjustment works well for early 1984 but, as the variance rate increases and goes above the mean level later in the year, the model no longer prices options very well. We find that the model with $\lambda^* = 0$ works better for the entire year.

We use at-the-money calls to estimate σ_t, and then we use that estimate to price all the calls and puts on that day. We then compare these theoretical model prices to the bid-ask quotes from CSFB and calculate the size of the deviations outside the bid-ask spread. Many of the theoretical prices fall within the bid-ask spread and the corresponding deviations are zero. We have 101 days of prices for 1984, and the total number of calls and puts is 1,574. We calculate both the mean squared error and the mean absolute deviation for each model. In the random variance model, σ_t is a variable that changes randomly and we use option prices to compute the ISD. For our analysis of the models, we use a random variance model with the mean-reverting process estimated in Section III, and a random variance model in which $\ln\sigma$ follows a random walk. The random walk for volatility has $a = 0$ and $\rho = 1$, and our historically-based sample estimate for σ_ε^2 is 0.1315, with a standard error of 0.2052. Our first test is a comparison of the random variance model and the Black-Scholes model, using historical estimates for the fixed parameters in both models. In the Black-Scholes model, σ is a fixed parameter, and we use the sample standard deviation calculated from $\Delta\ln S_t$ for the last 6 months of 1983. Because it is possible that we do not have a good sample estimate of σ, we also examine the Black-Scholes model using a constant σ, computed as the average of the ISD's that are calculated from the Black-Scholes model and revised every trading day. Our second test is a comparison of the random variance model with the Black-Scholes model in which the ISD is revised every trading day. The Black-Scholes model with revised estimates of volatility is the model that is regularly applied, and it can be viewed as a less expensive approximation for the random variance model.[7]

The results for all five models are contained in Table 14-3. First, we compare the random variance model with the Black-Scholes model using either a historical σ or a constant σ. These applications of the Black-Scholes model perform very poorly: the mean squared error and the mean absolute deviation are several orders of magnitude greater. We also find that the random variance model with a mean-reverting volatility process performs better than the random variance model in which $\ln\sigma$ is a random walk. For our second test, we compare the random variance model and the Black-Scholes model with an ISD that is revised daily. We find that the Black-Scholes model with a changing ISD outperforms the random variance model: for the random variance model, the root mean squared error is 1-1/2 times greater, and the mean absolute deviation is roughly twice as large, but the differences in Swiss centimes are not large. We have two possible interpretations for the superior performance of the Black-Scholes model with ISD's revised daily: (1) the Black-Scholes model may serve as a good approximation for whatever the true underlying model is; and (2) the market maker and the traders are using variations of the Black-Scholes formula with daily revisions in the variance rate.

In Table 14-4, we present some simple regression tests for biases in the two best-fitting option pricing models (the Black-Scholes model with revised ISD's and the random variance model with a mean-reverting volatility process). We examine three biases that have been documented in the literature on stock options: the strike price bias, the time-to-maturity bias, and the volatility bias.

TABLE 14-3   Call Options and Put Options on the $/Swiss Franc Exchange Rate, 1984 1574 Options

Pricing Errors as Differences between Model Prices and the Bid-Ask Spread		
	Mean Squared Error	Mean Absolute Deviation
Random Variance Model, (Mean-reverting volatility process)	0.125	0.204
Random Variance Model, (Random walk for $\ln\sigma$)	1.431	0.895
Black-Scholes Model, (ISD revised daily)	0.056	0.104
Black-Scholes Model, (Historical σ)	21.384	3.128
Black-Scholes Model, (Constant σ)	24.725	3.151

Note: Whenever the model price falls within the bid-ask spread, the pricing error is zero.

TABLE 14-4   Regression Tests for Option Pricing Biases: The Strike Price, Time-to-Maturity, and Volatility Biases

		α_0	$t(\alpha_0)$	α_1	$t(\alpha_1)$	R^2
Panel A: Calls (820 Observations)						
$e_{it} = \alpha_0 + \alpha_1 M_{it}$	Black-Scholes	0.01164	5.24	0.6021	8.23	0.076
	Random Variance	0.08151	8.38	2.564	7.99	0.072
$e_{it} = \alpha_0 + \alpha_1 \tau_{it}$	Black-Scholes	0.502×10^{-2}	1.37	-0.349×10^{-4}	-1.45	0.003
	Random Variance	0.2059	14.16	-0.181×10^{-2}	-13.63	0.190
$e_{it} = \alpha_0 + \alpha_1 \hat{\sigma}_t$	Black-Scholes	0.169×10^{-2}	0.19	-0.2068	-0.15	0.000
	Random Variance	0.1144	4.82	-15.21	-3.59	0.016
Panel B: Puts (710 Observations)						
$e_{it} = \alpha_0 + \alpha_1 M_{it}$	Black-Scholes	0.01077	2.32	-0.3050	-1.52	0.003
	Random Variance	0.06651	3.31	-3.013	-3.47	0.017
$e_{it} = \alpha_0 + \alpha_1 \tau_{it}$	Black-Scholes	0.584×10^{-2}	0.64	0.564×10^{-4}	0.92	0.001
	Random Variance	0.2747	7.09	-0.142×10^{-2}	-5.43	0.040
$e_{it} = \alpha_0 + \alpha_1 \hat{\sigma}_t$	Black-Scholes	0.223×10^{-2}	0.10	1.697	0.52	0.000
	Random Variance	0.2480	6.13	-30.76	-4.41	0.027

Notes: e_{it} is the percentage pricing error as defined in the paper, $M_{it} = (e^{-r_f(T-t)}S_t - e^{-r_d(T-t)}X_i)/e^{-r_d(T-t)}X_i$, τ_{it} = time to maturity, and $\hat{\sigma}_t$ = implied standard deviation. Here we are comparing the Black-Scholes model with revised ISD's and the random variance model with mean-reverting volatility.

The pricing error is computed as the amount by which the model price falls outside the bid-ask spread, and we divide by the model price to get a percentage pricing error. When the model price falls inside the bid-ask spread, the pricing error and the percentage pricing error are both zero. The pricing error is negative when the model price is above the ask price, and it is positive when the model price is below the bid price. To examine the strike price bias, we compute

$$M_{it} = (e^{-r_f(T-t)}S_t - e^{-r_d(T-t)}X_i)/e^{-r_d(T-t)}X_i,$$

for the *i*th call on date *t* as the measure of the degree to which the option is in- or out-of-the-money. For puts, we use the negative of this measure. We run separate regressions of the percentage errors on M_{it}, time to maturity, and the estimated volatility (ISD).

We find that there are some very extreme outliers for out-of-the-money options with short times to maturity, and these observations are omitted in the regression tests. The only bias for the Black-Scholes model is a strike price bias in the pricing of calls: only the *t* statistic for the slope coefficient on M_{it} is statistically significant in Table 14-4. The Black-Scholes model tends to underprice in-the-money calls and overprice out-of-the-money calls. All three biases are present in the random variance model: the *t* statistics on the slope coefficients for M_{it}, time-to-maturity, and volatility are all statistically significant. The random variance model also tends to underprice in-the-money calls and overprice out-of-the-money calls. The results are the exact opposite for puts. The random variance model has a tendency to overprice long time-to-maturity options (both calls and puts) and underprice short time-to-maturity options. With respect to volatility, the random variance model tends to overprice options when volatility is high and underprice options when volatility is low.

In Figures 14-1–14-4, we plot the percentage pricing errors against the strike price measure so that we have pictures of the strike price bias.[8] In Figure 14-1, we see a slight bias in call prices for the Black-Scholes model. For the put options priced by the Black-Scholes model in Figure 14-2, we see larger percentage errors in pricing, and the magnitude of the errors increases for out-of-the-money options, but there is no evidence of a bias, up or down. For the calls and puts priced by the random variance model in Figures 14-3 and 14-4, we see larger pricing errors. In Figure 14-3 for calls, the random variance model appears to overprice out-of-the-money calls and underprice at-the-money and in-the-money calls. In Figure 14-4 for puts, the errors are much greater for out-of-the-money options, and there is a tendency for the model to underprice the out-of-the-money puts. The two models produce different theoretical prices, and we find that the Black-Scholes model prices are closer to the bid-ask quotes observed in the market.

These results suggest that the observed prices are much closer to prices generated by the Black-Scholes model than to prices generated by the random

FIGURE 14-1   Percent Pricing Errors for Call Options with the Black-Scholes Model versus the Strike Price

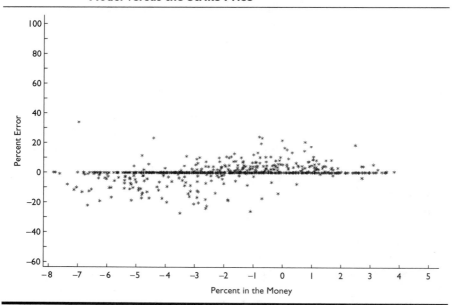

FIGURE 14-2   Percent Pricing Errors for Put Options with the Black-Scholes Model versus the Strike Price

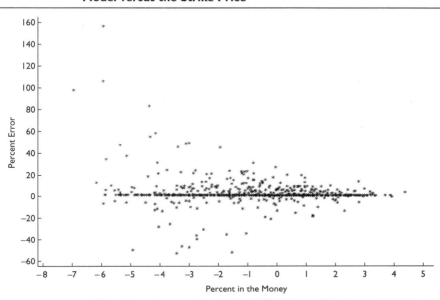

variance model. To examine the mispricing by the random variance model more closely, we compute theoretical prices for both models and compare these prices for different types of calls in Table 14-5. We examine two different cases: one in which volatility is below the mean-reverting level of 0.00696, and a second case in which volatility is above the mean-reverting level. In the table, we present ratios of the random variance price to the Black-Scholes price. For the comparison, we set the σ in the Black-Scholes model so that it yields the same price as the random variance model on a call option that is at-the-money and has a time-to-maturity of 4-1/2 months. For low volatility, we find that the random variance model, relative to the Black-Scholes model, overprices long maturity calls and underprices short maturity calls. The strike price bias varies depending on the time-to-maturity: if volatility is low, the random variance model underprices out-of-the-money calls that have short maturities and over-prices out-of-the-money calls with long maturities. In Panel B, the comparisons are reversed when volatility is high. When volatility is low, we expect volatility to gradually increase in the random variance model, whereas we expect it to remain constant in the Black-Scholes model. When volatility is high, we expect it to decrease in the random variance model.

If market prices are being generated by Black-Scholes traders, then we would expect pricing biases for the random variance model that are consistent

FIGURE 14-3   Percent Pricing Errors for Call Options with the Random Variance Model versus the Strike Price

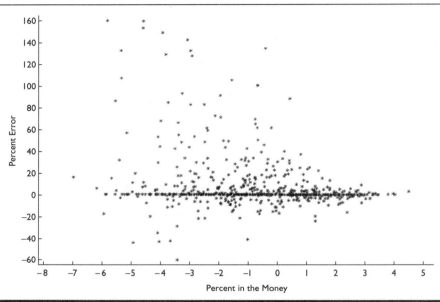

with Table 14-5. To sort out the interactions between volatility, strike price, and time-to-maturity, we split the sample into two parts according to the implied volatility for the random variance model. In our sample, implied volatility in the random variance model is below the mean-reverting level for the first 9 months and above the mean-reverting level for the last 3 months. We run the following regression for each sample

$$e_{it} = \alpha_0 + \alpha_1 M_{it} + \alpha_2 \tau_{it} + \alpha_3 D_{it} M_{it} + u_t,$$

where D_{it} is a dummy variable with zero for a short time-to-maturity and one for a long time-to-maturity. When volatility is low, our analysis predicts that $\alpha_1 < 0$, $\alpha_2 < 0$, and $\alpha_3 > 0$. When volatility is high, our analysis predicts that the signs of the coefficients should be reversed: $\alpha_1 > 0$, $\alpha_2 > 0$, and $\alpha_3 < 0$. These two regressions for call options are presented in Table 14-6. For the first 9 months when volatility is low, the slope coefficients are all statistically significant and have the signs predicted by our analysis above. For the last 3 months when volatility is high, α_1 and α_2 are statistically significant and have the predicted signs, but α_3 has the wrong sign and is not statistically significant. The mispricing by the random variance model is consistent with the analysis in Table 14-5.

The prices on the European currency options in our sample conform well to the Black-Scholes model with implied volatilities revised each day, and the

FIGURE 14-4   Percent Pricing Errors for Put Options with the Random Variance Model versus the Strike Price

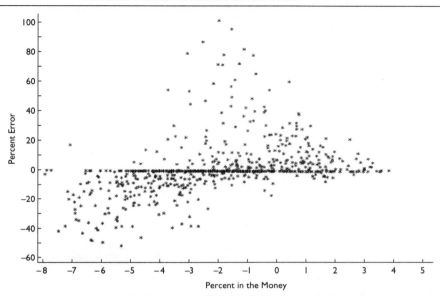

random variance model produces prices that differ significantly from the Black-Scholes prices. This observation suggests that there may be some trading opportunities available. If volatility is changing randomly, a trader with a random variance model may be able to identify mispriced options. To test this implication, we use the random variance model to compute net gains for a hedged position with the call options and the foreign currency. In the random variance model, both exchange rate and volatility risk need to be hedged and we accomplish this by taking positions in two options and the foreign currency. Our trading rule proceeds as follows. On each day, price the options with the random variance model and look for model prices that fall outside the bid-ask spread. Buy or sell the call option that has the largest deviation outside the bid-ask spread. If the model price for the call is below the bid, sell it; if the model price is above the ask, buy it. Then take an opposite position in a second call. If we need to sell a second call, use one that has a model price below the midpoint of the bid-ask spread. If we need to buy a second call, use one that has a model price above the midpoint of the bid-ask spread. Finally, take a position in the foreign currency to hedge exchange rate risk.

The hedged position becomes

$$C(S, \sigma, t, T_1) + w_1 S_t + w_2 C(S, \sigma, t, T_2),$$

and the hedge ratios are

TABLE 14-5 **A Comparison of Theoretical Prices between the Random Variance Model with Mean-Reverting Volatility and the Black-Scholes Model with Constant Volatility (Ratios of the Random-Variance Model Price to the Black-Scholes Model Price)**

Panel A: Low Volatility: $\sigma_{RV} = 0.0048797$, $\sigma_{BS} = 0.0064378$

Strike Price (francs)	Time-to-Maturity (Calendar Days)				
	30	68	135	200	270
2.00	1.00	1.00	1.01	1.02	1.04
2.05	0.99	0.99	1.00	1.03	1.05
2.10	0.95	0.96	1.00	1.04	1.07
2.15	0.82	0.90	1.00	1.06	1.10
2.20	0.63	0.84	1.01	1.09	1.14
2.25	0.47	0.81	1.04	1.14	1.20
2.30	0.42	0.83	1.12	1.22	1.29

Panel B: High Volatility: $\sigma_{RV} = 0.0099257$, $\sigma_{BS} = 0.0087564$

Strike Price (francs)	Time-to-Maturity (Calendar Days)				
	30	68	135	200	270
2.00	1.01	1.01	1.00	0.99	0.98
2.05	1.02	1.02	1.00	0.98	0.97
2.10	1.04	1.03	1.00	0.98	0.96
2.15	1.10	1.05	1.00	0.97	0.95
2.20	1.20	1.09	1.00	0.96	0.94
2.25	1.40	1.15	1.01	0.96	0.93
2.30	1.79	1.25	1.04	0.96	0.92

$S = 2.15$ Swiss Francs/$

Note: The σ for the Black-Scholes models is set so that the option with a strike price of 2.15 and a time-to-maturity of 135 days has a Black-Scholes price equal to the random variance model price.

$$w_1 = -\frac{\partial C(S, \sigma, t, T_1)}{\partial S} - w_2 \frac{\partial C(S, \sigma, t, T_2)}{\partial S},$$

$$w_2 = -\frac{\dfrac{\partial C(S, \sigma, t, T_1)}{\partial \sigma}}{\dfrac{\partial C(S, \sigma, t, T_2)}{\partial \sigma}}.$$

The positions are established with actual prices, and the random variance pricing function is used to calculate the derivatives for the hedge ratios. The net gain on the zero-investment hedge is

$$[C(t + 1, T_1) - C(t, T_1)] + w_1[S_{t+1}(1 + r_f) - S_t]$$
$$+ w_2[C(t + 1, T_2) - C(t, T_2)] - r_d[C(t, T_1) + w_1 S_t + w_2 C(t, T_2)].$$

TABLE 14-6   Regression Tests for Random Variance Model Call Options Stock Price and Time-to-Maturity Biases for Different Levels of Volatility

Panel A: Early Period, Low σ		
	Estimate	t-Statistic
α_0	0.2578	13.02
α_1	−3.176	−5.15
α_2	−0.001975	−7.97
α_3	5.386	6.56
580 observations $R^2 = 0.32$		

Panel B: Later Period, High σ		
	Estimate	t-Statistic
α_0	−0.01311	−1.84
α_1	0.6173	2.69
α_2	0.0002258	2.93
α_3	0.3151	1.13
240 observations $R^2 = 0.11$		

$$e_{it} = \alpha_0 + \alpha_1 M_{it} + \alpha_2 \tau_{it} + \alpha_3 D_{it} M_{it} + \mu_{it}$$

$$D_{it} = 0 \quad \text{if } \tau_{it} \leq 90 \text{ trading days (130 calendar days)}$$
$$= 1 \quad \text{if } \tau_{it} > 90 \text{ trading days}$$

Note: The sample of percentage pricing errors for the random variance model is split between the low volatility period and the high volatility period. $D_{it} M_{it}$ is an interaction variable for the combined effect of time-to-maturity and strike price.

The midpoint of the bid-ask spread is used to compute these gains. The average bid-ask spread for calls in our sample is 0.59 Swiss centimes, which is relatively large. Here, we are computing potential net gains for a market maker or a trader who can trade inside the bid-ask spread. The hedged positions are formed on each trading day on which mispriced options are found. The random variance model identifies mispriced options for all but two days. The average net gain is 0.2587 Swiss centimes, and the sample standard deviation is 0.4778. The t statistic for the sample mean is 5.33 so that it is statistically significant, but the average net gain is more than offset by the bid-ask spread. These results indicate that there are no trading opportunities for a small investor who must buy at the ask and sell at the bid. The results, however, do indicate that there is mispricing in the market and that there are some profit opportunities for a market maker or a trader who can transact inside the bid-ask spread. Each call option contract is for $50,000, and typical prices are around 5 Swiss centimes, which represents a contract cost of 2,500 Swiss francs. The average net gain is equal to 129.4 Swiss francs, or 5.2 percent of the typical contract cost. The cumulative gain, defined as the average net gain per contract times the number of mispriced contracts traded, is 12,548.50 Swiss francs.

A similar trading strategy has been examined for the Black-Scholes model with standard delta hedging (buy or sell a call and hedge with a position in the foreign currency). With the Black-Scholes model, we find trading opportunities on only 79 out of 99 trading days in our sample. The average net gain is 0.2170 with a sample standard deviation of 0.4974, and the t-statistic is 3.88, which is statistically significant. The average net gain of 0.2170 per dollar is 108.5 Swiss francs per contract, or 4.3 percent of the typical contract price. The cumulative gain for this strategy is 8,573 Swiss francs, which is much less than the cumulative gain for the random variance model.

SUMMARY AND CONCLUSIONS

We apply recent results on random variance option pricing to the pricing of European foreign currency options, and we use actual prices on European currency options from Geneva to compare the performance of this model with the modified Black-Scholes model. We find that the actual prices on calls and puts conform more closely to the Black-Scholes model if we allow the variance rate to be revised every day. When we use a constant variance rate, we find that the Black-Scholes model performs very poorly. Even though we find that the Black-Scholes model outperforms the random variance model, we do find much evidence from both the option prices and the foreign exchange rate series to support the notion that volatility changes randomly. A hedged trading strategy with the random variance model produces profits that are statistically and economically significant, but these profits are more than offset by the bid-ask spread. There is some evidence of mispricing in this market, but the magnitude of the mispricing is not large enough for a small investor who must transact at the bid-ask spread to earn abnormal profits.

REFERENCES

Biger, N., and J. C. Hull. "The Valuation of Currency Options." *Financial Management,* 12 (Spring 1983), 24–28.

Black, F., and M. Scholes. "The Pricing of Options and Corporate Liabilities." *Journal of Political Economy,* 81 (May 1973), 637–659.

Bodurtha, J., and G. Courtadon. "Efficiency Tests of the Foreign Currency Market." *Journal of Finance,* 41 (March 1986), 151–162.

———. "Tests of an American Option Pricing Model on the Foreign Currency Options Market." *Journal of Financial and Quantitative Analysis,* 22 (June 1987), 153–168.

Bollerslev, T. "A Conditionally Heteroskedastic Time Series Model for Speculative Prices and Rates of Return." *Review of Economics and Statistics,* 69 (Aug. 1987), 542–547.

Boyle, P. P. "Options: A Monte Carlo Approach." *Journal of Financial Economics,* 4 (May 1977), 323–338.

Boyle, P. P., and D. Emanuel. "Discretely Adjusted Option Hedges." *Journal of Financial Economics,* 8 (Sept. 1980), 259–282.

Chesney, M. "Prix d'Equilibre et Efficience sur le Marché Suisse des Options sur Devises." *Finance,* 7 (Dec. 1986), 149–167.

Chesney, M., and H. Loubergé. "The Pricing of European Currency Options: Empirical Tests Based on Swiss Data." *Aussenwirtschaft,* Heft II/III (1987), 213–228.

Cox, J. C., J. E. Ingersoll, and S. A. Ross. "An Intertemporal General Equilibrium Model of Asset Prices." *Econometrica,* 53 (March 1985), 363–384.

———. "A Theory of the Term Structure of Interest Rates." *Econometrica,* 53 (March 1985), 385–408.

Cox, J. C., and M. Rubinstein. *Options Markets.* Englewood Cliffs, NJ: Prentice-Hall (1985).

Galai, D. "The Components of the Return from Hedging Options against Stocks." *Journal of Business,* 56 (Jan. 1983), 45–54.

Garman, M., and S. Kohlhagen. "Foreign Currency Option Values." *Journal of International Money and Finance,* 2 (Dec. 1983), 231–237.

Grabbe, J. "The Pricing of Call and Put Options on Foreign Exchange." *Journal of International Money and Finance,* 2 (Dec. 1983), 239–254.

Hansen, L. P. "Large Sample Properties of Generalized Method of Moments Estimators." *Econometrica,* 50 (July 1982), 1029–1054.

Hull, J., and A. White. "The Pricing of Options on Assets with Stochastic Volatilities." *Journal of Finance,* 2 (June 1987a), 281–300.

———. "Hedging the Risks from Writing Foreign Currency Options." *Journal of International Money and Finance,* 6 (June 1987b), 131–152.

Johnson, H., and D. Shanno. "Option Pricing when the Variance Is Changing." *Journal of Financial and Quantitative Analysis,* 22 (June 1987), 143–152.

Macbeth, J., and L. Merville. "An Empirical Examination of the Black-Scholes Call Option Pricing Model." *Journal of Finance,* 34 (Dec. 1979), 1173–1186.

Rubinstein, M. "Nonparametric Tests of Alternative Option Pricing Models Using All Reported Trades and Quotes on the 30 Most Active CBOE Option Classes from August 23, 1976 through August 31, 1978." *Journal of Finance,* 40 (June 1985), 455–480.

Shastri, K., and K. Tandon. "Arbitrage Tests of the Efficiency of the Foreign Currency Options Market." *Journal of International Money and Finance,* 4 (Dec. 1985), 455–468.

———. "Valuation of Foreign Currency Options: Some Empirical Tests." *Journal of Financial and Quantitative Analysis,* 21 (June 1986), 145–160.

Scott, L. O. "Option Pricing when the Variance Changes Randomly: Theory, Estimation, and an Application." *Journal of Financial and Quantitative Analysis,* 22 (Dec. 1987), 419–438.

———. "Random Variance Option Pricing: Empirical Tests of the Model and Delta-Sigma Hedging." Working Paper, Univ. of Illinois (March 1988).

Wasserfallen, W., and H. Zimmerman. "The Wiener Process, Variance Measurement and Option Pricing—Evidence from Intra-Daily Data on Foreign Exchange." Working Paper, Univ. of Bern and Hochschule St. Gallen (Oct. 1986).

Whaley, R. E. "Valuation of American Call Options on Dividend-Paying Stocks: Empirical Tests." *Journal of Financial Economics,* 10 (March 1982), 29–58.

Wiggins, J. B. "Option Values under Stochastic Volatility: Theory and Empirical Estimates." *Journal of Financial Economics,* 19 (Dec. 1987), 351–372.

ENDNOTES

1. To get $d\sigma$ in Equation (2), let $x = \ln\sigma$ and $dx = \beta(\bar{a} - x)dt + \gamma dz_2$. Now apply Ito's lemma to $\sigma = e^x$.

2. In Section IV, we present an estimate that is close to zero.

3. With the antithetical variate method, we use each simulation as well as the negative of each simulated random variable. We have 2,000 simulations of V, but only 1,000 are independent simulations.

4. We started with four years of data and then went back to November 1979 in order to run the sample size up to 1,024 for the estimation of ρ in the ARMA (1,1) model. We use a frequency domain estimator for the ARMA model and this requires the Fourier transform of the data series. We use the fast Fourier transform, which works more efficiently, with sample sizes that are multiples of two such as 1,024.

5. The official middle rates are midpoints of bid-ask quotes for the Eurodollar and Euro-Swiss franc rates. Continuously compounded interest rates are used in the option pricing models. The interest rates are first converted to continuous time rates. When the option maturity falls between the maturity dates for the Euro-currency deposits, we interpolate to get rates for the option maturity.

6. We actually use 1,024 simulations on the Cray supercomputer.

7. One test that we have not performed is to compare the Black-Scholes model with a revised (or best fit) volatility parameter and the random variance model with revised (or best fit) parameters for the volatility process. Computing implied parameter values for the volatility process from option prices would be a very expensive procedure, even for a supercomputer.

8. The extreme outliers also have been omitted in the graphs.

PART SIX

Barrier, Binary, and Average Currency Options

15

On Pricing
Barrier Options

PETER RITCHKEN

oyle and Lau (hereafter BL) [1994] have illustrated how a naive application of the binomial option pricing algorithm can lead to significantly
biased estimates in the prices of a variety of barrier, capped, and vulner-
able options, even when the number of time steps is large. The source of the
problem arises from the location of the barrier with respect to adjacent layers
of nodes in the lattice. BL show that if the layers of the lattice are set up so that
the barrier falls between layers of the lattice, the errors may be quite significant.

To avoid these errors, they constrain the time partition so that the resulting
lattice has layers that are as close as possible to the barrier. While this procedure
reduces the size of errors, refining the partition size may not necessarily produce
more precise results. Moreover, the BL procedure may be difficult to implement
if the barriers are time-varying or if there are multiple barriers.

This article provides a simple and highly efficient algorithm that can be
used to price and hedge options that have single barriers that are either at
constant levels or time-varying as well as contracts that are subject to multiple
barriers. First, a lattice is constructed to pass through the barrier points exactly.
Second, the stock price partition and the time partition are decoupled. As a
result, *regardless* of the time partition, the lattice will have the property that
layers of the lattice pass exactly through the barrier points.[1]

This decoupling ensures that as the number of time partitions increases,
layers of the lattice always exist that pass through the barriers, and the option
prices converge smoothly to the true price. This feature is particularly attractive
to a manager of a book of contracts containing barriers because it permits a
time partition to be chosen independently of the contract.

Finally, if no barriers are present, the algorithm produces European and
American call option prices at least as efficiently as the usual binomial lattice

The author thanks Garry de Jager, Paul Laux, and Ivilina Popova for useful discussions and comments.

approach does. Indeed, the algorithm includes the usual binomial lattice as a special case, and the existence of barriers actually reduces the number of computations required.

TRINOMIAL MODELS FOR OPTION PRICING

It is well-known that trinomial and higher-order multinomial lattice procedures can be used as an alternative to the usual binomial lattice.[2] Here we briefly review the trinomial lattice implementation provided by Kamrad and Ritchken [1991].

Assume the underlying asset follows a geometric Wiener process, which for valuation purposes has drift $\mu = r - \sigma^2/2$, where r is the riskless rate, and σ is the instantaneous volatility. Then, with s (t) representing the price at date t, we have

$$\ln\{s(t + \Delta t)\} = \ln\{s(t)\} + \xi(t),$$
$$\text{with } s(0) \text{ given} \tag{1}$$

where $\xi(t)$ is normal with mean $\mu\Delta t$ and variance $\sigma^2\Delta t$. Let $\xi^a(t)$ be the approximating distribution for $\xi(t)$ over the period $[t, t + \Delta t]$. $\xi^a(t)$ is a discrete random variable with

$$\xi^a(t) = \begin{cases} \lambda\sigma\sqrt{\Delta t} & \text{with probability } p_u \\ 0 & \text{with probability } p_m \\ -\lambda\sigma\sqrt{\Delta t} & \text{with probability } p_d \end{cases} \tag{2}$$

where $\lambda \geq 1$ and p_u, p_m, and p_d are

$$p_u = \frac{1}{2\lambda^2} + \frac{\mu\sqrt{\Delta t}}{2\lambda\sigma} \tag{3A}$$

$$p_m = 1 - 1/\lambda^2 \tag{3B}$$

$$p_d = \frac{1}{2\lambda^2} - \frac{\mu\sqrt{\Delta t}}{2\lambda\sigma} \tag{3C}$$

λ can be viewed as a parameter that controls the gap between layers of prices on the lattice, and is referred to as the stretch parameter. Notice that if $\lambda = 1$, $p_m = 0$, and the lattice collapses to the usual binomial lattice. The advantage of this trinomial representation is that the extra parameter λ allows us to decouple the time partition from the state partition.[3] For ordinary options, Kamrad and Ritchken show that selecting λ so that the probability of a horizontal move is about one-third produces very rapid convergence in prices, and is computationally more efficient than a binomial lattice with twice as many time partitions.

PRICING BARRIER OPTIONS

For barrier options, for any given time partition, Δt, we can choose the stretch parameter λ such that the barrier is hit exactly. To make matters specific, consider the down-and-out call option with b representing the knock-out barrier. With the stretch parameter, λ, tentatively set at one, we compute the number of consecutive down moves that leads to the lowest layer of nodes above the barrier, b. This value, n_0, say, is the largest integer smaller than η, where η is given by

$$\eta = \frac{\ln(s(0)/b)}{\sigma\sqrt{\Delta t}} \tag{4}$$

If η is an integer, then we shall maintain λ at the level of one. In most cases η is not an integer. In this case, redefine the stretch parameter, λ, such that

$$\eta = n_0\lambda \tag{5}$$

Under this construction $1 \leq \lambda < 2$. With this specification of λ, the trinomial approximation will result in a lattice that will produce a layer of nodes that coincides with the barrier. In particular, n_0 successive down moves will take the price to the boundary.

Table 15-1 shows the convergence values for the down-and-out call option for the case parameters used by BL. For each time partition, the value of the stretch parameter is reported. Then the trinomial prices for the standard and the down-and-out calls are presented. The final column shows the prices as computed on a binomial lattice.

Notice the very rapid convergence of the down-and-out prices. Indeed, with just 50 time partitions, the accuracy is comparable to that achieved by a binomial lattice with 3,000 time partitions. Notice also that the speed of convergence for the standard European call option on the trinomial lattice is similar to that of the down-and-out option.

Table 15-2 compares the numerical values produced by the trinomial lattice with those produced by the binomial lattice for the selected time increments used by BL. The main reason that our results are more precise is that in our lattice the barrier is hit exactly, regardless of the time partition, while in BL the barrier may not be reached in an exact number of steps.

The results presented here are typical for barrier contracts. Similar results hold for knock-outs with rebates, such as capped call options, and other simple barrier contracts.

To establish the hedge parameters for these contracts, we follow Pelsser and Vorst [1994], who discuss numerical issues associated with computing the hedge parameters under the binomial lattice. They show that much more accurate values for delta and gamma can be obtained from a binomial lattice by extending it *backward* in time two steps, so that option values are obtained at t = 0 for stock prices above and below s(0).

TABLE 15-1   Convergence Rate for Down-and-Out Call Options

Number of Time Partitions (n)	Stretch Parameter (gl)	Trinomial European Call	Trinomial Down-and-Out	Binomial Down-and-Out
25	1.0813	11.6433	6.0069	8.8486
50	1.5292	11.6526	5.9942	7.2405
75	1.8729	11.6628	5.9899	6.3001
100	1.0813	11.6595	5.9977	7.5045
150	1.3243	11.6512	5.9976	6.5612
200	1.0195	11.6589	5.9986	7.2307
400	1.0813	11.6580	5.9977	6.6505
800	1.0195	11.6574	5.9974	6.6040
1,000	1.1398	11.6575	5.9972	6.1002
2,000	1.0746	11.6575	5.9970	6.1449
3,000	1.0768	11.6574	5.9969	6.0542
4,000	1.0521	11.6573	5.9969	6.0998
Accurate Value		11.6573	5.9968	5.9968

Case Parameters
$S_0 = 95$
Strike Price $= 100$
$\sigma = 25\%$ per year
$T = 1$ year
$r = 10\%$ per year
Barrier $= 90$

TABLE 15-2   Comparison of Revised Binomial and Trinomial Down-and-Out Option Prices

Number of Time Partitions	Revised Binomial*	Trinomial
85	6.020	5.9889
192	6.006	5.9967
342	5.998	5.9973
534	6.000	5.9973
Accurate Value	5.9968	5.9968

*The revised binomial prices are taken from Boyle and Lau [1994].

    For the trinomial lattice, however, it is not necessary to extend the lattice back in time for two time increments; rather, extending the lattice back just one period permits option prices to be obtained for stock prices above and below the initial price. Application of Equations (4) and (5) of Pelsser and Vorst then provides the delta and gamma values. The theta value is easily computed since a horizontal move is permitted in the lattice.

PRICING BARRIER OPTIONS WITH EXPONENTIAL BOUNDARIES

This algorithm is extremely efficient for pricing contracts subject to single-level barriers. Actually, if the barrier is an exponential function of time, then a minor modification to the algorithm is necessary to ensure that, at all time points, if the barrier can be reached, it is reached exactly.

Specifically, assume the barrier is given by $b(t) = b_0 e^{at}$. The trinomial moves are chosen:

$$\xi^a(t) = \begin{cases} \lambda_u \sigma \sqrt{\Delta t} & \text{with probability } p_u \\ (\lambda_u - \lambda_d)\sigma\sqrt{\Delta t}/2 & \text{with probability } p_m \\ -\lambda_d \sigma \sqrt{\Delta t} & \text{with probability } p_d \end{cases} \qquad (6)$$

Matching the first two moments (i.e., mean and volatility) of the risk-neutral returns distribution leads to the expressions for the probabilities

$$p_u = \frac{2 - \lambda_d(\lambda_u - \lambda_d) - a(\lambda_u - 3\lambda_d)}{(\lambda_u - \lambda_d)^2} \qquad (7A)$$

$$p_m = -\frac{4(\lambda_u \lambda_d + (\lambda_u - \lambda_d)a - 1)}{(\lambda_u + \lambda_d)^2} \qquad (7B)$$

$$p_d = \frac{2 + \lambda_u(\lambda_u - \lambda_d) - a(3\lambda_u - \lambda_d)}{(\lambda_u + \lambda_d)^2} \qquad (7C)$$

where $a = \mu\sqrt{\Delta t}/\sigma$.

The parameter λ_u is chosen so that after an integer number of successive moves the barrier is hit exactly. The parameter λ_d is selected so that the change $(\lambda_u - \lambda_d)\sigma\sqrt{\Delta t}/2$ exactly mirrors the change in the boundary value over the time increment, Δt. That is,

$$(\lambda_u - \lambda_d)\sigma\sqrt{\Delta t} = a\Delta t$$

or

$$\lambda_d = \lambda_u - \frac{a}{\sigma}\sqrt{\Delta t} \qquad (8)$$

Figure 15-1 shows the lattice near the boundary.

Barrier options with both constant and exponential barriers are encountered in the over-the-counter markets. There are also many contracts that have time-varying barriers. Unfortunately, if the knock-out boundary is neither constant nor exponential, a simple recombining trinomial lattice with state independent transition probabilities cannot easily be constructed that has the property that the barriers always fall on specific layers of the lattice. For such cases, the barrier may frequently fall between layers of the lattice, and the error in the resulting local transition probabilities may lead to large option pricing errors. Similarly, if there are multiple barriers, the lattice procedure may fail.

For example, consider a double knock-out option that provides a payout at the expiration date only if an upper boundary has not been reached and if a

FIGURE 15-1   Lattice Construction with an Exponential Barrier

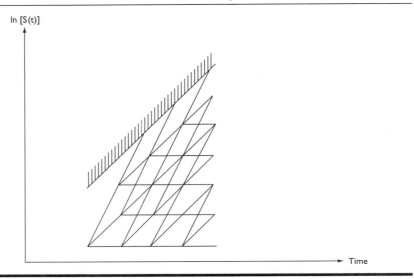

The trinomial increments are chosen so that the paths reconnect. Also, the middle jump is selected so that the change equals the change in the logarithm of the boundary.

lower threshold has not been attained. Such contracts are often referred to as trading range options. In general, our procedure cannot be applied to such problems because it cannot be guaranteed that a path-reconnecting lattice with constant transition probabilities can be constructed to hit both barriers exactly.

PRICING COMPLEX BARRIER OPTIONS

An alternative trinomial lattice for simple barriers readily generalizes to handling cases where the barrier is time-varying and where there are multiple barriers. Rather than requiring state-independent transition probabilities; this approach permits the probabilities of transitions to vary according to location in the lattice. The lattice will still reconnect, however.

To make matters specific, reconsider our down-and-out call option with a barrier imposed at b. For the moment, assume the stretch parameter, λ, is chosen exogenously. Figure 15-2 shows the lattice near the boundary.

From the point A, the usual next move is to point A^+, A, or A^-. The barrier is just below the point A^-. The stock price partition is $\lambda \sigma \sqrt{\Delta t}$, and for convenience we refer to the layer of nodes along the lattice at this level as layer A. At all layers above layer A, the transition probabilities are defined by Equation (2). For all nodes at layer A, we permit the usual up move to layer A^+ and the horizontal move, but we change the down move so that the barrier is hit exactly.

FIGURE 15-2   Lattice Construction with a Jump Adjustment Near the Barrier

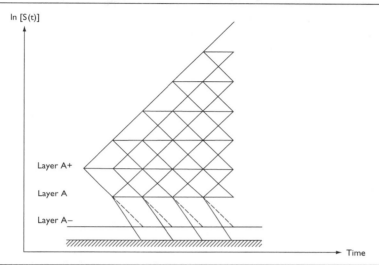

At all nodes in all layers other than layer A, the usual trinomial procedures is in effect. For nodes in layer A, the down jump is adjusted so as to hit the barrier exactly. The transition probabilities at those nodes are given by Equations (10A–10C).

To formalize the intuition provided in Figure 15-2, let $\gamma\lambda\sigma\sqrt{\Delta t}$ denote the change in the logarithmic return, given a down move at any node in layer A. Note that by construction $1 \leq \gamma < 2$. γ represents the "additional stretch" that is required to extend the down move so as to hit the barrier. Clearly, by extending the down move, the formulas for the probabilities of the three moves need to be changed so that locally the means and variances match their respective moments of the underlying process.[4]

Specifically, let $\xi^a(t|A)$ denote the approximating normal random variable at this node. We have

$$\xi^a(t|A) = \begin{cases} \lambda\sigma\sqrt{\Delta t} & \text{with probability } p_u^* \\ 0 & \text{with probability } p_m^* \\ -\gamma\lambda\sigma\sqrt{\Delta t} & \text{with probability } p_d^* \end{cases} \qquad (9)$$

where $1 \leq \gamma < 2$.

Matching up the drift and variance equations for these nodes leads to

$$p_u^* = \frac{b + a\gamma}{1 + \gamma} \qquad (10A)$$

$$p_m^* = 1 - p_d^* - p_u^* \qquad (10B)$$

$$p_d^* = \frac{b - a}{\gamma(1 + \gamma)} \qquad (10C)$$

where $a = \mu\sqrt{\Delta t}/\lambda\sigma$ and $b = 1/\lambda^2$.

At nodes at all other layers, the approximating random variable is given by Equation (2). Note that if the barrier is above the stock price (as in an up-and-out option), an adjustment needs to be made at the layer of nodes preceding the highest layer below the barrier. Denoting these nodes by B, the appropriate transitions and probabilities are:

$$\xi^a(t|B) = \begin{cases} \eta\lambda\sigma\sqrt{\Delta t} & \text{with probability } p_u^* \\ 0 & \text{with probability } p_m^* \\ \lambda\sigma\sqrt{\Delta t} & \text{with probability } p_d^* \end{cases} \tag{11}$$

where

$$p_u^* = \frac{b - a}{\eta(\eta - 1)} \tag{12A}$$

$$p_m^* = 1 - p_u^* - p_d^* \tag{12B}$$

$$p_d^* = \frac{a\eta - b}{\eta - 1} \tag{12C}$$

with a and b defined as earlier. Here η represents the "additional" stretch that permits the barrier to be attained with an up move from a node at layer B. Again, if the barrier is time-varying, the value of λ may vary from period to period.

In general, we always identify the node at which an additional stretch parameter is defined to be the second-lowest node above the barrier price, if the barrier is below the stock price, or the second-highest node below the barrier price, if the barrier is above the stock price. It can be shown that for any γ, $1 \leq \gamma < 2$, and η, $1 \leq \eta < 2$, with Δt suitably small, the values $p_u^* \geq 0$, $p_m^* \geq 0$, and $p_d^* \geq 0$. This condition implies that the lattice is stable, and in the limit converges to the desirable process.

To illustrate the procedure, consider our down-and-out option. The strike is 100, the barrier is at 90, the underlying volatility is 30%, and the current stock price is \$95. Assume the time partition is $\Delta t = 0.001$, and the stretch parameter is taken arbitrarily as $\lambda = 1.10$. Then the sequence of "unadjusted" down moves is $s_0 = 95$, $s_1 = 94.01$, $s_2 = 93.038$, $s_3 = 92.072$, $s_4 = 91.116$, $s_5 = 90.170$, and $s_6 = 89.234$ where $s_i = s_0 e^{-i\lambda\sigma\sqrt{\Delta t}}$. Layer A corresponds to the stock price $s_4 = 91.116$. At this node a "stretched down move" is defined so as to hit the barrier at 90. In particular, γ is defined so that:

$$s_4 e^{-\gamma\lambda\sigma\sqrt{\Delta t}} = 90$$

Solving for γ yields $\gamma = 1.18107$. The probabilities of moves from this stock price are then given by Equations (10A–10C)), while at all other price levels the transition probabilities are given by Equations (3A–3C).

Table 15-3 shows the convergence of prices using this procedure for the down-and-out option considered earlier. The value for λ is chosen so that the probability of a horizontal move at all layers except A is one-third ($\lambda = 1.2247$). The rate of convergence using this state-dependent algorithm is quite similar to the convergence rate using the previous (state-independent) trinomial lattice.

TABLE 15-3   Convergence of Down-and-Out Call Options*

Number of Time Patrons (n)	Down-and-Out Call Option Price (Trinomial)	Down-and-Out Call Option Price (Binomial)
50	5.9847	7.2405
75	5.9736	6.3001
100	5.9666	7.5045
150	5.9957	6.5612
200	5.9923	7.2307
400	5.9957	6.6505
800	5.9946	6.6040
1,000	5.9964	6.1002
2,000	5.9965	6.1449
3,000	5.9967	6.0542
4,000	5.9969	6.0998
Accurate Value	5.9968	5.9968

*The case parameters are shown in Table 15-1. The stretch parameter, $\lambda = 1.2247$, is chosen so that the probability of a horizontal jump is one in three.

For comparison purposes, the last column shows prices computed using a binomial lattice.

Table 15-4 shows the values of the same down-and-out option computed using 1,000 time partitions but for different λ values. Notice that regardless of the value of λ in the interval [1, 2] the option values are quite stable. Notice too that λ can equal one. In this case, throughout the lattice, binomial moves

TABLE 15-4   Down-and-Out Option Prices for Different Lattices*

Stretch Parameter (λ)	Down-and-Out Option Price
1	5.9965
1.1	5.9970
1.2	5.9962
1.3	5.9966
1.4	5.9948
1.5	5.9957
1.6	5.9961
1.7	5.9967
1.8	5.9929
1.9	5.9939
2.0	5.9946
Accurate Value	5.9968

*All results are based on 1,000 time partitions. The case parameters are shown in Table 15-1.

occur except near the boundary where a trinomial adjustment has to be made according to Equation (9).

This trinomial lattice with state-dependent transition probabilities has an advantage over the previous trinomial lattice, in that it can be used to price barrier options that have time-varying boundaries. In particular, along the "edges" of the lattice near the barrier the values of γ at successive nodes need not be the same.

PRICING OPTIONS WITH MULTIPLE BARRIERS

To illustrate the use of the state-dependent trinomial lattice, consider the problem of pricing and hedging a double knock-out option. Assume U and D are the upper and lower knock-out barriers of the call option with strike X. Clearly, D $\leq s_0 \leq$ U. First, the value of λ is chosen so that the upper boundary U coincides exactly with a layer of nodes. Then an adjustment to the lattice as described in Section IV is made at the layer of nodes that falls just above the lower boundary. The state probabilities are given by Equation (2) throughout the lattice except at the layer of nodes that precedes the lower boundary. At this location, the transition probabilities are given by Equations (10A–10C).

Table 15-5 shows the convergence rate for a double knock-out when an upper barrier of U $=$ 140 is placed on our previous down-and-out call. In this

TABLE 15-5   Convergence Rate for Double Knock-Out European Call Option

Number of Time Parameters (n)	Knock-Out Option
50	1.4181
75	1.4277
100	1.4414
150	1.4464
200	1.4502
400	1.4543
800	1.4564
1,000	1.4568
2,000	1.4576
3,000	1.4579
4,000	1.4580
5,000	1.4580

Case Parameters
$S_0 = 95$
Strike Price $= 100$
$s = 25\%$ per year
$T = 1$ year
$r = 10\%$ per year
Lower Knock-Out Boundary $= 90$
Upper Knock-Out Boundary $= 140$

example, prices converge using about 1,000 time partitions. Notice that, with multiple barriers, the computational effort for 1,000 time partitions is actually less than that required for a standard European option because nodes above and below the knock-out levels do not need to be searched.

Table 15-6 shows the sensitivity of the option price to a change in the upper knock-out level. As the knock-out level is raised, the value of the contract converges to that of the down-and-out option.

PRICING BARRIERS WHEN THE UNDERLYING IS VERY CLOSE TO THE BARRIER

When the option is very close to the barrier, there are some difficulties in using the lattice procedure. Indeed, ensuring the lattice is hit precisely may require a very small time step. As a result, the number of time partitions until expiration may be exorbitant.

Table 15-7 compares the true price of a European knock-out to that computed on a lattice when the stock price is close to the barrier. The table indicates the smallest number of time steps necessary to hit the barrier for the first time. Notice that even when one time step takes the price to the barrier, good approximations can be obtained. For prices very close to the barrier, however, 5,000 time partitions are not enough to obtain a price. In this case there is a very significant probability that the option will be knocked out, and for many specific contracts, approximating the price by an analytical model for European knock-outs may suffice. In general, pricing and hedging barrier options very close to the boundary remain problematical.

TABLE 15-6   Sensitivity of Double Knock-Outs to Change in Upper Barrier*

Upper Barrier	Knock-Out Price
110	0.0007
120	0.0906
130	0.5740
140	1.4568
160	3.4601
180	4.8433
200	5.5353
300	5.9949
400	5.9972
∞	5.9972

*The case parameters for the double knock-out are shown in Table 15-5. All calculations are based on 1,000 time partitions.

TABLE 15-7   Behavior of Barrier Option Prices Near the Boundary*

Stock Price	# of Time Steps						True Price
	500	1,000	2,000	3,000	4,000	5,000	
94.0	4.863	4.864	4.864	4.864	4.864	4.864	4.864
	(3)	(5)	(7)	(8)	(10)	(11)	
93.0	3.700	3.701	3.702	3.701	3.701	3.702	3.719
	(2)	(3)	(5)	(6)	(7)	(8)	
92.0	2.504	2.506	2.506	2.506	2.506	2.506	2.507
	(1)	(2)	(3)	(4)	(5)	(5)	
91.5	1.894	1.894	1.895	1.895	1.895	1.895	1.896
	(1)	(1)	(2)	(3)	(3)	(4)	
91.0	—	1.274	1.274	1.275	1.275	1.274	1.274
		(1)	(1)	(2)	(2)	(2)	
90.5	—	—	—	—	0.642	0.642	0.642
					(1)	(1)	
90.4	—	—	—	—	—	0.5148	0.5150
						(1)	
90.3	—	—	—	—	—	—	0.3869

*The last column gives the true price of the European contract computed using the analytical solution. Under each price, the minimum number of consecutive down moves that takes the price to the barrier is reported. Notice that even when one move takes the option to the barrier, reasonable estimates are obtained. If the stock price is very close to the barrier, then 5,000 partitions may not be sufficient to price the contract. In this example, if the price moves below $90.4, 5,000 partitions are not sufficient. Actually, a run with 5,000 partitions takes less than twenty seconds on a Pentium desktop computer.

EXTENSIONS TO HIGHER DIMENSIONS

The lattice procedures generalize naturally to higher dimensions. Kamrad and Ritchken [1991], for example, discuss lattice techniques with k state variables. For example, they establish a model in two dimensions, in which the price can at each time step move to five possible values. (Their model includes the four-step model of Boyle, Evnine, and Gibbs [1989] as a special case.)

The advantage of the five-step process is that it again permits the space increments for prices to be decoupled from the time increments. As a result, the stretch parameter can be chosen so as to ensure the barrier lines up with a layer (plane) of prices on the pyramid.

We provide details here of the use of this lattice procedure in pricing knock-outs that have payouts depending on two state variables. An example of such a contract is given by Heynen and Kat [1994]. They report that Bankers Trust has structured a call option on a basket of Belgian stocks that is knocked out if the Belgian franc (a second-state variable) appreciates by more than 3.5%. The authors call these contracts "outside" knock-outs to distinguish them from ordinary single-state variable knock-outs.

Since such contracts are quite common, they provide some analytical pricing models for some European contracts. When one values such contracts using lattice-based procedures, the problem of lining up the barrier along a plane of nodes again becomes important.

Toward the goal of developing an algorithm for handling this problem, let $\{S_1(t), S_2(t)\}$ define the asset pair at time t. Assume the joint density of the two underlying securities is bivariate lognormal. Let $\mu_i = r - \sigma_i^2/2$, and σ_i^2 be the instantaneous mean and variance for asset i (i = 1, 2), and let ρ be the correlation coefficient.[5] Without loss of generality, assume that the stock underlying the option is stock 1, and the knock-out is based on the level of stock 2. As before, for each asset we have over [t, t + Δt]

$$\ln S_i(t + \Delta t) = \ln S_i(t) + \zeta_i(t)$$

where $\zeta_i(t)$ is a normal random variable with mean $\mu_i \Delta t$ and variance $\sigma_i^2 \Delta t$. The instantaneous correlation between $\zeta_1(t)$ and $\zeta_2(t)$ is ρ. The joint normal random variable $\{\zeta_1(t), \zeta_2(t)\}$ will be approximated by a pair of multinomial discrete random variables having the distribution:

$\zeta_1^a(t)$	$\zeta_2^a(t)$	Probability
$\lambda\sigma_1\sqrt{\Delta t}$	$\lambda\sigma_2\sqrt{\Delta t}$	p_1
$\lambda\sigma_1\sqrt{\Delta t}$	$-\lambda\sigma_2\sqrt{\Delta t}$	p_2
$-\lambda\sigma_1\sqrt{\Delta t}$	$\lambda\sigma_2\sqrt{\Delta t}$	p_3
$-\lambda\sigma_1\sqrt{\Delta t}$	$\lambda\sigma_2\sqrt{\Delta t}$	p_4
0	0	p_5

where

$$p_1 = \frac{1}{4}\left\{\frac{1}{\lambda^2} + \frac{\sqrt{\Delta t}}{\lambda}\left(\frac{\mu_1}{\sigma_1} + \frac{\mu_2}{\sigma_2}\right) + \frac{\rho}{\lambda^2}\right\}$$

$$p_2 = \frac{1}{4}\left\{\frac{1}{\lambda^2} + \frac{\sqrt{\Delta t}}{\lambda}\left(\frac{\mu_1}{\sigma_1} - \frac{\mu_2}{\sigma_2}\right) - \frac{\rho}{\lambda^2}\right\}$$

$$p_3 = \frac{1}{4}\left\{\frac{1}{\lambda^2} + \frac{\sqrt{\Delta t}}{\lambda}\left(-\frac{\mu_1}{\sigma_1} - \frac{\mu_2}{\sigma_2}\right) + \frac{\rho}{\lambda^2}\right\}$$

$$p_4 = \frac{1}{4}\left\{\frac{1}{\lambda^2} + \frac{\sqrt{\Delta t}}{\lambda}\left(-\frac{\mu_1}{\sigma_1} + \frac{\mu_2}{\sigma_2}\right) - \frac{\rho}{\lambda^2}\right\}$$

$$p_5 = 1 - \frac{1}{\lambda^2}$$

and $\lambda \geq 1$.

Now, the stretch parameter λ can be chosen so that all the nodes on a particular layer in the S_2 dimension fall exactly on the barrier. In particular, if the barrier is b_{02}, then λ can be chosen according to the criteria developed in

Equations (4) and (5), using the state-independent Markov chain method, or by Equations (9) and (10A–10C), using the more general state-dependent Markov chain approximation.

CONCLUSION

We have addressed the problem of pricing barrier options using lattice procedures. If simple binomial models are used, large errors may result even when the time partition is quite small. These errors arise because near the barrier, the local means and variance approximations are imprecise. By making sure the layers of the lattice coincide with the barriers, this bias is reduced. We show how specific trinomial models can be used to price many types of barrier contracts.

Applications of these models are of obvious interest to traders of exotic options. The models should also be of interest to researchers who want to consider default risk in their positions.

Finally, application of these models to problems involving deposit insurance guarantees could be of interest. In particular, recent guidelines call for increased regulation as the level of a bank's assets deteriorates, or passes through different barriers. Applications of these barrier models should reveal the effects of alternative regulatory policies on the value of the deposit guarantee.

REFERENCES

Boyle, P. "A Lattice Framework for Option Pricing with Two State Variables." *Journal of Financial and Quantitative Analysis,* 35, 1 (1988), pp. 1–12.

Boyle, P., J. Evnine, and S. Gibbs. "Valuation of Options on Several Underlying Assets." *Review of Financial Studies,* 2 (1989), pp. 241–250.

Boyle, P., and S. H. Lau. "Bumping Up Against the Barrier with the Binomial Method." *Journal of Derivatives,* 1, 4 (1994), pp. 6–14.

de Jager, G. "Option Pricing with Implicit Finite Difference Methods and Large Scale Bounded Multinomials." School of Finance, Queensland University of Technology, Queensland, Australia, 1994.

Heynen, R., and H. Kat. "Crossing Barriers." *Risk Magazine,* 7, 6 (June 1994), pp. 192–195.

Hull, J., and A. White. "Valuing Derivative Securities Using the Explicit Finite Difference Method." *Journal of Financial and Quantitative Analysis,* 23, 3 (1990), pp. 237–252.

Kamrad, B., and P. Ritchken. "Multinomial Approximating Models for Options with k-State Variables." *Management Science,* 37, 12 (1991), pp. 1640–1652.

Madan, D., F. Milne, and H. Shefrin. "The Multinomial Option Pricing Model and its Limitations." *Review of Financial Studies,* 2 (1989), pp. 251–265.

Pelsser, A., and T. Vorst. "The Binomial Model and the Greeks." *Journal of Derivatives,* Spring 1994, pp. 45–49.

ENDNOTES

1. This decoupling property is not present in the binomial lattice. Indeed, for the binomial, once the time partition is determined, so is the space partition.

2. For a discussion of multinomial lattices, see Boyle [1988], Kamrad and Ritchken [1991], Hull and White [1990], and Madan, Milne, and Shefrin [1989]. For a comparison of these lattice procedures and implicit and explicit finite difference methods, see de Jager [1994].

3. Actually, de Jager [1994] demonstrates that a multinomial lattice procedure can be established that has identical spacing to any finite difference scheme's stock price step and time step, yet requires less computational effort.

4. For time-varying barriers, the value of γ varies from period to period.

5. If one of the underlyings is a foreign exchange rate, then $\mu_i = (r_d - r_f) - \sigma^2/2$, where r_d and r_f are the domestic and foreign rates, respectively.

16

Pricing and Hedging Double-Barrier Options: A Probabilistic Approach

HÉLYETTE GEMAN
MARC YOR

INTRODUCTION

Barrier options have become increasingly popular over the last few years. Less expensive than the equivalent standard options, they may be the appropriate hedge in a number of situations. For instance, a down-and-in put with a low barrier offers an inexpensive protection against a big downward move of the underlying asset; in the same manner, an up-and-out call on an index may enhance at a cheap cost an already existing long position in the index.

The pricing of "single barrier" options is not difficult in the standard Black and Scholes framework. An arbitrage approach leads to a fairly elementary mathematical problem and closed-form solutions have been available for some time. For instance, in his seminal paper of 1973, Merton presented a pricing formula for an option whose pay-off is restricted by a floor knock-out boundary; in 1979, Goldman, Sosin and Gatto offered closed-form solutions for all types of barrier options. The problem of double-barrier options which we address in this article is more difficult and, to our knowledge, no simple formula currently exists. Consequently, practitioners who trade these instruments rely heavily on the use of simulations to obtain option prices. Simulation is indeed an effective and

The authors are very grateful to Alexander Eydeland for his crucial help in inverting the main Laplace transform in the paper.

Reprinted with permission from *Mathematical Finance;* Vol. 6:4; Hélyette Geman and Marc Yor; 1996; Blackwell Publishing, Malden, MA.

simple tool that is readily applicable to the problem of valuing some of the most complex contracts. However, Fu, Madan and Wang (1995) show that for continuous time Asian options, and suspect that for other continuous time path-dependent options as well, naive simulations based on pricing strategies are expensive, inefficient and inaccurate. They even find that decreasing the standard error with more replications only serves to increase the confidence in the wrong valuation. Lastly, Geman and Eydeland (1995) show the remarkable superiority of an exact approach over Monte-Carlo simulations when delta hedging of Asian options is at stake.

Our goal is to adopt the same type of "exact" pricing methodology in the case of double-barrier options as the one we followed for Asian options. We use the standard risk-neutral valuation techniques and the Markov property as well as the Cameron-Martin theorem to obtain a simple expression of the Laplace transform of the option price. As is the case for the double-barrier options traded in the markets, we will only consider the situation of fixed boundaries.

PRICING DOUBLE-BARRIER OPTIONS

A double-knock option is characterized by two barriers L (lower barrier) and U (upper barrier); the option knocks out if either barrier is touched. Otherwise, the option gives at maturity T the standard Black and Scholes pay-off $\max(0, S(T) - k)$, where k, the strike price of the option, satisfies $L < k < U$.

The distribution of the range of Brownian motion was studied as early as 1941 by Bachelier while the trivariate joint distribution of $(I_t = \inf_{u \le t} W_u, L_t = \sup_{u \le t} W_u, W_t)$ has been known for some time (see e.g. Freedman (1971) or Revuz-Yor (1994, p. 106)) and is expressed as

$$P(a \le I_t \le L_t \le b; W_t \in dx) = (2\pi t)^{-1/2} \sum_{k=-\infty}^{\infty} \left\{ \exp\left(-\frac{1}{2t} (x + 2k(b - a))^2\right) - \exp\left(-\frac{1}{2t} ((x - 2b) + 2k(b - a))^2\right) \right\} dx$$

This result and variants of it are found in many places in the probabilistic literature (see e.g., Doob (1949), Feller (1970), Shorack-Wellner (1986), Teunen-Goovaerts (1994)). It is this path which is followed by Kunitomo and Ikeda (1992) who propose pricing formulas expressed as theta function type series for European options whose pay-off is restricted by general curve boundaries.

In our setting, the uncertainty in the economy is represented by a filtered probability space (Ω, f, f_t, P), where f_t is the information available at time t and P is the objective probability. From the seminal papers by Harrison-Kreps (1979) and Harrison-Pliska (1981) we know that the no-arbitrage assumption implies the existence of a probability measure Q equivalent to P such that the discounted prices of the basic securities are Q-martingales. Under the probability Q, the dynamics of the price S(t) of the underlying asset are driven by the stochastic differential equation

$$\frac{dS_t}{S_t} = y dt + \sigma d\tilde{W}_t, \tag{1}$$

where $(\tilde{W}(t))$ is a Q-Brownian motion, σ is constant, and the risk-neutral drift is assumed to be a general constant. So, we can incorporate the case where the underlying instrument is a dividend-paying stock, a currency or a commodity. Equation (1) immediately gives

$$S(t) = S(0) \exp\left\{\left(y - \frac{\sigma^2}{2}\right)t + \sigma\tilde{W}(t)\right\}.$$

The call price is equal to

$$C_{L,U}(t) = e^{-r(T-t)}E_Q[(S(T) - k)^+ 1_{\Sigma_{L,U}>T}/\mathfrak{f}_t] \tag{2}$$

where $\Sigma_{L,U}$ is the first exit time of the process $(S_t)_{t\geq 0}$ out of the interval $[L, U]$. We can write for all $u \geq t \geq 0$

$$S(u) = S(t)S_1(u - t),$$

where $S_1(s) = \exp\{(y - \sigma^2/2)s + \sigma\hat{W}(s)\}$ and $(\hat{W}(s) = \tilde{W}(t + s) - \tilde{W}(t)$, $s \geq 0)$ is a new Bronian motion under Q. Denoting by $\hat{\Sigma}_{\alpha,\beta}$ the first exit time of the process $(S_1(s))_{s\geq 0}$ out of the interval $[\alpha, \beta]$, we obtain the immediate equality

$$1_{\Sigma_{L,U}>T} = 1_{\Sigma_{L,U}>t}1_{\hat{\Sigma}_{L/S(t),U/S(t)}>T-t}.$$

Since the variable $1_{\Sigma_{L,U}>t}$ is $\mathfrak{f}_t$ measurable, we can simplify for all $t < T$

$$E_Q[(S(T) - k)^+ 1_{\Sigma_{L,U}>T}/\mathfrak{f}_t] = 1_{\Sigma_{L,U}>t}E_Q[(S(t)S_1(T - t) - k)^+ 1_{\hat{\Sigma}_{L/S(t),U/S(t)}>T-t}/\mathfrak{f}_t].$$

Consequently, if the double-barrier call has not been knocked out prior to time t, its price at time t is equal to

$$C_{L,U}(t) = e^{-r(T-t)}S(t)E_Q[(S_1(\tau) - h)^+ 1_{\hat{\Sigma}_{m,M}>\tau}], \tag{3}$$

where $\tau = T - t$, $h = k/S(t)$, $m = L/S(t)$ and $M = U/S(t)$.

We now observe that, rather than computing the expectation in (3) it is easier to compute the quantity

$$\varphi_{m,M}^{(h)}(\tau) = E_Q[(S_1(\tau) - h)^+ 1_{\hat{\Sigma}_{m,M}<\tau}].$$

This will give, by difference with the Black and Scholes formula and an appropriate adjustment, the double-knock call price as

$$C_{L,U}(t) = S(t)BS(0, 1, \sigma, h, \tau) - e^{-rt}S(t)\varphi_{m,M}^{(h)}(\tau), \tag{4}$$

where $BS(0, 1, \sigma, h, \tau)$ denotes the price at time 0 of a standard call with maturity τ and strike price h written on an underlying stock which has value 1 at time 0 and volatility σ.

The quantity $\varphi_{m,M}^{(h)}(\tau)$ has a fairly simple expression when τ is replaced by an exponential variable independent of S_1 (the reader interested in this question can find in Appendix 2 a general discussion of the issue: why is it easier to handle a functional of a Brownian motion W at an independent exponential time rather than at a fixed time?). This leads us to consider in this specific case the following Laplace transform with respect to time:

$$\psi(\lambda) = \int_0^{+\infty} e^{-\lambda \tau} \varphi_{m,M}^{(h)}(\tau) d\tau. \tag{5}$$

Making the change of variables $u = \tau \sigma^2$, the right-hand side of (5) becomes

$$\int_0^\infty \frac{du}{\sigma^2} e^{-\lambda u/\sigma^2} \varphi_{m,M}^{(h)}\left(\frac{u}{\sigma^2}\right),$$

where, denoting $\hat{v} = y - \sigma^2/2$ and $W(u) = \sigma \hat{W}(u/\sigma^2)$, we obtain

$$\varphi_{m,M}^{(h)}\left(\frac{u}{\sigma^2}\right) = E\left[\left(\exp\left(W(u) + \hat{v}\frac{u}{\sigma^2}\right) - h\right)^+ 1_{\hat{\Sigma}_{m,M}<u/\sigma^2}\right].$$

Recalling the definition of

$$\hat{\Sigma}_{m,M} = \inf\{s : \exp(\sigma \hat{W}(s) + \hat{v}s) = m \text{ or } M\},$$

we can write equivalently

$$\sigma^2 \hat{\Sigma}_{m,M} = \inf\left\{x : \exp\left(\sigma \hat{W}\left(\frac{x}{\sigma^2}\right) + \frac{\hat{v}x}{\sigma^2}\right) = m \text{ or } M\right\}$$

$$= \inf\left\{x : \exp\left(W(x) + \frac{\hat{v}x}{\sigma^2}\right) = m \text{ or } M\right\},$$

where $(W(x))$ was introduced earlier.

We define $v = \hat{v}/\sigma^2 = 1/\sigma^2(y - \sigma^2/2)$ and introduce

$$\Sigma_{m,M}^{(v)} = \sigma^2 \hat{\Sigma}_{m,M}$$

where $\Sigma_{m,M}^{(v)}$ represents the first time m or M is reached by the process $X_t^{(v)} \equiv \exp(W(t) + vt)$. Hence,

$$\varphi_{m,M}^{(h)}\left(\frac{u}{\sigma^2}\right) \overset{\text{def}}{=} \varphi(u) \equiv E[\{X_u^{(v)} - h\}^+ 1_{\Sigma_{m,M}^{(v)}<u}],$$

and

$$\psi(\lambda) = \int_0^\infty \frac{du}{\sigma^2} e^{-\lambda u/\sigma^2} \varphi(u) = \frac{1}{\sigma^2} \Phi\left(\frac{\lambda}{\sigma^2}\right), \tag{6.a}$$

where the function Φ is defined as the Laplace transform of φ, i.e.,

$$\Phi(\theta) = \int_0^\infty du \, e^{-\theta u} \varphi(u) = E\left[\int_{\Sigma_{m,M}^{(v)}}^\infty e^{-\theta u}(X_u^{(v)} - h)^+ du\right]. \tag{6.b}$$

From now on, we will focus on the computation of $\Phi(\theta)$. Let us denote for simplicity $f(x) = (x - h)^+$ and $\Sigma = \Sigma_{m,M}^{(v)}$ and introduce the positive numbers a and b such that $m = e^{-a}$, $M = e^b$. By using the strong Markov property, we simplify the expression of $\Phi(\theta)$

$$\Phi(\theta) = E\left[e^{-\theta_\Sigma}E_{X_\Sigma^{(v)}}\left(\int_0^\infty e^{-\theta u}f(X_u^{(v)})du\right)\right] = E[e^{-\theta_\Sigma}(V_\theta^{(v)}f)(X_\Sigma^{(v)})], \qquad (7)$$

where

$$V_\theta^{(v)}f(x) = E_x^v\left[\int_0^\infty e^{-\theta u}f(X_u)du\right]$$

and E_x^v is the expectation relative to P_x^v, where P_x^v is the law of the process $(X_u^{(v)}, u \geq 0)$ originating in x. To avoid confusion between Brownian and geometric Brownian motions, we use $\hat{E}_z$ for the expectation with respect to $\hat{P}_z$, the Wiener measure of Brownian motion starting at z.

Denoting $g = V_\theta^{(v)}f$, and using the Cameron-Martin absolute continuity relationship between $(W_t + vt, t \geq 0)$ and $(W_t, t \geq 0)$, we obtain

$$E[e^{-\theta_\Sigma}g(X_\Sigma)] = \hat{E}_0\left[e^{-(\theta+v^2/2)T_{-a}}g(e^{-a})e^{-va}1_{T_{-a}<T_b}\right] + \hat{E}_0\left[e^{-(\theta+v^2/2)T_b}g(e^b)e^{vb}1_{T_b<T_{-a}}\right]$$

Introducing $\mu^2/2 = \theta + v^2/2$, it is straightforward to show (see e.g., Itô-Mc Kean (1965) or Revuz-Yor (1994)) that

$$\hat{E}_0\left(\exp\left(-\frac{\mu^2}{2}T_{-a}\right); T_{-a} < T_b\right) = \frac{\text{sh } \mu b}{\text{sh}(\mu(a+b))}$$

and

$$\hat{E}_0\left(\exp\left(-\frac{\mu^2}{2}T_b\right); T_b < T_{-a}\right) = \frac{\text{sh } \mu a}{\text{sh}(\mu(a+b))}.$$

This is classically obtained by applying Doob's optional sampling theorem to exponential martingales of Brownian motion at T_{-a} and T_b. Then, using the strong Markov property (see Itô-Mc Kean for details), equation (6) becomes

$$\Phi(\theta) = \frac{\text{sh } \mu b}{\text{sh}(\mu(a+b))}g(e^{-a})e^{-va} + \frac{\text{sh } \mu a}{\text{sh}(\mu(a+b))}g(e^b)e^{vb}. \qquad (8)$$

We need now to make explicit

$$g(e^z) = V_\theta^v f(e^z) \overset{\text{def}}{=} \hat{E}_z\left(\int_0^\infty e^{-\theta u}f(e^{W_u+vu})du\right).$$

Using again the Cameron-Martin relationship, we obtain

$$g(e^z) = e^{-vz}\hat{E}_z\left(\int_0^\infty \varphi_v(W_u)e^{-\mu^2u/2}du\right),$$

where

$$\varphi_v(y) = e^{vy}f(e^y) \text{ and } f(x) = (x - h)^+. \qquad (9)$$

The resolvent of Brownian motion (see e.g., Revuz-Yor, p. 93) is given for a general function φ by

$$U_{\mu^2/2}\varphi(z) = \int_0^{+\infty} dt\, e^{-\mu^2/2t} Y_z(\varphi(W_t)) = \frac{1}{\mu} \int_{-\infty}^{+\infty} e^{-\mu|z-y|} \varphi(y) dy. \tag{10}$$

In the case of the specific function φ_v defined in (9), formula (10) gives

$$U_{\mu^2/2}\varphi_v(z) = \frac{1}{\mu} \int_{lnh}^{+\infty} dy(e^{-\mu|z-y|})[e^{(v+1)y} - he^{vy}].$$

For notational simplicity, we introduce

$$g_1(e^z) \equiv e^{vz} g(e^z) = U_{\mu^2/2}\varphi_v(z).$$

Relation (8) becomes

$$\Phi(\theta) = \frac{sh(\mu b)}{sh[\mu(a + b)]} g_1(e^{-a}) + \frac{sh(\mu a)}{sh[\mu(a + b)]} g_1(e^b), \tag{11.a}$$

where $g_1(e^{-a})$ and $g_1(e^b)$ are shown, in Appendix 1, to be respectively equal to

$$g_1(e^{-a}) = \frac{h^{v+1-\mu}e^{-\mu a}}{\mu(\mu - v)(\mu - v - 1)} \tag{11.b}$$

and

$$g_1(e^b) = 2\left\{ \frac{e^{b(v+1)}}{\mu^2 - (v+1)^2} - \frac{he^{bv}}{\mu^2 - v^2} \right\} + \frac{e^{-\mu b}h^{v+1+\mu}}{\mu(\mu + v)(\mu + v + 1)}. \tag{11.c}$$

We recall that Φ depends on θ through $\mu = \sqrt{2\theta + v^2}$ and that $\psi(\lambda)$, the quantity of interest, is related to Φ by the formula

$$\psi(\lambda) = \frac{1}{\sigma^2} \Phi\left(\frac{\lambda}{\sigma^2}\right) \tag{6.a}$$

Using this formula and denoting $\mathcal{L}^{-1}$ for the inverse of the Laplace transform operator, it is immediate to see that

$$\{\mathcal{L}^{-1}\psi\}(\tau) = \{\mathcal{L}^{-1}\Phi\}(\sigma^2\tau)$$

a result which may be substituted into equation (4) to give the price at time t of the double-barrier call, namely

$$C_{L,U}(t) = S(t)\{BS(0, 1, \sigma, \tau, h) - e^{-r\tau}\{\mathcal{L}^{-1}\psi\}(\tau)\}, \tag{12}$$

where $BS(0, 1, \sigma, \tau, h)$ is the Black and Scholes price of a standard call with maturity $\tau = T - t$, strike price $h = k/S(t)$, assumed to be written on an underlying asset S such that $S(0) = 1$.

NUMERICAL APPLICATIONS

We use formula (11) and the methodology developed in Geman-Eydeland (1995) in order to compute the price of a double-barrier option in three different settings; in all cases, we compare our results with the prices obtained through Monte-Carlo simulations and with the prices given in Kunitomo and Ikeda

(1992) (See Table 16-1). In the three tests, we use the values $S(0) = 2$, $T = 1$ year. The standard deviation is computed on a sample of 200 evaluations, each evaluation being performed on 5000 Monte-Carlo paths.

It is remarkable that in all cases, the price obtained through our method is extremely close to the Kunitomo-Ikeda price. Moreover, in order for these two prices to lie within one standard deviation of the Monte-Carlo price, the Monte-Carlo simulations must be run using very small step sizes and many paths to make sure one barrier is not "hit but missed." The consequence is that the inversion of the Laplace transform requires an order of magnitude less operations than the Monte-Carlo simulations (e.g., it takes a fraction of a second to do it on a Sun Sparc 20 station). As a comparison, in the case of Asian options, Geman-Eydeland (1995) obtain a standard deviation as low as 0.001 for a sample of 50 evaluations, each of them being performed on 500 Monte-Carlo paths (and it is in the context of delta hedging that the inversion of the Laplace transform of the Asian option obtained in Geman-Yor (1993) proves definitely superior, both theoretically and computationally). Using Monte-Carlo methods, one faces a drastic change between the smoothing effect of the averaging feature of Asian options and the danger of hitting a barrier without knowing it in the case of double-knock options. It is not clear that all users of double-barrier options are fully aware of this problem.

A final manner to illustrate this point is to show that, as expected, the sensitivity of the option price to the step size in Monte-Carlo simulations becomes extremely high when the time remaining to maturity is short and the strike price close to one of the barriers.

We come back to the first column of the previous table with the same parameters except that $\tau = T - t = 1$ month and $S_0 = 2.4$. For a step size equal to $1/365$ year, Monte-Carlo gives an option value equal to 0.1930 with a standard deviation $= 0.073$; for a step size $1/4 \times 365$ year, the Monte-Carlo value becomes 0.1739 and the standard deviation 0.008. Hence, a one-day step gives a wrong result (the barrier may have been hit and "missed", and the option is overpriced).

Using the Geman-Yor approach, we obtain:

TABLE 16-1

	$\sigma = 0.2$ $r = 0.02$ $k = 2, L = 1.5, U = 2.5$	$\sigma = 0.5$ $r = 0.5$ $k = 2, L = 1.5, U = 3$	$\sigma = 0.5$ $r = 0.5$ $k = 1.75, L = 1, U = 3$
BS(0, 1, σ, τ, h)	0.892	0.2179	0.27646
$e^{-r\tau}(\mathcal{L}^{-1}\psi)(T)$	0.0687	0.2090	0.23838
G-Y price	0.0411	0.0178	0.07615
K-I price	0.041089	0.017856	0.076172
Monte-Carlo price (st. dev $= 0.003$)	0.0425	0.0191	0.0772

$\text{BS}(0, 1, \sigma, \tau, h) = 0.1681; \ e^{-r\tau}(L^{-1}\psi)(\tau) = 0.23015$

$\text{G.Y price} = 2.4 \times 0.1681 - 0.23015 = 0.17321$

HEDGING DOUBLE-BARRIER OPTIONS

Among the sensitivities of the option price to the different variables, the sensitivity to the underlying asset price is the first subject of concern for practitioners.

In order to compute the delta of the double-barrier option, we differentiate with respect to S(t) the expression of $C_{L,U}(t)$ established in formula (12) and obtain

$$\Delta = \frac{\partial C_{L,U}(t)}{\partial S(t)} = [\text{BS}(0, 1, \sigma, \tau, h) - e^{-r\tau}\{L^{-1}\psi\}(\tau)] - S(t)e^{-r\tau}\frac{\partial}{\partial S(t)}\{L^{-1}\psi\}(\tau) \qquad (13)$$

The quantity between brackets equals the call price divided by S(t). We now need to find the derivative with respect to S(t) of $\{\mathcal{L}^{-1}\psi\}(\tau)$.

To clearly exhibit the dependence in S(t) of the function ψ, we write $S(t) = x$; $\psi_x(\lambda) = 1/\sigma^2\Phi_x(\lambda/\sigma^2)$ and we express formula (11) in terms of x. Remembering that $m = e^{-a}$ and $M = e^b$, we obtain

$$\Phi_x(\theta) = \frac{M^\mu - M^{-\mu}}{e^{\mu(a+b)} - e^{-\mu(a+b)}} g_1(m) + \frac{m^{-\mu} - m^\mu}{e^{\mu(a+b)} - e^{-\mu(a+b)}} g_1(M)$$

$$= \frac{m^\mu(M^{2\mu} - 1)}{M^{2\mu} - m^{2\mu}} g_1(m) + \frac{M^\mu(1 - m^{2\mu})}{M^{2\mu} - m^{2\mu}} g_1(M),$$

where

$$g_1(m) = \frac{m^\mu h^{v+1-\mu}}{\mu(\mu - v)(\mu - v - 1)}$$

and

$$g_1(M) = 2\left\{\frac{M^{v+1}}{\mu^2 - (v+1)^2} - \frac{hM^v}{\mu^2 - v^2}\right\} + \left(\frac{h}{M}\right)^\mu \frac{h^{v+1}}{\mu(\mu + v)(\mu + v + 1)}.$$

Lastly, we need to write that $h = k/x$, $m = L/x$, $M = U/x$, which gives

$$\Phi_x(\theta) = \frac{U^{2\mu} - x^{2\mu}}{U^{2\mu} - L^{2\mu}}\left(\frac{L}{x}\right)^\mu\left(\frac{k}{x}\right)^{v+1}\left(\frac{L}{k}\right)^\mu \frac{1}{\mu(\mu - v)(\mu - v - 1)} + \frac{x^{2\mu} - L^{2\mu}}{U^{2\mu} - L^{2\mu}}\left(\frac{U}{x}\right)^\mu \frac{1}{x^{v+1}}$$

$$\times \left[2\left\{\frac{U^{v+1}}{\mu^2 - (v+1)^2} - \frac{kU^v}{\mu^2 - v^2}\right\} + \left(\frac{k}{U}\right)^\mu \frac{k^{v+1}}{\mu(\mu + v)(\mu + v + 1)}\right].$$

We can finally write

$$\Phi_x(\theta) = \frac{U^{2\mu} - x^{2\mu}}{x^{\mu+v+1}} \alpha(L, U, k) + \frac{x^{2\mu} - L^{2\mu}}{x^{\mu+v+1}} \beta(L, U, k),$$

where

$$\alpha(L, U, k) = \frac{L^{2\mu}k^{v+1-\mu}}{U^{2\mu} - L^{2\mu}} \frac{1}{\mu(\mu - v)(\mu - v - 1)},$$

$$\beta(L, U, k) = \frac{1}{U^{2\mu} - L^{2\mu}} \left[2\left\{ \frac{U^{\mu+v+1}}{\mu^2 - (v+1)^2} - \frac{kU^{\mu+v}}{\mu^2 - v^2} \right\} + \frac{k^{\mu+v+1}}{\mu(\mu + v)(\mu + v + 1)} \right],$$

$$\psi_x(\lambda) = \frac{1}{\sigma^2} \Phi_x\left(\frac{\lambda}{\sigma^2}\right),$$

$$\frac{\partial}{\partial x} \{\mathcal{L}^{-1}\psi_x\}(\tau) = \left\{ \mathcal{L}^{-1} \frac{\partial \psi_x}{\partial x} \right\}(\tau) = \left\{ \mathcal{L}^{-1} \frac{\partial \Phi_x}{\partial x} \right\}(\sigma^2\tau).$$

We are consequently led to a problem of Laplace inversion nearly identical to the one encountered for the call price and involving $\partial\Phi_x/\partial x$ instead of Φ_x, where

$$\frac{\partial \Phi_x}{\partial x}(\theta) = \left[-(\mu - v - 1)x^{\mu-v-2} - \frac{(\mu + v + 1)U^{2\mu}}{x^{\mu+v+2}} \right]\alpha(L, U, k)$$

$$+ \left[(\mu - v - 1)x^{\mu-v-2} + \frac{(\mu + v + 1)L^{2\mu}}{x^{\mu+v+2}} \right]\beta(L, U, k).$$

CONCLUSION

From these results, we can easily derive the prices of double knock in options, i.e., options which pay like a vanilla call if the underlying spot price touches a lower or higher barrier prior to expiration but pay nothing (or a fixed rebate) if neither barrier is hit prior to expiration. In the same manner, double-barrier digital options, which pay a fixed amount if some reference asset price has remained within a band over the lifetime of the option, may be obtained as a special case of the valuation problem addressed in this paper. As in Geman-Yor (1993), this approach is satisfactory from a theoretical standpoint since the methodology is the same for the call price and for its delta. For practical purposes, the computational time of the two quantities is equally low and hedging—the ultimate concern of practitioners—is achieved with the same accuracy as pricing, which is rarely the case for path-dependent options. Moreover, the danger inherent in Monte-Carlo methods applied to barrier and double-barrier options disappears in this approach.

APPENDIX I

Computation of $U_{\mu^2/2}\varphi(z)$

We recall that $\mu = \sqrt{2\theta + v^2}$, hence $\mu > v$. We are looking for a simple expression of $U_{\mu^2/2}\varphi(z)$. We know that

$$U_{\mu^2/2}\varphi(z) = \frac{1}{\mu}\int_{lnh}^{\infty} e^{-\mu|z-y|}[e^{(v+1)y} - he^{vy}]dy \overset{def}{=} H_{\mu}^{z}(lnh, v + 1) - hH_{\mu}^{z}(lnh, v),$$

where

$$H_{\mu}^{z}(lnh, m) = \frac{1}{\mu}\int_{lnh}^{\infty} e^{\mu|z-y|}e^{my}dy$$

In the case of $g_1(e^{-a}) \equiv U_{\mu^2/2}\varphi(-a)$, the integrals

$$K_{\mu}^{z}(lnh, m) \equiv \int_{lnh}^{+\infty} e^{-\mu|z-y|+my}dy \quad (m = v \text{ or } v + 1)$$

do not need to be split since $z = -a$ is smaller than lnh and one easily obtains

$$g_1(e^{-a}) = \frac{e^{-\mu(a+lnh)}e^{(v+1)lnh}}{\mu(\mu - v - 1)} - h\frac{e^{-\mu(a+lnh)}e^{vlnh}}{\mu(\mu - v)} = \frac{h^{v+1-\mu}e^{-\mu a}}{\mu(\mu - v)(\mu - v - 1)}.$$

For the computation of $g_1(e^{b}) = U_{\mu^2/2}\varphi(b)$, both integrals $\int_{lnh}^{+\infty} e^{-\mu|z-y|+my}dy$ ($m = v$ and $v + 1$) have to be split since $z = b$ is bigger than lnh; this leads to the following expression:

$$g_1(e^{b}) = \frac{1}{\mu}\left[\frac{e^{b(v+1)}}{\mu + v + 1} + \frac{e^{b(v+1)}}{\mu - v - 1} - \frac{e^{\mu(lnh-b)+(v+1)lnh}}{\mu + v + 1}\right]$$
$$- \frac{h}{\mu}\left[\frac{e^{bv}}{\mu + v} + \frac{e^{bv}}{\mu - v} - \frac{e^{\mu(lnh-b)+vlnh}}{\mu + v}\right]$$
$$= \frac{1}{\mu}\left\{e^{b(v+1)}\frac{2\mu}{\mu^2 - (v + 1)^2} - e^{\mu(lnh-b)+vlnh}\frac{h}{\mu + v + 1}\right\}$$
$$- \frac{h}{\mu}\left\{e^{vb}\frac{2\mu}{\mu^2 - v^2} - \frac{e^{\mu(lnh-b)+vlnh}}{\mu + v}\right\}$$
$$= 2\left\{\frac{e^{b(v+1)}}{\mu^2 - (v + 1)^2} - \frac{he^{bv}}{\mu^2 - v^2}\right\} + \frac{e^{-\mu b}h^{\mu+v+1}}{\mu(v + 1)(\mu + v + 1)}.$$

APPENDIX 2

Why are the laws of functionals of $X_t = \sigma W_t + vt$ (Brownian motion with constant volatility $\sigma > 0$ and drift v) such as $M_t = \sup_{u \leq t}X_u$ or $I_t = -\inf_{u \leq t}X_u$ simpler when the fixed time t is replaced by an exponential time τ independent of W? A first explanation stems from the lack of memory of the exponential variable; but a deeper answer may be given in terms of excursion theory, which implies for instance that $M_\tau - X_\tau$ and M_τ are independent. This property is also well-known to be a consequence of the Wiener-Hopf factorization, which is referred to by Rogers and Satchell (1991) when looking at high, low and closing stock prices. However, Rogers and Satchell observed in their paper that cross-moments such as $E[M_\tau I_\tau(M_\tau + I_\tau)(X_\tau + I_\tau)]$ are hard to compute in the case of a nonzero drift v. We show below that the distribution of the triple (X_τ, M_τ, I_τ)—a quantity of great interest throughout our paper—has a fairly simple expression;

its use may in particular allow to compute, at the cost of a multiple integral, the above-mentioned expectation.

Let us denote τ_θ an exponential time independent of X, with parameter $\theta^2/2$. Then, we have the formula

$$P(M_{\tau_\theta} \leq a, I_{\tau_\theta} \leq b, X_{\tau_\theta} \in dz) = \left(\frac{\theta^2}{\mu\sigma}\right)\varphi\left(\frac{a\mu}{\sigma}, \frac{b\mu}{\sigma}, \frac{z\mu}{\sigma}\right)\exp\left(\frac{vz}{\sigma^2}\right)dz$$

where $\mu = \sqrt{\theta^2 + (v^2/\sigma^2)}$ and

$$\varphi(a, b, x) = \frac{\sinh(|x|)}{\coth a + \coth b}\begin{cases}\coth x - \coth a, & \text{if } 0 < x < a \\ \coth|x| - \coth b, & \text{if } -b < x < 0\end{cases}$$

Proof.

1. The formula in the "reduced case" $\theta = 1$, $\sigma = 1$, $v = 0$ is found in Pitman-Yor (1992) and has been obtained using excursion theory.
2. We now show how to obtain the general formula, using essentially the Cameron-Martin relation between Brownian motions with zero and nonzero drift, and the scaling property of Brownian motion.
   (2i) We first show the formula in the case $\sigma = 1$.

We denote $W_t^{(v)} = W_t + vt$, $M_t^{(v)} = \sup\limits_{s \leq t} W_s^{(v)}$, $I_t^{(v)} = -\inf\limits_{s \leq t} W_s^{(v)}$

We have, for any measurable f: $R^+ \times R^+ \times R \to R$

$$\lambda_f \equiv E[f(M_{\tau_\theta}^{(v)}, I_{\tau_\theta}^{(v)}, W_{\tau_\theta}^{(v)})] = E\left[f(M_{\tau_\theta}, I_{\tau_\theta}, W_{\tau_\theta})\exp\left\{vW_{\tau_\theta} - \frac{v^2}{2}\tau_\theta\right\}\right]$$

$$= \frac{\theta^2}{2}\int_0^\infty dt \exp\left\{-\left(\frac{v^2 + \theta^2}{2}\right)t\right\}E[f(M_t, I_t, W_t)\exp(vW_t)]$$

$$= \frac{\theta^2}{\mu^2}E[f(M_{\tau_\mu}, I_{\tau_\mu}, W_{\tau_\mu})\exp(vW_{\tau_\mu})]$$

Thanks to the scaling with respect to τ_μ, i.e., $\tau_\mu \overset{\text{law}}{=} 1/\mu^2\tau_1$, we obtain

$$\gamma_f = \frac{\theta^2}{\mu^2}E\left[f\left(\frac{1}{\mu}M_{\tau_1}, \frac{1}{\mu}I_{\tau_1}, \frac{1}{\mu}W_{\tau_1}\right)\exp\left(\frac{v}{\mu}W_{\tau_1}\right)\right]. \tag{1}$$

We now use the Pitman-Yor result in the "reduced case" and (1) in order to derive

$$E[M_{\tau_\theta}^{(v)} \leq a, I_{\tau_\theta}^{(v)} \leq b; f(W_{\tau_\theta}^{(v)})] = \frac{\theta^2}{\mu^2}P\left(M_{\tau_1} \leq a\mu, I_{\tau_1} \leq b\mu; f\left(\frac{1}{\mu}W_{\tau_1}\right)\exp\left(\frac{v}{\mu}W_{\tau_1}\right)\right)$$

$$= \frac{\theta^2}{\mu^2}\int dx\varphi(a\mu, b\mu, x)f\left(\frac{x}{\mu}\right)\exp\left(\frac{v}{\mu}x\right)$$

$$= \frac{\theta^2}{\mu}\int dy\varphi(a\mu, b\mu, \mu y)f(y)\exp(vy) \tag{2}$$

which gives the result in the case $\sigma = 1$.

(2ii) To get the general formula, we write

$$\sigma W_t + vt \equiv \sigma\left(W_t + \frac{v}{\sigma} t\right)$$

We denote $M_{(1)}$, $I_{(1)}$, $W_{(1)}$ the random quantities in (1) where v is replaced by v/σ

$$E[\sigma M_{(1)} \le a; \sigma I_{(1)} \le b; f(\sigma W_{(1)})] = E\left[M_{(1)} \le \frac{a}{\sigma}; I_{(1)} \le \frac{b}{\sigma}; f(\sigma W_{(1)})\right]$$

$$= \int dy\psi\left(\frac{a}{\sigma}, \frac{b}{\sigma}, y\right)f(\sigma y) = \int \frac{dz}{\sigma} \psi\left(\frac{a}{\sigma}, \frac{b}{\sigma}, \frac{z}{\sigma}\right)f(z)$$

where ψ refers to the density function obtained in (2) but with v replaced by v/σ.

Hence our final quantity is

$$\frac{1}{\sigma} \psi\left(\frac{a}{\sigma}, \frac{b}{\sigma}, \frac{z}{\sigma}\right) \equiv \left(\frac{\theta^2}{\mu\sigma}\right)\varphi\left(\frac{a\mu}{\sigma}, \frac{b\mu}{\sigma}, \frac{z\mu}{\sigma}\right) \exp\left(\frac{vz}{\sigma^2}\right)$$

REFERENCES

Bachelier, L. (1941) "Probabilités des Oscillations Maxima," *Note aux Comptes Rendus des Séances de l'Académie des Sciences.*

Black, F. and M. Scholes (1973) "The Pricing of Options and Corporate Liabilities," *Journal of Political Economy,* 81, 637–654.

Chesney, M., Jeanblanc M. and M. Yor (1997) "Brownian Excursions and Parisian Barrier Options," 29, 165–184.

Doob, J. L. (1949) "Heuristic Approach to the Kolmogorov-Smirnov Theorems" *Annals of Mathematics Statistics* 20, 393–403.

Feller, W. (1970) "Introduction to Probability Theory and its Applications," Vol 2, 2nd edition, Wiley

Freedman, D. (1971) "Brownian Motion and Diffusion," Holden-Day.

Fu, M., D. Madan and T. Wang (1995) "Pricing Continuous Time Asian Options: A Comparison of Analytical and Monte Carlo Methods," Preprint, University of Maryland.

Geman, H. and A. Eydeland (1995) "Domino Effect: Inverting the Laplace Transform," RISK, April.

Geman, H. and M. Yor (1992) "Quelques relations entre processus de Bessel, Options Asiatiques et Fonctions Confluentes Hypergéométriques," *Notes aux Comptes Rendus de l'Academie des Sciences,* Sér. I., 471–474.

Geman, H. and M. Yor (1993) "Bessel Processes, Asian Options and Perpetuities," *Mathematical Finance,* 3, N°4, 349–375.

Goldman, M., H. Sosin and M. Gatto (1979) "Path Dependent Options: Buy at the Low, Sell at the High," *Journal of Finance,* 34, 111–127.

Harrison, J. M. and D. Kreps (1979) "Martingales and Arbitrage in Multiperiod Securities Markets," *Journal of Economic Theory* 20, 381–408.

Harrison, J. M. and S. R. Pliska (1981) "Martingales and Stochastic Integrals in the Theory of Continuous Trading," *Stoch. Proc. Appl.,* 11, 215–260.

Kunitomo, N. and M. Ikeda (1992) "Pricing Options with Curved Boundaries," *Mathematical Finance,* Vol. 2, N°4, 275-2.

Itô, K. and H. P. Mc Kean (1965) "Diffusion Processes and Their Sample Paths," Springer.

Merton, R. C. (1973) "Theory of Rational Option Pricing," *Bell. J. Econ. Manag. Sci.,* Vol 4, p. 141-183.

Pitman, J. and M. Yor (1992) "The laws of Homogeneous Functionals of Brownian Motion and Related Processes," Preprint, University of Berkeley.

Revuz, D. and M. Yor (1994) "Continuous Martingales and Brownian Motion," 2nd edition, Springer.

Rogers, L. C. G. and S. E. Satchell (1991) "Estimating Variance from High, Low and Closing Prices," *Annals of Applied Probability,* Vol 1., N°4, 504-512.

Shorack, G. R. and J. A. Wellner (1986) "Empirical Processes with Applications to Statistics," Wiley.

Teunen, M. and Goovaerts, M. (1994) "Double Boundary Crossing Result for the Brownian Motion," *Scand. Act. J.,* Vol 2.

17

One-Touch Double Barrier Binary Option Values

CHO H. HUI

INTRODUCTION

One-touch double barrier options are path-dependent options in which the existence and payment of the options depend on the movement of the underlying price through their option life. We discuss two types of one-touch double barrier binary options here: (1) up-and-done out binary option, and (2) American binary knock-out option. For the first type, the option vanishes if the underlying price hits the upper barrier or the lower barrier once in the option life. Otherwise, the option buyer receives a fixed payment at maturity. This option combines the characteristics of a European binary option and knock-out barrier options together. For the second type, the option vanishes if the underlying price hits a knock-out barrier, while it gives a fixed payment if another payment barrier is touched. This option can be considered as an American binary option with a knock-out barrier.

Single-barrier European option and binary option formulae are published by Rubinstein and Reiner (1991a, 1991b). Since the one-touch double barrier options are not combinations of these options, in the following section we develop their valuation formulae in a Black-Scholes environment. In the third section we shall study the relationships among the one-touch double barrier (knock-out and knock-in) binary options and their applications in financial market.

The author gratefully acknowledges useful discussions with William Kwok, Gladys Lang, Alan Mak, and Wilfred Ng.

Reprinted with permission from Routledge Ltd; *One-Touch Double Barrier Binary Option Values;* Cho H. Hui; *Applied Financial Economics;* No. 6; 1996.

OPTION VALUATION

Our objective is to value the option in a Black-Scholes environment (Black and Scholes, 1973). The underlying is assumed to follow a lognormal random walk, and the interest rate and dividend are taken to be continuous and constant over the option life. The valuation method is a risk-neutral valuation approach. Therefore, we start the deviation from the Black-Scholes equation

$$\frac{\partial f}{\partial t} + \frac{1}{2}\sigma^2 S^2 \frac{\partial^2 f}{\partial S^2} + (r - d)S \frac{\partial f}{\partial S} - rf = 0 \tag{1}$$

where f is the option value, S is the underlying price, t is the time, σ is the volatility, r is the risk-free interest rate and d is the dividend if the underlying price is a stock price. For a foreign exchange option, r is the interest rate of the term currency and d is the interest rate of the commodity currency.

Up-and-Down Out Binary Option

If S ever reaches the barriers, H_1 and H_2, then the option is worthless; thus on the lines H_1 and H_2 the option value is zero. The boundary conditions for $t < T$ (time to maturity) of an up-and-down out binary option with $H_2 > H_1$ are

$$f(H_1, t) = 0 \quad f(H_2, t) = 0 \tag{2}$$

We let the final payment of the option be R if S never hits the barriers. Therefore, the final condition of Equation 1 is

$$f(S, T) = R \quad H_1 < S < H_2 \tag{3}$$

In order to make Equation 1 dimensionless (Wilmott *et al.*, 1993), we put

$$S = H_1 e^x \quad t = T - \frac{2\tau}{\sigma^2} \quad f = H_1 e^{\alpha x + \beta \tau} u(x, \tau)$$

$$k_1 = \frac{2(r - d)}{\sigma^2} \tag{4}$$

where

$$\alpha = -\frac{1}{2}(k_1 - 1) \quad \beta = -\frac{1}{4}(k_1 - 1)^2 - \frac{2r}{\sigma^2} \tag{5}$$

Then the Black-Scholes equation is transformed into a standard diffusion equation (heat equation)

$$\frac{\partial u}{\partial \tau} = \frac{\partial^2 u}{\partial x^2} \quad 0 < x < \ln \frac{H_2}{H_1} \tag{6}$$

in which the boundary conditions are

$$u(0, \tau) = 0 \quad u\left(\ln \frac{H_2}{H_1}, \tau\right) = 0 \tag{7}$$

for $\tau > 0$ and the initial condition is

$$u(x, 0) = \frac{Re^{-\alpha x}}{H_1} \quad 0 < x < \ln \frac{H_2}{H_1} \tag{8}$$

This is a diffusion equation with homogeneous boundary conditions. We use the method of separation of variables to solve Equation 6. Therefore, $u(x, \tau)$ can be expressed as a series of eigenfunctions:

$$u(x, \tau) = \sum_{n=1}^{\infty} b_n(\tau) \sin\left(\frac{n\pi x}{L}\right) \tag{9}$$

where $b_n(\tau) = b_n e^{-(n\pi/L)^2 \tau}$ and $L = \ln(H_2/H_1)$.

Since the function of the initial condition and its first derivative are piecewise continuous, it is represented by its Fourier sine series, where

$$b_n = \frac{2R}{H_1 L} \int_0^L e^{-\alpha x} \sin\left(\frac{n\pi x}{L}\right) dx = \frac{2\pi n R}{H_1 L^2} \left[\frac{1 - (-1)^n L^{-\alpha}}{\alpha^2 + \left(\frac{n\pi}{L}\right)^2} \right] \tag{10}$$

Hence by combining the above results in Equations 9 and 10 and substituting back the changing variables and transformations into option value $f(S, t)$ as a function of S, H_1, H_2 and t, we obtain the option value as

$$f(S, t) = \sum_{n=1}^{\infty} \frac{2\pi n R}{L^2} \left[\frac{\left(\frac{S}{H_1}\right)^\alpha - (-1)^n \left(\frac{S}{H_2}\right)^\alpha}{\alpha^2 + \left(\frac{n\pi}{L}\right)^2} \right] \sin\left(\frac{n\pi}{L} \ln \frac{S}{H_1}\right) e^{-1/2[(n\pi/L)^2 - \beta]\sigma^2(T-t)} \tag{11}$$

The option value is the probability of the underlying price staying within the barriers in the option life with the discounting effect due to r and d.

The solution given by Equation 11 is exact. In order to judge whether a satisfactory approximation to the solution can be obtained by using only a few terms of the series, we must estimate its speed of convergence. The sine factors are all bounded as $n \to \infty$; therefore this series behaves similarly to the series

$$\sum_{n=1}^{\infty} n^{-1} e^{-n^2(T-t)}$$

We estimate the convergence of the series as

$$\sum_{n=1}^{\infty} n^{-1} e^{-n^2(T-t)} = \sum_{n=1}^{\infty} \frac{1}{n} \left[\frac{1}{1 + n^2(T-t) + \frac{n^4(T-t)^2}{2} + \ldots} \right] \leq \sum_{n=1}^{\infty} \frac{1}{n} \left(\frac{1}{n^2(T-t)} \right)$$

The factor $e^{-1/2(n\pi/L)^2 \sigma^2(T-t)}$ with $(T - t) > 0$ makes the series converge similarly to the series on the right-hand side of the inequality. The only concern is a large α making the factors $(S/H_1)^\alpha$ and $(S/H_2)^\alpha$ so huge that it is difficult to calculate the numerical solution in some extreme conditions. Otherwise all terms after the first few terms are almost negligible when $(T - t)$ is sufficiently large.

If we put one of the barriers, for example H_1, sufficiently far below the spot price S, the presence of the barrier H_1 will become insignificant. Thus the solution 11 will approach the value of a knock-out binary put option with both barrier and strike at H_2.

American Binary Knock-Out Option

In this option, if S ever reaches on barrier, H_2, then the option is worthless; thus on the line H_2 the option value is zero. If S ever reaches another barrier, H_1, the payment is R at the time of touching the payment barrier. Therefore, the boundary conditions for $t < T$ of an American binary knock-out option are

$$f(H_1, t) = R \quad f(H_2, t) = 0 \tag{12}$$

The option is worthless at maturity if the barrier H_1 is never touched, thus the final condition of Equation 1 is

$$f(S, T) = 0 \quad H_1 < S < H_2 \tag{13}$$

where we assume $H_1 < S < H_2$.

By using the same transformation in the previous section, we get a standard diffusion Equation 6 with boundary conditions as

$$u(0, \tau) = \frac{Re^{-\beta\tau}}{H_1} \quad u\left(\ln \frac{H_2}{H_1}, \tau\right) = 0 \tag{14}$$

and the initial condition is

$$u(x, 0) = 0 \quad 0 < x < \ln \frac{H_2}{H_1} \tag{15}$$

It is a diffusion equation with non-homogeneous time-dependent boundary conditions. Since the function in the boundary conditions is differentiable, the problem can be reduced to one with homogeneous boundary conditions. We subtract from u a function y that is chosen to satisfy the boundary conditions. Then the difference $w = u - y$ satisfies a problem with homogeneous boundary conditions but with a modified forcing term and initial condition. We thus find that if

$$y(x, \tau) = \frac{Re^{-\beta\tau}}{H_1}\left(1 - \frac{x}{L}\right) \tag{16}$$

then the boundary conditions of w become

$$w(0, \tau) = 0 \quad w(L, \tau) = 0 \tag{17}$$

which are now homogeneous and the initial condition is

$$w(x, 0) = \frac{R}{H_1}\left(\frac{x}{L} - 1\right) \tag{18}$$

Therefore, the equation is modified as

$$\frac{\partial w}{\partial \tau} = \frac{\partial^2 w}{\partial x^2} + \frac{R\beta}{H_1}\left(1 - \frac{x}{L}\right)e^{-\beta \tau} \tag{19}$$

with a non-homogeneous forcing term in the diffusion equation.

According to Sturm-Liouville theory (Churchill and Brown, 1985), w can be expressed by Equation 9 where the sine functions are the normalized eigenfunctions of the boundary value problem. Since the functions of the initial condition and the forcing term, and their first derivatives are piecewise continuous, they are represented by their Fourier sine series. The coefficients b_n are determined from the differential equation

$$b'_n + \frac{n\pi}{L}b_n = \gamma_n(\tau) \tag{20}$$

and the $\gamma_n(\tau)$ are the expansion coefficients of the non-homogeneous forcing term in term of the eigenfunctions. Thus we have

$$\gamma_n(\tau) = \frac{2}{L}\int_0^L \frac{R\beta}{H_1}\left(1 - \frac{x}{L}\right)e^{-\beta \tau}\sin\left(\frac{n\pi x}{L}\right)dx = \frac{2R\beta}{n\pi H_1}e^{-\beta \tau} \tag{21}$$

The initial condition is expanded as

$$b_n(0) = \frac{2}{L}\int_0^L \frac{R}{H_1}\left(\frac{x}{L} - 1\right)\sin\left(\frac{n\pi x}{L}\right)dx = -\frac{2R}{n\pi H_1} \tag{22}$$

By combining the results in Equations 21 and 22, the solution of Equation 20 is

$$\begin{aligned}
b_n(\tau) &= -\frac{2R}{n\pi H_1}e^{-(n\pi/L)^2\tau} + \frac{2R\beta}{n\pi H_1}\int_0^\tau e^{-(n\pi/L)^2(\tau-s)}e^{-\beta s}ds \\
&= \frac{2R}{n\pi H_1}\left[\frac{\beta e^{-\beta \tau} - \left(\frac{n\pi}{L}\right)^2 e^{-(n\pi/L)^2\tau}}{\left(\frac{n\pi}{L}\right)^2 - \beta}\right]
\end{aligned} \tag{23}$$

Thus the solution of the modified Equation 19 is

$$w(x, t) = \sum_{n=1}^\infty \frac{2R}{n\pi H_1}\left[\frac{\beta e^{-\beta \tau} - \left(\frac{n\pi}{L}\right)^2 e^{-(n\pi/L)^2\tau}}{\left(\frac{n\pi}{L}\right)^2 - \beta}\right]\sin\left(\frac{n\pi x}{L}\right) \tag{24}$$

We obtain the solution of the non-homogeneous boundary value problem Equation 6 from

$$u(x, \tau) = w(x, \tau) + y(x, \tau) \tag{25}$$

After putting back the changing variables and transformations, the value of the American binary knock-out option is

$$f(S, t) = R\left(\frac{S}{H_1}\right)^\alpha \left\{ \sum_{n=1}^{\infty} \frac{2}{n\pi} \left[\frac{\beta - \left(\frac{n\pi}{L}\right)^2 e^{-1/2[(n\pi/L)^2 - \beta]\sigma^2(T-t)}}{\left(\frac{n\pi}{L}\right)^2 - \beta} \right] \right.$$

$$\left. \times \sin\left(\frac{n\pi}{L} \ln \frac{S}{H_1}\right) + \left(1 - \frac{\ln \frac{S}{H_1}}{L}\right) \right\} \tag{26}$$

From the derivation, we find that the assumption $H_1 < S < H_2$ does not affect the result. Thus the same solution can be applied to the condition $H_1 > S > H_2$.

By splitting the sine series in Equation 26 into two parts, the first and second series behave similarly to the series $\sum_{n=1}^{\infty} n^{-3}$ and $\sum_{n=1}^{\infty} n^{-1} e^{-n^2(T-t)}$ respectively. The factor $e^{-1/2(n\pi/L)^2\sigma^2(T-t)}$ makes the second series converge. The same concern as in Equation 11 is a large α making the factor $(S/H_1)^\alpha$ too large to be handled by a computer, otherwise a satisfactory approximation to the solution can be obtained by using a few terms in the series without too much computation.

If we put the knock-out barrier H_2 sufficiently far away from the spot price S, the option will then behave as without the knock-out barrier. Thus the solution 26 will approach the value of an American binary option.

RELATIONSHIPS TO OTHER OPTIONS AND DISCUSSION

A reverse of an up-and-down out binary is an up-and-down exercise binary option. This option lets a buyer receive a fixed payment at the time of the underlying price touching one of the barriers (American style). It can be structured by buying two American binary knock-out options in which the payment and knock-out barriers of the two options are opposite to each other.

In single barrier options, it is easy to show that barrier options with a knock-in feature can be priced by buying an option without any knock-out feature and selling a knock-out option. The same approach can be used in one-touch double barrier binary options. For example, an American has a binary option with a knock-in barrier H premium equal to buying an American binary option and selling an American binary knock-out option with a barrier at H. All the options have the same payment barrier.

Since the payment of the one-touch double barrier binary option is binary, they are not ideal hedging instruments. However, they are suitable for investment. Recently structured accrual range notes are popular in the financial market. The notes are linked to either foreign exchanges, equities, or commodities. Up-and-down out binary options are used in these kind of notes. For example, a daily accrual USD-DEM exchange rate range note pays a fixed daily accrual interest if the exchange rate remains within the range H_1 and H_2. However, if the rate moves outside the range at any time, the coupon will stop accruing for the rest of the period. The note is structured by using the up-front deposit interest to buy a series of up-and-down out binary options with barriers H_1 and H_2 and maturity on each interest accrual day. This note is suitable for an investor who has a strong view of the USD-DEM exchange rate movement within a certain range. On the other hand, if an investor has a view that the underlying price will move outside a range, an up-and-down exercise binary option is suitable for him. Other creative investment products can be structured by using one-touch double barrier binary options.

REFERENCES

Black, F. and Scholes, M. (1973) The pricing of options and corporate liability, *Journal of Political Economics,* **81,** 637–54.

Churchill, R. V. and Brown, J. W. (1985) *Fourier Series and Boundary Value Problem,* International Student Edition (McGraw-Hill, New York).

Rubinstein, M. and Reiner, E. (1991a) Breaking down the barriers, *Risk Magazine,* **4(8),** 28–35.

Rubinstein, M. and Reiner, E. (1991b) Unscrambling the binary code, *Risk Magazine,* **4(9),** 75–83.

Wilmott, P., Dewynne, J. and Howison, S. (1993) *Option Pricing: Mathematical Models and Computation* (Oxford Financial Press, Oxford).

18

Pricing European Average Rate Currency Options

EDMOND LEVY

A verage rate (or 'Asian') options (AROs) are path-dependent contingent claims which settle against the arithmetic average of prices calculated over a given time interval. This type of claim is being offered in a variety of markets and is receiving a significant amount of interest from banks and investors alike.

The rationale for the presence of such an instrument differs from market to market. Bergman (1985), in his introduction, favors such contracts as they represent an attractive specification for thinly traded asset markets where price manipulation on or near a maturity date is possible. In markets where prices are prone to periods of extreme volatility the averaging performs a smoothing operation. For example, options on oil are typically settled against an average of daily or monthly fixings from *Platts European Marketscan*. In the foreign exchange market, the ARO is offered over-the-counter to clients as a means to hedge a stream of foreign currency flows against adverse currency movements. Such options have become increasingly popular as (not surprisingly) they can be considerably cheaper than a European option of a similar maturity and often more relevant to a treasurer's needs. The alternative strategy of entering into a strip of individual options is unnecessarily costly if all that is required to be hedged is the resultant average of exchange rates.

Under standard assumptions, the valuation of such options presents certain difficulties. Apart from trivial circumstances, options involving the arithmetic average will not have closed-form solutions if the conventional assumption of a

An earlier version of this paper was entitled 'The valuation of average rate currency options.' The author would like to thank Robert Benson, Ian Cooper, Mark Garman, Bob Nobay, R.J. O'Brien, and especially Stuart Turnbull for helpful comments. The paper has also benefited from suggestions by participants at the Financial Options Research Centre seminar programme at the University of Warwick and an anonymous referee.

Reprinted with permission from *Journal of International Money and Finance;* Vol. 11; Edmond Levy; *Pricing European Average Rate Currency Options;* 1992; Elsevier Science Ltd., Oxford, England.

geometric diffusion is specified for the underlying price process. For unlike options on the geometric average, the density function for the arithmetic average is not log normal and has no explicit representation.

The few papers examining the valuation of this type of instrument fall into three main groups. Firstly, there are those that advocate a numerical approach: Kemna and Vorst (1990) propose a Monte Carlo methodology which employs the corresponding geometric option as a control variate; Carverhill and Clewlow (1990) adopt the Fast Fourier Transform to evaluate numerically the necessary convolutions of density functions. These methods can be accurate but time-consuming especially when the number of prices in the average is large. In addition, this shortcoming is compounded for traders examining the sensitivity of large portfolios of AROs to pertinent market parameters. A second approach is to modify the solution to the geometric average option: for example, Ruttiens (1990) and Vorst (1990). Employing the solution to the corresponding geometric average problem improves the speed of calculation but results in models which can systematically (and at times significantly) overprice put options and/or underprice call options, giving rise to misleading signals and inefficiencies in the dynamic hedging requirements. Furthermore, the methodology on which such solutions are based yields formulae which only satisfy the put-call parity condition for arithmetic options on the expiry date of the option. The final approach, and one which this paper follows, is to approximate the density function for the arithmetic average.

The simulations carried out in this paper demonstrate that for volatilities typically experienced in foreign exchange markets, the distribution of an arithmetic average is well-approximated by the log normal distribution when the underlying price process follows the conventional assumption of a geometric diffusion. As a result, the problem reduces to the less complicated task of determining the necessary parameters for the log normal density function. The reported simulations emphasize that in applying this approach to other underlying asset prices, users should be aware that the approximation is only valid for a limited range of volatilities and option maturities.

Turnbull and Wakeman (1991) also recognize the suitability of the log normal as a first-order approximation. These authors apply the Edgeworth series expansion (around the log normal) to the problem of valuing the ARO, and provide an algorithm to compute moments for the arithmetic average. However, Turnbull and Wakeman overlook the fact that when only the first two moments are taken into account in the approximation, the accuracy of the log normal assumption is acceptable making redundant the need to include additional terms in the expansion involving higher moments. This observation is important as closed-form expressions for the first two moments of the arithmetic average are relatively simple to derive.

This paper uses a straightforward approach (termed below as the 'Wilkinson approximation') to approximate the arithmetic density function. This can be interpreted as the first term in the Edgeworth expansion referred to above. Its main virtue, is that a closed-form analytical approximation for the valuation of

AROs becomes possible which has the advantage of being, for typical ranges of volatility experienced, both accurate and easily implemented.[1] It is also shown how the approach can be extended to value other contingent claims involving the arithmetic average.

The paper is organized as follows. Section I outlines the option contract to be valued and the put-call parity condition for AROs. Section II introduces the 'Wilkinson approximation' and develops a formula for the valuation of the ARO. The performance of the approximation is examined in Section III via Monte Carlo simulations. Finally, the paper ends with a brief summary and some observations on possible modifications to the approach.

THE AVERAGE RATE OPTION

Let $S(t)$ be the spot price at time t, defined (as are all prices here) as units of domestic currency per unit of foreign currency. We suppose that the average is determined over the time interval $[t_0, t_N]$ and at points on this interval $t_i = t_0 + ih$ for $i = 0, 1, \ldots, N$ where $h = (t_N - t_0)/N$. The 'running average,' $A(t)$, is defined for a given point in time $t_0 \leq t \leq t_N$ by

$$A(t) = \frac{1}{m + 1} \sum_{i=0}^{m} S(t_i)$$

for $0 \leq m \leq N$, and $A(t) = 0$ for $t < t_0$. Thus $A(t_N)$ represents the arithmetic average of $N + 1$ prices taken at equal intervals of time h between t_0 and t_N. Typically this time interval is specified to be a day, a week, or a month.[2]

The ARO is characterized by the payoff function at time t_N given by Max$[A(t_N) - K, 0]$ for a call option, or Max$[K - A(t_N), 0]$ for a put option. Here, K is the strike price of the option. It will be helpful later on to define the variable $M(t) = [A(t_N) - A(t)(m + 1)/(N + 1)]$ denoting the undetermined component of the final average.

The put-call parity condition is ignored (or at best implicit) in papers which examine the pricing of AROs, yet the condition is fundamental to the consistency of a pricing methodology. As for other European option claims, the condition is independent of volatility and should be embodied in all valuation models.

Define r_d and r_f as, respectively, the domestic and foreign (continuously compounding) interest rates and assume them constant. We also assume frictionless markets.[3] Consider a position of being long one call option and short one put option each with strike K. This is equivalent to a position which pays

$$\frac{1}{N + 1} \sum_{i=0}^{N} S(t_i) - K$$

units of domestic currency at time t_N. Suppose during the averaging period at some time $t = t_m + \xi h$, $0 \leq m \leq N$, we wish to value this position. At this time the uncertainty in the position is due only to the unknown spot prices

$S(t_i)$, $i = m + 1, \ldots, N$ which can be hedged in the forward market.[4] Arrange at time t to sell forward $1/N + 1\, e^{-r_d(t_N - t_i)}$ units of foreign currency for delivery at t_i for $i = m + 1, \ldots, N$. Note that the value of such a hedge is zero at t. Subsequently, at each t_i, these forward positions are closed at the prevailing spot rates $S(t_i)$ for net value

$$\frac{1}{N + 1}\, e^{-r_d(t_N - t_i)}[F(t, t_i) - S(t_i)],$$

where, $F(t, t_i)$ denotes the arbitrage-free forward price for foreign exchange at $t_m + \xi h$ for delivery at t_i given by

$$F(t, t_i) = S(t_m)e^{(r_d - r_f)(t_i - t_m - \xi h)}$$

These flows may be placed on deposit (or borrowed) for $(t_N - t_i)$ realizing a total value of

$$\frac{1}{N + 1} \sum_{i = m+1}^{N} [F(t, t_i) - S(t_i)].$$

Finally, setting off this amount against the maturity value of the call and put position, we have a known domestic currency amount which can be discounted at the risk-free rate to give

$$V(t) = e^{-r_d(t_N - t)}\left[\frac{1}{N+1} \sum_{i=0}^{m} S(t_i) + \frac{S(t)}{N+1} \sum_{i=m+1}^{N} e^{(r_d - r_f)(t_i - t)} - K\right]$$

$$= e^{-r_d\tau}\left\{\frac{m+1}{N+1} A(t) + \frac{S(t)e^{g(1-\xi)h}}{N+1} \frac{[1 - e^{g(N-m)h}]}{1 - e^{gh}} - K\right\},$$

where, $g = (r_d - r_f)$ and $\tau = (t_N - t)$ and where we have made use of $(t_i - t) = (i - m - \xi)h$. It follows that if $C(t)$ and $P(t)$ denote the value of, respectively, the call and put options at t, then to avoid the possibility of arbitrage we require

$$C(t) - P(t) = V(t). \tag{1a}$$

A similar argument in the case of $t < t_0$ results in

$$C(t) - P(t) = e^{-r_d\tau}\left\{\frac{S(t)}{N+1} \frac{[e^{g(t_0 - t)} - e^{g(t_0 - t + h(N+1))}]}{1 - e^{gh}} - K\right\}. \tag{1b}$$

Thus if an ARO call option is valued, we may use expressions (1) to value the corresponding put option.

A PRICING FORMULA

In the remainder of this paper, we will assume that the spot price process is the familiar geometric diffusion

$$dS(t) = \mu S(t)dt + \sigma S(t)dz,$$

where dz is a Wiener process, and μ and σ are constant. Applying the risk-neutrality transformation of Cox and Ross (1976), we may characterize the value of the ARO as:

$$C[S(t), A(t), t] = e^{-r_d\tau}E^* \text{ Max}[A(t_N) - K, 0], \tag{2}$$

where E^* is the expectation operator conditioned on $[A(t), S(t)]$ at time t under the risk-adjusted density function so that $S(t)$ is now described by the diffusion

$$dS(t) = gS(t)dt + \sigma S(t)dz. \tag{3}$$

For $\eta > t$, (3) implies that $\ln S(\eta)$ is normally distributed with mean $\ln S(t) + (g - 1/2\sigma^2)(\eta - t)$ and standard deviation $\sigma\sqrt{(\eta - t)}$.

For values of $K \neq 0$, the evaluation of (2) is not straightforward as it requires knowledge of the conditional distribution of $M(t) = [A(t_N) - A(t)(m + 1)/(N + 1)]$. Specifically, $M(t)$ is a sum of correlated log normal random variables. Although expressions for the moment generating function, mean, and variance for the sum of two log normal variates exist,[5] closed-form expressions for the density function of sums of log normals are not possible. As a result, unlike conventional European options which do possess closed-form solutions, solving (2) will require numerical procedures.[6]

There is however a large body of evidence suggesting that the distribution of such sums is well-approximated by another log normal distribution.[7] Let us, for the moment, take $\ln M(t)$ as normally distributed with unknown mean $\alpha(t)$ and variance $\nu(t)$.[2] Then a simple approach to determining these parameters is to make use of the moment generating function for $X(t) = \ln M(t)$, $\Psi_x(k)$, given by

$$\Psi_x(k) = E^*[M(t)^k] = e^{k\alpha(t) + 1/2k^2\nu(t)^2}. \tag{4}$$

Thus we see that the first two moments of $M(t)$ are jointly complete and sufficient statistics for $\alpha(t)$ and $\nu(t)$. Regarding (4) for $k = 1$ and $k = 2$ as simultaneous equations in the unknown $\alpha(t)$ and $\nu(t)$ yields the following expressions:

$$\alpha(t) = 2 \ln E^*[M(t)] = \frac{1}{2} \ln E^*[M(t)^2], \tag{5a}$$

$$\nu(t) = \sqrt{\ln E^*[M(t)^2] - 2 \ln E^*[M(t)]}. \tag{5b}$$

Such a procedure has previously been employed in the field of communication engineering and is sometimes referred to as the 'Wilkinson approximation.'[8]

Accepting that $M(t)$ is distributed as log normal with mean $\alpha(t)$ and variance $\nu(t)^2$ given by (5), we can immediately evaluate (2) and express the call option as:

$$C[S(t), A(t), t] = e^{-r_d\tau}\{E^*[M(t)]N(d)_1 - [K - A(t)(m + 1)/(N + 1)]N(d_2)\}, \tag{6}$$

where

$$d_1 = \frac{\dfrac{1}{2} \ln E^*[M(t)^2] - \ln[K - A(t)(m + 1)/(N + 1)]}{\nu(t)}$$

$d_2 = d_1 - \nu(t)$,

$\nu(t)$ is given by (5b), and $N(\cdot)$ is the cumulative normal distribution function. Expression (6) is the solution to a European option paying $\text{Max}[M(t) - K^*, 0]$ at time t_N where $K^* = [K - A(t)(m + 1)/(N + 1)]$ and $\ln M(t)$ is distributed as $N[\alpha(t), \nu(t)]$. Thus the strike price of our ARO is reduced by the known component of $A(t_N)$.[9] Closed-form expressions for $\mathbf{E}^*[M(t)]$ and $\mathbf{E}^*[M(t)^2]$ are derived in the Appendix.

The value for the corresponding put option, $P[S(t), A(t), t]$, can be found either by using the above expression for the call option and put-call parity (expression (1)) or by evaluating $e^{-r_d\tau}\mathbf{E}^* \text{Max}[K^* - M(t), 0]$ under the assumption that $M(t)$ is distributed as log normal with parameters $\alpha(t)$ and $\nu(t)$ given by (5). Both approaches yield:[10]

$$P[S(t), A(t), t] = e^{-r_d\tau}\{\mathbf{E}^*[M(t)][N(d_1) - 1] - [K - A(t)(m + 1)/(N + 1)][N(d_2) - 1]\}.$$

A simple extension of the ideas here is the valuation of the 'floating ARO' or 'average strike option.' This is an option whose payoff on maturity is $\text{Max}[A(t_N) - S(t_N), 0]$. That is, the strike price of the ARO is the spot rate on maturity [or alternatively, the strike price of a conventional European option is $A(t_N)$]. To provide a reliable approximation to the valuation of such an option, we assume $\mathbf{X}(t) = [\ln A(t_N), \ln S(t_N)]$ is approximately bivariate normal and hence the option valuation problem can be solved in the manner of Margrabe (1978).

To determine the necessary parameters to value this option, extend the Wilkinson approximation to vector processes. Under the bivariate lognormal distribution assumption, we use of the moment generating function for $\mathbf{X}(t)$, $\Psi_x(k_1, k_2)$, to produce sets of simultaneous equations. The moment generating function for $\mathbf{X}(t)$ is:

$$\Psi_x(k_1, k_2) = \mathbf{E}^*[A(t_N)^{k_1}S(t_N)^{k_2}] = e^{\alpha_1 k_1 + \alpha_2 k_2 + 1/2(\nu_1^2 k_1^2 + 2\rho\nu_1\nu_2 k_1 k_2 + \nu_2^2 k_2^2)}.$$

Substituting $(k_1, k_2) = (0, 1)$ and $(0, 2)$ yields $\alpha_2 = \ln S(t) + (g - 1/2\sigma^2)\tau$ and $\nu_2 = \sigma\sqrt{\tau}$ as parameters for $\ln S(t_N)$. For $(k_1, k_2) = (1, 0)$ and $(2, 0)$ the mean, α_1, and standard deviation, ν_1, for $\ln A(t_N)$ are determined as:

$$\alpha_1 = 2 \ln \mathbf{E}^*[A(t_N)] - \frac{1}{2} \ln \mathbf{E}^*[A(t_N)^2],$$

$$\nu_1 = \sqrt{\ln \mathbf{E}^*[A(t_N)^2] - 2 \ln \mathbf{E}^*[A(t_N)]}.$$

Finally, the covariance term, $\rho\nu_1\nu_2$, is determined as

$$\rho\nu_1\nu_2 = \ln \mathbf{E}^*[A(t_N)S(t_N)] - (\alpha_1 + \alpha_2) - \frac{1}{2}(\nu_1^2 + \nu_2^2),$$

having substituted $(k_1, k_2) = (1, 1)$. The expression for $\mathbf{E}^*[A(t_N)S(t_N)]$ is derived in the Appendix. Those for $\mathbf{E}^*[A(t_N)]$ and $\mathbf{E}^*[A(t_N)^2]$ may be readily found using $A(t_N) = A(t) + M(t)$.

The expressions for $\alpha(t)$ and $\nu(t)$ in (5) represent reliable estimates for the mean and standard deviation of ln $M(t)$ to the extent that $M(t)$ is approximately log normally distributed. Some idea as to the seriousness of the error in the approximation, and hence the reliability of these estimates, can be gauged by comparing the Wilkinson approximation with outcomes generated using Monte Carlo methods.

EMPIRICAL RESULTS

In this section we investigate the approximation error in the Wilkinson procedure and evaluate the adequacy of the ARO pricing equation (expression (6)) using Monte Carlo methods.

The empirical moments for ln $M(t)$ are compared with those implied by the Wilkinson approximation. If $X(t) = \ln M(t)$ has mean $\alpha(t)$ and variance $\nu(t)^2$ then, under our assumption, the kth moment of $X(t)$ is given by

$$\mathbf{E}^*[X(t)^k] = \left[\frac{\partial^k \Psi_x(\phi)}{\partial \phi^k}\right]_{\phi=0},$$

where $\Psi_x(\phi) = \exp(\phi\alpha(t) + 1/2\phi^2\nu(t)^2)$ is again the moment generating function for $X(t)$. The approximation for $\alpha(t)$ and $\nu(t)$ can be examined by substituting the discrete-form expressions for the first two moments of $M(t)$ given in the Appendix.

From a practical viewpoint, only discrete averages are relevant. However, as a simplification to ease computations, and to provide upper bounds (for $t \leq t_0$) to the approximate values, we might substitute continuous-form expressions lim $\mathbf{E}^*[M(t)]$ and lim $\mathbf{E}^*[M(t)^2]$ as $N \to \infty$:

$$\lim \mathbf{E}^*[M(t)] = \frac{S(t)}{(t_N - t_0)g}(e^{g\tau} - 1) \text{ for } t > t_0, \tag{7a}$$

and

$$\lim \mathbf{E}^*[M(t)] = \frac{S(t)e^{g(t_0-t)}}{(t_N - t_0)g}(e^{g(t_N-t_0)} - 1) \text{ for } t \leq t_0, \tag{7b}$$

$$\lim \mathbf{E}^*[M(t)^2] = \frac{2S(t)^2}{(t_N - t_0)^2(g + \sigma^2)}\left[\frac{e^{(2g+\sigma^2)\tau} - 1}{(2g + \sigma^2)} - \frac{e^{g\tau} - 1}{g}\right] \text{ for } t > t_0, \tag{8a}$$

and

$$\lim \mathbf{E}^*[M(t)^2] = \frac{2S(t)^2e^{(2g+\sigma^2)(t_0-t)}}{(t_N - t_0)^2(g + \sigma^2)}$$
$$\times \left[\frac{e^{(2g+\sigma^2)(t_N-t_0)} - 1}{(2g + \sigma^2)} - \frac{e^{g(t_N-t_0)} - 1}{g}\right] \text{ for } t \leq t_0. \tag{8b}$$

This will also allow us to consider in these experiments the rate of convergence to the continuous values as $N \to \infty$ and thus the importance of allowing for discretization when valuing average options. The tables below refer to moments for ln $M(t)$ implied by the discrete and continuous approximations as WD and WC, respectively, with the empirical moments from the Monte Carlo outcomes denoted by MC.

The distribution for ln $M(t)$ is examined for values of $N = 4, 32$, and 256, and a range of values for σ between 0.10 and 1.00. Simulations of $M(t)$ were achieved by generating a sequence of spot rates $S(t_i)$ for $i = 1, 2, \ldots, N$ using the following expression:

$$S(t_i) = S(t_{i-1})e^{(r_d - r_f - 1/2\sigma^2)b + \omega_i\sigma\sqrt{b}},$$

where ω_i is distributed as normal with zero mean and unit variance.

Monte Carlo estimates for $\alpha(t)$ and $\nu(t)$ were calculated by averaging 10000 replications of ln $M(t)$. In each replication, $r_d = 0.08$, $r_f = 0.16$, $S(t) = 1.5$, $t = t_0 - 0.001$ (thus the current timepoint is a fraction before the first fixing), and $\tau = 1$. To reduce the standard error of the estimates further, moments of the logarithm of the corresponding geometric average were employed as control variates for the moments of ln $M(t)$.

Tables 18-1, 18-2, and 18-3 present a sample of outcomes of these experiments. The tables display the first four moments of ln $M(t)$ together with their standard errors (in parentheses). In addition, statistics γ_1 and γ_2 are presented which test for, respectively, the null hypotheses of zero skewness and zero kurtosis (see Madansky, 1988, p. 37). Under the null, both statistics are distributed as normal with zero mean. For γ_1 the asymptotic standard error under the null hypothesis with 10000 replications is 0.0245, whilst that for γ_2 is 0.0490.

The results indicate that, for values of σ less than 0.20, the discrete Wilkinson approximation is very accurate. Beyond this value for σ the approximation deteriorates across all values of N. Secondly, the continuous Wilkinson approx-

TABLE 18-1   Analysis of Moments for $X(t) = \ln M_N(t)$, $N = 4$

Moment	$\sigma = 0.20$			$\sigma = 0.50$			$\sigma = 0.80$		
	MC	WD	WC	MC	WD	WC	MC	WD	WC
$E[X(t)]$	0.3601	0.3600	0.3592	0.3307	0.3283	0.3240	0.2772	0.2642	0.2554
	(4×10^{-5})			(3×10^{-4})			(7×10^{-4})		
$E[X(t)^2]$	0.1412	0.1413	0.1421	0.1794	0.1829	0.1884	0.2429	0.2732	0.2858
	(3×10^{-5})			(3×10^{-4})			(0.0012)		
$E[X(t)^3]$	0.0593	0.0593	0.0604	0.1114	0.1094	0.1151	0.1937	0.1796	0.1857
	(2×10^{-5})			(4×10^{-4})			(0.0020)		
$E[X(t)^4]$	0.0264	0.0263	0.0273	0.0812	0.0772	0.0844	0.2129	0.2141	0.2366
	(2×10^{-5})			(6×10^{-4})			(0.0044)		
γ_1	0.1222			0.3072			0.5075		
γ_2	0.0297			0.1998			0.3504		

Notes: MC = Monte Carlo estimate (standard error in parentheses).
WD = Wilkinson discrete approximation.
WC = Wilkinson continuous approximation.

TABLE 18-2   Analysis of Moments for $X(t) = \ln M_N(t)$, $N = 32$

Moment	$\sigma = 0.20$			$\sigma = 0.50$			$\sigma = 0.80$		
	MC	WD	WC	MC	WD	WC	MC	WD	WC
$E[X(t)]$	0.3593	0.3593	0.3592	0.3262	0.3247	0.3240	0.2665	0.2568	0.2554
	(3×10^{-5})			(2×10^{-4})			(5×10^{-4})		
$E[X(t)^2]$	0.1419	0.1420	0.1421	0.1839	0.1876	0.1884	0.2618	0.2838	0.2858
	(2×10^{-5})			(3×10^{-4})			(0.0010)		
$E[X(t)^3]$	0.0603	0.0603	0.0604	0.1147	0.1142	0.1151	0.1963	0.1848	0.1857
	(2×10^{-5})			(3×10^{-4})			(0.0016)		
$E[X(t)^4]$	0.0272	0.0272	0.0273	0.0845	0.0833	0.0844	0.2285	0.2329	0.2366
	(1×10^{-5})			(5×10^{-4})			(0.0032)		
γ_1	0.0786			0.1991			0.2977		
γ_2	-0.0051			0.0231			0.1792		

Notes: See Table 18-1.

TABLE 18-3   Analysis of Moments for $X(t) = \ln M_N(t)$, $N = 256$

Moment	$\sigma = 0.20$			$\sigma = 0.50$			$\sigma = 0.80$		
	MC	WD	WC	MC	WD	WC	MC	WD	WC
$E[X(t)]$	0.3593	0.3592	0.3592	0.3254	0.3241	0.3240	0.2641	0.2556	0.2554
	(4×10^{-5})			(2×10^{-4})			(5×10^{-4})		
$E[X(t)^2]$	0.1420	0.1421	0.1421	0.1851	0.1883	0.1884	0.2648	0.2856	0.2858
	(2×10^{-5})			(3×10^{-4})			(0.0010)		
$E[X(t)^3]$	0.0604	0.0604	0.0604	0.1160	0.1150	0.1151	0.1975	0.1856	0.1857
	(2×10^{-5})			(3×10^{-4})			(0.0017)		
$E[X(t)^4]$	0.0274	0.0273	0.0273	0.0861	0.0843	0.0844	0.2319	0.2361	0.2366
	(2×10^{-5})			(5×10^{-4})			(0.0035)		
γ_1	0.0720			0.1896			0.2840		
γ_2	0.0127			0.0299			0.1415		

Notes: See Table 18-1.

imation (WC) is found to be acceptable for values of $N > 30$. This implies that the value of an ARO with weekly fixings is likely to have a similar value to one with daily fixings.[11] Finally, the tests for lack of skewness are comprehensively rejected. Values for γ_1 indicate a general tendency for the right hand tail of the distribution to be heavier than the left hand tail. The tests for kurtosis, however, are significant only for $\sigma > 0.40$ for $N = 4$ and $\sigma > 0.60$ for $N = 32$ and $N = 256$.

Apart from the evidence for the presence of skewness, these results are very encouraging. In the foreign exchange market, options are rarely quoted with an implied annualized volatility (σ) greater than 20 percent. However, the experiments clearly demonstrate the unreliability of the procedure for average options on an underlying asset whose volatility is in excess of 30 percent. To assess the significance of the evidence for skewness on valuation, we now examine the performance of the pricing formula itself.

To determine values for the call option, experiments (each of 10000 replications) of $e^{-r_d \tau} \text{Max}[A(t_N) - K, 0]$ were generated with $S(t) = 1.5$, $r_d = 0.15$, $r_f = 0.10$, and $(t_N - t_0) = 1$. The results are presented in Tables 18-4, 18-5, and 18-6 for; $t = t_0 - 0.5$, t_0, and $t_0 + 0.5$; $\sigma = 0.10$, 0.20, and 0.30; and $N = 4$, 12, and 256. In each experiment, the replications were averaged and an estimated standard error calculated (the maximum standard error corresponding to σ and N is reported in the tables). Following Kemna and Vorst (1990), the corresponding geometric average rate option was used as a control variate to improve the accuracy of each estimated option value. In order to assess the behaviour of the Wilkinson approximation in the region of the tails of the distribution for $M(t)$, we examined AROs over a range of values for K.

The standard errors indicate that the Monte Carlo estimates of the ARO values are accurate to within 0.0001 with 95 percent confidence. As expected from the above analysis of the distribution for $M(t)$, the Wilkinson approximation (WD) is generally good across all values for N and K for $\sigma \leq 0.20$. There is a slight tendency for the approximation to undervalue out-of-the-money calls

TABLE 18-4 Average Rate Call Option Values, 10000 Replications

$t = t_0 - 0.5$		$N = 4$		$N = 12$		$N = 256$		$N \to \infty$
σ	$K/S(t)$	MC	WD	MC	WD	MC	WD	WC
	1.2	0.0039	0.0038	0.0040	0.0040	0.0041	0.0041	0.0041
	1.1	0.228	0.0228	0.0232	0.0232	0.0.235	0.0235	0.0235
0.10	1.0	0.0814	0.0815	0.0818	0.0819	0.0821	0.0822	0.0822
	0.9	0.1831	0.1832	0.1832	0.1832	0.1832	0.1833	0.1833
	0.8	0.3012	0.3012	0.3012	0.3012	0.3011	0.3011	0.3011
Std error		20×10^{-5}		1.7×10^{-5}		1.6×10^{-5}		
	1.2	0.0326	0.0325	0.0334	0.0333	0.0340	0.0338	0.0338
	1.1	0.0662	0.0661	0.0671	0.0671	0.0677	0.0677	0.0677
0.20	1.0	0.1220	0.1222	0.1231	0.1231	0.1236	0.1237	0.1237
	0.9	0.2036	0.2038	0.2042	0.2044	0.2046	0.2048	0.2048
	0.8	0.3065	0.3067	0.3067	0.3069	0.3069	0.3071	0.3071
Std error		7.6×10^{-5}		6.4×10^{-5}		5.3×10^{-5}		
	1.2	0.0729	0.0727	0.0742	0.0741	0.0750	0.0750	0.0750
	1.1	0.1110	0.1112	0.1126	0.1127	0.1134	0.1136	0.1137
0.30	1.0	0.1645	0.1650	0.1661	0.1664	0.1669	0.1673	0.1673
	0.9	0.2342	0.2363	0.2367	0.2374	0.2376	0.2381	0.2382
	0.8	0.3243	0.3252	0.3254	0.3259	0.3260	0.3264	0.3264
Std error		1.7×10^{-4}		1.5×10^{-4}		1.3×10^{-4}		

Notes: MC = Monte Carlo estimate; Std error = maximum standard error for MC corresponding to σ and N. WD = Wilkinson discrete approximation; WC = Wilkinson continuous approximation; $S(t)$ = 1.5; $A(t) = 0$; $r_d = 0.15$; $r_f = 0.10$; $t_N = t_0 = 1$.

TABLE 18-5   Average Rate Call Option Values, 10000 Replications

$t = t_0$		$N = 4$		$N = 12$		$N = 256$		$N \to \infty$
σ	$K/S(t)$	MC	WD	MC	WD	MC	WD	WC
	1.2	0.0001	0.0001	0.0001	0.0001	0.0001	0.0001	0.0001
	1.1	0.0038	0.0038	0.0042	0.0042	0.0045	0.0044	0.0044
0.10	1.0	0.0481	0.0482	0.0489	0.0490	0.0494	0.0495	0.0495
	0.9	0.1622	0.1622	0.1622	0.1622	0.1622	0.1622	0.1622
	0.8	0.2911	0.2911	0.2911	0.2911	0.2910	0.2910	0.2910
Std error		2.0×10^{-5}		1.7×10^{-5}		1.6×10^{-5}		
	1.2	0.0062	0.0060	0.0067	0.0065	0.0071	0.0068	0.0068
	1.1	0.0248	0.0247	0.0261	0.0259	0.0270	0.0267	0.0268
0.20	1.0	0.0753	0.0755	0.0772	0.0774	0.0781	0.0784	0.0785
	0.9	0.1694	0.1696	0.1703	0.1707	0.1710	0.1714	0.1714
	0.8	0.2914	0.2915	0.2916	0.2917	0.2917	0.2918	0.2918
Std error		7.1×10^{-5}		6.2×10^{-5}		5.6×10^{-5}		
	1.2	0.0235	0.0231	0.0249	0.0243	0.0259	0.0251	0.0252
	1.1	0.0517	0.0515	0.0540	0.0537	0.0551	0.0550	0.0551
0.30	1.0	0.1034	0.1038	0.1061	0.1067	0.1077	0.1084	0.1085
	0.9	0.1858	0.1864	0.1882	0.1890	0.1893	0.1905	0.1905
	0.8	0.2958	0.2961	0.2966	0.2974	0.2974	0.2982	0.2982
Std error		1.7×10^{-4}		1.4×10^{-4}		1.3×10^{-4}		

Notes: See Table 18-4. A(t).

and overvalue in-the-money calls. For the case of $\sigma = 0.10$, the accuracy is to within 0.007 percent of the underlying spot price. For $\sigma = 0.20$ the greatest error is 0.02 percent of the underlying spot price and for $\sigma = 0.30$ it is 0.06 percent.

The precision of this formula improves as the ARO contract tends in nature to a conventional European option. This occurs (more quickly for small values of N) as the ARO reaches maturity, or for AROs where the averaging period $(t_N - t_0)$ is much smaller than the option horizon $(t_N - t)$. Imprecision primarily occurs for deep in-the-money options and large values of σ. The simulations indicate, however, that fine accuracy is generally secured for $\sigma\sqrt{\tau} \leq 0.20$. Further simulations (not reported) indicate that the interest differential, g, has little or no bearing on the success of the Wilkinson approximation. Finally, the tables demonstrate the success of the continuous time limit expressions (7) and (8) (denoted in the tables as *WC*) for evaluating AROs with daily fixings.

A curious feature displayed by these tables is the comparative cheapness of AROs with different values of N. We know that conventional European options are relatively more expensive than otherwise identical AROs. This is largely explained by the fact that the variance of an average is smaller than the variance of the underlying price process. However, compare two AROs, daily and quarterly fixings (say), both with one year maturity and identical strike prices. In

TABLE 18-6 Average Rate Call Option Values, 10000 Replications

$t = t_0 + 0.5$		N = 4		N = 12		N = 256		N → ∞
σ	K/S(t)	MC	WD	MC	WD	MC	WD	WC
	1.2	0.0000	0.0000	0.0000	0.0000	0.0000	0.0000	0.0000
	1.1	0.0000	0.0000	0.0000	0.0000	0.0000	0.0000	0.0000
0.10	1.0	0.0185	0.0185	0.0172	0.0172	0.0164	0.0164	0.0164
	0.9	0.1497	0.1497	0.1486	0.1486	0.1480	0.1480	0.1479
	0.8	0.2889	0.2889	0.2878	0.2878	0.2871	0.2871	0.2871
Std error		1.0×10^{-5}		8.0×10^{-6}		8.0×10^{-6}		
	1.2	0.0000	0.0000	0.0000	0.0000	0.0000	0.0000	0.0000
	1.1	0.0010	0.0009	0.0006	0.0006	0.0005	0.0004	0.0004
0.20	1.0	0.0307	0.0307	0.0288	0.0288	0.0275	0.0276	0.0275
	0.9	0.1498	0.1498	0.1486	0.1487	0.1480	0.1480	0.1480
	0.8	0.2889	0.2889	0.2878	0.2878	0.2871	0.2871	0.2871
Std error		3.9×10^{-5}		3.1×10^{-5}		2.8×10^{-5}		
	1.2	0.0005	0.0004	0.0003	0.0002	0.0002	0.0001	0.00001
	1.1	0.0057	0.0057	0.0045	0.0044	0.0039	0.0037	0.0036
0.30	1.0	0.0430	0.0431	0.0406	0.0406	0.0388	0.0390	0.0389
	0.9	0.1508	0.1508	0.1495	0.1496	0.1486	0.1488	0.1488
	0.8	0.2889	0.2889	0.2878	0.2878	0.2871	0.2871	0.2871
Std error		8.5×10^{-5}		6.8×10^{-5}		6.1×10^{-5}		

Notes: See Table 18-4. A(t).

general, we should expect an ARO to be cheaper than an otherwise identical ARO with larger N because a relatively higher proportion of the exposure is taken out by the first fixing. Thus the quarterly ARO will initially be less expensive than the daily ARO. However, with one quarter remaining and assuming $A(t)$ is identical for both AROs, the quarterly ARO is a European option on $S(t_N)/5$ with strike K^*. The payout on the daily ARO, however, is still determined by the difference between the average of prices over this remaining period and K^* and thus will be less expensive. In general, as the maturity date approaches, *ceteris paribus,* a given ARO will always subsequently become more expensive than one with larger N.

In sum, under typical market conditions, the Wilkinson approximation provides a quick and accurate method for valuing AROs in foreign exchange and has the further benefit of ensuring that put-call parity is maintained. The approach is simple to implement and circumvents the need for time-consuming numerical procedures.

SUMMARY AND OBSERVATIONS

This paper has introduced a convenient and accurate method for valuing average rate currency options. The approach relies on the assumption that the distribution of sums of log normal variates is itself well approximated at least to a first order by the log normal. Our simulations have shown that this assumption is acceptable particularly for values of $\sigma\sqrt{\tau}$ less than 0.20. For larger values the accuracy of the pricing formula deteriorates and we might consider modifying the approach to estimating the necessary parameters by correcting the Wilkinson estimates.

Augmenting the pricing formula along the lines of Turnbull and Wakeman (1991) is one way to correct for the effects of higher volatility. Some useful results that should help in formulating correction factors are given in Fenton (1960) and Janos (1970). Fenton proposes that, where interest is in the tails of the distribution one should pay more attention to higher moments. Thus a better approximation for higher volatility conditions could be achieved by equating higher moments in equation (4), say $k = 3$ and $k = 4$. Janos shows that the behavior of the logarithm of the tail of the distribution of sums of log normals is dominated by that term with largest logarithmic variance. His results therefore suggest that we should concentrate attention to the distribution of $S(t_N)$ when correcting the tails. Lastly, further improvements could be made by adopting the more precise procedures in Schwartz and Yeh (1982). These ideas no doubt will lead to more satisfactory approximations to the valuation of AROs but their further consideration is beyond the scope of this paper. It is hoped that the results here provide some direction and encouragement for future research.

APPENDIX

In this appendix we provide expressions of $\mathbf{E}^*[M(t)]$, $\mathbf{E}^*[M(t)^2]$, and $\mathbf{E}^*[A(t_N)S(t_N)]$ conditional on time t when $S(t)$ satisfies the diffusion (3).

Let ξh be the time interval from the last spot rate fixing at t_m for some m, $0 \le m \le N$. Thus ξ is defined as $\xi = (t - t_m)/h$. Then from the definition for $M(t)$, we have

$$\mathbf{E}^*[M(t)] = \frac{1}{N+1} \sum_{i=m+1}^{N} \mathbf{E}^*[S(t_i)]$$

$$= \frac{1}{N+1} \sum_{i=m+1}^{N} S(t) e^{g(i-m-\xi)h} = \frac{S(t)}{N+1} e^{g(1-\xi)h} \left[\frac{1 - e^{g(N-m)h}}{1 - e^{gh}} \right].$$

For $t < t_0$, $\mathbf{E}^*[M(t)]$ is given as:

$$\mathbf{E}^*[M(t)] = \frac{S(t)}{N+1} e^{g(t_0 - t)} \left[\frac{1 - e^{g(N+1)h}}{1 - e^{gh}} \right].$$

We can express $\mathbf{E}^*[M(t)^2]$ for $t \ge t_0$ as

$$\mathbf{E}^*[M(t)^2] = \frac{1}{(N+1)^2} \sum_{i=m+1}^{N} \sum_{j=m+1}^{N} \mathbf{E}^*[S(t_i)S(t_j)].$$

The expectation term in this expression is given by

$$\mathbf{E}^*[S(t_i)S(t_j)] \;=\; e^{g(i+j-2\xi)b+\sigma^2[\mathrm{Min}(i,j)-\xi]b}S(t)^2,$$

and hence (after some tedious algebra) we can evaluate $\mathbf{E}^*[M(t)^2]$ as

$$\mathbf{E}^*[M(t)^2] \;=\; \frac{S(t)^2}{(N+1)^2}\, e^{-2\xi(g+1/2\sigma^2)b}(A_1 - A_2 + A_3 - A_4),$$

where

$$A_1 = \frac{e^{(2g+\sigma^2)b} - e^{(2g+\sigma_{2)(}^{}\,{}_{\;\;-}^{N}\,{}^{m}_{\;\;+1)}^{h}}}{(1-e^{gb})(1-e^{(2g+\sigma^2)b})},$$

$$A_2 = \frac{e^{[g(N-m+2)+\sigma^2]b} - e^{(2g+\sigma^2)(N-m+1)b}}{(1-e^{gb})(1-e^{(g+\sigma^2)b})},$$

$$A_3 = \frac{e^{(3g+\sigma_{2)}^{}{}^{h}} - e^{[g(N-m+2)+\sigma^2]b}}{(1-e^{gb})(1-e^{(g+\sigma^2)b})},$$

$$A_4 = \frac{e^{2(2g+\sigma^2)b} - e^{(2g+\sigma^2)(N-m+1)b}}{(1-e^{(g+\sigma^2)b})(1-e^{(2g+\sigma^2)b})}.$$

For $t < t_0$

$$\mathbf{E}^*[M(t)^2] \;=\; \frac{S(t)^2}{(N+1)^2}\, e^{(2g+\sigma^2)(t_0-t)}(B_1 - B_2 + B_3 - B_4),$$

where

$$B_1 = \frac{1 - e^{(2g+\sigma^2)(N+1)b}}{(1-e^{gb})(1-e^{(2g+\sigma^2)b})},$$

$$B_2 = \frac{e^{g(N+1)b} - e^{(2g+\sigma^2)(N+1)b}}{(1-e^{gb})(1-e^{(g+\sigma^2)b})},$$

$$B_3 = \frac{e^{gb} - e^{g(N+1)b}}{(1-e^{gb})(1-e^{(g+\sigma^2)b})},$$

$$B_4 = \frac{e^{(2g+\sigma^2)b} - e^{(2g+\sigma^2)(N+1)b}}{(1-e^{(g+\sigma^2)b})(1-e^{(2g+\sigma^2)b})}.$$

Finally, for $t \geq t_0$, $\mathbf{E}^*[A(t_N)S(t_N)]$ can be found as follows

$$
\begin{aligned}
\mathbf{E}^*[A(t_N)S(t_N)] &= \frac{m+1}{N+1}A(t)\mathbf{E}^*[S(t_N)] + \frac{1}{N+1}\sum_{i=m+1}^{N}\mathbf{E}^*[S(t_i)S(t_N)]\\
&= \frac{m+1}{N+1}A(t)S(t)e^{g(N-m-\xi)b} + \frac{S(t)^2}{N+1}\sum_{i=1}^{N-m}e^{g(i+N-m-2\xi)b+\sigma^2(i-\xi)b}\\
&= \frac{m+1}{N+1}A(t)S(t)e^{g(N-m-\xi)b}\\
&\quad + \frac{S(t)^2}{N+1}e^{g(N-m+1-2\xi)b+\sigma^2(1-\xi)b}\left[\frac{1-e^{(g+\sigma^2)(N-m)b}}{1-e^{(g+\sigma^2)b}}\right].
\end{aligned}
$$

REFERENCES

Barakat, Richard, 'Sums of Independent Lognormally Distributed Random Variables,' *Journal of the Optical Society of America,* March 1976, **66:** 211-216.

Bergman, Yaacov Z., 'Pricing Path Contingent Claims,' in Haim Levy, ed., *Research in Finance,* Vol. 5, JAI Press Inc., 1985, 229-241.

Carverhill, Andrew P., and Les J. Clewlow, 'Flexible Convolution,' *Risk,* April 1990, **3:** 25-29.

Cox, John C., and Stephen A. Ross, 'The Valuation of Options for Alternative Stochastic Processes,' *Journal of Financial Economics,* September 1976, **3:** 145-166.

Fenton, Lawrence F., 'The Sum of Log-Normal Probability Distributions in Scatter Transmission Systems,' *IRE Transactions on Communications Systems,* March 1960, **CS-8:** 57-67.

Garman, Mark B., and Steven W. Kohlhagen, 'Foreign Currency Option Values,' *Journal of International Money and Finance,* December 1983, **2:** 231-237.

Grabbe, J. Orlin, 'The Pricing of Call and Put Options on Foreign Exchange,' *Journal of International Money and Finance,* December 1983, **2:** 239-253.

Hamdan, M. A., 'The Logarithm of the Sum of Two Correlated Log-normal Variates,' *Journal of the American Statistical Association,* March 1971, **66:** 105-106.

Janos, William A., 'Tail of the Distribution of Sums of Log-Normal Variates,' *IEEE Transactions on Information Theory,* May 1970, **IT-16:** 299-302.

Kemna, A. G. Z., and A. C. F. Vorst, 'A Pricing Method for Options Based on Average Asset Values,' *Journal of Banking and Finance,* March 1990, **14:** 113-129.

Levy, Edmond, 'Asian Arithmetic,' *Risk,* May 1990, **3:** 7-8.

Madansky, Albert, *Prescriptions for Working Statisticians,* Springer-Verlag New York Inc., 1988.

Margrabe, William, 'The Value of an Option to Exchange One Asset for Another,' *Journal of Finance,* March 1978, **33:** 177-186.

Marlow, N. A., 'A Normal Limit Theorem for Power Sums of Independent Random Variables,' *Bell System Technical Journal,* November 1967, **46:** 2081-2089.

Nasell, I. E. O., 'Some Properties of Power Sums of Truncated Normal Random Variables,' *Bell System Technical Journal,* November 1967, **46:** 2091-2110.

Naus, J. I., 'The Distribution of the Logarithm of the Sum of Two Log-Normal Variates,' *Journal of the American Statistical Association,* June 1969, **64:** 655-659.

Ritchken, Peter, L. Sankarasubramanian, and Anand M. Vijh, 'The Valuation of Path Dependent Contracts on the Average,' unpublished manuscript, School of Business Administration, University of Southern California, September 1990.

Ruttiens, Alain, 'Classical Replica,' *Risk,* February 1990, **3:** 33-36.

Schwartz, Stuart C., and Y. S. Yeh, 'On the Distribution Function and Moments of Power Sums with Log-Normal Components,' *Bell System Technical Journal,* September 1982, **61:** 1441-1462.

Turnbull, Stuart M., and Lee Macdonald Wakeman, 'A Quick Algorithm for Pricing European Average Options,' *Journal of Financial and Quantitative Analysis,* September 1991, **26:** 377-389.

Vorst, Ton, 'Analytic Boundaries and Approximations of the Prices and Hedge Ratios of Average Exchange Rate Options,' unpublished manuscript, Econometric Institute, Erasmus University Rotterdam, February 1990.

Walmsley, Julian K., *The Foreign Exchange Handbook,* New York: John Wiley, 1983.

ENDNOTES

1. Ritchken et al. (1990) have recently independently advanced a similar approach to value the ARO. Their paper does not allow for an underlying asset which pays a dividend (the foreign rate of interest for currency AROs).

2. Ritchken et al. (1990) and Carverhill and Clewlow (1990) define the average as determined in the interval $[t_0, t_N]$ but at points on this interval $t_i = t_0 + ih$ for $i = 1, \ldots, N$. Thus the first fixing is at time t_1 with $N - 1$ remaining.

3. That is, no transaction costs, unrestricted borrowing or lending at a given interest rate, and continuous trading.

4. For our purposes, it is reasonable to assume that markets are continuously arbitraged. Thus synthetic forward prices can always be constructed by appropriate positions in the foreign exchange and money markets (see, for example, Walmsley, 1983).

5. See for example, Naus (1969), Hamdan (1971), and Schwartz and Yeh (1982).

6. Garman and Kohlhagen (1983) and Grabbe (1983) examine the valuation of conventional European currency options.

7. For example, Janos (1970), Barakat (1976), and Schwartz and Yeh (1982).

8. Marlow (1967) and Nasell (1967) refer to an unpublished work in 1934 by R. I. Wilkinson at Bell Telephone Laboratories. As an alternative to (5), we could have adopted the procedure in Schwartz and Yeh (1982), who provide exact expressions for the mean and variance of the logarithm of the sum of two log normal variates. Their approach can be applied sequentially to determine more precise estimates for $\alpha(t)$ and $\nu(t)$ if needed.

9. Levy (1990) approximates $A(t_N)$ by the log normal using continuous time expressions.

10. The term $e^{-r_d \tau} \{ \mathbf{E}^*[M(t)] + A(t)(m + 1)/(N + 1) \}$ is the value at time t of the 'averaging claim' considered by Bergman (1985). Note however that, given the above argument determining the put-call parity condition, we do not require $S(t)$ to be described by an Itô process to value this claim, only that the spot rates be defined at the points where the averaging rates are collected.

11. This finding is also noted in Turnbull and Wakeman (1991).

PART SEVEN

Quantos Options and Equity Warrants with Special Currency Features

19

Understanding Guaranteed Exchange-Rate Contracts in Foreign Stock Investments

EMANUEL DERMAN
PIOTR KARASINSKI
JEFFREY S. WECKER

DEFINING THE CONTRACTS

An ordinary foreign stock forward contract is an agreement to buy a stock on a certain date at a certain delivery price in a specified currency. On the delivery date the contract's value is the difference between the stock's price and the delivery price in the foreign currency, converted to dollars at the *prevailing* spot exchange rate.

In the same way, the value on the delivery date of a *guaranteed exchange-rate forward contract* on a stock is the difference between the stock's price and the delivery price in the foreign currency, but the difference is converted to dollars at a *predetermined* exchange rate.

More formally, a guaranteed exchange-rate (GER) forward contract on a foreign stock is an agreement to receive on a certain date the stock's prevailing price in exchange for a predetermined foreign-currency delivery price, with both prices converted to dollars at a predetermined exchange rate.

Similarly, a GER call (put) option on a foreign stock gives you the right to receive (deliver) by a certain date the stock's price in exchange for a predetermined foreign-currency delivery price, with all prices converted to dollars at a predetermined exchange rate.

Payoffs for GER forward and option contracts are independent of the foreign exchange rate. Therefore the contracts allow you to capture a foreign stock's return in your own currency.

The theoretical value of a GER contract is independent of the actual value of the exchange rate at any instant during its life. But surprisingly, the contract's value *is* influenced—albeit subtly—by the expected co-variance between the exchange rate and the stock price. We explain this below.

VALUING A FORWARD CONTRACT

The Method

The GER forward is a derivative security whose dollar value depends upon the foreign-currency price of the underlying stock. As with other derivatives, the traditional way to think about the contract's value is to look at how to hedge its *dollar value* against small moves in the price of the underlying stock. Let's look at this step-by-step.

You can hedge the forward against movements in the stock's price by shorting an appropriate number of shares of the stock. But this introduces exchange-rate risk since the dollar value of the short position depends on the exchange rate. To neutralize this risk, you keep the cash proceeds of the short sale invested in the foreign currency; a move in the exchange rate alone then has an equal and opposite effect on the dollar value of the short stock and long foreign currency positions. In this way, you can set up a three-part portfolio (the GER forward, the short stock position, and the foreign currency) whose dollar value will not change if either the foreign stock price or the foreign exchange rate changes in the next instant by a small amount.

This portfolio is therefore momentarily riskless. Assuming that the market does not allow riskless arbitrage, the portfolio must instantaneously earn the U.S. riskless rate. Consequently, you can value the portfolio by discounting its expected payoff *as if* you lived in a world where all investments, whatever their risk, were expected to earn this riskless rate.[1]

Because the GER forward is part of the portfolio, you can also calculate its value as though you lived in that world. You can pretend to live in it from a mathematical point of view by adjusting the centers of the probability distributions of your risky securities at future times so that their expected returns are riskless. Then it is a straightforward matter to value the contracts by discounting their expected payoffs.

Note that we are using hedging to value the contract. We hedged the GER contract against stock price moves by taking a short position in the foreign stock. We then hedged the sensitivity of the dollar value of this foreign stock to exchange-rate moves by taking a long position in the foreign currency. Therefore, the contract's value can depend upon the *properties of the probability distribution* of the future values of the exchange rate, even though it is insensitive to the *current value* of the exchange rate.

Let's apply this method to a GER forward on a German stock. The following defines our notation:

t = time to delivery
$S(0)$ = stock price in German marks today
$S(t)$ = stock price in marks at delivery
D = continuous dividend rate of the stock
$X(t)$ = spot dollar value of the mark at delivery
K = stock's delivery price in marks
X_0 = value of the mark in dollars used to convert the GER payoffs to dollars
$F(0)$ = dollar value of the GER forward today
$S_F(t)$ = stock's GER forward price in marks
$r_\$$ = U.S. riskless interest rate
r_g = German riskless interest rate
σ_s = estimated return volatility of the stock's price in marks
σ_x = estimated return volatility of the mark's value in dollars
σ_{xs} = estimated covariance between returns of the mark in dollars and the stock price in marks
ρ_{xs} = estimated correlation coefficient $\sigma_{xs}/(\sigma_x\sigma_s)$

At delivery t years from now, the dollar value of the forward contract's payoff is

$$(S(t) - K)X_0 = S(t)X_0 - KX_0 \tag{1}$$

Notice that the payoff is converted to dollars at the guaranteed rate.

The value of the GER forward contract today, $F(0)$, is the discounted expected value of the contract's dollar payoffs in equation (1) in the simplified world where all investments are expected to earn the U.S. riskless rate $r_\$$. To calculate the expected value of equation (1), we must center the future probability distributions of the dollar value of the mark and the dollar value of the German stock so that the expected returns on these investments are $r_\$$.

Centering the Probability Distribution

We begin by assuming that the mark and the stock have lognormally distributed probability distributions at future times in the simplified world with riskless expected returns. Let the dollar value of the mark at delivery, $X(t)$, be lognormally distributed with a volatility σ_x and a mean growth rate r_x. Similarly, let the stock price in marks, $S(t)$, be lognormally distributed with volatility σ_s and a mean growth rate r_s. Initially we don't know what values to assign to the two growth rates r_x and r_s in the simplified world. But we do know that our dollar-based investments in two assets, the mark and the stock, must have mean growth rates equal to the riskless rate $r_\$$ in this world. We can use these two constraints to pin down the values of r_x and r_s.

First let's fix r_x by calculating the expected growth rate of an investment in the German mark. An investment of $X(0)$ dollars gets you one mark today which you can invest at the German riskless ratee r_g. In addition, the value of a mark in this world is expected to grow at a rate r_x. Your total dollar investment therefore grows at an expected rate $r_x + r_g$. You now need to center the mark's probability distribution by choosing r_x so that this total growth rate is $r_\$$. In other words, choose r_x so that

$$r_\$ = r_x + r_g \tag{2}$$

Therefore, you must choose the center of the probability distribution for $X(t)$ so that the growth rate r_x is

$$r_x = r_\$ - r_g \tag{3}$$

Now let's fix r_s in this world by calculating the expected growth rate of an investment in the German stock. Suppose you buy one share of the stock today by paying $S(0)X(0)$ dollars for $S(0)$ marks worth of stock converted to dollars at today's exchange rate $X(0)$. If the stock pays dividends at a continuous rate D, you can reinvest them and own e^{Dt} shares of stock at delivery, each worth $S(t)$ marks. The dollar value of your position is $e^{Dt}S(t)X(t)$. Notice that it depends upon the product of two lognormally distributed variables $S(t)$ and $X(t)$. Its expected value is

$$E[e^{Dt}S(t)X(t)] = e^{(D+r_s+r_x+\sigma_{xs})t}S(0)X(0) \tag{4}$$

where σ_{xs} is the expected covariance between the returns on the stock and the mark. σ_{xs} affects the expected value because the mean of the product of two probability distributions differs from the product of their means. As you did with the mark's distribution, you now center the $S(t)$ probability distribution by choosing r_s so that the value of your initial investment in the stock is expected to grow at the riskless rate $r_\$$ to the value $e^{r_\$ t}S(0)X(0)$. This means that the exponent in equation (4) must satisfy

$$r_\$ = D + r_s + r_x + \sigma_{xs} \tag{5}$$

You can satisfy this by centering the $S(t)$ distribution so that

$$r_s = r_\$ - r_x - D - \sigma_{xs} \tag{6}$$

You can substitute for r_x from equation (3) to show that

$$r_s = r_g - D - \sigma_{xs} \tag{7}$$

In the simplified world where we calculate option prices by discounting expected payoffs, equation (7) is the growth rate for the stock value $S(t)$ in marks.

Finding the Value

Let's summarize our results. You can find the fair dollar value of the GER forward or option by discounting the expected value of its dollar-valued payoffs at the U.S. riskless rate. However, you must center the log-normal probability distributions of the mark and the stock so that the expected return on any investment is equal to the U.S. riskless rate.

The required lognormal distribution for the mark has volatility σ_x and mean

$$E[X(t)] = X(0)e^{(r_\$ - r_g)t} \tag{8}$$

The required distribution for the stock has volatility σ_s and mean

$$E[S(t)] = S(0)e^{(r_g - D - \sigma_{xs})t} \tag{9}$$
$$= S(0)e^{(r_g - D')t} \tag{10}$$

where

$$D' = D + \sigma_{xs} \tag{11}$$

The stock price in marks is expected to grow at a rate that is reduced by D', the sum of the real dividend rate and the covariance between the returns on the mark and the stock. In this world, it's as though the stock pays out additional dividends at a rate σ_{xs}. Note, for future use, that $X_0 S(t)$ has a lognormal distribution with the same volatility as $S(t)$ and the same additional dividend rate.

Now that you know the stock's probability distribution at delivery, you can calculate today's discounted expected value of the GER forward's payout in equation (1) by using equation (10) to obtain the value

$$F(0) = E[S(t)X_0 - KX_0]e^{-r_\$ t} \tag{12}$$
$$= [S(0)X_0 e^{(r_g - D')t} - KX_0]e^{-r_\$ t} \tag{13}$$

We define the forward price $S_F(t)$ for delivery at time t as the value in marks of the GER delivery price K that makes the forward contract's value $F(0)$ equal to zero:

$$S_F(t) = S(0)e^{(r_g - D')t} \tag{14}$$

By comparing equations (10) and (14), you can see that the forward price is simply the expected value of the stock in the simplified world.

Remarks

The GER forward price in equation (14) is almost the same as that of an ordinary mark-denominated forward contract whose forward price is $S(0)e^{(r_g - D)t}$ marks. The key difference is that the GER forward price uses the effective dividend rate D' rather than the true dividend rate D. Thus, it depends upon σ_{xs} (the expected covariance of the mark's return with the stock's return in marks), even though it does not depend upon the value of the mark at any particular time during the contract's life.

Note that either an increase in r_g or a decrease in σ_{xs} causes the forward price in (14) to increase.

When the covariance is positive, D' is greater than D. In this case the forward price of the GER forward is lower than that of an ordinary (non-GER) forward contract with forward price $S(0)e^{(r_g - D)t}$ in the German market. It's as though the stock were simply paying a higher average dividend rate $D' = D + \sigma_{xs}$.

The reduced forward price for a positive covariance makes sense intuitively if you think about the following argument. A positive covariance means that, on average, the mark is expected to strengthen relative to the dollar when the stock price in marks rises. Because of this, an ordinary forward whose delivery price is specified in marks and whose payout is converted to dollars at the spot exchange rate at delivery has a greater expected dollar value than a guaranteed exchange-rate forward. So you should expect a lower forward delivery price if the exchange rate is guaranteed.

VALUING AN OPTION

You can now easily value a GER put or call with a strike price of K German marks. The payoff of the put with European-style exercise is

$$max[X_0 K - X_0 S(t), 0] \tag{15}$$

This is the same as the payoff of a put struck at KX_0 dollars on an imaginary stock whose price distribution is that of $X_0 S(t)$ with volatility σ_s and mean growth rate $r_g - D'$. The dollar value of the put P_0 is the present value of the expected payoff in equation (15):

$$P_0 = E[max[X_0 K - X_0 S(t), 0]]e^{-r_s t} \tag{16}$$

Its value is

$$P_0 = [KN(-d_2) - S(0)e^{(r_g - D')t}N(-d_1)]X_0 e^{-r_s t} \tag{17}$$

where the first term represents the probability of the put being in the money, and the second is the expected value of the stock when the put is in the money. Here $N(\ )$ is the cumulative lognormal distribution and

$$d_1 = \frac{ln(S(0)/K) + (r_g - D' + \sigma_s^2/2)t}{\sigma_s\sqrt{t}} \tag{18}$$

$$d_2 = d_1 - \sigma_s\sqrt{t} \tag{19}$$

It's easy to verify that a portfolio consisting of a long call and a short put, both struck at K marks with guaranteed exchange rate X_0, is equivalent to a GER forward and has the same value as the forward in equation (13).

American-style GER options can be valued on a binomial tree by using the standard Cox-Ross-Rubinstein method applied to a stock with price distribution given by $X_0 S(t)$, strike $X_0 K$ dollars, and dividend rate D', and then considering the possibility of early exercise at each binomial node.

AN EXAMPLE

To get a feel for the prices of GER options, and to compare them with the prices of plain foreign stock options, walk through the following example with us.

Suppose that today we write two one-year European options on a German stock: (1) a plain option whose strike and payoff are in marks; and (2) a GER option with payoff in dollars. Both options are struck at the current stock price of S marks per share. The guaranteed exchange rate X_0 is equal to the current exchange rate X.

We assume that: (1) the stock pays no dividends; (2) the annual volatility of the stock's return in marks is 20%; (3) the annual volatility of the dollar/mark exchange rate's return is 10%; and (4) the U.S. interest rate is 9% per year, continuously compounded.

We show in Table 19-1 put and call prices, as a percentage of the current stock price, for both a plain option and a GER option. We look at three continuously compounded German interest rates: 7%, 9%, and 11% per year, and at five values of the correlation coefficient ρ_{xs}.

As we noted in the "Remarks" section, an increase in German interest rates or a decrease in the correlation coefficient, all else equal, causes the GER forward price $S_F(0)$ in equation (14) to increase. As a result, the call is more likely to be in-the-money at expiration, and its price increases. Similarly, the put price decreases.

APPENDIX: AN ALTERNATIVE APPROACH

Introduction

Another way to explain the pricing of a guaranteed exchange-rate option is to use a hedging argument. With this argument we show that a GER option on

---

TABLE 19-1 Guaranteed Exchange-Rate European Option Values as a Percentage of the Underlying Stock's Price

Correlation Coefficient	$r_\$ = 9\%$ $r_g = 7\%$		$r_\$ = 9\%$ $r_g = 9\%$		$r_\$ = 9\%$ $r_g = 11\%$	
	Put	Call	Put	Call	Put	Call
1.0	5.35	10.04	4.69	11.31	4.08	12.68
0.5	5.01	10.66	4.37	11.99	3.79	13.40
0.0	4.69	11.31	4.08	12.68	3.52	14.15
−0.5	4.37	11.99	3.79	13.40	3.26	14.92
−1.0	4.08	12.68	3.52	14.15	3.02	15.71
Plain Option	4.78	11.54	4.08	12.68	3.45	13.87

one share of a German stock is equivalent to an option on one share of a three-part synthetic dollar security.

The security's price is equal to the price of a German stock in marks converted to dollars at the guaranteed exchange rate. Its price return volatility is equal to the mark price return volatility of the German stock. But its dividend payments differ from those of a German stock. We show how.

One share of this synthetic security is a portfolio consisting of positions in: (1) shares of a German stock; (2) dollars; and (3) marks. We find the exact amount of each of these three components. Once we know them, we find the amount of dividends the synthetic security pays.

In the end we have a simple recipe for pricing and hedging GER options: Using your plain stock option calculator, you find the price and delta of a plain option on the synthetic dollar security struck at the GER option strike converted to dollars at the guaranteed exchange rate. The price is your GER option price. To hedge the GER option, you short "delta" shares of the synthetic security.

Hedging a GER Option

Let **A** be a German stock whose price in marks at time t is $S(t)$. Assume it pays no dividends.

Consider a GER option on stock **A** struck at K marks per share with guaranteed exchange rate X_0 dollars per mark. Write O for the dollar price of this option. This price is independent of the current exchange rate. How can we hedge this option?

Write O_Δ for the option's dollar delta due to the change in **A**'s price in marks. When S changes by the small amount ΔS marks, the option price changes by $O_\Delta \Delta S$ dollars.

To hedge the GER option's dollar delta we short:

$$\frac{1}{X} O_\Delta$$

shares of **A**.

To hedge the exchange rate risk of the short position in stock **A** we add marks to our hedge portfolio in the amount:

$$\frac{1}{X} O_\Delta S$$

Creating the Synthetic Security

Now we construct a dollar security $\mathbf{A}_{syn}$. We want to design it so that an option on one share of $\mathbf{A}_{syn}$ struck at $X_0 K$ dollars per share has the same value as a GER option on one share of **A** struck at K marks per share with guaranteed exchange rate X_0.

For this to be true these two options must have the same intrinsic value at any point in time before expiration, for any future price behavior of **A**. Therefore the price of $\mathbf{A}_{syn}$ must always be equal to the price of $\mathbf{A}$ in marks converted to dollars at the fixed exchange rate X_0.

Write $S_{syn}(t)$ for the dollar price of $\mathbf{A}_{syn}$ at time t. It is given by:

$$S_{syn}(t) = X_0 S(t)$$

Write $O_{\Delta syn}$ for the $\mathbf{A}_{syn}$ option's dollar delta due to the change in the price of $\mathbf{A}_{syn}$. It is related to O_Δ:

$$O_\Delta = X_0 O_{\Delta syn}$$

To hedge an $\mathbf{A}_{syn}$ option, or its equivalent GER option on $\mathbf{A}$, we need to short $O_{\Delta syn}$ shares of $\mathbf{A}_{syn}$. We can obtain the same result by shorting $O_{\Delta syn}$ shares of a fund where one share represents a portfolio of:

(1) $\dfrac{X_0}{X}$ $\mathbf{A}$ shares, and   (2) $\dfrac{X_0}{X}$ S marks borrowed.

In either case we must short the same number of shares. If we hedge by shorting $\mathbf{A}_{syn}$ shares, the price is S_{syn}. If we hedge by shorting fund shares, the shares are worthless.

We can create a riskless portfolio worth S_{syn} dollars by combining one share of $\mathbf{A}_{syn}$ with a short position in one share of the fund described above. This portfolio is equivalent to a position in S_{syn} dollars. Likewise, one share of $\mathbf{A}_{syn}$ is equivalent to a portfolio composed of one share of the fund plus a position in S_{syn} dollars.

Thus we can create one share of $\mathbf{A}_{syn}$ by:

- investing $X_0 S(t)$ dollars at the U.S. interest rate;
- borrowing $X_0/X(t)S(t)$ marks at the German interest rate; and
- using the borrowed marks to buy $X_0/X(t)$ shares of stock $\mathbf{A}$.

We must adjust these three components as the price of $\mathbf{A}$ and the \$/DM exchange rate change, and as we pay and receive interest. At any point in time, the portfolio is worth $X_0 S(t)$ dollars.

Now that we've shown how to construct $\mathbf{A}_{syn}$ we can view a GER option on $\mathbf{A}$ as a plain option on $\mathbf{A}_{syn}$. To price this plain option we need the price return volatility of $\mathbf{A}_{syn}$, which, by construction, is equal to the mark price return volatility of $\mathbf{A}$. We also need to find out about $\mathbf{A}_{syn}$'s dividend payments.

The Synthetic Security's Dividends

To find $\mathbf{A}_{syn}$'s dividend payments over a short period of time, we begin by finding its total return. This total return has two components: gain due to change in price and dividend payments.

Let's find $\mathbf{A}_{syn}$'s total return over a short time period Δt as the price of $\mathbf{A}$ changes by ΔS, as the exchange rate changes by ΔX, and as we pay and receive interest. This total return is the sum of total returns on each of $\mathbf{A}_{syn}$'s three components.

The net dollar amount of the interest rate payment received over time Δt is:

$$X_0 S(t)(r_\$ - r_g)\Delta t$$

If the exchange rate changes by ΔX, the profit on the borrowed marks is:

$$-\frac{X_0}{X} S(t)\Delta X$$

The total gain on the position in stock $\mathbf{A}$ is due to the change in $\mathbf{A}$'s dollar price. This change $\Delta(XS)$ has three parts:

$$\Delta(XS) = X\Delta S + S\Delta X + \Delta X\Delta S$$

The first part is due to $\mathbf{A}$'s price change assuming a fixed exchange rate. The second part is due to a change in the exchange rate assuming a fixed mark price for $\mathbf{A}$. The third part is a cross-over term.

We find $\mathbf{A}_{syn}$'s total return by combining gains on each of its three components:

$$X_0 \Delta S + X_0 S\left\{r_\$ - r_g + \frac{1}{\Delta t}\frac{\Delta X}{X}\frac{\Delta S}{S}\right\}\Delta t$$

The first part of this total return, $X_0 \Delta S$, is due to the change in $\mathbf{A}_{syn}$'s share price. The second part is the amount of dividends paid.

Thus, over a short time period Δt, one $\mathbf{A}_{syn}$ share pays a dividend whose dollar amount is:

$$X_0 S\left\{r_\$ - r_g + \frac{1}{\Delta t}\frac{\Delta X}{X}\frac{\Delta S}{S}\right\}\Delta t$$

This dividend is the net amount of dollars taken from one $\mathbf{A}_{syn}$ share in the process of adjusting the amount of each of its three components.

Assume that the return of the mark's value in dollars and of $\mathbf{A}$'s price in marks have a joint normal probability distribution and are correlated.

The annualized volatilities of returns are σ_x for the mark's dollar price and σ_s for $\mathbf{A}$'s price. The correlation coefficient of these two returns is ρ_{sx}.

Given these assumptions, as our time interval Δt approaches zero, we obtain[2]

$$\frac{1}{\Delta t}\frac{\Delta X}{X}\frac{\Delta S}{S} = \sigma_s\sigma_x\rho_{sx}$$

Finally, we find that $\mathbf{A}_{syn}$ pays a continuous dividend at a fixed rate D_{syn}:

$$D_{syn} = r_\$ - r_g + \sigma_s\sigma_x\rho_{sx}$$

Depending on the spread between U.S. and German interest rates, and on the correlation term, this dividend rate can be positive or negative.

It's easy to extend our analysis to a dividend-paying German stock. For a stock **A** paying a continuous dividend at a fixed rate D, the corresponding synthetic dollar security $\mathbf{A}_{syn}$ pays dividends at a rate:

$$D_{syn} = D + r_\$ - r_g + \sigma_s \sigma_x \rho_{sx}$$

ENDNOTES

1. F. Black and M. Scholes, "The Pricing of Options and Corporate Liabilities," *Journal of Political Economy* 81 (May/June 1973), pp. 637–654. See also, for example, John Hull, *Options, Futures and Other Derivative Securities* (Prentice-Hall, 1989), pp 95–99.

2. For a more detailed explanation, see Hull, p. 176.

20

The Perfect Hedge: To Quanto or Not to Quanto

CHRISTOPHER D. PIROS

C an an investor completely eliminate the currency risk of an asset denominated in foreign currency? If the future value of the asset is known, then simply selling that value in the forward market will achieve a perfect hedge over the specified horizon. But if the asset has an uncertain foreign value this will not work. A perfect hedge *can* be achieved, however, by using an instrument which explicitly allows a contingent, i.e. stochastic, amount of foreign currency to be converted at a pre-specified exchange rate. Such "quantity-adjusting" arrangements are generically termed "Quantos."

Quantos were originally developed in the late 1980's to address the needs of investors who wanted to participate in the explosive rally in the Japanese stock market without being exposed to movements in the Yen. The prototypical instrument was a quanto'ed warrant with terminal payoff of the form

$$Q \, \mathrm{Max}[S^* - K^*, \, 0] \tag{1}$$

where S^* is the foreign value of a stock index, K^* the foreign currency denominated strike price, and Q is the pre-specified exchange rate expressed in the investor's domestic currency per unit of foreign currency, e.g. USD/Yen.[1] Currency conversion will occur only if the owner of the warrant chooses to exercise it. If $S^* > K^*$ the warrant is worth exercising independent of what may have happened to the market exchange rate. Otherwise the warrant expires worthless. Hence, the *domestic* currency payoff on the warrant depends only on the *foreign* currency value of the underlying asset and the pre-specified exchange rate, Q.

By design the holder of the quanto'ed warrant has a call on the foreign stock index but does not bear any currency risk. It is useful to contrast this

---

This paper expands on material presented at the 1994 North American Derivatives Summit held at Boca Raton in October 1994. Thanks are due to Richard Hawkins, Robin Stelmach, Ned Stiker, and Lorne Whiteway for helpful comments on an earlier draft.

Reprinted by permission of Christopher D. Piros, Massachusetts Financial Services, Boston, MA.

warrant with two types of warrants which do entail currency risk. The first type is simply an ordinary warrant denominated in the foreign currency. That is, its terminal payoff in the foreign currency is given by Max[S* − K*, 0]. As with the quanto'ed warrant the exercise decision is independent of the exchange rate. But the foreign currency payoff must be converted at the prevailing terminal exchange rate, X, to obtain the domestic currency payoff. The owner bears the currency risk. The second type of warrant entails a strike price, K, fixed in the domestic currency and a terminal payoff in domestic currency given by Max[XS* − K, 0]. Here the decision to exercise depends not only on the foreign currency value of the asset but also upon the exchange rate.

In the early 1990's the investor's focus shifted away from Japanese toward European bond markets. Convergence of interest rates within the European Monetary System, expectations of declining rates, and the proliferation of derivative/structured vehicles led domestic investors to venture abroad once again. But many of these investors could not manage or were prohibited from bearing currency risk. Again, the solution was to buy quanto'ed assets.

As we will see below the quanto feature can increase or decrease the value of an asset. It is probably prudent, however, for investors to assume that they will usually pay (rather than be paid) for the privilege of having a perfect hedge. Investors who cannot bear currency risk have no choice but to accept this as a cost of entering foreign markets. Should investors who can and do manage currency risk use quantos?

In order to shed light on the costs and benefits of quantos this paper examines the valuation and replication of a simple quanto'ed asset. The next section illustrates some key points in the context of a single period example with discrete price movements. Section II extends the analysis to lognormally distributed price movements in continuous time. Section III considers hedging with forward contracts as an alternative to the quanto. Simulation is used to examine the residual risk arising from standard, but imperfect, hedging techniques. The final section raises some practical reasons for preferring an imperfect hedge. An appendix presents the mathematical details of the lognormal model including useful results linking the value of a quanto'ed contingent claim directly to the value of the same claim in foreign currency terms.[2]

A SINGLE PERIOD EXAMPLE

Consider investing in a foreign asset which will take one of three possible foreign currency values at the end of the period. Corresponding to each outcome is an exchange rate for converting the foreign currency back into the domestic currency. Table 20-1 summarizes possible outcomes for a risky asset and a riskless foreign deposit. The top portion shows the outcomes in foreign currency terms while the bottom portion shows the exchange rate and the domestic currency outcomes for each of the foreign assets. In addition, the table shows the outcomes for a riskless domestic deposit and for a unit of the foreign cur-

TABLE 20-1 Possible Outcomes in Foreign and Domestic Currency Terms

| | Foreign Currency Values | | | |
	Initial Value	Outcome 1	Outcome 2	Outcome 3
Foreign Risky Asset	100	122.57	107	84.12
Foreign Deposit	100	107	107	107

| | Domestic Currency Values | | | |
	Initial Value	Outcome 1	Outcome 2	Outcome 3
Exchange Rate	1	1.0036	0.8728	1.1598
Foreign Risky Asset	100	123.01	93.39	97.56
Foreign Deposit	100	107.38	993.39	124.10
Domestic Deposit	100	107	107	107
FX Sold Forward	0	−.0036	.1272	−.1598

rency sold forward. Since the foreign and domestic interest rates are assumed to be the same in this example (compare the riskless assets) the forward exchange rate is the same as the initial spot rate, i.e. unity.

Suppose we hedge the foreign assets by selling the foreign currency forward. In particular, suppose we gross up the initial value of each asset by the foreign interest rate and sell that amount (107) forward. That is, for hedging purposes, we assume that each foreign asset earns the foreign riskless rate over the period. Table 20-2 shows the domestic currency outcomes under this strategy. As should be expected the riskless foreign deposit is perfectly hedged. Its hedged domestic currency value is the same as its foreign currency value in each possible outcome. The risky asset is not perfectly hedged. Comparing the first rows of Tables 20-1 and 20-2 shows that the hedge is exact only for the second outcome. In this case the final value of the asset assumed for hedging purposes (107) turns out to be correct. Under the first outcome the terminal value of the asset is much larger than assumed in the hedge (122.57 vs. 107) but the exchange rate does not change very much (from 1.0000 to 1.0036) so the hedge works quite well. The result is a gain of 0.06 (123.63 − 122.57) relative to a perfect hedge. Under the third outcome, however, the hedging error is quite

TABLE 20-2 Outcomes Using Simple Forward Hedge

| | Domestic Currency Values | | | |
	Initial Value	Outcome 1	Outcome 2	Outcome 3
Foreign Risky Asset	100	122.63	107	80.47
Foreign Deposit	100	107	107	107

substantial. Here the asset drops in value (from 100 to 84.12) while the exchange rate appreciates (from 1.0000 to 1.1598). The investor sold too much foreign currency forward. With an appreciating currency this results in a loss of 3.65 (84.12 − 80.47) relative to a perfect hedge.

How can we create a perfect hedge, i.e. a quanto'ed asset? We want to create an asset with *domestic* currency payoffs that are the same as the *foreign* currency payoffs of the foreign risky asset. That is, we must match the last three entries in the top row of Table 20-1 but we must do it in domestic currency terms. Basic algebra suggests that this will require at least three instruments—one for each of the three possible outcomes. We will use the risky asset, domestic deposits, and forward contracts. As shown in Table 20-3 the portfolio which creates a quanto'ed asset consists of 0.9379 units of the foreign risky asset, 0.0704 units of the domestic deposit, and a sale of 0.9336 units of the foreign currency forward. This portfolio costs 100.83 in domestic currency whereas the risky asset itself can be purchased for 100. Hence, the quanto feature costs 0.83.

It should not be surprising that the quanto feature has a positive value in this example. Recall that the simple forward hedge worked well for two of the three possible outcomes. In the third case it resulted in a substantial loss relative to a perfect hedge. The quanto eliminates that loss. Hence, it has positive value.

Note that the forward hedge failed when the underlying asset value and the exchange rate moved sharply in opposite directions. Such divergent moves always result in a loss relative to a perfect hedge. If the asset value rises and the exchange rate falls, the investor will have sold too little foreign currency forward and will be forced to sell the remainder at a weaker exchange rate. If, as in Outcome 3 above, the asset value falls while the exchange rate rises, the investor will have sold too much foreign exchange forward and will be forced to buy back the excess at a higher price. **If the foreign currency asset value and the exchange rate are negatively correlated, then, on average, they move in opposite directions and (all else the same) the quanto feature will have positive value. The converse holds if the correlation is positive.** In this case the investor would, on average, have the opportunity to sell

TABLE 20-3   Creating a Quanto'ed Asset

	Quantity	Initial Value	Outcome 1	Outcome 2	Outcome 3
			Domestic Currency Values		
Quanto Payoff			122.57	107	84.12
Replicating Portfolio					
Foreign Risky Asset	.9379	93.79	115.37	87.59	91.50
Domestic Deposit	.0704	7.04	7.53	7.53	7.53
FX Sold Forward	.9336	0.00	−0.33	11.88	−14.91
Total		**100.83**	122.57	107	84.12

additional currency at high exchange rates and buy back currency at low exchange rates. Since the quanto eliminates this profit opportunity it has a negative value.

A MORE GENERAL MODEL

Let us now assume that the value of the foreign risky asset (S*) and the exchange rate (X) have a joint lognormal distribution. Consider a general quanto with terminal payoff at time T given by

$$Qg(S^*(T)) \tag{2}$$

for some function g(). As shown in the appendix, the value, V, of this instrument must satisfy a certain partial differential equation subject to the condition that $V(S^*, T) = Q g(S^*(T))$. The appendix also shows that this instrument can be dynamically created/replicated by a portfolio containing

$$\Delta = (1/X)V_{S^*} \tag{3}$$

shares of the risky asset, [V − ΔXS*] invested in the domestic riskless asset, and [ΔS* Exp(r*τ)] units of the foreign currency sold forward τ(= T − t) years. V_{S^*} is the partial derivative of V with respect to S*.

Three aspects of the replicating portfolio should be noted. First, Δ includes an exchange rate adjustment reflecting the fact that V and S* are denominated in different currencies. Otherwise, Δ is simply analogous to an option delta. Second, the amount invested in the domestic riskless asset indicates the amount of implicit leverage in the structure. A quanto'ed call option or other levered instrument will entail a negative investment in the riskless asset, i.e. [V − ΔXS*] < 0. Third, the amount of foreign currency sold forward is equal to the foreign value of the shares held, [ΔS*], grossed up at the foreign riskless rate. Thus, the quanto entails a fully hedged position in the foreign risky asset.

Also note that, in general, three instruments are required in the replicating portfolio. There is some confusion in the literature on this point. Dravid, Richardson, and Sun (1993, p. 38) state that only two instruments—the underlying foreign asset and the domestic riskless asset—are needed to replicate a quanto since the exchange rate drops out of the valuation formula (see below). This is incorrect. A portfolio containing only the foreign risky asset and the domestic riskless asset would be subject to exchange rate risk. Such a portfolio cannot replicate a quanto. To eliminate the currency risk another foreign denominated instrument must be included in the portfolio. In theory the foreign riskless asset could be used as the third instrument rather than a forward contract. For practical purposes, however, forwards are a more natural choice since the forward market is a more cost efficient method of adjusting exposure to the foreign currency.

In order to focus clearly on the quanto feature we will restrict attention to the simplest case—a perfectly hedged version of the foreign asset itself. In this case $g(S^*) = S^*$. As shown in the appendix the value of the quanto'ed asset is given by

$$V = QS^* \mathrm{Exp}[(r^* - r - \rho\sigma_s\sigma_x)\tau] \tag{4}$$

where ρ is the correlation between the asset price and the spot exchange rate, σ_s and σ_x are the respective volatilities, and r and r* are the interest rates. Note that the exchange rate, X, does not appear in the valuation formula. This reflects the fact that the quanto feature does indeed eliminate currency risk.

A clearer understanding of the quanto's value can be obtained by using the fact that the forward exchange rate, F, is equal to $(X \exp[(r - r^*)\tau])$. Substituting into equation (4) yields

$$V = [XS^*][Q/F] \mathrm{Exp}[-\rho\sigma_s\sigma_x\tau] \tag{5}$$

This expression has three components. The first component is the domestic currency value of the underlying asset, [XS*]. All else equal, the higher this value the more the quanto'ed version of the asset is worth. The second factor is the ratio of the pre-specified exchange rate, Q, to the prevailing forward rate. Clearly, it is advantageous to have locked in a rate greater than the prevailing forward rate. The third component is an adjustment factor reflecting the correlation between the foreign asset value and the exchange rate. As discussed in the previous section a negative (positive) correlation results in a higher (lower) value for the quanto'ed asset.

The value of the quanto feature alone can be obtained by subtracting the domestic value of the unhedged asset, XS*, from equation (5). Dividing by XS* then gives the value of the quanto feature as a fraction of the unhedged asset value.

$$[Q/F] \mathrm{Exp}[-\rho\sigma_s\sigma_x\tau] - 1 \tag{6}$$

If the foreign asset and the exchange rate are uncorrelated ($\rho = 0$), the quanto feature has a positive value only if it allows currency conversion at an exchange rate exceeding the forward rate, i.e. only if Q is greater than F. If, for example, the quanto allows conversion at a rate 3% higher than the forward rate, then the quanto feature is worth 3% of the underlying asset value. This makes intuitive sense. One has sold the foreign currency forward via the quanto and could buy it back at the prevailing forward rate for 3% less.

When the foreign asset and the exchange rate are correlated the value of the quanto feature reflects not only the premium/discount relative to the forward rate but also the expected gain or loss from eliminating hedging errors. As noted in the previous section, if the exchange rate and the foreign asset value are positively correlated, a simple forward hedge tends to generate opportunities for the investor to sell excess foreign currency at high prices and/or to buy additional foreign currency at low rates. An investor would have to be paid to enter into an at-the-money (i.e. $Q = F$) quanto under these conditions. On the other hand, if the correlation is negative, an investor would be willing to pay a positive amount for an at-the-money quanto because it eliminates losses which would arise from being forced to sell excess currency at low exchange rates and buy additional currency at high exchange rates.

Table 20-4 illustrates the cost of the quanto feature as a percent of the value of the underlying asset. Reading across each row shows that the quanto increases in value by 1% as the contract exchange rate, Q, rises 1% relative to the forward, F. Reading down each column indicates that, given the assumed parameter values, the cost of the quanto increases by about 38 basis points (0.38) for each 0.25 decline in correlation. With moderately strong negative correlation of -0.5 an at-the-money quanto (Q/F $=$ 1.0) costs 75 basis points.

For the special case of a quanto'ed version of the foreign asset itself, i.e. $g(S^*) = S^*$, the replicating portfolio entails holding

$$\Delta_S = [Q/F] \; Exp[-\rho\sigma_s\sigma_x\tau] = V/(XS^*) \tag{7}$$

shares of the risky asset. The total cost of the shares is $(\Delta_S XS^*) = V$. Hence, the whole value of the quanto'ed asset is invested in the risky asset and none in the domestic riskless asset.[3] As the forward exchange rate (F) declines we must buy additional shares. This is a reflection of the fact that as the exchange rate falls the quanto gains value relative to the unhedged asset. Conversely shares must be sold as the exchange rate increases since the quanto underperforms the unhedged asset. Over time the number of shares to be held converges to unity. If correlation is positive (negative) shares will be purchased (sold) as time passes.

QUANTOS VERSUS FORWARD HEDGING

Perfect hedging requires adjusting both the number of shares held and the currency hedge. This is not, however, what portfolio managers typically do. The number of shares held is usually kept constant while the forward currency po-

TABLE 20-4   Cost of Quanto Feature: Percent of Underlying Asset Value[5]

Correlation	Ratio of Contract Exchange Rate to Forward Rate (Q/F)				
	0.98	0.99	1.00	1.01	1.02
1.00	−3.46	−2.47	−1.49	−0.50	0.48
0.75	−3.10	−2.11	−1.12	−0.13	0.86
0.50	−2.73	−1.74	−0.75	0.25	1.24
0.25	−2.37	−1.37	−0.37	0.62	1.62
0.00	−2.00	−1.00	0.00	1.00	2.00
−0.25	−1.63	−0.63	0.38	1.38	2.38
−0.50	−1.26	−0.25	**0.75**	1.76	2.77
−0.75	−0.89	0.12	1.13	2.14	3.15
−1.00	−0.52	0.50	1.51	2.53	3.54

sition is adjusted to maintain the desired degree of hedging. Thus a "fully hedged" portfolio is subject to some degree of slippage.

How much slippage is induced by failure to adjust the position in the underlying asset? Is simple forward hedging an effective substitute for purchasing (or creating) a quanto? Table 20-5 summarizes a set of simulations designed to address these questions. One thousand sequences of 365 daily asset prices and exchange rates were generated from a joint lognormal distribution. The asset price and exchange rate have 15% and 10% volatilities, respectively, and a -0.5 correlation. Results are shown for eight simulations which differ in two respects: the frequency of hedge adjustment (1, 7, 14, or 28 day intervals) and whether the underlying asset position is adjusted along with the currency hedge.[4] Slippage due to imperfect hedging is measured as the difference between the terminal value of the simulated position and the ending value of the underlying asset converted at the initial forward rate, i.e. a quanto'ed asset with $Q = F$. In the table this error is expressed as a percent of the initial asset value.

The top half of the table shows the slippage arising from dynamic replication of the quanto'ed asset, i.e. adjusting both the underlying asset position and the forward hedge as specified in the previous section. As shown in the first column the quanto'ed asset is replicated quite well on average even if the hedge positions are only adjusted every 28 days. The mean error with monthly adjustment is only -0.03% while weekly or daily adjustment is virtually perfect on average. The dispersion of outcomes around the mean declines sharply as we move from monthly to daily rebalancing. The standard deviation drops from 0.53% to 0.10%. Similarly, the range of outcomes for daily adjustment (-0.40, 0.26) is much tighter than for monthly rebalancing (-2.60, 1.15). Thus, while slippage cannot be completely eliminated, frequent rebalancing results in very accurate replication.

TABLE 20-5 Hedging Error as a Percent of Underlying Asset Value

Hedge Frequency (Days)	Adjusting FX and Underlying Positions			
	Mean	Standard Deviation	Maximum	Minimum
28	−0.03	0.53	1.15	−2.60
14	−0.02	0.37	0.86	−1.39
7	0.00	0.27	0.76	−1.07
1	0.00	0.10	0.26	−0.40
	Adjusting FX Position Only			
28	−0.81	1.21	3.34	−9.18
14	−0.81	1.18	3.05	−8.24
7	−0.79	1.17	2.44	−8.10
1	−0.79	1.16	2.48	−8.14

The bottom part of the table reports the results obtained by adjusting only the forward currency hedge position. One share of the underlying asset is held at all times. Otherwise the procedure is the same as for the full replication strategy. On average this approach underperforms the quanto'ed asset by about 0.80% for each rebalancing frequency. Note that this is roughly the value of the quanto feature given the assumed parameter values (Table 20-4 shows a value of 0.75%). Unfortunately the dispersion of outcomes does not shrink much as we increase the frequency of hedge adjustment. The standard deviation of the error is 1.16% even for daily rebalancing. The range of errors is quite wide and the distribution of errors is heavily skewed toward underperformance. With daily adjustment the strategy underperformed by as much as 8.14% and outperformed by as much as 2.48%.

These simulations indicate that the average cost of hedging is about the same with or without a quanto. Buying the quanto feature entails an initial payment. Dynamic replication achieves the same result. Forward hedging alone avoids the upfront payment but, on average, this advantage is just offset by slippage on the hedge. Thus, based solely on *expected* outcomes forward hedging alone is an effective substitute for buying the quanto feature. But it clearly entails substantial risk of underperformance. In principle, a risk averse investor should therefore prefer a fairly priced quanto to the alternative of forward hedging.

TO QUANTO OR NOT TO QUANTO

The appeal of a perfect hedge is obvious. So why *not* quanto?

In setting the price at which to offer a quanto a dealer will charge a risk premium to compensate for potential slippage in creating the quanto. The potential error, and hence the risk premium, may be substantial if: (1) transaction costs prevent frequent adjustment of the hedge positions, (2) gap moves occur in the underlying asset value and/or exchange rate, or (3) the correlation between asset price and exchange rate is unstable. Of course the dealer will also build in a profit margin. Hence, some investors may prefer to bear the risk of an imperfect hedge rather than pay the dealer's asking price for a perfect hedge.

The fixed time horizon inherent in a quanto provides a second reason for eschewing it. A quanto provides a perfect hedge only over the pre-specified horizon. Unwinding a quanto early exposes the investor to potentially adverse changes in parameter values. In particular, an increase in correlation will decrease the value of the quanto feature. A sufficiently large increase in correlation would require the investor to *pay* to get rid of a previously valuable quanto! Thus the quanto loses some of its appeal if, as is usually the case for active managers, the holding period of the underlying asset is uncertain.

Quantos combine a currency decision (full hedging) with an investment in the underlying asset. Suppose an investor changes his mind about hedging after buying the quanto'ed asset. That is, the underlying asset is still attractive but now so is the foreign currency. The quanto could be sold and replaced with the unhedged asset but this could entail substantial transaction costs. Alternatively, currency exposure could be added by simply taking a long forward position in the foreign currency. But this means retaining an unnecessary perfect hedge and hence wasting the quanto's remaining "time value." Either way the investor is likely to incur costs which would not have arisen if the original hedge had been done with a simple forward contract. Hence, unless hedging is a once-and-for-all decision it may be preferable to accept an imperfect hedge in exchange for flexibility in hedging decisions.

It may make sense to quanto some assets but not others. For example, if investment policy calls for a fully hedged position in certain "core" assets it could make sense to quanto these assets even if, for the reasons discussed above, more actively managed assets are not quanto'ed. In general, however, one must question the rationale for quanto'ing a particular asset, e.g. a structured note, if the bulk of the portfolio is exposed to currency risk through unhedged and/or imperfectly hedged positions.

So, should you quanto? As with most risk/return tradeoffs, there is no universal prescription. Each investor must weigh the costs and benefits.

APPENDIX: MATHEMATICS OF THE LOGNORMAL MODEL

The dynamics of the foreign risky asset price and the exchange rate are given by

$$dS^* = \mu_s S^* dt + \sigma_s S^* dZ_s \tag{A1}$$

$$dX = \mu_x X dt + \sigma_x X dZ_x \tag{A2}$$

where $E\{dZ_s dZ_x\} = \rho$. By Itô's Lemma[6] the domestic currency value of the foreign risky asset, $S = XS^*$, follows

$$dS = (\mu_s + \mu_x + \rho\sigma_x\sigma_s)Sdt + \sigma_s SdZ_s + \sigma_x SdZ_x \tag{A3}$$

For simplicity we assume that foreign and domestic interest rates are constant. The value of domestic and foreign bank accounts, denoted by B and B* respectively, evolve according to

$$dB = rBdt \tag{A4}$$

$$dB^* = r^* B^* dt \tag{A5}$$

The (domestic currency) value of a forward contract to deliver, at time T, one unit of the foreign currency versus the domestic currency at an exchange rate of X_f is

$$V_{fwd} = (X_f - F) \exp[-r\tau] \tag{A6}$$

where F, the current forward exchange rate, is given by

$$F = X \exp[(r - r^*)\tau] \tag{A7}$$

and $\tau = (T - t)$. Note that equation (A6) states the value of the forward contract from the perspective of an investor who is short the foreign currency. Applying Itô's Lemma implies that this value evolves according to

$$dV_{fwd} = rV_{fwd}dt - \exp(-r\tau)\{(\mu_x - r + r^*)Fdt + \sigma_x FdZ_x\} \tag{A8}$$

Consider a general quanto with terminal payoff at time T given by $[Qg(S^*(T))]$. Q is the exchange rate at which currency conversion, if any, will take place. The stochastic amount of currency to be converted is given by the function $g(S^*)$. Let $V = V(S^*, t)$ be the domestic currency value of this asset at time $t \leq T$. Clearly, $V(S^*, T) = Qg(S^*(T))$. Applying Itô's Lemma implies that the dynamics of V are given by

$$dV = [V_t + V_{S^*}\mu_S S^* + (1/2)V_{S^*S^*}\sigma_S^2 S^{*2}]dt + V_{S^*}\sigma_S S^* dZ_s \tag{A9}$$

where V_t, V_{S^*}, and $V_{S^*S^*}$ are partial derivatives. Note that V depends on the foreign asset price but not on the exchange rate. Since its terminal (and only) payoff is independent of the market exchange rate the value at earlier times, $t < T$, is also independent of the prevailing exchange rate. This is consistent with the fact that the purpose of the quanto feature is to remove currency risk.

Two different, but equivalent, approaches can be used to derive the partial differential equation which must be satisfied by the value of the quanto, V. The first approach makes use of the fact that in the absence of arbitrage opportunities asset price ratios must be martingales. The second approach is to show that the quanto can be replicated by a portfolio. This approach is more cumbersome but has the advantage of providing the replicating portfolio as a by-product. Both approaches will be shown here—the first to obtain the partial differential equation and the second to obtain the replicating portfolio.

A key result of modern financial theory is that in the absence of arbitrage there exists a probability distribution (the "risk neutral distribution") under which the ratio of any two asset prices denominated in the same currency must be a martingale. That is, the expected change in these ratios must be zero. For present purposes it suffices to impose this condition on three ratios: (V_{fwd}/B), (XS^*/B), and (V/B). This is done by applying Ito's Lemma to each ratio and setting the resulting drift term equal to zero. This yields the following conditions

$$(V_{fwd}/B) \text{ a martingale} \Rightarrow \mu_x = r - r^* \tag{A10}$$

$$(XS^*/B) \text{ a martingale} \Rightarrow \mu_s = r^* - \rho\sigma_x\sigma_s \tag{A11}$$

$$(V/B) \text{ a martingale} \Rightarrow rV = V_t + V_{S^*}(r^* - \rho\sigma_x\sigma_s)S^* + (1/2)V_{S^*S^*}\sigma_S^2 S^{*2} \tag{A12}$$

The last of these conditions, (A12), is the partial differential equation which V must satisfy subject to the boundary condition $V(S^*, T) = Qg(S^*(T))$.

Now consider forming a portfolio containing $\Delta = [(1/X)V_{S^*}]$ shares of the foreign asset, $[V - \Delta S]$ units of the domestic bank account, and $[\Delta S^* \text{Exp}(r^*\tau)]$ units of the foreign currency sold forward at the prevailing forward rate (i.e. $X_f = F$). The cost of this portfolio is V. We want to show that it replicates the quanto. Suppose we buy the portfolio and finance it by selling the quanto. Over the next instant the value of the position changes by

$$\Delta dS + [V - \Delta S]rdt + [\Delta S^* \text{ Exp}(r^*\tau)]dV_{fwd} - dV$$
$$= \Delta\{(\mu_s + \mu_x + \rho\sigma_x\sigma_s)Sdt + \sigma_sSdZ_s + \sigma_xSdZ_x\} + (V - \Delta S)r$$
$$- [\Delta S^* \text{ Exp}((r^* - r)\tau)]\{(\mu_x - r + r^*)Fdt + \sigma_xFdZ_x\}$$
$$- [V_t + V_{s^*}\mu_sS^* + (1/2)V_{s^*s^*}\sigma_s^2S^{*2}]dt + V_{s^*}\sigma_sS^*dZ_s$$
$$= [rV - V_t - (r^* - \rho\sigma_x\sigma_s)V_{s^*}S^* - (1/2)V_{s^*s^*}\sigma_s^2S^{*2}]dt \qquad (A13)$$

Since the stochastic terms drop out this is a riskless position. Absence of arbitrage requires that a zero cost, riskless position neither gains nor loses value over time. Setting the change equal to zero yields the same partial differential equation as before. Since V satisfies this differential equation the specified portfolio does replicate the quanto.

To obtain the value of the quanto, V, we must solve the partial differential equation derived above. In many interesting cases it is possible to obtain the solution directly from the value of a foreign currency denominated asset. Let $h(S^*, t)$ be the value of a contingent claim denominated in the foreign currency. If $h(S^*, t)$ satisfies

$$r^*h = h_t + r^*S^*h_{s^*} + (1/2)h_{s^*s^*}\sigma_s^2S^{*2} \qquad (A14)$$

subject to $h(S^*, T) = g(S^*(T))$, then

$$V(S^*, t) = Q\Phi(\tau)h[\Theta(\tau)S^*, t] \qquad (A15)$$

where

$$\Phi(\tau) = \text{Exp}[(r^* - r)\tau] \qquad (A16)$$

$$\Theta(\tau) = \text{Exp}[-\rho\sigma_x\sigma_x\tau] \qquad (A17)$$

This result can be verified by direct substitution into the differential equation for V. Thus, if we know the value of a contingent claim denominated in the foreign currency we can obtain the value of the corresponding quanto simply by applying the transformation given in equations (A15)–(A17).

This transformation can be understood by separating it into two parts. Multiplying $h(S^*, t)$ by Q converts the value of the claim to the domestic currency. But Q is really a *forward* exchange rate since it applies at the expiration of the quanto. The corresponding "spot" rate is $[Q\Phi(\tau)]$. Hence, the first step in the transformation is to multiply the value of the foreign denominated claim by this spot exchange rate. The second step adjusts the underlying asset value, S^*, to reflect an implicit dividend yield paid continuously at the rate $(\rho\sigma_x\sigma_s)$. This dividend yield arises from the interaction of the foreign asset price and the exchange rate. If $\rho > 0$, exchange rate movements tend to reinforce the performance of the foreign asset in domestic currency terms. Conversely, the performance tends to be mitigated if $\rho < 0$. Replacing S^* with $[\Theta(\tau)S^*]$ as in equation (A15) takes account of the implicit dividend yield.

Two instruments of particular interest are priced below.

Case I: Quanto'ed Version of the Foreign Risky Asset

The foreign currency value of the foreign risky asset is simply S^*. Formally we have

$$h(S^*, t) = g(S^*) = S^* \tag{A18}$$

Applying the transformation in equations (A15)–(A17) yields the value of the quanto'ed asset.

$$V(S^*, t) = QS^* \, \text{Exp}[(r^* - r - \rho\sigma_x\sigma_s)\tau] \tag{A19}$$

Case 2: Quanto'ed European Call Option

The terminal payoff for a foreign currency denominated call option on the foreign risky asset is given by

$$g(S^*) = \text{Max}[S^* - K^*, 0] \tag{A20}$$

The value of this option, in foreign currency, is given by the standard Black-Scholes formula. That is

$$h(S^*, t) = S^*N(d) - K^* \exp(-r^*\tau)N(d - \sigma_s\sqrt{\tau})$$
$$\text{where} \quad d = [\text{Ln}(S^*/K^*) + (r + .5\sigma_s^2)\tau]/[\sigma_s\sqrt{\tau}] \tag{A21}$$

Applying the transformation gives the value of a quanto'ed call.

$$V(S^*, t) = Q \, \text{Exp}(-r\tau)\{S^* \, \text{Exp}[(r^* - \rho\sigma_x\sigma_s)\tau]N(b) - K^*N(b - \sigma_s\sqrt{\tau})\}$$
$$\text{where} \quad b = d - \rho\sigma_x\sqrt{\tau} \tag{A22}$$

REFERENCES

Astrom, K. J. *Introduction to Stochastic Control Theory.* New York: Academic Press, 1970.

Dravid, Ajay, Matthew Richardson, and Tong-sheng Sun. "Pricing Foreign Index Contingent Claims: An Application to Nikkei Index Warrants." *Journal of Derivatives,* 1 (Fall 1993), pp. 33–51.

ENDNOTES

1. Following common convention, a superscript * indicates that the variable is denominated in the foreign currency. Throughout the paper, exchange rates are stated in domestic currency per unit of foreign currency.

2. These results are probably known to those who develop quanto pricing models at dealer firms. To my knowledge, however, they have never been published. The appendix makes them accessible to investors for the first time.

3. This is a special case in which only two instruments are needed in the replicating portfolio. Note, however, that it is the domestic riskless asset which drops out and not, as suggested by Dravid et. al., the forward hedge. One might be tempted to say that only one instrument, the hedged foreign asset, is needed. However, this implicitly assumes that the foreign asset can be traded on a hedged basis. In general this is not the case. Hence, the foreign asset and the forward hedge are distinct positions.

4. The same sequence of asset prices and exchange rates was used in each run. Hence, differences in the degree of slippage are not due to different sample paths. Simulations were also run with correlation of $+0.5$. The results were qualitatively the same.

5. The parameter assumptions are $\tau = 1.0$, $\sigma_S = .15$, $\sigma_X = .10$.

6. See Astrom (1970, p. 74) for a statement of Itô's Lemma.

21

Pricing Foreign Index Contingent Claims: An Application to Nikkei Index Warrants

AJAY DRAVID
MATTHEW RICHARDSON
TONG-SHENG SUN

G lobalization of capital markets continues. Beyond well-established global links through currency and bond markets, equity and derivative markets have become internationalized.

Many foreign stocks are traded on the New York Stock Exchange (NYSE), either directly or through American Depository Receipts (ADRs), and the equities of several U.S. firms are listed on exchanges abroad. Trading in Nikkei Stock Average index futures began on the Singapore International Monetary Exchange (SIMEX) in September 1986, while put warrants on the Nikkei index have been traded on the Toronto Stock Exchange since February 1989.[1] Since then, put and call warrants and futures contracts on Japanese, British, and other foreign stock indexes have been introduced on the American Stock Exchange (AMEX) and other U.S. exchanges.

Pricing of these foreign stock index derivative securities, known to practitioners as *quantos,* presents some complications. In particular, the payoffs to

The authors thank Kobi Boudoukh, Jack Glen, Chris Leach, Angelo Melino, Sanjiv Sharma, Suresh Sundaresan, and especially David Bates, Bruce Grundy, and Peter Carr for helpful comments and discussion. We also thank Milind Shrikhande, Ryan Wierck, and Ching Wang for their capable research assistance, and Tom McCusker for providing data and helpful comments. An earlier version of this article titled "Options on Two Risky Assets: Nikkei Index Warrants" received the American Association of Individual Investors Award for Best Paper on Investments at the June 1992 WFA Meetings. Support from the Weiss Center for International Research at the Wharton School and the Columbia Futures Center is gratefully acknowledged.

these securities are contingent on two assets—the foreign stock index and the exchange rate.

Consider, for example, warrants written on the Nikkei index currently traded on the AMEX.[2] For these warrants, both the strike price and the underlying asset (the Nikkei index) are denominated in the foreign currency (yen). Clearly, the yen payoff to these warrants depends on the level of the Nikkei index. At the same time, the domestic currency (U.S. dollar) payoffs are calculated by converting these yen payoffs at some yen/dollar exchange rate. Thus the dollar prices of the warrants depend on the exact specification of this exchange rate, which generally involves the spot exchange rate prevailing on the payoff date. We call these "flexible-rate options." Other traded warrants specify a fixed exchange rate at which the payoff is to be converted. These are termed "fixed-rate options." This additional dependence on the exchange rate makes pricing and hedging these contingent claims an interesting issue.

This article makes several contributions. We derive partial differential equations (PDEs) for general contingent claims and describe a test methodology to evaluate pricing models for such contingent claims. Prices of fixed-rate options are shown to be independent of the current level of the exchange rate, but to depend on the parameters of the exchange rate dynamics. Prices of flexible-rate warrants depend on the current level of the exchange rate, but are independent of exchange rate dynamics.

Our replicating options portfolios for American and European options are different in terms of their riskless borrowing or lending component. Predicted prices for the American warrants on the Nikkei index can be obtained by numerically solving the appropriate PDE for comparison to observed prices.[3]

CONTINGENT CLAIMS ON FOREIGN INDEXES

The dollar payoff to a contingent claim on a foreign index depends on the prices of two assets: the underlying foreign index and the exchange rate. We derive the general partial differential equation for this case and describe an empirical estimation methodology for testing the ensuing model prices.

The General Partial Differential Equation

Following the usual convention, we use an asterisk to identify all foreign currency-denominated variables. Hence, let S_t^* denote the price at time t of the underlying asset, i.e., the foreign index, and Y_t the spot exchange rate specified in dollars per unit of the foreign currency. Define the dollar price of the underlying asset by $S_t \equiv S_t^* Y_t$. Suppose that r_t and r_t^* are the instantaneous U.S. and foreign interest rates, and δ_t is the instantaneous proportional dividend payout rate of the underlying asset.

As shown by Cox and Ross [1976], and more rigorously by Harrison and Kreps [1979], under the risk-neutral probability (or the martingale measure), for U.S. investors S_t, Y_t, and S_t^* must satisfy the stochastic differential equations:

$$dS = (r - \delta)Sdt + \sigma_H, SdZ^{(s^*)} + \sigma_y SdZ^{(y)} \tag{1}$$

$$dY = (r - r^*)Ydt + \sigma_y YdZ^{(y)} \tag{2}$$

$$dS^* = (r^* - \delta - \rho\sigma_{s^*}\sigma_y)S^*dt + \sigma_s S^*dZ^{(s^*)} \tag{3}$$

where σ_s, and σ_y are the instantaneous volatilities of the underlying asset and the exchange rate, and $Z^{(s^*)}$ and $Z^{(y)}$ are two standard Brownian motions with correlation coefficient ρ.[4]

Under the risk-neutral probability, for U.S. investors, the expected dollar rate of return on any asset traded in the U.S., including S_t, must equal the U.S. riskless interest rate r. In order to apply this argument to S_t, we must first assume that international capital markets are frictionless. Consequently, although the dollar price of the foreign index is not directly traded in the U.S., investors here can trade it indirectly through the currency market and the foreign stock market.

More specifically, to invest in the dollar price of the foreign index S_t, U.S. investors first convert S_t dollars into the quantity S_t/Y_t of foreign currency, which they invest in the foreign index. In such frictionless international capital markets, under the risk-neutral probability, the expected dollar rate of return on S_t must equal the U.S. riskless interest rate.

Similarly, the expected dollar rate of return on Y_t must also be r under the risk-neutral probability. To invest in the foreign currency, U.S. investors first convert dollars into foreign currency and then invest in riskless foreign bonds. The instantaneous mean in Equation (2) for Y_t reflects the fact that dollars converted into foreign currency are held in riskless foreign bonds and pay interest at the rate of r^*.

By way of contrast, the expected *foreign currency* rate of return on S_t^* for U.S. investors does not equal r because the underlying asset is not denominated in dollars. For foreign investors, the expected rate of return on S_t^* will be the foreign riskless interest rate r'' under the risk-neutral probability. For U.S. investors, however, the expected rate of return on S_t^* is generally not t^* and is subject to exchange rate risk because U.S. dollars are the numeraire.

The instantaneous return on the dollar price S_t is the sum of the instantaneous returns on the foreign index S_t^* and the foreign currency Y_t, adjusted by the covariance between the foreign index and the foreign currency.[5] Other things being equal, the return on the dollar price will be higher (lower) when the correlation between the foreign index and the foreign currency is positive (negative). U.S. investors concerned only with dollar returns are therefore willing to accept a lower foreign currency return on S_t^* when the correlation is positive, while requiring a higher return when the correlation is negative.

In this sense, we can say that the negative of the covariance between the exchange rate and the underlying foreign stock is a measure of the "currency premium" demanded by U.S. investors who consume in dollars. When the foreign currency and the foreign index are not correlated, U.S. investors do not demand this currency premium, and the expected dollar rate of return on the underlying foreign asset will be the foreign riskless interest rate.[6]

Note that these conclusions are valid under very general assumptions about asset price dynamics, as long as the stochastic volatilities and interest rates satisfy certain regularity conditions. In order to perform simple empirical tests of our model and to provide some intuition for the results that follow, however, we make standard Black-Scholes [1973] assumptions henceforth. Specifically, we assume that the instantaneous variances, covariance, dividend payout rate, and both domestic and foreign interest rates are known and constant. Further, when estimating the parameters, we also assume that the instantaneous means are constant so that both the underlying foreign stock index and the exchange rate follow geometric Brownian motions.

Let $F(S_t^*, Y_t, \tau)$ be the price at time t of a contingent claim expiring at time $t + \tau$ with payoff based on the foreign currency price of the underlying and the exchange rate between t and $t + \tau$. By the standard technique of using the contingent claim, the foreign index, and the foreign riskless bond to construct a riskless hedge portfolio, it can be shown that F must satisfy the fundamental three-variable PDE.[7]

$$-\frac{\partial F}{\partial \tau} + \frac{1}{2}\sigma_{S^*}^2 S^{*2}\frac{\partial^2 F}{\partial S^{*2}} + \frac{1}{2}\sigma_y^2 Y^2 \frac{\partial^2 F}{\partial Y^2} + \rho\sigma_{S^*}\sigma_y S^* Y \frac{\partial^2 F}{\partial S^* \partial Y}$$
$$+ (r^* - \delta - \rho\sigma_{S^*}\sigma_y)S^* \frac{\partial F}{\partial S^*} + (r - r^*)Y\frac{\partial F}{\partial Y} - rF = 0. \qquad (4)$$

The boundary conditions of the PDE are specified according to the contractual provisions of the contingent claim to be priced. In general, numerical techniques must be employed to solve the PDE. If the contingent claim's payoff depends only on the foreign currency price of the index and the exchange rate at time $t + \tau$, however, it is possible to derive a closed-form pricing formula (as is the case for European options and forward contracts).

Under the risk-neutral probability, the dollar price of a European contingent claim will equal its expected payoff at expiration discounted at the U.S. risk-free rate. More specifically,

$$F(S_t^*, Y_t, \tau) = e^{-r\tau}E_t[F(S_{t+\tau}^*, Y_{t+\tau})$$

where $E_t[\cdot]$ is the conditional expectation at time t with respect to the risk-neutral probability. We can use properties of bivariate normal random variables to evaluate this conditional expectation since the solutions to Equations (2) and (3) are (see, e.g., Arnold [1974, Theorem 8.4.2]):

$$Y_{t-\tau} = Y_t \exp\left[\left(r - r^* - \frac{\sigma_y^2}{2}\right)\tau + \sigma_y(Z_{t+\tau}^{(y)} - Z_t^{(y)})\right] \qquad (5)$$

$$S_{t+\tau}^* = S_t^* \exp\left[\left(r^* - \delta - \rho\sigma_{S^*}\sigma_y - \frac{\sigma_{S^*}^2}{2}\right)\tau + \sigma_{S^*}(Z_{t+\tau}^{(S^*)} - Z_t^{(S^*)})\right] \qquad (6)$$

Estimation Methodology

Testing whether a contingent claim pricing model explains observed prices is tantamount to checking whether the values (numerical or analytical) predicted by the model are equal to observed prices in a statistical sense. For example, consider the Nikkei index warrants traded on the AMEX. Because these options are American, we need to substitute values for the parameters and solve the PDEs, thereby obtaining model values for the option prices. The difficulty with this approach is that some of the model parameters are not observable.

In general, the pricing equations resulting from (4) involve three unobservable parameters: σ_{s^*}, the Nikkei index volatility; σ_y, the exchange rate volatility; and ρ, the correlation between these variables. Because these parameters are estimated with error, the model prices will also be affected by estimation errors. It is still possible to test deviations between the model and the actual prices using the maximum likelihood methodology developed in Lo [1986].

Using this method, we can construct confidence bands around the model prices, and check whether observed prices lie within these bands.[8] This procedure has a number of advantages. First, the tests can be performed on any particular date with a single contingent claim price observation. This is important because foreign index derivatives started trading fairly recently, and long independent time series of observed prices are not available.

Second, the methodology does not require analytical solutions. The partial derivatives and function values needed are simply evaluated numerically. Thus, model prices of complex securities like American put warrants on the Nikkei index can be statistically compared to the observed prices of these securities.

FOREIGN INDEX OPTIONS

For options on a foreign index, both the strike price and the underlying asset are denominated in the foreign currency. Clearly, the payoffs to these options depend on the level of the index relative to the strike price. The corresponding domestic currency payoffs are obtained by converting the foreign currency payoffs at one of two possible exchange rates according to the terms of the option contract.

Payoffs on "flexible-rate" options are converted at the spot exchange rate prevailing on the payoff date. In this case, the dollar payoff to the option buyer depends not only on the level of the foreign index, but also on the exchange rate on the exercise date. Holding such an option is therefore equivalent to holding a position in the foreign currency as well as the foreign stock index.

A "fixed-rate" option contract specifies a fixed exchange rate at which option payoffs can be converted into the domestic currency. Although it appears that the payoff and hence the price of such options should be independent of the exchange rate, this is not necessarily the case. While the level of the exchange rate does not come into the picture, the covariance between the exchange rate and the underlying foreign stock index is found to be a determinant of the option price.

By specifying the appropriate boundary conditions, we first derive the prices of fixed-rate and flexible-rate European options. Traded options are almost always American rather than European, so we discuss numerical solutions for American options using the general PDE with the appropriate boundary conditions.

We obtain an interesting simplification of the PDE in both cases: the exchange rate drops out so that the PDE involves two variables rather than three. This result also implies that the replicating portfolios for both types of options will contain only two assets rather than three. Finally, we study the sensitivity of prices to the option parameters, and compare them to the well-known standard Black-Scholes results.

Flexible-Rate and Fixed-Rate Option Prices

We consider first flexible-rate options, whose dollar payoffs depend on the spot exchange rate prevailing on the expiration date. Under the risk-neutral probability, the dollar value of the option today is its expected dollar payoff at expiration, discounted at the U.S. risk-free rate. Let $c(S^*_t, Y_t, K^*, \tau)$ denote the price at time t of a flexible-rate European call option expiring at $t + \tau$ with strike price K^*, and $\Delta_c(S^*_t, Y_t, K^*, \tau)$ denote its delta, i.e.,

$$\Delta_c = \frac{\partial c}{\partial S^*} (S^*_t, Y_t, K^*, \tau).$$

The call option price, derived in the appendix, and its delta are:

$$c(S^*_t, Y_t, K^*, \tau) = Y_t[S^*_t e^{-\delta\tau}N(d_1) - K^*e^{-t^*\tau}N(d_1 - \sigma_{S^*}\sqrt{\tau})] = Y_t c^*(S^*_t, K^*, \tau)$$
$$\Delta_c(S^*_t, Y_t, K^*, \tau) = Y_t e^{-\delta\tau}N(d_1) > 0 \tag{7}$$

where

$$d_1 = \frac{\ln(S^*_t/K^*) + (r^* - \delta)\tau}{\sigma_{S^*}\sqrt{\tau}} + \frac{1}{2} \sigma_{S^*}\sqrt{\tau}.$$

Similarly, the price and delta at time t of a European put option with the same strike price and expiration are:

$$p(S^*_t, Y_t, K^*, \tau) = Y_t[K^*e^{-t^*\tau}N(-d_1 + \sigma_{S^*}\sqrt{\tau}) - S^*_t e^{-\delta\tau}N(-d_1)] = Y_t p^*(S^*_t, K^*, \tau)$$
$$\Delta_p(S^*_t, Y_t, K^*, \tau) = -Y_t e^{-\delta\tau}N(-d_1) < 0. \tag{8}$$

The dollar prices of the flexible-rate options are simply the prices of identical options in the foreign country (c^* and p^*) converted into dollars at the current exchange rate. To see this, suppose that a European call option with strike price K^* expiring at $t + \tau$ is traded in the foreign country. The payoff to this call upon exercise is $\max[S^*_{t+\tau} - K^*, 0]$. The exercise value in dollars of the flexible-rate European call equals this exercise value of the foreign option, converted into dollars at the exchange rate prevailing on the expiration date. In frictionless international capital markets, the dollar prices of the two options must be the same, i.e., $c = Y_t c^*$.

Next, consider fixed exchange rate options, whose payoffs can be converted into U.S. dollars at a pre-specified exchange rate $\bar{Y}$. Let $c(S_t^*, \bar{Y}, K^*, \tau)$ denote the price at time t of a fixed-rate European call option expiring at $t + \tau$ with strike price K^*. The call option price, which is derived in the appendix, and its delta are:

$$c(S_t^*, \bar{Y}, K^*, \tau) = \bar{Y}[S_t^* e^{-(r-r^*+\delta+\rho\sigma_S\cdot\sigma_y)\tau} N(d_2) - K^* e^{-r\tau} N(d_2 - \sigma_{S^*}\sqrt{\tau})]$$
$$\Delta_c(S_t^*, \bar{Y}, K^*, \tau) = \bar{Y} e^{-(r-r^*+\delta+\rho\sigma_S\cdot\sigma_y)\tau} N(d_2) > 0 \tag{9}$$

where

$$d_2 \equiv \frac{\ln(S_t^*/K^*) + (r^* - \delta - \rho\sigma_S\cdot\sigma_y)\tau}{\sigma_{S^*}\sqrt{\tau}} + \frac{1}{2}\sigma_{S^*}\sqrt{\tau}.$$

Similarly, the price and delta at time t of a European fixed-rate put option with the same strike price and expiration are:

$$p(S_t^*, \bar{Y}, K^*, \tau) = \bar{Y}[K^* e^{-r\tau} N(-d_2 + \sigma_{S^*}\sqrt{\tau}) - S_t^* e^{-(r-r^*+\delta+\rho\sigma_S\cdot\sigma_y)\tau} N(-d_2)] \tag{10}$$

$$\Delta_p(S_t^*, \bar{Y}, K^*, \tau) = -\bar{Y} c^{(r-r^*+\delta+\rho\sigma_S\cdot\sigma_y)\tau} N(-d_2) < 0, \tag{11}$$

At first glance, the fixed-rate option prices appear to be different from their standard Black-Scholes counterparts. The reason is that the foreign index S_t^* is denominated in the foreign currency, so that its expected rate of return is not equal to r under the risk-neutral probability.

Recall that the expected rate of return on S_t^* is equal to $r^* - \delta - \rho\sigma_S\cdot\sigma_y$. Thus, if we set the expected return on the underlying foreign index equal to the U.S. riskless interest rate, i.e., when $r^* - \delta - \rho\sigma_S\cdot\sigma_y = r$, the fixed-rate pricing formulas revert to the standard Black-Scholes expressions.

Some observations are in order. First, flexible-rate option prices depend on the current level of the exchange rate, while fixed-rate option prices do not. Also, only the foreign riskless interest rate and the volatility of the foreign stock index are important parameters for flexible-rate options. On the other hand, both domestic and foreign interest rates, as well as the covariance between the innovations in the index and exchange rate, are determinants of fixed-rate option prices.

Replicating Portfolios and Currency Risk

To replicate the payoff to an option written on a foreign stock or index, investors generally need to use three assets: the underlying asset, U.S. riskless bonds, and foreign riskless bonds. In the case of both our flexible-rate and fixed-rate options, an interesting simplification of this general result can be obtained.

To replicate flexible-rate options, whether European or American, only the foreign riskless bonds and the underlying foreign stock are needed. For example, the dynamics of $c(S_t^*, Y_t, K^*, \tau)$ can be duplicated by continuously holding Δ_c

(S_t^*, Y_t, K^*, τ) units of the foreign stock and shorting $[\Delta_c(S_t^*, Y_t, K^*, \tau)S_t^* - c(S_t^*, Y_t, K^*, \tau)]$ foreign riskless bonds.

This is clear from the fact that the dollar prices of flexible-rate options are simply the prices of identical options in the foreign country, converted into dollars at the current exchange rate. Hence, prices of flexible-rate options depend on the current level of the exchange rate, since the investor converts dollars into foreign currency only once, at the current exchange rate.

They are independent, however, of the parameters of the exchange rate dynamics, since there is no need to convert dollars continuously into the foreign currency. Consequently, prices of flexible-rate American options can be obtained by first numerically solving the standard Black-Scholes two-variable PDE to obtain option prices denominated in the foreign currency, and then converting these into dollars at the current exchange rate.

For fixed-rate options as well, investors need only two assets to replicate their payoffs: the foreign stock and U.S. riskless bonds. For example, the dynamics of $c(S_t^*, \bar{Y}, K^*, \tau)$ can be duplicated by continuously holding $\Delta_c(S_t^*, \bar{Y}, K^*, \tau)$ units of the foreign stock and shorting U.S. riskless bonds equal to $[\Delta_c(S_t^*, \bar{Y}, K^*, \tau)S_t^* - c(S_t^*, \bar{Y}, K^*, \tau)]$.

To see this, note that hedging these options is in essence no different from hedging options on any domestic stock. The only difference is that while investors can directly take long or short positions in the domestic stock, they now need to go to the foreign currency market in order to take and adjust their positions. Thus, investors need to convert dollars continuously into the foreign currency, or vice versa, in order to adjust their positions in the underlying foreign stock.

Consequently, option prices depend on the parameters of the exchange rate dynamics as indicated by the presence of the covariance term. Yet because their payoffs do not depend on the level of the exchange rate, the prices of fixed-rate options are independent of this factor.

One practical implication of the simplified replicating portfolios is that we can obtain foreign currency prices for fixed-rate American options by numerically solving the two-variable PDE (12) rather than the three-variable Equation (4):

$$-\frac{\partial F^*}{\partial \tau} + \frac{1}{2}\sigma_{S^*}^2 S^{*2}\frac{\partial^2 F^*}{\partial S^{*2}} + (r^* - \delta - \rho\sigma_{S^*}\sigma_y)S^*\frac{\partial F^*}{\partial S^*} - rF^* = 0. \tag{12}$$

Dollar prices are then obtained by converting the foreign currency prices into dollars at the fixed exchange rate, i.e., $F^*(S_t^*, \tau)\bar{Y}$.

Sensitivity to Option Parameters

Compared to the standard Black-Scholes equity option formula, the prices of European options on a foreign index possess a number of new and interesting features. Of particular interest is the fact that changes in various parameters have different effects on fixed-rate versus flexible-rate options. Sensitivity results for the parameters are summarized in Table 21-1, and some key results are discussed here.

Time to Expiration (Theta):

From the usual Black-Scholes equity option pricing formula, a standard call's price unambiguously increases with time to expiration when no dividends are paid. An interesting result here is that the price of a fixed-rate call option increases unambiguously with time to expiration only if $r^* - \delta - \rho\sigma_{s^*}\sigma_y \geq r$. Otherwise, the sign of theta is indeterminate.

This can be understood in terms of the replicating portfolio, which consists of a long position in the foreign index and a short position in U.S. riskless bonds. Under the risk-neural probability, the foreign stock index is expected to appreciate at the rate $r^* - \delta - \rho\sigma_{s^*}\sigma_y$, while the U.S. riskless bond appreciates at the rate r. If $r^* - \delta - \rho\sigma_{s^*}\sigma_y \geq r$ the long position will appreciate more than the short position, and the call value increases with time to expiration.

The arguments also show that it is never optimal to exercise an American fixed-rate call option prior to expiration if $r^* - \delta - \rho\sigma_{s^*}\sigma_y \geq r$, although early exercise may be optimal otherwise.

Interest Rates (RHO)

For fixed-rate calls, the sign of the partial derivative with respect to the U.S. rate r, popularly known as rho, is negative. In the usual Black-Scholes framework,

TABLE 21-1 Sensitivity to Option Parameters of European Call and Put Options Written on a Foreign Stock Index with Time to Maturity τ and Strike Price K

Option Parameter	Sensitivity of Call Price		Sensitivity of Put Price	
	Fixed-Rate	Flexible-Rate	Fixed-Rate	Flexible-Rate
Exchange Rate (Y_t)	0	>0	0	>0
Time to Maturity (τ)*	>0 if $r^* - \delta - \rho\sigma_s\sigma_y \geq r$, $\gtreqqless 0$ Otherwise	>0 if $\delta = 0$ $\gtreqqless 0$ Otherwise	$\gtreqqless 0$	$\gtreqqless 0$
U.S. Risk-Free Rate (r)*	<0	0	<0	0
Japanese Risk-Free Rate (r^*)	>0	>0	<0	<0
Asset Volatility (σ_{s^*})*	>0 if $\rho \leq 0$ $\gtreqqless 0$ if $\rho > 0$	>0	>0 if $\rho \geq 0$ $\gtreqqless 0$ if $\rho < 0$	>0
Exchange Rate Volatility (σ_y)	Sign Opposite to correlation	0	Sign Same as Correlation	0
Correlation (ρ)	<0	0	>0	0

*These sensitivities are commonly known as the option theta, rho, and vega (or kappa), respectively.

Notes: The instantaneous volatilities of the underlying asset S^* and the exchange rate Y are σ_{s^*} and σ_y, respectively, and the correlation between them is ρ. Domestic and foreign interest rates are denoted by r and r^*. Foreign currency payoffs are convertible into dollars at either a fixed exchange rate $\bar{Y}$ or the spot exchange rate on the exercise date $Y_{t+\tau}$.

under the risk-neutral probability, a change in r does not affect today's present value of the stock price received at expiration, although the call holder benefits from the decrease in the present value of the strike price paid. Hence, call rho is positive.

This is not true for the fixed-rate call options. As in Black-Scholes, an increase in r will still result in a lower present value of the exercise price. The present value of the underlying asset is now lower, since its rate of appreciation is not r. This decrease dominates the lower present value of the exercise price because at maturity only in-the-money options are exercised. Hence, fixed-rate calls decrease in value as r increases.

In contrast, when the foreign risk-free rate r^* increases, the fixed-rate call price increases. As r^* increases, the index appreciates at this faster rate, while there is no change in the present value of the exercise price. Thus, the holder of the call benefits.

The prices of flexible-rate European options are given by standard Black-Scholes formulas, evaluated in Japan and converted into dollars at the current exchange rate. Therefore, the foreign risk-free rate r^* plays the role of the domestic risk-free rate r in the standard Black-Scholes formulas. Accordingly, an increase in r^* results in an increase (decrease) in call (put) prices. On the other hand, the U.S. rate r now has no effect on option prices.

Volatilities (Vega or Kappa)

From the discussion of the replicating portfolio, recall that the prices of flexible-rate options are independent of the parameters related to the exchange rate, σ_y, and ρ. Clearly, the effect of the foreign index volatility σ_{s^*} on flexible-rate options is exactly the same as in the standard Black-Scholes case.

For fixed-rate options, the three parameters—volatilities of the foreign index and the exchange rate, and the correlation coefficient—affect the option price via the covariance term $\rho\sigma_{s^*}\sigma_y$. Recall that the negative of the covariance is a measure of the currency premium of the foreign index for investors concerned with dollar returns. An increase in the covariance decreases the call price since it lowers the dollar rate of appreciation of the index. Hence, an increase in the correlation coefficient ρ results in a decrease in the call price. Similarly, when ρ is positive (negative), an increase in the exchange rate volatility σ_y decreases (increases) the currency premium and hence the call price.

With respect to an increase in the volatility of the index σ_{s^*}, there are two effects on the fixed-rate option price. The first is the usual effect of an increase in the instantaneous variance of the underlying asset, which always increases an option's value. The second is the effect on the currency premium. When ρ is negative, an increase in σ_{s^*} increases the currency premium and reinforces the first positive effect on the call price.

On the other hand, when ρ is positive, the second effect is to the detriment of a call holder. These two effects oppose each other, and the sign of the net effect cannot be determined unambiguously.

APPLICATION: NIKKEI INDEX WARRANTS

In recent years, U.S. investors have become increasingly interested in the Japanese stock market. Part of this can be attributed to Japan's emergence as one of the leading world economies and the corresponding 300% rise in the Nikkei index during the 1984–1989 period. Until January 1990, however, individual investors in the U.S. did not have convenient access to Nikkei index derivatives, which would have facilitated hedging against or speculating on a decline in the index.[9]

On January 12, 1990, the first Nikkei put warrants to be traded in the U.S. were issued by Goldman Sachs (on behalf of the Kingdom of Denmark) and began trading on the American Stock Exchange. Several additional issues followed thereafter, leading to six put and two call warrants being traded on the AMEX. An important feature of these warrants is that some use flexible rather than fixed exchange rates to convert yen payoffs into dollars. This and other features are summarized in more detail in Table 21-2.[10]

The empirical results of our option pricing analysis of Nikkei index warrants are generated using American option prices found by solving the appropriate PDEs numerically. These model prices are compared to observed prices using the estimation methodology described.

TABLE 21-2   Summary of Key Features of the Eight Nikkei Index Warrants Traded on the AMEX

Ticker[a]	DXA	SXA	SXO	BTB	PXB	EXW	SXZ	PXA
Type	Put	Put	Put	Put	Put	Put	Call	Call
Expiration Date	1/03/93	1/19/93	2/16/93	1/16/93	4/08/93	4/22/93	4/06/93	4/08/93
Strike Index (yen)[b]	37,517	36,821	37,471	37,206	29,249	29,425	28,443	29,249
Exchange Rate[c]	145.325	145.520	144.554	Flexible	159.80	158.84	158.800	Flexible
Divisor[d]	5	5	5	2	5	5	15	10
Strike Index ($)[e]	51.63	50.61	51.84	Flexible	36.61	37.05	11.94	Flexible
Limit Exercise[f]	Yes	Yes	Yes	No	Yes	Yes	Yes	Yes
Extraordinary Event Clause[g]	Yes	Yes	Yes	Yes	Yes	Yes	Yes	Yes

[a]Respectively. Kingdom of Denmark/Goldman Sachs, Salomon, Salomon, Bankers Trust/Merrill Lynch, Paine Webber, A/S Eksportfinans, Salomon, and Paine Webber.
[b]The closing level of the Nikkei index on the valuation date, which is the next Tokyo business day following the exercise date. The exercise date is the New York business day on which an exercise notice is tendered prior to 3 pm.
[c]For flexible-rate warrants, this will be the yen buying rate at close of trading on the valuation date.
[d,e]This is computed by dividing the strike index in yen by the exchange rate and the divisor.
[f]This provides an escape clause for warrant holders who have tendered an exercise notice, in the event that the Nikkei index on the valuation date closes at a significantly different level from that on the exercise date.
[g]This provides an escape clause for the issuers of the warrants in the case of "calamitous event."

Specifically, the maximum likelihood estimates of the parameters are computed using the 100 most recent observations on the Nikkei index and the exchange rate. Sampling error in these estimators implies sampling error in the model prices, which can be used to construct confidence intervals around each day's estimated model price.[11] It is then possible to test the model by checking whether observed prices fall between the model's confidence bands.

Data Description

We collect the following data over the calendar year 1990 from the Bloomberg Financial Markets quote system: 1) daily open and close prices for all eight Nikkei index warrants traded on the AMEX; 2) daily exchange rate data; and 3) interest rate data.[12] Since the warrants have long expirations (three years) relative to the nine months or less for standard equity options, it is not easy to identify the appropriate risk-free interest rates to use. We use the yield on U.S. Treasury Strips maturing in February 1993 as our estimate of the U.S. risk-free rate r.

Despite the obvious problems, we are constrained to use the yield on the benchmark Japanese long-term government bond as a proxy for r*. Finally, open and close levels of the Nikkei index for the same period are provided by the Susquehanna Investment Group.

The Immediate Exercise Arbitrage Bound Puzzle

Our results are summarized graphically in Figures 21-1 through 21-8. We graph observed prices relative to model prices with corresponding 95% confidence bands for each of the eight warrants. Note that the band in each graph represents the model price plus or minus 1.96 standard errors. On occasion, the band reduces to a single line: these are the days on which the model indicates that the option is selling for its immediate exercise value.[13]

As a test of the quality of the data, we checked the immediate exercise arbitrage bound for all warrants. On a number of days during March to May and August to December, the model prices of the four put options—DXA, SXA, SXO, and BTB—were equal to their exercise value, $S^* - K^*$, converted at the appropriate fixed or flexible rate. Surprisingly, there were several instances when the observed price was below the exercise value. If investors were to purchase the warrants and exercise them immediately, it appears as though they would have earned arbitrage profits.

For example, the price of the DXA fixed-rate put on October 1 was $21.25, but its exercise value (and our model price) was $23.80. While this date represents one of the most extreme violations of the immediate exercise arbitrage bound, there are actually quite a few such observations, as shown in Figures 21-1–21-8.

There are at least two plausible explanations for these discrepancies: nonsynchronous prices and transaction costs. First, the model price is calculated

**FIGURE 21-1   Observed and Model Prices for DXA Fixed-Rate Nikkei Put
                Warrants**

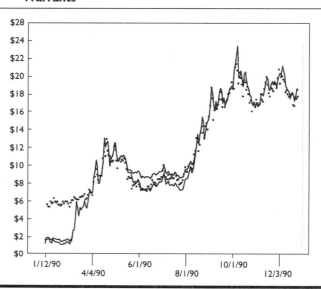

Observed prices (denoted by the symbol "∎") are shown relative to 95% confidence bands obtained from
model prices by adding and subtracting 1.96 standard errors.

using the opening level of the Nikkei index the next morning in Tokyo, while
the actual settlement value of the warrants is based on the closing level of the
Nikkei index the next Tokyo business day.[14] Depending on the day of the week
that the warrant is exercised, and any intervening holidays in New York or
Tokyo, the delay between the decision to exercise and the settlement date on
which the exercise value is determined can vary from one to several calendar
days.

Warrant holders therefore face some risk as a result of adverse movements
in the Nikkei index. It is possible that the low price reflects this added risk if
investors perceive that it is difficult (or costly) to hedge. In that case, prices of
the warrants would be based on the forecast level of the Nikkei index at the
close of the settlement date. Thus, on October 1, the market may have anticipated a sharp increase in the Nikkei index during the next trading day in Japan.

This explanation cannot explain all the deviations, though. First, futures
contracts on the Nikkei index are traded on the Chicago Mercantile Exchange,
so this anticipated increase could have been hedged in the futures market. Second, the issuers of most warrants have incorporated a limit option clause under
which the warrants will not be exercised if the Nikkei index moves 500 points
or more against the warrant after it has been tendered. Even if investors find it
difficult to hedge against movements in the Nikkei index, the limit option is

**FIGURE 21-2   Observed and Model Prices for SXA Fixed-Rate Nikkei Put
Warrants**

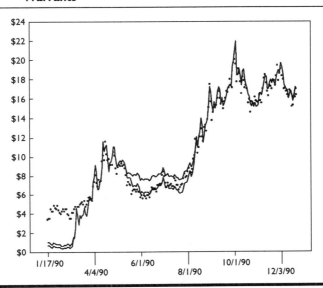

Observed prices (denoted by the symbol "■") are shown relative to 95% confidence bands obtained from
model prices by adding and subtracting 1.96 standard errors.

supposed to reduce their risk. Because we find that the only warrant without
the limit option (the flexible-rate put BTB) behaves like the others, the limit
option does not appear to have an important effect on pricing.

The second explanation for the apparent violations of the immediate exercise arbitrage bound is the presence of transaction costs, which, if high
enough, could eliminate the apparent arbitrage bound violations. For example,
the end-of-day prices we collected are not identified as bid or ask prices. Since
the bid-ask spread for these securities is at least $0.125, a significant portion of
the deviation may be attributable to this problem.

Since spreads are inversely related to volume, we plot the average daily
volume (number of contracts) for four of the warrants during our sample period
(see Figures 21-9–21-12). While there is evidence that trading activity in these
warrants was low during some periods in 1990, it seems unlikely from Figures
21-9–21-12 that bid or ask errors can completely explain the arbitrage bound
puzzle, especially in the August to October 1990 period.

Summary of Results

Beyond the few violations of the no-arbitrage condition, the model fares well
throughout most of the sample period. Specifically, comparing observed prices

**FIGURE 21-3   Observed and Model Prices for SXO Fixed-Rate Nikkei Put
Warrants**

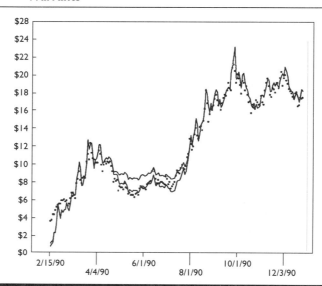

Observed prices (denoted by the symbol "■") are shown relative to 95% confidence bands obtained from
model prices by adding and subtracting 1.96 standard errors.

to model prices produces encouraging results for the put warrants issued in
early 1990 (the fixed-rate puts DXA, SXA, and SXO and the flexible-rate put
BTB). Figures 21-1 through 21-4 show that the observed price generally lies
within the statistical bounds.

For the four warrants issued later in April 1990, Figures 21-5 through 21-8
show slightly more serious deviations between model and observed prices. Nevertheless, after about the first week of trading, prices for the two fixed-rate puts
(PXB and EXW) generally lie within the bounds until August 1990.

Finally, deviations between observed and model prices for each of the eight
warrants do not appear to be related to whether the warrant is in- or out-of-the-
money. For example, with respect to the fixed-rate puts PXB and EXW, the model
does much better when the warrants are out-of-the-money (the period 5/90–
8/90 in Figures 21-5 and 21-6). In contrast, for the DXA, SXA, SXO, and BTB
puts, the model performs well when the warrants are in-the-money (the period
6/90–8/90 in Figures 21-1–21-4). No differences in mispricing are discernible
between the fixed-rate and flexible-rate put warrants.

On the other hand, the model fares worst relative to the market in pricing
both the fixed-rate call warrant SXZ and the flexible-rate call PXA. There is
overpricing until August 1990, with slight underpricing after that date. For the
put warrants, there are essentially two periods of mispricing. The first occurs

FIGURE 21-4   Observed and Model Prices for BTB Flexible-Rate Nikkei Put Warrants

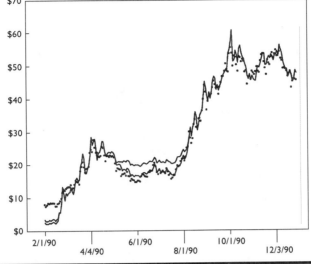

Observed prices (denoted by the symbol "■") are shown relative to 95% confidence bands obtained from model prices by adding and subtracting 1.96 standard errors.

in January when the puts were first issued. The second mispricing is with the later issued puts (PXB and EXW) and occurs for a few months after August 1990.

Explanation of Results

The explanation of mispricing of the calls may lie in the fact that trading volume for the two call warrants is much lower than put volume, as shown in Figures 21-9 through 21-12. Daily volume for both call warrants is never higher than about 200,000, while almost all the fixed-rate puts trade in the 200,000 to 1,000,000 range during the second half of 1990. This lower volume could be indicative of higher bid-ask spreads. Thus, there are reasons to question the quality of the observed price data for the calls.

Volatility Estimates

For the most part, the prices of all the put warrants are either within the bounds or at least close to the bounds in Figures 21-1–21-6. The most notable exception is during the first few weeks of trading for the four originally issued puts. There is a systematic tendency for the model to underprice the warrants.[15]

We believe most of the pricing deviations can be attributed to historical estimates of the volatilities and correlation. Recall that historical volatility is

FIGURE 21-5   Observed and Model Prices for PXB Fixed-Rate Nikkei Put Warrants

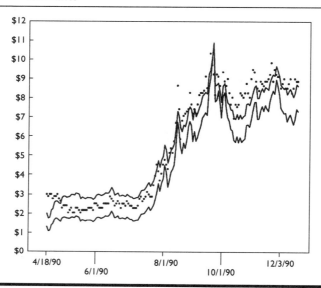

Observed prices (denoted by the symbol "■") are shown relative to 95% confidence bands obtained from model prices by adding and subtracting 1.96 standard errors.

estimated from the most immediate past 100 daily observations. Figure 21-13 graphs this "rolling" historical estimate of the volatility of the Nikkei index over the sample period. Although the daily estimates are highly autocorrelated, it is apparent that there is a sharp increase in volatility from about 9% to 25% during April 1990.[16]

In contrast to our January 1990 historical estimate of 9%, the volatility of the Nikkei has generally been in the range of 25%–30% during the late 1980s. In pricing the warrants, investors may have used this higher estimate of volatility. In order to examine this conjecture, we compute the volatility implied by the warrant prices during 1990. While there is variation across the warrants and over time, the implied volatility for the most part lies in the range from 20% to 40% (see, for example, the DXA put's implied volatility given in Figure 21-13).

The same story explains why model prices are closer to observed prices after late April 1990. Whether the puts were in the money (DXA, SXA, SXO, and BTB in Figures 21-1–21-4) or out of the money (PXB and EXW in Figures 21-5 and 21-6), prices generally lie within the statistical bounds. Not coincidentally, this is about the time that the historical Nikkei volatility estimate reaches (and stays) around the 25% to 30% level.

As further evidence, note that the second major deviation between ob-

FIGURE 21-6   Observed and Model Prices for EXW Fixed-Rate Nikkei Put Warrants

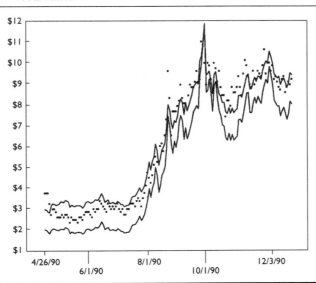

Observed prices (denoted by the symbol "■") are shown relative to 95% confidence bands obtained from model prices by adding and subtracting 1.96 standard errors.

served and model prices for the warrants occurs after August 1990. In particular, the EXW and PXB fixed-rate puts, which are in the money (but not deep enough to be exercised), are underpriced by our model during this time. Figure 21-13 also shows another increase in historical volatility starting shortly after August 1990, which was the start of a very unusual period, the Gulf crisis.

This type of unexpected event was almost certainly not incorporated into the market's implied volatility estimates prior to August—the implied volatility jumps to over 40% at this time, while our historical volatility estimate continues to lag behind the implied volatility until the two become roughly equal at about 35% in December 1990.

Thus, there are strong reasons to believe that the underpricing of the warrants in these two subperiods is attributable to differences in historical and implied volatility estimates.

Additional Issues

There are a few additional issues that arise uniquely in this setting. First, Nikkei index warrant holders need to contend with credit risk. Unlike standard options guaranteed by the Options Clearing Corporation, these warrants are unsecured obligations issued by various institutions. It is therefore plausible to expect some

**FIGURE 21-7   Observed and Model Prices for SXZ Fixed-Rate Nikkei Call
                 Warrants**

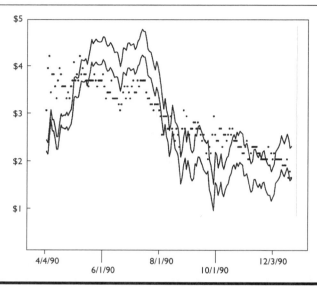

Observed prices (denoted by the symbol "■") are shown relative to 95% confidence bands obtained from
model prices by adding and subtracting 1.96 standard errors.

risk premium in the observed prices of the warrants, depending on investor
perceptions about the creditworthiness of the issuer. In the 1990 sample, however, this does not appear to be important, as there is no systematic tendency
for the model to overprice the warrants.

Second, in order to protect themselves in the event of abnormal market
conditions, the issuers of most Nikkei warrants incorporate a clause that pre-
vents the exercise of warrants under certain circumstances. The specific definition of these "extraordinary events" varies across warrants. Generally, it is
defined as the suspension, absence, or material limitation of trading on the
Tokyo Stock Exchange of some (usually seventy-five or more) or all of the Nikkei
stocks, an outbreak or escalation of international or national hostilities, the occurrence of natural calamities, and so on. The terms of most of the warrants
specify an alternative cash settlement value (which is never greater than the
normal settlement value) in the event of extended abnormal market conditions.

In order to assess the impact of such clauses on warrant prices, we would
need estimates of the probability of the occurrence of extraordinary events. It
appears reasonable, however, to assume that this probability is very low.[17] The
effect of this clause, if any, should be to lower observed prices, although this
does not appear to be the case in our sample.[18]

FIGURE 21-8 Observed and Model Prices for PXA Flexible-Rate Nikkei Call Warrants

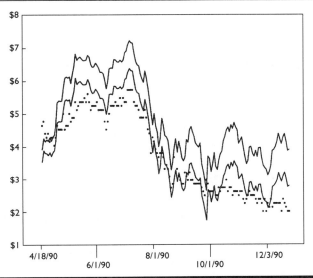

Observed prices (denoted by the symbol "■") are shown relative to 95% confidence bands obtained from prices by adding and subtracting 1.96 standard errors.

Assumptions and Future Research

In applying our analysis to actual data, we make two fairly strong assumptions regarding the Nikkei index warrants. The first is that the Nikkei index and the exchange rate follow geometric Brownian motions.[19] We note that mispricing seems to occur when historical volatility estimates are low relative to future historical estimates. Caveats aside, Figure 21-13 further suggests that implied volatility estimates 1) are greater than historical estimates; 2) provide an accurate assessment of future historical volatility estimates; and 3) are somewhat inversely related to the level in the index. This implies that there may be an advantage to exploring the effect of stochastic volatility in future analyses of the Nikkei index warrants.

The second strong assumption is that interest rates are constant.[20] Since the warrants were issued with three years to maturity, violations of this assumption may have more important consequences than we normally find with short-lived options. It is not clear to us, however, that more general interest rate specifications could explain the two periods of mispricing identified.[21]

We conjecture that the basic set-up and intuition for the various types of instruments (fixed-rate and flexible-rate contingent claims) will carry through to more complex environments. In our application to Nikkei index warrants,

FIGURE 21-9   Trading Volume for DXA Fixed-Rate Nikkei Put Warrants

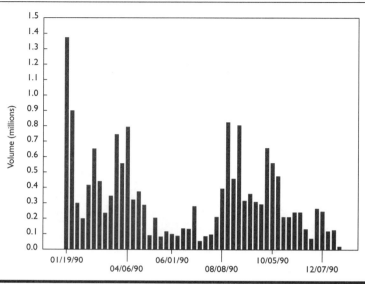

The average daily trading volume for each week is shown.

FIGURE 21-10   Trading Volume for BTB Flexible-Rate Nikkei Put Warrants

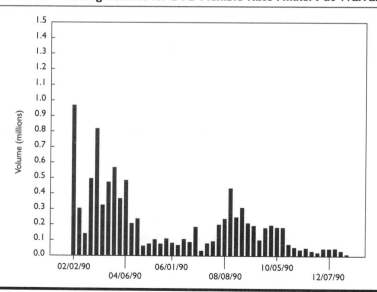

The average daily trading volume for each week is shown.

FIGURE 21-11   Trading Volume for PXB Fixed-Rate Nikkei Put Warrants

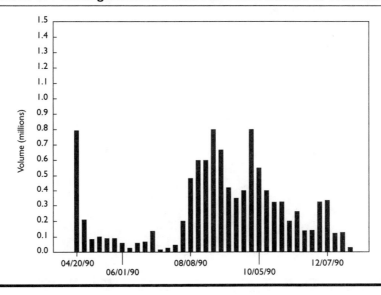

FIGURE 21-12   Trading Volume for PXA Flexible-Rate Nikkei Call Warrants

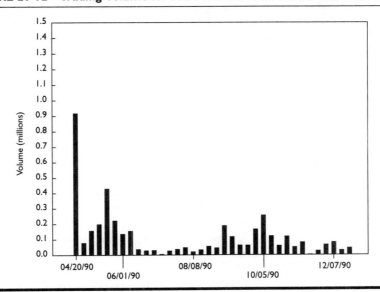

The average daily trading volume for each week is shown.

FIGURE 21-13 **Nikkei Stock Average Index: Level, Historical, and Implied Volatilities**

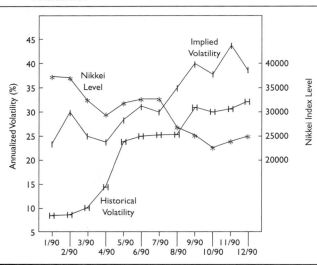

Mid-month values of the Nikkei index level (denoted by the symbol "a"), the volatility of the Nikkei implied from the prices of DXA fixed-rate put warrants (denoted by the symbol "I"), and 100-day rolling estimates of hisorical Nikkei volatility (denoted by the symbol "H") are shown.

however, volatility appears to play an important role in our understanding of the periods in which the model misprices the warrants.

It remains an open question whether more complex models of volatility will ex ante improve the pricing over all periods. We hope to explore this in future research.

SUMMARY

The introduction of foreign index derivative securities in financial markets raises some interesting pricing issues. For quantos and similar derivatives whose payoff depends on the price of an asset denominated in one currency, with payment in a different currency, even under the usual distributional assumptions, prices depend on dynamics of both the index and the exchange rate.

Our general framework for evaluating these derivative securities theoretically and empirically results in explicit formulas for fixed-rate and flexible-rate options on a foreign index. An interesting simplification is possible: the exchange rate separates out of the PDE so that a two-variable (rather than three-variable) PDE needs to be solved numerically, implying that the replicating portfolios for both fixed-rate and flexible-rate options need contain only two assets rather than three.

As an empirical application, we study Nikkei index warrants traded on the AMEX. We compare the numerical prices of American options found by solving the appropriate PDEs to the observed prices of these warrants, and analyze the deviations that we uncover.

APPENDIX

We apply a lemma to derive the prices of flexible-rate and fixed-rate European call options, (7) and (9).[22] The derivation for European put option prices is similar.

Lemma: Let x_1 and x_2 be standard normal random variables with correlation coefficient ρ. Then, for arbitrary constants a, b, c, d, and k,

$$E[e^{cx_1 + dx_2} I(ax_1 + bx_2 \geq k)] = e^{(c^2 + d^2 + 2\rho cd)/2} N\left(\frac{ac + bd + \rho(ad + bc) - k}{\sqrt{a^2 + b^2 + 2\rho ab}}\right),$$

where $I(\cdot)$ denotes the indicator function that takes the value 1 if the expression in parentheses is true and 0 otherwise, and $N(\cdot)$ the cumulative standard normal distribution.

We consider first flexible-rate options, whose dollar payoffs depend on the spot exchange rate prevailing on the expiration date. Under the risk-neutral probability, the dollar price at time t of the European call option expiring at t $+ \tau$ with strike price K^* is its expected dollar payoff at expiration, discounted at the U.S. risk-free rate. Therefore

$$c(S_t^*, Y_t, K^*, \tau)$$
$$= e^{-r\tau} E_t\{Y_{t+\tau} \max[S_{t+\tau}^* - K^*, 0]\} = e^{-r\tau} E_t\{Y_{t+\tau}[S_{t+\tau}^* - K^*]I(S_{t+\tau}^* \geq K^*)\}$$
$$= e^{-r\tau} E_t\{Y_{t+\tau}[S_t^* e^{[r^* - \delta - \rho\sigma_{S^*}\sigma_y - \sigma_{S^*}^2/2]\tau + \sigma_{S^*}[z_{t+\tau}^{(S^*)} - z_t^{(S^*)}]} \geq K^*)\}$$
$$= Y_t S_t^* e^{(-\delta - \rho\sigma_{S^*}\sigma_y - \sigma_{S^*}^2/2 - \sigma_y^2/2)\tau} E_0\{e^{\sigma_{S^*}\sqrt{\tau}z_t^{(S^*)} \sigma_y\sqrt{\tau}z_t^{(Y)}} I(Z_t^{(S^*)} \geq \rho\sigma_y\sqrt{\tau} + \sigma_{S^*}\sqrt{\tau} - d_1)\}$$
$$\quad - Y_t e^{(-r^* - \sigma_y^2/2)\tau} K^* E_0\{e^{\sigma_y\sqrt{\tau}z_t^{(Y)}} I(Z_t^{(S^*)} \geq \rho\sigma_y\sqrt{\tau} + \sigma_{S^*}\sqrt{\tau} - d_1)\}$$
$$= Y_t[S_t^* e^{-\delta\tau} N(d_1) - K^* e^{-r^*\tau} N(d_1 - \sigma_{S^*}\sqrt{\tau})]$$

where

$$d_1 \equiv \frac{\ln(S_t^*/K^*) + (r^* - \delta)\tau}{\sigma_{S^*}\sqrt{\tau}} + \frac{1}{2}\sigma_{S^*}\sqrt{\tau}.$$

We use Equations (5) and (6) and the fact that $Z_{r+\tau} - Z_t$ has the same distribution as $\sqrt{\tau}Z_1$ for any standard Brownian motion Z.

Next, consider fixed-rate options, whose payoffs are converted into U.S. dollars at a prespecified exchange rate $\bar{Y}$. The price at time t of the flexible-rate European call option with the same strike price and expiration is:

$$
\begin{aligned}
c(S_t^*, \bar{Y}, K^*, \tau) &= e^{-r\tau}E_t\{\bar{Y}\max[S_{t+\tau}^* - K^*, 0]\} = e^{-r\tau}\bar{Y}E_t\{[S_{t+\tau}^* - K^*]I(S_{t+\tau}^* \geq K^*)\} \\
&= e^{-r\tau}\bar{Y}E_t\{[S_{t+\tau}^* - K^*]I(S_t^* e^{[r^* - \delta\rho\sigma_S\cdot\sigma_Y - \sigma_S^2\cdot/2]\tau + \sigma_S\cdot[z_{t+\tau}^{(S^*)} - z_t^{(S^*)}]} \geq K^*)\} \\
&= e^{-r\tau}\bar{Y}S_t^* e^{(r^* - \delta - \rho\sigma_S\cdot\sigma_Y - \sigma_S^2\cdot/2)\tau}E_0\{e^{\sigma_S\cdot\sqrt{\tau}z_t^{(S^*)}}I(Z_1^{(S^*)} \geq \sigma_S\cdot\sqrt{\tau} - d_2)\} \\
&\quad - e^{-r\tau}\bar{Y}K^*E_0\{I(Z_1^{(S^*)} \geq \sigma_S\cdot\sqrt{\tau} - d_2)\} \\
&= \bar{Y}[S_t^* e^{-(r - r^* + \delta + \rho\sigma_S\cdot\sigma_Y)\tau}N(d_2) - K^* e^{-r\tau}N(d_2 - \sigma_S\cdot\sqrt{\tau})],
\end{aligned}
$$

where

$$
d_2 = \frac{\ln(S_t^*/K^*) + (r^* - \delta - \rho\sigma_S\cdot\sigma_Y)\tau}{\sigma_S\cdot\sqrt{\tau}} + \frac{1}{2}\sigma_S\cdot\sqrt{\tau}.
$$

REFERENCES

Arnold, Ludwig. *Stochastic Differential Equations: Theory and Applications.* New York: Wiley-Interscience, 1974.

Babbel, David, and Laurence Eisenberg. "Quantity-Adjusting Options and Forward Contracts." Working paper, Rodney L. White Center for Financial Research. The Wharton School of the University of Pennsylvania, 1991.

Bailey, W., and W. Ziemba. "An Introduction to Japanese Stock Index Options." In W. Bailey, W. Ziemba, and Y. Hamao, eds., *Japanese Financial Markets Research.* Amsterdam: North Holland, 1990.

Black, Fischer, and Myron Scholes. "The Pricing of Options and Corporate Liabilities." *Journal of Political Economy,* 81 (1973), pp. 637-654.

Clyman, Dana. "Anatomy of an Anomaly, or What I Know About Fixed Exchange Rate Nikkei Put Warrants." Working paper, Harvard University, 1991.

Cox, John, and Stephen Ross. "The Valuation of Options for Alternative Stochastic Processes," *Journal of Financial Economics,* 3 (1976), pp. 145-166.

Derman, Emanuel, Piotr Karasinski, and Jeffrey Wecker. "Understanding Guaranteed Exchange-Rate Contracts in Foreign Stock Investments." International Equity Strategies, Goldman, Sachs & Co., 1990.

Dravid Ajay, Matthew Richardson, and Alastair Craig. "Explaining Overnight Variation in Japanese Stock Returns: The Information Content of Derivative Securities." Working paper, The Wharton School of the University of Pennsylvania, 1993.

Gruca, E., and Peter Ritchken. "Exchange-Traded Foreign Warrants." Working paper, Case Western Reserve University, 1991.

Harrison, J. Michael, and David Kreps. "Martingales and Arbitrage in Multiperiod Securities Markets." *Journal of Economic Theory,* 20 (1979), pp. 381-408.

Hull, John, and Alan White. "The Pricing of Options on Assets with Stochastic Volatilities." *Journal of Finance,* 42 (1987), pp. 281-300.

Lo, Andrew. "Statistical Tests of Contingent-Claims Asset-Pricing Models." *Journal of Financial Economics,* 17 (1986), pp. 143-173.

Melino, Angelo, and Stuart Turnbull. "Pricing Foreign Currency Options with Stochastic Volatility." *Journal of Econometrics,* 45 (1990), pp. 239-265.

Reiner, Eric. "Quanto Mechanics." *Risk,* 5 (1992), pp. 59-63.

Rubinstein, Mark. "Two Into One." *Risk,* 4 (1991), pp. 49-53.

Rumsey, John. "Pricing Cross-Currency Options." *Journal of Futures Markets,* 11 (1991), pp. 89-93.

Shaw, Julian, Edward Thorp, and William Ziemba. "Convergence to Efficiency of the Nikkei Put Warrant Market of 1989-91." Working paper, University of British Columbia, 1992.

Wei, Jason. "Pricing Options on Foreign Assets When Interest Rates are Stochastic." Working paper, University of Toronto, 1992.

Wiggins, James. "Option Values Under Stochastic Volatility: Theory and Empirical Estimates." *Journal of Financial Economics,* 19 (1987), pp. 351-372.

ENDNOTES

1. The Nikkei Stock Average Index, sponsored by Nihon Kcizai Shimbun, Inc., consists of 225 common stocks traded on the First Section of the Tokyo Stock Exchange (TSE). These are among the most actively traded stocks on the TSE.

2. For practical purposes, these warrants are identical to options, and we use these two terms interchangeably.

3. Derman, Karasinski, and Wecker [1990], Babbel and Eisenberg [1991], Gruca and Ritchken [1991], Rubinstein [1991], and Reiner [1992] have derived theoretical results along similar lines. Wei [1992] examines the case of stochastic interest rates. Gruca and Ritchken [1991] use prices of traded Nikkei warrants to predict next day's Tokyo opening level of the Nikkei index. Clyman [1991] investigates the existence of arbitrage opportunities implied by Nikkei warrant prices, particularly during the first few weeks of trading on the AMEX. In a similar vein, Shaw, Thorp, and Ziemba [1992] address the issue of convergence to efficiency of the market for these warrants in both Toronto and New York. Bailey and Ziemba [1990] contains an excellent discussion of some of the institutional aspects of foreign index warrants. Finally, Rumsey [1991] focuses on volatility estimation for a particular class of "cross-currency" options.

4. Let $B_t \equiv \exp\{\int_0^t r_t dt\}$, the value at time t of one dollar deposited at time 0, and B_t^* be similarly defined. Then for U.S. investors $YS^* \exp\{\int_0^t \delta_t dt\}/B$ and YB^*/B are martingales under the risk-neutral probability, which implies (1) and (2). Equation (3) follows from Itô's Lemma.

5. For any $\tau > 0$,

$$E_t\left[\frac{S_{t+\tau}}{S_t}\right] = E_t\left[\frac{S_{t+\tau}^*}{S_t^*}\right]E_t\left[\frac{Y_{t+\tau}}{Y_t}\right] + COV_t\left[\frac{S_{t+\tau}^*}{S_t^*}, \frac{Y_{t+\tau}}{Y_t}\right]$$

6. As pointed out to us by Peter Carr, the asymmetry between domestic and foreign equities is related to Siegel's paradox in international economics. The problem can easily be formulated from a foreign investor's point of view. Let Y_t^* denote the spot exchange rate specified in the foreign currency per dollar. Then the dollar price of the foreign index S_t is S_t^*/Y_t^*. For foreign investors, the counterparts to (1)-(3) arc

$$dS = (r - \delta + \sigma_{y^*}^2 - \rho^*\sigma_{s^*}\sigma_{y^*})Sdt + \sigma_s\text{-}SdW^{(S^*)} - \sigma_{y^*}SdW^{(y^*)}$$

$$dY^* = (r^* - r)Y^*dt + \sigma_{y^*}Y^*dW^{(y^*)}$$

$$dS^* = (r^* - \delta)S^*dt + \sigma_s\text{-}S^*dW^{(S^*)}$$

where $W^{(s^*)}$ and $W^{(y^*)}$ are two standard Brownian motions with correlation coefficient ρ^*. It can be shown that $\rho^*\sigma_{y^*} = -\rho\sigma_y$.

7. In fact, the PDE applies only for values of S^*, Y, and t where early exercise is not optimal.

8. Details of the calculation of standard errors are available upon request.

9. Institutional investors could trade Nikkei futures contracts on the Osaka Securities Exchange (OSE) or the SIMEX, warrants on the Nikkei index on the OSE, and put warrants on the Nikkei index on the Toronto Stock Exchange, as well as options on the underlying stocks and the stocks themselves. Although individual investors could have traded Nikkei put warrants in Toronto, they would have needed to open accounts in Canada in order to do so since the warrants were not approved by the SEC.

10. Although the first warrants to be issued have expired, the AMEX has recently announced its intention to permit the introduction of new issues. Meanwhile, options on the AMEX's own Japan Index, designed to replicate the Nikkei index, are also being traded.

11. We repeated all our tests using a much shorter twenty-five-day window and obtained basically similar results.

12. In order to verify the accuracy of the data, prices and trading volumes of the warrants on twenty randomly selected days were checked against data published in the *Wall Street Journal*. Except for two minor discrepancies in trading volumes, no errors were found.

13. Note that warrant prices and the pricing errors are highly correlated from one observation to the next. In evaluating statistical significance across any time series on the options, therefore, the results need to be interpreted cautiously.

14. Note that warrant prices are obtained at 9:30am EST and 4:00pm EST, while the open and close for the Nikkei occur at 7:00pm EST and 1:00am EST. Clearly, using today's closing price of a warrant in conjunction with the same day's close for the Nikkei would exacerbate the problem, since the Nikkei quote is fifteen hours old. Using today's opening price of warrants reduces the gap to eight and one-half hours, which is still quite large. The closest alignment that can be obtained is to use closing prices of warrants with the next day's opening level of the Nikkei, which represents a time lag of only three hours. Even though the opening level of the Nikkei is not available at the time the warrants stop trading in New York, there is evidence that there are spillover effects from U.S. capital markets into Japanese markets. See, for example, Dravid, Richardson, and Craig [1993]. Although additional research is needed in order to resolve this issue, we perform two separate sets of tests. First, we use closing warrant prices and the next day's opening Nikkei index. Then, we repeat the tests using closing warrant prices and the same day's Nikkei close. We find no systematic differences between the results.

15. Note that the warrants were issued in fixed supply. As widely reported in the press, initial demand for these warrants was extremely high. Trading volume figures corroborate this story. If investors believed that the warrants could not be replicated easily and costlessly, it is conceivable that "excess demand" could have driven observed prices well above model prices. The fact that these relatively high prices were sustained for over a month suggests that this is not the entire explanation.

16. Of course, this raises questions about the validity of our assumptions regarding the stochastic processes of stock returns and exchange rates. As partial vindication, we offer the evidence that the volatility of the exchange rate is much less variable, ranging between about 8% and 12% during our sample period. The correlation coefficient is also relatively constant.

17. The prospectuses of some warrants state that no circumstances that would qualify as extraordinary events occurred during the period between October 1986 and April 1990, which includes the months of October 1987 and October 1989. Nor did the outbreak of the Gulf War trigger this clause.

18. Of course, it is also possible that the effect, if any, is offset by that of some other factor, such as the credit risk.

19. There is evidence that exchange rate processes may be characterized by stochastic volatility, and that stock prices perhaps follow jump-diffusion processes or may also exhibit stochastic volatility. See, for example, Hull and White [1987] and Wiggins [1987] and others for the effects of stochastic volatility on stock and index options, and Melino and Turnbull [1990] and others for its effects on foreign currency options.

20. In this context, given that the dynamics of exchange rates are related to interest rates via interest rate parity, constant interest rates imply sharp restrictions on these dynamics.

21. Wei [1992] discusses the pricing of options on foreign assets under stochastic interest rates. In most cases, he finds that the impact on option prices of using constant rather than stochastic interest rates is quite small.

22. The proof of the lemma is available upon request.

Index